Rockets and People

Volume IV: *The Moon Race*

ISBN 978-0-16-089559-3

For sale by the Superintendent of Documents, U.S. Government Printing Office
Internet: bookstore.gpo.gov   Phone: toll free (866) 512-1800;   DC area (202) 512-1800
Fax: (202) 512-2104 Mail: Stop IDCC, Washington, DC 20402-0001

ISBN 978-0-16-089559-3

Rockets and People

Volume IV: *The Moon Race*

Boris Chertok

Asif Siddiqi, Series Editor

The NASA History Series

National Aeronautics and Space Administration

Office of Communications
History Program Office
Washington, DC
NASA SP-2011-4110

Library of Congress Cataloging-in-Publication Data

Chertok, B. E. (Boris Evseevich), 1912–
    [Rakety i lyudi. English]
    Rockets and People: The Moon Race (Volume IV) / by
Boris E. Chertok ;
    [edited by] Asif A. Siddiqi.
    p. cm. — (NASA History Series) (NASA SP-2011-4110)
  Includes bibliographical references and index.
    1. Chertok, B. E. (Boris Evseevich), 1912– 2. Astronautics—
Soviet Union—Biography. 3. Aerospace engineers—Soviet Union—
Biography. 4. Astronautics—Soviet Union—History.
I. Siddiqi, Asif A., 1966– II. Title. III. Series. IV. SP-2011-4110.
TL789.85.C48C4813 2011
629.1'092—dc22

I dedicate this book

to the cherished memory

of my wife and friend,

Yekaterina Semyonova Golubkina.

Contents

Series Introduction

In an extraordinary century, Academician Boris Yevseyevich Chertok has lived an extraordinary life. He has witnessed and participated in many important technological milestones of the 20th century, and in these volumes, he recollects them with clarity, humanity, and humility. Chertok began his career as an electrician in 1930 at an aviation factory near Moscow. Thirty years later, he was one of the senior designers in charge of the Soviet Union's crowning achievement as a space power: the launch of Yuriy Gagarin, the world's first space voyager. Chertok's 60-year-long career, punctuated by the extraordinary accomplishments of both Sputnik and Gagarin, and continuing to the many successes and failures of the Soviet space program, constitutes the core of his memoirs, *Rockets and People*. In these four volumes, Academician Chertok not only describes and remembers, but also elicits and extracts profound insights from an epic story about a society's quest to explore the cosmos.

Academician Chertok's memoirs, forged from experience in the Cold War, provide a compelling perspective into a past that is indispensable to understanding the present relationship between the American and Russian space programs. From the end of World War II to the present day, the missile and space efforts of the United States and the Soviet Union (and now Russia) have been inextricably linked. As such, although Chertok's work focuses exclusively on Soviet programs to explore space, it also prompts us to reconsider the entire history of spaceflight, both Russian and American.

Chertok's narrative underlines how, from the beginning of the Cold War, the rocketry projects of the two nations evolved in independent but parallel paths. Chertok's first-hand recollections of the extraordinary Soviet efforts to collect, catalog, and reproduce German rocket technology after World War II provide a parallel view to what historian John Gimbel has called the Western "exploitation and plunder" of German technology after the war.[1] Chertok describes how the Soviet design team under the famous Chief Designer Sergey Pavlovich Korolev quickly outgrew German missile technology. By the late 1950s, his team produced the majestic R-7, the world's first intercontinental ballistic missile. Using this rocket, the Soviet Union launched the first Sputnik satellite on 4 October 1957 from a launch site in remote central Asia.

The early Soviet accomplishments in space exploration, particularly the launch of Sputnik in 1957 and the remarkable flight of Yuriy Gagarin in 1961, were benchmarks of the Cold War. Spurred by the Soviet successes, the United States formed a governmental agency, the National Aeronautics and Space Administration (NASA), to conduct civilian space exploration. As a result of Gagarin's triumphant flight, in 1961, the Kennedy administration charged NASA to achieve the goal of "landing a man on the Moon and returning him safely to the Earth before the end of the decade."[2] Such an achievement would demonstrate American supremacy in the arena of spaceflight at a time when both American and Soviet politicians believed that victory in space would be tantamount to preeminence on the global stage. The space programs of both countries grew in leaps and bounds in the 1960s, but the Americans crossed the finish line first when Apollo astronauts Neil A. Armstrong and Edwin E. "Buzz" Aldrin, Jr., disembarked on the Moon's surface in July 1969.

Shadowing Apollo's success was an absent question: What happened to the Soviets who had succeeded so brilliantly with Sputnik and Gagarin? Unknown to most, the Soviets tried and failed to reach the Moon in a secret program that came to naught. As a result of that disastrous failure, the Soviet Union pursued a gradual and consistent space station program in the 1970s and 1980s that eventually led to the *Mir* space station. The Americans developed a reusable space transportation system known as the Space Shuttle. Despite their seemingly separate paths, the space programs of the two powers remained dependent on each other for rationale and direction. When the Soviet Union disintegrated in 1991, cooperation replaced competition as the two countries embarked on a joint program to establish the first permanent human habitation in space through the International Space Station (ISS).

Academician Chertok's reminiscences are particularly important because he played key roles in almost every major milestone of the Soviet missile and

---

1. John Gimbel, *Science, Technology, and Reparations: Exploitation and Plunder in Postwar Germany* (Stanford: Stanford University Press, 1990).

2. U.S. Congress, Senate Committee on Aeronautical and Space Sciences, *Documents on International Aspects of the Exploration and Uses of Outer Space, 1954–1962*, 88th Cong., 1st sess., S. Doc. 18 (Washington, DC: GPO, 1963), pp. 202–204.

space programs, from the beginning of World War II to the dissolution of the Soviet Union in 1991. During the war, he served on the team that developed the Soviet Union's first rocket-powered airplane, the BI. In the immediate aftermath of the war, Chertok, then in his early 30s, played a key role in studying and collecting captured German rocket technology. In the latter days of the Stalinist era, he worked to develop long-range missiles as deputy chief engineer of the main research institute, the NII-88 (pronounced "nee-88") near Moscow. In 1956, Korolev's famous OKB-1 design bureau spun off from the institute and assumed a leading position in the emerging Soviet space program. As a deputy chief designer at OKB-1, Chertok continued with his contributions to the most important Soviet space projects of the day: the Vostok; the Voskhod; the Soyuz; the world's first space station, Salyut; the Energiya superbooster; and the Buran space shuttle.

Chertok's emergence from the secret world of the Soviet military-industrial complex, into his current status as the most recognized living legacy of the Soviet space program, coincided with the dismantling of the Soviet Union as a political entity. Throughout most of his career, Chertok's name remained a state secret. When he occasionally wrote for the public, he used the pseudonym "Boris Yevseyev."[3] Like others writing on the Soviet space program during the Cold War, Chertok was not allowed to reveal any institutional or technical details in his writings. What the state censors permitted for publication said little; one could read a book several hundred pages long comprising nothing beyond tedious and long personal anecdotes between anonymous participants extolling the virtues of the Communist Party. The formerly immutable limits on free expression in the Soviet Union irrevocably expanded only after Mikhail Gorbachev's rise to power in 1985 and the introduction of *glasnost'* (openness).

Chertok's name first appeared in print in the newspaper *Izvestiya* in an article commemorating the 30th anniversary of the launch of Sputnik in 1987. In a wide-ranging interview on the creation of Sputnik, Chertok spoke with the utmost respect for his former boss, the late Korolev. He also eloquently balanced love for his country with criticisms of the widespread inertia and inefficiency that characterized late-period Soviet society.[4] His first written works in the *glasnost'* period, published in early 1988 in the Air Force journal *Aviatsiya i kosmonavtika* [*Aviation and Cosmonautics*], underlined Korolev's central role

---

3. See, for example, his article "Chelovek or avtomat?" ["Human or Automation?"] in the book M. Vasilyev, ed., *Shagi k zvezdam* [*Footsteps to the Stars*] (Moscow: Molodaya gvardiya, 1972), pp. 281–287.
4. B. Konovalov, "Ryvok k zvezdam" ["Dash to the Stars"], *Izvestiya* (1 October 1987): 3.

in the foundation and growth of the Soviet space program.⁵ By this time, it
was as if all the patched up straps that held together a stagnant empire were
falling apart one by one; even as Russia was in the midst of one of its most
historic transformations, the floodgates of free expression were transforming
the country's own history. People like Chertok were now free to speak about
their experiences with candor. Readers could now learn about episodes such
as Korolev's brutal incarceration in the late 1930s, the dramatic story behind
the fatal space mission of *Soyuz-1* in 1967, and details of the failed and abandoned Moon project in the 1960s.⁶ Chertok himself shed light on a missing
piece of history in a series of five articles published in *Izvestiya* in early 1992
on the German contribution to the foundation of the Soviet missile program
after World War II.⁷

Using these works as a starting point, Academician Chertok began working
on his memoirs. Originally, he had only intended to write about his experiences from the postwar years in one volume, maybe two. Readers responded so
positively to the first volume, *Rakety i lyudi* [*Rockets and People*], published in
1994, that Chertok continued to write, eventually producing four substantial
volumes, published in 1996, 1997, and 1999, covering the entire history of
the Soviet missile and space programs.⁸

---

5. B. Chertok, "Lider" ["Leader"], *Aviatsiya i kosmonavtika* no. 1 (1988): 30–31 and no.
2 (1988): 40–41.

6. For early references to Korolev's imprisonment, see Ye. Manucharova, "Kharakter
glavnogo konstruktora" ["The Character of the Chief Designer"], *Izvestiya* (11 January 1987):
3. For early revelations on *Soyuz-1* and the Moon program, see L. N. Kamanin, "Zvezdy
Komarova" ["Komarov's Star"], *Poisk* no. 5 (June 1989): 4–5, and L. N. Kamanin, "S zemli na
lunu i obratno" ["From the Earth to the Moon and Back"], *Poisk* no. 12 (July 1989): 7–8.

7. *Izvestiya* correspondent Boris Konovalov prepared these publications, which had the
general title "U Sovetskikh raketnykh triumfov bylo nemetskoye nachalo" ["Soviets Rocket
Triumphs Had German Origins"]. See *Izvestiya*, 4 March 1992, p. 5; 5 March 1992, p. 5;
6 March 1992, p. 5; 7 March 1992, p. 5; and 9 March 1992, p. 3. Konovalov also published a
sixth article on the German contribution to American rocketry. See "U amerikanskikh raketnykh
triumfov takzhe bylo nemetskoye nachalo" ["American Rocket Triumphs Also Had German
Origins"], *Izvestiya* (10 March 1992): 7. Konovalov later synthesized the five original articles
into a longer work that included the reminiscences of other participants in the German mission
such as Vladimir Barmin and Vasiliy Mishin. See Boris Konovalov, *Tayna Sovetskogo raketnogo
oruzhiya* [*Secrets of Soviet Rocket Armaments*] (Moscow: ZEVS, 1992).

8. *Rakety i lyudi* [*Rockets and People*] (Moscow: Mashinostroyeniye, 1994); *Rakety i lyudi:
Fili Podlipki Tyuratam* [*Rockets and People: Fili Podlipki Tyuratam*] (Moscow: Mashinostroyeniye,
1996); *Rakety i lyudi: goryachiye dni kholodnoy voyny* [*Rockets and People: Hot Days of the Cold
War*] (Moscow: Mashinostroyeniye, 1997); *Rakety i lyudi: lunnaya gonka* [*Rockets and People:
The Moon Race*] (Moscow: Mashinostroyeniye, 1999). All four volumes were subsequently
translated and published in Germany.

My initial interest in the memoirs was purely historical: I was fascinated by the wealth of technical arcana in the books, specifically projects and concepts that had remained hidden throughout much of the Cold War. Those interested in dates, statistics, and the "nuts and bolts" of history will find much that is useful in these pages. As I continued to read, however, I became engrossed by the overall rhythm of Academician Chertok's narrative, which gave voice and humanity to a story ostensibly about mathematics and technology. In his writings, I found a richness that had been nearly absent in most of the disembodied, clinical, and often speculative writing by Westerners studying the Soviet space program. Because of Chertok's storytelling skills, his memoir is a much-needed corrective to the outdated Western view of Soviet space achievements as a mishmash of propaganda, self-delusion, and Cold War rhetoric. In Chertok's story, we meet real people with real dreams who achieved extraordinary successes under very difficult conditions.

Chertok's reminiscences are remarkably sharp and descriptive. In being self-reflective, Chertok avoids the kind of solipsistic ruminations that often characterize memoirs. He is both proud of his country's accomplishments and willing to admit failings with honesty. For example, Chertok juxtaposes accounts of the famous aviation exploits of Soviet pilots in the 1930s, especially those to the Arctic, with the much darker costs of the Great Terror in the late 1930s when Stalin's vicious purges decimated the Soviet aviation industry.

Chertok's descriptive powers are particularly evident in describing the chaotic nature of the Soviet mission to recover and collect rocketry equipment in Germany after World War II. Interspersed with his contemporary diary entries, his language conveys the combination of joy, confusion, and often anticlimax that the end of the war presaged for Soviet representatives in Germany. In one breath, Chertok and his team are looking for hidden caches of German matériel in an underground mine, while in another they are face to face with the deadly consequences of a soldier who had raped a young German woman (Volume I, Chapter 21).[9] There are many such seemingly incongruous anecdotes during Chertok's time in Germany, from the experience of visiting the Nazi slave labor camp at Dora soon after liberation in 1945, to the deportation of hundreds of German scientists to the USSR in 1946. Chertok's massive work is of great consequence for another reason—he cogently provides context. Since the breakup of the Soviet Union in 1991, many participants have openly written

---

9. For the problem of rape in occupied Germany after the war, see Norman M. Naimark, *The Russians in Germany: A History of the Soviet Zone of Occupation, 1945–1949* (Cambridge, MA: The Belknap Press of Harvard University Press, 1995), pp. 69–140.

about their experiences, but few have successfully placed Soviet space achievements in the broader context of the history of Soviet science, the history of the Soviet military-industrial complex, or indeed Soviet history in general.[10] The volumes of memoirs compiled by the Russian State Archive of Scientific-Technical Documentation in the early 1990s under the series *Dorogi v kosmos* [*Roads to Space*] provided an undeniably rich and in-depth view of the origins of the Soviet space program, but they were, for the most part, personal narratives, i.e., fish-eye views of the world around them.[11] Chertok's memoirs are a rare exception in that they strive to locate the Soviet missile and space program in the fabric of broader social, political, industrial, and scientific developments in the former Soviet Union.

This combination—Chertok's participation in the most important Soviet space achievements, his capacity to lucidly communicate them to the reader, and his skill in providing a broader social context—makes this work, in my opinion, one of the most important memoirs written by a veteran of the Soviet space program. The series will also be an important contribution to the history of Soviet science and technology.[12]

In reading Academician Chertok's recollections, we should not lose sight of the fact that these chapters, although full of history, have their particular

---

10. For the two most important histories of the Soviet military-industrial complex, see N. S. Simonov, *Voyenno-promyshlennyy kompleks SSSR v 1920-1950-ye gody: tempy ekonomicheskogo rosta, struktura, organizatsiya proizvodstva i upravleniye* [*The Military-Industrial Complex of the USSR in the 1920s to 1950s: Rate of Economic Growth, Structure, Organization of Production and Control*] (Moscow: ROSSPEN, 1996), and I. V. Bystrova, *Voyenno-promyshlennyy kompleks sssr v gody kholodnoy voyny (vtoraya polovina 40-kh – nachalo 60-kh godov)* [*The Military-Industrial Complex of the USSR in the Years of the Cold War (The Late 1940s to the Early 1960s)*] (Moscow: IRI RAN, 2000). For a history in English that builds on these seminal works and complements them with original research, see John Barber and Mark Harrison, eds., *The Soviet Defence-Industry Complex from Stalin to Khrushchev* (Houndmills, U.K.: Macmillan Press, 2000).

11. Yu. A. Mozzhorin et al., eds., *Dorogi v kosmos: Vospominaniya veteranov raketno-kosmicheskoy tekhniki i kosmonavtiki, tom I i II* [*Roads to Space: Recollections of Veterans of Rocket-Space Technology and Cosmonautics: Volumes I and II*] (Moscow: MAI, 1992), and Yu. A. Mozzhorin et al., eds., *Nachalo kosmicheskoy ery: vospominaniya veteranov raketno-kosmicheskoy tekhniki i kosmonavtiki: vypusk vtoroy* [*The Beginning of the Space Era: Recollections of Veterans of Rocket-Space Technology and Cosmonautics: Second Issue*] (Moscow: RNITsKD, 1994). For a poorly translated and edited English version of the series, see John Rhea, ed., *Roads to Space: An Oral History of the Soviet Space Program* (New York: Aviation Week Group, 1995).

12. For key works on the history of Soviet science and technology, see Kendall E. Bailes, *Technology and Society Under Lenin and Stalin: Origins of the Soviet Technical Intelligentsia, 1917–1941* (Princeton, NJ: Princeton University Press, 1978); Loren R. Graham, *Science in Russia and the Soviet Union: A Short History* (Cambridge, U.K.: Cambridge University Press, 1993); and Nikolai Krementsov, *Stalinist Science* (Princeton, NJ: Princeton University Press, 1997).

perspective. In conveying to us the complex vista of the Soviet space program, he has given us one man's memories of a huge undertaking. Other participants of these very same events will remember things differently. Soviet space history, like any discipline of history, exists as a continuous process of revision and restatement. Few historians in the 21st century would claim to be completely objective.[13] Memoirists would make even less of a claim to the "truth." In his introduction, Chertok acknowledges this, saying, "I...must warn the reader that in no way do I have pretensions to the laurels of a scholarly historian. Correspondingly, my books are not examples of strict historical research. In any memoirs, narrative and thought are inevitably subjective." Chertok ably illustrates, however, that avoiding the pursuit of scholarly history does not necessarily lessen the relevance of his story, especially because it represents the opinion of an influential member of the postwar scientific and technical intelligentsia in the Soviet Union.

Some, for example, might not share Chertok's strong belief in the power of scientists and engineers to solve social problems, a view that influenced many who sought to transform the Soviet Union with modern science after the Russian Revolution in 1917. Historians of Soviet science such as Loren Graham have argued that narrowly technocratic views of social development cost the Soviet Union dearly.[14] Technological hubris was, of course, not unique to the Soviet scientific community, but absent democratic processes of accountability, many huge Soviet government projects—such as the construction of the Great Dnepr Dam and the great Siberian railway in the 1970s and 1980s—ended up as costly failures with many adverse social and environmental repercussions. Whether one agrees or disagrees with Chertok's views, they are important to understand because they represent the ideas of a generation who passionately believed in the power of science to eliminate the ills of society. As such, his memoirs add an important dimension to understanding the *mentalité* of the Soviets' drive to become a modern, industrialized state in the 20th century.

Chertok's memoirs are part of the second generation of publications on Soviet space history, one that eclipsed the (heavily censored) first generation published during the Communist era. Memoirs constituted a large part of the second generation. In the 1990s, when it was finally possible to write candidly

---

13. For the American historical discipline's relationship to the changing standards of objectivity, see Peter Novick, *That Noble Dream: The "Objectivity" Question and the American Historical Profession* (Cambridge, U.K.: Cambridge University Press, 1988).

14. For technological hubris, see for example, Loren Graham, *The Ghost of the Executed Engineer: Technology and the Fall of the Soviet Union* (Cambridge, MA: Harvard University Press, 1993).

about Soviet space history, a wave of personal recollections flooded the market. Not only Boris Chertok, but also such luminaries as Vasiliy Mishin, Kerim Kerimov, Boris Gubanov, Yuriy Mozzhorin, Konstantin Feoktistov, Vyacheslav Filin, and others finally published their reminiscences.[15] Official organizational histories and journalistic accounts complemented these memoirs, written by individuals with access to secret archival documents. Yaroslav Golovanov's magisterial *Korolev: Fakty i Mify* [*Korolev: Facts and Myths*], as well as key institutional works from the Energiya corporation and the Russian Military Space Forces, added richly to the canon.[16] The diaries of Air Force General Nikolay Kamanin from the 1960s to the early 1970s, published in four volumes in the late 1990s, also gave scholars a candid look at the vicissitudes of the Soviet human spaceflight program.[17]

The flood of works in Russian allowed Westerners to publish the first works in English. Memoirs—for example, from Sergey Khrushchev and Roald Sagdeyev—appeared in their English translations. James Harford published his 1997 biography of Sergey Korolev based upon extensive interviews with veterans of the Soviet space program.[18] My own book, *Challenge to Apollo: The Soviet*

---

15. V. M. Filin, *Vospominaniya o lunnom korablye* [*Recollections on the Lunar Ship*] (Moscow: Kultura, 1992); Kerim Kerimov, *Dorogi v kosmos (zapiski predsedatelya Gosudarstvennoy komissii)* [*Roads to Space (Notes of the Chairman of the State Commission)*] (Baku, Azerbaijan: 1995); V. M. Filin, *Put k 'Energii'* [*Path to Energiya*] (Moscow: 'GRAAL,' 1996); V. P. Mishin, *Ot sozdaniya ballisticheskikh raket k raketno-kosmicheskomu mashinostroyeniyu* [*From the Creation of the Ballistic Rocket to Rocket-Space Machine Building*] (Moscow: 'Inform-Znaniye,' 1998); B. I. Gubanov, *Triumf i tragediya 'energii': razmyshleniya glavnogo konstruktora* [*The Triumph and Tragedy of Energiya: The Reflections of a Chief Designer*] (Nizhniy novgorod: NIER, four volumes in 1998–2000); Konstantin Feoktistov, *Trayektoriya zhizni: mezhdu vchera i zavtra* [*Life's Trajectory: Between Yesterday and Tomorrow*] (Moscow: Vagrius, 2000); N. A. Anifimov, ed., *Tak eto bylo—Memuary Yu. A. Mozzhorin: Mozzhorin v vospominaniyakh sovremennikov* [*How It Was—Memoirs of Yu. A. Mozzhorin: Mozzhorin in the Recollections of His Contemporaries*] (Moscow: ZAO 'Mezhdunarodnaya programma obrazovaniya, 2000).

16. Yaroslav Golovanov, *Korolev: fakty i mify* [*Korolev: Facts and Myths*] (Moscow: Nauka, 1994); Yu. P. Semenov, ed., *Raketno-Kosmicheskaya Korporatsiya "Energiya" imeni S. P. Koroleva* [*Energiya Rocket-Space Corporation Named After S. P. Korolev*] (Korolev: RKK Energiya, 1996); V. V. Favorskiy and I. V. Meshcheryakov, eds., *Voyenno-kosmicheskiye sily (voyenno-istoricheskiy trud): kniga I* [*Military-Space Forces (A Military-Historical Work): Book I*] (Moscow: VKS, 1997). Subsequent volumes were published in 1998 and 2001.

17. The first published volume was N. P. Kamanin, *Skrytiy kosmos: kniga pervaya, 1960–1963 gg.* [*Hidden Space: Book One, 1960–1963*] (Moscow: Infortekst IF, 1995). Subsequent volumes covering 1964–66, 1967–68, and 1969–78 were published in 1997, 1999, and 2001 respectively.

18. Sergey N. Khrushchev, *Nikita Khrushchev and the Creation of a Superpower* (University Park, PA: The Pennsylvania State University Press, 2000); Roald Z. Sagdeyev, *The Making of a Soviet Scientist: My Adventures in Nuclear Fusion and Space from Stalin to Star Wars* (New York: John Wiley & Sons, 1993); James Harford, *Korolev: How One Man Masterminded the Soviet Drive to Beat America to the Moon* (New York: John Wiley & Sons, 1997).

Union and the Space Race, 1945–1974, was an early attempt to synthesize the wealth of information and narrate a complete history of the early Soviet human spaceflight program.[19] Steven Zaloga provided an indispensable counterpoint to these space histories in *The Kremlin's Nuclear Sword: The Rise and Fall of Russia's Strategic Nuclear Forces, 1945–2000*, which reconstructed the story of the Soviet efforts to develop strategic weapons.[20]

With any new field of history that is bursting with information based primarily on recollection and interviews, there are naturally many contradictions and inconsistencies. For example, even on such a seemingly trivial issue as the name of the earliest institute in Soviet-occupied Germany, "Institute Rabe," there is no firm agreement on the reason it was given this title. Chertok's recollections contradict the recollection of another Soviet veteran, Georgiy Dyadin.[21] In another case, many veterans have claimed that artillery general Lev Gaydukov's meeting with Stalin in 1945 was a key turning point in the early Soviet missile program; Stalin apparently entrusted Gaydukov with the responsibility to choose an industrial sector to assign the development of long-range rockets (Volume I, Chapter 22). Lists of visitors to Stalin's office during that period—declassified only very recently—do not, however, show that Gaydukov ever met with Stalin in 1945.[22] Similarly, many Russian sources note that the "Second Main Directorate" of the USSR Council of Ministers managed Soviet missile development in the early 1950s, when in fact, this body actually supervised uranium procurement for the A-bomb project.[23] In many cases, memoirs provide different and contradictory information on the very same event (different dates, designations, locations, people involved, etc.).

Academician Chertok's wonderful memoirs point to a solution to these discrepancies: a "third generation" of Soviet space history, one that builds

19. Asif A. Siddiqi, *Challenge to Apollo: The Soviet Union and the Space Race, 1945–1974* (Washington, DC: NASA SP-2000-4408, 2000). The book was republished as a two-volume work as *Sputnik and the Soviet Space Challenge* (Gainesville, FL: University Press of Florida, 2003) and *The Soviet Space Race with Apollo* (Gainesville, FL: University Press of Florida, 2003).

20. Steven J. Zaloga, *The Kremlin's Nuclear Sword: The Rise and Fall of Russia's Strategic Nuclear Forces, 1945–2000* (Washington, DC: Smithsonian Institution Press, 2002).

21. G. V. Dyadin, D. N. Filippovykh, and V. I. Ivkin, *Pamyatnyye starty* [*Memorable Launches*] (Moscow: TsIPK, 2001), p. 69.

22. A. V. Korotkov, A. D. Chernev, and A. A. Chernobayev, "Alfavitnyi ukazatel posetitelei kremlevskogo kabineta I. V. Stalina" ["Alphabetical List of Visitors to the Kremlin Office of I. V. Stalin"], *Istoricheskii arkhiv* no. 4 (1998): 50.

23. Vladislav Zubok and Constantine Pleshakov, *Inside the Kremlin's Cold War: From Stalin to Khrushchev* (Cambridge, MA: Harvard University Press), p. 172; Golovanov, *Korolev*, p. 454. For the correct citation on the Second Main Directorate, established on 27 December 1949, see Simonov, *Voyenno-promyshlennyy kompleks sssr*, pp. 225–226.

on the rich trove of the first and second generations but is primarily based on *documentary* evidence. During the Soviet era, historians could not write history based on documents since they could not obtain access to state and design bureau archives. As the Soviet Union began to fall apart, historians such as Georgiy Vetrov began to take the first steps in document-based history. Vetrov, a former engineer at Korolev's design bureau, eventually compiled and published two extraordinary collections of primary documents relating to Korolev's legacy.[24] Now that all the state archives in Moscow—such as the State Archive of the Russian Federation (GARF), the Russian State Archive of the Economy (RGAE), and the Archive of the Russian Academy of Sciences (ARAN)—are open to researchers, more results of this "third generation" are beginning to appear. German historians such as Matthias Uhl and Christoph Mick and those in the United States such as myself have been fortunate to work in Russian archives.[25] I would also note the enormous contributions of the Russian monthly journal *Novosti kosmonavtiki* [*News of Cosmonautics*] as well as the Belgian historian Bart Hendrickx in advancing the state of Soviet space history. The new work has opened opportunities for future research. For example, we no longer have to guess about the government's decision to approve development of the Soyuz spacecraft; we can see the original decree issued on 4 December 1963.[26] Similarly, instead of speculating about the famous decree of 3 August 1964 that committed the Soviet Union to competing with the American Apollo program, we can study the actual government

---

24. M. V. Keldysh, ed., *Tvorcheskoye naslediye Akademika Sergeya Pavlovicha Koroleva: izbrannyye trudy i dokumenty* [*The Creative Legacy of Sergey Pavlovich Korolev: Selected Works and Documents*] (Moscow: Nauka, 1980); G. S. Vetrov and B. V. Raushenbakh, eds., *S. P. Korolev i ego delo: svet i teni v istorii kosmonavtiki: izbrannyye trudy i dokumenty* [*S. P. Korolev and His Cause: Shadow and Light in the History of Cosmonautics*] (Moscow: Nauka, 1998). For two other published collections of primary documents, see V. S. Avduyevskiy and T. M. Eneyev, eds. *M. V. Keldysh: izbrannyye trudy: raketnaya tekhnika i kosmonavtika* [*M. V. Keldysh: Selected Works: Rocket Technology and Cosmonautics*] (Moscow: Nauka, 1988), and B. V. Raushenbakh, ed., *Materialy po istorii kosmicheskogo korablya 'vostok': k 30-letiyu pervogo poleta cheloveka v kosmicheskoye prostranstvo* [*Materials on the History of the 'Vostok' Space Ship: On the 30th Anniversary of the First Flight of a Human in Space*] (Moscow: Nauka, 1991).

25. Matthias Uhl, *Stalins V-2: Der Technolgietransfer der deutschen Fernlen-kwaffentechnik in die UdSSR und der Aufbau der sowjetischen Raketenindustrie 1945 bis 1959* (Bonn, Germany: Bernard & Graefe-Verlag, 2001); Christoph Mick, *Forschen für Stalin: Deutsche Fachleute in der sowjetischen Rüstungsindustrie 1945–1958* (Munich: R. Oldenbourg, 2000); Asif A. Siddiqi, "The Rockets' Red Glare: Spaceflight and the Russian Imagination, 1857–1957" (Ph.D. diss., Carnegie Mellon University, 2004).

26. "O sozdaniia kompleksa 'Soyuz' " ["On the Creation of the Soyuz Complex"], 4 December 1963, RGAE, f. 298, op. 1, d. 3495, ll. 167–292.

document issued on that date.[27] Academician Chertok deserves much credit for opening the doors for future historians, since his memoirs have guided many to look even deeper.

The distribution of material spanning the four volumes of Chertok's memoirs is roughly chronological. In the first English volume, Chertok describes his childhood, his formative years as an engineer at the aviation Plant No. 22 in Fili, his experiences during World War II, and the mission to Germany in 1945–46 to study captured German missile technology.

In the second volume, he continues the story with his return to the Soviet Union, the reproduction of a Soviet version of the German V-2 and the development of a domestic Soviet rocket industry at the famed NII-88 institute in the Moscow suburb of Podlipki (now called Korolev). He describes the development of the world's first intercontinental ballistic missile (ICBM), the R-7; the launch of Sputnik; and the first-generation probes sent to the Moon, Mars, and Venus.

In the third volume, he begins with the historic flight of Yuriy Gagarin, the first human in space. He discusses several different aspects of the burgeoning Soviet missile and space programs of the early 1960s, including the development of early ICBMs, reconnaissance satellites, the Cuban missile crisis, the first Soviet communications satellite *Molniya-1*, the early spectacular missions of the Vostok and Voskhod programs, the dramatic Luna program to land a probe on the Moon, and Sergey Korolev's last days. He then continues into chapters about the early development of the Soyuz spacecraft, with an in-depth discussion of the tragic mission of Vladimir Komarov.

The fourth and final volume is largely devoted to the Soviet project to send cosmonauts to the Moon in the 1960s, covering all aspects of the development of the giant N-1 rocket. The last portion of this volume covers the origins of the *Salyut* and *Mir* space station programs, ending with a fascinating description of the massive Energiya-Buran project, developed as a countermeasure to the American Space Shuttle.

It was my great fortune to meet with Academician Chertok in the summer of 2003. During the meeting, Chertok, a sprightly 91 years old, spoke passionately and emphatically about his life's work and remained justifiably proud of the achievements of the Russian space program. As I left the meeting, I was reminded of something that Chertok had said in one of his first public

---

27. "Tsentralnyy komitet KPSS i Sovet ministrov SSSR, postanovleniye" ["Central Committee KPSS and SSSR Council of Ministers Decree"], 3 August 1964, RGAE, f. 29, op. 1, d. 3441, ll. 299–300. For an English-language summary, see Asif A. Siddiqi, "A Secret Uncovered: The Soviet Decision to Land Cosmonauts on the Moon," *Spaceflight* 46 (2004): 205–213.

interviews in 1987. In describing the contradictions of Sergey Korolev's personality, Chertok had noted: "This realist, this calculating, [and] farsighted individual was, in his soul, an incorrigible romantic."[28] Such a description would also be an apt encapsulation of the contradictions of the entire Soviet drive to explore space, one which was characterized by equal amounts of hardheaded realism and romantic idealism. Academician Boris Yevseyevich Chertok has communicated that idea very capably in his memoirs, and it is my hope that we have managed to do justice to his own vision by bringing that story to an English-speaking audience.

ASIF A. SIDDIQI
Series Editor
October 2004

---

28. Konovalov, "Ryvok k zvezdam."

Introduction to Volume IV

IN THIS, THE FOURTH AND FINAL VOLUME OF HIS MEMOIRS, Boris Chertok concludes his monumental trek through a nearly 100-year life. As with the previous English-language volumes, the text has been significantly modified and extended over the original Russian versions published in the 1990s. The first volume covered his childhood, early career, and transformation into a missile engineer by the end of World War II. In the second volume, he took the story up through the birth of the postwar Soviet ballistic-missile program and then the launch of the world's artificial satellite, *Sputnik*. This was followed, in the third volume, by a description of the early and spectacular successes of the Soviet space program in the 1960s, including such unprecedented achievements as the flight of cosmonaut Yuriy Gagarin. The fourth volume concludes his memoirs on the history of the Soviet space program with a lengthy meditation on the failed Soviet human lunar program and then brings the story to a close with the events of the 1970s, 1980s, and 1990s.

In the summer of 1989, Soviet censors finally allowed journalists to write about an episode of Soviet history that had officially never happened: the massive Soviet effort to compete with Apollo in the 1960s to land a human being on the Moon. U.S. President John F. Kennedy had laid down the gauntlet in a speech in May 1961 to recover some of the self-confidence lost by the series of Soviet successes in space in the wake of *Sputnik*. Kennedy's challenge was embodied in an enormous investment in human spaceflight in the 1960s and culminated in the landing of NASA astronauts Neil A. Armstrong and Edwin E. "Buzz" Aldrin, Jr., on the surface of the Moon in 1969 during the *Apollo 11* mission.

Although a number of Western analysts and observers (not to mention U.S. intelligence analysts) suspected that the Soviets had been in the race to the Moon, Soviet spokespersons officially disavowed or rejected the notion that they had tried to preempt the Americans. This façade eventually cracked at the height of *glasnost* ("openness") in the late 1980s. In the summer of 1989, Soviet censors permitted the publication of a number of articles and books that admitted the existence of a *human* lunar program in the 1960s.[1] As more and more information emerged in the early 1990s, some salient features began to emerge: that the program had been massive, that it had involved the development of a super booster known as the N-1, that all efforts to beat the Americans had failed, and that evidence of the program had been whitewashed out of existence.[2]

It has become increasingly clear to historians that it would be impossible to understand the early history of the Soviet space program without accounting for the motivations and operations of the human lunar landing program. By the late 1960s, the N1-L3 project constituted about 20 percent of annual budget expenditures on Soviet space exploration; by some estimates, total spending on the Moon program may have been about 4 to 4.5 billion rubles, which roughly translated to about 12 to 13.5 billion dollars in early 1970s numbers.[3]

But beyond the numbers, the program was undoubtedly one of the most dramatic episodes in the history of the Soviet space program. During the eventful and troubled period that Chertok covers in this volume, from about 1968 to 1974, the Korolev design bureau, now led by the talented but flawed Vasiliy Mishin, stumbled from one setback to another. The heart of the program during these years was the giant N-1 rocket, a massive and continually evolving technological system whose development was hobbled by difficult compromises in technical approaches, fighting between leading chief designers, lack of money, and an absence of commitment from the Soviet military, the primary operator of Soviet space infrastructure.

Chertok begins his narrative with a discussion of the origins of the N-1 in the early 1960s and the acrimonious disagreement between Sergey Korolev, the

---

1. These included Lev Kamanin, "S zemli na lunu i obratno" ["From the Earth to the Moon and Back"], *Poisk* no. 12 (July 1989): 7–8; S. Leskov, "Kak my ne sletali na lunu" ["How We Didn't Fly to the Moon"], *Izvestiya* (18 August, 1989): 3; A. Tarasov, "Polety vo sne i nayvu" ["Flights in Dreams and Reality"], *Pravda* (20 October 1989): 4; and Grigoriy Reznichenko, *Kosmonavt-5 [Cosmonaut-5]* (Moscow: Politicheskoy literatury, 1989).

2. For some early revelations on the Soviet human lunar program, see M. Rebrov, "A delo bylo tak: trudnaya sudba proyekta N-1" ["But Things Were Like That: The Difficult Fate of the N-1 Project"], *Krasnaya zvezda* (13 January 1990); V. P. Mishin, "Pochemu my ne sletali na Lunu?" ["Why Didn't We Land on the Moon?"], *Znanie: seriya Kosmonavtika, Astronomiya* no. 12 (1990): 3–43; S. Leskov, *Kak my ne sletali na lunu [Why We Didn't Land on the Moon]* (Moscow: Panorama, 1991); I. B. Afanasyev, "Neizvestnyye korabli" ["Unknown Spacecraft"], *Znaniye: seriya Kosmonavtika, Astronomiya* no. 12 (1991): 1–64; R. Dolgopyatov, B. Dorofeyev, and S. Kryukov, "Proyekt N-1" ["The N-1 Project"], *Aviatsiya i kosmonavtika* no. 9 (1992): 34–37; and I. B. Afanasyev, "N-1: sovershenno sekretno" ["The N-1: Top Secret"], *Krylya rodiny* no. 9 (1993): 13–16, no. 10 (1993): 1–4, and no. 11 (1993): 4–5.

3. Asif A. Siddiqi, *Challenge to Apollo: The Soviet Union and the Space Race, 1945–1974* (Washington, DC: NASA SP-2000-4408, 2000), p. 838.

chief designer of spacecraft and launch vehicles, and Valentin Glushko, the chief designer of liquid-propellant rocket engines. On one level, theirs was a disagreement over arcane technical issues, particularly over the choice of propellants for the N-1, but at a deeper level, the dispute involved fundamental differences over the future of the Soviet space program. Korolev and Glushko's differences over propellants date back to the 1930s when Glushko had embraced storable, hypergolic, and toxic propellants for his innovative engines. By the 1940s, Korolev, meanwhile, had begun to favor cryogenic propellants and believed that a particular cryogenic combination, liquid hydrogen and liquid oxygen, was the most efficient way forward. Korolev was not alone in this belief. In the United States, NASA had invested significant amounts in developing such engines, but Glushko had an important ally on his side, the military. When Korolev and Glushko refused to come to an agreement, a third party, Nikolay Kuznetsov's design bureau in the city of Kuybyshev (now Samara), was tasked with the critical assignment to develop the engines of the N-1.

Having known both Korolev and Glushko, Chertok has much to say about the relationship between the two giants of the Soviet space program. Contrary to much innuendo that their relationship was marred by the experience of the Great Terror in the late 1930s, Chertok shows that they enjoyed a collegial and friendly rapport well into the 1950s. He reproduces a congratulatory telegram (in Chapter 3) from Korolev to Glushko upon the latter's election as a corresponding member of the Academy of Sciences. It obviously reflects a warmth and respect in their relationship that completely disappeared by the early 1960s as the N-1 program ground down in rancorous meetings and angry memos.

Chertok has much to say about the development of the so-called KORD system, designed to control and synchronize the operation of the 42 engines on the first three changes of the giant rocket (see Chapters 5 and 7, especially). One of the main challenges of developing the N-1's engines was the decision to forego integrated ground testing of the first stage, a critical lapse in judgment that could have saved the engineers from the many launch accidents.

Chertok's descriptions of the four launches of the N-1 (two in 1969, one in 1971, and one in 1972) are superb. He delves into great technical detail but also brings into relief all the human emotions of the thousands of engineers, managers, and servicemen and -women involved in these massive undertakings. His accounts are particularly valuable for giving details of the process of investigations into the disasters, thus providing a unique perspective into how the technical frequently intersected with the political and the personal. His account in Chapter 17 of the investigation into the last N-1 failure in 1972 confirms that the process was fractured by factional politics, one side representing the makers of the rocket (the Mishin design bureau) and other representing the engine makers (the Kuznetsov design bureau). Some from the former, such as Vasiliy Mishin, made the critical error of allying themselves with the latter, which contributed to their downfall. Historians have plenty of examples of the impossibility of separating out such technological, political, and personal factors in the function of large-scale technological systems, but Chertok's descriptions give a previously unseen perspective into the operation of Soviet "Big Science."[4]

Chertok devotes a lengthy portion of the manuscript (five chapters!) to the emergence of the piloted space station program from 1969 to 1971. We see how the station program, later called Salyut, was essentially a "rebel" movement within the Mishin design bureau to salvage something substantive in the aftermath of two failed launches of the N-1. These "rebels," who included Chertok himself, were able to appropriate hardware originally developed for a military space station program known as Almaz—developed by the design bureau of Vladimir Chelomey—and use it as a foundation to develop a "quick" civilian space station. This act effectively redirected resources from the faltering human lunar program into a new stream of work—piloted Earth orbital stations—that became the mainstay of the Soviet (and later Russian) space program for the next 40 years. The station that Mishin's engineers designed and launched—the so-called Long-Duration Orbital Station (DOS)—became the basis for the series of Salyut stations launched in the 1970s and 1980s, the core of the *Mir* space station launched in 1986, and eventually the *Zvezda* core of the International Space Station (ISS). In that respect, Chertok's story is extremely important; when historians write the history of ISS, they will have to go back to the events of 1969 and 1970 to understand how and why the Russian segments look and operate the way they do.

Chertok's account of the dramatic mission of *Soyuz-11* in the summer of 1971 is particularly moving. The flight began with an episode that would haunt the living: in the days leading up the launch, the primary crew of Aleksey Leonov, Valeriy Kubasov, and Petr Kolodin were replaced by the backup crew of Georgiy Dobrovolskiy, Vladislav Volkov, and Viktor Patsayev when Kubasov apparently developed a problem in his lungs. The original backup crew flew the mission and dealt with some taxing challenges such as a fire on board the station and personality conflicts, and then they were tragically killed on reentry when the pressurized atmosphere of the Soyuz spacecraft was sucked out due

---

4. For important literature on large-scale technological systems, see particularly Thomas P. Hughes, *Networks of Power: Electrification in Western Society, 1880–1930* (Baltimore: Johns Hopkins University Press, 1983); Wiebe E. Bijker, Thomas P. Hughes, and Trevor J. Pinch, eds., *The Social Construction of Technological Systems* (Cambridge, MA: MIT Press, 1987); and Thomas P. Hughes, *Rescuing Prometheus* (New York: Pantheon Books, 1998).

to an unexpected leak. The funeral of these three cosmonauts was made all the more painful for, only days before, Chertok had lost one of his closest lifelong friends, the engine chief designer Aleksey Isayev (see Chapter 16).

A chapter near the end of the manuscript is devoted to the cataclysmic changes in the management of the Soviet space program that took place in 1974: Mishin was fired from his post, the giant Korolev and Glushko organizations were combined into a single entity known as NPO Energiya, and Glushko was put in charge. These changes also coincided with the suspension of the N-1 program and the beginning of what would evolve in later years into the Energiya-Buran reusable space transportation system, another enormously expensive endeavor that would yield very little for the Soviet space program. Since the early 1990s, there have appeared many conflicting accounts of this turning point in 1974, but Chertok's description adds a useful perspective on the precise evolution from the death of the N-1 to the beginning of Energiya-Buran.[5] A recent collection of primary source documents on Glushko's engineering work suggests that Glushko came to the table with incredibly ambitious plans to replace the N-1 and that these plans had to be downsized significantly by the time that the final decree on the system was issued in February 1976.[6]

In a final chapter (Chapter 18) on the later years of the Soviet space program, Chertok picks through a number of important episodes to highlight the tension between human and automatic control of human spacecraft. These included the failed *Soyuz-2/3* docking in 1968, the short-lived flight of DOS-3 (known as *Kosmos-557*) in 1973, a series of failed dockings of crews flying to Salyut space stations (including *Soyuz-15* in 1974, *Soyuz-23* in 1976, and *Soyuz-25* in 1977) as well as successful dockings (including *Soyuz T-2* in 1980 and *Soyuz T-6* in 1982). All of these accounts underscore the enormous investments the Soviets made in rendezvous and docking systems and procedures that have paid off in the ISS era, when no Russian spacecraft has ever failed to ultimately dock with its target.

---

5. For other accounts on this period, see B. I. Gubanov, *Triumf i tragediya "Energii": razmyshleniya glavnogo konstruktora*, t. 4 [*The Triumph and Tragedy of Energiya: Reflections of a Chief Designer*, Vol. 4] (Nizhniy Novgorod: NIEP, 1999); V. M. Filin, *Put k "Energii"* [*Road to Energiya*] (Moscow: Logos, 2001); Bart Hendrickx and Bert Vis, *Energiya-Buran: The Soviet Space Shuttle* (Chichester, U.K.: Springer-Praxis, 2007); V. P. Lukashevich and I. B. Afanasyev, *Kosmicheskaya krylya* [*Space Wings*] (Moscow: OOO LenTa Stranstviy, 2009).

6. See the three-volume set titled *Izbrannyye raboty akademika V. P. Glushko* [*Selected Works of Academician V. P. Glushko*] (Khimki: NPO Energomash imeni akademika V. P. Glushko, 2008).

On the human dimensions of the Soviet space program, Chertok shows a rare ability to make small incidents both evocative and poignant. In Chapter 8, for example, he describes how, during a break while controlling a space mission in 1968, Chertok and his colleagues visited Sevastopol, the site of some of the most brutal fighting during World War II. When a war veteran noticed that Chertok had a "Hero of Socialist Labor" medal pinned on his lapel, he inquired as to why. Chertok explained that he had been honored for his role in the flight of Yuriy Gagarin. Given that Chertok's identity and job were state secrets, this was a rare moment of candor; bursting with pride, the war veteran eloquently equated the sacrifices made during the war with Soviet successes in space, a connection that many made during the 1960s.

I am often asked by interested readers about the relative worth of Chertok's memoirs in the literature on the history of the Soviet space program; in other words, where do these memoirs fit in the broader historiography? Chertok's memoirs stand as probably the *most* important personal account of the history of the Soviet space program. His ability to integrate technical detail, human yearning, high politics, and institutional history makes *Rockets and People* unusual for a memoir of the genre; the breadth of Chertok's recollections, covering nearly 100 years, makes it unique. As I have mentioned elsewhere, in the absence of any syncretic work by a professional historian in the Russian language on the history of the Soviet space program, the contents of *Rockets and People* represent probably the most dominant narrative available.[7] Its availability in both Russian and English means that it will have a significant and enduring quality. That Chertok's memoirs are taken to be important and reliable does not mean, however, that it is the *only* narrative of this history worth considering. In underscoring the significance of Chertok, we should also acknowledge the abundance of other memoirs by Soviet space veterans. Collectively considered, they provide an extremely rich resource for historians. If Chertok represents the starting point for future researchers, I would recommend some other memoirs as crucial both in filling in spaces unexplored by Chertok and in providing a counterpoint to Chertok, especially on those events considered controversial. In this category of essential memoirs, I would include those by the following individuals:

---

7. Asif A. Siddiqi, "Privatising Memory: The Soviet Space Programme Through Museums and Memoirs," in *Showcasing Space: Artefacts Series: Studies in the History of Science and Technology,* ed. Martin Collins and Douglas Millard (London: The Science Museum, 2005), pp. 98–115.

- Vladimir Bugrov, the designer under Korolev (*The Martian Project of S. P. Korolev*, 2006);[8]
- Konstantin Feoktistov, the cosmonaut who played a key role in the design of Vostok, Voskhod, Soyuz, and DOS (*Life's Trajectory*, 2000);[9]
- Oleg Ivanovskiy, the engineer and bureaucrat (*Rockets and Space in the USSR*, 2005);[10]
- Vyacheslav Filin, the designer under Korolev (*Recollections on the Lunar Vehicle*, 1992, and *The Road to Energiya*, 2001);[11]
- Boris Gubanov, the chief designer of the Energiya rocket (*The Triumph and Tragedy of Energiya: Reflections of a Chief Designer*, four volumes in 1999);[12]
- Aleksey Isayev, the rocket engine designer (*First Steps to Space Engines*, 1979);[13]
- Kerim Kerimov, the chairman of the State Commission (*Roads to Space*, 1995);[14]
- Sergey Khrushchev, the son of the Soviet Party Secretary (*Nikita Khrushchev: Crises and Rockets*, 1994);[15]
- Grigoriy Kisunko, the chief designer of antiballistic missile systems (*The Secret Zone*, 1996);[16]
- Sergey Kryukov, the leading designer of the N-1 rocket (*Selected Works*, 2010);[17]
- Vasiliy Mishin, the successor to Korolev (*From the Creation of Ballistic Missiles to Rocket-Space Machine Building*, 1998);[18]

---

8. V. Ye. Bugrov, *Marsianskiy proyekt S. P. Koroleva* (Moscow: Russkiye vityazi, 2006).

9. Konstantin Feoktistov, *Trayektoriya zhizni: mezhdu vchera i zavtra* (Moscow: Vagrius, 2000).

10. Oleg Ivanovskiy, *Rakety i kosmos v sssr: zapiski sekretnogo konstruktora* (Moscow: Molodaya gvardiya, 2005).

11. V. M. Filin, *Vospominaniya o lunnom korablye* (Moscow: Kultura, 1992); V. M. Filin, *Put k "Energii"* (Moscow: Logos, 2001).

12. B. I. Gubanov, *Triumf i tragediya "Energii": razmyshleniya glavnogo konstruktora* (four volumes) (Nizhniy Novgorod: NIEP, 1999).

13. A. M. Isayev, *Pervyye shagi k kosmicheskim dvigatelyam* (Moscow: Mashinostroyeniye, 1979).

14. Kerim Kerimov, *Dorogi v kosmos (zapiski predsedatelya Gosudarstvennoy komissii)* (Baku, Azerbaydzhan: 1995).

15. Sergey Khrushchev, *Nikita Khrushchev: krizisy i rakety: vzglyad iznutri* (two volumes) (Moscow: Novosti, 1994).

16. Grigoriy Kisunko, *Sekretnaya zona: ispoved generalnogo konstruktora* (Moscow: Sovremennik, 1996).

17. S. S. Kryukov, *Izbrannyye raboty: iz lichnogo arkhiva*, ed. A. M. Peslyak (Moscow: MGTU, 2010).

18. V. P. Mishin, *Ot sozdaniya ballisticheskikh raket k raketno-kosmicheskomu mashinostroyeniyu* (Moscow: Informatsionno-izdatel'skiy tsentr "Inform-Znaniye," 1998).

- Yuriy Mozzhorin, the head of the leading space research institute (*How It Was: The Memoirs of Yuriy Mozzhorin*, 2000);[19]
- Arkadiy Ostashev, the senior operations manager (*Testing of Rocket-Space Technology—The Business of My Life*, 2001);[20]
- Boris Pokrovskiy, the senior official in the communications network (*Space Begins on the Ground*, 1996);[21]
- Valentina Ponomareva, the female cosmonaut trainee (*A Female Face in Space*, 2002);[22]
- Vladimir Polyachenko, the leading designer under Vladimir Chelomey (*On the Sea and in Space*, 2008);[23]
- Vladimir Shatalov, the senior cosmonaut and cosmonaut manager (*Space Workdays*, 2008);[24]
- Vladimir Syromyatnikov, the docking system designer under Korolev (*100 Conversations on Docking and on Other Rendezvous in Space and on the Earth*, 2003);[25] and
- Vladimir Yazdovskiy, the senior space biomedicine specialist (*On the Paths of the Universe*, 1996).[26]

I would also include in this category volumes that collect the recollections of dozens of key actors in the Soviet missile and space programs:

- *Academician S. P. Korolev: Scientist, Engineer, Man* (1986);[27] and
- *Roads to Space* (three volumes in 1992 and 1994).[28]

---

19. Yu. A. Mozzhorin et al., eds., *Dorogi v kosmos: Vospominaniya veteranov raketno-kosmicheskoy tekhniki i kosmonavtiki* (two volumes) (Moscow: MAI, 1992); Yu. A. Mozzhorin et al., eds., *Nachalo kosmicheskoy ery: vospominaniya veteranov raketno-kosmicheskoy tekhniki i kosmonavtiki: vypusk vtoroy* (Moscow: RNITsKD, 1994); N. A. Anfimov, ed., *Tak eto bylo…: Memuary Yu. A. Mozzhorin: Mozzhorin v vospominaniyakh sovremennikov* (Moscow: ZAO "Mezhdunarodnaya programma obrazovaniya," 2000).

20. V. A. Polyachenko, *Na morye i v kosmosye* (St. Petersburg: Morsar Av, 2008).

21. B. A. Pokrovskiy, *Kosmos nachinayetsya na zemlye* (Moscow: Izdatelstvo Patriot, 1996).

22. V. Ponomareva, *Zhenskoye litso kosmosa* (Moscow: Gelios, 2002).

23. A. I. Ostashev, *Ispytatelniye raketno-kosmicheskoye tekhniki: delo moyey zhizni* (Moscow: A. I. Ostashev, 2001).

24. V. A. Shatalov, *Kosmicheskiye budni* (Moscow: Mashinostroyeniye, 2008).

25. V. S. Syromyatnikov, *100 Rasskazov o stykovke i o drugikh priklyucheniyakh v kosmose i na Zemle: chast 1: 20 let nazad* (Moscow: "Logos," 2003).

26. V. I. Yazdovskiy, *Na tropakh vselennoy: vklad kosmicheskoy biologii i meditsiny v osvoyeniye kosmicheskogo prostranstva* (Moscow: Firma "Slovo," 1996).

27. A. Yu. Ishlinskiy, ed., *Akademik S. P. Korolev: ucheniy, inzhener, chelovek* (Moscow: Nauka, 1986).

28. Yu. A. Mozzhorin et al., eds., *Dorogi v kosmos: Vospominaniya veteranov raketno-kosmicheskoy tekhniki i kosmonavtiki* (two volumes) (Moscow: MAI, 1992); Yu. A. Mozzhorin et al., eds., *Nachalo kosmicheskoy ery: vospominaniya veteranov raketno-kosmicheskoy tekhniki i kosmonavtiki: vypusk vtoroy* (Moscow: RNITsKD, 1994).

I'd like to conclude this final introduction with a few words on the implementation of this enormous project. Working on this series for the past eight years has been an extraordinary honor and pleasure for me. I owe a debt of gratitude to many for their hard work in bringing these stories to the English-speaking world. As before, I must thank NASA historian Steve Garber, who supervised the entire project at the NASA History Program Office. He also provided insightful comments at every stage of the editorial process. Former NASA Chief Historians Roger D. Launius and Steven J. Dick supported the birth of the project with firm hands, and their eventual successor, William P. Barry, enthusiastically brought it to its completion. Bill read the entire manuscript carefully and offered many useful suggestions. Thanks are due to Jesco von Puttkamer at NASA for his sponsorship of the project. He also facilitated communications between the two parties in Russia and the United States and tirelessly promoted *Rockets and People* at home and abroad. Without his enthusiasm, sponsorship, and support, this project would not have been possible. I'd also like to thank Nadine Andreassen at the NASA History Program Office for her support throughout the past eight years. NASA History Program Office intern Anna J. Stolitzka is also due some thanks.

We were very fortunate to have a capable team of translators at the award-winning Houston-based TechTrans International to facilitate this project. Their team included translators/editors Cynthia Reiser, Laurel Nolen, Alexandra Tussing, and Ksenia Shelkova, as well as document control specialists Lev Genson and Yulia Schmalholz.

Thanks also are due to those who handled the post-editorial stage of the work at the Communications Support Services Center (CSSC) at NASA Headquarters: editors George Gonzalez and Lisa Jirousek; designer Chris Yates; printing specialist Tun Hla; supervisors Gail Carter-Kane and Cindy Miller; and civil servant Michael Crnkovic.

Every one of these aforementioned individuals put in long, hard hours to ensure that we produced the best product possible.

I would like to thank David R. Woods and Alexander Shliadinsky for kindly contributing supplementary images for Volume IV. Unless otherwise noted, all images are from the collection of Chertok.

As the series editor, my job was first and foremost to ensure that the English language version was as faithful to Chertok's original Russian version as possible. At the same time, I also had to account for the stylistic considerations of English-language readers who may be put off by literal translations. The process involved communicating directly with Chertok in many cases and, with his permission, occasionally taking liberties to restructure a text to convey his original spirit. I also made sure that technical terms and descriptions of rocket and spacecraft design satisfied the demands of both Chertok and the English-speaking audience. Readers should be aware that all weights and measures are in the metric system; thus "tons" denotes metric tons (1,000 kg or 2,205 lbs) and not the English ton (2,240 lbs) or the American ton (2,000 lbs). Finally, I provided numerous explanatory footnotes to elucidate points that may not be evident to readers unversed in the intricacies of the Soviet space program, or Soviet history and culture in general. Readers should be aware that all of the footnotes are mine unless cited as "author's note," in which case they were provided by Chertok.

Asif A. Siddiqi
Series Editor
February 2011

A Few Notes About Transliteration and Translation

THE RUSSIAN LANGUAGE IS WRITTEN using the Cyrillic alphabet, which consists of 33 letters. While some of the sounds that these letters symbolize have equivalents in the English language, many have no equivalent, and two of the letters have no sound of their own, but instead "soften" or "harden" the preceding letter. Because of the lack of direct correlation, a number of systems for transliterating Russian (i.e., rendering words using the Latin alphabet), have been devised, all of them different.

Russian Alphabet	Pronunciation	U.S. Board on Geographic Names	Library of Congress
А, а	ă	a	a
Б, б	b	b	b
В, в	v	v	v
Г, г	g	g	g
Д, д	d	d	d
Е, е	ye	ye* / e	e
Ё, ё	yō	yë* / ë	ë
Ж, ж	zh	zh	zh
З, з	z	z	z
И, и	ē	i	i
Й, й	shortened ē	y	ĭ
К, к	k	k	k
Л, л	l	l	l
М, м	m	m	m
Н, н	n	n	n
О, о	o	o	o
П, п	p	p	p
Р, р	r	r	r
С, с	s	s	s
Т, т	t	t	t
У, у	ū	u	u
Ф, ф	f	f	f
Х, х	kh	kh	kh
Ц, ц	ts	ts	ts
Ч, ч	ch	ch	ch
Ш, ш	sh	sh	sh
Щ, щ	shch	shch	shch
Ъ	(hard sign)	"	"
Ы	guttural ē	y	y
Ь	(soft sign)	'	'
Э, э	ĕ	e	ĭ
Ю, ю	yū	yu	iu
Я, я	yă	ya	ia

*Initially and after vowels

For this series, editor Asif Siddiqi selected a modification of the U.S. Board on Geographic Names system, also known as the University of Chicago system, as he felt it better suited for a memoir such as Chertok's, where the intricacies of the Russian language are less important than accessibility to the reader. The modifications are as follows:

- The Russian letters "Ь" and "Ъ" are not transliterated, in order to make reading easier.
- Russian letter "ё" is denoted by the English "e" (or "ye" initially and after vowels)—hence, the transliteration "Korolev," though it is pronounced "Korolyov".

The reader may find some familiar names to be rendered in an unfamiliar way. This occurs when a name has become known under its phonetic spelling, such as "Yuri" versus the transliterated "Yuriy," or under a different transliteration system, such as "Baikonur" (LoC) versus "Baykonur" (USBGN).

In translating *Rakety i lyudi*, we on the TTI team strove to find the balance between faithfulness to the original text and clear, idiomatic English. For issues of technical nomenclature, we consulted with Asif Siddiqi to determine the standards for this series. The cultural references, linguistic nuances, and "old sayings" Chertok uses in his memoirs required a different approach from the technical passages. They cannot be translated literally: the favorite saying of Flight Mechanic Nikolay Godovikov (Vol. 1, Chapter 7) would mean nothing to an English speaker if given as "There was a ball, there is no ball" but makes perfect sense when translated as "Now you see it, now you don't." The jargon used by aircraft engineers and rocket engine developers in the 1930s and 1940s posed yet another challenge. At times, we had to do linguistic detective work to come up with a translation that conveyed both the idea and the "flavor" of the original. Puns and plays on words are explained in footnotes. *Rakety i lyudi* has been a very interesting project, and we have enjoyed the challenge of bringing Chertok's voice to the English-speaking world.

TTI TRANSLATION TEAM
Houston, TX
October 2004

List of Abbreviations

AAP	Apollo Applications Project
ABM	antiballistic missile
ABMA	Army Ballistic Missile Agency
AFU	antenna feeder unit
APAS	Androgynous-Peripheral Docking Assembly
APO	emergency spacecraft destruction
APR	emergency missile destruction system
ARS	emergency x-ray system
ASTP	Apollo-Soyuz Test Project
ATG	autonomous turbo generator
ATV	Automated Transfer Vehicle
AVD	emergency engine shutdown
BINS	strapdown inertial navigation system
BO	Living Compartment
BTsVM	on-board digital computing machine
BUS	rendezvous control unit
BV DPO	ignition assembly for approach and attitude-control engines
CEP	circular error probability
ChP	emergency event
CSM	Command and Service Module
DARPA	Defense Advanced Research Projects Agency
DO	control engine
DOS	Long-Duration Orbital Station
DP	remote switch
DRS	remote radio communications system
DUS	angular rate sensor
DZZ	Remote Sensing of Earth
EIIM	equivalent isotropically radiated power
EKhG	electrochemical generator
EO	Primary Expeditions

EPAS	Experimental Apollo-Soyuz Flight
ERD	electric rocket engine
ESTEC	European Space Research and Technology Center
EU	power plant
EYaRD	electric nuclear rocket engine
GAI	State Automobile Inspectorate
GDL	Gas Dynamics Laboratory
GEO	geostationary Earth orbit
GKNII VVS	Air Force State Red Banner Scientific-Research Institute
GKNPTs	State Space Scientific-Production Center
GKOT	State Committee on Defense Technology
GKRE	State Committee on Radio Electronics
GLONASS	Global Navigation Satellite System
GMKS	Global Meteorological Space System
GOGU	Main Operations Control Group
Gossnab	State Committee for Logistics
GP	State Enterprise
GPS	Global Positioning System
GR	Global Rocket
GRTs	State Rocket Center
GRU	Main Intelligence Directorate
GSKB	State Union Design Bureau
GSKB Spetsmash	State Union Design Bureau of Special Machine Building
GTsP	State Central Firing Range
GUKOS	Main Directorate of Space Assets
GURVO	Main Directorate of Missile Armaments
HEO	Human Exploration and Operations Mission Directorate
ICBM	intercontinental ballistic missile
IKI	Institute of Space Research
IKV	infrared vertical
ILS	International Launch Services
IPM	Institute of Applied Mathematics
IS	Satellite Fighter
ISS	International Space Station
ITMiVT	Institute of Precision Mechanics and Computer Technology
KB	Design Bureau
KB Khimmash	Design Bureau of Chemical Machine Building
KB Transmash	Design Bureau for Transport Machine Building
KB OM	Design Bureau of General Machine Building
KDU	correction engine unit
KGB	Committee for State Security

KIK	Command-Measurement Complex
KIS	monitoring and testing station
KLA	heavy space vehicle
KONRID	Engine Performance Monitoring System
KORD	Engine Operation Monitoring
KP	command post
KPP	airfield checkpoint
KRL	command radio link
KTDU	correcting braking engine unit
KV	shortwave
KVO	circular probable deviation
kW	kilowatt
LII	Flight-Research Institute
LK	Lunar Vehicle
LKI	flight-developmental testing
LM	Lunar Module
LOK	Lunar Orbital Vehicle
LV	Lunar Vehicle
MAI	Moscow Aviation Institute
MAP	Ministry of the Aviation Industry
MFTI	Moscow Physics and Technology Institute
MGU	Moscow State University
MIAN	Mathematics Institute of the Academy of Sciences
MIIGAiK	Moscow Institute of Engineers of Geodesy, Aerial Photography, and Mapping
MIK	Assembly and Testing Building
MIK KO	Assembly and Testing Building for Spacecraft
Minobshchemash	Ministry of General Machine Building
Minsredmash	Ministry of Medium Machine Building
MIRV	multiple independently targetable reentry vehicle
MIT	Moscow Institute of Thermal Technology
MKAD	Moscow Automobile Ring Road
MKB	Machine Building Design Bureau
MKB Fakel	Torch Machine Building Design Bureau
MKBS	Multipurpose Base/Station
MKTS	reusable space transportation system
MNTS-KI	Interdepartmental Scientific-Technical Council on Space Research
MO	Ministry of Defense
MOK	Multipurpose Orbital Complex
MOM	Ministry of General Machine Building

MOP	Ministry of the Defense Industry
MPSS	Ministry of the Communications Equipment Industry
MSM	Ministry of Medium Machine Building
MV	Mars-Venera
MVTU	Moscow Higher Technical School
NACA	National Advisory Committee for Aeronautics
NASA	National Aeronautics and Space Administration
NATO	North Atlantic Treaty Organization
NII	Scientific-Research Institute
NII IT	Scientific-Research Institute of Measurement Technology
NIIAP	Scientific-Research Institute of Automatics and Instrument Building
NIIERAT	Scientific-Research Institute for the Operation and Repair of Aviation Technology
NIIKP	Scientific-Research Institute of Space Instrumentation Building
NIIP	Scientific-Research and Testing Range
NIISchetmash	Scientific-Research Institute of Calculating Machines
NIITP	Scientific-Research Institute of Thermal Processes/ Scientific-Research Institute of Precision Instruments
NIItransmash	Scientific-Research Institute of Transport Machine Building
NIIYaF	Scientific-Research Institute of Nuclear Physics
NIOKR	scientific-research and experimental-design work
NIP	Ground Tracking Station
NIP-15	Ussuriysk tracking station
NIP-16	Center for Deep Space Communications
NITsEVT	Scientific-Research Center for Electronic Computer Technology
NKVD	People's Commissariat of Internal Affairs
NPO	Scientific-Production Association
NPO Geofizika	Geophysics Scientific-Production Association
NPO PM	Scientific-Production Association of Applied Mechanics
NPP	Scientific-Production Enterprise
NS-BS	normal stabilization-lateral stabilization
NZ	emergency supply
OAO	Joint-Stock Company
OKB	Experimental-Design Bureau
OKB MEI	Special Design Bureau of the Moscow Power Institute
OKB SD	Experimental Design Bureau for Special Engines
OPM	Department of Applied Mathematics
OPS	Orbital Piloted Station

OTI	technological firing test
OTR	operational and technical management
PAO	Instrumentation System Compartment
PELSHO	enamel-, lacquer- and silk-coated winding wire
PKO	antispace defense
PO	Production Association
POS	Permanent Orbital Station
PRO	antimissile defense
PUNA	science equipment control console
PVO	antiaircraft defense
PVO Strany	National Air Defense Forces
PVU	programmable timing instrument
p/ya	post office box
RKK	rocket-space complex
RKK	Rocket-Space Corporation
RLA	rocket flying apparatus
RNII	Reactive Scientific-Research Institute
RORSAT	Radar Ocean Reconnaissance Satellite
RSFSR	Russian Soviet Federated Socialist Republic
RVSN	Strategic Rocket Forces
SA	Descent Module
SALT	Strategic Arms Limitations Talks
SAS	emergency rescue system
SDI	Strategic Defense Initiative
ShPU	silo launch unit
SIO	effector system
SKD	rendezvous and correction engine
SKDU	approach and correction engine unit
SKTDU	approach and correction braking engine unit
SLBM	submarine-launched ballistic missile
SOI	Strategic Defense Initiative
SOUD	orientation and motion control system
Sovnarkhoz	Council of the National Economy
SSVP	docking and internal transfer system
STR	thermal control system
SUBK	on-board complex control system
SUS	descent control system
TASS	Telegraph Agency of the Soviet Union
TE	fuel cell
TKS	Transport-Supply Ship
TMK	Heavy Interplanetary Ship

TNA	turbopump assembly
TP	engineering facility
TsAGI	Central Aerohydrodynamics Institute
TsENKI	Center for the Operation of Ground Space Infrastructure Objects
TsIAM	Central Institute of Aviation Engine Building
TsKB	Central Design Bureau
TsKBEM	Central Design Bureau of Experimental Machine Building
TsKBM	Central Design Bureau of Machine Building
TsNIIKS	Central Scientific-Research Institute of Space Assets
TsNIImash	Central Scientific-Research Institute of Machine Building
TsSKB	Central Specialized Design Bureau
TsUKOS	Central Directorate of Space Assets
TsUP	Flight Control Center/Mission Control Center
UKP	universal space platform
UKSS	Universal Rig-Launch Complex
UNKS	Directorate of the Chief of Space Assets
US	Controlled Satellite
VA	Return Vehicle
VAB	Vehicle Assembly Building
VDNKh	Exhibition of Achievements of the National Economy
VLKSM	All-Union Leninist Communist Union of Youth
VMF	the Soviet Navy
VNII	All-Union Scientific-Research Institute
VNIIEM	All-Union Scientific-Research Institute of Electromechanics
VNIIT	All-Union Scientific-Research Institute of Television Technology
VNIIT	All-Union Scientific-Research Institute of Current Sources
VPK	Military-Industrial Commission/Military-Industrial Corporation
VSE	Vision for Space Exploration
VSK	cosmonaut's special visor/sight
VSNKh	Supreme Council of the National Economy
VVS	the Soviet Air Force
YaRD	nuclear rocket engine
ZAS	encrypted/secure communications system
ZEM	Factory of Experimental Machine Building
ZhRD	liquid-propellant rocket engine
ZIKh	M. V. Khrunichev Factory
ZIS	Stalin Factory
ZOMZ	Zagorsk Optical-Mechanical Factory

Introduction

Voice of the People...

On 20 July 1969, the first human being from the planet Earth set foot on the surface of the Moon. This person was a citizen of the United States of America.

"That's one small step for [a] man, one giant leap for mankind"—Neil Armstrong's words flew around the entire world beneath the Moon.

In August 1969, getting into a taxi, I told the driver my home address: "Academician Korolev Street."[1] En route, the elderly taxi driver let me know that he was aware of who lived in the "Korolev" apartments. Evidently he decided that it was all right to tell me what the "man on the street" was thinking: "Korolev is not with us anymore and the Americans have become the first to land on the Moon. Does that mean that they haven't found another mind like his among us?"

Until 1964, Nikita Khrushchev was so active that people associated our triumphant victories in space with his name. In January 1966, the world discovered that our success was primarily the result of the creative work of Academician Sergey Pavlovich Korolev. But after Korolev's death, once again everything happened "under the wise leadership of the Communist Party Central Committee."

For our people, who had grown accustomed to the cascade of achievements in Soviet cosmonautics, the Americans' brilliant success was a complete surprise. During the Cold War, the Soviet mass media made no mention of our work on a human lunar program. All of this was strictly classified. Reports on the Americans' outstanding space achievements were also more than modest, but not because they were classified. Television coverage of the first lunar landing in the history of humankind was broadcast worldwide, with the exception of the USSR and the People's Republic of China. In order to see the U.S. broadcast

---

1. The original 3rd Ostankino Street in Moscow was renamed Academician Korolev Street in January 1967, the first anniversary of Korolev's death.

that was available to the entire world, we had to drive over to NII-88 [the main Soviet missile and space research institute], which received the television footage via cable from the television center.[2] The television center in turn received the footage via the Eurovision channel, but a live broadcast was forbidden. Later, one of the television employees said that their request for a live broadcast had passed through the entire hierarchy, but eventually Central Committee Secretary Suslov had put a stop to it.[3]

For those of us involved in the Soviet lunar program, the Americans' achievements were not surprising. The open press wasn't our only source of information about the progress of the Americans' projects. After the death of our cosmonaut Vladimir Komarov on *Soyuz-1* in April 1967, we had an 18-month break in piloted flights.[4] During this interval, the Americans completed their first piloted flight of the Apollo program.[5] Our Soyuz launches resumed with maximum intensity. Three piloted Soyuzes lifted off before July 1969.[6] Our newspapers tried to write up these flights as enthusiastically as those of the first cosmonauts, beginning with Yuriy Gagarin. From 1961 through 1965, this enthusiasm was genuine and sincere. It emanated from our national soul and touched all social strata. The populace attributed the tragic death of Komarov in April 1967 to the death of Chief Designer Korolev. No one knew who was actually in charge of our space programs now. Only insiders were aware that thousands of our specialists at secret enterprises and at the now-famous Baykonur complex were preparing for a landing expedition to the Moon.

From 1957 through 1967, the Soviet Union was the clear leader in all space endeavors and had achieved universally recognized superiority in piloted space programs.[7] During the first decade of the Space Age, the Soviet Union's intellectual, industrial, and organizational potential enabled it to solve such top-priority challenges as developing the world's first intercontinental ballistic missile; launching the first artificial satellites; delivering to the Moon the first object from Earth (a pendant inscribed with the emblem of the Soviet Union); photographing the far side of the Moon; being the first to launch a human

---

2. NII—*Nauchno-issledovatelskiy institut* (Scientific-Research Institute).

3. Mikhail Andreyevich Suslov (1902–1982) was a powerful Soviet Politburo member responsible for ideological policing during the late Soviet era.

4. For the *Soyuz-1* disaster, see Boris Chertok, *Rockets and People, Vol. III: Hot Days of the Cold War*, ed. Asif A. Siddiqi (Washington, DC: NASA-SP-2009-4110, 2009), Chapter 20. The first Soviet human space mission after *Soyuz-1* was *Soyuz-3* in October 1968.

5. This was the *Apollo 8* mission in October 1968.

6. These were *Soyuz-3, -4*, and *-5*.

7. Most historians would argue that the lead tipped in favor of the United States sometime in 1966 with the achievements of the Gemini program.

being (Yuriy Gagarin) into space; being the first to launch a woman (Valentina Tereshkova) into space; conducting Aleksey Leonov's spacewalk; executing the soft landing of an automatic station on the Moon; televising the transmission to Earth of a panoramic shot of the lunar surface; achieving the first penetration into the atmosphere of Venus; and completing the world's first automatic docking of spacecraft. This list of our "firsts" is described in detail in numerous publications, in the memoirs of those involved, and in historical works.

After such a storybook succession of cosmic breakthroughs, it seemed completely natural that the next conquest to shake the imagination of Earthlings would be the landing of Soviet cosmonauts on the surface of the Moon and their safe return to Earth. But Americans turned out to be the first Earthlings on the Moon. Today, few are aware that it was not until 1964 that the top political leaders of the Soviet Union resolved to consider the landing of Soviet cosmonauts on the Moon no later than 1968 a task of utmost importance. The Soviet expedition to the Moon, which was conceived in Korolev's lifetime and supported by Khrushchev, simply never took place. Work on the Soviet N1-L3 program—the piloted landing expedition to the Moon—ended in 1974.

Everything that had to do with the N1-L3 program remained a secret until the late 1980s. The first publications, which primarily looked into the technical problems of this program, appeared in the early 1990s.[8] As for other aspects of the "Moon race," the authors of the majority of the publications I have read greatly simplified or distorted the actual situation in an attempt at a sensational revelation of secrets. And today, 40 years later, for many it remains an unanswered question: "Why wasn't there a Soviet person on the Moon?"[9]

In Volume III of my memoirs, the chapter "The Hard Road to a Soft Landing" provides insight into the initial phase of lunar exploration involving the Ye-6 program, the world's first soft landing of an automatic spacecraft on the lunar surface.[10] In this volume, I continue my story with the Soviet human lunar expedition programs. In the process, I attempt to weave my narrative over the background of the general history of the development of rocket and space technology, cosmonautics, and the military and political rivalry of the two superpowers. During the 20th century, the USSR and United States implemented global military technical programs on an unprecedented scale.

---

8. The first articles in the Soviet media confirming a human lunar landing program appeared in the summer of 1989. See Lev Kamanin, "S zemli na lunu i obratno" ["From the Earth to the Moon and Back"], *Poisk* no. 12 (July 1989): 7–8; Sergey Leskov, "Kak my ne sletali na lunu" ["How We Didn't Go to the Moon"], *Izvestiya* (18 August 1989): 3.

9. Chertok wrote this introduction in 2009.

10. See Chertok, *Rockets and People, Vol. III*, Chapters 13 and 14.

For this reason, a considerable portion of this volume is spent reminiscing about events that took place at the same time as the N1-L3 lunar program. Unfortunately, professional Moscow taxi drivers who are capable of expressing the opinion of the "man on the street" are a thing of the past, too.

Chapter 1
Rocket–Space Chronology (Historical Overview)

When comparing the economic and scientific-technical capabilities of the USSR and the United States, one can't help but wonder how the Soviet Union, which lost more than 20 million people during World War II and sustained inconceivably enormous material damage, overcame extraordinary economic difficulties and—in just two decades from 1956 through 1976—made an amazing breakthrough into space, forever leaving its mark on world history and in the annals of the 20th century.[1]

The most outstanding successes in the development of space technology and the highest rates of nuclear missile buildup both in the USSR and in the U.S. took place during the period from 1960 through 1975. During this same time, the so-called "Moon race" was also getting under way. The beginning and end of operations on the N1-L3 program coincided with the tensest periods of the nuclear arms race. Everything that happened after that, up to the end of the 20th and beginning of the 21st centuries, was, to a significant degree, predetermined during that very period. I am certain that an overwhelming majority of readers cannot imagine the true scale of the operations of the two superpowers in these areas. For this reason, I think it might be helpful, before getting into the memoir part of this volume, to start out with some historical information. This information, in the form of a list of the main projects, will provide some idea of everything that was happening in the rocket-space field. But it is also essential because the collective heroism of the intellectuals and workers who secured strategic parity for the Soviet Union has yet to be properly appreciated in historical works. If a similar list were also compiled for all the

---

1. Chertok's figure of "more than twenty million" has been borne out by recent studies. Most contemporary sources lean toward a figure of 26.6 million fatalities for Soviet losses (both civilian and military) during the war. See G. F. Krivosheyev, ed., *Grif sekretnosti snyat: poteri vooruzhennykh sil sssr v voynakh, boyevykh deystviyakh i voyennykh konfliktakh: statisticheskoye issledovaniye* [*Without the Stamp Secret: Losses of the USSR Armed Forces in War, Battle Actions and Military Conflicts: Statistical Research*] (Moscow: Voyenizdat, 1993).

other areas of scientific and technical progress in the defense industries, then today's readers would find an impressive picture.

The Soviet Union's centralized and authoritarian power system created a progressive, mobilization-economy system for science and the defense industry.[2] In the field of liberal arts and sciences, the Iron Curtain partially closed off Soviet society from the culture of the outside world. However, in the field of hard science and science-driven technologies, it was state policy to surpass world achievements by any means.

Contemporary Russia is experiencing an extreme ideological and system-wide crisis. If Russia still enjoys the respect of the world community, it is due to the scientific-industrial potential accumulated by the Soviet superpower, rather than her democratic achievements at the end of the 20th century.

In the process of developing strategic missile armaments and rocket-space systems, both we and the Americans, in the majority of cases, strove to achieve the very same ultimate objectives. However, the U.S. sailed toward these objectives over a magnificent expressway that war had not touched, and we were negotiating an unpaved, crater-pocked wilderness. Having spread out over a very broad front of scientific-technical progress with surprising speed, we pursued lofty goals and accomplished deeds comparable, in terms of heroism, with the feats of the wartime years.

After we launched the first artificial satellite, and especially after Gagarin's triumph, the safe, sound, and self-satisfied U.S. realized that its many-fold superiority in strategic nuclear weapons was clearly insufficient to win the Cold War. A lavish investment of billions of dollars into a national campaign to gain the upper hand in space ensued. We were ahead of the Americans in the space race, but we repeatedly lost to them in the strategic nuclear arms race.

"All for the front, all for victory!" This was the call that went out to all Soviet people during the war, no matter where they worked. Spurred on by this rallying cry, the Soviet economy gathered such dynamic energy that for many years after the war it continued to galvanize the most diverse social strata, united by the military-industrial complex, the army, militarized science, and even art.

The defense industry's managerial system was characterized by the strict centralization of Party and state leadership, which made it possible, by dint of the maximum concentration of financial, intellectual, and material resources, to develop new complex weapons systems within extremely tight timeframes.

---

2. "Mobilization economics" was a term used to describe the wartime Soviet policy of massive state direction of the Soviet economy to singular goals. This practice was modified for the postwar period to galvanize state resources for specific projects, usually of a military nature.

This is how the challenges of developing a broad spectrum of strategic nuclear weapons, ground-based nuclear missiles, atomic submarines, missile-carrying aircraft, and a surface naval missile fleet were met. Resolutions of the Central Committee and Council of Ministers were required to implement priority arms programs and to develop scientific-production facilities. The Military-Industrial Commission painstakingly prepared these resolutions.[3] As a rule, the technical gist of the programs remained strictly secret. The progress of the most crucial projects was discussed at sessions of the Politburo. The chief function of the Commission was to coordinate the activity of all the ministries and departments involved in the complete and mandatory execution of the task assigned to the general designer or general director of the production enterprise.

THE N1-L3 LUNAR ROCKET-SPACE COMPLEX was under development concurrently with dozens of other high-technology programs. The highest governmental agency that was monitoring work on the program was the Military-Industrial Commission under the auspices of the Presidium of the USSR Council of Ministers.[4] In 1965, the Ministry of General Machine Building (MOM) became the lead ministry responsible for program implementation.[5] Its primary "subcontractors" were the Ministry of Defense (MO), the Ministry of the Aviation Industry (MAP), the Ministry of Medium Machine Building (MSM), the Ministry of the Electronics Industry, the Ministry of the Radio Industry, the Ministry of Heavy Machine Building, the Ministry of the Defense Industry (MOP), the Ministry of the Communications Equipment Industry (MPSS), the Ministry of the Electrical Engineering Industry, and many others.[6]

Neither the VPK nor the lead ministry, much less the other ministries, had any specialized "main directorate" that dealt exclusively with the N1-L3 program.[7] OKB-1, headed by Chief Designer S. P. Korolev, remained the lead

---

3. The Military-Industrial Commission (VPK), established in December 1957, was a high-level governmental body that coordinated the activities of the Soviet defense industry and, essentially, was the epicenter of the Soviet military-industrial complex.

4. The more common name of this body was VPK—*Voyenno-promyshlennaya komissiya* (Military-Industrial Commission).

5. MOM—*Ministerstvo obshchego mashinostroyeniya*.

6. MO—*Ministerstvo oborony*; MAP—*Ministerstvo aviatsionnoy promyshlennosti*; MSM—*Ministerstvo srednego mashinostroyeniya*; MOP—*Ministerstvo oboronnoy promyshlennosti*; MPSS—*Ministerstvo promyshlennosti sredstv svyazi*. *Author's note*: Until 1965 there were state committees pertaining to the various branches of industry rather than ministries. The state committee chairmen had the rank of ministers.

7. "Main directorates" were functional units within a particular ministry responsible for specific areas of research, development, or production.

3

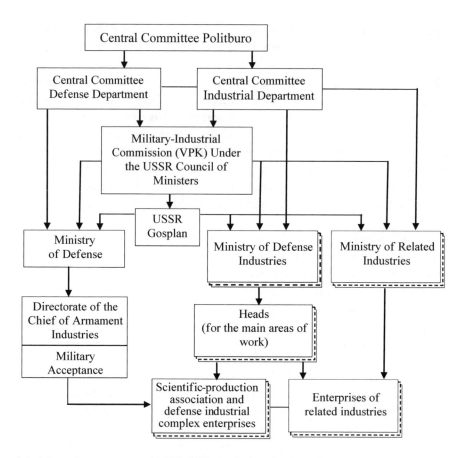

Administrative structure of USSR Military–Industrial Complex.

organization for N1-L3 development.[8] In March 1966, after Korolev's death, OKB-1 was renamed the Central Design Bureau of Experimental Machine Building (TsKBEM).[9] Chief Designer V. P. Mishin was in charge there until May 1974. The main subcontractors for engines, control systems, on-board and ground radio complexes, the ground-based launch complex, and dozens of other systems were the chief designers who had already fulfilled a multitude of other assignments and who continued to receive new projects pursuant to Central Committee and Council of Ministers decrees.

---

8. OKB—*Opytno-konstruktorskoye byuro* (Experimental-Design Bureau).
9. TsKBEM—*Tsentralnoye konstruktorskoye byuro eksperimentalnogo mashinostroyeniya.*

The production, optimization, and testing of launch vehicles, which were unprecedented in terms of their scale, required the construction of specialized shops, colossal assembly buildings, and launch complexes with numerous support services.

Although the N-1 rocket was developed under Cold War conditions, it was not intended for a possible preventive or retaliatory nuclear strike, and the prospects for using it for military purposes were very vague.[10] For this reason, the nation's top political leaders were ambivalent toward the development of this rocket and toward the whole lunar program.

In the early 1960s, the threat of a nuclear strike against the Soviet Union seemed entirely realistic. Although they had fallen behind in the space race, the Americans had held the lead in the development of strategic nuclear systems from the very beginning. Even the most glorious triumphs in space were no guarantee against a sudden switch from a "cold war" to a hot one.

According to data cited by Robert McNamara, U.S. superiority over the USSR in the field of strategic arms was overwhelming until the mid-1970s.[11] The table below provides some idea of only the quantitative side of the missile race dynamic.

People who are far-removed from technology in general, and nuclear missile technology in particular, cannot gain a sense of the true scale of this national feat of science and labor, which is concealed behind dry statistics. Colossal economic resources were invested into these projects, and millions of people participated in them. However, a well-organized system of secrecy, which had endured until recently, prevented an assessment of how much more difficult and costly it was than the Moon race. The majority of those involved weren't even aware of what a potentially lethal game they had been drawn into. Unlike the millions who toiled on the home front during World War II, these workers were unwitting of their cause.

When analyzing the piloted lunar expedition programs of the U.S. and USSR, one should take into consideration the crucial factor of the vastly superior U.S. postwar economy. By the 1960s, it enabled the U.S. to achieve a twentyfold advantage over the Soviet Union in terms of the total number of

---

10. The name of this rocket has been variously denoted as both "N-1" and N1." For the purposes of this volume, we use "N-1" when used alone and "N1" when used along with other designations, such as "N1-L3."

11. Chertok cites from a table published in the Russian translation: R. Maknamara, *Putem oshibok k katastrofe* (Moscow: Nauka, 1988). The original was published as Robert McNamara, *Blundering Into Disaster: Surviving the First Century of the Nuclear Age* (New York: Pantheon Books, 1986), pp. 154–155. Robert Strange McNamara (1916–2009) served as U.S. Secretary of Defense from 1961 to 1968.

Ratio between U.S. and USSR strategic nuclear forces (1960–1980)

Year	1960		1965		1970		1975		1980	
Warheads	U.S.	USSR	U.S.	USSR	U.S.	USSR	U.S.	USSR	U.S.	USSR
Missiles	60	some	1050	225	1800	1600	6100	2500	7300	5500
Bombs	6000	300	4500	375	2200	200	2400	300	2800	500
Total:	**6068**	**300**	**5550**	**600**	**4000**	**1800**	**8500**	**2800**	**10100**	**6000**
Delivery Systems	U.S.	USSR	U.S.	USSR	U.S.	USSR	U.S.	USSR	U.S.	USSR
Bombers	600	150	600	250	550	145	400	135	340	156
ICBMs	20	*some*	850	200	1054	1300	1054	1527	1050	1398
SLBMs	48	15	400	25	656	300	656	784	656	1028
Total:	**668**	**165**	**1850**	**475**	**2260**	**1745**	**2110**	**2446**	**2046**	**2582**
Ratio between U.S. and USSR strategic nuclear forces	20.2 : 1		9.2 : 1		2.2 : 1		3 : 1		1.6 : 1	

Notes:
ICBM: intercontinental ballistic missile
SLBM: submarine-launched ballistic missile

strategic nuclear weapons. Having secured such a margin of safety, the American administration could allow itself to spend a significant portion of the taxpayers' funds on the lunar program, which promised a real political victory over the Soviet Union. Striving to achieve a decisive upper hand in all types of missile armaments, the U.S. took the lead in more than the sheer number of ICBMs. For a long time, the U.S. maintained an advantage in target accuracy and was the first to develop missile systems using multiple independently targetable reentry vehicles (MIRVs).

FOR THE OPTIMIZATION of the N-1 rocket—the launch vehicle for the lunar landing expedition—we executed four experimental launches. Experts' assessments showed that most likely another four or five launches would have been required to bring the launch vehicle to the necessary degree of reliability. Usually hundreds of launches are conducted in the process of flight-developmental tests (LKI), both before combat missiles are put into service and afterwards to confirm their reliability.[12] All told, the Strategic Rocket Forces (RVSN) and Soviet Navy (VMF) conducted thousands of launches of combat missiles.[13]

Large-scale mass production of nuclear weapons and various missiles—intercontinental missiles, mobile missiles, so-called medium-range and short-range missiles, submarine-launched missiles—in and of itself was not the only deciding factor in achieving parity. It was missile *systems* that needed to be put into service, not missiles. For each medium-range and intercontinental missile, a launch silo needed to be built; systems for transport, remote monitoring, control, and launch needed to be developed; thousands of soldiers and officers needed to be trained; and then rocket regiments, divisions, and armies needed to be formed. For naval missiles, submarines needed to be redesigned and built. Each of them cost considerably more than the missiles they carried.

It took truly an incredible amount of work and an extreme amount of strain on the economy in order to bring the ratio between the strategic arms of the U.S. and USSR from 20.2:1 to 1.6:1 in 20 years! In so doing, an overwhelming portion of this heroic work was carried out at enterprises and in organizations that also performed assignments for the N1-L3 program. Having lost the Moon race, the Soviet Union achieved parity with the U.S. in nuclear missile armaments.

The triumphant space achievements of the USSR had a much greater psychological impact on the world community than the boastful reports about the number of U.S. Minuteman missiles and the capabilities of the U.S. bomber fleet. Our cosmonauts, who visited various countries, and our effectively delivered propaganda campaign demonstrated the advantages of the Soviet system. That is why the U.S. government wagered billions of dollars in the early 1960s and embraced the space program, figuring on surpassing the USSR not only in terms of nuclear might, but also through the awe-inspiring peaceful exploration of space.

There was one more sector of the broad front of the Cold War where the rivalry between the two powers went on with alternating success or, more accurately, almost on an equal footing. This was the direct use of space in the interests of defense and the armed forces. The first phase of the use of space for military purposes coincided with the period of the Moon race. In contrast with the so-called "peaceful" programs, this activity was classified, and until

---

12. In Russian engineering vernacular, the common abbreviation for the test launch phase for a new missile is LKI—*Letno-konstruktorskiye ispytaniya* (flight-development testing).

13. RVSN—*Raketnyye voyska strategicheskogo naznacheniya*; VMF—*Voyenno-morskoy flot*.

the late 1980s there were very few overt publications about the achievements in this field.

The most complete and historically authentic information about the Military Space Forces in the Soviet Union did not appear until 1997.[14] This is the definitive achievement of Lieutenant General Viktor Vyacheslavovich Favorskiy, the former deputy chief of the Main Directorate of Space Assets (GUKOS), and of Lieutenant General Ivan Vasilyevich Meshcheryakov, the former chief of the Central Scientific-Research Institute of Space Assets (TsNIIKS) No. 50.[15] It is regrettable that no similar work about the history of the Strategic Rocket Forces and strategic forces of the Navy has yet emerged.[16]

I believe that the reader will find it interesting to peruse the list of programs and developments in the field of rocket technology and cosmonautics in the Soviet Union. I have grouped them by head organizations rather than by subject matter. In so doing, I have limited myself to the 1960s and 1970s—the period of the Moon race. I begin with my own home organization.

OKB-1, later known as TsKBEM, then NPO Energiya, and currently S. P. Korolev RKK Energiya

1. From 1957 through 1960, flight tests were conducted, and in early 1960 the first R-7 intercontinental missile went into service.
2. On 12 September 1960, the updated R-7A missile went into service.

---

14. Chertok is referring to a three-volume set published by the Russian Military Space Forces on the history of the Soviet and Russian military space programs. These were published in Moscow under the general title of *Voyenno-kosmicheskiye sily (voyenno-istoricheskiy trud)* [*The Military Space Forces (A Military-Historical Work)*] in 1997, 1998, and 2001. The first two volumes were edited by V. V. Favorskiy and I. V. Meshcheryakov and published by the Military Space Forces, while the third was edited by V. L. Ivanov and published by the VVF Publishing House.

15. GUKOS—*Glavnoye upravleniye kosmicheskikh sredstv*; TsNIIKS—*Tsentralnyy nauchno-issledovatelskiy institut kosmicheskikh sistem*.

16. There have been a number of important histories of the Strategic Rocket Forces published in Russian. These include Yu. P. Maksimov, ed., *Raketnyye voyska strategicheskogo naznacheniya* [*Strategic Rocket Forces*] (Moscow: RVSN, 1992); I. D. Sergeyev, ed., *Khronika osnovnykh sobytiy istorii raketnykh voysk strategicheskogo naznacheniya* [*Chronicle of the Primary Events of the History of the Strategic Rocket Forces*] (Moscow: RVSN, 1994); Mikhail Pervov, *Mezhkontinentalnyye ballisticheskiye rakety SSSR i Rossii: kratkii istoricheskiy ocherk* [*Intercontinental Ballistic Missiles of the USSR and Russia: A Short Historical Account*] (Moscow: Mikhail Pervov, 1998). Works on the history of strategic missiles of the Soviet Navy have been rarer. For one of the few, see Yu. V. Apalkov, D. I. Mant, and S. D. Mant, *Otechestvennyye ballisticheskiye rakety morskogo bazirovaniya i ikh nositeli* [*Native Naval Ballistic Missiles and Their Carriers*] (St. Petersburg: Galeya Print, 2006).

3. From 1957 to 1970, the R-7A underwent modifications and development for use as a launch vehicle for the execution of various space programs. Working jointly with the Kuybyshev branch of OKB-1 and with related organizations, six main modifications were developed in two-, three-, and four-stage versions.[17] These were repeatedly updated.

4. Between 1959 and 1965, the R-9 (8K75) intercontinental missile was developed and put into service. From 1965 through 1979, missile systems using the R-9 missile were on combat alert. TsKBEM conducted tests on and participated in routine firings of these on-alert missiles.

5. The GR-1 (8K713) global missile was developed from 1962 through 1964. Just two missiles were fabricated, and a special launch complex with fully automated launch preparation was built. In developing the design for the GR-1, proposals were elaborated for the destruction of enemy combat satellites.

6. In 1959, scientific-research and design projects for the RT-1 (8K95) solid-propellant medium-range missile and RT-2 (8K98) intercontinental missile got under way. Flight tests for the RT-1 were conducted from 1962 through 1963. The RT-1 was not put into service.

   Flight testing for the RT-2 began in 1966, and in 1968 the RT-2 went into service. The modified RT-2P (8K98P) solid-propellant missile underwent flight testing from 1970 to 1971, and in 1972 it was put into service. In all, over the course of its flight testing and duty, 100 launches of the RT-2 and its RT-2P modification were conducted. Missile systems using RT-2 and RT-2P missiles were on duty for more than 15 years. The RT-2 missile was the first Soviet solid-propellant intercontinental ballistic missile. Aleksandr Nadiradze, the chief designer of the Moscow Institute of Thermal Technology, continued to develop solid-propellant missile technology.

7. From February 1960 through March 1966, development continued on the four-stage 8K78 launch vehicle using the R-7A for the exploration of Mars and Venus. In all, from 1962 through 1966, 19 interplanetary stations in four modifications were launched for the Mars-Venera (MV) program. Later, the projects in this field were handed over to the S. A. Lavochkin OKB, which was headed at that time by chief designer Georgiy Babakin.

8. In 1961, research began to develop an automatic spacecraft to perform a soft landing on the Moon and transmit panoramic shots of its surface to

---

17. Chertok is probably referring here to the Sputnik, Luna, Vostok, Voskhod, Soyuz, and Molniya variants of the launch vehicle. Each of these variants had many subvariants.

Earth. Flight tests, including an attempt at a soft landing on the Moon, were conducted from 1963 through 1966. During this period, 12 Moon launches took place. Only the last station executed the assignment completely.[18] It was developed jointly with the S. A. Lavochkin OKB, which then continued operations in this field.

9. From 1961 through 1965, research and development (NIOKR) was conducted on space communications systems.[19] The first launch of the *Molniya-1* experimental satellite took place in June 1964. In 1967, after seven launches and after the space communication system was put into operation, subsequent operations were handed over to OKB-10, which was located in Krasnoyarsk-26, the closed city of atomic scientists.

10. The Elektron satellite was developed over the course of 1962 and 1963. In 1964, four of these satellites were launched and used to gather data to model phenomena in space.

11. Automatic spy satellites equipped with cameras and special radio reconnaissance facilities were developed from 1959 through 1965. During this time, the first *Zenit-2* spy satellite was developed, underwent flight testing, and was put into service and the *Zenit-4* satellite was developed. In 1965, spy satellite projects were transferred to the OKB-1 branch in Kuybyshev.[20]

Piloted programs comprised a huge portion of OKB-1's and later TsKBEM's intellectual load.

12. The first phase of the piloted programs was the flights of Vostok spacecraft. From 1960 through 1963, four unpiloted spacecraft and the first six piloted spacecraft were successfully launched.

13. In 1964, after the experimental launch of the unpiloted 3KV (*Kosmos-47*) vehicle, a three-seat Voskhod spacecraft was launched with a crew of three.

14. On 22 February 1965, the experimental launch of the unpiloted *Kosmos-57* spacecraft occurred, and from 18 to 19 March, the flight of a two-seat piloted *Voskhod-2* vehicle took place. During the latter flight, the world's first spacewalk was performed.

15. From 1962 through 1963, the Soyuz design was developed for a piloted circumlunar flight. The scenario for this flight entailed using four launches of a launch vehicle based on the R-7: inserting into Earth orbit a piloted

---

18. For Chertok's accounts of these launches, see Chertok, *Rockets and People, Vol. III*, Chapters 13 and 14.

19. The common Russian abbreviation for the English term "research and development" is NIOKR—*nauchno-issledovatelskiye i opytno-konstruktorskiye raboty* (scientific-research and experimental-design work).

20. See Chertok, *Rockets and People, Vol. III*, Chapter 12.

7K vehicle, a 9K booster stage, and two 11K refuelers. To implement this idea, it was first necessary to solve the problem of automatic rendezvous and docking. The Soyuz design was completed in 1963. Considerable efforts were expended on selecting the Descent Module for the return to Earth at escape velocity and on developing a profile for guided descent.[21] This multiple-launch configuration of the Soyuz space complex was not successfully implemented. The most important results of the project were the development of a new type of piloted spacecraft, the 7K-OK, which inherited the name "Soyuz," and the solution to the problem of automatic rendezvous and docking. Completely new on-board motion control, radio communications, telemetry, integrated power supply, television, life-support, correcting engine, descent, landing, and emergency rescue control systems were developed for the spacecraft. OKB-1 developed the special ground complex 11N6110 for testing the new spacecraft.[22]

The first flight of an unpiloted Soyuz spacecraft (7K-OK No. 2— *Kosmos-133*) ended on 28 November 1966 with its emergency destruction during an attempt to return to Earth. The second unpiloted launch on 14 December 1966 (7K-OK No. 1) never got off the ground. The rocket burned up on the launch pad at Site No. 31. The third unpiloted vehicle (7K-OK No. 3—*Kosmos-140*) landed on the ice of the Aral Sea on 7 February 1967. The flight of the fourth, piloted *Soyuz-1* (7K-OK No. 4) ended tragically with the death of cosmonaut Vladimir Komarov.[23]

In October 1967 and April 1968, two pairs of Soyuzes (*Kosmos-186*, *-188* and *Kosmos-212, -213*) were launched to test the rendezvous and docking systems. The qualification flight of the unpiloted 7K-OK (*Kosmos-238*) vehicle took place from 28 August through 1 September 1968. Flights of piloted Soyuz vehicles started up again in October 1968 with the launch of *Soyuz-3*. During the period from January 1969 through June 1970, six more Soyuz vehicles were launched. This ended the flight-testing phase of the first version of the Soyuz vehicle.

16. In 1969, in conjunction with Long-Duration Orbital Station projects, development began on transport versions of the Soyuz spacecraft—7K-T (11F615A8) and 7K-TA (11F615A9).[24]

---

21. The usual Russian term for "escape velocity" is "second cosmic velocity." The "first cosmic velocity" is the velocity necessary to reach Earth orbit.
22. See Chertok, *Rockets and People, Vol. III*, pp. 476–477.
23. See Chertok, *Rockets and People, Vol. III*, Chapter 20.
24. These were transport vehicles for DOS and Almaz, respectively.

17. In 1973, the design process got under way on a modification of the Soyuz for docking with the American Apollo spacecraft.
18. In all, during the period from 1971 through 1975, 18 Soyuz spacecraft flights took place for various programs.
19. TsKBEM started developing Long-Duration Orbital Stations (DOS) in 1969.[25] By 1977, five DOS-7K Long-Duration Orbital Stations had been manufactured and launched: DOS No. 1 (*Salyut*), DOS No. 2 (was not inserted into orbit), DOS No. 3 (*Kosmos-557*), DOS No. 4 (*Salyut-4*), and DOS No. 5 (*Salyut-6*).
20. The history of Soviet piloted circumlunar flight programs is quite convoluted. The resolution of the Central Committee and USSR Council of Ministers, dated 3 August 1964, "On Work to Research the Moon and Outer Space" named OKB-52 (General Designer Vladimir Chelomey) as the head design bureau for circumlunar flight using the augmented UR-500K launch vehicle. The deadline was the first half of 1967.

From 1964 to 1965, the optimal version for the circumlunar flight was being selected from among three alternative configurations:

   a. *Soyuz-7K*, *-9K*, and *-11K* (OKB-1);
   b. UR-500K with piloted vehicle LK-1 (OKB-52); and
   c. UR-500K with booster stage Block D, adopted from the N1-L3 program, and a modified 7K vehicle (OKB-1 working jointly with OKB-52).

On 25 October 1965, the next resolution, "On Concentrating the Efforts of Industrial Design Organizations in Industry to Create a Rocket-Space System for a Circumlunar Flight and Preparing for the Subsequent Organization of a Landing of an Expedition on the Surface of the Moon," was issued. Despite its leading role and being loaded down with the N1-L3 program, OKB-1 received the assignment to perform the circumlunar flight using a piloted spacecraft and the UR-500K launch vehicle. This same resolution proposed that OKB-52 concentrate on developing the UR-500K launch vehicle and the booster rocket stage designed to support the circumlunar flight. Thus, OKB-52 was relieved of manufacturing the piloted spacecraft.[26]

OKB-1 was assigned to develop the piloted spacecraft for the circumlunar flight and the booster stage (on a competitive basis) using the UR-500K launch vehicle. The circumlunar flight program was conducted independently of the

---

25. DOS—*Dolgovremyennaya orbitalnaya stantsiya*.
26. The original piloted vehicle for circumlunar flight designed by OKB-52 was known as the LK-1.

development of the N-1 launch vehicle and also independently of the Lunar Orbital Vehicle (LOK) and the Lunar Vehicle (LK) for landing on the Moon.[27]

In December 1965, Korolev and Chelomey approved the "Fundamental Principles for the UR-500K–7K-L1 Rocket-Space Complex."

21. TsKBEM and collaborating organizations developed and manufactured 14 7K-L1 spacecraft for circumlunar flight. In all, from 1967 through 1970, there were 13 launches of UR-500K-L1 complexes in the unpiloted version. After a series of failed launches, they achieved satisfactory reliability.

Unlike the 7K-OK and the LOK of the L3 complex, the L1 control system did not have to perform rendezvous and docking tasks. For the first time, special 99K and 100K solar and stellar orientation sensors, plus a gyrostabilized platform, w ere installed on an orbital vehicle. The Scientific-Research Institute of Automatics and Instrument Building (NIIAP) was named the lead organization for the development of circumlunar flight control systems.[28] At the initiative of N. A. Pilyugin, the *Argon-11* on-board digital computer (BTsVM) was used for navigation and propulsion systems control for the first time.[29] S. A. Krutovskikh originally developed this system for airplanes at the Scientific-Research Center for Electronic Computer Technology (NITsEVT).[30] The working groups of the departments of my complex, under the supervision of B. V. Rauschenbach, I. Ye. Yurasov, and V. A. Kalashnikov, were tasked with developing orientation and navigation systems using the optical sensors developed at NPO Geofizika, the on-board control complex systems, emergency rescue systems, antenna-feeder systems, and emergency destruction systems for unpiloted flights. The control specialists at OKB-1, NIIAP, and NII-885 imbued the design with the experience they had gained from the development of Vostoks, Voskhods, the vehicles for the Mars and Venera missions, and the numerous Luna Moon-shot vehicles.

A large rocket-space system with a fundamentally new control system was actually developed. In addition to it, during the process of flight tests, Block D—the UR-500K's fourth stage—also underwent experimental development. This booster stage subsequently proved useful for other programs and was

---

27. LOK—*Lunnyy orbitalnyy korabl*; LK—*Lunnyy korabl.*

28. NIIAP—*Nauchno-issledovatelskiy institut avtomatiki i priborostroyeniya*—was one of the primary organizations developing guidance and control systems for the Soviet missile and space programs.

29. N. A. Pilyugin (1908–1982) was an original member of the Council of Chief Designers. As a chief designer, first at NII-885 and then at NIIAP, he oversaw the development of several generations of guidance systems for Soviet missiles, launch vehicles, and spacecraft. The common Russian abbreviation for digital computer is BTsVM—*Bortovaya tsifrovaya vychislitelnaya mashina* (on-board digital computing machine).

30. NITsEVT—*Nauchnyy institut tsifrovoy elektronnoy vychislitelnoy tekhniki.*

put into service. However, after the flight of *Apollo 8* [in 1968], there was no sense in performing a piloted circumlunar flight, and the decision was made to suspend further L1 operations. The UR-500K-L1 program did not fulfill its main mission, a piloted circumlunar flight. Fundamentally new developments were, however, further refined in subsequent space programs.

22. Beginning in 1960, OKB-1, and later TsKBEM, conducted research and developed designs for a landing expedition to Mars. The 1960 scenario called for the use of electrical rocket engines and a nuclear reactor as power sources. OKB-1 formed a special subdivision for this field of work. In 1965, studies began on a project for an expedition to Mars using the N-1 launch vehicle. The Mars expedition complex was supposed to have been assembled in near-Earth orbit by means of several launches of the N-1 launch vehicle.

   Dozens of scientific-research institutes, design bureaus, and institutes of higher learning were enlisted to develop the nuclear power plants for the heavy interplanetary spacecraft. OKB-1 had the lead role in this project. From 1960 through 1975, a one-of-a-kind experimental facility was created for these purposes. Research and development showed that it would be realistically possible to create nuclear power plants using reactors with thermionic converters with an electric output of up to 550 kilowatts.

23. Beginning in 1959, at OKB-1 and later at TsKBEM, a scientific, design, and production facility was created for the integrated development of spacecraft control systems, antenna-feeder units, power supply systems, actuator assemblies for motion control in space, on-board life-support systems, and docking assemblies. At the same time, spaceflight control methods and methods for training test-engineers for spaceflights were being developed.

24. Despite the fact that a number of industry organizations had been successfully involved in the development of liquid-propellant rocket engines (ZhRDs), OKB-1 created its own design and process facility for the production of low-thrust engines.[31] It developed and introduced six types of power plants for booster rockets and for spacecraft control.

25. And finally, the N1-L3 rocket-space complex to fly two cosmonauts to the Moon, land one cosmonaut on the lunar surface, and return to Earth was developed at OKB-1 and later at TsKBEM. This is the program that I shall tell about in this volume.

---

31. The common Russian abbreviation for liquid-propellant rocket engine is ZhRD— *Zhidkostnyy raketnyy dvigatel.*

From the list cited above, it is clear that for the lead organization OKB-1, headed by Korolev, and later for TsKBEM under Mishin's leadership, the N1-L3 program, despite its large scale, was only one of 20 programs!

During Korolev's time, OKB-1 had three branches. Branch No. 1 was the territory of TsNII-58, which was transferred to OKB-1 in 1959. Branch No. 2 was created in Krasnoyarsk and Branch No. 3 in Kuybyshev (now Samara). The latter two branches eventually became independent rocket-space organizations. The first chiefs of the branches during Korolev's lifetime were his deputies Chertok, Reshetnev, and Kozlov, respectively.

OKB-1 Branch No. 2, later known as OKB-10, then NPO PM (Krasnoyarsk-26), currently Federal State Unitary Enterprise "Academician M. F. Reshetnev Scientific-Production Association of Applied Mechanics"[32]

Branch No. 2 was formed in 1958 at the initiative of Korolev to set up production of R-11M (8A61) tactical missiles for the ground forces. OKB-1 Deputy Chief Designer Mikhail Reshetnev, the missile's lead designer, was appointed chief of Branch No. 2.[33] In 1961, Branch No. 2 became the independent OKB-10, which was located in Krasnoyarsk-26, the closed city of atomic scientists. Reshetnev was placed in charge of OKB-10 and became its chief designer. In 1966, OKB-1 handed over its work on the *Molniya-1* communications satellite and all work related to communications satellites to OKB-10. OKB-10, subsequently the Scientific-Production Association of Applied Mechanics (NPO PM), became the nation's primary developer of communication and navigation satellites.[34] Here is a list of its projects:

1. Medium-class launch vehicle for the insertion of satellites up to 1,000 kilograms into medium elliptical and circular orbits. Developments began in 1962 (used design inventory of OKB-586 in Dnepropetrovsk).[35]
2. *Strela* (Arrow) system satellites for official communications. From 1962 through 1970, four modifications were developed and put into operation.

---

32. Since Chertok's original writing, the name of the organization has changed again. In early 2010, it was known as OAO "ISS"—*imeni Akademika M. F. Reshetnev* (or Open Joint Stock Company Academician M. F. Reshetnev Information Satellite Systems).

33. A "lead designer" (*vedushchiy konstruktor*) was a different position than a "chief designer." In a Soviet-era design bureau, a lead designer was typically responsible for design support during the experimental production phase of a new weapons system.

34. NPO PM—*Nauchno-proizvodstvennoye obedineniye prikladnoy mekhaniki*.

35. This was the 11K65M light launch vehicle, better known as the *Kosmos-3M*, derived from OKB-586's R-14 intermediate range ballistic missile.

3. *Molniya-1* (Lightning-1) high-elliptical orbit satellite. Mastery of production and upgrading for broadcasting television programs. Beginning of development—1968. Put into service in 1975.
4. *Molniya-2* television communications satellite. Beginning of development—1967. Put into service in 1972.
5. *Tsiklon* (Cyclone) system navigation and communications satellite. Beginning of development—1966. Put into service in 1972.
6. *Molniya-3* communications satellites. Developed for long-range telephone and telegraph communications, for transmission of television programs to *Orbita* (Orbit) system stations, and for the needs of the Ministry of Defense. Put into service in 1974.
7. *Raduga* (Rainbow) geosynchronous television communications satellite. Beginning of development—1970. First launch took place on 22 December 1975.
8. The *Sfera* (Sphere) system geodesic and topographical survey satellite. Put into service in 1973.
9. National, special departmental, and governmental communications systems and navigation systems for the Navy produced using NPO PM developments. The following systems that were put into service should go down in the history of cosmonautics:
    * the *Orbita* national space-based telephone communications and Central Television broadcast relay system;
    * the *Korund* (Corundum) integrated system of space-, air-, and ground-based governmental communications networks;
    * the *Sfera* complex updating the geodesic survey of the continents;
    * the *Tsiklon* navigation and long-range two-way radio communication support system with active relay for submarines and surface ships; and
    * the *Strela* standardized official communications space system using standardized satellites.
10. *Tsikada* (Cicada) space navigation system providing global navigation support for naval and civilian vessels. Its development began in 1974 based on the *Tsiklon* system.

NPO PM developments were extremely important in providing effective information support for the armed forces and creating a single national communications and television broadcast system.

From the author's archives.

Dmitriy Kozlov (left) and Boris Chertok at a meeting in Samara (formerly Kuybyshev).

OKB-1 Branch No. 3, later known as TsSKB (in Kuybyshev, now Samara), currently GNPRKTs "TsSKB-Progress"[36]

Branch No. 3 was formed under the auspices of Kuybyshev aviation Factory No. 1, which soon thereafter was renamed the Progress Factory. Beginning in 1957, instead of aircraft, the factory was supposed to start up series production of R-7 and R-7A combat missiles. R-7 missile lead designer Dmitriy Kozlov was named chief of Branch No. 3. He faced the difficult task of setting up the series production of combat missiles and launch vehicles for the first spacecraft. Considering the crucial nature of this sector of operations, in 1961, Korolev named Kozlov his deputy chief designer. In 1964, on Korolev's recommendation, the government approved a decree calling for the *Zenit-2* and *Zenit-4* spy satellite projects to be transferred to Branch No. 3 and the Progress Factory. In 1966, Kozlov became the first deputy chief of TsKBEM and the chief and chief designer of the TsKBEM Kuybyshev branch.

In 1974, the branch was spun off as an independent organization—the Central Specialized Design Bureau (TsSKB). Dmitriy Kozlov was appointed as its chief and chief designer. From 1983 through 2003, he was general designer of TsSKB, the head design bureau for the development of space complexes

---

36. TsSKB—*Tsentralnoye spetsializirovannoye konstruktorskoye byuro* (Central Specialized Design Bureau); GRKNPTs—*Gosudarstvennyy nauchno-proizvodstvennyy raketno-kosmicheskiy tsentr* (State Scientific-Production Rocket-Space Center).

for strategic photographic and optical-electronic reconnaissance, cartography, exploration of Earth's natural resources, ecological monitoring, and also medium-class launch vehicles based on the R-7A missile. Dmitriy Ilyich Kozlov is a two-time Hero of Socialist Labor and corresponding member of the USSR Academy of Sciences (now the Russian Academy of Sciences).[37]

The Progress Factory thereafter became the head enterprise for the series production of all modifications of launch vehicles based on the R-7, of R-9 combat missiles, of spacecraft developed at TsSKB, and of N-1 launch vehicles.

Here I shall list only the main projects of Branch No. 3 and TsSKB from 1960 through 1975.

1. Branch No. 3 was responsible for management of production setup, modernization, and design follow-through on R-7, R-7A, and R-9 combat missiles.

2. From 1966 through 1974 and later, the branch was independently in charge of development of three- and four-stage launch vehicles using the R-7A missile. Branch No. 3 (and later TsSKB) became the head organization for the development of the USSR's only rocket for the piloted program, and D. I. Kozlov was the chief designer of all versions of launch vehicles derived from the R-7A. Right up until 2003, the three-stage Soyuz-U rocket was the only single-use ballistic launch vehicle in the world that was trusted to insert piloted spacecraft into space.[38]

3. In 1964, design development began on a second generation of photoreconnaissance satellites—*Zenit-4*. It was put into service in late 1965. From 1965 through 1967 alone, 55 launches of *Zenit-2* and *Zenit-4* satellites took place.

4. In 1970, the *Zenit-2M* photoreconnaissance satellite went into service and in 1971, the *Zenit-4M*. Subsequently, the Zenits were modified four more times.[39]

5. In 1972, a special precision cartography satellite—*Zenit-4MK*—was developed.

6. In 1970, development began on the next generations of *Yantar* (Amber) reconnaissance spacecraft. By all parameters, this model of spacecraft surpassed the Zenits. They provided detailed high-resolution surveillance of small objects, supplied a great degree of real-time information acquisition, and performed cartographic and topographic missions.

---

37. Chertok wrote these words prior to Kozlov's death on 7 March 2009.

38. In October 2003, a Chinese CZ-2F (Long March-2F) rocket launched the piloted *Shenzhou 5* spacecraft into orbit with Chinese astronaut Yang Liwei.

39. These later variants included the *Zenit-4MK*, *Zenit-4MT*, *Zenit-6U*, and *Zenit-8* models.

7. *Zenit-Resurs* spacecraft for the exploration of natural resources, *Foton* (Photon) spacecraft for scientific research, and *Bion* spacecraft for bio-medical research were developed from 1968 through 1975 using Zenits.

8. Between 1968 and 1971, the Ministry of Defense ordered the development of the 7K-VI piloted military spacecraft. Subsequently, this field of endeavor was transferred from Branch No. 3 to TsKBEM. This development laid the foundation for the development of the 7K-S piloted spacecraft, which replaced the first generation of Soyuz (7K-OK) spacecraft.[40]

I shall not provide such a detailed list of the projects conducted in the entire rocket-space industry. The list cited below contains only the main projects of the other head organizations.

OKB-52, later known as TsKBM, currently OAO VPK NPO Mashinostroyeniya and Khrunichev Factory (ZIKh)[41]

Submarine-launched cruise missiles constituted the main thrust of the postwar work at OKB-52, where General Designer Vladimir Nikolayevich Chelomey was in charge. In October 1960, a government decree attached OKB-23 to OKB-52 as its Branch No. 1. Until that time, well-known designer of heavy bombers Vladimir Mikhaylovich Myasishchev headed OKB-23. The production facilities of OKB-52 became the M. V. Khrunichev Factory (ZIKh) in Fili—one of the best enterprises of the aviation industry. The personnel of ZIKh and OKB-23 demonstrated a high degree of manufacturing refinement and discipline, which was often lacking in recently created enterprises of the rocket industry. Chelomey—two-time Hero of Socialist Labor and full member of the USSR Academy of Sciences—remained the permanent chief of TsKBM until his death in 1984.[42]

From 1960 through 1975, OKB-52 worked in the following areas:

1. The design bureau developed the UR-100 (8K84) combat intercontinental ballistic missile. The first modification went into service in July 1967. After this, the UR-100 underwent several upgrades. More than 1,000

---

40. The 7K-S variant of the Soyuz was the basis for the 7K-ST model, better known as the Soyuz-T, which started flying crews in 1980.

41. TsKBM—*Tsentralnoye konstruktorskoye byuro mashinostroyeniya* (Central Design Bureau of Machine Building); OAO VPK NPO Mashinostroyeniya—*Otkrytoye aktsionernoye obshchestvo 'Voyenno-promyshlennaya korporatsiya Nauchno-proizvodstvennoye obedineniye mashinostroyeniya'* (Joint-Stock Company Military-Industrial Corporation Scientific-Production Association of Machine Building); ZIKh—*Zavod imeni M. V. Khrunicheva* (M. V. Khrunichev Factory).

42. Chelomey received two Hero of Socialist Labor awards, in 1959 and 1963. He became a full member of the Academy of Sciences in 1962.

UR-100 missiles in silo launchers constituted the main offensive force of the Strategic Rocket Forces (RVSN).[43]

2. The production of UR-100s, their upgrading, and their operational support constituted ZIKh's main workload until the mid-1970s. A modification (of the UR-100) known as the UR-100K (RS-10 or 15A20) went into service in December 1972. The next modification, the UR-100U, which went into service in September 1974, had a nose cone containing three warheads with a TNT equivalent of 350 kilotons each. At a maximum range of 10,000 kilometers, the inertial control system provided a circular error probability (CEP) of 900 meters.[44] Between 1972 and 1974, the new UR-100N missile was developed, and in 1975 it was put into service. It was equipped with six individually targeted warheads with a TNT equivalent of 0.75 megatons each. During the 1980s, it was replaced with the modified UR-100NU, which is still in service today.

The UR-100N and UR-100NU intercontinental ballistic missiles, which are relatively inexpensive and simple to operate, were mass-produced and placed in lightly protected silos. According to Chelomey's concept, in the event of a nuclear attack on the Soviet Union, there must always be enough missiles on hand for a retaliatory strike.

3. The *Taran* (Ram) project, which called for the use of the UR-100 as an antiballistic missile, was developed from 1964 to 1965. It was never implemented.

4. After the UR-100, launch vehicle projects cropped up one after the other: the medium-class UR-200, heavy-class UR-500, and super-heavy UR-700. A small series of UR-200 launch vehicles underwent flight tests from 1963 to 1964. Chelomey proposed using the UR-200 as an all-purpose launch vehicle for various payloads. The UR-200 carrying a nuclear warhead was capable of reaching distances in excess of 12,000 kilometers. Among the payloads developed at OKB-52 for the UR-200 were the IS (Satellite Fighter) maneuvering spacecraft, satellites for global naval reconnaissance, and even satellites capable of striking ground targets.[45]

---

43. *Author's note*: Most domestic Soviet missiles had four or even five names: military, industrial, international (as mentioned in treaties), U.S., and NATO designations. For example: UR-100K, 15A20, RS-10, SS-11, and Sego, respectively.

44. The Russian term for CEP is KVO—*Krugovoye veroyatnoye otkloneniye* (circular probable deviation).

45. IS—*Istrebitel sputnikov*. The first IS spacecraft were launched in 1963 and 1964 as *Polet-1* and *Polet-2*.

Operations on the UR-200 stopped in 1965. By that time, Yangel's R-16 intercontinental ballistic missile had been put into service, and by all parameters the new heavy R-36 had surpassed the UR-200.

5. The draft plan of the two-stage UR-500 launch vehicle was completed in 1963.[46] At the firing range, fundamentally new ground-based launch systems for this missile were built. Military builders were blamed for disrupting the N-1 schedule: construction on the large Assembly and Testing Building (MIK), the launch site, and the residential area dragged on.[47] They were forced to throw all their efforts onto the "left flank"—the open "western front" where Chelomey's engineering facility and launch sites were under construction. This "left flank" 70 kilometers northwest of the city of Leninsk was the location of two launch sites with four UR-500 launchers, an engineering facility with two MIKs, and a residential area for 10,000 people.

According to our traditions, even for the first experimental launches of a launch vehicle, we created an expensive payload. Using a third-stage hull, OKB-52 manufactured the *Proton* satellite—a heavy space laboratory designed to study cosmic rays and to interact with super-high-energy particles. The block of science equipment containing detectors for all types of space particles was developed under the supervision of Academician Sergey Nikolayevich Vernov at the Moscow State University's Scientific-Research Institute of Nuclear Physics.[48]

The first launch of the two-stage UR-500 took place on 16 July 1965.

6. In addition to the scientific equipment, *Proton-1* was equipped with a power plant with solar arrays, telemetry systems, spatial orientation indicators, an on-board control complex with sequencer (PVU), a command radio link, and a thermal control system.[49]

Flight-developmental tests (LKI) of the two-stage UR-500 Proton rocket ended on 6 July 1966 with the launch of the *Proton-3* space station. Three out of the four launches were successful. The third launch failed during the second-stage operational segment.[50]

---

46. In the Soviet research and development process, the "draft plan" (*eskiznyy proyekt*) represents a multivolume set of documents describing in detail a vehicle's basic design and performance elements.

47. MIK—*Montazhno-ispytatelnyy korpus.*

48. Sergey Nikolayevich Vernov (1910–1982) was a famous Soviet physicist specializing in the physics of cosmic rays. From 1960 to 1982, he served as director of the Scientific-Research Institute of Nuclear Physics (NIIYaF) of Moscow State University (MGU). He became a full member of the Academy of Sciences in 1968.

49. The literal Russian term for a sequencer is PVU—*programmno-vremennoye ustroystvo* (programmable timing instrument).

50. This launch took place on 24 March 1966.

7. The three-stage UR-500K was developed in response to the aforementioned decree of 3 August 1964 and in accordance with Khrushchev's admonition, "Don't let the Americans have the Moon!" The decree named OKB-52 as the top executor of the piloted circumlunar flight program. The deadline: 1966 to the first half of 1967. There remained only two and a half years from the day that Khrushchev signed the decree until the piloted circumlunar flight. Understanding the vulnerability of the highly complex Soyuz program for circumlunar flight, after the successful launch of the two-stage UR-500, Korolev instructed his designers to study the possibility of using stockpiled inventory from the piloted vehicle of the Soyuz program and the Block D upper stage of the N1-L3 program.

After the overthrow of Nikita Khrushchev in October 1964, the top governmental officials had the opportunity to exercise some common sense. The Military-Industrial Commission, the head ministries, and the defense department of the Communist Party Central Committee understood that it was an unjustifiable dissipation of efforts to pursue two circumlunar flight projects—Korolev's Soyuz using a three-stage *Semyorka* and Chelomey's using the UR-500K launch vehicle. In August 1965, the VPK recommended that Korolev and Chelomey resolve the issue of whether it would be possible to unify the piloted vehicles for the circumlunar flight and use the UR-500K rocket in the Soyuz system program. The result of this difficult joint operation of OKB-1 and OKB-52 was the development of a version of the launch vehicle in which the third stage of the UR-500K rocket fell into the ocean rather than inserting the circumlunar flight vehicle into orbit. The Block D booster stage, adapted from N1-L3, provided the acceleration to leave Earth orbit and achieve escape velocity. In all, from March 1967 through December 1970, there were 25 launches of the UR-500 and UR-500K rockets.[51] Today, the UR-500K under the name Proton is one of the most reliable heavy launch vehicles.

8. After the first successful launches of the UR-500, OKB-52's initiative in cosmonautics was not limited to ideas of circumlunar flight. In 1965, Chelomey and his deputies Gerbert Yefremov and Arkadiy Eydis proposed creating an Orbital Piloted Station (OPS) for integrated surveillance and reconnaissance. The Main Intelligence Directorate (GRU) was extremely interested in this.[52] It was assumed that the presence of cosmonauts on

---

51. Of these 25 launches, at least 12 failed due to malfunctions in the main rocket or the Block D upper stage.

52. OPS—*Orbitalnaya pilotiruyemaya stantsiya*; GRU—*Glavnoye razvedyvatelnoye upravleniye*. The GRU was the primary military intelligence agency of the Soviet armed forces.

board a spy spacecraft and their involvement in obtaining information using optical, television, radar, and high-resolution cameras would help to make a qualitative leap compared with specialized unpiloted spy satellites. The Almaz (Diamond) orbital station was developed. We subsequently proposed using its first hulls for the Salyut Long-Duration Orbital Stations (DOS).

The first Almaz launch took place on 3 April 1973. The three-stage UR-500K, which underwent development testing with launches for the L1 and DOS programs, inserted it into orbit. However, the station malfunctioned before a piloted vehicle could lift off to meet up with it. For reasons of secrecy, the Almaz was called *Salyut-2* so there would be no doubt that it had the same peaceful purpose as our DOS—the first in the Salyut series. Almaz launches ended in 1976 due to an expansion of international collaboration and concentration of efforts on a single type of Salyut piloted Long-Duration Orbital Station. The Almaz spacecraft that were inserted into space were called *Salyut-2, -3,* and *-5.* The DOSes were referred to as *Salyut-1, -4, -6,* and *-7* all the way up until the *Mir* station.

Chelomey's successor Chief Designer Gerbert Yefremov (left) and Boris Chertok.

From the author's archives.

9. MOM supported the design that Chelomey proposed for the UR-700 super-heavy launch vehicle. The only work that OKB-52 performed on this project was on its draft plan. However, Glushko at OKB-456 began working on engines for the UR-700 and got as far as the manufacture of prototype models.[53] A design was developed for an engine operating on such propellant components as nitrogen tetroxide and unsymmetrical dimethyl hydrazine with a thrust of 640 tons. This engine was proposed for use with the first stage of the UR-900 super-heavy launch vehicle.[54] But the design for this launch vehicle failed to find support.

---

53. These were the RD-270 engines, developed between 1962 and 1970.
54. Chertok is probably in error here and means the UR-700 launch vehicle.

10. Between 1968 and 1973, US (Controlled Satellite) model satellites for a naval space reconnaissance and target designation system were developed and put into service.[55]

11. Despite its broad range of developments in the field of strategic combat missiles and space technology, OKB-52 continued to produce new models of naval cruise missiles. In 1965, due to successes in the development of naval ballistic missiles, operations were halted on submarine-launched cruise missiles for striking land-based targets. OKB-52 concentrated its efforts on the production of antiship missiles—first designed for surface launch and then for underwater launch. In 1968, the world's first *Ametist* (Amethyst) antiship cruise missile launched from underwater was put into service on submarines. In 1972, the more advanced *Malakhit* (Malachite) cruise missile was put into service. Both missiles used solid-propellant engines. In 1969, OKB-52 began developing long-range antiship missiles using turbojet and ramjet engines, including ones armed with nuclear warheads.

New generations of cruise missiles have gone into service on nuclear submarines outside the timeframe we are examining here. However, for the sake of history it is important to note that Vladimir Chelomey, while putting forward new designs of super-heavy launch vehicles, did not stop arming the Navy with small cruise missiles.

OKB-586, now known as GP M. K. Yangel KB Yuzhnoye and Yuzhmash Factory (Dnepropetrovsk)[56]

I have already discussed the creation of the rocket-building enterprise in Dnepropetrovsk in my previous books. To recap, beginning in 1954, the chief designer and later the general designer of OKB-586 was Mikhail Kuzmich Yangel.

The main managerial staff of OKB-586 from 1949 to 1952 was made up of NII-88 staff members, including individuals from Korolev's OKB-1, which was part of NII-88 until 1956. I will also remind the reader that in

Former Chief Designer Vladimir Utkin (Yangel's successor) and Boris Chertok (right).

From the author's archives.

---

55. US—*Upravlyayemyy sputnik*. In the West, these satellites were known as the Radar Ocean Reconnaissance Satellite (RORSAT).

56. GP—*Gosudarstvennoye predpriyatiye* (State Enterprise).

1951 Yangel worked as chief of department No. 5 of OKB-1, and I was his deputy. Before moving to Dnepropetrovsk, Yangel was briefly the deputy of Chief Designer Korolev and later director of NII-88.[57] Yangel passed away in 1971. Vladimir Fedorovich Utkin replaced him as general designer. Both general directors were two-time Heroes of Socialist Labor, and both were academicians.[58] Yangel became an Academy of Sciences member in 1966, and Utkin in 1984. From 1990 through 2000, Vladimir Utkin was director of TsNIImash (formerly NII-88).[59]

The first director of Factory No. 586 was Leonid Vasilyevich Smirnov. Under his management the factory mastered the series production of Korolev's R-1, R-2, R-5, and R-5M rockets and Yangel's R-12, R-14, and R-16 rockets. In 1961, Aleksandr Maksimovich Makarov replaced him in the post of director of Yuzhmash. The list of developments cited below spans the period of time when Makarov ran the factory.

1. The R-12 (8K63) medium-range strategic ballistic missile was put into service in 1959; its upgraded modification, the R-12U in a silo-based version, was put into service in 1963. The R-12 is considered a record-holder: in all, more than 2,300 missiles were manufactured, and the R-12U remained in service for 30 years.

2. The R-14U medium-range strategic missile is a modification of the R-14 missile. Its first launch took place in 1962. It went into service in 1963. The missile was supposed to be dismantled by 1990 in accordance with a treaty regarding medium- and short-range missiles.[60]

3. After the disaster of 24 October 1960, the R-16 (8K64) missile was modified.[61] Its flight tests resumed in February 1961. In 1963, the upgraded silo-based version of the R-16U went into service. It was taken out of service in 1975.

4. The second generation of the R-36 (8K67) intercontinental strategic missile gave rise to an entire line of Soviet heavy intercontinental strategic rockets carrying super-powerful warheads (the TNT equivalent of 18 to 25 megatons). The R-36 went into service in 1967. This rocket was equipped with Glushko's engines, which operated on high-boiling components, just as its precursors

---

57. Yangel served as director of NII-88 from May 1952 to October 1953.

58. The "Hero of Socialist Labor" was the highest national honor bestowed to civilian citizens during the Soviet era. It was first awarded in 1938. Yangel received his awards in 1959 and 1961, while Utkin received his in 1969 and 1976.

59. TsNIImash—*Tsentralnyy nauchno-issledovatelskiy institut mashinostroyeniye* (Central Scientific-Research Institute of Machine Building).

60. The last six R-14 missiles were destroyed as per the terms of the Intermediate-Range Nuclear Forces Treaty by 21 May 1990.

61. For the R-16 disaster, see Boris Chertok, *Rockets and People, Vol. II: Creating a Rocket Industry*, ed. Asif A. Siddiqi (Washington, DC: NASA SP-2006-4110, 2006), Chapter 32.

had.[62] The missile's control system was produced at OKB-692 in Kharkov (later NPO Elektropribor) under the supervision of General Director and Chief Designer Vladimir Sergeyev.[63] It was retired in the late 1970s.

5. The R-36M intercontinental strategic missile (15A14), or RS-20A, which inherited all the best features of the R-36, was the third generation for OKB Yuzhnoye. It became the most powerful in its class. Flight testing began in 1973, and in 1975 the R-36M missile went into service. A fundamentally new proposal came out: arm the missile with a 24-megaton monoblock warhead or with eight independently targetable reentry vehicles, each with a 0.9-megaton warhead. The missile's flight and preparation control system was developed using an on-board computer. An advanced gyrostabilized platform equipped with a full set of inertial navigation command instruments made it possible to ensure a high degree of target kill accuracy. According to flight-test data, the CEP was 430 meters. The North Atlantic Treaty Organization (NATO) called this missile Satan.

   Yangel and Utkin developed the R-36M missile according to the concept "fewer but better is best." The sophisticated and heavy missiles were substantially better than the initial R-36. They had great resistance to the destructive factors of a nuclear explosion, had better protected silo launchers (ShPU), and had a high degree of combat readiness.[64] A fundamentally new concept was the use of a so-called "mortar launch" from a container.[65]

6. The RS-16A intercontinental strategic missile, or MR-UR-100 (15A15). This missile is distinguished by a high degree of automatic control over all the launch systems and an increased capability to overcome the enemy's antiballistic missile systems.[66] The RS-16A missile went into service in 1975.

7. Mobile missile systems using heavy tank chassis and railroads. These systems were also produced at KB Yuzhnoye, although in terms of their tactical performance data, they were inferior to the mobile missile systems that Aleksandr Nadiradze developed.

8. Two lines of *Kosmos*-series launch vehicles for small spacecraft were developed from 1959 to 1967 on the basis of R-12 and R-14 rockets. The light

---

62. The R-36 first stage used a single RD-251, and the second stage used a single RD-252.

63. Vladimir Grigoryevich Sergeyev (1914–2009) served as chief designer of OKB-692 from 1960 to 1986. He succeeded Boris Mikhaylovich Konoplev (1912–1960), who was killed in the R-16 disaster in 1960.

64. ShPU—*Shakhtnaya puskovaya ustanovka.*

65. "Mortar launch" describes the practice of shooting the missile out of its silo, mortar fashion, by a piston driven by the expansion of gases from a solid propellant charge inside the piston. The missile's main engines fire only after ejection of the missile from the silo, several meters aboveground.

66. The equivalent Russian term for antiballistic missile (ABM) systems is PRO— *Protivoraketnaya oborona* (antimissile defense).

Kosmos-2 launch vehicle was launched from 1961 through 1977. The heavier launch vehicle, the last model of which was named *Kosmos-3M*, has been used from 1967 to the present. It first went into series production at the Krasnoyarsk Machine Building Factory (design support was handed over to OKB-10), and later at PO Polet in Omsk.[67]

9. The *Tsiklon* line of launch vehicles with a mass up to 3 tons. It was produced on the basis of R-36 and R-36P rockets. Testing began in 1967 for a two-stage model and in 1977 for a three-stage model. They are used for various space programs to this day.

10. R-56 super-heavy launch vehicle. From 1964 to 1965, Yangel developed a draft plan incorporating Glushko's high-boiling component engines with up to 640 tons of thrust. The proposal aimed to develop alternatives to Chelomey's UR-700 and Korolev's N-1. Operations were ceased during the draft plan phase.

In addition to combat missiles and launch vehicles, OKB-586 began to design various spacecraft. Chief Designer Vyacheslav Kovtunenko, subordinate to the general designer [Yangel], managed the majority of the developments. The main areas of endeavor of KB-3, which he headed and which was part of KB Yuzhnoye, were electronic reconnaissance spacecraft, monitoring and calibrating complexes, and target satellites.

11. *Tselina* (Virgin Land) electronic reconnaissance satellites for surveillance and detailed observation were developed for the Navy beginning in the mid-1960s jointly with the TsNII-108 Radio Engineering Institute. The *Tselina* electronic reconnaissance space complex went into service in the mid-1970s.

12. DS-P1-Yu, DS-P1-I, and *Tayfun* (Typhoon) monitoring and calibrating space complexes for the experimental development and testing of antimissile and antispace defense (PRO and PKO).[68] They were produced from 1967 through 1973.

13. The *Lira* (Lyre) auxiliary spacecraft was developed as a target for testing IS satellite fighters. It went into service in 1973.

14. Block Ye was the propulsion system for the LK lunar landing vehicle of the L3 complex. The project was conducted in accordance with the governmental resolution on the N1-L3 program per design specifications approved by OKB-1. The Block Ye underwent flight testing as part of the LK mockup during three launches using the 11A511L (based on the R-7A) launch vehicle.[69]

---

67. PO—*Proizvodstvennoye obyedineniye* (Production Association).
68. PKO—*Protivokosmicheskaya oborona*.
69. These launches were carried out in 1970 and 1971 under the *Kosmos* label.

S. A. Lavochkin Factory and NPO, now known as S. A. Lavochkin Scientific-Production Association or NPO imeni Lavochkina (Khimki)

The design bureau and Factory No. 301 of illustrious aviation designer Semyon Lavochkin switched over from developing airplanes to producing antiaircraft missiles in 1947. The transfer in 1949 of Georgiy Babakin's staff from NII-88 to Lavochkin contributed to the success in this field. In 1965, Georgiy Babakin was appointed chief designer of Lavochkin's firm. Korolev trusted him and handed over the projects for automatic interplanetary vehicles for the exploration of the Moon, Mars, and Venus for him to continue.

The design bureau and factory, transformed into NPO Lavochkin, were transferred from the Ministry of the Aviation Industry to the Ministry of General Machine Building.[70] Nowadays, this is the head organization for the development of spacecraft for the exploration of the Moon and planets of the solar system.[71] When developing automatic spacecraft, the most complex aspect is ensuring the reliability of the control system, radio communication, and data transmission. Per government decrees, NII-885, KB Geofizika, NII-944, NPO Elas, the All-Union Scientific-Research Institute (VNII) for Power Sources, and a number of other organizations that had cooperated earlier on the development of L3 systems participated in the development of these systems.[72]

From 1966 through 1975, NPO Lavochkin developed 10 types of spacecraft, which maintained the Soviet Union's superiority in solving fundamental scientific problems. Here is a list of accomplishments:

* soft landing on the surface of the Moon;
* delivery to the Moon of the Lunokhod self-propelled lunar exploration vehicle;
* exploration of the Moon from an orbital satellite;
* delivery of lunar soil to Earth by an automatic spacecraft;
* exploration of Venus from an orbital satellite;
* landing of an automatic spacecraft on the surface of Venus;
* exploration of Mars from an orbital satellite;
* landing of an automatic spacecraft on the surface of Mars; and
* research on the physics of the Sun and on geomagnetic and radiation conditions.

---

70. NPO Lavochkin was established in 1974 by combining the design bureau with the factory.

71. It should be noted that the last Soviet or Russian spacecraft that went beyond Earth orbit (*Fobos-1* and *-2*) were launched in 1988. The last attempt took place in 1996 when the Mars-8 spacecraft failed to leave Earth orbit.

72. VNII—*Vsesoyuznyy nauchno-issledovatelskiy institut.*

A formidable experimental facility for the developmental testing of automatic spacecraft was set up at NPO Lavochkin. The organizer of the design school for this most crucial scientific research was Georgiy Babakin, who received the title Hero of Socialist Labor and was elected Corresponding Member of the USSR Academy of Sciences.[73] Each of the interplanetary developments and the results of the explorations of the Moon, Venus, and Mars performed using spacecraft developed at the NPO Lavochkin have been broadly discussed in the mass media and in special literature. As a rule, though, no mention was made of the failed interplanetary program launches in those days.

After Babakin's death in 1971, Korolev's close associate Sergey Sergeyevich Kryukov became chief designer. Under his supervision, projects for the development of more advanced interplanetary spacecraft continued. NPO Lavochkin remains the only space organization in Russia after OKB-1 that developed automatic interplanetary spacecraft.

SKB-385, now known as Joint-Stock Company V. P. Makeyev State Rocket Center (OAO GRTs imeni V. P. Makeyeva) (Miass)[74]

From 1960 to 1975, the nation's leadership devoted exceptional attention to achieving nuclear parity with the help of not only ground-based missile systems, but also nuclear submarine–launched missile systems. Former OKB-1 lead designer Viktor Makeyev was in charge of these projects. I wrote about the beginning of work on ballistic missiles for submarines in Volume II of *Rockets and People*.[75] Viktor Makeyev was in charge of SKB-385 in the city of Miass in the Ural Mountains. In addition to all of his other achievements, Makeyev's integrated systemic approach to the process of designing a large and complex system should be considered one of his defining achievements.

The chief designer of a missile was in charge of a complex that, in addition to the missile itself, comprised the launcher, the shipboard computer system controlling the missile firing, the missile checkout equipment, the data-control system processing the firing data, etc. The chief designer was also responsible for preparing for and conducting launches. For this reason, governmental decrees instructed Makeyev to develop a system rather than a missile.

The four head organizations that Korolev (followed by Mishin), Yangel (and after him, Utkin), Chelomey, and Nadiradze oversaw produced surface-to-surface missile systems for the Strategic Rocket Forces. The cooperative

---

73. He received both honors in 1970.
74. GRTs—*Gosudarstvennyy raketnyy tsentr* (State Rocket Center).
75. Chertok, *Rockets and People, Vol. II*, Chapters 14 and 15.

network that Viktor Makeyev oversaw was virtually the exclusive producer of strategic missile systems to arm nuclear submarines. In terms of the numerous parameters, especially the control system, a submarine-launched missile system is more complex than a land-based missile system.

The first independent development of SKB-385 under Makeyev's leadership was the single-stage R-13 missile with a firing range of up to 600 kilometers. The missile was the foundation of the D-2 system, which went into service in 1961 and remained in operation until 1973.

The first missile that SKB-385 produced specifically for subsurface launch was the R-21 of system D-4. The first launch of a missile from a submerged submarine took place on 10 September 1960, 40 days after the launch of the U.S. Polaris missile from a submerged submarine.[76] The D-4 system with its R-21 missile went into service in May 1963. However, it was appreciably inferior to the U.S. Polaris A-1 systems with a firing range of 2,200 kilometers and the Polaris A-2 with a range of 2,800 kilometers. In 1962, development began on the D-5 system, which was meant to bridge the qualitative gap between the missile armaments of Soviet and U.S. nuclear submarines. The D-5 system's R-27 missile control system provided inertial navigation using a gyrostabilized platform that had sensitive navigation elements mounted along three axes. The missile was equipped with a homing warhead for firing against naval targets. Isayev, who developed the engine for this missile, called it the "sinker"—in the initial models the engine was "sunk" within a recess in the fuel tank.[77] Later, the "sinker" was also developed for an oxidizer tank.

The D-5 system with the R-27 missile went into service in 1968. In 1974, the D-5U with R-27U missile, equipped with either a single warhead or three independently targetable warheads, went into service. A modification of the R-27U missile was also developed. Its warhead had a homing system for striking pinpoint targets on the shore and surface ships.

In 1974, system D-9 with the first R-29 naval intercontinental missile went into service. Eighteen *Murena*-class submarines were equipped with this system. The R-29 missile gave rise to three modifications with independently targetable warheads. All three were given the designation RSM-50. A stellar correction system was developed to control the missiles of the D-9 system. This substantially improved the system's firing accuracy.

---

76. The first launch of a Polaris missile from a submerged submarine, the USS *George Washington*, took place on 20 July 1960.

77. This was the 4D10 engine, which comprised a main sustainer with a thrust of 23 tons and two side verniers with a thrust of 3 tons.

In 1971 under Makeyev's leadership, development began on the D-19 system with R-39 missiles, which received the designation RSM-52. The payload of this missile had 10 independently targeted warheads. The D-19 system went into service on *Akula*-class heavy nuclear submarine cruisers.

In all, during Makeyev's lifetime, his design bureau developed seven basic models of submarine-launched missiles.[78] Six of these had several modifications each. The missile systems and submarines were modified accordingly. All told, over the 15 years from 1960 through 1975, hundreds of launches were conducted for the developmental testing of naval missile systems before putting them into service, to train personnel, and to check out the missiles in operation.

Makeyev was twice awarded the title Hero of Socialist Labor.[79] He was elected a corresponding member of the USSR Academy of Sciences in 1968 and full member in 1976. Those who headed up design projects for submarines and missile system control systems also became academicians and Heroes of Socialist Labor.

Today, the submarines that comprised the naval fleet during that period have outlived their service life. The thousands of missiles that were on them need to be destroyed. By the late 1990s, in Severodvinsk alone, more than 150 nuclear submarines were decommissioned because they had reached the end of their service life.[80] They were disarmed and destroyed in accordance with international agreements. In and of itself, this figure provides an impression of the colossal work, in terms of both volume and cost, performed to achieve superiority over the U.S. in the field of strategic ballistic missile submarines.

Moscow Institute of Thermal Technology (MIT), originally known as NII-1[81]

Until the end of his life, Chief Designer Aleksandr Davidovich Nadiradze was in charge of the Moscow Institute of Thermal Technology, which joined the Ministry of the Defense Industry system after 1964. The primary focus of this organization was the production of short-range tactical missile systems for the infantry.

The experience that OKB-1 had gained developing RT-2 solid-propellant rockets, and the achievements of industry, which mastered the production of

---

78. These were the R-13 missile (of the D-2 system), the R-21 (D-4), the R-27 and variants (D-5), the R-29 and variants (D-9), the R-29R and variants (D-9R), the R-39 and variants (D-19), and the R-29RM and variants (D-9RM).

79. He was awarded the Hero of Socialist Labor in 1961 and 1974.

80. Severodvinsk is a city in Arkhangelsk Oblast situated in the delta of the Northern Dvina River. It is the center of a massive defense-industrial infrastructure responsible for the construction and repair of submarines.

81. MIT—*Moskovskiy institut teplotekhniki.*

effective composite solid propellants, enabled Nadiradze to develop first short-range, and then medium-range, missiles that were supposed to replace the R-5M, R-12, and R-14 liquid-propellant rockets. The main advantage of the new missile systems was their abandonment of the silo-based launcher and use of a mobile deployment mode. Mobile launchers could be covertly relocated, and the uncertainty of their whereabouts offered substantially increased viability.

The design process for the short-range *Temp-2S* system began in the late 1960s. One of the most difficult tasks was the development of a control system that ensured a high-degree of combat readiness and precision when the launch site changed. *Temp* and *Temp-2S* were the first mobile systems using solid-propellant ballistic missiles to be put into service. The missiles of these systems were the first to be destroyed by the end of the 20th century in accordance with U.S. demands during offensive arms reduction talks.[82]

The development and testing of medium-range *Pioner* (Pioneer) missiles (factory index 15Zh45) lasted for more than six years. In March 1976, the *Pioner* mobile missile system (or RSD-10) went into service for the Strategic Rocket Forces. NATO declared these Soviet missiles the "menace of Europe" and assigned them the index SS-20.[83]

The governmental decree assigned NIIAP the task of developing the inertial control system for the *Pioner*. In the early 1970s, NIIAP was overloaded with control system projects for N1-L3 and for Chelomey's and Yangel's new generation of intercontinental ballistic missiles. Nevertheless, Chief Designer Pilyugin gave his consent for the development of the system for the *Pioner* despite the objections of the minister of general machine building.[84]

The self-propelled launcher carrying the *Pioner* missile was placed on a Minsk Automobile Factory special six-axle tractor truck. The industry delivered more than 500 *Pioner* mobile missile systems to the Strategic Rocket Forces. The wealth of experience gained by MIT from operating the *Pioner* systems enabled them to switch to the production of *Topol* (Poplar) mobile solid-propellant intercontinental ballistic missile systems. A list of them goes beyond the limits of the period of time we are studying here. However, the successes in this field made it possible to drastically reduce the production and

---

82. The *Temp-2S* missiles were declared operational in 1976 but then removed from duty by 1986 as a result of the Strategic Arms Limitations Talks (SALT) II treaty signed by the U.S. and the USSR in 1979.

83. The "SS-20" designation was actually assigned by the U.S. Department of Defense. The NATO name for the SS-20 was "Sabre."

84. Chertok is referring to Sergey Aleksandrovich Afanasyev, the minister of general machine building from 1965 to 1983.

upgrading of stationary liquid-propellant combat missile systems. Aleksandr Nadiradze became a full member of the USSR Academy of Sciences in 1981 and was twice awarded the title Hero of Socialist Labor.[85]

NII-627, later known as All-Union Scientific-Research Institute of Electromechanics (VNIIEM), now known as the Scientific-Production Enterprise All-Russian Scientific-Research Institute of Electromechanics with the A. G. Iosifyan Factory (NPP VNIEM)[86]

Beginning in 1947, NII-627 was in charge of developing on-board electrical equipment for the rapidly growing field of rocket technology and later space technology. As far back as during World War II, the institute had assembled a staff of first-class scientists and engineers in the field of electrical machines, electromechanical devices, and electroautomatic control engineering.

The scientific potential and experience accumulated during its 12-year association with leading rocket-space organizations, plus the initiative and irrepressible energy of the institute's director, Andronik Iosifyan, enabled NII-627 to take on the role of lead organization for the production of space-based meteorological systems. A governmental decree on 30 October 1961 named NII-627 as the lead organization for the development of the *Meteor* spacecraft. The Main Directorate of the Hydro-meteorological Service (under the auspices of the USSR Council of Ministers) and the Ministry of Defense served as the customers.

In 1964, the first *Meteor* satellite was manufactured. From 1964 through 1967, four satellites underwent flight testing. As experience was gained, the spacecraft became more advanced. From 1967 to 1971, a global space meteorological system was produced based on *Meteor*, then *Meteor-2*, and *Meteor-3* satellites. The next advancement in this field was the development of the *Meteor-Priroda* satellite for conducting research and meteorology observations and ecological monitoring.[87]

In addition to the lead organization, VNIIEM, specialized organizations that had already been involved in the programs of OKB-1 and its branches, and also OKB-52, participated in the creation of meteorological satellites. OKB Geofizika developed the sensitive elements for the attitude-control systems; VNII-380 (subsequently VNIIT) developed the television system for observing

---

85. He was awarded the Hero of Socialist Labor in 1976 and 1982.
86. VNIIEM—*Vsesoyuznyy nauchno-issledovatelskiy institut elektromekhaniki.*
87. The first *Meteor-Priroda* satellite was launched in 1974.

Earth's surface and transmitting color images of it; and NII-648 (later NIITP) developed the orbital monitoring and command transmission radio complex.[88]

VNIIEM was the only organization that independently developed spacecraft outside the Ministry of General Machine Building system. However, launch vehicles were manufactured and preparation at the cosmodrome and liftoff were carried out through the efforts of the Ministry of Defense and Ministry of General Machine Building.

THE NINE ORGANIZATIONS LISTED ABOVE were the lead organizations responsible for achieving the ultimate goal: putting the final product into service, into operation, or fulfilling unique assignments for fundamental research. A cooperative network comprising dozens of scientific-research institutes and design bureaus and hundreds of factories worked for these lead organizations. They, too, had their own lead entities in their respective fields:

From the author's archives.
Valentin Glushko in a photo probably taken in the 1970s.

- OKB-456 (V. P. Glushko NPO Energomash) and OKB-2 (A. M. Isayev KB Khimmash) were the lead organizations for the development of liquid-propellant rocket engines;[89]
- NII-885 (Russian Scientific-Research Institute of Space Instrument Building) was the head organization for the radio system;
- NIIAP (N. A. Pilyugin Scientific-Production Center for Automatics and Instrument Building) was the head organization for autonomous control systems;

---

88. VNIIT—*Vsesoyuznyy nauchno-issledovatelskiy institut televizionnoy tekhniki* (All-Union Scientific-Research Institute of Television Technology); NIITP—*Nauchno-issledovatelskiy institut tochnykh priborov* (Scientific-Research Institute of Precision Instruments).

89. *Author's note*: The contemporary names of these enterprises are given in parentheses. The Isayev organization is now formally part of the M. V. Khrunichev State Space Scientific-Production Center (GKNPTs im. M. V. Khrunicheva).

- GSKB Spetsmash (V. P. Barmin Design Bureau of General Machine Building) was the head organization for the ground complex;[90] and
- NII-648 (Scientific-Research Institute of Precision Instruments) was the head organization for command radio links and rendezvous radio systems.

Each of these organizations in turn had its own collaborative system set up. Each head general designer was at the top of the pyramid. The pyramids were built on the common foundation of the manufacturing industry, regardless of the field—radio electronic, electrical, instrumentation, optical, mechanical engineering, metallurgical, chemical, etc.

The atomic industry was another story, isolated in the Ministry of Medium Machine Building (MSM). Almost all of its lead design bureaus, scientific-research institutes, and factories were located in closed cities.[91] They developed a special warhead for each model of missile. The MSM surpassed other industry ministries of the military-industrial complex in terms of its intellectual and manufacturing power.

The common foundation for all the pyramids was a powerful base—the Ministry of Defense. It was the Ministry of Defense that financed, built, and equipped the rocket-space firing ranges Kapustin Yar, Baykonur, and Plesetsk, as well as the sea-based firing ranges; the ministry also developed a universal Command and Measurement Complex (KIK), including its own control centers and ballistics centers.[92] In all, the Ministry of Defense system had more than 20 launch pads just for inserting spacecraft into space. This was not much compared with the thousands of combat missile launchers, but combat launchers were single-use and "on alert," while space rocket launch facilities could be reused. They were used for hundreds of launches. In 1973 alone, the total number of space launches exceeded 100.

Ground Tracking Stations (NIPs), consolidated under a single command authority; a common timing system; and a common control, communications, and data transmission and processing system, formed the foundation of the KIK.[93]

---

90. GSKB Spetsmash—*Gosudarstvennoye soyuznoye konstruktorskoye byuro spetsialnogo mashinostroyeniya* (State Union Design Bureau of Special Machine Building).

91. "Closed cities" were first established in the Soviet Union in the late 1940s. These locations were off-limits to regular Soviet citizens and were usually centered around military or scientific facilities.

92. KIK—*Komandno-izmeritelnyy kompleks*.

93. NIP—*Nazemnyy izmeritelnyy punkt*.

Sixteen NIPs were created on the territory of the USSR, including seven at the firing ranges.[94] In addition, shipborne and airborne stations performed the role of NIPs. All told, as many as 15 naval vessels composed a command and measurement complex. At first, naval transport vessels retrofitted and equipped with the necessary systems were used, and then they were replaced with specially designed ships using the latest achievements in radio electronics and antenna technology—these ships were the *Academician Sergey Korolev*, the *Cosmonaut Yuriy Gagarin*, the *Cosmonaut Vladimir Komarov*, and others.

The Command and Measurement Complex, the firing ranges, and the military NIIs were subordinate to the military-space command, which in turn was subordinate to the Commander-in-Chief of the Strategic Rocket Forces. By the late 1970s, permanently operating systems had been put into service to provide the strategic forces with the space information needed to employ nuclear missiles. The space forces implemented measures that enabled the armed forces to achieve strategic parity with the U.S. not only in terms of nuclear arms, but also in terms of the efficiency and precision of their employment!

Large military-space systems were produced on the basis of automatic spacecraft developments:

- a network for photographic surveillance and cartography using *Zenit*, *Yantar-2K*, and *Yantar-1KFT* satellites;
- the *Tselina-2* radio-technical surveillance complex;
- an integrated system of communications satellites using the *Molniya-2*, *Molniya-3*, and *Raduga* spacecraft;
- the Global Meteorological Space System (GMKS) consisting of the *Meteor-2* and *Meteor-3* spacecraft;[95]
- the *Tsikada* space navigation system;
- the *Tayfun* calibration complex;
- the *Strela* space-based official communications system;
- a system to provide the branches of the armed forces with real-time local and global weather information; and
- a system for real-time meteorological reconnaissance of regions scheduled to be photographed by space-based photosurveillance facilities.

The development of an efficient military acceptance system should be considered a great achievement of the Ministry of Defense. Historically, the Institute of Military Acceptance had been in existence since the time of Peter I.

---

94. The Soviet Union had three space-launch firing ranges: NIIP-5 (at Tyuratam), NIIP-52 (at Mirnyy near Plesetsk), and GTsP-4 (at Kapustin Yar).

95. GMKS—*Globalnaya meteorologicheskaya kosmicheskaya sistema.*

Matters of quality and reliability in the rocket-space industry were under the control of military representatives at all stages of the engineering process—from the draft plans until the hardware was released into service. The military acceptance engineering cadres weren't just brought in to perform inspections when fulfilling orders for the armed forces. They actively participated in production processes and in all types of testing of launch vehicles and space technology for scientific and economic missions.

So that I will not be chided because the list of projects of the rocket-space industry head organizations cited above is incomplete, I shall once again remind the reader that I have intentionally confined myself to listing those projects that were contemporary with the N1-L3 program. Therefore, I shall not mention developments that were completed before 1960 or begun after 1974.

I am deliberately not mentioning the sophisticated antiaircraft and antiballistic missile systems. This special field deserves serious scientific historical research. Even given these temporal and thematic limitations, this list provides an idea of the scale, the nomenclature, and the material and intellectual contributions that dramatically changed the military-political situation in the world.

One more important factor contributed to the achievements of Soviet military-industrial technology: almost all types of missile and space technology, as well as strategic nuclear assets, were developed with the highly active participation of the USSR Academy of Sciences. Almost all the chief designers of the leading organizations of the rocket and nuclear industry were Academy members. As a rule, the president of the Academy of Sciences was appointed chairman of the expert commissions that the nation's top political leadership tasked with drawing up the proposals for the selection of strategic weapons. Fundamental academic research and the applied science of the industry ministries enriched one another.

Chapter 2

U.S. Lunar Program

The history of our N1-L3 lunar program can be compared with the U.S. Apollo-Saturn program. Later, the American program came to be called simply "Apollo," like the lunar vehicle. Comparing the technology and operational organization for the lunar programs in the U.S. and the USSR, one is compelled to pay tribute to the efforts of the two superpowers in their realization of one of the greatest engineering projects of the 20th century.

So, let's take a brief look at what was happening in the U.S.[1] As soon as it was founded in February 1956, the Army Ballistic Missile Agency (ABMA) dealt with the production of long-range ballistic missiles. The Redstone Arsenal in Huntsville, Alabama, which is a center for practical missile developments, was part of the agency. One of the arsenal's directors was Wernher von Braun, who headed a staff of German specialists who were transferred from Germany to the U.S. in 1945. That same year, 127 German prisoners of war from Peenemünde started to work under von Braun's supervision. In 1956, in addition to them, 1,600 Americans were working at the Redstone Arsenal. Incidentally, by 1955, having obtained American citizenship, 765 German specialists were working in various branches of the U.S. defense industry. The majority of them had come to the U.S. from West Germany voluntarily and worked on a contractual basis.

The first Soviet satellites stunned the U.S. and made Americans ask themselves whether they were really the front-runners of human progress. Indirectly, the Soviet satellites helped to strengthen the authority of the German specialists in America. Von Braun convinced the American military leadership that only a launch vehicle that was considerably more powerful than the one that had inserted the first Soviet satellites and the first lunar vehicles would be able to surpass the level of the Soviet Union.

---

1. We have preserved the spirit and content of Chertok's original narrative on the U.S. space program as much as possible so as to convey Chertok's *perception* of American achievements rather than the reality of events in the U.S.

Von Braun had dreamed of super-heavy rockets for interplanetary expeditions even before the first artificial satellite was launched. In 1953, von Braun and Willy Ley published the results of the research and the basic design data for a three-stage launch vehicle intended for the creation of a large orbital station and for piloted expeditions to the Moon. One of its versions was designed for a mission with a crew of 25. The vehicle's launch mass exceeded 7,000 metric tons.[2]

Von Braun's team spent its first years working for the U.S. Army under conditions of rivalry between the Army, Air Force, and Navy. After the launch of the second Soviet satellite, the U.S. Secretary of Defense ordered the ABMA to begin preparation for the launch of an artificial satellite using the Jupiter-C rocket that von Braun's team had developed.[3] It was a version of the Redstone rocket with three additional solid-propellant stages. Von Braun requested 60 days for this task. General John Medaris, his boss, who was quite familiar with von Braun's optimism and enthusiasm, gave him 90 days. The team of rocket specialists managed to fulfill their assignment in 84 days! On 31 January 1958, *Explorer 1*—the first U.S. satellite—went into orbit. America had entered the space race.

Before the launch of the first Soviet artificial satellite, the attitude of the U.S. military toward spaceflight was cool, to say the least. In September 1957, von Braun's team was working at the Redstone Arsenal on developing intermediate-range combat missiles.

I shall cite an excerpt from the memoirs of Ernst Stuhlinger—one of von Braun's closest associates:

> *Von Braun's satellite project was brought to a complete halt by order of the secretary of defense. My urgent appeal that von Braun go to the Department of Defense requesting one more time that they allow him to continue with our satellite project was to no avail.*
>
> *"Please, leave me alone," he said. "You know very well that my hands are tied."*
>
> *Then on 27 September, I went to see General Medaris, our commanding officer at the Redstone Arsenal.*
>
> *"A Russian satellite is going to be in orbit soon. Aren't you going to try one more time to ask the Secretary of Defense for permission to work on our satellite? It will be an incredible shock for our nation if they are in space first!"*

---

2. Wernher von Braun and Willy Ley, *Start in den Weltraum: Ein Buch uber Raketen, Satelliten und Raumfahrzeuge* [*Launching into Space: A Book About Rockets, Satellites, and Space Launch Vehicles*] (Frankfurt am Main: S. Fischer, 1959).

3. The Secretary of Defense at the time was Neil H. McElroy.

"Listen," said the general, "Don't get all worked up! You know how complicated it is to build and launch a satellite. Those people won't be able to do that…. Go back to your laboratory and don't worry!"

A week later the first Sputnik was in orbit. Anyone who had even the simplest radio receiver could listen to its soft "beep-beep!" The shock for our nation was enormous. Von Braun asked me:

"Has the general spoken with you since this happened? I think he owes you an apology."

"Yes," I answered, "But all he said was: 'Those damned bastards!'" Von Braun had a different reaction.

"The Russians have taught us Americans a free lesson. We had better capitalize on it!" he said and added:

"The majority of Americans committed serious errors in judgment. They were unable to recognize the enormous psychological effect of having an artificial Moon ever present in the sky. The majority of Americans really underestimated the outstanding capabilities of the Russian directors of the space project, their scientists, engineers, and technical specialists. They also didn't know how to properly determine the scientific and production capabilities of a nation, even one under a totalitarian government."[4]

IN DECEMBER 1957, VON BRAUN PROPOSED A DESIGN for a heavy rocket, the first stage of which had an engine cluster with a total thrust at Earth's surface of 680 tons (the reader will recall that the R-7 five-engine cluster had a thrust of 400 tons).

In August 1958, impressed by the roaring success of our third satellite, the U.S. Defense Department's Advanced Research Projects Agency (DARPA) consented to finance the development of a design for the Saturn heavy launch vehicle.[5] Subsequently, launch vehicles of varying capacities and configurations were given the name Saturn with different alphanumeric designations. They were all built for a common program with a single final objective—to produce a heavy launch vehicle that far surpassed the achievements of the Soviet Union.

---

4. Ernst Stuhlinger (1913–2008) was a guidance systems expert who worked with von Braun both in Germany and later in the United States. At NASA, he worked at the Marshall Space Flight Center until his retirement in 1975. The excerpt is probably from Ernst Stuhlinger and Frederick I. Ordway III, *Wernher von Braun, Crusader for Space: A Biographical Memoir* (Malabar, FL: Krieger, 1994).

5. DARPA was known as ARPA from its founding in January 1958 to March 1972, when "Defense" was added to the designation. In August 1958, ARPA provided initial funding for a powerful launch vehicle named Juno V, which later evolved into the Saturn.

The company Rocketdyne received the order for the development of the H-1 engine for the heavy rocket in September 1958, when it became obvious that the Americans had fallen behind. To speed up operations, the decision was made to make a relatively simple engine, achieving, above all, a high degree of reliability rather than record-setting specific indices. The H-1 engine was produced within a record-setting short period of time. On 27 October 1961, the first launch of the Saturn I rocket took place. It had a cluster of eight H-1 engines, each with a thrust of 75 tons. The initial plans for the production of heavy rockets in the U.S. had nothing to do with a peaceful lunar program.

Commander in Chief of the U.S. Strategic Air Command General Thomas S. Power, supporting the allocation of funds to the space programs, declared: "Whoever is first to make their claim in space will own it. And we simply cannot allow ourselves to lose this contest for supremacy in space."[6]

Other U.S. military officials also spoke rather candidly, declaring that whoever controls space will control Earth. Despite President Dwight D. Eisenhower's obvious aversion to supporting the hysterical hype regarding the "Russian threat" from space, the general public demanded that measures be taken to get ahead of the USSR. Congressmen and senators demanded decisive actions, arguing that the U.S. was running the risk of complete annihilation by the USSR. Under these conditions, one can only marvel at the resoluteness of Eisenhower, who insisted that space must not under any circumstances be used for military purposes.

On 29 July 1958, President Eisenhower signed the National Aeronautics and Space Act, authored by Senator Lyndon B. Johnson. This act defined the basic programs and administrative structure for space exploration. A professional military man, General Eisenhower clearly defined the civilian orientation of operations in space. The act stated that space exploration must be developed "in the name of peace for all mankind." Later, these words were engraved on a metal plaque that the crew of *Apollo 11* left on the Moon.[7]

But first, the National Advisory Committee for Aeronautics (NACA) was transformed into the National Aeronautics and Space Administration (NASA). This enabled the government of the United States to create a new, powerful government organization within a brief period of time. Subsequent events showed that appointing Wernher von Braun as director of the design and testing complex in Huntsville, Alabama, and making him responsible

---

6. General Thomas S. Power headed the U.S. Strategic Air Command from 1957 to 1964.

7. The actual inscription on the plaque read: "Here men from the planet Earth first set foot upon the Moon—July 1969, A.D.—We came in peace for all mankind."

for developing heavy launch vehicles was crucial for the success of the lunar program. On 21 October 1959, Eisenhower held a meeting during which the decision was made to transfer the Redstone Arsenal to NASA. On 15 March 1960, the president signed a directive transforming the Huntsville center into the George C. Marshall Space Flight Center. The transfer took place on 1 July 1960, and Wernher von Braun officially became the director and sole manager of the Center.[8]

This event was particularly significant for von Braun personally. His affiliation with the Nazi party had tainted him in the eyes of American democratic society, but despite this, he had been given a high degree of trust. Finally he had been given the opportunity to fulfill his dream of human interplanetary flight, which had been under discussion back in Peenemünde! In 1944, the Gestapo had arrested Wernher von Braun and Helmut Gröttrup simply for talking about interplanetary flight, thus taking their time away from work on the V-2.

The successes of Soviet cosmonautics didn't leave the Americans time to catch their breath for a calm reorganization and recruitment of personnel. Scientific research organizations from the NACA, the Army, and the Navy were hastily transferred to NASA. In December 1962, this federal agency had more than 25,000 people working for it, and of these employees, 9,240 had degrees in science or engineering. Scientific research centers, flight-testing centers, the Jet Propulsion Laboratory, large testing complexes, and specialized manufacturing plants were immediately subordinated to NASA. New centers began to be set up.

In Houston, Texas, a government center for the development of manned spacecraft was created.[9] The headquarters for the development and launch of the Gemini and future Apollo spacecraft was located here.

A group of three men appointed by the President of the United States was in charge of NASA. In Soviet terms, these three men fulfilled the function of general designer and general director of all of NASA. The U.S. administration tasked NASA with attaining superiority over the USSR in the next few years in all crucial areas of space utilization and exploration. The organizations composing NASA were entitled to recruit other government organizations, universities, and private industrial corporations.

---

8. The ABMA was subordinated to NASA on 1 July 1960 and renamed the George C. Marshall Space Flight Center on 8 September 1960.

9. The Manned Spacecraft Center officially opened for work in September 1963. It was renamed the Lyndon B. Johnson Space Center in February 1973.

During World War II, President Franklin D. Roosevelt had created a powerful governmental organization to develop atomic weaponry.[10] Young President Kennedy now used this experience. He strengthened NASA in every way possible and monitored its work to see that the national goal was achieved: overtake the USSR no matter what.

Von Braun convinced the NASA leadership that the only effective response to the Soviet Union would be to develop more-powerful heavy rockets. NASA gambled on "von Braun's brigade" to develop a super-powerful launch vehicle. The first stage of the new Saturn I launch vehicle was designed to use kerosene and liquid oxygen. The Marshall Space Flight Center proved capable of manufacturing it on its own. It was proposed that liquid hydrogen and liquid oxygen—revolutionary components for those times—be used in the second and third stages. In addition, the third liquid-hydrogen stage required guaranteed reliability for repeated firings to accelerate toward the Moon.

In January 2007, NASA's leading historian on cosmonautics, Dr. Jesco von Puttkamer, gave a speech entitled "My Years Working with von Braun's Team on the Saturn Project" in Moscow at the Korolev Lectures.[11] Von Puttkamer has

From the author's archives.

been responsible for the publication of the volumes of my book *Rockets and People* at NASA Headquarters.

I shall cite an excerpt from his speech: "In von Braun's view, to be an effective leader, which means to be both planner and doer, a manager should 'keep his hands dirty at the work bench.' This approach derived directly from the 'Arsenal' concept first used at Peenemünde, then also encountered at ABMA. By always being in the forefront and immersing himself intimately in the whole vehicle, with all its minute

Wernher von Braun shown at the base of a Saturn V launch vehicle.

---

10. Chertok is referring to the Manhattan Project.

11. Dr. Jesco von Puttkamer, as of 2011, is stationed at NASA Headquarters in the Human Exploration and Operations (HEO) Mission Directorate, where he holds special responsibilities as a Russia expert for the Russian segment of the International Space Station (ISS).

technical working-level details, von Braun constantly set an example himself. In my 45 years with NASA (as of now), I have never met anyone else who came even close to him in that respect."

This is a German writing about a German. But I heard approximately the same opinion about von Braun as a director from Jerry Clubb, a 100-percent American who worked at Marshall Space Flight Center during the development of the Saturn V launch vehicle and the lunar landing expeditions.[12] According to the testimonials of von Puttkamer and Jerry Clubb, von Braun's lifestyle represented the highest degree of technical expertise.

Reading or listening to testimonials about von Braun's working style and methods, I compared them with my own personal experience and close acquaintance with S. P. Korolev and yet again realized what a decisive role an individual plays in history. What these two now legendary but very different leaders from the epoch of the development of the first rockets and the conquest of space had in common was the exceptional ability to create a unified first-class creative team in which each individual felt valued and strove to demonstrate his or her best qualities.[13]

New ideas that had been generated "at the grass roots," at the level of frontline workers, quickly reached the chief designer. He gave them an objective evaluation or called for additional elaboration. As a rule, both here and there, promising long-range plans were developed with such enthusiasm that the authors had no doubt that it would be possible to implement them. Von Braun's and Korolev's "teams" never abandoned their leaders in difficult situations.

American politicians and historians did not hide the fact that the National Aeronautics and Space Administration was created in response to the gauntlet that the Soviet Sputniks had thrown down. Unfortunately, neither we, the Soviet rocket scientists, nor the top political leadership of the Soviet Union appreciated back then the crucial importance of these actions by the U.S. administration. The main mission of the cooperative network under the aegis of NASA was a national program to land an expedition on the Moon before the end of the 1960s. Expenditures on this mission in the first years already amounted to three-quarters of the entire NASA budget.

Gagarin's flight was a very strong incentive for speeding up the U.S. lunar program. After 12 April 1961, the world had no doubt about the Soviet Union's

---

12. Jerry Clubb was the NASA representative at RKK Energiya for joint operations on the ISS. Previously, he had worked at the Marshall Space Flight Center on the Apollo-Saturn project.

13. For the most critically acclaimed biography of von Braun, see Michael J. Neufeld, *Von Braun: Dreamer of Space, Engineer of War* (New York: Alfred Knopf, 2007).

supremacy in space. The intimidating (to the Americans) slogan "the Russians are coming" was used in America as proof of the military superiority of the USSR over the U.S. After 12 April 1961, the young U.S. President John F. Kennedy frantically searched for an answer to the question, is there any field in which we can catch up with the Russians? He understood that he needed to maintain his own leadership and return the American people's confidence and pride in their country and the respect that had been lost overseas.

On 20 April 1961, Kennedy sent a memorandum to Vice President Lyndon B. Johnson calling on him, as chairman of the National Aeronautics and Space Council, to conduct a general assessment of achievements in space exploration and to answer the question, "Do we have a chance to beating the Soviets by putting a laboratory in space, or by a trip around the moon, or by a rocket to go to the moon and back with a man? Is there any other space program which promises dramatic results in which we could win?"[14]

Lyndon B. Johnson was an avid proponent of developing a project for landing a human being on the Moon. President Kennedy's request spurred him to active consultations with NASA, the Defense Department, various agencies, committees, and finally with von Braun, whose work he held in very high esteem. Von Braun answered the questions concerning the U.S. national space program in great detail and cogently. He assured Johnson, "We have an excellent chance of beating the Soviets to the first landing of a crew on the moon.... With an all-out crash program, I think we could accomplish this objective in 1967/68."[15]

After intensive negotiations, meetings, and consultations, President Kennedy reached a decision, and on 25 May 1961, he addressed Congress and in fact all Americans. In his speech he said: "Now it is time to take longer strides—time for a great new American enterprise—time for this nation to take a clearly leading role in space achievement, which in many ways may hold the key to our future on Earth.... I believe that this nation should commit itself to achieving the goal, before this decade is out, of landing a man on the Moon and returning him safely to the Earth. No single space project in this period

---

14. For the complete memo that Chertok quotes from, see "John F. Kennedy, Memorandum for Vice President, April 20, 1961" in *Exploring the Unknown: Selected Documents in the History of the U.S. Civil Space Program, Vol. 1: Organizing for Exploration*, ed. John M. Logsdon with Linda J. Lear, Jannelle Warren-Findley, Ray A. Williamson, and Dwayne A. Day (Washington, DC: NASA SP-4407, 1995), pp. 423–424.

15. For the complete letter, see "Wernher von Braun to the Vice President of the United States, April 29, 1961," in *Exploring the Unknown, Vol. 1*, pp. 429–433.

will be more impressive to mankind, or more important for the long-range exploration of space; and none will be so difficult or expensive to accomplish."[16]

Congress approved the decision to send an American to the Moon almost unanimously. The mass media showed broad support.

Soon after Kennedy's address, Keldysh paid a visit to Korolev at OKB-1 to discuss our comparable program.[17] He said that Khrushchev had asked him: "How serious is President Kennedy's announcement about landing a man on the Moon?"

"I told Nikita Sergeyevich," said Keldysh, "that technically the mission can be accomplished, but it will require a very large amount of resources. They will have to be found at the expense of other programs. Nikita Sergeyevich was obviously worried and said that we would revisit this issue very soon."

At that time we were the indisputable leaders in world cosmonautics. However, the U.S. had already passed us in the lunar program because right away it was proclaimed a national cause: "For all of us must work to put him [the first man on the Moon] there." "Space dollars" had begun to penetrate into almost every area of the American economy. Thus, the entire American public was in control of the preparations for a landing on the Moon. Unlike the Soviet space projects, the U.S. lunar program was not classified.

The U.S. mass media did not cover up the fact that Yuriy Gagarin's flight on 12 April 1961 had shocked the nation. Americans were afraid that the rocket that had carried Gagarin was capable of delivering an enormously powerful hydrogen bomb to any point on the globe. One has to give President Kennedy credit. He was able to find a quick response, reassure a nation, and simultaneously mobilize it to achieve great feats.

Titov's flight on 6 August 1961 struck another blow against American public opinion. But the lunar "psychotherapy" had already begun to take effect. On 12 September 1962, speaking at Rice University, Kennedy declared: "We choose to go to the moon in this decade and do the other things, not because they are easy, but because they are hard, because that goal will serve to organize and measure the best of our energies and skills, because that challenge is one

---

16. "John F. Kennedy, Excerpts from 'Urgent National Needs,' Speech to a Joint Session of Congress, May 25, 1961," in *Exploring the Unknown, Vol. 1*, pp. 453–454.

17. Mstislav Vsevolodovich Keldysh (1911–1978) served as President of the USSR Academy of Sciences from 1961 to 1975.

that we are willing to accept, one we are unwilling to postpone, and one which we intend to win, and the others, too."[18]

In 1941, Hitler assigned von Braun the top-secret national mission of developing the V-2 ballistic missile—the secret "weapon of vengeance" for the mass annihilation of the British. In 1961, President Kennedy openly, in front of the entire world, once again entrusted von Braun with a national mission—to develop the most powerful launch vehicle in the world for a piloted flight to the Moon.

For the liquid-propellant rocket engine (ZhRD) of the first stage of the new multistage Saturn V rocket, von Braun proposed using components that were already well mastered—liquid oxygen and kerosene. On the second and third stages, he proposed a new pair of components—liquid oxygen and liquid hydrogen. Two factors stand out here. First, there were no proposals to use high-boiling components (like nitrogen tetroxide and dimethylhydrazine) for the new heavy rocket despite the fact that at that time, the Titan II heavy intercontinental missile was being designed to run on these high-boiling components. Second, right off the bat, as opposed to some time in the future, they proposed using hydrogen for the other stages. By proposing hydrogen as a propellant, von Braun showed his appreciation for the prophetic ideas of Konstantin Tsiolkovskiy and Hermann Oberth.[19] Moreover, for one of the versions of the Atlas rocket, the Centaur second stage with a liquid-propellant rocket engine operating on oxygen and hydrogen was already being developed. The Centaur was later also successfully used as the third stage of the Titan III rocket. Pratt & Whitney developed the RL-10 liquid-hydrogen propellant engine for the Centaur. It had a thrust of just 6.8 tons. This was the first liquid-propellant rocket engine with what was, for that time, a record specific thrust of 420 units.[20]

In 1985, the encyclopedia *Kosmonavtika* [*Cosmonautics*] made its debut. Its editor-in-chief was Academician Valentin Glushko. In this publication,

---

18. John F. Kennedy, "Address at Rice University on Nation's Space Effort" (speech, Rice University, Houston, TX, 12 September 1962), *http://www.jfklibrary.org/Research/Ready-Reference/ JFK-Speeches/Address-at-Rice-University-on-the-Nations-Space-Effort-September-12-1962.aspx* (accessed 2 March 2011).

19. Historians consider the Russian Konstantin Eduardovich Tsiolkovskiy (1857–1935) and the Romanian-German Hermann Oberth (1894–1989) to be two of the three major pioneers of rocketry and space exploration. Tsiolkovskiy, Oberth, and the American Robert Goddard (1882–1945) all came to the same conclusions regarding the use of high-energy cryogenic propellants, such as liquid hydrogen and liquid oxygen, as the most efficient for use in rockets.

20. The specific impulse (change in momentum per unit amount of propellant used) of the original RL-10 engine was 433 seconds.

Glushko paid tribute to liquid-hydrogen propellant rocket engines and to the work of the Americans. The article entitled "Liquid-propellant Rocket Engine" states: "Given the same [launch vehicle] launch mass, [liquid-propellant rocket engines operating on oxygen and hydrogen] were capable of inserting on orbit a payload that was three times greater than that of [liquid-propellant rocket engines] operating on oxygen and kerosene."[21]

However, early in his career developing liquid-propellant rocket engines, Glushko had a negative attitude toward the idea of using liquid hydrogen as a propellant. In his book *Rockets, Their Design and Application*, Glushko provided a comparative analysis of rocket propellants for a case of motion in space described by a Tsiolkovskiy formula. Summarizing his calculations, the analysis of which is not part of my task here, the 27-year-old RNII engineer wrote in 1935: "Thus, a rocket with hydrogen propellant will have greater speed than a rocket of the same weight operating on gasoline, only if the weight of the propellant exceeds the weight of the rest of the rocket by more than 430 times.... From this we see that the notion of using liquid hydrogen as a propellant must be abandoned."[22]

Judging by the fact that he later signed off on a decree calling for, among various other measures, the development of a liquid-propellant rocket engine operating on liquid hydrogen, Glushko had understood his youthful error at least by 1958. Unfortunately, the USSR was behind the U.S. in practical developments of liquid-hydrogen rocket engines at the very beginning of the Moon race. Over time, this gap widened, and ultimately it proved to be one of the factors that determined the substantial advantage of the U.S. lunar program.

Glushko's negative attitude toward pairing oxygen and hydrogen as propellant components for liquid-propellant rocket engines was one reason that Korolev, and especially Mishin, harshly criticized him. Among rocket fuels, the pairing of oxygen and hydrogen as propellant components ranked in second place behind fluorine-hydrogen fuel. The announcement that Glushko was creating a special branch for testing fluorine engines on the shore of the Gulf of Finland caused particularly strong feelings. Mishin ranted, "He could poison Leningrad with his fluorine."

---

21. V. P. Glushko, ed., *Kosmonavtika: entsiklopediya* [*Cosmonautics: An Encyclopedia*] (Moscow: Sovetskaya entsiklopediya, 1985), p. 528.

22. G. E. Langemak and V. P. Glushko, *Rakety, ikh ustroystvo i primeneniye* [*Rockets, Their Design and Application*] (Moscow-Leningrad: ONTI NKTP, 1935). RNII—*Reaktivnyy nauchno-issledovatelskiy institut* (Reactive Scientific-Research Institute)—was the main government-sponsored organization that developed rockets in the Soviet Union in the 1930s.

To be fair, I must mention that, after becoming general designer of NPO Energiya, during the development of the Energiya-Buran rocket-space complex, Glushko decided to create a second stage using an oxygen-hydrogen engine. A government resolution entrusted the development of the Energiya's second-stage oxygen-hydrogen engine to OKB Khimavtomatiki Chief Designer Aleksandr Konopatov. He fulfilled this assignment, but it took place 15 years after the Americans landed on the Moon.[23]

RELIABILITY AND SAFETY WERE THE STRICT CONDITIONS for all phases of the U.S. lunar program. They were achieved as a result of thorough ground-based developmental testing so that the only optimization performed in flight was what couldn't be performed on the ground given the level of technology at that time. The Americans succeeded in achieving these results thanks to the creation of a large experimental facility for performing ground tests on each stage of the rocket and all the modules of the lunar vehicle. It is much easier to take measurements during ground-based testing. Their accuracy is increased, and it is possible to analyze them thoroughly after the tests. The very high costs of flight-testing also dictated this principle of the maximum use of ground-based experimental development. The Americans made it their goal to reduce flight-testing to a minimum.

Our scrimping on ground-based development testing confirmed the old saying that if you buy cheaply, you pay dearly. The Americans spared no expense on ground-based developmental tests and conducted them on an unprecedented scale. They built numerous firing test rigs for the developmental testing of both single engines and all the full-scale stages of the flight rockets. Each series-produced engine underwent standard firing tests at least three times before flight: twice before delivery and a third time as part of the corresponding rocket stage. Thus, engines that were intended for one-time use according to the flight program were actually multiple-use engines.

One must keep in mind that to achieve the required reliability, both we and the Americans had two basic types of tests. The first are conducted on a single prototype unit (or on a small number of articles) in order to demonstrate how reliably the design executes its functions in flight; at the same time, the unit's actual service life is determined. The second are conducted on each flight article in order to guarantee that they have no random production defects or flaws from the series production process.

---

23. This cryogenic engine was the RD-0120 (or 11D122) with a vacuum thrust of 190 tons. Its first flight test was in 1987 during the first launch of the Energiya launch vehicle.

The first category of tests includes development tests during the design phase. These are the so-called design-development tests (in American parlance—qualification tests) performed on test articles. In this case, when testing individual engines, we and the Americans operated more or less the same way. For the second category, entailing the acceptance testing of engines, rocket stages, and a number of other items, in terms of procedures, it took 20 years, during the development of the Energiya rocket, before we were able to catch up with the Americans. A broad spectrum of tests, which could not be shortened for the sake of deadlines, made it possible to achieve a high degree of reliability for the Saturn V rocket and the Apollo spacecraft.

THE TRANSFER TO VON BRAUN'S GERMAN TEAM of all technical management over launch-vehicle production in its entirety played a decisive role in the success of the American lunar program. Even in the gyroscope technology for the inertial navigation systems, they used two-gimbal gyrostabilized platforms, which were based on earlier developments for A-4 rockets, which the Germans had not managed to realize during the war.

The third-stage Instrument Unit contained the main portion of the flight control equipment. This compartment housed the rocket's "brain." The German specialists of the "von Braun team," who utilized the latest breakthroughs of American electronics, achieved a fundamentally new development. After the basic design issues and the experimental development had been resolved, production of the entire Instrument Unit was handed over to IBM.

FIRING RIG TESTS ON EACH STAGE were combined with the flight tests. Flight testing began with the brief flight of Saturn I rocket number SA-1 as early as 22 October 1961. Only its first stage was operational, and this launch confirmed the viability of von Braun's concept of clustering powerful engine units. On 9 November 1967, a full-scale Saturn V lunar rocket executed the first unpiloted flight in automatic mode. During this flight, the Americans tested the refiring of the third stage in space after it had been in orbit for 3 hours. For the first time, they tested out the return of the Apollo Command Module into the atmosphere at a velocity corresponding to the lunar return velocity.

Failures, explosions, and fires on the test rigs occurred. The most horrible disaster was the fire during ground testing of the Apollo spacecraft: three astronauts perished on the launch pad on 27 January 1967.[24]

---

24. Chertok is referring to the *Apollo 1* fire that killed astronauts Virgil I. "Gus" Grissom, Edward H. White II, and Roger B. Chaffee.

It is worth noting that the Americans developed the structure and equipment of the Apollo spacecraft itself independently, without the input of von Braun's team.

Soon after the assassination of President Kennedy, at one of our routine meetings concerning the lunar operations schedule, Korolev disclosed some information that he said our top political leaders had at their disposal. Supposedly, the new American President, Lyndon B. Johnson, did not intend to support the lunar program at the same pace and on the scale that NASA proposed. Johnson was inclined to spend more money on intercontinental ballistic missiles and economize on space.

However, our hopes that the Americans would cut back on space programs did not pan out. New U.S. President Lyndon B. Johnson sent a letter to Congress, giving an account of the projects in the field of aerospace performed in the U.S. in 1963. In this letter he said: "Nineteen sixty-three was a year of continued success in the exploration of space. It was also a year of thorough re-examination of our space program in terms of the interests of national security. Consequently, a course to achieve and maintain our supremacy in space exploration in the future has been broadly endorsed…. The achievement of success in space exploration is crucial for our nation if we want to maintain superiority in the development of technology and effectively contribute to strengthening peace throughout the world. However, to achieve this goal will require the expenditure of considerable material resources."

Even Johnson recognized that the U.S. lagged behind the USSR "due to the relatively late start of operations and the lack of enthusiasm for space exploration in the beginning." He noted: "During that period our chief rival was not standing still and physically continued to set the pace in some fields…. However, our remarkable success in the development of large rockets and complex spacecraft is convincing proof that the United States is on its way to new successes in space exploration and is catching up completely in this field…. If we have made it our goal to achieve and maintain superiority, then we must keep up our efforts and maintain our enthusiasm."

Listing the achievements of 1963, Johnson felt it was necessary to mention: "The Centaur rocket has been successfully launched.[25] It is the first rocket using high-energy fuel. One in a series of tests on the first stage of the Saturn rocket with a thrust of 680,000 kilograms-force has been successfully conducted. It is the biggest of the launch vehicle first stages tested to date.

---

25. The first Centaur launch (a failure) was on 8 May 1962. The first successful launch as part of an Atlas Centaur was on 27 November 1963.

By late 1963 the U.S. has developed more powerful rockets than the USSR has at this time."

Switching directly to the lunar program, Johnson noted that in 1963 nine mockups of the Apollo spacecraft had already been manufactured, the spacecraft propulsion systems and numerous test rigs were being developed, and an escape system in the event of an explosion on the launch pad was undergoing testing.

A similar report about operations on Saturn rockets confirmed our sketchy information about the successful fulfillment of this program. In particular, the report mentioned that the J-2 hydrogen engine designed for the second stage of the Saturn V launch vehicle had successfully undergone factory tests and the first deliveries of these engines had begun.[26] Finally, the report removed all doubt as to the selection of the model of rocket for the lunar expedition: "At this time, the most powerful Saturn V launch vehicle, designed to deliver two men to the surface of the Moon, is in the developmental phase."

Then the members of Congress were told in detail about the structure and parameters of the Saturn V, its lunar mission flight plan, the production status of the test rigs and launch facilities, and the development of the means for transporting the gigantic rocket.

A comparison of the status of operations on the respective lunar programs in the U.S. and USSR in early 1964 shows that we were at least two years behind on the project as a whole. In regard to engines, at that time we had not developed oxygen-kerosene liquid-propellant engines with a thrust on the order of 600 tons and powerful oxygen-hydrogen liquid-propellant engines at all.

The information that had come to us through open channels over the course of 1964 confirmed that operations on the lunar program were not preventing the Americans from developing combat missiles. Our foreign intelligence service gathered more details. The scale of operations for the construction of new assembly shops for the Saturn V and Apollo, test rigs, launch complexes on Cape Canaveral (later the Kennedy Space Center), and launch and flight control centers made a strong impression on us.[27] Lunar program developers and von Braun's entire team, which had developed the Saturn series, no longer had anything to do with intercontinental ballistic missiles.

Leonid Voskresenskiy told me his most pessimistic thoughts on this subject after several serious conversations with Korolev and then with Georgiy Tyulin

---

26. The first extended-duration firing test (lasting 8 minutes) of the J-2 engine occurred on 27 November 1963.

27. The original Launch Operations Center at Cape Canaveral was renamed the John F. Kennedy Space Center in December 1963 after Kennedy's assassination.

and Mstislav Keldysh.[28] He wanted to persuade them to demand more vigorously that funding be increased, first and foremost, to develop a firing test rig for the full-scale first stage of a future rocket. He received no support from Korolev. Voskresenskiy told me, "If we disregard the Americans' experience and continue to build a rocket, hoping that if it doesn't fly the first time, then maybe it will fly the second time, then we're up the creek without a paddle. We did a full-scale burn for the R-7 rocket on the rig in Zagorsk, and even then it took four attempts for it to take off.[29] If Sergey continues this game of chance, I'm getting out of it." The drastic deterioration of Voskresenskiy's health might also have explained his pessimism. However, his inborn tester's intuition, which amazed his friends time after time, proved to be prophetic.

In 1965, the "Americanese," as Korolev used to say, had already performed development tests on reusable engines for all the stages of the Saturn V and had moved on to their series production. This was critical for the launch vehicle's reliability.

Single-handed creation of the Saturn V design itself proved to be beyond the power of even the most powerful aviation corporations in the U.S. For this reason, the design stage and manufacture of the launch vehicle were divided up among the leading aviation corporations: Boeing manufactured the first stage; North American Aviation, stage two; Douglas Aircraft, stage three; and IBM, the world's largest producer of electronic computers, delivered the Instrument Unit and the hardware that it contained. The Instrument Unit contained a two-gimbal gyrostabilized platform, which performed the function of a coordinate system platform. It controlled the rocket's spatial position and navigational measurements (using a digital computer).

The launch complex was developed at the Kennedy Space Center on Cape Kennedy (now Canaveral).[30] The rockets were assembled within a building of imposing dimensions.[31] This structural-grade steel building is used to this day. It is 160 meters high, 160 meters wide, and 220 meters long. Next to the assembly site, 5 kilometers from the launch site, is the four-story mission

---

28. Leonid Aleksandrovich Voskresenskiy (1913–1965) was one of Korolev's most senior deputies. During his stint as deputy chief designer at OKB-1, from 1954 to 1963, he led missile-testing operations at Kapustin Yar and Baykonur on behalf of Korolev's design bureau. Georgiy Aleksandrovich Tyulin (1914–1990) was a senior defense industry manager who, in his many different positions in the 1950s, 1960s, and 1970s, was one of the key administrators of the Soviet missile and space programs.

29. Zagorsk (now known as Sergeyev Posad) was the location of NII-229, the largest rocket engine static test center in the Soviet Union.

30. Cape Canaveral was known as Cape Kennedy from 1963 to 1973.

31. Chertok is referring here to the Vehicle Assembly Building (VAB).

control center, where, in addition to all the necessary services, there are also cafeterias and even a gallery for visitors and distinguished guests.

The launch took place from a launch pad, but not one like ours. It was arrayed with computers for conducting tests, equipment for the fueling system, an air conditioning system, ventilation, and water supply systems. During launch preparation, 114-meter-tall mobile service towers with two high-speed elevators were used. The rocket was transported from the assembly site to the launch site in a vertical position on a crawler transporter that had its own diesel generator power plants. The mission control center had a control room that accommodated more than 100 people sitting at electronic screens.

All subcontractors were subject to the most stringent reliability and security requirements, which encompassed all phases of the program—from the design phase until the spacecraft was inserted into its flight trajectory to the Moon.

DEVELOPMENTAL FLIGHTS OF THE APOLLO LUNAR VEHICLES began with the use of an unpiloted version. Experimental models of the Apollo spacecraft were tried out in unpiloted mode using the Saturn I and Saturn IB launch vehicles. For these purposes, from May 1964 through January 1968, five Saturn I launches and three Saturn IB launches took place. Two launches of the Apollo spacecraft carrying no crew took place on 9 November 1967 and on 4 April 1968 using a Saturn V launch vehicle.

When the crewless *Apollo 4* was launched on the Saturn V launch vehicle on 9 November 1967, a boost maneuver towards Earth was executed at a velocity of more than 11 kilometers per second from an altitude of 18,317 kilometers! The unpiloted experimental development phase of the launch vehicle and spacecraft was completed in 1968.

Launches of spacecraft carrying crews began considerably later than called for by the initial plan. The day of 27 January 1967 became the darkest in the history of the U.S. lunar program. At Cape Kennedy, three astronauts inside the *Apollo 1* spacecraft atop the Saturn IB launch vehicle perished in a fire. The tragedy of the situation was intensified by the fact that neither the crew nor the ground personnel were able to quickly open the hatch. Gus Grissom, Ed White, and Roger Chaffee either burned to death or suffocated. The cause of the fire turned out to be the atmosphere of pure oxygen that was used in the Apollo life-support system. As fire specialists explained it to us, in an atmosphere of pure oxygen everything burns, even metal. That is why all it took was a spark from electrical equipment, which would be harmless in a normal atmosphere. It took 20 months to perform fire-prevention modifications on the Apollo spacecraft.

In our piloted spacecraft, beginning with the Vostoks, we used a gas composition that did not differ from normal air. Nevertheless, after what happened in America, in connection with our Soyuzes and L3, we launched studies that culminated in the development of standards for materials and designs that ensured fire safety.

A crew executed the first piloted flight in the *Apollo 7* Command and Service Module, which was inserted into Earth orbit by a Saturn IB in October 1968. The spacecraft without its Lunar Module was thoroughly checked out during an 11-day flight.

In December 1968, a Saturn V inserted *Apollo 8* on a flight trajectory to the Moon. This was the world's first flight of a crewed spacecraft to the Moon. *Apollo 8* completed 10 orbits around the Moon. In flight, the navigation and control system was checked out on the Earth-Moon flight leg, during orbit around the Moon, on the Moon-Earth flight leg, and then during the entry of the Command Module carrying the crew into Earth's atmosphere at reentry velocity, ensuring the accuracy of splashdown in the ocean.

In March 1969, the Lunar Module and Command and Service Module underwent joint testing in near-Earth orbit on *Apollo 9*. The Americans checked out methods for controlling the entire lunar complex as an assembled unit and verified communications between the vehicles and the ground, as well as the procedures for rendezvous and docking. The Americans performed a very risky experiment. Two astronauts in the Lunar Module undocked from the Command and Service Module, separated from it, and then tested the rendezvous and docking systems. If a failure had occurred in those systems, the crewmembers in the Lunar Module would have been doomed. But everything went smoothly.

It seemed that now everything was ready for a landing on the Moon. But lunar descent, liftoff, and navigation for rendezvous in orbit around the Moon had still not been tested. The Americans used one more complete Apollo-Saturn complex. They held a "dress rehearsal" on *Apollo 10* in May 1969, during which they checked out all the phases and operations except the actual landing on the lunar surface.

In a series of flights, step by step, the range of procedures tested under actual conditions leading to a reliable lunar landing gradually increased. Over the course of seven months, Saturn V launch vehicles lifted four piloted vehicles into orbit, making it possible to check out all the hardware, eliminate defects that were discovered, train all of the ground personnel, and instill confidence in the crew who had been entrusted to carry out this great mission.[32] For comparison, one should keep in mind that it would be almost an impossible

---

32. In reality, before *Apollo 11*, the Saturn V launched *three* crews into orbit (*Apollo 8*, *Apollo 9*, and *Apollo 10*).

task to carry out four piloted Shuttle flights to the International Space Station in seven months' time, let alone the Moon!

By the summer of 1969, everything had been tested except the actual landing and activities on the lunar surface. The *Apollo 11* team had concentrated all of its time and attention on these remaining tasks. On 16 July 1969, Neil Armstrong, Michael Collins, and Edwin "Buzz" Aldrin lifted off on *Apollo 11* to go down in the history of cosmonautics forever. Armstrong and Aldrin spent 21 hours, 36 minutes, and 21 seconds on the surface of the Moon. In July 1969, all of America celebrated, just as the Soviet Union had in April 1961.

After the first lunar expedition, America sent six more! Only one of the seven lunar expeditions proved unsuccessful. Due to a malfunction on the Earth-Moon leg of the flight, the crew of *Apollo 13* was forced to abort its landing on the Moon and return to Earth. This failed flight gave us engineers even more cause for admiration than the successful lunar landings. Officially, this was a failure, but it demonstrated high margins of reliability and safety. In December 1972, *Apollo 17* executed the last lunar expedition on the 12th Saturn V. The United States spent around 25 billion dollars (at 1972 monetary rates) on the entire program (at the time I am writing this chapter, this would be at least 125 billion).

Having created the world's most powerful launch vehicle, Wernher von Braun left his team and transferred to work at NASA Headquarters in Washington, DC. Two years later, he retired from NASA and went to work in private industry. On 16 June 1977, von Braun passed away at the age of 65 after an operation for colon cancer.

Thirteen piloted flights on Saturn rockets, developed under the technical management of von Braun's German team, are convincing proof of the high reliability and safety that technology and the political will of government leaders in the 20th century could provide. At a roundtable discussion in 1997 dedicated to the 40th anniversary of the launch of the first *Sputnik*, Ernst Stuhlinger, a veteran of von Braun's team, cited the words of von Braun in a conversation with a friend shortly before he died: "If I had had the opportunity to meet and talk with any one of the many pioneers of space who helped to make space flight a reality over the course of the last 80 to 100 years, then I would have picked Sergey Korolev."

Chapter 3

N1–L3 Lunar Program Under Korolev

Someday, not before the mid-21st century, I believe that historians will argue about whose idea it was to use atomic energy for interplanetary rocket flight. In the early 1950s, after rocket scientists began to have access to the operating principles of nuclear reactors, ideas emerged for using the energy of nuclear reactors to convert rocket engine propellant into high-temperature gas. An indisputable advantage of a nuclear rocket engine (YaRD) is its lack of oxidizer.[1] Liquid propellant is converted into gas, the temperature of which is much higher than in the combustion chambers of liquid-propellant rocket engines. When this high-temperature gas is discharged from the reaction nozzle, thrust is generated. According to the thinking of these enthusiasts, the nuclear reactor would replace the conventional liquid-propellant rocket engine combustion chamber.

At NII-1, the scientific chief of which was Mstislav Keldysh at that time, Vitaliy Iyevlev was the initiator and head of operations on nuclear rocket engines.[2] In 1957, he reported on this subject to Igor Kurchatov, Anatoliy Aleksandrov, and Aleksandr Leypunskiy.[3] These people were able to make decisions without waiting for instructions from higher up. At their initiative, within an unprecedentedly short period of time, a one-of-a-kind graphite reactor was constructed at the Semipalatinsk nuclear test site. The initial successes

---

1. YaRD—*Yadernyy raketnyy dvigatel.*
2. Vitaliy Mikhaylovich Iyevlev (1926–) is a well-known Russian specialist in the theory of engines, heat exchange, and the theory of the turbulent boundary layer. Much of his work was focused on the hydrodynamics of high-temperature gas flows.
3. Igor Vasilyevich Kurchatov (1903–1960) was a Soviet physicist most well known for being the leader of the Soviet atomic bomb project. Anatoliy Petrovich Aleksandrov (1903–1994), who for a while was Kurchatov's deputy, contributed to the Soviet nuclear project before eventually serving as president of the USSR Academy of Sciences from 1975 to 1986. Aleksandr Ilyich Leypunskiy (1903–1972) played a significant role in the development of Soviet civilian nuclear reactors in the postwar period.

provided the impetus for the subsequent steps toward the development of a nuclear rocket engine.

The U.S. also announced that it was funding research for the development of a rocket with a nuclear engine. This information also reached the nuclear energy enthusiasts in the USSR. We could not lag behind in these matters.

Research work in this field began at the Institute of Atomic Energy under Kurchatov, at OKB-456 under Glushko, at NII-1 under Keldysh, and at OKB-670 under Bondaryuk.[4] On 30 June 1958, the first Central Committee and Council of Ministers decree calling for the development of a heavy-lift rocket using a nuclear rocket engine was issued. This same decree called for the development of heavy-lift rockets with liquid-propellant engines using cryogenic high-energy components—oxygen and hydrogen. Kurchatov, Korolev, Keldysh, Aleksandrov, and Glushko actively participated in drawing up the decree. Although Glushko had never undertaken any developments for liquid-propellant engines using hydrogen, the idea of a nuclear rocket engine interested him. At his design bureau in Khimki he organized design work in this field jointly with NII-1.

At OKB-1, Korolev assigned Mishin, Kryukov, and Melnikov to look into the possibility of producing a rocket with a nuclear rocket engine.[5] Throughout 1959, they performed calculations, estimates, and layouts for various models of heavy launch vehicles with oxygen-hydrogen liquid-propellant engines on the first stage and nuclear rocket engines on the second. The decree of 30 June 1958 formalized these studies. A draft plan of a rocket using a nuclear rocket engine was developed at OKB-1 and approved by Korolev on 30 December 1959.

The design called for using six R-7 first-stage blocks as the rocket's first stage. The second stage—the central block—was essentially a nuclear reactor in which propellant was heated to a temperature in excess of 3,000 kelvins. OKB-456 proposed using ammonia as the propellant, while OKB-670 proposed using a mixture of ammonia and alcohol. The engine itself comprised four nozzles through which streams of gases escaped, having been intensely heated by the nuclear reaction.

The draft plan examined in detail several versions of rockets with nuclear engines. The most impressive was a super rocket with a launch mass of 2,000 tons and a payload mass of up to 150 tons in Earth orbit. The first stage of

---

4. Mikhail Makarovich Bondaryuk (1908–1969) was a prominent Soviet engine designer who specialized in ramjet engines. He served as chief designer of OKB-670 from 1950 to 1969.

5. Sergey Sergeyevich Kryukov (1918–2005) and Mikhail Vasilyevich Melnikov (1919–1996) were two of Korolev's leading deputies during the 1950s and 1960s. Vasiliy Pavlovich Mishin (1917–2001) was Korolev's "first deputy," i.e., "first among the deputies," from 1946 to 1966, before succeeding him.

this "super rocket" carried the number of liquid-propellant rocket engines that enabled it to obtain a total launch thrust of 3,000 tons. For this, Glushko proposed developing a liquid-propellant engine using toxic high-boiling components with a thrust of from 500 to 600 tons. Korolev and Mishin categorically rejected this version and used only Nikolay Kuznetsov's oxygen-kerosene liquid-propellant rocket engines in the design.[6] His NK-9 engine for the first stage of the global rocket (GR) with a thrust up to 60 metric tons was still in its initial stage of development.[7] Fifty of these engines were required for the first stage of the rocket with a nuclear engine! This alone made the design of the nuclear super rocket rather unrealistic.

At an early stage, the draft plan proposed a hybrid rocket with a launch mass of 850 to 880 tons that would insert a payload of 35 to 40 metric tons into orbit at an altitude of 300 kilometers. The first stage of the rocket, with a block structure similar to that of the R-7 rocket, was composed of six liquid-propellant rocket engine blocks. The central block was a nuclear-chemical rocket.

Despite the top-secret nature of all the work on nuclear rocket engines, the engineers remained extremely optimistic about the exceptional efficiency of nuclear power for rockets. Rumors that emanated not only from Kurchatov's institute, but also from Keldysh's NII-1, heated up the nuclear boom. Tupolev was working on the design of an airplane for which an aircraft nuclear power plant was being developed.[8] Such an airplane would be capable of supersonic speed and unlimited flight range.

Almost simultaneously, both we and the Americans were spending great amounts of resources on research in this field and conducting experimental work with various reactors. However, to this day, nuclear rocket engines have obtained no practical use in aviation or in rocket technology. And complete disappointment has replaced the optimism kindled by examples of the successful use of atomic energy on submarines, icebreakers, and heavy warships. But it took a while for attitudes toward nuclear rocket engines to cool, and in 1959 Korolev, who had access to Tupolev's work, was still chiding his deputies

---

6. Nikolay Dmitriyevich Kuznetsov (1911–1995) headed a major design bureau in Kuybyshev (now Samara) between 1949 and 1994 (now known as the N. D. Kuznetsov Samara Scientific-Technical Complex) that developed many of the most efficient and reliable jet engines for the Soviet aviation industry.

7. "Global rocket" (*Globalnaya raketa*) was a generic Russian term for orbital bombardment systems. The Korolev, Yangel, and Chelomey design bureaus each proposed several orbital bombardment systems in the early 1960s, only one of which, Yangel's R-36-O, reached the flight-testing stage.

8. This was Tupolev's experimental Tu-119 aircraft, a modification of the more well-known Tu-95 strategic bomber.

From the author's archives.

Two rocket engine designers: Aleksey Isayev (left) and Valentin Glushko.

for insufficient zeal in the nuclear field, saying that they mustn't let an airplane with a nuclear engine come out before a rocket with a nuclear engine.

However, the overwhelming majority of design engineers were in agreement on the fact that it was quicker, more reliable, and safer to develop heavy-lift rockets only using liquid-propellant rocket engines, while nuclear rocket engines would find an application in the distant future. The Americans demonstrated in practice the advantages of liquid hydrogen by producing the Saturn I rocket with a second stage that ran on hydrogen. At that time, our leading chief designers of liquid-propellant rocket engines—Glushko, Isayev, and Kosberg—were carrying on heated debates on the problems of producing liquid-propellant rocket engines using hydrogen.

Opponents and skeptics of the use of liquid hydrogen exaggerated the difficulties of its practical usage. Supposedly, the low density of liquid hydrogen would require the creation of inordinately large fuel tanks, which would increase the rocket's dimensions. The rocket specialists told the engine specialists that that wasn't their problem. Then the engine specialists were afraid that at a temperature of −235°C all the metals would become brittle. Impact strength would supposedly drop by 30 percent. Under these conditions, the use of pyrotechnic valves could not be allowed. Even schoolchildren knew that a mixture of hydrogen and oxygen was an explosive gas and during the fueling process the least bit of sloppiness would cause an explosion. Just imagine, the skeptics fretted, that the hydrogen leaks out imperceptibly and saturates the area around the launch site. All it will take is the slightest initiator and a fuel-air explosion will take place. Whoever doesn't die from the shock wave will suffocate from lack of oxygen and burn up with the hydrogen. I mention only the main arguments, but many more objections explained our lag in the production of liquid-propellant rocket engines using hydrogen.

After all manner of discussions and consultations, the Military-Industrial Commission (VPK) began to draw up a decree hoping to speed up work on high-power rockets and, consequently, on high-performance engines. Korolev personally inserted a demand for the development of liquid-hydrogen-propellant engines into the draft text.

On 23 June 1960, the Central Committee and USSR Council of Ministers decree "On the Creation of Powerful Launch Vehicles, Satellites, Spacecraft, and the Mastery of Cosmic Space in 1960–1967," which had been coordinated with the Ministry of Defense and the ministers and State Committee chairmen of all the necessary defense industries, was issued. This was the first attempt to confirm the prospects for the development of cosmonautics at the very highest level in the form of a seven-year plan. To some extent, the decree was a response to Brezhnev's visit to OKB-1.[9] By that time, Khrushchev felt it was advisable to plan the development of the entire economy in seven-year increments rather than the Stalinist five-year plans.

For history, the content of the decree can serve to illustrate that political figures are not the only ones who make unrealistic, populist promises. Back then, no one dared challenge Khrushchev's announcement that "our generation will live under communism." Khrushchev himself probably sincerely believed that would be the case. This remained on his conscience, and none of us was required to take an oath that we actually promised to live to see communism.

The "top secret—of special importance" decrees were a different story. They contained much more specific deadlines and spelled out the names of the responsible administrators. They were the ones who had proposed writing down unrealistic deadlines for their own organizations in the government plans. The administrators were the chiefs of large staffs, and by that time they were already experienced chief designers. The ministers, who had drawn up the decrees, had passed through the grueling school of managing industry during wartime. They remembered quite well that disrupting deadlines that Stalin had set or failing to fulfill promises could cost your life. Now they all signed their names to unrealistic promises.

The decree called for the development from 1961 through 1963 of the new N-1 high-power launch vehicle with liquid-propellant rocket engines that

---

9. See Boris Chertok, *Rockets and People, Vol. II*, pp. 553–555.

would be capable of inserting into orbit a satellite with a mass of 40 to 50 tons and accelerating a payload with a mass of 10 to 20 tons to escape velocity. Next, on the basis of this rocket, from 1963 through 1967, the plan was to develop a launch vehicle that would insert into Earth orbit a payload with a mass of 60 to 80 tons and accelerate a 20- to 40-ton payload to escape velocity. At the same time, this decree ordered "the use of newly developed [nuclear rocket engines], engines running on new chemical energy sources, and low-thrust electric rocket engines on stage two and subsequent stages." The decree stipulated developing high-thrust liquid-hydrogen engines, autonomous control and radio control systems, and experimental facilities for these projects and the performance of scientific research work. On 9 September 1960, Korolev signed the report "On the Possible Characteristics of Space Rockets Using Hydrogen," which demonstrated the advantages of hydrogen.

Let's return to the figure of an 80-ton payload in Earth orbit. That's the maximum figure that all the chief designers combined took a stab at. Nobody at the top dictated this figure by government directive to Korolev, Keldysh, the other chiefs, and all the aides, deputies, planners, and designers. It so happened that we ourselves did not dare go any further.

In the history of the Moon race, this was our first design error. As painful as it is to admit, Korolev, Keldysh, and the entire Council of Chiefs all committed this conceptual error. What we should have taken into consideration was what we actually needed to land on the Moon and return to Earth, rather than what we could demand of the launch vehicle within the timeframe stipulated in the directive. We should have begun our calculation of tons from the surface of the Moon, not Earth.

But there were two extenuating circumstances. For one thing, Korolev and all of us deputies could be excused by the fact that in 1960 we did not yet consider a piloted landing expedition to the Moon to be our main, top-priority mission and we had not imagined all the problems that we would have to deal with. Secondly, back then, Korolev was already thinking about the possibility of a multilaunch lunar flight plan. By assembling the spacecraft in Earth or lunar orbit, the critical mass of the payload could be doubled or even tripled.

In September 1960, during a large "convention" of chief designers at the firing range before the first launches of the four-stage 8K78 launch vehicles carrying the 1M spacecraft for the exploration of Mars, a standing-room-only meeting took place.[10] During this session, we discussed the status of the draft

---

10. OKB-1 carried out two launches of 1M Mars probes on 10 and 14 October 1960. Both failed to reach Earth orbit.

development of the "N-1 phase one integrated rocket system." While discussing the mass of the payload that would be inserted into orbit, Mikhail Tikhonravov gave the most radical presentation. He proposed that, in selecting our launch vehicle version, we proceed from the assumption that in-orbit assembly was the primary means for ensuring the payload's requisite mass.

The universal triumph of 12 April 1961 threatened to decrease the zeal of designers and scientists in the military field. At the initiative of the Central Committee and the Ministry of Defense, a new decree soon appeared: "On Revising Plans for Space Objects Dedicated to the Fulfillment of Defense Goals."

It is significant that this decree appeared on 13 May, on a significant day for USSR rocket technology. On 13 May 1946, the first decree calling for the organization of operations for the production of long-range ballistic missiles in general and the R-1 missile in particular was issued. Fifteen years later, on 13 May 1961, the order went out to produce the N-1 rocket in 1965.

We were actually quite serious that we would produce it in 1965! Perhaps not for a landing expedition to the Moon, but certainly for defense and other purposes. Overconfidently, we sought to produce the desired rather than the feasible. Of course, the authorities encouraged us to behave like that. However, the failure to meet deadlines for long-range projects is an international phenomenon.

From the author's archives.

In the early 1950s, Wernher von Braun published in the open press his vision of a heavy three-stage rocket to provide vehicle traffic between satellites and spacecraft in Earth orbit, to construct a permanent orbital station with a mass of 400 metric tons, and to launch interplanetary spacecraft. For his rocket, von Braun proposed a launch mass of 7,000 tons, a height of 80 meters, and a diameter of 20 meters. The first stage was to have 51 engines with a thrust of 275 tons each. The second stage was to have 22 engines, and the third—5

The Saturn V rocket shown here exiting the Vehicle Assembly Building (VAB) on the Crawler-Transporter.

engines each with 55 metric tons of thrust. In 1953, von Braun asserted that the creators of a structure such as this and an orbital station faced fewer problems than the inventors of the atomic bomb had faced in 1940. Von Braun surmised that the flight of such a rocket would take place in 1977. Ten years later, the same von Braun argued that it was not necessary to produce such a rocket and that a launch mass of 3,000 tons, which his Saturn V launch vehicle had, was quite adequate to land an expedition on the Moon.

Decrees aimed at long-range developments with knowingly unrealistic deadlines caused a rush of new enthusiasm in the various design teams. The awareness of being involved in great achievements and of drawing the attention of the nation's top leadership boosted the ambitions of everyone who was responsible for fulfilling the Central Committee and Council of Ministers decrees.

On 25 May 1961, 12 days after the Kremlin signing of the top-secret, high-importance decree, President Kennedy quite openly appealed to the American people on the very same subject. I am certain that espionage intrigues were beside the point here. The idea of producing heavy rockets and expeditions to the Moon "hung in the air," as the saying goes. After Gagarin's feat, this had to be the next historical step for humankind.

In the preceding chapter I wrote that the U.S. publicly announced this historic step as a national mission. In 1964, from the congressional podium, President Lyndon B. Johnson exhorted Americans "to keep up their efforts and enthusiasm." Every American had to know that their country was preparing for a flight to the Moon. In the Soviet Union all programs and plans of operations for piloted flights to the Moon were classified, and for that reason, only those involved on the front lines of the secret programs with access to the ongoing projects showed real enthusiasm. It is amazing that all the "top" designers, who drew up and signed the decrees, believed that absolute secrecy was every bit as necessary as when producing new combat missiles. At that time, we had no specific ideas regarding the possible use of the Moon, even in the distant future, for military purposes.

All three of the aforementioned decrees [from 1958, 1960, and 1961], signed by First Secretary of the Central Committee and Chairman of the USSR Council of Ministers Khrushchev, assigned the leading role in the development of the new heavy launch vehicle to OKB-1 and, consequently, to Chief Designer Sergey Korolev. The conflicts between Korolev and Glushko in their views on the prospects for developing heavy launch vehicles had escalated by that time. At first Glushko was critical, and then openly hostile, to Korolev during the selection of propellant components for the new liquid-propellant engines. For the first stage of the new heavy rocket, all of the proposals from OKB-1 called for the use of a liquid-propellant rocket engine that ran on liquid oxygen and kerosene. Subsequent stages called for the use of engines that ran on liquid hydrogen and, finally, in the distant future, nuclear rocket engines. However, despite the wealth of experience that Glushko and his design team had accumulated since 1946 in the production of oxygen-kerosene engines, and despite the creation in Khimki of a one-of-a-kind test rig facility for liquid-propellant rocket engines that used oxygen, Glushko stubbornly proposed using high-thrust liquid-propellant rocket engines operating on high-boiling components—nitrogen tetroxide and unsymmetrical dimethyl hydrazine—for the future heavy rocket. Glushko's position can be explained by the fact that during this time he was developing high-boiling component engines for Yangel's and Chelomey's intercontinental ballistic missiles. A large experimental facility for these engines had been created in Khimki.

The discord between Korolev and Glushko over propellant components, which had arisen during the period from 1959 to 1960 in connection with the design of the R-9A rocket, also affected the personal relationships of the two pioneers of Soviet rocket technology.[11] Glushko did not forgive Korolev for recruiting aviation industry engine-building organizations to produce powerful liquid-propellant rocket engines: Lyulka's OKB-165, which was developing a liquid-hydrogen engine, and Kuznetsov's OKB-276, which was producing an engine that ran on liquid oxygen and kerosene.[12] This was a direct affront to Glushko—Korolev's old comrade-in-arms from the RNII, the design bureau in Kazan, the Institute Nordhausen, and the Council of Chief Designers, where Glushko ranked second after Korolev.

As a rule, historians of cosmonautics mention the disagreements between Korolev and Glushko either indirectly or not at all. The true causes of this acrimonious conflict, which many of my contemporaries and I witnessed, and which we were obliged to take sides on because of our duties, have not been sorted out to this day. I cannot agree with the explanation that Glushko's towering ambition caused the downfall of our operations on powerful liquid-propellant rocket engines in the 1960s. Supposedly, he envied Korolev and, dreaming of rising above him and all the chief designers of rockets, he wanted to prove, "Hey, look here, I am an engine expert; without me you can't do anything, and I'm the only one who can help you out."

---

11. As finally produced, the R-9A missile used Glushko's RD-111 engine on the first stage and Kosberg's RD-0106 (or 8D715P) engine. Both used liquid oxygen and kerosene.

12. Arkhip Mikhaylovich Lyulka (1908–1984) was an aviation designer who is credited with developing the first double jet turbofan engines. His former organization is now a part of NPO Saturn.

While discussing the problems of engines for the first stage of the N-1, at all levels, Glushko declared that it would not be particularly difficult for his organization to develop engines with a thrust as high as 600 tons using high-boiling components: nitrogen tetroxide and unsymmetrical dimethyl hydrazine. At the same time, the creation of an engine of this size and capacity running on liquid oxygen and kerosene, in Glushko's opinion, would take way too much time.

In the U.S., von Braun was the one who came up with the idea for using liquid hydrogen for the Saturn launch vehicle series. The NASA leadership approved it, and in a relatively short time the U.S. aviation industry was able to produce high-thrust liquid hydrogen engines. The American experience, and later our own experience in Voronezh, showed that there was nothing supernatural in the hydrogen engine manufacturing process.

Alas! Korolev's will and even Central Committee and government decrees proved insufficient for the oxygen-hydrogen liquid-propellant rocket engines under development for the N1-L3 program to be produced in time to take their place on the "lunar" rocket.

I worked with Korolev for 20 years, and with Glushko from 1974 until he died. I was a deputy to both of them. I'm very well acquainted with Mishin, who remained an ardent opponent of Glushko's high-boiling component concept (and Glushko reciprocated the opposition). I often met, both at and outside of work, with engine specialists who were Glushko's deputies, old and young, colleagues who sincerely respected him. They all considered Glushko to be a very complex human being, sometimes excessively fault-finding and demanding not only in dealing with his immediate subordinates, but also with subcontractors. At the same time, nobody doubted his technical prowess, erudition, general refinement, and ability to quickly identify the main issue in the heap of complicated day-to-day problems in large systems.

In the interests of business, Korolev sought to avoid conflicts, tried to meet people halfway, and if any hope remained, he tried to persuade everyone all the way up to the highest government officials. Glushko made it a point to only defer to the highest-ranking leaders—the Party General Secretary and members of the Politburo. Relationships with ministers certainly did not always turn out to his benefit. Ustinov, who was very attentive to Glushko's ideas and proposals, was an exception.[13] While he was logically methodical in

---

13. Dmitriy Fedorovich Ustinov (1908–1984) was probably the most important Soviet administrative figure involved in the Soviet space program during the Cold War. Through various posts in both the government and Communist Party over a span of nearly 40 years, he was instrumental in both setting Soviet space policy and executing it.

most of his creative work, Glushko, especially in cases involving the selection of propellants, sometimes engaged in actions that were logically inexplicable.

In March 1961, Korolev sent Glushko an official letter. In essence, it contained a question rather than a complaint: "OKB-456's unexpected position concerning the use of supercooled liquid oxygen for the R-9A rocket is incomprehensible and difficult to explain. You have apparently forgotten that in our joint report to the Central Committee in April 1959, which you signed, the main and only version of the R-9A called specifically for the use of supercooled liquid oxygen and kerosene. All this time, the design and experimental work, in which your representatives have participated, by the way, was conducted on the R-9A with the intention of using supercooled oxygen."

Instead of a calm, businesslike discussion of an issue so vital not only for the R-9A rocket, but also for the entire future of cosmonautics, Korolev and Glushko were exchanging letters that were anything but amicable, copies of which they were sending to the ministers and VPK. Lev Grishin, who was a deputy minister at that time, attempted to bring Korolev and Glushko together in his office for a private meeting during the summer of 1960.[14] Mishin and I were present during the conversation. With his innate sense of humor, Grishin very calmly said that in a matter such as selecting a type of liquid-propellant engine and propellant components for rockets, letters to the Central Committee were not the best way to solve the problem. "Why drag Khrushchev into matters that he tasked us to solve? Khrushchev trusts us, but it turns out we don't trust each other."

A heart-to-heart conversation didn't pan out. Glushko began to speak very calmly, but in the process he stepped on Korolev's pride, accusing him of "playing footsie" with the aviation industry, where he, Korolev, wanted to have new, obedient, but completely incompetent liquid-propellant rocket engine developers. Korolev exploded. Tit for tat, both began to fling such insults at each other that Grishin, Mishin, and I quickly left the office. Completely despondent, we stood out in the corridor for about 20 minutes.

"I'm worried they'll get into a fistfight there…," Grishin fretted. But both chief designers, red as boiled lobsters, came flying out of the office without looking at each other, or at us, as if they didn't realize where they were, and bolted out of the ministry. Korolev didn't want to see anyone and got in his car and drove away without offering Mishin or me a ride. Grishin summed

---

14. Lev Arkhipovich Grishin (1920–1960) was deputy chairman of the State Committee of Defense Technology from 1958 to 1960. He died as a result of injuries sustained during the R-16 disaster on 24 October 1960.

up the situation, saying, "It seems to me that two members of the Russian intelligentsia just parted company after exhausting their entire repertoire of obscenities." After this absolutely wild altercation, I don't recall Korolev having a single warm, friendly conversation with Glushko.

The State Memorial Museum of Cosmonautics contains a globe of the world—a gift from V. P. Glushko to S. P. Korolev with the following inscription: "I send you this globe, Sergey, with the profound hope that one day we will see the living Earth at the same size with our own eyes. 25.4.1952." This same museum contains an original telegram that Glushko received from Korolev on 25 October 1953. Below is a reproduction of the text from a Xerox copy that was kindly provided to me:

```
MOSCOW GORKOGO NO.43 APT 94
TO GLUSHKO VALENTIN PETROVICH
KAPUSTIN YAR 11:50
I EMBRACE YOU WARMLY FROM THE BOTTOM OF MY
HEART MY DEAREST FRIEND AND CONGRATULATE
YOU ON YOUR ELECTION TO THE USSR ACADEMY
OF SCIENCE STOP I RECALL THE MOUNTAINS
OF WORK THE DIFFICULTIES THE BITTERNESS
OF FAILURE AND JOY OF ACHIEVEMENT STOP I
WISH YOU MUCH GOOD HEALTH AND STRENGTH FOR
GREAT NEW TRIUMPHS FOR THE GOOD OF OUR
BELOVED SOVIET MOTHERLAND STOP I SEND MY
GREETINGS TO YOUR MAMA MAGDA AND A STRONG
HANDSHAKE TO YOU
YOUR SERGEY KOROLEV
```

In October 1953, Korolev and Glushko were simultaneously elected corresponding members of the USSR Academy of Sciences.

I was on an expedition to the State Central Firing Range (GTsP) in Kapustin Yar with Korolev.[15] At that time, the second phase of the flight tests on the R-5 rocket was under way.[16] The rocket was equipped with a new engine

---

15. GTsP—*Gosudarstvennyy tsentralnyy poligon*. Until the launch of the R-7 ICBM from Tyuratam in 1957, all Soviet long-range ballistic missiles were launched from the Kapustin Yar firing range, located southeast of the major city of Volgograd in Astrakhan Oblast.

16. The second phase of testing of the R-5 rocket spanned from 30 October to 9 December 1953. The R-5, with a range of 1,200 kilometers, was the first "strategic" rocket developed by the Soviets.

developed by Glushko, which ran on liquid oxygen and ethyl alcohol.[17] In terms of its performance specifications, it greatly surpassed the preceding engines for the R-1 and R-2 rockets, which were basically reproductions of the German V-2 rocket engines. Glushko was also supposed to be at the firing range, but because of their elections to the Academy of Sciences, Korolev decided that one of them should stay in Moscow—just in case....

The news of their election brightened Korolev's mood so much that no amount of flight headaches could dampen his joy. Glushko was still the person with whom he had to share these feelings. The words "my very best friend" were undoubtedly sincere and came from the bottom of his heart. Just seven years later, Korolev was no longer able to call Glushko "my very best friend."

Korolev's proposal to recruit Kuznetsov and Lyulka, chief designers of aircraft turbojet engines, to develop powerful liquid-propellant rocket engines [in the early 1960s] was accepted by Khrushchev and codified in decrees.

Glushko was the nation's universally recognized chief authority on liquid-propellant rocket engines. Forty years later, it seems to me that he made a big mistake by refusing in the early 1960s to develop powerful oxygen-kerosene and oxygen-hydrogen engines. It took us 20 years to overtake the U.S. in this field with the production of the Energiya rocket! Glushko finally produced an oxygen-kerosene engine, about which Korolev did not even dare to dream in the early 1960s, when he occupied Korolev's place as general designer of NPO Energiya.[18]

The schism in the chief designers' camp over engines for intercontinental ballistic missiles and the new heavy rockets widened. Two new chief designers—Yangel and Chelomey—joined the dispute between the two pillars of Soviet rocket technology. Korolev's monopoly in heavy launch vehicles threatened their active participation in future space programs. A powerful attack began on the government bureaucracy from various sides, as did criticism of earlier decisions.

Consequently, yet another decree appeared, signed by Khrushchev on 16 April 1962: "On the Creation of Models of Intercontinental Ballistic Missiles, Global Rockets, and Launch Vehicles for Heavy Space Payloads." This decree proposed limiting N-1 operations to the draft plan phase and a cost assessment of the rocket system. At the same time, it called for the development of a three-stage global orbital rocket on the basis of our R-9A, but using the new NK-9 engines being developed at Korolev's initiative by Nikolay Kuznetsov

---

17. This was the RD-103 engine.
18. Glushko headed the development of the RD-170 engines for the Energiya booster. This was his first liquid-oxygen-based engine since the 1960s.

in Kuybyshev, rather than using Glushko's engines. The document also called for the production of Yangel's new super-heavy R-56 rocket.

Then, on 29 April 1962, a decree was issued in which OKB-52, i.e., Chelomey, was tasked with developing the UR-500—the future Proton. The expert commission under the chairmanship of Academy of Science President Keldysh was not supposed to give its recommendations until it had reviewed the draft plans. The decrees made no mention of organizing operations specifically oriented toward piloted flights to the Moon.

THROUGHOUT 1962, THE SELECTION OF THE DESIGN AND LAUNCH MASS for the N-1 launch vehicle continued. According to Korolev's concept, it would perform numerous scientific and defense missions and by no means just deliver an expedition to the Moon. In a letter to Sergey Kryukov, chief of the design department, Korolev wrote: "Work with M. V. Melnikov to determine the required weight for a flight using ERDs [electric rocket engines] to carry out the primary missions: Moon, Mars, Venus (i.e. the TMK)."[19]

The Ministry of Defense was not interested in super-heavy launch vehicles. At the same time, without the consent of military officers to directly participate in the development of such a launch vehicle, the expert commission could not approve the draft plan.

Korolev approved the draft plan of the rocket space systems based on the N-1 on 16 May 1962. The plan was issued in accordance with the decree of 23 June 1960 mentioned above and officially responded to the latest decree of April 1962. It contained 29 volumes and eight appendices. The draft plan, which all of Korolev's deputies, myself included, signed, assigned the following primary objectives:

a. Insert heavy space vehicles (KLA) into orbit around Earth to study the nature of cosmic radiation, the origins and development of the planets, solar radiation, the nature of gravity, and the physical conditions on the nearest planets, and to discover organic life-forms under conditions different from those on Earth, etc.[20]

b. The insertion of automatic and piloted heavy satellites into high orbits to relay television and radio broadcasts, for weather forecasting, etc.

---

19. ERD—*Elektricheskiy raketnyy dvigatel*; TMK—*Tyazhelyy mezhplanetnyy korabl* (Heavy Interplanetary Ship). Chertok's excerpt is taken from S. P. Korolev, "Zametki po N-I" ["Notes on the N-I"] in *S. P. Korolev i ego delo: svet i teni v istorii kosmonavtiki* [*S. P. Korolev and His Work: Light and Shadow in the History of Cosmonautics*] (Moscow: Nauka, 1998), pp. 355–356.

20. KLA—*Kosmicheskiy letatelnyy apparat*.

c. When necessary, the insertion of heavy automatic and piloted military stations capable of staying in orbit for long periods of time and making it possible to perform a maneuver for the simultaneous orbital insertion of a large number of military satellites.

The plan declared the main phases for the further exploration of space:

- Execute circumlunar flight of a spacecraft with a crew of two or three cosmonauts;
- Insert a spacecraft into lunar orbit, land on the Moon, explore its surface, and return to Earth;
- Conduct an expedition to the lunar surface to study the soil and topography and to search for a site for a research facility on the Moon;
- Build a research facility on the Moon and set up transport systems between Earth and the Moon;
- Conduct a flight with a crew of two or three cosmonauts around Mars and Venus and return to Earth;
- Conduct expeditions to the surface of Mars and Venus and select sites for research facilities;
- Build research facilities on Mars and set up transport systems between Earth and other planets; and
- Launch automatic spacecraft to explore circumsolar space and the distant planets of the solar system (Jupiter, Saturn, etc.).

Even 45 years later, the text cited above seems like an amazing cascade of missions capable of captivating thousands of enthusiasts. It is unfortunate that not only were none of these missions ever announced to the public, or even to the scientific community, but they were also shrouded under a "top secret" classification. One might ask us, "In 1962, did you really not understand that, aside from a lunar landing and the dispatching of automatic stations, the remaining phases should have been planned for the 21st century?" Korolev and everyone who signed the list of prospective missions had hoped to impart to them the status of State plans. However, in the higher echelons of power, aside from Khrushchev himself, there were no romantics who would be enthralled with interplanetary expeditions.

The draft plan proposed a three-stage N-1 launch vehicle with a launch mass of 2,200 tons capable of inserting a satellite with a mass of up to 75 tons into a circular orbit with an altitude of 300 kilometers. All three stages of the rocket were designed for Kuznetsov's liquid-propellant rocket engines using liquid oxygen and kerosene. The first stage—Block A—would be equipped with 24 engines each with 150 tons of thrust at liftoff. The second stage—Block B—and the third—Block V—had eight and four engines, respectively. Blocks A and B were equipped with Kuznetsov's virtually identical

NK-15 engines.[21] Block V would have NK-9 engines with 40 tons of thrust (*sorokatonniki*).[22]

Back when the R-7 was still in the design phase, Mishin came out with the idea of controlling the rocket by boosting and throttling diametrically opposed engines. At that time, his idea was not met with approval: Glushko disagreed with regulating engine thrust over a broad range, which required diametrically opposed engines to create control moments by means of varying thrust.

On the N-1, 24 engines arranged around its 15-meter diameter made it possible to implement this idea, especially since the OKB-276 engine specialists did not oppose it. For them, the aircraft engine developers, the requirement of regulating thrust within the broadest limits was completely natural.

The structural layout of the rocket proposed in the draft plan was unconventional. Since the days of the R-2, we had been proud of the fact that we had been the first to implement the concept of integral tanks: the metal tanks were load-bearing and at the same time formed the outer shell of the rocket. All of our combat missiles and launch vehicles were constructed using this principle, as were the Americans'. Kryukov's designers were studying a rocket model that used fuel and oxidizer tanks as a load-bearing structure. Beginning with the R-2 rocket, this principle had worked splendidly. The dimensions of the tanks of the first and second stages for the N-1 prevented them from being delivered from the Progress Factory in Kuybyshev to the firing range by rail, by ship, or by air.

A factory for the welding of the tanks, and the manufacture and assembly of all three stages of the rocket, had to be built at the firing range. The thickness of the metal of the load-bearing tanks was selected taking into consideration the internal pressure and the static and dynamic loads on the structure of the entire rocket. The technology at that time could not ensure the weld reliability and strength on a shell of that thickness. For this reason, after heated arguments, the designers persuaded Korolev to forgo what had become the traditional rocket technology design principle of integral tanks. The structural layout of the rocket was an external load-bearing shell with thinner-walled spherical fuel tanks, engines, and all the systems arranged inside it.

To weld the spherical tanks, Boris Paton, director of the Ye. O. Paton Institute of Electric Welding, proposed a new technology and special welding equipment. But in this case, the dimensions of the spherical tanks precluded

---

21. Block B used NK-15V engines, the "v" standing for *vysotnyy* or "altitude."

22. This nickname is derived from the Russian word *soroka* meaning "forty" and *tonn* meaning "ton."

their transportation from the factory to assemble them at the firing range. The tanks would have to be manufactured right at the cosmodrome.

By no means had everything been considered in the design layout of the rocket and its control system. Arguments continued over the methods for delivering the untransportable parts. According to the decree, flight development tests were supposed to begin in 1965. Over the three years that remained before this deadline, they would first have to build a modern rocket-assembly plant on the barren steppes and then master a new tank-welding process, assemble the stages, and put the entire rocket as a whole there. All sorts of rocket assembly operations and testing, except for firing tests, would have to be performed for the first time at the firing range. This meant that, among other things, they would have to build a residential town for the new factory's workers and specialists.

It was proposed that the project for the military be implemented in two phases. First, on the basis of the second and third stages, produce a separate N-11 rocket with a launch mass of 750 tons, capable of inserting a satellite with a mass up to 25 tons into Earth orbit. Then produce the actual super-heavy three-stage N-1 rocket with a launch mass of 2,200 tons. Despite its obvious logic, this proposal to begin operations on the N-11 ultimately found no support from expert commissions, from the military, or in subsequent decrees.

In history, one should not resort to the "what ifs," but I am not a historian and I can allow myself to conjecture how everything would have unfolded if our 1962 proposal had been enacted. There is no doubt that we would have produced the N-11 considerably sooner than the first N-1 flight model. We could have conducted developmental testing on the second and third stages of the rocket on the firing rigs near Zagorsk at NII-229 (as later happened).[23] The launch systems that were constructed for the N-1 would have been simplified to be used for the N-11 during the first phase. We missed a real opportunity to produce an environmentally clean launch vehicle for a 25-metric-ton payload. To this day, world cosmonautics has a very acute need for such a clean launch vehicle. But at that time, that idea could have interfered with Chelomey's proposals for the UR-500 and Yangel's proposals for the R-56.

---

23. Scientific-Research Institute-229 (NII-229) was the primary facility dedicated to testing liquid-propellant rocket engines in the Soviet Union. It is known today as the Scientific-Research Institute of Chemical Machine Building (NIIkhimmash).

Today, as I write this in 2007, Roscosmos is attempting to correct this historic error, having called for the development of the Angara launch vehicle in the Federal Space Program in the 21st century.[24]

The lunar landing expedition was still not the launch vehicle's primary mission in the draft plan [in 1962]. The mated configuration of two vehicles (lunar orbital vehicle and the landing LK) and booster Blocks G and D was very prosaically referred to as L3. Actually, there was not yet a design for the L3 vehicle in 1962. Moreover, to avoid getting anyone riled up, as S. P. sometimes used to say, we intentionally did not calculate the distribution of the masses for the lunar complex, and in particular, the requisite mass of the lunar (landing) vehicle to perform a landing with a maneuver, a reliable liftoff from the lunar surface, and subsequent rendezvous with the orbital vehicle.

At the plenary session of the expert commission Korolev reported that the draft presented only the N-1 launch vehicle without the payload. He listed the missions that such a launch vehicle would carry out in the following order:

- Defense missions, including a permanent system (several hundred satellites) for tracking, detecting, and destroying enemy missiles;
- Scientific missions;
- Human exploration of the Moon and closest planets of the solar system (Mars and Venus); and
- Global communications and radio and television broadcast relay.

It is interesting that the first mission on this list predated the development of the Strategic Defense Initiative (SDI) concept, which the Americans started 20 years later![25] And 10 years after that, in 1995, the U.S. sponsored an effort to create a system of several hundred satellites for the purposes of global communications. In 1962, in his report, Korolev referred to a similar system as an "orbital belt." The hundreds of satellites comprising this belt could have been used for global monitoring and to observe everything happening on Earth and in near-Earth space.

In the end, two rather large global personal communications systems were deployed, Iridium and Globalstar, in which, all told, more that 100 satellites are

---

24. Roscosmos (or Roskosmos) is the convenient short form for the Federal Space Agency of the Russian Federation.

25. The Russian abbreviation for SDI is SOI—*Strategicheskaya oboronnaya initsiativa.*

operating. The historical paradox is that to create this orbital belt, the Americans used Russian and Ukrainian launch vehicles: the Proton, Zenit, and Soyuz.[26]

EVEN THOUGH A SINGLE UR-500 ROCKET was not yet ready in 1962, the decision to develop it was one of the reasons why the expert commission did not support OKB-1's proposal on the N-11 rocket. In July 1962, the expert commission approved our draft plan for the N-1 launch vehicle capable of inserting a satellite with a payload mass of 75 tons into circular orbit at an altitude of 300 kilometers. Academy of Sciences President M. V. Keldysh approved the findings of the expert commission on the N-1 project, which named defense rather than lunar missions as the primary tasks for the N-1. The VPK kept a very attentive eye on the status of operations on the N-1. Despite the general background of success in the piloted space programs, the triumphant press conferences, and lavish postflight receptions at the Kremlin, Khrushchev once again reminded us of the N-1.

On 24 September 1962, a new Central Committee and Council of Ministers decree on the N-1 came out. The main purpose of the document consisted of the approval of the basic operations and the beginning of flight-developmental tests of the launch vehicle in 1965. Despite the fact that the main chief designers had worked with Korolev on the document's text under the supervision of Deputy Chairman of the State Committee on Defense Technology (GKOT) Georgiy Tyulin, its specified deadlines for wrapping up the work in the various phases prompted many ironic comments among the main authors.[27]

In the preceding decrees of 1960 and 1961, we were ordered to produce the N-1 in 1965. In April 1962, the same government and Central Committee and the same First Secretary of the Central Committee Khrushchev proposed that we limit ourselves strictly to the draft plan. The very cool attitude of the Ministry of Defense toward the N-1 project and the influence of Yangel's and Chelomey's proposals on Khrushchev resulted in the appearance of this interim decree. A year before this decree came out, Leonid Smirnov, the director of

---

26. A total of 98 Iridium satellites have been launched using American Delta II, Russian Proton-K, or Chinese CZ-2C launch vehicles. A total of 72 Globalstar satellites were launched by a variety of launch vehicles, including the American Delta 7420, the Ukrainian Zenit-2, and the Russian Soyuz-U and Soyuz-FG launch vehicles.

27. GKOT—*Gosudarstvennyy komitet po oboronnoy tekhnike*. The GKOT was the Khrushchev-era incarnation of the old Ministry of the Defense Industry, which oversaw the postwar missile program.

Dnepropetrovsk Factory No. 586, was named deputy chairman of GKOT, and soon thereafter, minister of the USSR—GKOT chairman.[28]

Considering the nation's very difficult economic situation and Khrushchev's eagerness to find funding for residential construction, agricultural improvements, and the production of fertilizers, he could have halted the funding of the N-1 altogether. In the spring of 1962 Khrushchev was still wavering, but the decree of 24 September showed that the wavering ended in the autumn. The new decree ordered that rig testing of the third-stage on-board engines end in 1964, and of the second- and first-stage engines in 1965. The rig testing of the engines integrated into stages and propulsion systems was to end in the first quarter of 1965. Completion of the launch site construction, its startup, and beginning of flight tests—all were to happen in 1965.

Vladimir Barmin, who was stubbornly against signing his initials to what was in his opinion an absurd plan, approached Korolev and stridently declared:

"According to the government decree, I officially have the right to sign the certificate of clearance for the first launch at the launch site with all its systems and facilities on 31 December. Until this document appears, you, Sergey Pavlovich, do not have the right to deliver the flight rocket to the launch pad. And there won't be anything to transport it on because, at your recommendation, I also have the right to clear the erector for it no later than 31 December. You understand that the builders and I will use our rights in full. What does that leave us for preparation and launch? Zero point zero seconds right on New Year's!"

Many similar sarcastic remarks were expressed as well in the offices of the VPK, Council of Ministers, and even in the Central Committee. But in the "halls of power" they threw up their hands—these deadlines were coordinated with Korolev, and he not only didn't protest, but he even declared that no one had given us the right to revise the dates for the beginning of flight-developmental testing, which had been set by previous decisions of the Central Committee and Council of Ministers.

Besides the unrealistic deadlines, there was in fact one more serious problem, which evoked a pained reaction from Korolev. With Korolev's consent, an item on the construction of a rig for technological firing tests (OTI) for the first stage had been crossed out of the draft of the latest decree at some stage during the coordination process.[29] When the draft plan was issued, Voskresenskiy temporarily came to terms with this, but now he went on an

---

28. Smirnov became chairman of GKOT in June 1961.
29. OTI—*Ognevyye tekhnologicheskiye ispytaniya*.

all-out offensive: he demanded the construction of rigs for full-scale testing of each stage, including the first stage with all 24 of its engines.

Korolev and Voskresenskiy had fundamentally different opinions on matters of experimental operations. Korolev wanted to completely avoid the need to build new and very expensive firing test rigs for the rocket stages. He hoped that the firing test rigs for all the stages could be limited to single-unit firing tests on engines after adapting the already existing rigs of NII-229. Voskresenskiy stubbornly insisted on designing and constructing the rigs, making it possible to conduct firing tests on the rocket stages under conditions that were as close to real as possible.

Novostroyka director Gleb Tabakov supported Voskresenskiy.[30] *Novostroyka* was the unclassified name of the former branch of NII-88 in the Zagorsk area.[31] After becoming independent, this branch was later called NII-229, and then NIIkhimmash.

Tabakov and I had been colleagues at one time—in 1949 we both worked as deputy chief engineers at NII-88. Before that, I often bumped into Tabakov when he was taking higher engineering courses at the Moscow Higher Technical

School (MVTU) where I taught a course in control systems.[32] Later I ran into him at *Novostroyka* near Zagorsk when we were conducting firing rig tests on rockets. Beginning in 1948, Tabakov worked as chief engineer at *Novostroyka*, then after a break for design work, he returned to *Novostroyka* in 1956 as director. In 1958, Tabakov became my neighbor on 3rd Ostankinskaya Street, and so our families also became acquainted.

Gleb Tabakov had a storied career in the Soviet space program, beginning as director of NII-229 and ending as a deputy minister of general machine building.

From the author's archives.

30. Gleb Mikhaylovich Tabakov (1912–1995) served as director of NIIkhimmash from 1958 to 1963. He later became a deputy minister at the Ministry of General Machine Building.
31. *Novostroyka* means "new construction project" in Russian.
32. MVTU—*Moskovskoye vyssheye tekhnicheskoye uchilishche.*

Voskresenskiy and I—particularly Voskresenskiy—formed very trusting relationships with Tabakov. He often told us: more than 10 years' experience developing firing rigs, putting them into operation, conducting firing tests, fighting fires and explosions, "plus common sense" cry out for and demand full-scale firing rig tests for the first stage of the N-1, but.... That's when the "buts" started. It wasn't possible to build such a rig at NII-229. That is to say, it would be possible to build such a grandiose structure, but there was no way to deliver the first stage there. In actuality, the first stage of the N-1 rocket would first be manufactured and then assembled in the new "large" MIK at the firing range. It was not transportable. For that reason, they also needed to build a firing test rig at the firing range near the launch sites and use all their available fueling, measurement, launch control, security, and other services.... But if you manufacture the first stage for the sake of performing tests on it right at *Novostroyka*—that means another factory needs to be built! So wouldn't it be better if one of the two launch sites at the firing range were used as a firing test rig? But that requires time and finances. Tabakov would talk calmly, simply acknowledging this departure from the experience and traditions that had emerged in rocket technology, while Voskresenskiy would fly into a rage, without regard for the authority of Mishin, Korolev, or the government leaders standing over all of us.

A structural diagram of the lunar landing expedition had not yet been selected before the end of 1963. Initially our designers proposed a version with a good mass margin. It called for a three-launch configuration with assembly of the space rocket with a total launch mass of 200 tons (including fuel) in near-Earth assembly orbit. The payload mass for each of the three N-1 launches did not exceed 75 tons. The mass of the system for the flight to the Moon in this version reached 62 metric tons, which was almost 20 tons more than the corresponding mass of Apollo. The mass of the system executing the landing on the Moon's surface was 21 tons in our proposals, while it was 15 tons for Apollo. But, on the other hand, we had not just three launches in our configuration, but four. It was proposed that a crew of two to three be inserted into space on rocket 11A511—that is what the future rocket based on the R-7A was named in late 1963.[33] The Progress Factory was supposed to manufacture it for piloted launches of 7K (Soyuz) spacecraft.

---

33. The 11A511 was a three-stage launch vehicle derived from the R-7 ICBM that was used for the early Soyuz launches. Later derivations such as the 11A511U, 11A511U2, and 11A511FG were used for Soyuz piloted launches from the 1970s onwards. Since that time, the launch vehicle took the name of its most famous payload and has been generically called the Soyuz rocket.

From the author's archives.

Two giants of the Soviet missile and space program: Valentin Glushko (left) and Mikhail Yangel.

Theoretically, the three-launch configuration would enable us to compensate for the large number of advantages of the American design, which used hydrogen fuel for the second and third stages of the Saturn V launch vehicle. Of course, in terms of cost-effectiveness and general system reliability at that time, we were losing.

If Korolev had exhibited his inherent firmness in the subsequent defense of this configuration when the project was passing through all the levels of bureaucracy, the history of the N-1 might have been different. However, the situation developed in such a way that he was forced to compromise in order to simplify and reduce the costs of the project. The opposition from Chelomey, Glushko, Yangel, and the Ministry of Defense proved to be too powerful.

On 17 March 1964, Korolev met with Khrushchev. Mishin, Nikolay Kuznetsov, and Pilyugin accompanied him. In his report to Khrushchev about the status of work on the N-1 project, Korolev put particular emphasis on the need to develop hydrogen and nuclear engines and to optimize docking. According to Mishin and Pilyugin, on the whole, Khrushchev supported proposals for the promotion of lunar operations, but he displayed absolutely no enthusiasm for the idea of stepping up operations on hydrogen and nuclear engines.

After the meeting with Khrushchev, there were no subsequent decisions to revive the operations. The VPK and State Committees (or ministries) were preoccupied with implementing the programs of Chelomey, Yangel, and Makeyev for the series production of combat missiles and preparing the UR-500 for flight tests. As for OKB-1, all of the attention of VPK and State Committee on Defense Technology officials was directed at ensuring the launch of the three-seat Voskhod vehicle and determining the causes for the streak of failures of the four-stage 8K78. And really, how is a highly placed official supposed to react to complaints about insufficient funding for a program involving a lunar expedition in the distant future, if this very pushy chief designer has had four failures in a row during launches of automatic stations to Venus and for the soft landing of automatic vehicles on the Moon on 21 March, 27 March, 2 April, and 20 April?[34]

A week after the failed launch of Ye-6 No. 5 (20 April 1964), I was in Korolev's office to explain the causes of the failure in the power supply system between Blocks I and L and to explain the reason why a heated argument had flared up between Iosifyan and Pilyugin over the root cause.[35] I was expecting to be grilled and accused of poor quality control on our part. However, instead of this, Korolev began to speak, with a pessimism that was rare for him, about the very difficult situation surrounding all of our future plans. State Committee and VPK officials were not monitoring the progress of operations on the N-1 at the majority of our subcontractors at all. The Ministry of Defense had practically cut off funding for the construction at the launch site and engineering facility. He continued, "Our old friend Kalmykov, to whom you are partial, is not only not involved with the production of N-1 systems, but he even proposed to Smirnov that these operations be postponed for a couple of years because the radio electronic industry is overloaded with more important defense orders."[36]

Korolev told me for the first time that Glushko actively supported Chelomey in his development of the super-heavy UR-700 rocket, promising to produce engines with 600 tons of thrust running on nitrogen tetroxide and unsymmetrical dimethyl hydrazine. According to Korolev, Glushko had

---

34. There were several failures of the 8K78 launch vehicle (later known as the Molniya launch vehicle) in 1964. The launches were 21 March (Ye-6 lunar probe), 27 March (3MV-1 Venus test probe), 2 April (3MV-1 deep space probe), and 20 April (Ye-6 lunar probe).

35. See Chertok, *Rockets and People, Vol. III*, pp. 383, 396, 399.

36. Valeriy Dmitriyevich Kalmykov (1908–1974) headed the Ministry of the Radio Engineering Industry in its various incarnations from 1954 to 1974. As such, he oversaw many of the institutes and design bureaus in charge of developing guidance systems for the Soviet missile and space programs. Leonid Vasilyevich Smirnov (1916–2001) was chairman of the Military-Industrial Commission (VPK). He served in that position for nearly two decades, from 1963 to 1985, thus being at the apex of the Soviet military-industrial complex for much of the late Cold War.

not only agreed to make powerful engines for Chelomey, but he was also taking the liberty of criticizing the design and layout of the N-1. Supposedly, somewhere among the top brass the opinion already existed that Korolev and Glushko had been the first to produce the R-7 using a cluster configuration, and now Korolev was rejecting this progressive path for the N-1 and Glushko considered this a mistake.

"Under these circumstances we need to reconsider the concept of the three-launch profile with a landing on the Moon. The whole time they will accuse us of having a complicated, unreliable, and expensive version compared with the Americans' single-launch profile. But the Americans already have a hydrogen engine and it's already flying, while all our engine specialists have for the time being are promises," concluded Korolev.

AMONG THE MINISTERS/STATE COMMITTEE CHAIRMEN who were VPK members, only Kalmykov found time to seriously study the situation with the future payloads for the N-1 and with the lunar vehicles in particular.

In 1963, the organizations of chief designers Pilyugin, Ryazanskiy, Bykov, and Rosselevich were subordinate to the State Committee on Radio Electronics (GKRE), which Minister Kalmykov headed.[37] In April 1963, instead of making a soft landing, *Luna-4* flew past the Moon due to a control system error. I wrote about this in detail in *Hot Days of the Cold War*, volume III of my memoirs.[38] Soon after the investigation into the actual causes, Kalmykov telephoned Korolev and asked him whether he would have any objection to my coming over to see him in order to acquaint him in depth with control problems for a soft landing on the Moon. Not only did Korolev not object, but right then and there he scheduled me to visit Kalmykov and at the same time to tell him about our problems with Ryazanskiy and Pilyugin as far as their inactivity in developing a radio complex and control system for the lunar landing expedition vehicles.

When I was one on one with Kalmykov, to my surprise he confessed that rather than wanting to find out why the spacecraft flew past the Moon on 6 April 1963, he was more interested in the state of affairs with the designs of the vehicles and their systems for the execution of a piloted landing expedition

---

37. GKRE—*Goskomitet po radioelektronike*. Nikolay Alekseyevich Pilyugin (1908–1982), Mikhail Sergeyevich Ryazanskiy (1909–1987), Yuriy Sergeyevich Bykov (1916–1970), and Igor Aleksandrovich Rosselevich (1918–1991) were leading chief designers in the Soviet missile and space program who were responsible for the development of guidance and communications systems.

38. Chertok, *Rockets and People, Vol. III*, pp. 385–388.

in 1967.[39] Korolev and the chief designers directly subordinate to Kalmykov had proposed this date in the draft decree that they had prepared. I was not prepared for this turn in the topic of our conversation and began by telling him what the Americans were doing, rather than by describing our developments. In the course of our casual conversation, Kalmykov realized that at this point we not only had a poor grasp of control technology, but we had not even decided who was responsible for what and, most importantly, who would be general designer of the entire control systems complex.

Kalmykov had gotten a very good feel for what sort of complex this would be and what sorts of problems it would entail during the development of air defense (PVO) and missile defense systems (PRO) while working with such headstrong chief designers as Raspletin and Kisunko.[40] After Kalmykov had pulled out of me an approximate list of problems that needed to be solved, he asked: "Tell me frankly, forgetting for a minute that I am a minister, a member of the Central Committee and all that—you want to do all of this in three years so that in 1967, the 50th anniversary of the Revolution, you can have a fully tested system, and on 7 November, after returning from the Moon, our cosmonauts can stand on Lenin's Mausoleum [and watch the parade go by]? Is this really what you thought?"

I confessed that I wasn't certain that this date was realistic, but if a later date were proposed, we would risk having the project prolonged indefinitely.

"This is not a reason," objected Kalmykov. "I have already consulted with Ryazanskiy and Pilyugin. I believe that everyone, and your OKB-1 first and foremost, needs not three years, but six or seven years. Considering the actual work load on the industry, you all deserve to have monuments erected to you in your lifetime if our cosmonauts fly to the Moon and return safely before 1970."

Soon after this conversation with Kalmykov, Korolev telephoned me on the direct line. He was so angry he almost shouted: "Kalmykov sent a letter to Smirnov and to the Central Committee. He is proposing that the dates for the development of the lunar vehicles and spacecraft for the N-1 in general be postponed indefinitely. I will not let this stand!" And Korolev actually personally composed and sent a letter protesting Kalmykov's position to the same recipients.

---

39. The lunar flyby spacecraft is a reference to *Luna-4*, which failed to reach the surface of the Moon.

40. These abbreviations are the common terms in Russian for air defense and antiballistic missile systems. Their literal translations are PVO—*Protivovozdushnaya oborona* (antiaircraft defense) and PRO—*Protivoraketnaya oborona* (antimissile defense). Grigoriy Vasilyevich Kisunko (1918–1998) and Aleksandr Andreyevich Raspletin (1908–1967) were major chief (and later general) designers responsible for the development of Soviet antiballistic missile and air defense missile systems, respectively.

MY NEIGHBOR BUSHUYEV ON 3RD OSTANKINSKAYA STREET, known today as Academician Korolev Street, had the habit of stepping out for a breath of fresh air late in the evening before going to bed.[41] Usually he called me up requesting that I keep him company. On such evening strolls around Ostankino, which in those days was not yet polluted by automobile exhaust, we shared our thoughts more calmly and in greater depth than under our hectic work conditions. Korolev had placed the main design responsibility for the L3 on Bushuyev. His designers Feoktistov, Ryazanov, Frumkin, Sotnikov, and Timchenko managed to put two and two together and convince him that the situation with mass for future lunar vehicles in a single-launch scenario was already critical.[42] In this regard, Bushuyev had very pointed squabbles with Mishin, who at that time did not consider the Moon to be a primary objective and did not wish to listen to proposals for launch vehicle modifications.

"If, with this launch mass," lamented Bushuyev, "we could use hydrogen on the second and third stages, then instead of 75 tons, we would have at least all of 100 tons in Earth-orbit."

This figure of 100 tons was mentioned in the draft plan as what we could look forward to when hydrogen engines were introduced on the second and third stages. This was understood up and down the chain of command, but for the time being none of the engine specialists had developed liquid-hydrogen rocket engines, and the leadership at that time couldn't order them to.

That's when Bushuyev and I arrived at a seditious thought. If the nation were ruled by "Uncle Joe" and someone reported to him that new liquid-hydrogen rocket engines needed to be developed to solve a problem that he had assigned, you can bet that he would call in everyone he needed, set deadlines, ask how he could help—and we would have engines as good as the Americans'.[43] Like everyone else, great scientists, and especially chief designers, are not without sin and are not free of vanity. If you combine that with fear and give them everything they ask for to enhance the design bureau and production facility, they could work wonders. Stalin understood this and used it to the full extent.

---

41. Konstantin Davidovich Bushuyev (1914–1978) was one of Korolev's most senior deputies. As deputy chief designer of OKB-1 from 1954 to 1972 (and then chief designer from 1972 to 1978), Bushuyev oversaw the development of piloted spaceships at the design bureau.

42. Konstantin Petrovich Feoktistov (1926–2009), Yuriy Mikhaylovich Frumkin, Yevgeniy Fedorovich Ryazanov (1923–1975), Boris Ivanovich Skotnikov, and Vladimir Aleksandrovich Timchenko (1931–2005) were senior designers at OKB-1 who were in charge of designing human spacecraft.

43. Western media coined the nickname "Uncle Joe" to refer to Stalin during World War II.

DESIGNING THE L3 VEHICLES AND ROCKET STAGES and also developing the plans for the lunar expedition began in earnest in late 1963. Over the following two years the engineering drawings of the actual rocket were released and the predraft plans of the lunar vehicles appeared.

Dozens of government officials needed to grasp the immense production and technical scale of the entire lunar program, to determine the gross volumes of capital construction, and to make preliminary calculations of the total required expenditures. The economics of those years did not require very precise calculations. Nevertheless, the veteran *Gosplan* economists, with whom Korolev usually consulted, warned that the actual figures of the required expenditures would not make it past the Ministry of Finance and *Gosplan*.[44] In addition to expenditures on the nuclear-missile shield, the USSR needed to find funding for the new proposals for Chelomey's and Yangel's heavy-lift rockets. This was the most aggravating thing. Even the officials understood what a disadvantage it was to disperse funding for super-heavy launch vehicles. "But even that's not the most important thing," said Korolev once after his latest meeting in the offices of the Council of Ministers. "On Khrushchev's command, all of them are feverishly searching for a couple of billion rubles for agriculture."

The figures that had been submitted to the Central Committee and Council of Ministers were understated. The officials from the State Committee on Defense Technology, Council of Ministers, and *Gosplan* made it clear that it was not a good idea to frighten the Politburo with documents calling for many billions of rubles. Otherwise, Chelomey and Yangel would start arguing that their projects were much cheaper. Georgiy Pashkov, who had a great deal of experience with *Gosplan* politics, advised: "Turn out production of at least four launch vehicles per year and get everyone you need involved in the work, but according to a single timetable. And then we'll issue yet another decree. There is hardly anyone who would decide to shut down a project of that scale. It's going to work—we'll find the money!"[45]

Ustinov tasked NII-88 to conduct an objective comparative assessment of the lunar exploration capabilities of the N-1 (whose military index was 11A52), UR-500 (8K82), and R-56 (8K68) to sort out the design controversies of Korolev, Chelomey, and Yangel. The calculations of Mozzhorin and his specialists showed

---

44. *Gosplan—Gosudarstvennyy komitet po planirovaniyu* (State Committee for Planning) was a government-level body responsible for economic planning during the Soviet era. Prior to 1948, the body was known as the State Planning Commission.

45. Georgiy Nikolayevich Pashkov (1909–1993) headed the so-called second department at *Gosplan*, responsible for the Soviet ballistic missile program, from 1946 to 1951. Later in his career he rose to become a deputy chairman of the Military-Industrial Commission (VPK).

that to ensure absolute superiority over the U.S., a 200-ton rocket complex should be assembled in Earth orbit using three N-1 rockets.[46] This would require three N-1 rockets or 20 UR-500 rockets. In this case, we could manage a lunar landing of a vehicle weighing 21 metric tons and return a vehicle weighing 5 tons to Earth. All the economic calculations were in favor of the N-1. Despite the positive assessment of the leading institute [NII-88], Korolev firmly decided to move forward only with the single-launch format.

"While the going is good, do a study of a two-launch scenario with your designers," I recommended to Bushuyev during our next evening stroll. "Mozzhorin is right. We won't manage to overtake the Americans using a single-launch scenario now, and with a two-launch scenario, we might be two or three years behind them, but we can land five or six people on the Moon instead of two and throw a real party up there for the whole universe."

Bushuyev didn't support my idea. That sort of study couldn't be conducted without the knowledge of Mishin and Korolev, and he would end up in serious trouble. Korolev demanded that the designers study ways to increase the load-bearing capacity of the N-1 launch vehicle alone. After that came a series of proposals for modifications of the launch vehicle, first and

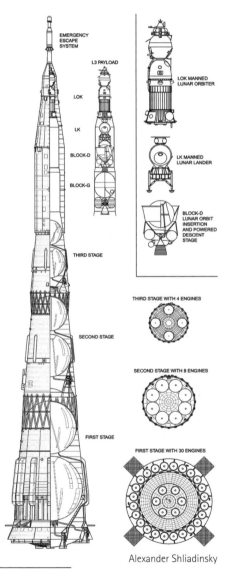

EMERGENCY ESCAPE SYSTEM

L3 PAYLOAD

LOK

LK

BLOCK-D

BLOCK-G

THIRD STAGE

SECOND STAGE

FIRST STAGE

LOK MANNED LUNAR ORBITER

LK MANNED LUNAR LANDER

BLOCK-D LUNAR ORBIT INSERTION AND POWERED DESCENT STAGE

THIRD STAGE WITH 4 ENGINES

SECOND STAGE WITH 8 ENGINES

FIRST STAGE WITH 30 ENGINES

The final configuration of the N-1 rocket (with the six extra engines on the first stage).

Alexander Shliadinsky

46. At the time, Yuriy Aleksandrovich Mozzhorin (1920–1998) was director of NII-88 (later known as TsNIImash), the leading research institute of the Soviet missile and space program. In this position he played a key role in developing long-term policy for the Soviet space program.

foremost, the installation of six more engines on the first stage and, unlike the Americans' layout, the appearance of fourth and fifth stages—Block G and Block D for the boost to the Moon. The launch mass of the N1-L3, taking the new proposals into account, had grown to 2,750 tons. All the measures made it possible to increase the in-orbit payload mass from 75 tons to 93 tons. But we still needed to work and work on these ideas!

Under these circumstances, the deadlines specified in the decrees for the beginning of flight-developmental tests in 1965 looked absurd. Everyone up and down the chain of command understood this. We needed an official reason to revise the deadlines and, finally, a decision about the main mission for the super-heavy N-1 launch vehicle that was under development. On 19 June 1964, the Central Committee and Council of Ministers issued a decree allowing the deadlines for the beginning of flight-developmental tests to be postponed to 1966.

Ryazanskiy had this to say about that: "Fox terriers get their tails docked when they're puppies. But in our case, so that it won't be so painful, they're going to chop off a little piece every year."

Everyone knew that shifting the deadline back a year wouldn't save us—common sense called for the deadlines for the beginning of flight-developmental tests to be moved back at least three years. But no one dared go to the Central Committee and then to the Politburo with such seditious proposals. This same decree calling for a technical and scientific expert review of controversial issues established a council on the N-1 complex under the chairmanship of Keldysh.

On 23 June 1964, Korolev convened the Council of Chief Designers to discuss operations on the N-1 in view of the latest decree. In his introductory speech, Korolev outlined the state of affairs, taking the opportunity to say that the two design schools of engine specialists had not helped in the selection of the type of liquid-propellant rocket engine and had delayed the design process.

Korolev informed them that there was a chance that another decree would come out, which would finally say that a landing expedition to the Moon was the main mission for the N-1. Then, going up to a poster, he briefly discussed and showed what the whole rocket complex would look like for the flight to the Moon. The three-stage N-1 launch vehicle would insert the upper stage—the payload—into Earth orbit. The following were installed under the fairing of the upper stage: Block G, which would initiate acceleration toward the Moon; Block D, which would accelerate and brake to make the transition into lunar orbit and brake to descend from lunar orbit; and two vehicles—the Lunar Orbital Vehicle (LOK) and the Lunar (landing) Vehicle (LK). Each of the vehicles had its own propulsion system. On the LOK this was Block I, and on the LK—Block Ye. An Emergency Rescue System (SAS) was mounted over the fairing.[47] The mass of this system was also included in the total mass of the launch vehicle's payload.

Keldysh, who had nodded off, woke with a start and remarked that our greatest shortcoming was the fact that there was no hope that the liquid-hydrogen engine would appear in the coming year. In his opinion, the chief designers of engines, who had not fulfilled the preceding government decisions with regard to the hydrogen problem, bore the responsibility for this lack of progress. Korolev stood up for the engine specialists and said that we were already developing a hydrogen block for the upper stages. This would be the booster block instead of Blocks G and D to set the spacecraft on a trajectory toward the Moon. He noted that "We are conducting the design with reference to Isayev's hydrogen engines with 7 to 8 tons of thrust. Lyulka's OKB-165 is working on an engine for the third stage with up to 40 tons of thrust." If we managed to build a third stage using these engines, we would get rid of all our mass deficit problems for the lunar expedition.

Glushko did not miss the opportunity to remind us that three years ago he had proposed developing a launch vehicle that ran on high-boiling propellant components.

"Today we would already have closed-loop configuration engines with 150 tons of thrust each for all of the stages," he declared.[48]

Keldysh suddenly pounced on Glushko: "Valentin Petrovich, you have had more opportunity to develop powerful oxygen-kerosene and oxygen-hydrogen engines than the others. Returning to conversations about high-boiling components for the N-1 today means killing the project completely. All the decisions on that matter have been made. We don't have time for arguments about the selection of engines for the N-1. We must clearly define the priority objective for the launch vehicle—this landing expedition to the Moon. We need to immediately nail down the number of cosmonauts—two or three, the entire expedition plan, and revisit the problem of reliability. First and foremost, I'm concerned about reliability issues."

"Reliability is exactly what I had in mind," Glushko retorted to Keldysh very calmly. "The engine that we developed for the UR-500 has been optimized and has already been handed over for series production."[49]

---

47. SAS—*Sistema avariynogo spaseniya*.

48. A "closed-loop" or "closed-cycle" rocket engine, typically known in the West as a staged combustion cycle engine, provides higher efficiency than the standard "open-cycle" liquid-propellant rocket engines because in a "closed-cycle" engine, *all* of the engine's gases and heat pass through the combustion chamber. The first prototype "closed-cycle" rocket engine was developed at NII-1 in the late 1950s. The first operational engine was the 11D33 used on the 8K78 launch vehicle's Block I stage.

49. That engine was the RD-253 (or 11D43).

Pilyugin felt compelled to remind us that in addition to the engines there was also the control system: "We must unequivocally understand that we still have to develop a system for the flight to the Moon with controlled landing and return, and not simply some sort of all-purpose system. I request that Sergey Pavlovich provide us with comprehensive baseline data for the upper blocks and the vehicles. This is new work for us."

Barmin also spoke up: "We have managed to speed up construction of the launch site lately. There are a lot of problems there. But keep in mind that we have made no provisions for hydrogen. If you decide to use it, even if only for the booster block, for us this will be a new assignment, new funding, and new deadlines."

In closing, Korolev asked the Council to make the following decisions:

- Approve the configuration proposed by OKB-1 for the N-1 heavy launch vehicle;
- Consider a landing expedition to the Moon to be the launch vehicle's primary mission;
- Use liquid oxygen and kerosene as the propellant components for the launch vehicle's rocket blocks, but at the same time speed up work on hydrogen propellant; and
- Task all project participants with studying the plans and schedules stemming from the decree of 19 June, and in a month convene once again to consider one more decree, which would be issued in conjunction with our proposal about the lunar expedition as a primary objective.

Everyone present nodded in approval, but Glushko, despite Keldysh's reprimand, said that if a protocol would be drawn up on this meeting, then he had a dissenting opinion regarding the reliability of the engines under development at OKB-276. This comment was directed at Nikolay Kuznetsov, who responded that he had never rejected the advice and assistance of OKB-456 and would be very grateful if, to speed up the optimization process, Valentin Petrovich would make available his advice and test rigs. Glushko gave no response, and on that note, Korolev closed the Council session.

On behalf of all the chiefs, Korolev and Keldysh asked for VPK Chairman Leonid Smirnov to resolve the matter about the primary objective at the governmental level. Smirnov was in no hurry to approach Khrushchev on his own. It was high time to face up to the radical decisions on a whole gamut of problems—deadlines, construction of the factory and launch complexes, production of the lunar vehicles, and finally crew training. Korolev and Keldysh, with Ustinov's support, approached Khrushchev: "Are we going to fly to the Moon or not?" These were Khrushchev's instructions: "Don't let the Americans have the Moon! Whatever resources you need, we'll find them."

The Americans prompted the decision. This appeal fell on fertile soil. On their desks VPK leaders had copies of "white TASS," which had reported about the flight of the heavy Saturn I rocket, which inserted the main unit of the lunar orbital vehicle into geocentric orbit for a trial run on 28 May.[50]

On 3 August 1964, a decree was issued that mentioned for the first time that the N-1 rocket's most crucial objective in space exploration was to explore the Moon by landing expeditions on its surface and then returning them to Earth. The second most important item of the decree was new deadlines. The year 1966 remained in place as the starting date for flight-developmental tests, and a new date appeared for the expedition to the Moon—1967 to 1968.

This decree was the first to name the main chief designers and organizations that would be responsible not only for the N-1 launch vehicle, but also for the entire N1-L3 complex (the designation L3 denoted the part of the complex that was needed only for the flight to the Moon).

- OKB-1 was the lead organization for the system as a whole and for the development of Blocks G and D (including the engines for Block D) and the lunar orbital and lunar landing vehicles;
- OKB-276 (N. D. Kuznetsov) was responsible for developing the engine of Block G;
- OKB-586 (M. K. Yangel) was tasked with developing the rocket Block Ye of the lunar vehicle and the engine for this block;
- OKB-2 (A. M. Isayev) was responsible for developing the propulsion system (tanks, pneumohydraulic systems, and engine) of Block I of the lunar orbital vehicle;
- NII-944 (V. I. Kuznetsov) was assigned to develop the control system for the lunar complex;
- NIIAP (N. A. Pilyugin) was tasked with developing the motion control system for the lunar landing and lunar orbital vehicles;
- NII-885 (M. S. Ryazanskiy) was responsible for the radio measuring complex;

---

50. This was the launch of SA-6, which put the first Apollo boilerplate spacecraft into orbit. "White TASS" represented one of three types of TASS news during the Soviet era. Green or blue TASS was intended for the public and comprised extremely sanitized versions of domestic and international news. White TASS—the equivalent of secret news—included very candid accounts of domestic and international events prepared only for governmental ministries and Communist Party offices. Red TASS was top-secret information, i.e., completely unexpurgated information from foreign news agencies, delivered only to the topmost individuals of the government and Party structure (including the Politburo).

- GSKB Spetsmash (V. P. Barmin) was responsible for the L3 system ground-based equipment complex;[51] and
- OKB MEI (A. F. Bogomolov) was tasked with developing the mutual measurement monitoring system for vehicle rendezvous in lunar orbit.[52]

The addendum to the decree containing a complete list of all those involved in developing systems for the L3 was a bulky document that showed that "no one and nothing was forgotten." Nevertheless, baffled questions about the detailed breakdown of work—who issued requirements, to whom, and for which systems—continued to be asked, and answers to them were written in all sorts of individual resolutions and protocols for another three years.

Once the text of the government decree had been received, Korolev decided to convene a wide-ranging technical review meeting in his office right away to explain to everyone what we had come up with and what we would ask of those involved in the project. This meeting took place on 13 August 1964. All the chief designers; chiefs of the State Committees' main directorates; Council of National Economy (*Sovnarkhoz*) chairmen involved in the program; officials from the VPK and Central Committee; officials from the Air Force Command, rocket forces, and Ministry of Defense space assets; representatives of the Academy of Sciences; and directors of NII-4, NII-88, and the firing range were invited.[53] Ryabikov, Pashkov, Zverev, Afanasyev, and Tyulin attended the meeting.[54]

In his opening comments, Korolev remarked that this was the first representative-level gathering for the lunar program. And the reason for this was the latest decree of 3 August, which challenged us with a crucial government mission. We, OKB-1, were the head organization, but each of us was personally

---

51. GSKB Spetsmash—*Gosudarstvennoye soyuznoye konstruktorskoye byuro spetsialnogo mashinostroyeniya* (State Union Design Bureau of Special Machine Building).

52. OKB MEI—*Osoboye konstruktorskoye byruo Moskovskogo energeticheskogo instituta* (Special Design Bureau of the Moscow Power Institute). Aleksey Fedorovich Bogomolov (1913–2009) served as chief designer of OKB MEI from 1952 to 1988.

53. *Sovnarkhoz—Soviet narodnogo khozyaystva.* In 1957, Khrushchev introduced the *Sovnarkhoz* system, whereby governmental ministries were replaced by local economic planning organs all over the Soviet Union. This attempt to decentralize the Soviet economy was rolled back in 1965 after Khrushchev's ouster.

54. At the time, these four men were senior managers of the Soviet defense industry. Their positions in 1964 were as follows: Vasiliy Mikhaylovich Ryabikov (first deputy chairman of the USSR *Sovnarkhoz*), Georgiy Nikolayevich Pashkov (deputy chairman of the Military-Industrial Commission), Sergey Alekseyevich Zverev (chairman of the State Committee for Defense Technology), Sergey Aleksandrovich Afanasyev (chairman of the Russian Soviet Federated Republic *Sovnarkhoz*), and Georgiy Aleksandrovich Tyulin (first deputy chairman of the State Committee for Defense Technology).

From the author's archives.

These men were the principal architects behind the design of the N–1. From left to right, Yakov Kolyako, Sergey Kryukov, and Pavel Yermolayev. Here, they are shown looking over a drawing of the L–1 circumlunar spacecraft.

responsible for that part of the system specified in the decree. Next, Kryukov and Bushuyev, referring to posters, presented the schematic diagram of the N1-L3, its basic performance data, and its flight program. It was difficult for Bushuyev to deliver his report. The draft plan of the lunar vehicles had not yet been completed, the specifications had not been drawn up for the subcontractors, and the whole plan for the flight to the Moon was still very rough.

At the risk of overloading my memoirs with details, I nevertheless feel that I need to discuss the main issue and, in particular, provide a description of the lunar expedition rocket-space complex. The N1-L3 rocket space complex consisted of the three-stage N-1 rocket and the L3 lunar complex. The N-1 was a three-stage rocket with transverse division of structurally similar stages. Intermediate trusses connected the stages, ensuring the free escape of gases when the engines of the subsequent stage started up.

Liquid-propellant rocket engines operating on oxygen and kerosene developed at OKB-276 were used on all three stages of the rocket. The rocket's load-bearing structure was a braced shell taking up the external loads. Spherical propellant tanks were housed inside this frame. In all the stages, the fuel tanks were in front. The first-stage (Block A) propulsion system comprised

24 NK-15 engines with a thrust of 150 tons each on the ground. Kryukov reported that we were conducting a study to see if the number of engines on the first stage could be increased to 30. Six engines would be mounted around an inner ring, and the 24 engines on the outer ring would remain in their places. The second stage (Block B) had eight of the same type of engines, but with NK-15V high-altitude nozzles. The third stage (Block V) had four NK-19 engines with high-altitude nozzles. All the engines would operate on a closed-loop configuration, i.e., with after-burning of the gas after passing through the turbopump assembly.

The instruments of the control and telemetry systems were arranged in special compartments in their respective stages. The main instruments of the control system for the three stages were in the third-stage instrument compartment. The accepted aerodynamic layout made it possible to minimize the requisite control moments and to control pitch and yaw by using the principle of thrust offset of opposing engines on the first and second stages. Special control nozzles would be used for roll control. The special KORD diagnostic system was being developed to monitor engine operation.[55] This system would issue an engine shutdown command when signs of possible failure occurred. The diametrically opposite engine would shut down simultaneously. Unlike all contemporary rockets, the electric energy source was an alternating current turbo generator.

The rocket's stages and compartments were very large. For that reason, the factory/manufacturers would produce only transportable parts. The welding of tanks and blocks and the assembly of the entire rocket were to be carried out in the Assembly and Testing Building, which was then under construction at the firing range. There would actually be a branch of the Kuybyshev-based Progress Factory—the main rocket manufacturing plant—at the firing range.

In order to insert a payload with a mass of 90 to 93 tons into Earth orbit at an altitude of 200 kilometers, we were undertaking a series of measures, the most important of which was mounting six more engines on the first stage. The height of the rocket including the L3 nose cone was 105.3 meters. The launch mass was 2,820 tons. The mass of the oxygen was 1,730 tons, and the mass of the kerosene was 680 tons. The L3 system consisted of the rocket booster Blocks G and D; the LOK (the vehicle itself and the rocket Block I) and the LK (the vehicle itself and the rocket Block Ye); the payload fairing,

---

55. The expansion for the KORD system has been variously described as *Kontrol i otklyucheniye rabotayushchego dvigatelya* (Operating Engine Monitoring and Shutdown) and **Kontrol raboty dvigateley** (Engine Operation Monitoring).

which would be jettisoned upon reaching specified acceleration loads; and the emergency rescue system propulsion system.[56]

The LOK consisted of the Earth-descent module and the habitation module, on which were mounted a special compartment containing the docking and attitude control engines and the docking system assembly, the Instrumentation System Compartment (PAO), and the power compartment, containing the rocket Block I and a power plant (EU) and three electrochemical generators (EKhG) for the power supply system using hydrogen-oxygen fuel cells.[57] The LOK habitation compartment would serve simultaneously as an

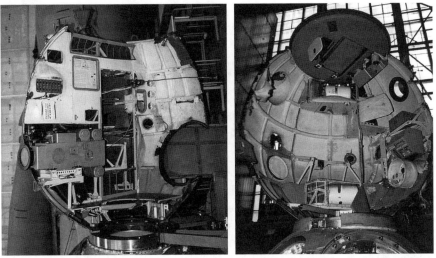

David R. Woods

This shows the LOK's Habitation Compartment (or Orbital Module) at the Moscow Aviation Institute (MAI). The Compartment was cut in half for the benefit of engineering students at MAI. The left half shows the circular hatch where the LK pilot would exit and return for the surface phase of the mission. To the left of that is a large–format camera for photography during the lunar orbital phase. The large rectangular opening is where one of the two spacesuits would be carried. The other half shows the rack for the other suit, controls for the various camera systems on the right, and the rendezvous and docking control panel at the top.

---

56. It was common terminology to refer to each propulsion stage of a complete rocket system as a "block." Thus, in the case of the N1-L3 system, the first three stages of the N-1 were known as Block A, Block B, and Block V (A, B, and V being the first three letters of the Cyrillic alphabet). The L3 payload itself comprised several propulsion stages. These were Block G (a stage for translunar injection), Block D (a stage for lunar orbit insertion and powered descent from lunar orbit), Block I (the propulsion stage of the lunar orbiter), and Block Ye (the propulsion stage of the lunar lander).

57. PAO—*Priborno-agregatnyy otsek*; EU—*Energoustanovka*; EKhG—*Elektrokhimicheskiy generator*.

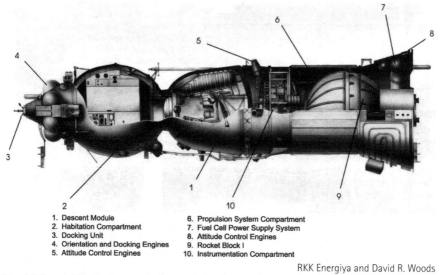

1. Descent Module
2. Habitation Compartment
3. Docking Unit
4. Orientation and Docking Engines
5. Attitude Control Engines
6. Propulsion System Compartment
7. Fuel Cell Power Supply System
8. Attitude Control Engines
9. Rocket Block I
10. Instrumentation Compartment

RKK Energiya and David R. Woods

The LOK was the Soviet equivalent of the Apollo Command and Service Module and served as the living quarters of the two-person crew during most of the lunar trip.

airlock chamber when a cosmonaut was transferring through open space into the lunar vehicle before descent to the Moon and during return. Cosmonauts would execute the entire journey from Earth to the Moon without spacesuits. They would don spacesuits before transferring from the LOK to the LK.

The LK consisted of the pressurized cosmonaut cabin, a compartment with attitude control engines and "passive" docking assembly of the instrument compartment, the lunar landing unit, and the rocket Block Ye. Storage batteries mounted on the exterior provided power for all the LK systems. For the first time in our space program, landing control would be conducted using an on-board digital computer and partial backup would be provided by a manual system, which would enable the cosmonaut to execute a limited maneuver to select a landing site.

The N1-L3 flight would be executed according to the following program:

- Insertion of L3 into Earth orbit by the N-1 launch vehicle, where the readiness of all L3 systems to depart for the Moon is tested over a 24-hour period;
- Boost of L3 onto Earth-Moon flight trajectory by Block G. In so doing, the engine of the Block G completely exhausts its fuel supply, after which Block G is jettisoned;
- Reboost using Block D until the designated velocity is attained, and then two trajectory corrections and deceleration, followed by insertion of the L3 system into lunar orbit. The flight time to the Moon will be three and a half days, and the time spent in lunar orbit will be no more than four days;

- Transition using Block D from circular orbit to elliptical orbit;
- Transfer of one of the cosmonauts from the LOK to the LK through open space;
- Separation from LOK of lunar landing system—Block D and LK;
- Orientation of system using Block D and deceleration for descent from orbit;
- Separation of Block D and its escape maneuver to the side to avoid collision with the LK;
- Deceleration for landing using Block Ye, maneuver to select landing site, and landing on Moon;
- Egress of cosmonaut onto lunar surface, performance of specified exploration, collection of soil samples, and return to the LK. Time of stay on the lunar surface no more than 24 hours;
- Liftoff of the LK from the Moon using Block Ye, rendezvous and docking with the LOK, transfer of cosmonaut from the LK to the LOK through open space, and jettisoning of the LK;
- Acceleration of the LOK using Block I on Moon-Earth trajectory, performance of one to two correction maneuvers. Flight time—three and a half days; and

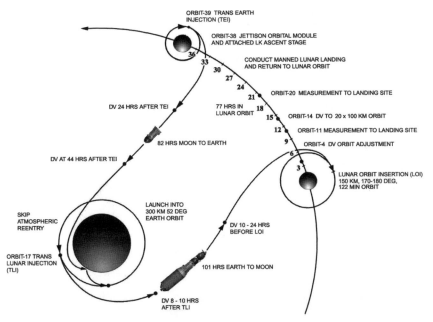

David R. Woods

This simplified graphical description of the Soviet lunar landing profile using a single N-1 rocket highlights details of the Earth-to-Moon and Moon-to-Earth segments. This schematic is based on a plan issued in January 1970.

- Separation of the LOK Descent Module, its entry into Earth's atmosphere at reentry velocity, gliding descent, and landing on USSR territory.

Total time of expedition: 11 to 12 days.

THE MAJORITY OF THOSE ATTENDING THE MEETING were learning about the N1-L3 complex and the flight configuration for the first time and with great interest. Questions followed:

"Aren't we afraid to let the cosmonaut descend to the lunar surface alone?"

"What if he falls and can't return to the LK? What decision will the commander who has remained in orbit make?"

"Why are the Americans planning to have two astronauts land on the Moon, and we're only going to have one cosmonaut?"

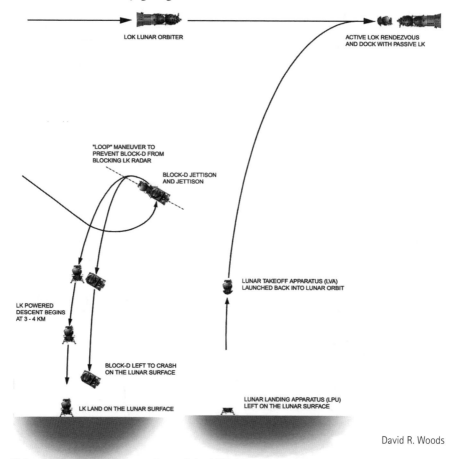

David R. Woods

This graphic shows the operations of the LOK, LK, and Block D near the lunar surface. The Lunar Takeoff Apparatus lifts off the lunar surface after a short stay and enters lunar orbit, where it acts as a passive target for the LOK.

But other questions were the most difficult: "In what phase of development are all the blocks, vehicles, and systems? When will the general plan and schedule of operations come out? When will the developers receive all the baseline data? What experimental facilities are being provided and when will the factories receive the working documentation for production?"

So that there would be no doubts, Korolev himself answered all the questions, sometimes humorously, but for the most part seriously, trying to show that the success of the entire program depended on each person there.

This first, very broad meeting on the N1-L3 program was held when preparation was under way for the flight of the three-seat *Voskhod*. It ended on an optimistic note, despite the fact that in August 1964, there was still no detailed design of the system as a whole. A design that more or less made sense finally appeared in December 1964. Keldysh's expert commission quickly reviewed and approved it.

Decrees and subsequent orders from GKOT obliged us to issue specifications to all project participants before the end of 1964. This was extremely difficult, since we had to lay down conditions for assignments without yet really understanding what answers we wanted to receive. In these cases, groups of brainstorming enthusiasts helped to formulate the work statement and guided us along the path of decision. The most heated debates flared up between the customers and the contractors when, after stipulating principles and parameters, the time came to specify the mass. Under pressure from Mishin and Korolev, who were responsible for the launch vehicle's performance characteristics, and from Bushuyev, who was responsible for the design of the lunar vehicles, the designers—rocket specialists and vehicle specialists—occupied an irreconcilable position in the struggle to reduce the mass of the systems. All the developers of on-board systems listed in the decrees, without exception, demanded that the mass limits be increased. Sometimes they haggled for tons, sometimes for tens of grams. However, the total amount of excess weight for all the systems and assemblies, which for the time being was only on paper, already looked appalling.

Nowhere in our previous experience had the mass of the manufactured systems matched what was stipulated in the designs. Frequently, after production and modifications based on test results, the mass approved during the design process was exceeded by as much as 100 percent.

Chapter 4
A Difficult Conversation with Korolev

In mid-December 1964, I tore myself away from our futile searches for and arguments about ways to reduce the mass of the L3 and immersed myself in frenetic production and testing work. We were preparing for the launch of the third Molniya (the previous launches were failures) and a Voskhod with a cosmonaut performing a spacewalk, and for communication sessions with an automatic interplanetary station on its way to Mars with solar arrays that had failed to open.[1] Noisy colleagues were sitting in my office smoking when the rapid jingle of a direct call from Korolev rang out. Everyone in my office quieted down and listened to my responses.

"Are you alone?"

"No, Sergey Pavlovich, my office is full and I'm surrounded by a cloud of smoke."

"Here's the thing: tell everybody to get out, open the windows, and air the place out. I'm on my way over there to curse at you, and I mean it!"

"But, why come over to my smoky office? I'll hurry over right now."

"No, I want to curse at you on your territory. Make sure no one will bother us."

"What should I brace myself for, should I ask anyone to join the conversation?"

"I don't need to see anyone but you. The conversation is going to be difficult for both of us!"

There was nothing left for me to do but to follow instructions. Intrigued by the purpose of S. P.'s sudden visit, the crowd left my office.

OKB-1's ninth Party conference had taken place on 10 November. In his speech, Korolev criticized me and my deputies for technical errors we had

---

1. The third *Molniya-1* satellite was launched on 23 April 1965. See Chertok, *Rockets and People, Vol. III*, pp. 500–504. The Mars probe was *Zond-2*, launched on 30 November 1964.

committed recently.[2] Could it be he felt he needed to speak with me more harshly in private?

"It's a good thing that Zoya Grigoryevna is on duty today as my receptionist," I thought. S. P. had the habit of finding fault with disorder in the reception rooms when he visited the offices of his deputies. Sometimes he would test the secretaries by giving them tasks and checking to see how quickly and precisely they carried them out. It was a disaster if something rubbed him the wrong way. Rather than berate the secretary, he chewed out the one in charge of the office and advised him to either retrain or replace the secretary. But Korolev himself had hired Zoya Grigoryevna for the job. She was the wife of a staff colleague at RNII, rocket propellant specialist Nikolay Chernyshev.[3] Before Korolev's arrest in 1938, they had lived in the same building on Konyushkovskaya Street. The Korolev, Pobedonostsev, and Chernyshev families were friends. After Chernyshev's sudden death in 1953, Korolev offered Zoya Grigoryevna a job at OKB-1. Thus, she became Bushuyev's secretary, and when he was moved to our first territory, she remained in her post in the reception room, which was shared by two offices—Rauschenbach's and mine.[4]

I warned Zoya Grigoryevna that S. P. was on his way over, that he was very angry, and he should be received as amiably as possible. While S. P. called for a car to pick him up and made his way to our second territory, we managed to air out our offices and the reception room, posted a lookout in the adjacent hallway to drive away loiterers, and a small group gathered in Rauschenbach's office in case I needed help in my conversation with S. P.

Looking out my window and seeing an approaching ZIS, I decided to go out into the hallway to meet S. P., but Zoya Grigoryevna advised me: "Stay

---

2. Criticism of Chertok is evident in the published version of the proceedings. See "Stenogramma vystupleniya na IX partkonferentsii OKB-1 [1964 g.]" [Stenogram report of the 9th Party Conference of OKB-1 (1964)] in *S. P. Korolev i ego delo: svet i teni v istorii kosmonavtiki: izbrannye trudy i dokumenty* [*S. P. Korolev and His Works: Light and Shadow in the History of Cosmonautics: Selected Works and Documents*], ed. B. V. Rauschenbach and G. S. Vetrov (Moscow: Nauka, 1998), pp. 465–471.

3. Nikolay Gavrilovich Chernyshev (1906–1953) was a noted pioneer of Soviet liquid-propellant rocketry, having worked in the interwar years at the Gas Dynamics Laboratory (GDL), the Reactive Scientific-Research Institute (RNII), and KB-7. After the war, he worked at the military NII-4 institute until his death.

4. Boris Viktorovich Rauschenbach (1915–2001) was one the pioneers in the development of control systems for Soviet spacecraft. He worked with Korolev at RNII during the interwar years, but after the war he worked as a scientist at NII-1 under Mstislav Keldysh developing concepts for the spacecraft control systems. In 1960, Rauschenbach transferred to work under Korolev at OKB-1, where he remained until 1973. He became a Corresponding Member of the Academy of Sciences in 1966 and a full member in 1986.

in the office."[5] She greeted Korolev in the reception room with a lovely smile. He had to pause and ask questions showing that he did not forget old friends and abandon them in time of need. Korolev stayed less than a minute in the reception room, but when he entered my office he was hardly furious, as I had expected him to be. His tired face had an expression of conciliation.

For a few moments his eyes, usually attentive to his company, looked somewhere off in space. It seemed that he was trying to recall why he was here. But this only lasted a few seconds. Sergey Pavlovich approached my desk, saw a thick volume—the report on the Americans' Saturn project—and immediately his demeanor changed. He slowly paced about my office, looking things over and entering a new "coordinate system." Then a long conversation took place. I read so much nonsense now in my old notebooks, but this meeting I reconstruct from memory. I'd say that over the entire course of 20 years working together, this was the only one-on-one meeting I ever had with him in my office that lasted so long.

Over the phone, S. P. had warned me that he wanted to chew me out. Now he had either forgotten or changed his mind, but the conversation began very amicably. So many problems tormented him that he needed to talk, to think out loud, and to take people whom he trusted into his confidence. On one of my evening strolls along 3rd Ostankinskaya Street, I learned that Korolev had spoken with Bushuyev and Voskresenskiy before me about the same thing. Perhaps, they said, he had also met with Mishin and with Okhapkin.[6]

I must interrupt my account of my meeting with Korolev to explain the urgency of the issues that were about to be discussed. After the three-launch scenario was rejected, a very serious "weight crisis" developed for the entire lunar expedition program.[7] It was not just the chief designer's deputies and leading design engineers who were grumbling about very strong pressure from Korolev; the subcontractors' chief designers were, too. After a detailed study of the crisis situation that had formed during the very first phase of development of the lunar vehicles, Korolev started looking for ways to save the project. In so doing, he started at the very bottom. Here he discovered what appeared at first glance to be insurmountable difficulties inherent to the project. But, at the same time, there were redeeming features. The most radical was the installation of an additional six engines on the first stage of the N-1 rocket.

---

5. The ZIS suffix was added to all automobiles that were produced by the ZIS—*Zavod imeni Stalina* (Stalin Factory).

6. Sergey Osipovich Okhapkin (1910–1980) was one of Korolev's most senior deputies at OKB-1.

7. *Author's note*: At that time the term "weight" was used; the term "mass" came into use later.

In and of themselves, the engines with all their systems also constituted tons of metal, but they added 900 tons of thrust, the thrust of Chelomey's entire *Pyatisotka* at that time.[8] It was necessary to modify the pneumohydraulic and electrical systems of the first stage, manufacture additional instruments, upgrade the engine control algorithms, increase the capacity of the tanks, review the ballistic analysis, remake the bottom shield, and take into consideration a whole array of odds and ends that come to light during any serious modification of such a complex system.

According to preliminary calculations, the totality of these measures increased the mass of the spacecraft to be inserted into orbit to 93 tons. Compared with 75 tons in 1962, this was significant progress. Korolev knew from experience that relaxing the rigid weight discipline would lead to unchecked weight increases in dozens of systems, which would bring the gains made from all the measures to naught. The situation was complicated by the fact that the Progress Factory—the lead factory for the manufacture of the N-1—had already built up some production inventory. If the factory was informed that it would have to make modifications and needed to wait for new drawings, then this would also affect the already missed production deadlines for the first launch vehicle. Okhapkin and Kozlov, who supervised the work at the Progress Factory, proposed introducing the measures in a phase-by-phase plan: the in-orbit payload mass would not reach approximately 93 tons until the rocket's fourth flight model.[9]

Despite the current events, the latest piloted Voskhod launches, and the development of the Soyuz—a circumlunar flight project using a "Baron Münchausen plan"—S. P. tried to be up to date on all the N-1 modifications. He demanded that margins be sought everywhere, to the point of changing the orbital inclination and altitude.

The meeting with Korolev described below took place during a period when numerous measures were being developed to save the project from the fierce criticism of experts. Despite the completely benevolent attitude of Keldysh, who headed the expert commission, the most meticulous of its members, especially the rocket design specialists, criticized the fact that the "rocket transports air," and there's nothing left over for payload. You may laugh about it, but there were development engineers who proposed purging all the air from the tubular structural elements before liftoff, thereby gaining a few kilograms of payload.

---

8. *Pyatisotka* is the Russian noun form of the number "500" and was the nickname for Chelomey's UR-500 rocket.

9. Dmitriy Ilich Kozlov (1919–2009) was the chief of OKB-1's Branch No. 1 based in Kuybyshev (now Samara) where the N-1 was manufactured at the colocated Progress Factory.

The initial version of the proposals for the N-1 called for three crewmembers to participate in the lunar expedition. However, while drafting the decree that came out in August 1964, it was determined that the three-cosmonaut configuration simply wouldn't work with our launch vehicle. Assessing the situation with a clear eye, Bushuyev's design engineers came to the firm conviction that we could only carry out the expedition using a "2 + 1" configuration. In this case, "2 + 1" did not equal three: two cosmonauts would fly to the Moon in the LOK, and after the vehicle transferred to lunar orbit, just one of them would perform a spacewalk, enter the LK landing vehicle, and descend to the surface of the Moon. He would stroll around on the Moon in sublime solitude, and, a couple of hours later, return to orbit to dock with the LOK, and once again spacewalk over to his waiting comrade. After this, they would undock the LK and jettison it to the Moon, and the LOK, using its propulsion system, would return to Earth.

To coordinate the developments of the control system for the L3 vehicles and for the landing and liftoff rocket blocks and the rendezvous and docking system, OKB-1 and the organizations of Pilyugin, Ryazanskiy, Bogomolov, Bykov, and Khrustalev created integrated brigades.[10] The assignment of these brigades was to "search for weight" so that there would be enough for the "2 + 1" configuration. When I assembled plenary sessions of specialists, it turned out that each time we strayed farther from the limits that Bushuyev's design engineers had given us. The situation seemed catastrophic.

BUT NOW I'LL RETURN TO THE CONVERSATION with Korolev in my office. The first subject of our meeting was, of course, the L3. I remember his request/ultimatum quite well: "Boris, give me back 800 kilograms."

Grabbing a previously prepared weight report with numerous handwritten amendments, I tried to demonstrate that "giving back" was out of the question. All the systems for which my departments were responsible already required more than 500 kilograms above our allotment. And there was still so much documentation that hadn't been issued, dozens of expert commission recommendations that hadn't been implemented, and not a single bit of experimental work had been completed yet! The automatic landing of the LK was the least developed part of the program. For reliability, we needed triple or, at least, double redundancy, diagnostics, and good communications with Earth, and all of this meant weight and more weight.

---

10. Vladimir Aleksandrovich Khrustalev headed TsKB-598, later known as TsKB Geofizika, which was responsible for developing optical sensors for Soviet spacecraft and missiles.

Korolev was not about to look at the weight report. He interrupted my explanations and calmly repeated, this time looking me straight in the eye (he had a real knack for this): "All the same, give me back 800."

Without allowing me once again to switch to a forceful defense, S. P. said that he had held a very difficult discussion with Keldysh. He [Keldysh] didn't believe that we had yet solved the weight problem for landing even one cosmonaut on the Moon. For that reason, in Keldysh's opinion, the design as a whole still had loose ends. Chelomey, who had his own alternative design proposals, was putting pressure on Keldysh.[11]

Tyulin was forming a new ministry, but evidently they weren't going to appoint him minister of his own ministry.[12] "Uncle Mitya" had his own people, and now in the Politburo you couldn't get past Ustinov.[13] The only one there who really knew what we were doing was Khrushchev. Now he's gone, and all those who had seized power were not yet accustomed to making independent decisions. The military officials couldn't understand at all why it was necessary to fly to the Moon. It's a big headache that since Nedelin, "infantry" marshals had been in command of space.[14] The Air Force should have piloted programs—they had a better understanding of human capabilities. Incidentally, Air Force Commanders-in-Chief were being appointed, as a rule, from the ranks of combat pilots. They knew human capabilities, but it was difficult for them to get a sense of the scale of space systems.

"The 'Americanese' don't hesitate to say that the master of space will be the master of the world," continued S. P.[15] "They have greater opportunities than we do. We are poorer, and therefore our leaders, especially the military, must be wiser."

S. P. expressed these thoughts as if verifying his reasoning to justify his demand to "give back 800 kilograms." Now, in his opinion, I knew everything and I understood everything, and by hook or by crook I must bring the weight reports down by 800 kilograms in the design materials. It turned

---

11. Chelomey proposed an alternative plan for a piloted lunar landing using the heavy-lift UR-700 launch vehicle.

12. The new Ministry of General Machine Building (MOM) was established in March 1965, soon after this conversation, to manage the Soviet missile and space programs.

13. "Uncle Mitya" (*dyadya Mitya*) was the nickname for then-chairman of the Supreme Council of the National Economy (VSNKh) of the USSR Council of Ministers, Dmitriy Fedorovich Ustinov.

14. This is a reference to the domination of Soviet space activities by artillery (i.e., infantry) officers since the formation of the Strategic Rocket Forces under the command of Marshal Mitrofan Ivanovich Nedelin (1902–1960) in 1959.

15. Korolev is paraphrasing a comment by then-President Lyndon B. Johnson that "whoever controlled 'the high ground' of space would control the world."

out that he wanted to get 800 kilograms less than the limit stipulated in Bushuyev's design materials! This was completely unrealistic. But I wasn't about to argue. I knew that S. P. was "padding" his request. Feigning annoyance, he said that because of such obstinate people as Voskresenskiy and me, in our current situation they might cut back appropriations for the N-1. Then the "Americanese" would certainly pass us. They are getting billions for the Saturn V. The president is monitoring the program personally, while our program is divided between aviation, rockets, and agriculture. Now, after Nikita, Brezhnev is going to support Yangel. The Ukraine has a stranglehold on this Central Committee Presidium.[16]

Here, I remember saying that perhaps this was a good thing—Pilyugin wouldn't be able to cope with the N-1 without the Kharkov instrumentation group, and we also had the Kievpribor Factory working for us in Kiev.[17] We would also have a difficult time without its help. As for Yangel, I reminded Korolev of the quip the military officers had come up with: "Korolev works for TASS, Chelomey's [work] goes down the toilet, and Yangel's is for us."

S. P. had already heard this aphorism, but it clearly offended him to hear it repeated. His mood darkened. His facial expression, the glint in his eyes, and the position of his head always betrayed Korolev's mood and state of mind. He did not have Glushko's ability to maintain a completely impenetrable and imperturbable appearance regardless of his inner state.

"What stupidity," said Korolev, "and military men from Dnepropetrovsk [where Yangel's design bureau was located] started it. And they've got no grounds to poke fun at Chelomey. He's got Myasishchev's magnificent aviation designers and an aviation factory with production culture the likes of which Dnepropetrovsk has never dreamed.[18] That's precisely where Chelomey's main strength lies, rather than any special relationship he has with Nikita Sergeyevich."

When Korolev mentioned the factory, I couldn't restrain myself and boasted: "The factory in Fili set me up in life and even provided me with a wife."[19]

---

16. Chertok is referring to the coterie of people surrounding Brezhnev who were either from Ukraine or worked there and who later came to dominate Soviet Party and government positions during the Brezhnev era. Yangel's design bureau, OKB-586 (now KB Yuzhnoye), and its associated factory are located in Dnepropetrovsk, Ukraine.

17. Kharkov and Kiev are major cities in Ukraine.

18. Chelomey's OKB-52 acquired a number of important branches in the early 1960s. The most important was Branch No. 1, a design bureau previously known as OKB-23 and headed for nearly a decade by the famous Soviet aviation designer Vladimir Mikhaylovich Myasishchev (1902–1978).

19. The "factory in Fili" is a reference to the M. V. Khrunichev Factory (ZIKh) colocated with OKB-52's Branch No. 1 located in the Moscow suburb of Fili.

"Did your Katya really work there, too?"

"Yes, all my personnel forms mention that."

"I haven't studied your personnel forms, but don't forget to say hi to Katya for me."

After that little breather, Korolev returned to his thoughts about Chelomey's projects.

"Now that they've given Nikita the boot, officials whom Chelomey has really annoyed have decided to show him who's boss. Ustinov and Smirnov talked Keldysh into heading a commission to investigate the work of OKB-52. I advised him not to, but he consented. Look what's happening. Keldysh is chairman of the expert commission on the N-1, he was chairman of the commission on Yangel's combat missiles, and now he has been assigned the role of inspector over all of Chelomey's work. He has taken on a very large responsibility. It will be interesting to see how he will act with the circumlunar flight project using the UR-500.[20] After all, the deadline for that was just recently set for the first quarter of 1967. God willing, the rocket will fly for the first time in a year, and in two years they're already planning a piloted circumlunar flight. I think that we should join forces with regard to the vehicle, rather than fritter away our strength. Now, since we're soon going to be in the same ministry, maybe we can make some arrangement. In any event, I gave Kostya [Bushuyev] the assignment to look into whether it would be possible to adapt a 7K from a Soyuz [launch vehicle] to a UR-500 launcher. After all, honestly, I am not very convinced that your beloved Mnatsakanyan will make a system that will go through three dockings in a row without a hitch."[21]

"Sergey Pavlovich! According to information from our 'fifth column,' Chelomey hasn't really gotten moving on the vehicle yet, while our landing on the Moon is set for a year after the circumlunar flight, and we have to make not just one, but two completely new vehicles."

"That's why you have to give me back 800 kilograms," he said very sternly.

Suddenly Korolev brightened up.

"But still, Yangel is doing a great job. I honestly didn't expect that he would voluntarily shut down his R-56 project and agree to make Block Ye for us. You

---

20. Chelomey's circumlunar program involved the use of a three-stage UR-500 rocket and the LK-1 spacecraft.

21. This is a reference to OKB-1's original circumlunar program, which involved a 7K crewed spacecraft, several orbital propellant tankers, and a translunar stage. This early plan involved at least three dockings in a row in Earth orbit before the crew headed to the Moon. Armen Sergeyevich Mnatsakanyan (1918–1992) was a chief designer at NII-648 where he oversaw the development of Soviet orbital rendezvous systems.

and Pilyugin must quickly decide who will provide the baseline control data so that Yangel's work will under no circumstances be delayed."

"Right before you arrived I broke up a big free-for-all here in my office having to do with the allocation of projects between us and Pilyugin. Everything worked out fine regarding the launch vehicle, but when it came to the vehicles, especially the LK, there were heated debates. We still haven't come to an agreement as to who will make the integrated test rigs."

At the mention of the test rigs, Korolev once again started talking about Voskresenskiy. He was outraged with Leonid's behavior regarding the construction of a test rig for full-scale firing tests of the N-1's first stage. The rough estimates that Voskresenskiy made with the assistance of the design institute and NII-229 in Zagorsk showed that the production of this rig would cost a hundred million and would take at least three to four years. At least a year would be spent in the coordination and design process. As a result, no testing would begin before 1968. And here's another question: where would it be built? If we built it in Tyuratam, the primary construction of the large MIK and launch site were still in their embryonic stages there. There were enough funds for materials, and that's precisely the excuse the military builders were using for their own falling behind.

"I paid a special visit to Dymshits," continued Korolev, "to discuss funding.[22] He is, you know, deputy chairman of the Council of Ministers and chief of *Gossnab*.[23] I thought he could do anything. Ustinov himself advised me to meet with him. Ustinov said, 'In such cases personal contacts are more reliable than decrees.'"

"So what happened?"

"The meeting went just fine. He inquired about the N-1 in great detail. It's true, he didn't understand why we or the Americans needed to fly to the Moon so urgently. Dymshits is a smart but very tired Jew. He miraculously survived under Stalin and supported Khrushchev's idea about councils of national economy (*Sovnarkhozy*). Now they were eliminating them and restoring complete centralization of control and supply only from Moscow. There were once again shakeups at *Gossnab* and *Gosplan*, reconsiderations of the allocation of appropriations and funds, and everyone tried to grab the biggest

---

22. Veniamin Emmanuilovich Dymshits (1910–1993) was a deputy chairman of the USSR Council of Ministers from 1962 to 1985 and chairman of the USSR *Sovnarkhoz* from 1962 to 1965.

23. *Gossnab—Gosudarstvennyy komitet po materialno-tekhnicheskomu snabzheniyu* (State Committee for Logistics). Dymshits served as chairman of *Gossnab* from 1965 to 1976. *Gossnab*'s primary duty was to provide logistical support to ensure proper functioning of the Soviet economy (distributing products to Soviet consumers, supporting interindustry communications, etc.).

piece of the pie. They hinted to Dymshits that he had given way too much to the rocket specialists and it was time to restore ship building and aviation after the toll Khrushchev had taken on them."[24]

As he told me about his meeting with Dymshits, Korolev looked at me searchingly and suddenly recalled the 1953 "Doctors' Plot."[25] For the first time, S. P. confessed that back then he had had a great deal of trouble defending me against the personnel officers who were getting out of hand, especially since he too was still somewhat tainted.[26]

"Even Ustinov, who knew you well, said that he would help, but if they put any more pressure on him, he was not omnipotent. Then there was a call on the 'Kremlin line.' Boris, you can't even guess who called, and I'll never tell you. Among other things, this person told me that I shouldn't worry about you. Nobody's going to touch you. I'm telling you this 11 years after the fact, but who called—that I won't tell you."

To this day I haven't unraveled the mystery and I haven't confided with anyone on this subject. The circumstances were too convoluted and complicated in the upper echelons of power. But that is a completely different subject.

S. P. never hinted to anyone and never implied that he required some sort of reciprocity for his good deeds. All he required was work with full commitment, enthusiasm, and decency. S. P. had a knack for discerning and appreciating honest and decent people. He drew people to himself based on their professional qualities, and in his inner circle he appreciated this same cultured integrity. At one time it seemed to me that Voskresenskiy was more a kindred spirit to him than the other deputies. Actually, S. P. appreciated Leonid not just for his exceptional qualities as an investigative tester. He loved him as a man of integrity and a comrade with whom he could "scout around." And all of a sudden, Leonid comes out publicly against the N-1 program of operations that Korolev had approved.

During one of our evening strolls along 3rd Ostankinskaya Street, Voskresenskiy joined Bushuyev and me. Leonid was genuinely surprised by the stance that all of us deputy chiefs had taken. He took Korolev's rejection

---

24. During Khrushchev's time, the aviation industry was slighted in favor of massive investment into the missile industry. A number of major aviation industry enterprises were either closed down or redirected to work on missiles.

25. The "Doctors' Plot" was orchestrated by Stalin in 1953 to blame nine doctors, six of them Jewish, for planning to poison the Soviet leadership. Their arrest was a pretext for the future persecution of Jews in the Soviet Union. Fortunately, after Stalin's death in March 1953, all the accused were released.

26. Because Chertok is Jewish, Korolev was under pressure to marginalize Chertok in the institutional work at NII-88, a pressure he tried to resist.

(with Mishin's active support) of the construction of a full-scale firing test rig so personally that during this evening stroll that's all he would talk about. Leonid, who had quite recently recovered from a heart attack, appealed to my experience, conscience, and common sense, saying that if the decision on the test rig failed to come through, he would no longer be on good terms with Korolev. He was prepared to go on fishing trips and mushroom hunts with us, but he would refuse to be involved in N-1 projects.

Since Korolev started the conversation about Voskresenskiy, already knowing about their damaged relationship, I changed the subject to the monitoring, diagnostics, and engine shutdown system (KORD). The development of this system had forced my comrades and me to delve into the state of affairs with Kuznetsov's new engines. I expressed my misgivings to Korolev regarding the deadlines for the experimental testing of the entire KORD system for the simple reason that the very hardware that we were supposed to be performing diagnostics on and save from a catastrophic explosion was still so unreliable that it was difficult to select a stable parameter for diagnostics. We were firmly convinced that the KORD system, on the whole, needed to be a lot more reliable than each individual engine, especially all 30 on the first stage.

"In this sense," I said, "conducting firing rig tests on the entire fully-assembled first stage is a better way to verify and confirm reliability."

I tried to start my pitch in favor of the test rig, but S. P. once again scowled, and his mood darkened. "You and Leonid think that I don't understand the rig's benefits. Don't defend Leonid! I asked you to give up 800 kilograms, and don't bring up the issue of the test rig. We can't pose that question now, we don't have the right to, if we want to produce the N-1. You all want to be squeaky clean, you demand rigs, experimental testing, reliability, but I, Korolev, don't allow you this! Look, we're putting in equipment for the manufacture of the second and third stages at Tabakov's facility in Zagorsk. After modifying the existing rigs, they can be tested there. It's unrealistic to build a test rig for the first stage."

I was afraid that now our calm conversation would fall apart, S. P. would stand up and leave. Despite this danger, I nevertheless took a chance and insisted that S. P. pay some attention to the status of the KORD system's development. He promised to have a word with Kuznetsov about the final proposals for the diagnostics program very soon.

"I just ask that you make sure, Sergey Pavlovich, that when any emergency condition is determined, we will need 4 to 5 hundredths of a second to shut down the engine along with Pilyugin's control system. If the engine is going to explode in thousandths of a second, there's nothing we can do."

Korolev smiled sadly. He was well aware of the state of affairs with the experimental testing of engines at Kuznetsov's facility. I had heard fragmentary information from our engine specialists and KORD system experts that the engine was going through its phase of childhood diseases. The Kuybyshev developers had no experience with liquid-propellant rocket engines. They were just learning and were still far from the level of the Khimki specialists.[27]

Without a pause the conversation switched to the current Ye-6 program: a soft landing on the Moon.

"How are things with Morachevskiy on the next Ye-6?" asked Korolev.[28]

I was ready to roll on this subject and wanted to explain in detail about our efforts and the progress on this project, but once again S. P. stopped me.

"We absolutely must not let the Americans make the first soft landing. Look what's happening: we have already conducted five launches and only reached the Moon once. Your beloved astronavigation didn't help us out. By the way, what's going on with Lisovich and those nice 'star' ladies who worked in his shop?"[29]

I told him everything that I knew about them, jumping on the chance to remind S. P. that he had inquired about these ladies back in 1949 and now they were 15 years older. And then I started to justify myself: "The Americans have also had five failures with their Rangers and it wasn't until their seventh launch that they obtained an image of the lunar surface.[30] And they aren't planning a soft landing until October 1965 with the Surveyor."[31]

"If we work like that," countered S. P., "then in 1966 our soft landing will fail too. Keep in mind, from now on, I am not about to forgive you for an astronavigation failure. Any day now, Keldysh is getting ready to hear in his Council once again about the state of affairs on the Moon, Mars, and Venus projects.[32] I am arranging for you or Kostya [Bushuyev] to report."

---

27. Kuznetsov's OKB-276 was located in Kuybyshev while Glushko's OKB-456 was located in Khimki.

28. Valentin Leonidovich Morachevskiy led the development of stellar navigation systems for Soviet spacecraft.

29. For details on these lunar launches, see Chertok, *Rockets and People, Vol. III*, Chapters 13 and 14. Izrael Meyerovich Lisovich was involved in the development of stellar navigation systems.

30. Ranger was a NASA program designed to obtain close images of the lunar surface as the probes plummeted down from altitude. *Ranger 7* returned the first images in July 1964.

31. NASA's robotic *Surveyor 1* accomplished the first successful U.S. soft landing on the Moon on 2 June 1966.

32. This is a reference to the Interdepartmental Scientific-Technical Council on Space Research (*Mezhvedomstvennyy nauchno-tekhnicheskiy sovet po kosmicheskim issledovaniyam*, MNTS-KI), an interagency body attached to the Presidium of the USSR Academy of Sciences, which directed the future research agenda of Soviet space science research.

"I'll report, but there is a reason why our people are losing enthusiasm for the Ye-6 and MV. If we transfer all the work to Babakin next year, then naturally the main incentive disappears—the prospect of being involved with this achievement.[33] All our people will have left will be the failed launches."

S. P. retorted that the point of honor for us was to ensure a soft landing ourselves and as soon as possible. "Let Babakin continue to work on other automatic spacecraft. Mars and Venus are programs that will go on for many years. People need to understand that. After the Moon, we'll need to use the N-1 to insert heavy automatic spacecraft in orbit toward Mars and Venus, and beyond. And what about the TMK—the Heavy Interplanetary Ship?[34] Do you really think that has no prospects? We can't manage it all. Lavochkin's factory is going to transfer into our new ministry; let it develop these projects to the full extent of its capacity."[35]

"I like Babakin. You've been on friendly terms with him for a long time; you're not about to hide anything from him. Keep in mind, I know that too. Explain everything to the people. They will understand," said S. P. as consolation to me.

Then we once again talked about the reliability of the Ye-6 and the dates for the upcoming launch. S. P. said that he personally would travel to Simferopol as soon as there appeared to be hope for a soft landing.[36]

Korolev was right on the verge of leaving when it seemed something occurred to him and he said: "Keldysh telephoned me. He wants to hear the state of affairs with the L3 control system one more time in the expert commission. I told him that I wouldn't be able to be there. You and Kostya go. I've already told Pilyugin about it; he's not about to complain about us. Don't you stir anything up. It's very important now for us to show that there are no disagreements and everything should work out. Keep in mind there are "friends" who are just waiting for an opportunity to bark that all our work is coming apart at the seams. Incidentally, Keldysh is now in over his head. His task is to make sure that the Academy of Sciences comes to no harm under the new [Brezhnev] regime. He had a smooth-running relationship with Khrushchev. Nikita even forgave Keldysh for exposing Lysenko and for the failure of his best

---

33. Georgiy Nikolayevich Babakin (1914–1971) was appointed chief designer of the Lavochkin Design Bureau in 1965 and, soon after, inherited all lunar and interplanetary programs from Korolev's OKB-1.

34. In the early 1960s, Korolev's designers devoted significant resources to studying piloted interplanetary spacecraft. These concepts were generically known as the TMK.

35. Here, the new ministry in question was the Ministry of General Machine Building, established in March 1965.

36. A major deep space tracking station known as NIP-10 was located at Simferopol in Crimea. The early Soviet lunar and deep space probes were tracked from here.

friend—Nuzhdin—to enter the Academy during the most recent elections. Keldysh had the courage to listen to Sakharov rather than Khrushchev, who asked him not to offend Lysenko.[37] Now Keldysh is complaining that in the new Politburo he doesn't understand very well with whom he is dealing. So don't worry, for the time being Keldysh doesn't have time for us!"

These were Korolev's parting words on that very long day. S. P. smiled almost imperceptibly, struggled to get up from the deep armchair, and went out into the reception room. Remembering Zoya Grigoryevna's warning, I did not see him out. As soon as Korolev's ZIS pulled away, everyone whom I had asked to leave before the meeting crowded back into my office. Having patiently waited for more than 2 hours, my comrades demanded that I give them a report.

As I was editing this chapter for the new edition of my memoirs, I recalled the words of Yuriy Mozzhorin, which he managed to tell me in 1996 after that year's Korolev Lectures.[38]

"You described Korolev as if you, his deputies, knew about the flaws and unreliability of the N1-L3 design, and he, Korolev, stubbornly refused to look into it. As director of NII-88 at that time, at the personal request of Uncle Mitya

[Ustinov], I tried to gain an understanding of all the lunar problems, including what motivated people, on whom much depended, in their attitude toward the Moon. I was convinced that Korolev, perhaps

Boris Chertok and A. K. Medvedeva, the scientific secretary of the Korolev Readings.

From the author's archives.

---

37. This is a reference to the Trofim Denisovich Lysenko (1898–1976), the infamous Soviet agronomist whose ideologically driven vendetta against Soviet geneticists in the late 1940s gravely and deleteriously affected the state of Soviet science. The careers of many Soviet biologists were destroyed as a result. Khrushchev was sympathetic to Lysenko's idiosyncratic scientific theories, and his ideas were only officially discredited after Khrushchev's fall in 1964. Keldysh was one of the leading opponents of "Lysenkoism" in the Academy of Sciences. Nikolay Ivanovich Nuzhdin was a protégé of Lysenko whose candidacy for full membership of the Academy was opposed by many of the leading lights of Soviet science including Academician Andrey Dmitriyevich Sakharov (1921–1989), the physicist considered the "father" of the Soviet hydrogen bomb.

38. The "Korolev Lectures," officially known as the "Academic Readings on Cosmonautics, Dedicated to the Memory of Academician S. P. Korolev and Other Prominent Native Scientist-Pioneers in the Mastery of Cosmic Space." Sponsored by the Russian Academy of Sciences, they are held each year in late January and early February.

better than we, felt and understood the general situation. Those 800 kilograms that he demanded from you were a test of your loyalty to his policy. He needed a super-heavy-lift launch vehicle and as soon as possible. Even if we didn't fulfill the mission in a one-launch version, then at least we were testing out the launch vehicle. And then we could come out with new robust proposals for the Moon and Mars."

Chapter 5
N1–L3 Control

We always had heated debates centered around the assignment and supervision of work concerning motion control, electronic systems, and radio systems. My comrades at work were split into two camps. The most aggressive enthusiasts had already experienced the joy of creative satisfaction during the independent development of systems for robotic spacecraft and Vostoks. The successes of the first years of the Space Age gave my closest colleagues courage and confidence in their strengths and capabilities.

Why farm out interesting work, they asked, if we understand better than others what needs to be done and how to do it? It's easier to do it ourselves than to explain what we want to a new person at an outside firm.

These enthusiasts included department chiefs Viktor Legostayev, Yevgeniy Bashkin, Oleg Babkov, Yuriy Karpov, and Petr Kupriyanchik. They had not only experienced the pangs of creation, but had also tasted the first fruits of secret celebrity. Those who stood closer to the problems of the launch vehicle—Viktor Kalashnikov, Oleg Voropayev, Leonid Alekseyev, Lev Vilnitskiy, and Viktor Kuzmin—held the "pro-Pilyugin" position. They felt we needed to have a share-and-share-alike relationship with Nikolay Pilyugin's firm and with all others we might be able to recruit.[1]

From the author's archives.

Petr Kupriyanchik was a department chief at TsKBEM who worked under Chertok on the design of spacecraft control systems.

---

1. Chertok is referring here to the distribution of responsibility in the development of control systems. Pilyugin's firm, known as the Scientific-Research Institute of Automatics and Instrument Building (NIIAP), was responsible for guidance and control systems for the majority of Soviet ground-based long-range ballistic missiles and space launch vehicles, but Chertok's department at OKB-1 had a significant role in the evolution of such systems, especially for Soviet spacecraft.

I felt particularly strong pressure from the design departments and the factory. They were overloaded with routine work on Mars, Venera, and Ye-6 systems; R-9, RT-1, RT-2, and GR combat missiles; and piloted vehicles. In the shops of the instrument factory, hundreds of sophisticated instruments, antenna-feeder units, control surface actuators, and thousands of cables of every description were being manufactured simultaneously.

Korolev often intervened in our disputes. He didn't dampen the enthusiasm of the most aggressively disposed portion of my staff, who sought to seize everything they could, but he did convince them that one cannot do everything. Pilyugin and his powerful staff should be used to the greatest extent possible rather than pushed away. This was his imperative demand, which he expressed to Boris Rauschenbach and me in the form of an ultimatum.[2]

Finally, as 1964 was drawing to a close, a distribution of work assignments for N1-L3 was devised, which for the most part continued throughout the next decade of the program's existence. Pilyugin was the head chief designer of the N-1 launch vehicle control system. A government decree put this in writing. My complex [at OKB-1] was given responsibility for assembling all the baseline data needed to develop the control system and handing it over to Pilyugin.[3] The baseline data on aerodynamics and gas dynamics, mass and inertial loads, centers of gravity, external disturbances, necessary control moments, the effect of liquids in the tanks, structural flexibility, engine characteristics, and many other parameters of a large rocket system needed to be converted into a system of differential equations. Voropayev's department was responsible for this mental processing. The multivolume calculations that were modestly referred to as the launch vehicle's mathematical model could only be performed using computers that had only just begun to appear in our computer center. Back then, the first computers were distributed by government decision. Korolev and Mishin personally, wherever they could, pushed through decisions on the procurement of computers for OKB-1. The leadership of the computer center was entrusted to the "chief ballistics expert"—Svyastoslav "Svet" Lavrov. Junior engineer Vladimir Stepanov was in charge of bringing the first computer "monsters" on line and servicing them.

Thanks to the initiative and perseverance of Vladilen Finogeyev, head of the integrated department at NIIAP—as Pilyugin's new organization split off

---

2. Rauschenbach was the chief of the control systems department (subordinate to Chertok) at OKB-1.

3. Thematic divisions within OKB-1 were known as "complexes." In 1966, OKB-1 had at least 10 complexes, each headed by a deputy chief designer. Chertok headed Complex 3, which was responsible for control systems.

From the author's archives.

Shown here are the developers of the control system for the N-1 at Pilyugin's organization (NIIAP): B. P. Tkachev, V. I. Nikiforenko, A. V. Skripitsyn, V. P. Finogeyev, and V. M. Bessonov.

from NII-885 was then called—in two years they rolled out the integrated stand for the N-1 launch vehicle control system. A web of cables interconnected the hundreds of different-caliber instruments for all the systems installed on the launch vehicle. That's how the working model of the full control system looked.

In the launch vehicle control system, I was responsible for developing all the drives for Kuznetsov's engines that controlled thrust and for all the types of control surface actuators that might be needed for any of the stages and lunar vehicles. Andronik Iosifyan's firm developed the on-board 5-kilowatt power plant for all the launch vehicle's electrical systems.[4] Iosifyan and his deputy, Nikolay Sheremetyevskiy, very actively promoted this new idea. They undertook the development of the turbo generator, which would replace the set of heavy storage batteries. Arkhip Lyulka designed the high-speed turbine for it.

The reliability prediction specialists were filled with superstitious fear at the thought of 36 engines on the launch vehicle's three stages. They were completely crushed when the proposal to install six *more* engines on Block A [first

---

4. This firm was the All-Union Scientific-Research Institute of Electromechanics (VNIIEM).

stage] came out. The statistics of the last few years showed that even among the well-tested engines of missiles that had been put into service, the frequency of failures caused by propulsion systems was at least two per 100 launches. Now they would have to figure the reliability for the N-1 with 42 engines. Consequently, for the N-1 there would certainly be at least one failure every two launches. To protect against the catastrophic consequences of engine failures, back in 1960 the decision was made to develop a system that monitored engine operation, performed diagnostics, and shut down the engine when signs of an emergency situation arose. We called it KORD (Engine Operation Monitoring [System]). Pilyugin refused to develop it for understandable reasons: "We are not engine specialists and we can't be responsible for the failure of a liquid-propellant engine. God forbid that we shut down dozens of good engines and send the rocket flying abroad."

Once again Korolev gave me an ultimatum: "If you can't persuade Pilyugin and can't find another reliable contractor—develop KORD yourself."

I assembled my "small council of small chiefs," as Kalashnikov joked, and we ascertained by a poll that there were "no fools" as far as we could see and we would have to make this system ourselves. I put Kalashnikov in charge of development and assigned the electrical and circuitry problems to Viktor Kuzmin's department and the construction of instruments to Semyon Chizhikov's and Ivan Zverev's departments. Nikolay Kuznetsov's engine specialists specified the emergency criteria. And, working with these criteria, it was up to us to develop sensors and electrical instruments that would process information and manage to shut down the engine before an explosion occurred, inevitably resulting in a fire and loss of the rocket. The task of selecting the emergency criteria in this system proved to be complicated and very contentious. A special laboratory was set up to develop the KORD system, whose chief Yuriy Kunavin and a small number of young colleagues bore such an important responsibility for the fate of the N-1 that we felt it "ponderously, crudely, and tangibly" on the very first launch.[5]

We once again realized that even under the most favorable conditions, subcontracting organizations do not want to develop emergency systems. It was that way with the emergency missile destruction (APR) and emergency spacecraft destruction (APO) systems, the emergency rescue system (SAS) and emergency landing system, and now with the KORD system.[6] If the emergency

---

5. The phrase in quotes is a reference to a 1930 poem ("At the Top of My Voice") by famous Russian poet and playwright Vladimir Vladimirovich Mayakovskiy (1893–1930).

6. APR—*Avariynyy podryv rakety*; APO—*Avariynyy podryv kosmicheskikh obyektov*; SAS—*Sistema avariynogo spaseniya*.

system performed its task properly, then no one would say thank you, because thanks are not in order for an accident. And if the emergency system were to be erroneously activated, then there would be hell to pay—the system itself might cause the destruction of a rocket or a spacecraft. I can remember at least two such tragic events—the failure during the attempted launch of the first Soyuz on 16 December 1966 and the failure of the first N-1 rocket.[7] I shall tell about the latter event later on.

When it came to the very complex problems of controlling the flight of the L3 lunar vehicle, which consisted of rocket Blocks G and D and the LOK and LK spacecraft, it turned out that my staff received a sizable portion of the work. My comrades grumbled that our branch was doing the lion's share of the total volume of control work for the entire lunar complex, while according to the decrees, Pilyugin's staff was considered to be the head team. I countered such conversations by suggesting that anyone who wasn't satisfied with the work assignments could transfer from Chief Designer Korolev to Chief Designer Pilyugin. I must say that I found no takers.

Vladilen Finogeyev and Mikhail Khitrik were quite helpful to me in coordinating the work assignments. Formalism and the bureaucratic approach were foreign to these two absolutely outstanding engineers, very decent men, and future deputies of Pilyugin.[8] They talked Pilyugin into taking on as much of the work as possible. Their efforts paved the way for us to work jointly in harmony, without any serious conflicts. They proposed an arrangement in which NIIAP developed the L3 complex control system for the flight segments during which the engines of Blocks G, D, Ye, and I were in operation; the automatic control equipment for propulsion systems; and the means to maintain control during the braking maneuvers to leave lunar orbit and decrease velocity for the descent segment. They also took on control of the automatic soft landing, control of the LK during liftoff from the lunar surface and insertion into lunar orbit in the vicinity of the LOK, and a system to control descent during return to Earth at reentry velocity.

We still backed up the automatic lunar landing system with manual control. Rauschenbach solved this problem very cleverly on paper and in graphic models. Legostayev and Khitrik coordinated the automatic and manual dynamics, while Savchenko invented the optics needed to select a landing site on the surface of the Moon.

---

7. For Chertok's account of the second (and aborted) attempt to launch a Soyuz spaceship in December 1966, see Chertok, *Rockets and People, Vol. III*, pp. 607–618.

8. Vladilen Petrovich Finogeyev (1928–) would later go on to serve as deputy minister of the defense industry between 1970 and 1981.

From the author's archives.
The theory of the motion control system of the N-1 rocket was developed by scientists at NIIAP: A. G. Glazkov (left) and M. S. Khitrik.

The distribution of responsibilities among the radio firms was relatively easy. The fierce struggle between the *Kontakt* (Contact) and *Igla* (Needle) rendezvous radio systems for a spot in the lunar program continued for several years. It clearly convinced us of the benefit of healthy competition even under conditions of strictly centralized planning. It is difficult to say what the fate of the *Kontakt* system would have been if our lunar program had been successfully implemented. The small staff that took on this project at OKB MEI under the supervision of radio enthusiast Petr Kriss demonstrated infinite capabilities in inventing new technical systems using old principles of radio physics.

For some time the fate of the main sources of electrical power for the lunar vehicles remained unclear. The option of using fuel cells (TE) or electrochemical generators (EKhG) started to be aggressively "promoted."[9] Nikolay Lidorenko (of VNIIT[10]) proposed his option first. At OKB-1, in view of the complexity of the problem of oxygen and hydrogen supplies, we entrusted Viktor Ovchinnikov's team, which was experienced in cryogenic technology and hydraulic automatic equipment, to oversee these orders and to develop a pneumohydraulic system. Along the way, the projects changed hands among

9. TE—*Toplivnyy element;* EKhG—*Elektrokhimicheskiy generator.*
10. VNIIT—*Vsesoyuznyy nauchno-issledovatelskiy institut istochnikov toka* (All-Union Scientific-Research Institute of Current Sources).

three EKhG development firms, until finally one of the atomic energy enterprises in the Urals found a brilliant solution to this problem.[11]

It wasn't until February 1965 that the VPK authorized the ministries to develop and coordinate a plan for the production of the L3 lunar system. The date of August 1965 was set for the draft plan as a whole. As for the schedule for the development and manufacture of the L3 complex, the VPK did not approve it in 1965 or in 1966.

Unlike conventional plans, where the design documentation is released *before* the working documentation, in planning the N1-L3 production schedule, the development of the draft plan for the system as a whole was scheduled for completion in August 1965, and the working documentation—in April through June 1965.[12] This meant that we would prepare and issue the baseline data to our designers and subcontracting organizations before the release of the multivolume draft plan. The date for the manufacture of the experimental units, the first models of the systems, and the mockups and engineering models of the launch vehicle was the second quarter of 1966. "All of 1966" was set aside for the experimental development of the engines, new blocks, systems, and vehicles. The schedule also called for flight development testing (LKI) of the N1-L3 complex in 1966.

Intelligent people worked in the offices of the VPK. They understood full well that the proposed document contained a lot of "phony" dates, and not wanting to put their own superiors on the spot, they were in no hurry to present the plan schedule for approval.

Throughout 1965, I had to meet more often than usual with Pilyugin, his deputies, and leading specialists. NIIAP developed the control system for the N-1 launch vehicle more quickly than the others. For them, however, as for the many other organizations involved, the development was one of a kind. Pilyugin demanded from his developers that the main criterion for the development of the system must be reliability, regardless of OKB-1's "hysterics" regarding weight. Wherever possible, there must be triple redundancy!

The N-1's triple-redundant flight control system had three gyrostabilized platforms, nine longitudinal accelerometers (instead of three), and 18 normal

---

11. This organization was the Ural Electrochemical Combine.

12. In the typical sequence of events in the Soviet R&D system, weapons makers first issued a multivolume "draft plan" that represented the most complete design specification for the vehicle. This was followed by the issuance of "design documentation" (detailed schematics of each element of the system) followed by the "working documentation" (which allows engineers, technicians, and workers to begin to produce an experimental model of the vehicle). Chertok is noting that, in the case of N1-L3, the actual design of the vehicle wasn't finished before rushing ahead to the stage of prototype manufacture.

stabilization and lateral stabilization accelerators (NS-BS), in addition to three on-board digital computers with peripheral devices and code-analog and analog-code converters.[13] All of the command and measurement circuitry operated on the "two out of three" voting principle. Due to the very heavy vibro-acoustic and temperature loads anticipated in the area of the launch vehicle's propulsion system, the automatic control equipment for each engine had additional backup. In this case, the entire cable network had redundancy, and in addition, the most crucial circuit nodes also had part-by-part redundancy. The total number of instruments developed by NIIAP alone exceeded 200, while the mass of the cable network, according to various data, ranged from 3 to 5 tons.

Pilyugin loved to boast about the scope of work on the launch vehicle control system: "We have to manufacture all of this almost simultaneously—for the integrated stand, for type tests, for the first engineering model of the rocket, and for the first flight model. Over the course of a year, just for the N-1 (not counting all the other orders) I have to manufacture more than 2,000 new instruments. My factory does not have the capacity for this. But others will not take it up because there is still no tried-and-true documentation. But I'm not about to be the first to raise a ruckus about it. We will not be last. We'll see how you meet your deadlines with the new engines and who debugs their part quicker."

These were the sorts of conversations that went on about the launch vehicle. And designers and the factory still had to manufacture the equipment for the lunar vehicles as soon as possible. As Roman Turkov, the director of our factory, loved to say in 1965, "We haven't gotten in gear yet."[14]

When some new idea captivated Pilyugin, he could talk about it glowingly and at great length, disregarding the fact that we had come over with the tough assignment of coordinating dozens of designs.

Pilyugin telephoned to have them bring him the "latest thing" in gyroscopic technology—the floating angular rate sensor. "The weight and dimensions of Vitya Kuznetsov's platforms are going to sink us all! Look here, we made everything on floats and it's all half the size and weighs half as much."

Indeed, during the period from 1965 to 1967, NIIAP began to independently develop and manufacture gyrostabilized platforms and accelerometers—sensitive instruments for measuring accelerations. Despite the government decree, at Pilyugin's initiative, NIIAP's gyro platforms were installed on the

---

13. NS-BS—*Normalnaya stabilizatsiya-Bokovaya stabilizatsiya.*
14. Roman Anisimovich Turkov (1901–1975) served as director of OKB-1's experimental production facility until 1966.

N-1 (and later on the L3) rather than those platforms produced at Viktor Kuznetsov's NII-944. This added fuel to the fire of disagreement over technical matters between Pilyugin and Kuznetsov. My comrades and I had to observe a strict "benevolent" neutrality. Kuznetsov's gyroscopic instruments were not only installed on all of our previous rockets and spacecraft, but they had already been developed for a new spacecraft—the Soyuzes.

During the second half of 1965, my comrades and I visited NIIAP almost every week to coordinate dozens of technical issues. Sipping tea and munching on biscuits in Pilyugin's office, we arrived at the off-the-record conclusion that if the engines were ready, then we could still somehow manage to launch the launch vehicle in 1968, but the LOK and LK—no way! The conversations once again returned to the volume of production work and burdening of the factories. We often departed from the hospitable Nikolay Alekseyevich without having reached any sort of agreement, but with promises from both sides "to think about it for another week, and then give each other a phone call."

THE WEIGHT OF THE N-1 CONTROL SYSTEM was a major issue of discussion in late 1965. On Monday, 20 December 1965, Pilyugin telephoned me on the Kremlin line: "Boris! Come on over. There's something I need to talk to you about. Keldysh was interrogating me about the L3 weights. Someone filled his head with the idea that the weight deficit is greater than what you and Bushuyev are reporting. He wants to investigate and he's called for a session of the expert commission on Wednesday. I telephoned Sergey [Korolev], and he said that you are going to report about the work assignments and at the same time, 'among other things,' about the weights too. I'm only going to report on my part, and I'm not about to talk about deadlines. That's the wrong place."

Nikita Khrushchev, and Leonid Brezhnev after him, considered Academy of Sciences President Mstislav Keldysh the most competent and objective scientist, standing above departmental interests and personal ambitions. Keldysh's authority was so great that they put him in charge of the widest range of expert commissions—from selecting combat missile systems to measures to save Lake Baikal.[15]

As chairman of various expert commissions on rocket-space technology and of the Interdepartmental Scientific-Technical Council on Space Research, he was forced to conduct a myriad of closed sessions on this subject, and as

---

15. In 1971, the Communist Party took firm steps to limit pollution in Lake Baikal, the world's oldest and deepest lake. The Party took these steps after much protest by locals and others who were concerned by pollution largely caused by a nearby pulp and cellulose mill.

president of the Academy of Sciences, he held public press conferences.[16] Keldysh's primary workplace was considered to be the president's office in the palatial building of the Presidium of the Academy of Sciences at 14 Leninskiy Prospekt. However, Keldysh held meetings on rocket-space matters in the small office of the director of the Institute of Applied Mathematics on Miusskaya Square. This was one of the "secure" institutes. Within its walls one could talk about top-secret projects. This was forbidden in the Academy Presidium building because, among other reasons, foreign scientists, foreign delegations, and the press visited it. Keldysh would arrive at Miusskaya Square in the afternoon, spending the first very difficult and troublesome half of the day at the Academy of Sciences on Leninskiy Prospekt. This time he convened the meeting of the expert commission that Korolev had warned me about when he demanded: "Give me back 800 kilograms."

Bushuyev, Rauschenbach, and I arrived a little bit before the appointed time of three o'clock, and I tacked up a poster displaying information about the distribution of L3 work assignments. Opening up the expert commission meeting, Keldysh said: "Korolev authorized Boris Yevseyevich to give us a report on the distribution of work assignments and on the status of developments on the L3 systems. The main issue, which disturbs all of us, is weight. I request that in your report you tell us what is really going on according to the latest figures."

I knew full well that you had to get up pretty early to fool Keldysh, but nevertheless decided to draw out the report so that there would be no time left for serious discussion of the weight reports. Before our departure Korolev had instructed Bushuyev and me: "Two dozen curious individuals will be gathered there. Don't get into a discussion with Keldysh about our weight problems in front of them—under any circumstances! If it becomes difficult, Kostya [Bushuyev] must help you out. He didn't study at a diplomatic school for nothing." Korolev did not pass up the opportunity to take a jab at Bushuyev, who had been enticed into diplomatic service before beginning his space career.

I began to talk about the number of systems and the distribution of responsibility between the main contractors. In the interests of history I shall cite its main content.

I noted that OKB-1 was performing the role of the lead organization but at the same time independently was developing a number of systems for the L3

---

16. The Interdepartmental Scientific-Technical Council on Space Research was an advisory body of the Academy of Sciences that brought together representatives from many different branches of the Soviet space industry to deliberate on the future directions of the civilian space program. Keldysh headed the body from its inception in 1960 until his death in 1978.

lunar complex. By agreement with NIIAP, we had taken on the development of systems with which we already had experience.

I noted that OKB-1 was developing the following systems:

1. The attitude control system for the entire L3 complex.
2. The LOK attitude control system.
3. The LK attitude control system.
4. The LOK-LK rendezvous control system.
5. The autonomous manual attitude control and navigation system.

I added that Geofizika (TsKB-589) and the Ministry of the Defense Industry's Arsenal Factory in Kiev were developing the sensitive elements—the optical-electronic devices—for all of these systems. The *Kontakt* radio system developed at OKB MEI would be used for the rendezvous of the two spacecraft. In order to draw out the time and pay a compliment to Keldysh, I said: "Boris Viktorovich Rauschenbach is responsible for these five items. Since his transfer to us at the initiative of you and Sergey Pavlovich, his staff has tripled in size. If there are any questions on this part, Boris Viktorovich can brief you in greater detail."

The Lunar Vehicle (LK), the Soviet version of the American Apollo Lunar Module (LM), shown here in an assembly shop. The lander is positioned on a trusslike circular dolly set underneath the base.

From the author's archives.

Unfortunately, there were no questions, and I continued the list:

6. The control system that would run the LOK and LK on-board systems and instruments in accordance with the flight program, the integrated electrical circuit, and the on-board cable network. This system would receive, transmit, and process the on-board systems' control commands in order to execute the logical operations that would run the on-board equipment.
7. The vehicles' integrated power system. Electrochemical generators developed by a *Minsredmash* factory would serve as the electric power source (EKhG) for the LOK, and silver-zinc batteries developed by the All-Union

Scientific-Research Institute of Current Sources (VNIIT) would power the LK.[17]

8. The antenna-feeder units for all radio systems except the *Kontakt* system and radio altimeter.

9. The ground testing equipment for the LOK and LK at the factory, engineering facility, and launch site.

I CONTINUED, STATING THAT NIIAP and their cooperative network were developing and manufacturing the following:

1. The motion control system for flight segments when the engines of Blocks G, D, I, and Ye would be in operation. This system would provide stabilization about the center of mass and control the motion of the center of mass.

2. The control automatics for propulsion systems, including the apparent velocity control automatics.

3. The motion control system during braking segments for lunar deorbiting, deceleration during descent, and soft lunar landing.

4. The control system for lunar liftoff and lunar orbital insertion in the area of rendezvous with the LOK.

5. The system for the controlled descent to Earth at reentry velocity.

6. The gyrostabilized platforms for all segments when the following would be operational: the motion and attitude-control system, accelerometers controlling accelerations about all three axes, and the on-board computer.

FURTHERMORE, NII-885 WAS DEVELOPING THE FOLLOWING:

1. An integrated radio system providing transmission of control commands and trajectory measurements to the spacecraft during all flight segments.

2. Telemetry systems and telemetry transmission lines.

3. Television-image transmission equipment (jointly with NII-380).

4. Equipment for the transmission of voice and telegraph signals (jointly with NII-695).

5. An Earth-seeking radio direction-finding system for orientation of pencil-beam antennas.

6. An altimeter and computer providing measurements and control during the lunar vehicle's landing segments.

---

17. *Minsredmash* was the abbreviation for *Ministerstvo srednego mashinostroyeniya* (Ministry of Medium Machine Building), the ministry that oversaw the nuclear weapons and nuclear energy industry during the post-Stalin era.

I noted that NII-695 was developing the following:
1. The autonomous communication system between cosmonauts when one of them would egress onto the lunar surface and perform a spacewalk while transferring from one vehicle to the other.
2. The radio system for descent module search after its return to Earth.

OKB MEI was developing the new *Kontakt* relative-motion parameter measurement system. I noted that because of its smaller mass and layout advantages, we had decided to use this system instead of *Igla*, which was developed for the Soyuzes.

I informed those assembled that draft plans had been issued for all of the aforementioned systems. The working documentation had been partially developed, but not a single system was yet in production for the flight version. Taking into consideration the production cycle and subsequent debugging in the developers' shops and on our experimental units, in the best-case scenario it would be possible to deliver the systems for the flight vehicles and blocks in late 1967. Thus, flight testing of the vehicles and L3 blocks would begin no sooner than 1968.

I had taken a forbidden tack. One was "not supposed" to mention 1968 in official meetings. According to decrees, and also Korolev's and Keldysh's promises, flight testing was supposed to begin in 1967 when the 50th anniversary of the Great October Socialist Revolution would take place.

The meeting started to get noisy—to start a discussion about deadlines was dangerous for everyone. Keldysh understood this very well and, without asking me any questions, he said, "Let's hear what Nikolay Alekseyevich [Pilyugin] and then Mikhail Sergeyevich [Ryazanskiy] have to say. First and foremost, the fate of the control systems depends on them."

Bearing in mind my *faux pas*, Pilyugin and Ryazanskiy reported in optimistic tones about the state of affairs, bypassing the problem of masses and deadlines. But both men felt they needed to turn the expert commission's attention to problematic issues that still had to be resolved. Pilyugin brought up his achievements in the field of gyro platforms and accelerometers on floating gyroscopes and said that he had established close contact with the Scientific-Research Center for Electronic Computer Technology (NITsEVT) for the development of on-board digital computers.[18]

"We know how to control rockets and satellites without using on-board digital computers," remarked Pilyugin, "but for a descent to the Moon we

---

18. NITsEVT—*Nauchno-issledovatelskiy tsentr elektronnoy vychislitelnoy tekhniki.*

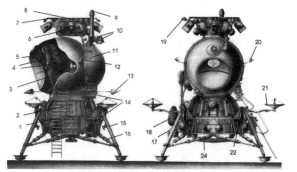

Landing and Surface Configuration   Ascent Configuration

1. Lunar Landing Aggregate - LPU	10. Alignment Sensors	19. Omni-Directional Antennas
2. Rocket Block E	11. Instrumentation Compartment	20. Rendezvous System Antennas
3. Cosmonaut Cabin	12. TV Camera	21. TV Antennas
4. Life Support System Equipment	13. Omni-Directional Antennas	22. Pressing Engine
5. Visual Observation Port For Landing	14. Power Supplies	23. Main engine
6. Block Of Attitude Control Engines	15. Support Leg With Shock Absorber	24. Reflector
7. Thermal Control System Radiator	16. Strut With Shock Absorber	25. Backup Engine
8. Docking Mechanism	17. Landing Radar Locator	
9. Targeting Sensor	18. Strap-On Instrumentation Compartment	

RKK Energiya & David R. Woods

These three views of the LK provide a good sense of the main systems of the Soviet lunar lander. The on-board LK propulsion system is used for the final phase of descent plus ascent from the surface back to lunar orbit. The propulsion system consists of a variable-thrust primary system that can be throttled for landing, plus a fixed-thrust backup system for emergency return to lunar orbit should the primary system fail.

must have one. Without a computer we could burn up so much fuel trying to land that there wouldn't be enough for the return trip."

Ryazanskiy supported Pilyugin with regard to the on-board digital computer, saying that for NII-885 the most complex problem was the lunar altimeter, the measurements of which must be processed by a high-speed computer. After back-and-forth banter about the reality of producing a computer within the necessary timeframe Keldysh asked what was going on with the EKhG—the so-called "fuel cells."

"The thing is," said Keldysh, "that Slavskiy called me and complained that one of his Sverdlovsk factories supposedly is being dragged into the 'lunar adventure,' but he, the minister of Medium Machine Building, doesn't know anything about this and is asking us not to count on them very much for the time being."[19]

---

19. Yefim Pavlovich Slavskiy (1898–1991) was head of the Ministry of Medium Machine Building (*Minsredmash*), i.e., the industrial ministry in charge of the Soviet atomic energy branch. He served in this position from 1957 to 1986.

This information came as a complete surprise to Bushuyev and me. The day before, Viktor Ovchinnikov and Mikhail Melnikov, who had supported him by means of his connections at the Ministry of Medium Machine Building (MSM), reported to Korolev that in Sverdlovsk everything had been arranged and we would receive much more reliable EKhGs than [Nikolay] Lidorenko's firm was offering.

We promised Keldysh "to look into it and report back."

We looked into it about 10 days later and could hardly stop laughing. Here is what Ovchinnikov, who was responsible for the EKhG negotiations, told us. They really had come to an agreement with one very reliable design bureau of an atomic industry plant in the Urals. The nuclear engineers were very interested in the problem of obtaining electric energy from liquid oxygen and liquid hydrogen, and also providing breathing oxygen and clean drinking water for the cosmonauts. In order to authorize the agreement they needed the blessing of the MSM—the atomic ministry. The officials didn't object but said that it would be good if someone from outside reported about this interesting work to Slavskiy, and it would be bad if he were the last to hear about it.

A rather complicated relationship had formed between Korolev and Slavskiy. Myriad problems had cropped up since the time when, under the leadership of [Korolev's deputy] Mikhail Melnikov and with the very active support of Vasiliy Mishin, we had set up a large branch dealing with electric nuclear rocket engines (EYaRD).[20] These problems required the involvement of professionals from atomic firms under the nuclear ministry. The MSM bureaucracy was very anxious about Korolev's "independent activities" [in nuclear energy].

Korolev felt that at the present time it was premature to turn to the all-powerful Slavskiy. But then Melnikov decided to battle his way through to the ministry of the atomic industry on his own. Someone in the bureaucracy helped him, and he wound up in Slavskiy's office. The rather short and thin Melnikov boldly went on the attack against the tall, powerful minister and former swashbuckling soldier of Budennyy's.[21] Slavskiy listened to Melnikov's long speech in which he described the future of atomic technology in cosmonautics, his problems and requests for MSM regarding electric nuclear rocket engines, and thanked him for beginning operations on the fuel cell. In closing,

---

20. EYaRD—*Elektricheskiy yaderno-raketnyy dvigatel.*

21. Slavskiy served under the famous Marshal S. M. Budennyy in the 1st Cavalry Army during the Russian Civil War.

Melnikov committed an unforgivable mistake—he switched to the issue of controlled thermonuclear reaction.

"We have achieved great success," he boasted, "in mastering deep vacuum technology. Your specialists haven't mastered this technology—let us teach them."

Ovchinnikov found out about the meeting's finale from the aide who was in the office at that time. At this point, according to the aide, Yefim Pavlovich [Slavskiy] turned red in the face, stood up to the full extent of his imposing height and, pointing toward the door, he said:

"And you can go f—— yourself…."

Melnikov understood his mistake by the time he reached the reception area, where the aide consoled him and explained that this kind of treatment from Slavskiy is a good sign.

"He has made a mental note of everything and will certainly help."

Evidently Slavskiy's telephone call to Keldysh followed this "conversation."

Everyone was already rather tired when Keldysh asked a question that I really didn't want to answer: "Well now, Boris Yevseyevich, the time has come to have a look at what's happening with weights. Please brief the commission on the latest data."

I could not conceal from the expert commission that now, while we were coordinating work assignments, issuing working documentation, and designing new systems, the most sensitive issue remained not the hardware, but its weight. Keldysh was demanding that I specify the actual numbers of the weight deficit. I did not wish to frighten the experts and did my best to avoid a direct answer. Finally, having lost patience and become irritable, Keldysh said: "Boris Yevseyevich, if you do not know what is really going on with the systems' weights, then at least give us a hint as to who at OKB-1 is capable of answering this question. If there are no such people, it means that nobody has a grip on this project and everything is happening willy-nilly. But I don't believe this. Don't make me complain to Sergey Pavlovich."

Bushuyev decided that it was time to come to my rescue.

"Mstislav Vsevolodovich, we have every gram under the strictest control. The designers in my department are responsible for the weight report. We are keeping track of all the systems, and Chertok does not have the right to exceed the limits allotted him."

Keldysh smiled knowingly and stopped tormenting us. But this didn't make our lives any easier.

Chapter 6
We're Behind, but We're Not Giving In

From 1963 to 1965, Dmitriy Ustinov was chairman of the Supreme Council of the National Economy (VSNKh) and first deputy chairman of the USSR Council of Ministers.[1] Having dove into the problems of coordinating the work of the Councils of the National Economy, which exercised regional authority over industry, Ustinov had temporarily stepped away from the management of rocket-space technology. After Khrushchev's ouster the VSNKh was phased out. Its functions were transferred to the Council of Ministers and to the reinstated industry ministries.

Ustinov had not been actively involved in the overthrow of Nikita Khrushchev, but in terms of his "specific gravity" after the "October Revolution of 1964," he could certainly count on the post of Chairman of the Council of Ministers. However, many members of the new Brezhnev Politburo were apprehensive about Ustinov's strong-willed nature and the possible consequences of offering him the second position in the Party and government hierarchy.[2] Instead, Aleksey Kosygin was named chairman of the Council of Ministers. Kosygin had not been involved in the plot against Khrushchev and was non-threatening because, involved in economics, he was not interested in political leadership. Ustinov was offered the honorary post of Central Committee secretary for defense matters. He was a candidate to become a Politburo member, while Minister of Defense Rodion Malinovskiy was a Politburo member.

---

1. The Supreme Council of the National Economy was a short-lived body established by Nikita Khrushchev in 1963 to coordinate Soviet industry. It was an extra layer of bureaucracy that was eventually abolished in 1965, a year after Khrushchev's overthrow. During its brief period of existence, the VSNKh was headed by Ustinov. The governmental body was modeled after a similarly named council that was much more powerful and longer-lasting that operated between 1917 and 1932.

2. The "first position" was usually considered the General Secretary of the Central Committee of the Communist Party, i.e., in the Party hierarchy.

Central Committee General Secretary Brezhnev headed the Defense Council.[3] The ministers of all the branches of industry were subordinate to the Council of Ministers. Anastas Mikoyan, Nikolay Podgornyy, Andrey Kirilenko, and other members of the Politburo could feel more secure with this alignment of forces in the upper echelons of power.[4]

Some strictly secret "water cooler" anecdotes and jokes circulated after Khrushchev's downfall. Supposedly at the Plenum of the Central Committee, some delegates from Odessa spoke out against Nikita Sergeyevich's removal from his post as General Secretary of the Central Committee: "Odessa will survive without meat, but we can't live without jokes." Historians, meanwhile, came up with this quip: "There was Russia before Peter (*dopetrovskaya*), then there was Russia under Peter (*petrovskaya*), and now there's Russia under Dnepropetrovsk (*dnepropetrovskaya*).[5] This last joke referred to the new makeup of the Politburo, where former Party leaders from Dnepropetrovsk played a decisive role.

Having ended up in the post of Central Committee secretary for defense issues, Ustinov actually didn't meddle in the affairs of the Ministry of Defense.[6] The Minister of Defense and Chief of the General Staff preferred to deal directly with Brezhnev. Ustinov focused all of his energy on the defense industry [rather than the military] and was quite familiar with all of its branches. Between him and the ministries was VPK Chairman Leonid Smirnov, whom Ustinov had promoted.[7]

---

3. The Defense Council was a highly secret body attached to the Politburo that was responsible for all top-level defense policies in the Soviet Union. It was established in February 1955 by Nikita Khrushchev and usually headed by the General Secretary of the Central Committee of the Communist Party, i.e., Khrushchev, then Leonid Brezhnev, then Yuriy Andropov, then Konstantin Chernenko, and finally Mikhail Gorbachev. It was abolished in March 1991.

4. Anastas Ivanovich Mikoyan (1895–1978) was an extremely influential Soviet diplomat who served under Stalin and then survived into the Khrushchev era before retiring in 1965. Nikolay Viktorovich Podgornyy (1903–1983) served as the token President of the Supreme Soviet from 1965 to 1977, while Andrey Pavlovich Kirilenko (1906–1990) was a leading Party member and member of the Politburo from 1962 to 1982 with broad responsibilities for supervising Soviet industry.

5. This is a pun that employs the Russian adjectival form of Peter (*petrovskaya*) referring to Peter I (the Great) (1672–1725), who is credited with the modernization of Russia in his day. Dnepropetrovsk is a major city in Ukraine from where a large of number of senior Party leaders (including Leonid Brezhnev) hailed. This group was often known as the "Brezhnev mafia."

6. Ustinov's new post, the Secretary of the Central Committee for Defense Industry and Space Affairs, effectively made him the topmost policy-making official in the Soviet space program, a post that would be higher than a NASA Administrator (since managerial issues were left to specific ministers). The Minister of Defense position was closer in analogy to the Secretary of Defense in the United States.

7. Smirnov was one of Ustinov's key protégés, having benefited from the latter's patronage through the years. In 1963, Smirnov was appointed chairman of the powerful Military-Industrial Commission (VPK). He served in that position for nearly two decades until 1985.

The leaders of the shipbuilding and aviation industries did not forget the active support that Ustinov had rendered to Khrushchev in the development of missiles at the expense of naval submarines and bomber aviation.[8] Ustinov had to seek out new ways to work with the industry. Officially, he did not have the authority to order or forbid or permit. However, the Central Committee was the Central Committee—all the ministers understood that. The personal fates of the minister, his deputies, chiefs of the main directorates, and directors of large enterprises depended on the offices of the Central Committee and its defense department. The manager of the Department of the Defense Industry, Ivan Serbin, was now officially subordinate to Ustinov. However, this "unsinkable" official of the Central Committee bureaucracy was feared more than Ustinov himself. The Central Committee offices did not prepare any resolutions or decisions concerning the defense industry. That was done by the VPK and offices of the Council of Ministers. But not a single government resolution was issued without the Central Committee's thorough review and blessing.

After the death of Korolev, our letter to the Central Committee about the appointment of Mishin as chief designer prevented Ustinov from putting Georgiy Tyulin in this post.[9] He, Ustinov, had prepared everything. All that remained was to obtain the signatures of the other Central Committee secretaries and to brief Brezhnev. With our appeal we had short-circuited the established system for appointing chiefs. We had not even consulted with Ustinov and had not warned him. Perhaps for this reason, and possibly due to other circumstances, for the first year and a half he "had no time for" the N-1.

ONE AFTER ANOTHER, INTELLIGENCE REPORTS AND SURVEYS—"white TASS" articles reporting on the Americans' successes—appeared. In August 1966, the U.S. press reported on the second successful flight of the Saturn IB carrying an experimental model of the Apollo.[10] Ustinov appealed directly to MOM Minister Sergey Afanasyev and to USSR Academy of Sciences President Mstislav Keldysh with a proposal to review the state of affairs with the lunar program and to determine why we were lagging behind the Americans and failing to meet the deadlines stipulated by the resolutions of the Central Committee and

---

8. In the late 1950s and early 1960s, Khrushchev had reduced the size and funding of the Soviet aviation and naval industries to divert resources to develop ballistic missiles.

9. See Chertok, *Rockets and People, Vol. III*, pp. 537–539.

10. This was AS-202 involving the launch on 25 August 1966 of an Apollo Command and Service Module (CSM-011) on a suborbital flight.

Council of Ministers. Ustinov assigned TsNIImash chief Yuriy Mozzhorin to prepare a detailed and objective report.[11]

In December 1966, Mishin was on vacation, and Sergey Okhapkin was performing the duties of chief designer of TsKBEM (as OKB-1 was now known). It was an unpleasant surprise for him to be invited to give a presentation about the status of operations on the N-1 project at a Central Committee meeting in Ustinov's office. He asked Bushuyev, Kryukov, and me to provide him with all the necessary reference materials for the report. I advised Okhapkin, either through the minister or directly, to persuade Ustinov to postpone the meeting until Mishin returned from vacation. He answered: "I have already tried to do that. They insinuated that, on the contrary, Ustinov wants to conduct the conversation in Mishin's absence."

Okhapkin knew better than others the state of affairs regarding the launch vehicle's design development. But he depicted what was going on with the vehicles and their systems as utterly a "total failure." I suggested, "You can't say 'total failure,' you need to say that, through the fault of subcontractors, operations on the vehicles are 'under threat of missing deadlines.' "

From our TsKBEM, only Okhapkin was invited to the meeting. From among the other chiefs, Pilyugin and Barmin, who enjoyed Ustinov's special favor, were invited. Keldysh, Smirnov, Afanasyev, Tyulin, Serbin, Strogonov, and Pashkov also participated in the meeting.[12] After citing American information sources, Ustinov said that the Americans are rigorously executing their plan and had already announced the commencement of Saturn V flights in July 1967 and the beginning of piloted flights in 1968. According to him, we had become bogged down with the circumlunar flight programs, we were missing deadlines for the 7K (or Soyuz) vehicles, and it was unclear when we intended to begin flight-developmental testing (LKI) on the N-1 launch vehicle. He, Ustinov, asked Mozzhorin—the director of the head institute of the rocket-space industry—not only to honestly speak about the status of operations, but also to give an objective evaluation.

According to the accounts of Okhapkin and Mozzhorin himself, the report he gave was in a completely different style than that to which Ustinov was accustomed. First, Mozzhorin made his colleagues, who knew the fundamentals of economics and information about the state of affairs in our industry

---

11. TsNIImash (Central Scientific-Research Institute of Machine Building) was the main policy-making institution in the Soviet space industry.

12. Besides Keldysh, the other six men mentioned (Smirnov, Afanasyev, Tyulin, Serbin, Strogonov, and Pashkov) were all senior officials in the government or Party hierarchy of the Soviet defense industry.

and among the subcontractors, honestly assess the scope of the operations. Many years later, Mozzhorin recounted that he had prepared himself very thoroughly, knowing that the report would provoke outraged surprise rather than calm discussion.

Mozzhorin put up posters that very clearly displayed the year-by-year schedules of expenditures that would be needed to support a lunar landing expedition, compared with the actual funds that the state budget was capable of setting aside for all cosmonautics programs. From Mozzhorin's posters and report, one could deduce that, even with the most heroic efforts, it would be impossible to implement the project in 1968. It would be possible to assign tasks for the beginning of flight-developmental testing in 1969, but this would require new decisions to dramatically increase funding for this project. The existing plans and timelines for the N-1 at this time were unrealistic.

In addition to everything else, Mozzhorin believed that significantly greater resources needed to be spent on ground developmental testing than had previously been assumed. It was wrong to approach testing a rocket like the N-1, using the rocket method of testing reliability in flight, when the number of failed launches didn't matter. By spending perhaps a greater percentage of funding on ground developmental testing, in the final analysis, we would manage to lower costs rather than raise the cost of the program as a whole.

Mozzhorin's report caused an explosion of outrage. For the first time at such a level, officially, a leader of a head institute had, in no uncertain terms, declared that plans dictated by the Central Committee of the Communist Party of the Soviet Union were unrealistic. Ustinov was more indignant than anyone. Airing a report like this to the Politburo threatened his personal authority. They might ask him: "And where were you all this time, Comrade Ustinov? After all, you were both minister of the defense industry *and* VPK chairman."[13]

Keldysh and Serbin supported the perturbed Ustinov. Mozzhorin was nearly branded an enemy of the people, as in the old days. Keldysh was worked up because, as chairman of the expert commission on the N1-L3 project, such figures had not been available to him and he had approved the clearly underestimated expenditures that were shown in our drafts. According to established practice, we made everything cheaper on paper so as not to frighten the minister of finance and *Gosplan*. Everyone knew about this practice but pretended that no one was being deceived.

---

13. From 1946 to 1957, Ustinov was minister of the defense industry; from 1957 to 1963, he was chairman of the VPK.

As a first step, Keldysh proposed reviewing Ministry of Defense expenditures on spy satellites and other military space needs and reducing them in favor of the N-1. He reluctantly proposed doing the same thing with Babakin's automatic stations for scientific space exploration. However, Mozzhorin had foreseen these proposals. He showed on each poster that the total funding for all the space programs taken together was just one-fifth of the amount that needed to be added on to the expenditures for the N-1. Even if funding were found from other sources, at this time it was not really possible to trim the cycles of construction, production, and subsequent reliability testing. He told us to assume that at the beginning of next year, by some miracle, full-scale funding would begin for the needs of all the operations' participants. In that case, in terms of the turnaround time for such a system, based on the available inventories of stock and experience, we'd still need at least three years before we could begin flight-developmental testing. Consequently, if there were full funding *and* the necessary funds were transferred for construction and production, we would be looking at the end of 1969 or more likely 1970!

Ustinov was a very experienced manager. Having suppressed his initial flash of outrage and wanting to calm himself and the others, he posed the following question to Okhapkin: "And you, the prime contractors, what do you think about this?"

After returning from the meeting, Okhapkin told us: "What could I say? My back was already drenched with sweat. I knew that this question was coming and I answered: 'Dmitriy Fedorovich, if they help us, then we will fulfill the work within the deadlines set by the Central Committee.' "

Outwardly, Ustinov seemed satisfied with the response. He did not dare question Barmin, who had spent enormous amounts on the construction of grandiose launch facilities. Barmin then said that inwardly he agreed with Mozzhorin but decided that if they weren't going to ask, he would remain silent.

Turning to Afanasyev, Ustinov proposed that the minister get to the bottom of the "unhealthy attitude" of the director of the industry's head institute. Mozzhorin was not so naïve that he had not familiarized his minister with the figures beforehand. Afanasyev gave his word that he would "get to the bottom of things" with Mozzhorin. Afanasyev and Mozzhorin understood that Ustinov and Keldysh were playing up their indignation. In actual fact, they had a better grasp of the general situation than the others, but out of "instructional" considerations they could act no other way.

During the last two years of his administration, Khrushchev managed to significantly reduce expenditures on conventional weapons, the construction of large surface ships, the production of heavy bombers, and the army in general. Now, in order to please the military officials who supported him in 1964, Brezhnev was supposed to correct Khrushchev's "mistakes." Under these conditions, Ustinov was leery of coming out with proposals to increase funding for the lunar landing expedition project, the necessity of which the marshals could not comprehend at all.

After finding out the details of the meeting, we once again realized that if the actual status of the programs stipulated by the decrees of the nation's higher political leadership did not coincide with what they desired, then even individuals with extensive experience in technology like Ustinov could bring down their wrath on the one who dares speak the truth. Even Keldysh, the chairman of the interdepartmental expert commission on N1-L3, who had realized a year ago that we were in a very difficult "weight" crisis from which we had yet to find a way out, supported the indignant Ustinov, rather than Mozzhorin!

When Okhapkin called us together and gave us a detailed account of the meeting in the Central Committee, Konstantin Bushuyev, who was responsible for design work for the lunar vehicles; Dmitriy Kozlov, who was responsible for monitoring design compliance during manufacture of the launch vehicle at the Progress Factory and who had just flown in from Kuybyshev; and I let it be known that we thought Mozzhorin was right. Before it was too late, we needed to draw up proposals with his input for new deadlines and arrangements. Taking advantage of Mishin's absence, Bushuyev even went so far as to say that we needed to draw up proposals for an alternative two-launch scenario. I stated that my friend Bushuyev, who was now proposing a two- and even three-launch scenario, was allotting values in his weight reports for the entire control system that were one and a half times less than those we were aware of from American data. Our control system was supposed to perform the very same functions as the system of the future American lunar expedition. We could reduce the mass, but only at the expense of reliability.

Bushuyev forcefully declared that the launch vehicle, which could insert just 85 tons into orbit, would not allow him to give weight limits for systems "on demand." We had to honestly admit that the rocket was not suited for landing a human being on the Moon.

Kryukov, cut to the quick, said that his departments had completed all the design work for the installation of an additional six engines on the first stage. This and other measures would make it possible to bring the in-orbit mass up to 95 tons. Kozlov reproached Okhapkin for not having mentioned at the meeting that the installation of 30 engines on the first stage instead of 24, regardless of any measures, would move the deadlines for the readiness of the first launch vehicle flight model back another year. We had agreed to have 30 engines installed on the first stage beginning with the first N-1 flight model, No. 3L. The first two engineering models of the rocket—for static tests and fit operations at the launch site—would have to be modified "during testing."

ALMOST 2,000 ENTERPRISES AND ORGANIZATIONS were involved in one way or another with the preparation of the Soviet landing expedition to the Moon. Two years—from 1966 to the beginning of 1969—had become the most intense period in this program, and despite the avalanche of problems, the people involved remained optimistic. The successes of the Vostoks and Voskhods, the entry into service of one combat missile after another, the operation of the Molniya communications satellites, and the automatic docking of the Soyuzes inspired hope for success.

Everything we had tackled under Korolev had panned out. But he had been there when things had panned out. How would it be now without him and his efforts? In 1966, Mozzhorin had predicted the beginning of flight-developmental testing no earlier than 1969. It really did begin in 1969. The Americans spent three and a half years on flight-developmental testing (before the first landing on the Moon) if you consider the first flight of the Saturn IB carrying the unmanned model of the main Apollo vehicle as the beginning of testing. If we had come up with a more realistic schedule in 1966, we should have set the deadline for accomplishing the mission in 1972!

I sensed in myself and realized in my comrades that in the general breakdown of our time and attention, the N1-L3 was not our top priority. The 7K-OK and 7K-L1, the Molniyas, the R-9, and solid-propellant RT-2s had flown. Each flight brought new worries. An event such as the death of Komarov had a decelerating effect on the N1-L3 program, if only because the management of TsKBEM and many of the subcontracting organizations cut themselves completely off from N1-L3 project issues for months. Myriad, various smaller headaches also ripped us away from the lunar program. Incidents that individually received a minimum of attention combined into a stream capable of disrupting the most realistic planning. And nevertheless, the scope of operations over the entire front began to bring visible results.

Hills and valleys were few and far between in the topography of the Tyuratam steppe. Site No. 2 and its hotels rose up barely perceptibly over the surrounding countryside. Old-timers knew that if you looked from the top stories of buildings, all you could see for dozens of kilometers to the northwest was bare desert steppe. In 1964, despite the "hue and cry" about insufficient funding, this desert was converted into a colossal construction site. By 1967, hundreds of permanent structures had sprouted up. The enormous assembly factory building, which we called the big MIK and a few smart alecks called the "big barn," was the centerpiece of the industrial landscape. Crowded all around it were all kinds of entry gates, transformer sheds, and warehouses. There were paved roads and railway lines. In the west, a large residential town of five-story buildings went up. Insulated water lines stretched along the roadways and, to the north, high-voltage power transmission towers advanced toward the launch complexes. There, the launch site teemed with its own construction activity. Around the clock, dump trucks traveled over the dusty steppe roads and motorized cranes and heavy hauling equipment crept along. In 1967, engineering equipment was installed in the big MIK and production activity began. Staff workers and engineers in white shop coats replaced the dusty construction workers.

THE LARGEST-SCALE EXPERIMENTAL WORK BEING DONE at that time was the experimental integrated developmental testing of the propulsion systems. At NII-229, Gleb Tabakov, whose face had grown markedly drawn from the sheer volume of work that fell upon him, not only had to manage the firing tests of the propulsion systems, but also had to set up the manufacture of the second- and third-stage rocket blocks. Because the N-1 launch vehicle stages couldn't be transported, the tanks of the second and third stages, which had been stipulated for firing rig tests, were welded on the grounds of NII-229. The Progress Factory set up its production there.

The firing rig tests took place in the specially retrofitted "facility No. 2," which until then had served as the firing rig for tests on the *Semyorka*. EU-15 was the experimental unit that simulated Block B, the second stage. When its eight engines were started up, a total thrust of 1,200 tons was generated.

It wasn't until 23 June 1968 that the first firing took place. This was the most powerful firing test that the rig and the surrounding environment had experienced since the *Novostroyka* facility had begun operation in 1948. Unit EU-16, which also held four engines, simulated the third stage—Block V. This made it possible to conduct three firing tests by early 1969. Block A with its 30 engines remained untested on the ground. Firing rig tests on individual engines under the supervision of Nikolay Kuznetsov at OKB-276 were supposed to prove the reliability of the first stage.

Mishin could not conceal his pleasure over the fact that once upon a time he had persuaded Korolev to give Nikolay Kuznetsov the requirements for the unique parameters to perfect the liquid-propellant rocket engine. Indeed, compared with the parameters of the Saturn V oxygen-kerosene engines, the NK-15 engines of the N-1 first stage had very high indices. The specific impulse—the main characteristic of a liquid-propellant rocket engine—was 294 seconds for the NK-15 on the ground and 331 seconds at high altitudes. The Saturn V first-stage engines had a specific impulse of 266 seconds on the ground and 304 seconds in space. To achieve these indices, Kuznetsov had to bring the pressure in the combustion chamber to 150 atmospheres. The Saturn V F-1 engines had just 70 atmospheres of pressure in the combustion chamber.

OKB-276 was considered one of the nation's leading design bureaus for the development of turbojet aircraft engines. Nikolay Kuznetsov and his specialists did not think that it would be particularly difficult for such a highly quali-fied staff to develop these relatively simply designed "pots," which is what the liquid-propellant rocket engines seemed like. However, life showed that the main reasons why unreliable engines appeared on the first N-1s were a complete lack of design experience and production discipline for liquid-propellant rocket engines, no experimental facilities, and, above all, no firing rigs.

Mishin sent our engine specialists Raykov, Yershov, and Khaspekov on temporary assignment [to OKB-276] in Kuybyshev to provide continuous supervision, monitoring, and assistance. Raykov—my neighbor in building No. 5 on Academician Korolev Street—told me when he was in Moscow that in the new engines it was very difficult to achieve stable combustion in the combustion chambers. At such a high pressure they needed to find a way to get the oscillation energy out of the chamber. They already understood this at OKB-276. The greatest difficulties showed up where they didn't expect them—in the turbopump assembly. It would seem that, of all places, in the turbojet OKB it would be easier to deal with a turbine and pumps than with a combustion chamber, injector assemblies, and burnt-through nozzles.[14] Sometimes they observed instantaneous flame erosions of the oxygen pump that could not have been foreseen using any measurement techniques. The flame erosion process lasted less than one-hundredth of a second from the moment it began until the engine was completely destroyed. It was not as necessary to have methods for the early warning of a defect as it was to preclude the very possibility of this phenomenon. An engine explosion in flight inevitably would lead to destruction in the immediate surroundings. An armor shield could not be installed in the aft section.

"Your KORD isn't likely to help there," Raykov told me. "Your boys have installed a KORD device on Kuznetsov's rigs, and it often comes to the rescue, but it can't save engines from explosions like these."

"Along with military acceptance," explained Raykov, "we are obliged to accept engines using the KONRID" system, which has been approved by Mishin and Kuznetsov and coordinated with military acceptance.[15] Using this system, engines are issued in batches of six. From each batch, a military inspector selects two engines for firing tests. If they pass the tests, then the other four engines from this batch are shipped off for assembly in rocket blocks without any firing tests. The engines are strictly for one-time usage. After firing

---

14. OKB-276's primary work profile was to design and manufacture turbojet engines for Soviet civilian and military jets.

15. KONRID—*Sistemoy kontrolya rabotosposobnosti dvigateley* (Engine Performance Monitoring System).

tests on such an engine, it is no longer fit to be installed on a rocket. This is the fundamental distinction between Kuznetsov's engines and the Americans'. Each rocket engine installed on the Saturn has previously undergone three firing tests without overhaul.

"Who can guarantee," I asked, "that there isn't some technological defect lurking in those four engines that will manifest itself only under the conditions of a real firing mode with all its vibrations, temperatures, mechanical and acoustical loads, and other delights that rockets have to offer?"

"That is precisely the danger of such a system, that there is no absolute guarantee. I argued that to Mishin, but for the time being he could recommend only making the selection more rigorous. We need to have batches of eight engines and select four of them for firing tests," answered Raykov.

"That means," Raykov continued, "in order to put 30 engines plus 8 plus 4 on the rocket—42 in all—we need to manufacture, test-fire, and then throw out another 42 engines? According to the resolution for LKI [flight-developmental testing], we're supposed to use up 12 rockets. So the series production factory is supposed to manufacture around 500 flight engines. So we'll be left with engines, but we'll lose the shirts off our backs and any other accessories!

"We've already persuaded Kuznetsov's boys in Kuybyshev, on the sly for the time being, to urgently begin modifying the engine so that it can be used multiple times, so that it will endure at least three or four runs without overhaul. But this won't happen soon—it will take a couple of years."

"And in the meantime?"

"In the meantime we'll be carrying on using the KONRID method. The latest hypothesis for the sudden explosions, which they speak about only in a whisper, is a shifting of the oxygen pump rotor. Under large loads, off-nominal axial and radial shifting greater than the gap between the rotor and the housing is possible. In an atmosphere of pure oxygen, all it takes is for the rotor to scrape against the housing and an explosion is guaranteed."

"But perhaps everything is much simpler. What if there is dirt or 'foreign objects' in the tanks on the firing rig—this would also cause explosions."

"We tested that. We intentionally threw metallic shavings and even nuts (which supposedly could turn up in the tanks) into the turbopump assembly.[16] And nothing happened! The turbopump assembly swallowed them up without a cough."

---

16. The common Russian abbreviation for turbopump assembly is TNA—*Turbonasosnyy agregat.*

I had this gloomy conversation in 1967 with Raykov, whose eyes were rimmed with the dark circles of fatigue. I was tormenting him with questions in order to find out about the effectiveness of the KORD system. If we were to determine the readiness of the lunar launch vehicle only through the development tests on the propulsion systems, then based on this indicator, by 1968, the N-1 would be five years behind the Saturn V.

Chapter 7
KORD and ATG

Back at the very beginning of the N-1 launch vehicle design process, the need to create a diagnostics system to monitor the operation of the more than 40 engines of the N-1's three stages was obvious. This system differed from the telemetry system monitoring the parameters of the propulsion systems in that not only did it identify the status of this or that parameter, but it also issued a command to the control system to shut down the engine if the parameters it was monitoring exceeded the permissible limits.

The inescapable need to develop the KORD system using our own resources was becoming more and more obvious since all the subcontracting organizations to whom we had offered this project immediately understood the degree of responsibility it involved, its labor intensity, and the lack of prospects in terms of any credit for a job well done. After many hours of discussion with very close comrades, we decided to assign conceptual development of the electrical circuitry and its optimizing to Viktor Kuzmin's department and the design implementation and manufacturing application to Ivan Zverev's department. A VPK decision assigned the series production of KORD system electronics to the Zagorsk Optical-Mechanical Factory (ZOMZ) using our technical documentation.[1]

After studying the structure of Nikolay Kuznetsov's equipment, our electronics engineers decided that they were fully capable of rescuing a propulsion system from a fire, explosion, and other disasters if the engine specialists concisely formulated the criteria for the pre-emergency state. After insistent appeals from Korolev, Chief Designer Kuznetsov finally specified which engine parameter deviations would cause the KORD system to respond. In the process of this work, Kuznetsov and his specialists changed both the list of parameters that were to be monitored and the critical values that would prompt the KORD system to transmit the engine shutdown command to the control system.

---

1. ZOMZ—*Zagorskiy optiko-mekhanicheskiy zavod.*

Initially, four parameters were selected for diagnostic control of the engines of the first flight model of the N-1 launch vehicle: the temperature of the gas downstream from the turbopump turbine, the pressure pulsation in the gas generator, the rotation speed of the main shaft of the turbopump, and the pressure in the combustion chamber. When these parameters exceeded the limits set by the engine specialists, the KORD system would issue a command prompting the control system, based on its own algorithm, to completely shut down the suspect engine.

Each of the 42 engines had its own monitoring equipment consisting of primary sensors, an electronic block of amplifiers, a communication line, and a system control block linked with the engine control automatics system. The primary sensors—converters of physical values into electrical signals— measured the critical parameters. Thus, for example, a triple-redundant membrane-type contact sensor was especially developed to monitor pressure. For other control channels, they developed generator-type sensors: piezo-electric transducers in the pressure pulsations channel, induction sensors in the rotational speed channel, and rapid-response thermocouples in the temperature channel.

The amplifier/converter block performed the general coordination and conversion of measurements into commands. This was a rather complex electronic instrument made up of 1,600 elements. Various organizations developed all of the sensors from 1962 through 1963, and our engineers debugged them on firing rigs during tests of the first-, second-, and third-stage engines.

The mandatory and most stringent requirement for an emergency system is that it must be on the lookout for and respond only to an emergency flag. Issuing a false signal in flight could cause a healthy engine to be shut down, and for the first stage, a second, diametrically opposite engine as well.

The N-1 launch vehicle had a 25 percent margin in terms of thrust-to-weight ratio. This allowed two pairs of liquid-propellant rocket engines to malfunction even during liftoff. After receiving an engine failure signal, the control system was supposed to augment the power of the working engines and increase the total operating time of the first stage. On the second stage, when emergency signals were received, no more than two engines could be shut down; and on the third stage, one.

The most difficult problem during the development testing of the system was protecting the KORD system against interference. During tests at the engineering facility in the big MIK, interference—voltage up to 15 volts at a frequency of 1,000 Hertz—was detected on the system's power buses. This dangerous interference came from the rocket's main electric power source—the special turbo generator. To shield against this interference we introduced a block of capacitors, which bypassed the source and made sure that the interference was reduced to 1 volt. We relaxed too early—1,000 Hertz soon came back to haunt us under "aggravating circumstances."

Subsequent events showed that much of what had happened during the first flight could have been discovered if there had been a full-scale firing rig to test the first stage with the nominal cable network and nominal power sources and control system.

DURING PREVIOUS PROJECTS involving the development of rocket systems and spacecraft, Korolev had always encouraged business contacts between managers strengthened by personal long-lasting friendship. When Pilyugin or I was asked to resolve something related to the integration of propulsion systems with control systems and actuators, we easily came to terms with Glushko, Kosberg, Isayev, or their specialists. We quickly found common ground, and then for the sake of "formality" we filled out the appropriate protocols.

The deputies of all the chief designers were on familiar "*ty*" terms with one another, and in difficult situations they made arrangements among themselves about how best to "handle" one chief designer or another for the quick acceptance of a decision that they had coordinated.[2]

Nikolay Kuznetsov and his engine experts, who had become part of our cooperative network, were new to us. Moved by the desire to bring us together, Korolev invited his closest deputies—Mishin, Bushuyev, Okhapkin, and me—over to the "Korolev cottage" on 3rd Ostankinskaya Street. We were sure that we were in for more shoptalk. But it turned out that it was Nina Ivanovna who was hosting us rather than S. P., and the main guests of this companionable dinner were Mr. and Mrs. Kuznetsov. We arrived without our wives, and Nina Ivanovna realized the gaffe that S. P. had committed, but it was too late to correct his mistake.

At the dinner table, S. P. tried in every way possible to sustain the dying conversations about culinary achievements, the latest movies (which hardly anyone had seen), the theaters that almost none of us had visited, the weather, and mushrooms. No matter how hard the mistress of the house tried, all one had to do was mention rocket engine matters and the conversation livened up. Kuznetsov said something about the construction of firing rigs away from his factory; Mishin extolled the one-of-a-kind engine parameters used for the development; I waited for a convenient moment to talk about the omnipotence of the KORD system, which was capable of saving this one-of-a-kind

---

2. The Russian language has two different ways to express the second-person singular: *vy* for formal or unfamiliar relationships, and *ty* for informal, familiar relationships.

engine; and Bushuyev diplomatically attempted to switch the conversation to Kuznetsov's latest achievements in the development of aircraft turbojet engines.

On our way home Okhapkin was the first to speak his mind: "S. P. arranged this dinner to bring us together with Kuznetsov. He feels that after the rift with Glushko a void has formed in our personal contacts with the engine corporation and he understands that if worse comes to worst, we can weld our own tanks and rivet the shell, but the engines will determine everything."

Bushuyev agreed and added: "But Chertok would have been better off keeping his mouth shut about his KORD. He hinted too soon about the inevitability of engine failures."

"Time will tell," I said.

WHILE THE KORD SYSTEM WAS BEING DEBUGGED and put through test runs on the rigs in Kuybyshev, many changes were introduced to it. The KORD system was sometimes forgiven for unauthorized shutdowns, but in general the engine experts had faith in it.

Kalashnikov, Kuzmin, and Kunavin came to me with disturbing news. They had just received a phone call from Kuybyshev and were told that an explosion had taken place on the rig and the engine was destroyed. So, the KORD system was unable to prevent this event. Raykov reported on the incident to Mishin, convincing him that the engines had a defect that could lead to destruction so rapidly that the KORD system wouldn't even have time to register the parameters' deviation from the norm.

In early 1967, by decision of the VPK, an interdepartmental commission was created to determine the reliability of the engines, to make the decision to start up their series production, and to clear them for installation on the first flight models of the rocket. Deputy Chief Valerian Levin of the P. I. Baranov Central Institute of Aviation Engine Building (TsIAM) headed the commission, and Glushko was one of its members.[3] It seemed that the commission could give an objective assessment of the new engines, which had such unique performance characteristics for that time. As Raykov recounted to me, at one of the commission sessions Glushko spoke out to the effect that no diagnostics and monitoring system was capable of healing "rotten engines."

Actually, the KORD system couldn't save a rocket from the split-second process of an engine explosion. It also had its own flaws that we discovered too late. One of them is the previously mentioned sensitivity to spurious electrical

---

3. TsIAM—*Tsentralnyy institut aviatsionnogo motorostroyeniya imeni P. I. Baranova.*

pickup at a frequency of 1,000 Hertz, which from time to time exceeded the emergency signal in the KORD system.

"You and Andronik [Iosifyan] thought up this primary alternating current source instead of the reliable storage batteries that we've been flying with all our lives. And now we are going to take the blame," the testers reproached me. These reproaches were justified.

Here I must tell about one more unique development that we undertook solely for the sake of the N-1. Recalling my prewar research on an alternating current system for heavy bombers, back in 1960 I figured how much mass we could save on current sources and power cables if we did away with traditional storage batteries and installed a special generator driven by one of the turbopump assemblies of the main liquid-propellant rocket engines.

In order to go anywhere with this proposal I needed Pilyugin's consent and support. The main electric power consumer on board a heavy launch vehicle was the control system, and its chief designer, Pilyugin, would have to do away with conventional power sources. I was almost certain that Pilyugin would have a negative attitude—why should he take on yet another "headache" with a system in which, as it is, everything needed to be done from scratch? First off, I presented my proposals to Georgiy Priss, who was considered the head guru of on-board electrical complex circuitry at NIIAP, and to Serafima Kurkova, who managed the laboratory for on-board power source systems at NIIAP.

To my surprise and great pleasure, they had arrived at similar ideas on their own. There was no argument over authority, especially since the only organization that could be responsible for the new electric power system was VNIIEM. It didn't take long to persuade Andronik Iosifyan to take on the task of developing the powerful alternating current power source. Right off the bat, Andronik invited his deputy for science matters, Nikolay Sheremetyevskiy, and Yevgeniy Meyerovich, Naum Alper, and Arkadiy Platonov, people with whom I was very familiar from the institute, and assigned the task to accept the proposal and begin work immediately! Working together, OKB-1 and NIIAP would need to determine the parameters and the outputs, select the voltages and the frequency, and figure out how to turn the generator. He decided he needed to have his own drive rather than get mixed up with the engine experts.

Thirty-five years later I admire the enthusiasm of Iosifyan, Sheremetyevskiy, and other VNIIEM specialists—their work was literally at a boil. They quickly rejected the idea of using the turbopump assembly of the main engines. They decided to make an independent autonomous system. After debates and months of calculations, VNIIEM came up with a draft plan, which revealed that the optimal version would be a three-phase on-board turbo generator operating on 60 volts and at a frequency of 1,000 Hertz. The generator turbine must run on various gas components—compressed air, nitrogen, or helium—products available in abundance on board a rocket. Such a source did not require the development of a capricious "ground-to-spacecraft" power transfer system; it was reusable and made it possible to precisely maintain frequency and voltage.

Doubling the supply voltage substantially reduced the mass of the on-board cable network. Creating a one-of-a-kind turbo generator also required a one-of-a-kind turbine. The Saturn Factory, which was headed by Arkhip Lyulka, was located on the bank of the Yauza River, just 10 minutes' drive from my house. When I drove out to see Chief Designer Lyulka—Hero of Socialist Labor, Stalin Prize laureate, and corresponding member of the Academy of Sciences—with a kind and crafty smile, he asked whether I'd come to persuade him to develop a liquid-hydrogen engine for the third stage of the N-1.[4]

"Korolev will do a better job of that than I," was my reply.

"Perhaps you remember how we used to gulp down that *bilimbaikha* in the Urals?" Lyulka asked me.[5]

He clearly wanted to know why I had shown up first thing in the morning, even before I could come out with my explanation. When I explained what had brought me to the office of the esteemed chief designer of aircraft turbojet engines, he was somewhat disappointed. Developing such low-power turbines—that was no problem, but there would be a lot of trouble with them. To fan his interest I talked a lot about reliability, the precision control of the rotation speed, the low mass—but he had already grasped all of this just fine on his own.

"We can make the turbine," Lyulka said. "Just let your boys come up with how you're going to make it turn and you figure out how much and what kind of gas it will take. That's where the problem will be—not in my little wheel."

Lyulka agreed to do this work. And subsequently, beginning in 1962, VNIIEM developed autonomous turbo generators (ATGs) for the N-1 in very close collaboration with the Saturn Factory.[6] Korolev assigned the OKB-1 engine specialists to develop the assemblies' pneumohydraulic delivery systems, compressed gas tanks, heat exchangers, filters, and pneumatic valves. At our OKB-1, Petr Shulgin's department took on these responsibilities. Korolev,

---

4. In the early 1960s, Lyulka's OKB-165 had been contracted to develop a 40-ton-thrust engine (the 11D57) for application on an upper stage of the N-1 rocket.

5. Lyulka is referring to their wartime experience when the NII-1 institute had been evacuated to Bilimbay in the Urals. There, they would cook an unappetizing concoction of brown noodles cooked in boiling water (without any fat), which they named after their new home. Here and later, Lyulka's diction as reproduced by Chertok in his original manuscript is in Ukrainian.

6. ATG—*Avtonomnyy turbogenerator*.

Pilyugin, Iosifyan, and Lyulka solemnly approved the technical specifications for the whole system.

During the development process, the idea of a simple turbo generator became overgrown with pressure regulators, valve blocks, throttles, dual frequency-regulator channels, helium heat exchangers, and an electropneumatic converter of an electrical signal into regulating pressure. Compared to this, a contactless alternating current synchronous generator and direct current generator proved to be the simplest and most reliable devices. Frequency and voltage regulators and the pneumohydraulic mechanisms that surrounded them caused a lot more trouble during test runs than the main issue—the turbine and two electric motors.

The VNIIEM branch in Istrinsk had set up an integrated test stand to test out all the assemblies jointly with the nominal "working fluid" feed system. Each N-1 rocket had two turbo generator sources—one on Block A to supply all the first-stage consumers and a second on Block V for the second and third stages.

At the same time that the on-board turbo generators were being produced, VNIIEM was developing their on-the-ground equivalent, including a block that contained a network frequency converter, transformers, and rectifier units. During the testing process, the ground-based equivalent made it possible, without consuming the on-board reserves of compressed air or helium, to feed 60 and 40 volts of alternating current at a frequency of 1,000 Hertz and 28 volts of direct current on board.

For the development tests alone, the project teams at VNIIEM and Saturn manufactured 22 "air version" turbo drives, which ran for almost 3,000 hours, and 17 "helium version" drives, which ran for 1,000 hours, for a flight time of just 12 minutes! The reliability margin was enormous. The individual turbo drives ran for more than 8,500 flight cycles.

At my request, one of the lead developers of the system at VNIIEM, Vladimir Averbukh, compiled a briefing paper in which he listed the primary individuals involved in the system's development—developmental engineers and testers. VNIIEM alone had more than 90 of these individuals working there, not counting the production workers and machine operators—the on-the-spot manufacturers of assemblies "in metal." Not counting the production engineers, Lyulka had 15 engineer specialists at the Saturn Factory who were the hands-on creators of the air-helium turbo drive system. If you add to this list the people who worked at NIIAP on the electric power supply system (at TsKBEM on the rocket's design and pneumohydraulic system, telemetry, and test documentation) plus the military acceptance staff in all the organizations and firing range specialists assigned solely to this project, then it turns out that the implementation of a seemingly simple idea required the self-sacrificing creative work of more than 200 specialists. Once again, this does not count the "working class," which eventually cranked out the finished products.

My reason for dwelling in such detail on this instance was certainly not to boast about my part in the project. The experience of the subsequent flight tests on this system confirmed its reliability. One can consider this as the achievement of each individual participant in the development. But, first and foremost, this was a victory for VNIIEM managers Iosifyan and Sheremetyevskiy, who were unyielding in their demands for ground testing and conducted it on the proper scale, despite cries from higher up the chain of command—from the offices of the ministries and VPK—about missed deadlines.

Chapter 8
Once Again We're Ahead of the Whole World

During the last years of Korolev's life we could not foresee, overburdened as we were with a myriad of routine technical and organizational tasks, which of our undertakings would attain further development and which projects that seemed highly promising would prove to be dead ends. Forty years have passed. Given today's pace of scientific and technical progress, that is a considerable period of time.

Practically all airplanes, rockets, and spacecraft developed in the 1960s in the USSR and U.S. have long since become obsolete and removed from production. But there are also exceptions. The R-7 and Proton launch vehicles, the Soyuz spacecraft, and Molniya communications satellites are still alive in the world of cosmonautics. The American Atlas and Titan launch vehicles, retaining the basic designs of the 1950s and 1960s, continued to operate until the first years of the 21st century. After Korolev, the *Semyorka* (R-7) launch vehicle, the Soyuz spacecraft, and the Molniya communications satellite underwent numerous updates. This process is natural for any article of hardware. Nevertheless, the basic parameters, the look, and even the names remained the same.

One of the parameters determining the longevity of any rocket-space system is reliability. Despite obsolescence, it is this high degree of reliability up until the early 21st century that ensured the utilization of the *Semyorka* and Soyuzes.

Up until the end of the 20th century, the world had only two space transport systems capable of inserting a human being into space—our *Semyorka*, in conjunction with the Soyuz, and the American Space Shuttle. In 2003, China disrupted the American-Russian monopoly in piloted space systems for the first time. In October 2003, from its cosmodrome, China inserted a man into space in a Chinese spacecraft on a Chinese launch vehicle. Various mass media sources suggested that the Chinese Shenzhou spacecraft was very similar to the Russian Soyuz vehicle. Indeed, the Chinese had studied our Soyuz very well, but this in no way detracts from their own achievements. Our automakers have every opportunity to study the best automobiles in the world down to the tiniest detail. But for many decades they simply have not managed to reproduce anything even approaching contemporary Mercedes or Toyota models.

The history of the Soyuz series is rich with examples of successful engineering designs and just as many mistakes, which sometimes had tragic results. In this respect, it is quite instructive for all creators of space technology.

In 1966, KOROLEV's OKB-1 underwent a structural reorganization. We were given a new name—Central Design Bureau of Experimental Machine Building (TsKBEM). Minister Sergey Afanasyev approved the structure of TsKBEM, the main elements of which were issue-related "complexes" that combined a group of departments. A deputy chief designer was in charge of each complex. A ministerial order appointed Sergey Osipovich Okhapkin first deputy.[1] By early 1968, Okhapkin was up to his neck in N-1 issues—he had to be involved in the design of rocket stages, structural tests on the launch vehicle model, materials selection, aerodynamics, and a plethora of miscellaneous everyday matters. If a director is in charge of more than 1,000 individuals, a good half of whom are responsible for pending technical documentation, then everyday matters don't leave him time for the in-depth understanding of the strategic objectives of space politics.

After the edifying conversation that the minister held on 23 January 1968, Mishin fell ill for a short while.[2] His first deputy, Okhapkin, recognizing his responsibility, set aside the hundreds of drawings on Whatman paper and tracing paper awaiting his review, and the pile of correspondence, and invited Konstantin Bushuyev, Yakov Tregub, Viktor Klyucharev (who had been named factory director—in 1966, Roman Anisimovich [Turkov] retired), and me to come see him.[3] Okhapkin reminded us of the minister's observation that we were in the position of a rabbit facing a boa constrictor.

"Afanasyev saw the American space program as the boa constrictor," said Okhapkin. "But we have our own domestic, albeit smaller 'boas'—7K-OK, 7K-L1, N1-L3, and military-purpose RT-2s. If we have been unable up until now to cope with any one of them without missing deadlines by one or two years, then there's no way we can deal with four. Let's put our heads together and see how we can deal with these 'little boas'."

I can't reconstruct everything that we said back then word for word, but the gist was that our nation did not have a high-level managerial organization that could rationally select the most urgent tasks and distribute them among

---

1. A "first deputy" was the person ranked first among the deputies.

2. For more about the minister's "conversation" on 23 January 1968, see Chertok, *Rockets and People, Vol. III,* pp. 686–695.

3. The factory is a reference to the experimental production facility attached to TsKBEM that was colocated with the main design bureau.

Chelomey, Yangel, aviation, and us. There was a time when Khrushchev had personally convened the chiefs and determined who should do what, but even he could not bring peace between Korolev and Glushko, who had refused to develop the oxygen-kerosene engine for the N-1 rocket.

After sitting together an entire evening, we simply couldn't come up with any redeeming ideas. However, after calmly discussing the due dates for each project and the actual volume of work necessary for their successful implementation, we once again proved to one another their complete irreconcilability.

Each of us thought to himself: what would Korolev have done in this situation? He would have certainly come up with something, but what? It is amazing that even our awareness of impending failure did not take away our optimism. Perhaps the source of this optimism was precisely the vast amount of assignments of "critical government importance" that we had been saddled with. Ultimately, out of all the critical piloted space programs, history itself selected only two: Soyuzes and orbital stations. But at that time, in 1968, we didn't know this yet and didn't foresee that the Soyuzes would make up a transport system without which the orbital stations would not be able to exist. An enormous amount of work was invested in developing reliable Soyuzes. We worked on these spacecraft at the same time we were conducting operations on the L1 and N1-L3 lunar programs.

On 4 April 1968, the Americans launched an orbital vehicle, the sixth Apollo spacecraft, into high elliptical orbit on a Saturn V rocket. The goal was to check out the rocket-spacecraft system during orbital insertion, after acceleration to escape velocity, before entry into the atmosphere, and during landing.[4] Descriptions and photographs of the American Mission Control Center in Houston appeared in the press. Judging by the enormous presence of electronic computer technology and automatic data-processing and display facilities, they had gotten so far ahead of us that our comment about our own Center for Deep Space Communications in Yevpatoriya was: "It's the Stone Age, and we are cavemen admiring our cave drawings."

From the literature that we could obtain, which was available to the whole world but was "for official use only" for us, we knew that the American operators and flight control directors sat in an enormous hall, in comfortable seats, with each individual at an electronic monitor displaying essential data in real time. At any moment the flight director could request that any specialist tell him what data is displayed on his screen, listen to his report, and study the

---

4. This was the AS-502 launch (also known as *Apollo 6*). There were a number of anomalies on the mission, although none were serious enough to jeopardize the primary goals of the flight.

problem without creating a ruckus. In contrast, when we were controlling a flight, we sat on creaky chairs facing a wall covered with charts, grabbing for various telephone receivers, and we still made correct decisions.

We were motivated far more effectively by American achievements—the 10 successful piloted Gemini flights, American public announcements about their rendezvous and docking system tests scheduled for late 1968, and a piloted circumlunar flight—rather than being constantly urged on by "the brass."

The automatic docking of unpiloted vehicles *Kosmos-186* and *Kosmos-188*, which we had dedicated to the 50th anniversary of the October Revolution, was not a full-fledged gift.[5] Few knew about that. Annoying mechanical negligence during assembly at the engineering facility (TP) prevented complete retraction and mating of the electrical connectors of the two vehicles.[6] Adding insult to injury, one of the vehicles was destroyed by the emergency destruction system. Komarov's ashes pounded in our hearts and beseeched us: "Spare no effort in testing reliability!"[7]

Within our staff there were no arguments about whether we needed to repeat the experimental docking of two unpiloted 7K-OK vehicles, solidly executing the four phases—automatic rendezvous, docking, guided descent, and soft landing. There had not yet been any serious discussion of the program of subsequent operations. When disagreements cropped up with the Air Force representatives concerning the makeup of the future crews, I avoided arguments and said: "First, let's achieve reliability in the unpiloted mode, and then we'll come to an agreement."

At the engineering facility, work continued on the preparation of vehicles 7K-OK No. 7 and No. 8 and the latest Zond L1 No. 6 throughout February and March 1968. In volume three of my book *Rockets and People: Hot Days of the Cold War*, I mentioned that in 1968, my comrades and I had to celebrate Cosmonautics Day in the air en route from Moscow to the Crimea, and then in Yevpatoriya at NIP-16, the control center at that time, which was officially called the Center for Deep Space Communications. Based on the number of portraits and the mood, 12 April at NIP-16 had turned into a memorial day for Gagarin. Just a month ago he had been here with us for the last time.

The launch of the rocket carrying the active vehicle, 7K-OK No. 8, was scheduled for 1300 hours on 14 April. The next day, 15 April, they planned

---

5. See Chertok, *Rockets and People, Vol. III*, Chapter 22.

6. The common Russian abbreviation for the facility where the rocket and payload undergoes prelaunch processing is TP—*Tekhnicheskiy positsiya* (literally "technical station" or more generally "engineering facility").

7. The "ashes pounding in our hearts" is a quote from *The Legend of Thyl Ulenspiegel and Lamme Goedzak*, an 1867 novel by the Belgian novelist Charles De Coster (1827–1879).

to launch the passive vehicle, 7K-OK No. 7. The precise liftoff time of the passive vehicle was determined based on the trajectory parameters of the active vehicle. An analysis of the various nominal and off-nominal situations, debates about documentation and whether it conformed to what had actually been done, and a readiness check of all the flight control groups confirmed that "everything should pan out as long as they don't shove some rag between the vehicles' docking interfaces again." That was how the guys in Yevpatoriya bad-mouthed the assembly workers who had prepared the preceding pair of vehicles.

At exactly 1300 hours on 14 April, 7K-OK No. 8 lifted off. Communication with the cosmodrome was excellent. We received the same running commentary that was taking place in the bunker. After 530.9 seconds, spacecraft No. 8 entered Earth orbit. The first reports were soothing: everything that should have deployed, deployed.

At 1430 hours during the second orbit, active control from our center began. We had already been informed from Moscow that instead of the TASS report that had been prepared for publication announcing the launch of an automated Soyuz, they were providing low-key information about the latest launch of *Kosmos-212*.

During the second orbit, all 10 ground tracking stations reported good telemetry reception. Eight stations measured orbital parameters. GOGU Chief Pavel Agadzhanov polled each of the stations in succession.[8] They all reported the normal operation of all systems. During the third orbit, spacecraft No. 8 began normal spinning on the Sun. For the first time in seven Soyuz launches, we began to hope that everything would go according to the program despite the fact that, just to be on the safe side, even when the mission was a success, the Soyuzes would be called Kosmoses with the latest numbers attached.

At 1630 hours, at the recommendation of the ballistics specialists, the operational and technical management (OTR) made the decision to perform an orbital correction maneuver using the approach and correction engine unit (SKDU) to reduce the perigee altitude.[9] Performing orbital correction maneuvers was also a way to carry out general checkout procedures for all the on-board motion control systems.

---

8. GOGU—*Glavnaya operativnaya gruppa upravleniya* (Main Operations Control Group)—was the flight control team for Soviet piloted missions.

9. OTR—*Operativno-tekhnicheskoye rukovodstvo*; SKDU—*Sblizhayushche-korrektiruyushchaya dvigatelnaya ustanovka*. The SKDU was the main propulsion system of the Soyuz, consisting of a primary engine (the S5.60) and a backup engine (the S5.35). The system was designed by KB Khimmash under Chief Designer Aleksey Isayev.

Beginning with vehicle No. 7, all Soyuzes had 76K infrared vertical sensors installed on them. We should have done this on the very first vehicle. Our over-estimation of the infallibility of the ionic system prevented us from using such a natural, tried-and-true design on the *Zenit* [reconnaissance satellite] series.

The correction maneuver during the fifth orbit went as calculated. The apogee was increased by 6 kilometers, while the perigee was reduced by 22 kilometers. We had now reached the point where we needed to send a telegram to the cosmodrome with the official report granting clearance for the launch of the second vehicle.

On the morning of 15 April, after "silent" orbits, we were convinced that everything was okay on board. When we received the T-minus-2-hours alert from the cosmodrome, something pulled me into the room of the analysis group.

"If everything is going well, it means we missed something." I had only just recalled this law of rocket-space launches when it made itself apparent. I was hoping to receive assurances from Irina Yablokova, a specialist on storage battery power sources, that the obvious overcharging of the silver-zinc buffer batteries with a large amount of "solar current" during the "silent" orbits would not require a report to the State Commission. All of Boris Rauschenbach's available staffers, headed by Lev Zvorykin, were crowded together in the analysis group room arguing and gesticulating. Fretting, he began to explain that they had just discovered a serious glitch. Twice during solar inertial spin mode, the effectiveness of the attitude-control engines (DO) for roll control had been 10 times lower than the design value.[10] Perhaps the culprit was the main instrument of the attitude-control system—the ignition assembly for the approach and attitude-control engines (BV DPO), which issues the commands to the engines controlling the rendezvous process?[11] If that were the case, we were in danger of messing up the upcoming rendezvous. Zvorykin was so perplexed by this discovery that he proposed that I ask the State Commission to postpone the launch of No. 7 for 24 hours.[12] I was exasperated: "It's T minus 2 hours at the launch site! They've finished fueling the launch vehicle. Do you have any idea what you are saying? Hold the rocket for 24 hours with tanks full of oxygen?!"

---

10. DO—*Dvigatel orientatsii.*

11. BV DPO—*Blok vklyucheniya dvigateley prichalivaniya i orientatsii.* The basic 7K-OK Soyuz spacecraft's DPO (approach and attitude-control engines) were used for attitude control during rendezvous and docking. The system comprised 14 engines for docking and orientation (10 kilograms thrust) and eight for orientation (1 to 1.5 kilograms thrust).

12. State Commissions were ad hoc operational bodies that made all final decisions during flight testing of spacecraft and Soviet weapons systems. The Soviet government would appoint senior designers, military officers, and industry representatives to serve on a particular State Commission for every new weapons system (including spacecraft). They were usually dissolved after the testing regime was concluded.

Before reporting to Mishin at the cosmodrome, I tried to track down Rauschenbach and Legostayev over the high-frequency communication line. They hadn't flown anywhere and were following events from Podlipki. Zvorykin and his junior associate Pimenov began to explain themselves in an unbearably long conversation with Legostayev over the high-frequency line, during which the latter, breaking away from the phone, consulted with other on-duty analysts. I lost patience, snatched the receiver, and demanded an official and immediate statement from Rauschenbach authorizing the launch.

The analysts on the other end of the line debated and wavered. At this point I did not care about the overcharged batteries anymore. After running back to the control room, I barely had time to tell Agadzhanov about what had happened, and I found Feoktistov on the direct communication line at the command post at Site No. 2. After explaining the situation to him, I asked him to brief Mishin.[13] Feoktistov said that everyone was at the launch site; he promised to drive out to the "apron" and to find Mishin, but he for one thought that it was unacceptable to postpone the launch by 24 hours!

"These Rauschenbachers are always skeptical of something," concluded Feoktistov, "and no one will understand you."

Ten minutes later Yurasov was calling from the bunker. He immediately understood our misgivings.

"I'm going to find Vasiliy Pavlovich right now and bring him here," he said.

Five minutes later an aggravated Mishin was on the line. Technically, he had acted properly.

"Where is GOGU Chief Agadzhanov?" I handed the receiver to Agadzhanov.

Mishin demanded: "We're supposed to announce T minus 1 hour. I'm giving everyone 10 minutes. Either you send us a ZAS-telegram confirming readiness for launch or forbid us flat out and provide reasons.[14] In any event, you and Chertok will bear the responsibility."

Agadzhanov took the secret notepad for the encrypted communications system telegram and wrote the text confirming the readiness of the entire KIK (Command and Measurement Complex) and vehicle No. 8 to work with vehicle No. 7. He prepared the decoding of signatures and began polling the review team. All members were "in favor" except for Zvorykin, Dubov, and Pimenov.

---

13. Those responsible for this mission were located in three different places: Chertok and Agadzhanov were at NIP-16 at Yevpatoriya in Crimea; Mishin and Feoktistov were at Site No. 2 at the launch range at Tyuratam; and Rauschenbach and Legostayev were back at OKB-1 in Podlipki.

14. In Soviet times, Russians used the abbreviation ZAS-telegram—*Zakrytaya apparatura svyazi-telegram* (encrypted communications system telegram) as shorthand for encrypted telegrams.

I asked Mishin to give us 10 more minutes. He gave us 2. I used up 3 just determining that Rauschenbach and Legostayev were still wavering. These were moments when our people in Tyuratam, Yevpatoriya, and Podlipki had no time left for technical analysis of the situation and we needed to either immediately make a risky decision or abort the program. Agadzhanov handed me the notepad, which already contained nine signatures. I signed, and the telegram [approving the launch] was sent off then and there.

Kerim Kerimov, the chairman of the State Commission, called up Agadzhanov from the bunker: "Where have you been? We're announcing T minus 30 minutes. Why couldn't you get to the bottom of this? You have all the specialists over there. What kind of a situation are you putting me and the entire State Commission in?"

What could Agadzhanov say in his defense? The State Commission chairman was right. But now the telegram had been sent—the decision had been made.

Agadzhanov handed me the telephone and Kerimov repeated the very same questions to me. After hanging up, I tried to cheer up everyone who was standing around waiting for feedback: " 'Cavemen' who didn't have all the information at their disposal made correct decisions guided by their innate instincts."

After receiving instructional compliments from the firing range, Agadzhanov and I felt the urgent need to let off some steam, and right then and there we convened the operational and technical management for a public excoriation of Kravets and Zvorykin, the leaders of the analysis group.

At T minus 5 minutes, Kerimov requested that I be on the line at all times and report to him personally about the process after insertion, and he would relay my reports to everyone in the bunker.

At 1234 hours, we heard the "Liftoff" announcement. After what was now the standard 530 seconds for insertion came the announcement of entry into orbit, and then after 20 seconds of intense anticipation came the soothing message: "All elements have deployed." I reported to Kerimov that the *Igla* was activated on the active vehicle and was ready to work with the passive one.[15] Now all hope was on information from "35," which was the code name used in voice communications for NIP-15 in Ussuriysk.[16]

The well-being of dozens of people packed into the bunker at the cosmodrome's Site No. 1 and in the control room in Yevpatoriya completely depended on the speed with which the telemetry specialists in Ussuriysk could sort out

---

15. *Igla* was the name of the rendezvous radar system of the 7K-OK Soyuz spacecraft.

16. Ussuriysk, the location of the NIP-15 tracking station, is a city on the eastern seaboard of the Russian landmass, near Vladivostok, just 60 kilometers from the Pacific Ocean.

the information being sent from the two vehicles flying over them. At 1254 hours, Ussuriysk reported that its data indicated that we had radio lock-on and the distance between the vehicles when they left the coverage zone was just 335 meters and the relative approach rate was 2 meters per second. The vehicles left the coverage zone at 1253 hours.

"What a job we're doing!" Colonel Aleksandr Rodin boasted for all the telemetry specialists. "Just 1 minute for decoding, deliberation, and the report!"

Now, somewhere over the ocean for just the second time in the world, the process of rendezvous, final approach, and docking of unpiloted spacecraft was beginning and we had no way of monitoring it. I couldn't shake a feeling of aggravation over the incident caused by Zvorykin's recommendation that we postpone the launch. While we were in suspense awaiting the beginning of communication, I said: "The ballistics specialists have lined up the passive with the active so precisely that they're going to meet up even without the BV DPO." Zvorykin and his comrades hung their heads in silence. They would be the guilty ones no matter what. If the docking took place, they would be a laughingstock for playing it too safe. And if it failed, they would be asked sternly: "What happened there with you guys and why didn't you insist on postponing the launch? Your lack of principles has destroyed a good vehicle."

Yuriy Bykov had supplemented the *Zarya* system on both vehicles with a low-capacity shortwave telemetry line.[17] There was a faint glimmer of hope that the shortwave centers would receive information before the vehicles entered our station's coverage zone. If the three members of the operations and technical management who voted to postpone the launch were right, then the irreversible process of DPO fuel depletion would now occur and the active vehicle, which had appeared in our coverage zone, would only be able to execute a ballistic descent.

Kerimov and Mishin drove over from the bunker to the KP (command post) at Site No. 2 and requested reports: "Why is *Zarya* silent?"[18]

We were pestering the communications operators, although they would scream on their own as soon as *Zarya* detected signs of change in the shortwave signals. But they calmly responded: "No changes in 'parameter two.' Shortwave centers are receiving."

"Parameter two" was the code name of the channel for controlling the electrical connection of the two vehicles' interfaces. If the level jumped from

---

17. Yuriy Sergeyevich Bykov (1916–1970) was chief designer at NII-695 (later MNII Radiosvyazi), which designed the communications systems for Soviet piloted spacecraft. The common abbreviation for shortwave in Russian is KV (*korotkovolnovyy*).

18. KP—*kommandnyy punkt*.

zero to 100 percent, it meant that the vehicles had not only mated mechanically, but that they had actually connected electrically.

"At 1320 hours there are no changes," reported the chief of communications.

And then at 1321 hours, the situation quite clear, unable to restrain his excitement, he shouted over the public address system: "Three shortwave centers—Alma-Ata, Novosibirsk, and Tashkent—have reported: Parameter two—100 percent!"

Someone mumbled a muffled "hoorah," someone sobbed, but for the time being, even blabbermouths fell silent out of superstitious caution.

Two more shortwave centers confirmed: "We have parameter two at 100 percent."

And there on the screen of the jubilant television operators, obscurely through a mesh of interference, one could make out the contours of a stationary spacecraft. This was the hull of the passive vehicle in the field of vision of the active vehicle's television camera. There were applause, embraces, and handshakes. In short—there was universal jubilation. The television operators felt like the main heroes.

Amidst all the noise, the telemetry specialists' report came in confirming complete mechanical and electrical mating. Now the telemetry specialists were the heroes. In the general tumult, nobody remembered those who had developed and debugged the attitude-control, rendezvous, and docking systems. After all, they weren't the ones who had reported the earthshaking success. Let them sort out the recordings and prepare the report about the rendezvous and docking process.

Now everyone needed to quickly grab some lunch. The State Commission would be flying out to us [at Yevpatoriya]. We needed to prepare a detailed report about the rendezvous process before they arrived. I stayed behind so that I could congratulate everyone who had suffered through this experience on the high-frequency communication line in Podlipki. At 2100 hours, the photogenic, smiling "Academy of Sciences research associate" Viktor Pavlovich Legostayev appeared on our television screens. Wielding his pointer at the wall charts, he told the television viewers of the Soviet Union (and the broadcast was being relayed to all the countries of Eastern Europe over "Intervision") how the automatic hard docking of *Kosmos-212* with *Kosmos-213* took place.[19]

For some reason it was sad when, just 4 hours after such a long-awaited and exciting docking, we gave the command to undock and separate the vehicles.

---

19. Intervision was an Eastern European radio and TV broadcasting network established in 1960.

Each assumed its own orbit. Multiple orbits of work lay ahead of each of them to thoroughly check out their systems.

Mishin and Kerimov arrived. The future Soyuz cosmonauts also flew in to Yevpatoriya. Now began mundane, strenuous work with all sorts of tests. The developers of all the systems tried to track down a comment [from the mission transcripts] that, rather than bring yet another State Commission investigation, would prove that it was precisely their system that had conducted itself intelligently; it shouldn't be forgotten in future glamorous reports and stories about the docking.

On 16 April, newspapers published a TASS report that stated: "The second automatic docking is of great importance in space exploration." Measures enhancing the dynamics of the rendezvous process, which our specialists conducted in concert with the developers of *Igla*, proved to be effective. The misgivings of Zvorykin and his friends turned out to be unjustified. Compared with the preceding docking, the process had gone considerably more smoothly. Instead of 28 engine burns to accelerate, brake, and neutralize lateral velocity, in this case we had "just" 14.

On 17 April, discussing our first impressions about the docking processes with Legostayev over the high-frequency communications line, I thanked him and Rauschenbach both on my behalf and that of the State Commission for the substantial improvement of the rendezvous process, and I asked him to pass along our gratitude and congratulations to NII-648 for *Igla*. For my own part I added: "It's terrific that you didn't flinch when it came to the BV DPO." In response came the assurance, "you ain't seen nothing yet." To be on the safe side, he asked that all the BV DPO units that were still on the ground be thoroughly retested.

"Look how much work you've thrown at us. Don't think that you there in Yevpatoriya are the smartest. We're searching too, and maybe soon we'll come up with a way to do without it altogether," relayed Legostayev.

Alas! We weren't able to substantially simplify the BV DPO until the computer came on board. But we had to wait five more years for that!

The vehicles had flown for just 3 hours and 50 minutes in a hard-docked state. These were joyful orbits for everyone, sort of like the "victory laps" that a speed skater takes after winning a race. The difficult prelanding workdays had begun, interrupted by local emergencies. And once again Zvorykin's team stood out.

During the 51st orbit we were supposed to perform a test orbital correction maneuver of vehicle No. 8 in attitude-control mode using the infrared vertical (IKV) and the ionic system followed by solar inertial spin mode.[20] All

---

20. IKV—*Infrakrasnaya vertikal.*

the settings and commands for this mode proceeded normally on board, but the correction engine unit (KDU) failed to start up.[21]

Ten minutes after this first real emergency after 50 successful orbits, Zvorykin appeared, accompanied by his advisers.[22]

"We've got it," they reported. "We've got a device in the unit, in the amplifier of the ionic orientation system, to check the whole circuit. It polls the main circuit and, if it determines it's malfunctioning, it switches the control loop to the second backup circuit. That's how we backed up the ionic system for reliability. After receiving the system poll about the performance of the first ionic orientation circuit, this diagnostic system failed. The reliability monitoring system itself turned out to be unreliable."

"A fundamental rule was broken during the development of these instruments," is how I began my defense to Mishin. "They overlooked the fact that this circuit, which was supposed to determine the reliability of the other circuits, was itself unreliable! This is a conceptual error."

When Zvorykin and I reported to Kerimov after Mishin, Kerimov did not miss the opportunity to take a slight jab at us: "So I've been told that supposedly the Japanese press is writing that the 'second automatic docking is a testament to the superiority of Soviet electronic computer technology'."

It was very annoying. A mere test circuit wouldn't allow the functional primary one to operate. The traditional question followed: "What are we going to do?"

I proposed using manual control. We would replace the future cosmonaut with commands from the ground. We would hold a "circus with acrobatics," using the television services of Bratslavets and Krichevskiy. One of the television cameras was installed so that in attitude-control mode it could look at Earth just like a cosmonaut in the vehicle. Using the position of the horizon in the television camera's field of vision and also making note of Earth's course, we would monitor the position of the vehicle, having excluded the failed ionic system instrument from the readiness loop. After orientation using the infrared vertical and television, we would switch to gyroscopic stabilization. Before descent, we would avail ourselves of the other ionic system for acceleration. For the time being, it was in good working order. As had already been done, we would swing once around 180 degrees and fly "on gyroscopes," monitoring the image on the screen from

---

21. KDU—*Korrektiruyushchaya dvigatelnaya ustanovka*.

22. Chertok uses the abbreviation ChP—*chrezvychaynoye polozheniye* (literally "emergency event")—to denote an emergency.

the ground; we would have first loaded the settings for the calculated time of the firing of the correcting braking engines (KTDU).[23]

During the landing orbits the control room was overflowing with spectators. No one was asked to "clear out." We understood how personal the success and failure of any spacecraft system of the new generation was to each one there.

On 19 April, the active vehicle landed in guided descent mode. The "acrobatics" of the ionic system during acceleration, the orientation using the infrared vertical for pitch and roll, the 180-degree turn according to the previously loaded settings, and the hour-long gyrostabilized flight proceeded normally. We had had heated arguments—full of passion and feeling—over the development of this program, since we had feared going outside the limits of the emergency vehicle destruction "corridor."

When this method of orientation is used, errors in determining the moment to issue commands to begin the descent cycle or braking pulse could lead to significant deviations from the calculated time. In such cases, the APO is triggered. If we were to blow up such a good vehicle, after erring in dozens of settings, we would not be forgiven.

At five o'clock in the morning, Feoktistov and I tracked down Pavel Elyasberg over the high-frequency communications line at the NII-4 ballistics center and asked him to perform one more control calculation of all the descent parameters.[24] Our designated ballistics specialist, Zoya Degtyarenko, was already at NII-4. She came up with someone else from among the TsNIImash descent specialists. By 9 a.m., Elyasberg reassured us that "everything would be okay."

The passions calmed down, but the tension did not abate. The landing took place precisely according to schedule, although a strong wind in the touchdown area prevented the parachutes from pooling on the ground, and they dragged the Descent Module over the steppe for about 5 kilometers. The following day, the passive vehicle touched down more smoothly.

Search groups confirmed that in both cases the soft landing system had been actuated upon receiving a command from the gamma ray altimeter. This instrument was the first serious work of a young special design bureau organized by Professor Yevgeniy Yurevich at the Leningrad Polytechnic Institute. Oh, what a lot of trouble this altimeter would cause! We provided a command to jettison the parachutes so that they would not drag the Descent Module over

---

23. KTDU—*Korrektiruyushchaya tormoznaya dvigatelnaya ustanovka.*

24. NII-4 was a military research institution located in the Bolshevo suburb of Moscow. It served as a center to develop strategic and operational plans for the Strategic Rocket Forces and the Soviet military space program. The NII-4 ballistics center provided ballistics, tracking, and communications support for the Soviet human space program in the early days.

the steppe in a strong wind. We left out this command for vehicles No. 7 and No. 8. Nevertheless, some time after the forced "stroll" over the steppe, the parachute of vehicle No. 7 was jettisoned. It turned out that while it was dragging over the ground, static electricity accumulated in the parachute material, which then ignited the pyrocartridges.

On 21 April, TASS reported that "all vehicle systems functioned normally and showed a high degree of reliability." The main point in the TASS report was a prediction that was soon proven true: "The entire complex of operations…is a new major step in the creation of orbital stations and interplanetary spacecraft."

A new set of cosmonaut candidates showed up in Yevpatoriya, in addition to cosmonauts we knew well. Mishin picked a comparatively quiet time and organized an unofficial meeting "for sizing each other up." "We're always associating with future cosmonauts through Kamanin or at official conferences," he said. "Let them talk with us themselves." That was his reasoning behind the meeting. We agreed that our side would have four representatives—Mishin, Feoktistov, Kerimov, and myself. Hero of the Soviet Union Colonel Georgiy Beregovoy and Lieutenant Colonel Vladimir Shatalov met with us and spoke their minds.

These were certainly not the young lieutenants who had made up the first cosmonaut corps. Beginning in 1942, Beregovoy had fought as a pilot on the famous Il-2 fighter-bombers. He decided to fly into space, having a great deal of experience as a test pilot at the Air Force State Red Banner Scientific-Research Institute (GKNII VVS).[25] He was already 47 years old and did not aspire to go into space for the sake of glory. Shatalov was 41 years old. He had already waited his turn for five years in the cosmonaut corps.[26] After graduating from the Air Force Academy in 1956, Vladimir flew a great deal in a variety of airplanes.

Since the times of Korolev, we had been accustomed to the fact that the cosmonauts treated the technical management with pronounced respect. Shatalov, who was the first to speak his mind, did not exhibit this respect. He said that the plans, not just for the distant future, but for the immediate future as well, were completely unclear to them, the future cosmonauts. They were being kept in the dark about what the chief designers and their closest associates thought. They

---

25. GKNII VVS—*Gosudarstvennyy krasnoznamennyy nauchno-issledovatelskiy institut voyenno-vosdushnykh sil.*

26. Georgiy Timofeyevich Beregovoy (1921–1995) was selected for cosmonaut training on 25 January 1964 as a supplement to the 15 cosmonaut pilots and engineers selected earlier on 10 January 1963, which included Vladimir Aleksandrovich Shatalov (1927–). These men were slightly older and more experienced than the original "Gagarin Group" selected in 1960. Both Beregovoy and Shatalov went on to senior positions in the Air Force's management hierarchy for cosmonaut training.

needed to determine, not in a week, but in a year or even sooner, who would fly on what vehicle, and be bolder in recruiting them—experienced pilots—not just for flight training on a vehicle that was already ready, but for the actual development of the spacecraft, like they do in the field of aviation.

I liked Shatalov's blunt observations. They differed from the speeches of the obedient kids from Gagarin's class. He spoke fervently and was not afraid to step on our toes, having brought up the Americans' successes and the opportunities afforded their astronauts for training sessions on special simulators.

When Beregovoy had his turn to speak, he was less vehement than Shatalov. He said that the review team, State Commission, and other managers were too cautious. They needed to first begin launching new vehicles with a cosmonaut on board and not drag on for years with unpiloted launches. Then new space technology would be developed faster. In his opinion, Komarov's death was not a disaster. In aviation, over a year's time, at least a dozen crashes take place, and two dozen crashes occur during the testing of new aircraft. And there's nothing horrible in that. It's all to be expected. In aviation this is called an "air accident with grave consequences."

ON THE EVENING OF 20 APRIL, we conducted a ceremonial closing meeting of the operational and technical leadership. Agadzhanov emphatically called each of the systems testing managers up to report, while Volodya Suvorov, who had specially prepared for this festive event, having arranged spotlights around the entire hall, shot the first secret film about automatic docking at the Yevpatoriya mission control center (TsUP).[27] When Suvorov was still alive, I asked him if he could track down this film. He promised but didn't manage to do so. I simply haven't set aside time to search without him.

On 21 April, the State Commission and command of military unit 32103 rewarded all docking participants with an excursion to Sevastopol.[28] Setting out for the hero-city, everyone got dressed up. I pinned my Hero of Socialist Labor star to my lapel. Mishin complained that he wanted to go with us but

---

27. Vladimir Andreyevich Suvorov was the main movie cameraman responsible for taking films of the early Soviet piloted spaceflights. He began his career by taking films of the early Soviet nuclear explosions. The common abbreviation for "mission control center" is TsUP (*Tsentr upravleniya poletami*), literally "Flight Control Center."

28. "Military unit 32103" was the service designation for the staff of the Command and Measurement Complex (KIK). Sevastopol is a port city on the Black Sea in current-day Ukraine. During World War II (in 1941–1942), the city suffered a vicious German attack and siege. It was finally liberated by Soviet forces in 1944.

was unable to since he had to fly back to the firing range to participate in the latest 7K-L1 circumlunar flight.[29]

We visited all the sites; their very names would inspire anyone who knew the history of this truly Russian hero-city to pay tribute to the heroism of those who lie beneath its earth and at the bottom of the sea. There were a lot of tourists at Sapun Mountain outside the entrance to the city.[30] A middle-aged sailor in a pea jacket covered in military medals walked up to me. He was clearly "in his cups," but steady on his feet; he had something he had to say to a new person. After politely pointing to my gold star, he asked: "What's it for, buddy?"[31]

Instead of the usual evasive answer that I gave in such situations, I pulled out the award certificate booklet and showed it to him. He read aloud:

For outstanding services in developing rocket technology models and ensuring the successful flight of a Soviet cosmonaut into space, the Presidium of the Supreme Soviet of the USSR by Decree on 17 June 1961 has awarded YOU the title of Hero of Socialist Labor.
Chairman of the Presidium of the Supreme Soviet of the USSR
L. Brezhnev
Secretary of the Presidium of the Supreme Soviet of the USSR
M. Georgadze
Kremlin, 19 June 1961[32]

"Look who I've stumbled into," said the sailor after closing the booklet with particular reverence and returning it to me. "So, I guess you received this for Gagarin, and now the spacecraft are flying, docking, and landing without people—why is this?"

Violating official security regulations, I said that we control those flights here in the Crimea from Yevpatoriya. The spacecraft are undergoing tests, and soon people will be flying again.

---

29. Mishin directed the launch of 7K-L1 vehicle No. 7L on 23 April 1968. The spacecraft failed to reach Earth orbit.

30. Soviet troops began the bloody process of regaining Sevastopol from the Germans by storming Sapun Gora (Sapun Mountain) on 7 May 1944.

31. Chertok is referring here to his Hero of Socialist Labor pin.

32. Chertok was one among many from the Soviet space industry who were awarded the Hero of Socialist Labor on 17 June 1961 to honor them for their contributions to Yuriy Gagarin's flight on the *Vostok* spaceship. Mikhail Porfiryevich Georgadze (1912–1982) was Secretary of the Presidium of the Supreme Soviet from 1957 until his death. This position was largely ceremonial in nature.

"So then my friends did not drench this land with their blood in vain. You're really doing something there. I must tell you, when they retreated, and then we stormed this mountain, 1 hour of that pandemonium is worth many days there, in your space. How many heroes fell here for our Russian glory! Forgive me if I said something wrong. Take care."

I extended my hand and couldn't help but embrace him. Weaving a bit, he hurried off to look for his comrades.

WE RETURNED TO YEVPATORIYA LATE THAT EVENING, and that night (it was already 23 April), we gathered in anticipation of the L1 launch. The commentary came to us from Chelomey's bunker. Liftoff took place at a few seconds after 0201 hours. Separation of the spacecraft from the launch vehicle was supposed to take place 589 seconds into the flight. But the launch vehicle didn't make it that far. What bad luck we were having with the lunar programs! At 260 seconds the second-stage engines shut down and once again the emergency rescue system (SAS) worked excellently. The spacecraft was unscathed. I saw it in excellent condition several days later in shop No. 439. It landed 520 kilometers from the launch site. Three failures of the UR-500K launch vehicle proved the high reliability of the emergency rescue and landing system that we had developed for the L1.[33] As our confidence in the reliability of the SAS grew, our hope that a Soviet cosmonaut would fly around the Moon before the Americans waned. For the time being, our May Day present was just the docking of the *Kosmos-212* and *-213*. Why they couldn't be called "Soyuzes," if only in honor of the holiday, no one could really understand. This playing it safe was not a secrecy issue, but a political one.

The airplane that was supposed to transport the main contingent of people from the Crimea to Moscow had been delayed in Tyuratam. Mishin and Tyulin had counted on flying into Yevpatoriya on it. After the nighttime crash of the UR-500K, the aviation schedule had been disrupted. I flew to Moscow with cosmonaut Aleksey Leonov on a Tu-124—the brand new Air Force airplane equipped for the navigational training of the cosmonauts, which still had its pleasant, fresh-from-the-factory smell.[34]

Throughout the entire flight up until the landing at Chkalovskiy airfield, we argued about the role of a human being in the control of spacecraft. The cosmonauts saw me as one of the chief proponents of purely automatic control

---

33. The three failures took place on 28 September 1967, 22 November 1967, and 23 April 1968.

34. The Tu-124 was a short-range twin-jet passenger airliner that was introduced into service in 1962.

and, using examples of the two latest Kosmos flights, they argued that docking would have been more reliable if just one cosmonaut had been on each spacecraft.

All I had left as a defense was to refer to the Komarov tragedy. Whoever had been in his place still wouldn't have been able to open the solar array and pull the parachute out of the container. We made a mistake by deciding to let a human being fly before we had tested all the new vehicle's systems. The last two Kosmos flights confirmed that, with a few exceptions, everything had been tested out and the decision could be made to resume piloted flights.

The next day all of our comrades who had returned from the Crimea were greeted at work like heroes. Naturally—the second automatic rendezvous and automatic docking! This was an absolute victory for the control specialists. The Americans still didn't know how to do this. We were once again "ahead of the whole world."

Chapter 9

"Sort It Out, and Report on Your Endeavors"

Saturday, 21 December 1968, the weather was fine, but the mood was anything but festive. At NII-88 on a big screen we were watching the liftoff of a Saturn V carrying *Apollo 8*. Considering the complicated relay arrangement, the image quality was quite decent. Even on a television screen the liftoff was a sight to behold. When the first and second stages separated, everything was shrouded in billows of smoke and flame. It created the impression that an explosion had taken place, but seconds later the bright, pure plume rushed onward. We compared everything that we had seen with our own liftoffs and could not help but think about the launch of the first N-1 No. 3L coming up in February.

The next day, Sunday, I went cross-country skiing around the Botanical Garden. The snow wasn't deep, and from time to time my skis scraped the ground. I didn't experience the usual pleasure I got from the exertion of skiing.

Usually while skiing I managed to escape all burdensome thoughts and tried to look at things from an outside perspective. This time it didn't work. First I thought about Vladimir Shatalov and Aleksey Yeliseyev—they were supposed to fly in January, dock, and transfer from vehicle to vehicle. Then I thought about the upcoming difficult State Commission on the N-1—this was at the firing range—then I'd have to fly to Yevpatoriya. At the firing range and in Yevpatoriya, we'd meet with Babakin—the launch of two Veneras was coming up. On 20 January, there would be another L1 launch…. How would all of this go? But most of all, the February N-1 launch would not let my mind rest.

On Monday, 23 December, "Uncle Mitya" summoned the leadership of the "cuckoo's nest" (as we privately referred to Ustinov and the MOM building on Miusskaya Square, respectively) to his office. According to the shock waves that had reached us by that evening, the conversation boiled down to the standard questions and instructions: "How are we going to respond to the Americans? Sort it out and tell me what you're going to do. The main problem is how to shorten the timeframes. We have to report our proposals to the Politburo."

Having come out to see us after the hoopla in the Central Committee, Viktor Litvinov told us: "Dmitriy Fedorovich was complaining that the Americans

171

have borrowed our basic method of operation—plan-based management and networked schedules.[1] They have passed us in management and planning methods—they announce a launch preparation schedule in advance and strictly adhere to it. In essence, they have put into effect the principle of democratic centralism—free discussion followed by the strictest discipline during implementation."

According to Ustinov, we had let ourselves go. We had returned to the times of feudalism. Each ministry was a separate feudal fiefdom. Instead of working harmoniously, the chief designers were adopting aggressive stances against one another; they had even stopped listening to their own ministers. The Americans were concentrating enormous efforts. They had either 500,000 or 1,500,000 people working on the lunar program, and 20,000 companies. And a government organization—NASA—was organizing and managing all of this. We were presumptuous, Ustinov upbraided us, and it was time to make a sober assessment of the situation.

On Monday, Mishin called in sick and didn't show up at work. The minister instructed Litvinov to ask Sergey Okhapkin—the chief designer's first deputy—for proposals for the upcoming meeting at the VPK with Smirnov or in the Central Committee with Ustinov.

Okhapkin invited Konstantin Bushuyev, Sergey Kryukov, and me to consult about what to do. I recalled Saltykov-Shchedrin, who last century wrote, "Any administration acts through endeavors."[2] We needed to compose umpteen necessary and useful endeavors and propose them to the minister. He will cross out half of them because there won't be enough money or authority for all of them, but he'll take some sort of action on the other half and at least render moral support.

I proposed: "Let's consult with Pilyugin. He knows his way around the political scene better than we do now. He meets almost every other day with Keldysh, often with Yangel, the deputy Commander-in-Chief of the rocket forces spends an hour drinking tea with him, and Ustinov is betting on him to develop control systems for Nadiradze's rockets."[3]

We accepted this proposal as the "first action." Litvinov flared up: "What are you doing to me? I've been ordered to report to the minister this evening about your actions, and you're about to go on a field trip to see Pilyugin."

---

1. Valentin Yakovlevich Litvinov (1910–1983) served as a deputy minister of the Ministry of General Machine Building (MOM) from 1965 to 1973.
2. Mikhail Yevgrafovich Saltykov-Shchedrin (1826–1889) was a leading Russian satirist of the 19th century.
3. Aleksandr Davidovich Nadiradze (1914–1987) was chief designer at the Moscow Institute of Thermal Technology (MIT), where he led the development of long-range solid-propellant ballistic missiles, which eventually replaced the liquid-propellant ones developed under Korolev, Yangel, and Chelomey.

"Viktor Yakovlevich," reassured Okhapkin, "first of all, we're not going on a field trip, we're going for serious deliberation; and second, in a day or two, Vasiliy Pavlovich [Mishin] will be back on the job, and anyway, without him we won't deliver any actions to the minister."

Litvinov gave a wave of his hand and left for the factory floor. He could breathe easier there.[4]

Okhapkin telephoned Pilyugin on the "Kremlin line" and arranged for us to come over on the 25th after lunch. "We can't go see Pilyugin empty-handed; we need to have proposals, an outline, so that the conversation will be more concrete. I propose that we switch to the dual-launch scenario [for a lunar landing]," I said, having decided to take advantage of the good company for such a conversation.[5]

"But that means putting off the mission for four to five years," objected Bushuyev.

"We're already behind by at least three to four years. If we come out with a scenario in three years—in the best case—that is clearly worse than the current Apollo, then what good does this do anyone?"

After returning to my office, I convened a "small council" of my deputies and department chiefs, who to a great extent determined both the deadlines and weight reports. They did not always follow the instructions of management, but they had their own opinions in store. Rauschenbach, Kalashnikov, Karpov, Yurasov, Krayushkin, Vilnitskiy, Kuzmin, Chizhikov, Zverev, Penek, and Babkov came. The group, whose members often clashed with one another and got embroiled in heated arguments, supported me this time very keenly and harmoniously. Only Rauschenbach was skeptical and said: "This won't get past Mishin."

Yurasov retorted: "I will persuade Vasiliy Pavlovich."

The dual-launch scenario that I drew on the board, referring to my notebook to avoid using the secret notepad, was the subject of a heated discussion. I like this scenario even today. If humankind had possessed N-1 launch vehicles, then such a scenario could have been used for a long-duration expedition to the Moon even in the early 21st century. I shall give a brief account of the proposal as it has been preserved in my notebook.

---

4. For most of his early career, from 1944 to 1962, Litvinov had been director of one of the largest aviation and missile production facilities in the Soviet Union, Factory No. 1 (later known as the Progress Factory) in Kuybyshev.

5. At various times, such proposals involved either Earth-orbit rendezvous or lunar-orbit rendezvous mission profiles using two N-1 rockets.

The Saturn V inserts into Earth orbit a payload weighing 135 tons, of which 45 tons fly to the Moon, and of that amount, if one rounds off, 30 tons is in the primary payload (what we call the LOK—the Lunar Orbital Vehicle), and 15 tons is in the lunar module. En route the Americans perform a restructuring operation—the primary payload swings around and mates with the lunar module.[6] This is their first docking. They perform the second after liftoff from the Moon. And so the Americans have two dockings.

When we send off the N-1, then in the best-case scenario, instead of 45 tons to the Moon, we will be able to send just 30 tons. However, with the dual-launch plan, we'll be able to send 60 tons! Instead of restructuring with a docking en route to the Moon, we will perform a docking of a piloted LOK with the unpiloted LK in lunar orbit. We will necessarily develop a docking assembly with internal transfer—there will be no need to crawl through open space. Three cosmonauts will transfer to the new LK. One will remain in the LOK. In all, we'll need to send at least four or five cosmonauts. That will be sensational! The second docking, just as in the Americans' plan and in our current plan, will take place during the return from the Moon.

Each increment of payload needs to be designed so that when the launch vehicle's power generation increases, there would be the potential for expanding the missions. The control and navigation systems need to be backed up with manual operations. In the next two years, we absolutely must manage to develop a reliable computer for the LOK and for the LK.

We will begin to design both spacecraft all over again. We will make them more spacious and with reliable systems backup. The vehicles should stay in lunar orbit and on its surface for a total of at least 30 days. That is the only way that we will achieve technical and political advantage, by deliberately overtaking the Americans rather than just catching up. We can substantially increase the value of the lunar expedition if, before the piloted flights, we perform a preliminary launch with an automatic landing on the Moon in order to deliver part of the payload there and thus reduce the load of the subsequent piloted vehicles.

That is how the *three*-launch scenario shapes up. The first launch is an unpiloted transport vehicle, and then there is a two-launch piloted expedition. In this case, only the launch of the launch vehicle carrying the new LOK is piloted. It will carry four or five cosmonauts. They will dock in lunar orbit with the lunar module, which will have arrived there beforehand. The first unpiloted reconnaissance vehicle could drop an electric power plant with an output of 3 to 5 kilowatts, a radio station with a pencil-beam antenna for television

---

6. In NASA parlance, this was known as the transposition and docking maneuver.

broadcasts, and supplies of oxygen, water, and food for a month or so on the surface of the Moon in advance. The same flight could deliver a lunar rover. Such an automatic LK doesn't need a liftoff stage, and therefore the mass of the deliverable cargo is very great. The vehicle carrying the cosmonauts would land next to this first automatic vehicle.

To speed up the design process, we need to separate permanent modules that don't change from launch to launch and variable ones that depend on specific tasks. Permanent modules should perform all functions: orientation, navigation, on-orbit docking, return to Earth, descent, and landing. These functions need to be tested out in automatic and manual modes and in ground control mode "until they are perfect." We need to create the maximum comfort level in the LOK and LK for the crew in view of the amount of time they will be in orbit and on the surface of the Moon.

Having laid out these first, very general principles of the lunar program, I hoped to receive the moral support of my comrades. Discussion of this proposal and its details began immediately and turned up many full-fledged and alarming problems. First and foremost, we needed to make a decision and stop the development of modifications and new orbital vehicles, stop updating the L1, halt operations on the already obsolete LOK and LK, and make a really progressive leap. We needed to persuade Pilyugin to refine the launch vehicle control system. We also needed to speed up the development of a system with an on-board digital computer in order to have flexible trajectories. This would give us an additional 3 to 5 tons of payload and would increase the reliability of the launch vehicle, especially of Blocks G and D.[7] Nikolay Kuznetsov would need at least a year to debug the engines of all three stages!

My still quite crude proposal found such ardent support among my comrades that I tried to "back up."

"Don't cause a stir before it's time. We haven't discussed these proposals with Mishin. If word gets around about a new version, we risk disrupting our current work."

Yurasov and Bashkin were more excited than the others.

"We're in a real dead end in terms of weights. We're trying to pull the wool over the eyes of the expert commission in the hope that in time everything will sort itself out somehow. During the process of landing on the Moon, we need to give the cosmonaut the ability, if only for a minute, to hover, look around, and maneuver to select a spot so that he doesn't topple into some crater. For this

---

7. Block G and Block D were the translunar injection stage and lunar orbit injection stage, respectively. Block D also would perform the deorbit burn from lunar orbit.

we need propellant, and there is neither room nor weight for that. The same is true for the second docking, if the first one goes awry. There are no reserves!"

Everyone unanimously supported the idea but at the same time expressed apprehension that this wouldn't get past "the brass."

On 25 December, we met in Pilyugin's office. The conversation was long and tumultuous. We started at 3 p.m. and it was after 9 p.m. when we left, having drunk an incalculable number of cups of tea. Among those participating in the conversation on the eternal subject of "what to propose" were Pilyuginites Finogeyev and Khitrik.[8] He did not invite any other staff members. Finogeyev and Khitrik received my revolutionary proposals concerning the two-launch plan with interest and obvious sympathy, but Pilyugin showed no enthusiasm.

"Under the current circumstances, only Sergey [Korolev] could allow himself to deliver such proposals—and even then, only if Nikita [Khrushchev] were in power. But whom can we turn to today? Glushko claims that Kuznetsov's engines are rotten and that it's useless to make the N-1 using them. And instead of one rocket using 'rotten' engines, you propose launching three.

"Chelomey will be against it. After all, you didn't leave him anything, and you're even proposing that the L1 be shut down. You're not enticing Yangel with anything either. You want to do everything yourself. They will publicly announce that Mishin won't be able to cope with this work. Grechko is completely against it.[9] He now believes that our association with the Moon has been on the whole all for naught, and he's outraged that at the expense of the Ministry of Defense budget, they're paying expenses for naval telemetry ships, Crimean tracking stations, all the preparation at Baykonur, and cosmonaut training. Grechko believes that this is Ustinov's policy, and supposedly he stated flat out in the Defense Council that the Academy of Sciences and interested ministries should pay for space. He, Grechko, does not need the Moon.

"You figure that Nikita merely threatened that we can make rockets like sausages, but supposedly spared no expense for space. But they didn't provide money for the N-1 on a large scale until late 1964. And before that, Nikita wavered: is it necessary or not? Now [i.e., early 1969] we're about three years behind the Americans and we need to catch up in terms of missiles in silos, submarine-launched missiles, and the number of cosmonauts, and now you announce that we've been doing it all wrong and that we need to do everything differently for the Moon, so give us some more money.

---

8. Vladilen Petrovich Finogeyev (1928–) and Mikhail Samuilovich Khitrik were Pilyugin's two principal deputies.

9. Marshal Andrey Antonovich Grechko (1903–1976) served as USSR minister of defense from 1967 to 1976.

"Everyone whom Nikita had squeezed—sailors, shipbuilders, aviation—is now rushing to restore what had been wrecked while he was in office, and this is no small sum of money. And currently, to be honest, the Americans have three times more nuclear warheads on intercontinental ballistic missiles and submarines. That's where we need to catch up and move ahead. That's the only point that Ustinov agrees on with Grechko. But, once again, whose rockets will they be: Yangel's or Chelomey's? Uncle Mitya has outwitted everyone, he's dragging out Nadiradze, and I am helping him in this. We're ending up with an interesting system. Sergey started focusing on solid-propellant engines late, and Vasiliy came out against them; if their development had begun earlier, you wouldn't be involved with the Moon now, and everyone would be working for Grechko.

"The other day Tolubko was sitting in my office here.[10] He said that the generals were riled up: Afanasyev is now in charge of all rocket production, and they are diverting him to lunar problems. Let Keldysh deal with that.

"Sergey is the only one who could accept everything that Boris just proposed. He would have won over Keldysh and the two of them would have gone to Brezhnev. If they 'swung' Brezhnev, he would have brought up the discussion in the Defense Council or right in the Politburo. The problems are not so much technical as they are political. Someone needs to find the courage to say that we are not hurrying to the Moon, but instead we are going to settle down there in around five years the right way. But who is that brave? Nobody.

"Now there is no one to turn to with these proposals. Look at Kosygin, who proposed a good plan for industrial management, and they supported it verbally but then didn't let him do anything but experiment on taxi fleets.[11]

"Let's finish up the N-1 as it was conceived. Now the most important thing is for the first launch vehicle to fly. I am going to finish my system for the time being without a computer. But they've talked so much to Keldysh about Kuznetsov's engines that he has already complained to me in the Academy presidium, but he doesn't know what's to be done."[12]

We talked about all of this with interruptions and distractions.

---

10. Vladimir Fedorovich Tolubko (1914–1989), a friend of Pilyugin's, served as First Deputy Commander-in-Chief of the Strategic Rocket Forces from 1960 to 1968. Since the Rocket Forces had full operational control over the Soviet space program, he was closely involved in many key decisions of the period. Later in his career, from 1972 to 1985, Tolubko headed the Strategic Rocket Forces.

11. Aleksey Nikolayevich Kosygin (1904–1980) was the most powerful man in the Soviet government during the Brezhnev era, serving as chairman of the USSR Council of Ministers from 1964 to 1980. Yet, many of his initiatives were left unfulfilled, partly due to opposition from Party leaders.

12. Pilyugin was a member of the Academy's presidium, i.e., its highest deliberative body. This was an extremely rare honor accorded to only one or two chief designers in the missile and space industry.

PILYUGIN WAS A CREATIVE INDIVIDUAL who got carried away at any given time with some particular idea. We diverted him with our N1-L3 problems from his own musings about problems that were totally different and quite removed from the lunar expedition. Now he was absorbed in working on the control system for the *Temp* mobile missile system, the chief designer of which was Aleksandr Nadiradze. Pilyugin simply could not keep silent about his project. He didn't need our advice; he needed us as an audience that could appreciate the difficulty of the assignment. He demanded a great deal of himself and his specialists when it came to his philosophy of the creative process.

"Chelomey and Yangel are disputing whose rocket is better. But Nadiradze and I aren't developing a rocket, but a new weapons system. By the way, Sergey began to understand this when he first proposed the RT-2. You and Yangel both had proposals for mobile missiles come up, but it's interesting to work with Nadiradze because he has an integrated approach that many of our military men lack. We are helping him a lot now, although our ministry is clearly insinuating that if it weren't for Ustinov, they would forbid me to work for an outside agency.[13]

"Dmitriy Fedorovich, in my opinion, now has a better grasp of how good these mobile complexes are than the military. After all, this is much less expensive than building a silo for each missile, which a satellite will detect sooner or later. And now, submarines are always being followed by another submarine. But if our land-based mobile complexes are well camouflaged, no reconnaissance will detect them."

The project that had engrossed Pilyugin at that time was not a passing fancy, but a field that the NIIAP staff would be working on for decades. The Moscow Institute of Thermal Technology, which Aleksandr Nadiradze headed until the end of his life, developed the *Temp*, *Temp-2S*, *Pioner*, *Kuryer*, and finally the *Topol* and *Topol-M* mobile missile systems, which were supposed to become the main domestic strategic nuclear forces in the 21st century.[14]

"Our system is set up so that battlefield marshals become defense ministers. But in my opinion, if Ustinov were to be put in that post, it would make a lot more sense," said Pilyugin. His words proved to be prophetic. In 1976,

---

13. The "outside agency" alluded to here is the Ministry of the Defense Industry.

14. Nadiradze died in 1987. Probably the most famous of his creations was the *Pioner* intermediate range ballistic missile, better known in the West as the SS-20. The *Temp* (SS-12), *Temp-S* (SS-12M), and *Temp-2S* (SS-16) were early solid-propellant missiles developed in the late 1960s and mid-1970s. The *Topol* was the first ICBM developed by Nadiradze. The *Topol-M* ICBM was deployed for service duty in December 1988. An updated model of the *Topol-M* serves as the backbone of the Russian strategic Rocket Forces in the early 21st century. The *Kuryer* was never deployed.

Ustinov was appointed USSR Minister of Defense. Pilyugin said then what many of us were thinking: "The appointment is correct. It just would have been good to do this about ten years earlier."

Back then, Politburo member and Defense Minister Ustinov essentially could have become the second-ranking individual in the state leadership. Combining the knowledge and experience of industrial management with ascendancy over a great power's armed forces in a single individual, especially given the authority that Ustinov enjoyed in the scientific-technical sphere, he could have influenced the nation's history *if* he had continued an active life for another five years or so. But Ustinov survived Pilyugin by just two years.[15] Both of them were severely ill during the last year of their lives.

Here it is appropriate to write about how the missile projects in those days were distributed between ministries. Short-range tactical missiles for land-based troops were developed in the Ministry of the Defense Industry (MOP) system. The main developer of these missiles was the Moscow Institute of Thermal Technology, the chief designer of which was Aleksandr Nadiradze, and the main customer was the Commander-in-Chief of the Ground Forces.

Medium-range and intercontinental ballistic missiles equipped with nuclear warheads, and also ballistic missiles for submarines, were developed in the Ministry of General Machine Building system. The customers for these missiles, which were called strategic, were the Strategic Rocket Forces Commander-in-Chief and Commander-in-Chief of the Navy, respectively.

The Ministry of the Aviation Industry developed missiles for PVO (air defense) and PRO (missile defense) systems and for arming airplanes, and the customers were, respectively, the PVO and VVS Commanders-in-Chief.[16] Each of the ministries had its own internal cooperative network for the development of missile guidance and control systems.

Ministry of the Defense Industry organizations also developed control systems for Nadiradze's tactical missiles. There were projects enough for everyone. However, in the mid-1960s, with the very active support of Ustinov, Nadiradze went outside the bounds of his departmental framework and began to develop medium-range and then intercontinental missile systems. This was an area that had been allocated to MOM and the Strategic Rocket Forces (RVSN), but not to MOP and the Ground Forces. In so doing, it became clear that the MOP

---

15. Pilyugin died on 2 August 1982, while Ustinov passed away on 20 December 1984.

16. During the late Soviet era, the Soviet armed forces consisted of five services: the Ground Forces, the Air Force (VVS—*Voyenno-vozdushnyye sily*), the National Air Defense Forces (PVO Strany—*Protivovozdushnaya oborona strany*), the Navy (VMF—*Voyenno-morskoy flot*), and the Strategic Rocket Forces (RVSN—*Raketnyye voyska strategicheskogo naznacheniya*).

system did not have an organization capable of developing control systems for such complexes. Therefore, it was necessary to make use of the experience and power of MOM's main control system organization—Pilyugin's NIIAP. Thus, Ustinov found an optimal solution.

But in so doing, MOM's monopoly on the development of medium-range and intercontinental strategic missile complexes was broken. It turned out that the head organization for control systems, NIIAP, together with other instrument-building factories, was now obliged to work for MOP, the head ministry for Nadiradze's missile complexes. Meanwhile, Pilyugin was inundated with orders for his own chiefs: Mishin, Yangel, and Chelomey. But the truth was that nobody twisted Pilyugin's arm. He voluntarily agreed to work for another ministry without having asked for the approval of his own minister [i.e., Afanasyev], who couldn't have liked all of this.

WE DROVE OUT TO SEE PILYUGIN in Okhapkin's official car. Reckoning on a long conversation, we arranged to have the car and driver stay on the premises in a warm garage. After 8 p.m., Okhapkin remembered and started to fret: "We've just drunk our 10th glass of tea with toast and our driver is starving out there!"

Pilyugin himself telephoned the garage. They reassured him: "We're keeping the car from Podlipki warm. We've served the driver tea."

Pilyugin was very pleased that, even without his intervention, they had shown such hospitality.

Returning to the subject of our meeting, Pilyugin said that we also shouldn't particularly count on Keldysh. He was up to his ears with problems at the Academy. And relations had become even more strained with Suslov and the entire Central Committee staff because of Andrey Sakharov. There were some zealous types who were demanding that Keldysh make the decision in the presidium to expel Sakharov from the Academy. He argued that this was a gross violation of regulations. For the time being he seemed to have warded them off.[17]

We continued to argue, discussing Chelomey's and Yangel's programs more than our own problems, which was the reason we had driven out there. Finogeyev and Khitrik were to a great extent better informed than

---

17. Andrey Dmitriyevich Sakharov (1921–1989) was an eminent Soviet nuclear physicist whose concern about the destructive power and proliferation of nuclear weapons would later transform him into a dissident and human rights activist who was a thorn in the side of the Soviet regime throughout the 1960s and into the 1980s. Keldysh took some big risks and supported Sakharov at key points in the 1960s and early 1970s, incurring the wrath of senior Party functionaries such as Mikhail Andreyevich Suslov.

we. When it came to a discussion of the lunar landing plan, Khitrik listed so many yet-to-be-resolved tasks concerning control of the Lunar Vehicle alone that Bushuyev, who was supposed to find "weight" from the margin for all of this, said frankly: "I've got nothing left. You solve these problems at the expense of your own systems. Day after tomorrow I have to report to the VPK about what caused the failed landing of 7K-L1 No. 12—*Zond-6.*"

Pilyugin did not pass up an opportunity to take a dig: "Finally all the L1 systems activated without a glitch during the circumlunar flight, and you managed to shoot off the parachute when it was almost on the ground and crash the Descent Module. And you were dreaming that we were about to launch a human being on the L1!"

Indeed, the incident was extremely annoying. The launch of vehicle 7K-L1 No. 12 took place on 10 November 1968. The vehicle executed a circumlunar flight. It managed to take black-and-white and color photographs of the lunar surface from distances of 8,000 and 2,600 kilometers. The most important event was the return to Earth. For the first time in the history of 7K-L1 launches, a guided descent to the territory of the USSR was taking place during a return from the Moon at reentry velocity. The Descent Module came down just 16 kilometers from the launch site from which it had lifted off to the Moon.

For the long-suffering circumlunar flight control system of the L1 vehicle, this was a great and long-awaited success. But just before reaching the ground, once again a vexing slip-up occurred. The cords of the fully deployed parachute shot off at an altitude of 5,300 meters. Fortunately, when it hit the ground, the 10 kilograms of TNT in the APO system failed to

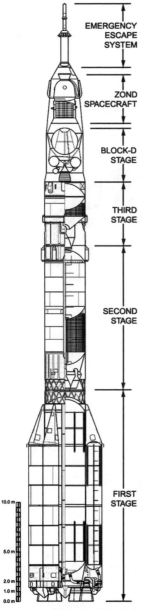

Alexander Shliadinsky

The cutaway of the Proton-K/L-1 stack clearly shows the Zond spacecraft and the Block D stage.

181

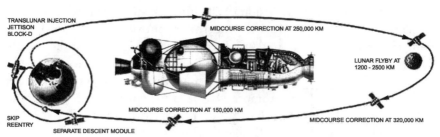

RKK Energiya & David R. Woods

The mission profile of the Zond circumlunar mission was relatively simple in comparison to a more complex lunar orbital mission.

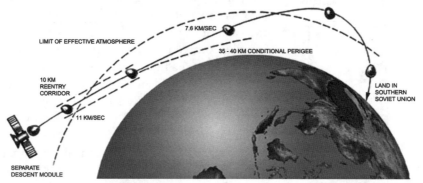

RKK Energiya & David R. Woods

This breakdown of the Zond reentry profile shows the double-dip reentry into Earth's atmosphere designed to reduce stresses on the Descent Module. The normal mode was to approach from the south with the first dip into the atmosphere over the Indian Ocean, followed by a second dip and landing in the southern Soviet Union. *Zond-8* used a northern approach with the first dip over the Soviet Union for more precise tracking, followed by a landing in the Indian Ocean.

explode. Bushuyev flew out to the crash site to lead the "minesweeping" of the Descent Module and recovery of the intact film.

"Konstantin Davidovich, if you could please tell us, after such a good flight, why did you crash the Descent Module?" Pilyugin insisted.

"Because," answered Bushuyev, "depressurization occurred." On the sixth day of the flight the pressure fell to 380 millimeters of mercury, and during descent it fell to just 25 millimeters.

"But why? After all, that could doom a crew!"

"It was an engineering error. There was a leak due to a bad seal in the edging strip around the hatch. After power was supplied to the landing system, a corona discharge occurred in the gamma-ray altimeter circuit due to the low pressure. It issued a false command to start up the soft landing engines and, simultaneously, to shoot off the parachute."

I felt partially responsible for the unforeseen occurrence of a corona discharge in the gamma-ray altimeter. This was a blatant oversight that I had committed along with my subordinates working on the landing system, which the Leningrad Polytechnic Institute OKB had supervised. Professor Yevgeniy Yurevich, the chief designer of the gamma-ray altimeter, admitted that no one had tested the electrical reliability of the system at low pressures. The gamma-ray altimeter was supposed to activate as the Descent Module neared the ground. The instrument was simply dead until the module reached an altitude of 5,000 meters. The pressure in the Descent Module was also supposed to be normal; otherwise the cosmonauts would die. It was all so logical that it never occurred to anyone to test out the altimeter at a pressure of 25 millimeters of mercury. Again and again we realized that in our technology, coincidences of the "not-in-your-wildest-dreams" variety do occur.

THE DAY AFTER OUR CONVERSATION AT PILYUGIN'S OFFICE, no one from the ministry harassed us regarding a lack of "actions."

On 27 December, Bushuyev gave his account of the L1 failure in the State Commission. Yurevich came forward with a confession, accepting full responsibility for the occurrence of the corona discharge. One complaint was lodged against me: the engineering specifications had mentioned high vacuum conditions, but nothing had been said about the pressures at which a corona discharge occurs.

Tyulin on the State Commission confined himself to a verbal castigation of Yurevich and TsKBEM, but there would be no retaliatory organizational consequences. The fact of depressurization aggravated everyone more than the corona discharge. They decided to execute the next unpiloted launch of vehicle 7K-L1 No. 13 with the objective of a circumlunar flight on 20 January 1969.

When Tyulin was already bringing the State Commission session to a close, Mrykin loudly asked: "But why should we launch No. 13 at all? After all, tomorrow three Americans are returning to the Earth after flying around the Moon. If, God forbid, something happens again [to our L1 spacecraft], our launch will be considered a failure of our lunar landing program." In their thoughts, the majority of the State Commission members agreed with Mrykin, but no one uttered a word in reply.

On 28 December, ministry leaders and our small group on the "special list" were granted the opportunity to watch the splashdown of *Apollo 8*, which had lifted off on 21 December. The vehicle consisted of a main section weighing 30 tons, which was supposed to have been inserted into selenocentric orbit carrying three astronauts. From our point of view, this event stole the thunder from our lunar program by the very fact that it was a piloted lunar orbital flight. This was the first instance of using the Saturn V rocket to launch a piloted vehicle.

Apollo 8 made 10 orbits around the Moon. Numerous television broadcasts followed the flight along its route to and around the Moon. Television viewers saw images of Earth, the Moon, the cabin interior, the crew at work, and activity in the mission control center.

We received the broadcast via the Eurovision channel. It didn't go over the airwaves but was transmitted via cable to TsNIImash. When the crew capsule entered the atmosphere, it passed over Siberia and China and splashed down in the Pacific Ocean 6 kilometers from the precalculated position where the aircraft carrier *Yorktown* was located. The splashdown, the search, the approach of the rescue boats, the placement of the pontoons under the spacecraft, the approach of the helicopters, and the evacuation and transport of the crew to the aircraft carrier took just an hour and a half.

The splashdown area had waves up to 2 meters high, and a drizzly rain was falling. In the dim predawn light the helicopter hovered over the Command Module and illuminated it with its searchlight. Judging by the television pictures, the astronauts were delivered on board the aircraft carrier hale and hearty, and during the festive reception on board the aircraft carrier they felt pretty well. Besides the subsequent landing expeditions to the Moon, the flight of *Apollo 8* was the greatest success in the entire history of American astronautics, showing the whole world that the U.S. had finally managed to overtake the Soviet Union in space.

On 30 December, at the demand of Ustinov, the VPK held an emergency session to discuss just one issue: "How can we respond to the Americans?" From our organization only Okhapkin was present. Mishin was ill. Okhapkin later told us: "Opening the session, Smirnov reminded us that on 3 August 1964, the Central Committee and Council of Ministers had adopted the resolution 'On Work on Researching the Moon and Cosmic Space.' According to this resolution, a vehicle launched by the UR-500K rocket was supposed to execute a circumlunar flight in the first half of 1967. Comrade Chelomey—OKB-52—was named prime contractor.[18] This same resolution called for the landing of a crew on the surface of the Moon from a vehicle inserted by the N-1 heavy launch vehicle, and the crew's return and landing on Earth sometime in 1967 or 1968. The prime contractor for the launch vehicle, the spacecraft, and the expedition as a whole was OKB-1 (Chief Designer Korolev), later TsKBEM (Chief Designer Mishin)."

---

18. This involved the use of Chelomey's LK-1 piloted spacecraft, later abandoned.

"After this, a whole series of VPK decisions appeared with further specifics on the programs. On 25 October 1965, the resolution 'On Concentrating the Forces of the Industry's Design Organizations on the Creation of a Rocket-Space Complex for Flight Around the Moon' came out. In fulfillment of these resolutions, the Military-Industrial Commission routinely made decisions calling for a circumlunar flight through the joint efforts of TsKBEM and OKB-52 sometime between late 1967 and early 1968.

"These projects had remained crucial for the entire space industry over the last three years. The first launches of the 7K-L1 vehicles for the circumlunar flight program took place in March 1967.[19] Since then, nine unpiloted 7K-L1 vehicles have been launched using the UR-500K launch vehicle.[20] However, either through the fault of the launch vehicle or of the spacecraft systems, a decision cannot yet be made to go ahead with a piloted flight. Flight tests on the N-1 launch vehicle have not even begun. Thus, all the deadlines stipulated in the resolutions do not correspond to reality."

Discussion of the 7K-L1 projects ended in the opening remarks. The main subject of this pre–New Year's VPK session was to approve the Ye-8-5 program—the delivery to Earth of lunar soil by an automatic spacecraft. Back in early 1968, Babakin had told me about this idea with his inherent enthusiasm and confidence that everything would pan out and we would deliver a little lunar soil to Earth, just around 100 grams, but before the Americans would bring back a dozen kilograms on their Apollos. The project had so many purely engineering problems that I expressed my doubt as to whether the problem could be solved in the upcoming year. Babakin's proposal seemed very bold, but it found support in the Central Committee as a backup scenario that was inexpensive.

Now, having become aware of the lack of prospects for the 7K-L1 and the vague deadlines for the N1-L3, even Keldysh spoke out in favor of accelerating the Ye-8-5 project: "We can show that our way of studying the Moon is through automatic spacecraft. We have no intention of foolishly risking human life for the sake of political sensation."

They made a tacit decision to give this explanation to the mass media.

---

19. These were Earth orbital test flights flown under the cover names *Kosmos-146* (10 March 1967) and *Kosmos-154* (8 April 1967).

20. Besides the two launches in March 1967, there were six further launches on 28 September 1967 (launch failure), 22 November 1967 (launch failure), 2 March 1968 (*Zond-4*), 23 April 1968 (launch failure), 15 September 1968 (*Zond-5*), and 10 November 1968 (*Zond-6*). Another spacecraft suffered an accident on the ground on 14 July 1968 prior to launch.

THE YEAR 1969 BEGAN WITH A JUMBLE OF EVENTS, among which the first launch of the N-1 rocket appeared to be far from the most important. In this situation it would seem that we needed to throw everything "to the devil" and use everything in our power (and we had an enormous arsenal) in order to cut the Americans off at the pass.

Fat chance! The behavioral algorithm loaded into our consciousness for adhering to Central Committee directives did not allow for showing such initiative. Other space programs had gained such kinetic energy and had been reinforced with such a number of Central Committee, Council of Ministers, and VPK resolutions and ministers' orders that a radical restructuring of plans was out of the question. Despite genuine space patriotism and the enormous potential of science and industry, Soviet cosmonautics had no true leader at the helm capable of turning around its development as decisively as Korolev had done in 1961.

After our long pre–New Year's conversation with Pilyugin I realized that even he, a true compatriot of Korolev, did not consider landing a crew on the Moon to be our main mission. Personally, most of his time was devoted to launching Nadiradze's solid-propellant missiles from mobile launching systems, the technology for MIRV (multiple independently targetable reentry vehicle) separation, the development of his own on-board computers, and a competitive system for remote control, monitoring, and launching of missiles. From time to time Pilyugin was so enthralled with the very development process that it was as if he had forgotten about the final objective.

However, there was no time left to indulge in grim reflections. At the beginning of the year we celebrated our latest victory in space: on 14 and 15 January we launched *Soyuz-4* carrying cosmonaut Vladimir Shatalov and *Soyuz-5* carrying cosmonauts Boris Volynov, Aleksey Yeliseyev, and Yevgeniy Khrunov. The Soyuz vehicles executed an automatic docking, after which Yeliseyev and Khrunov performed a spacewalk to Shatalov's vehicle. The cosmonauts carried out the risky trek through open space splendidly.

During these space operations, Tregub, Rauschenbach, Bushuyev, and I were at the control center in Yevpatoriya. After the launch of *Soyuz-5*, Mishin flew in with Kerimov and Minister Afanasyev. Of course, along with us there were dozens of leading specialists involved in this truly engrossing work who had a great deal of work left to do on the N1-L3 project. But during such events we all forgot about N1-L3. This included Minister Afanasyev, who was chairman of the State Commission on N1-L3.

The first piloted docking, which included a vehicle-to-vehicle spacewalk to boot, went very smoothly. Among all the flight participants, Shatalov stood out in particular for the organization and integrity of his reports and his work.

Shatalov's launch had been scheduled for 13 January. We did not believe that 13 was an unlucky number. This time the ancient superstition proved true. At 1030 hours Shatalov was comfortably settled into the spacecraft and had begun to communicate with the bunker. Everything was going fine. Right before the launch, when the launch site had already been cleared, the control console issued a report revoking the readiness status of the launch vehicle gyroscopes. At a temperature of –24 degrees [–11.2°F] and a slight wind, to begin replacing gyroscopes when there was a cosmonaut on board was risky. Shatalov was safely removed from the spacecraft. He was upbeat and joked that he had "performed the most precise landing." The gyroscopes were replaced, all the ground cables were rechecked, and the launch took place successfully the following day.

I followed these events with a large group of specialists and enthusiasts at Yevpatoriya based on scanty dispatches from the firing range. Vehicle rendezvous was conducted automatically. At a range of 100 meters in accordance with the program, Shatalov and Volynov switched to manual control. Approach and docking proceeded very precisely. The vehicles flew for more than 4 hours in a mated state.

Soyuz-4 executed a normal landing, while the landing of *Soyuz-5*, which carried cosmonaut Volynov, was off-nominal. The Instrument Systems Compartment (PAO) didn't want to separate when the electrical command was issued from the Descent Module.[21] It broke away only upon entry into the atmosphere. Descent was ballistic with great g-forces; the hull of the Descent Module was turned 180 degrees when it entered the atmosphere and almost burned up. After the ballistic descent, when the main parachute came out, its cords began to twist up. Before reaching the ground the cords untwisted, but the landing was very hard. However, miraculously, Volynov was alive and well. In this connection, local poets composed blank verse using the surnames of the crewmembers:

PoShatalis,	They swayed,
PoVolynili,	They dawdled,
Ni Khruna ne sdelali,	They didn't do a thing,
Yeli seli.	They barely landed.

---

21. The Soyuz was divided into three major sections, the Living Compartment (BO), the Descent Module (SA), and the Instrument-Systems Compartment (PAO), often called the Service Module in the West.

It was four days after Volynov's hard landing that the *Soyuz-4* and *-5* cosmonauts were exposed to mortal danger. On 22 January, Moscow fêted the new heroes. They were traveling to the traditional Kremlin banquet from Vnukovo Airport in a motorcade. Right at the Kremlin's Borovitskiy Gates, someone hoping to kill Brezhnev fired on the motorcade. He fired on the wrong vehicle. Eight shots were fired at the car carrying Beregovoy, Leonov, Nikolayev, and Tereshkova. Their driver was mortally wounded, and a motorcyclist in the motorcade escort detail received a minor injury. The celebration at the Kremlin took place as if nothing had happened. We found out about the incident much later and enjoyed ourselves at the Kremlin Palace as we had before. But our laughter didn't last long. The launch of N-1 No. 3L was approaching, literally hanging over us.

From the author's archives.

After the completion of the *Soyuz-4/5* mission, the cosmonauts met with various officials from TsKBEM, the military, and the government for an official portrait. Sitting in the front row (left to right) are K. A. Kerimov, A. N. Ponomarev, V. A. Shatalov, B. V. Volynov, Ye. V. Khrunov, A. S. Yeliseyev, V. P. Mishin, N. P. Kamanin, and V. D. Vachnadze. In the second row (left to right) are B. Ye. Chertok, B. A. Strogonov, M. I. Samokhin, S. O. Okhapkin, P. A. Agadzhanov, A. A. Leonov, I. P. Rumyantsev, A. I. Tsarev, unknown, V. M. Klyucharev, A. S. Smirnov, G. T. Beregovoy, and N. A. Terentyev. In the back row (left to right) are A. T. Karev, M. F. Besserezhnov, G. V. Sovkov, A. A. Nazarov, I. T. Bobyrev, B. A. Radionov, A. P. Pedan, and G. S. Titov.

Chapter 10

1969—The First N-1 Launch

On 18 January, in Yevpatoriya over lunch in the officers' dining hall, we "actively" celebrated Vasiliy Mishin's birthday and Boris Volynov's miraculous deliverance.[1] After a good meal, Mishin, Kerimov, Kamanin, Ponomarev, and Beregovoy flew out to the firing range to greet the cosmonauts and send them off to the Moscow festivities. The next morning we, too, flew home. When we returned to Moscow, having celebrated the happy ending of our tribulations a good bit on the airplane, I said to Bushuyev, "This is the 12th 7K-OK landing, and look at the unexpected tricks it threw at us. For the L3 we're going to design a different Descent Module and a different descent system. How many modules need to first execute a descent at reentry velocity for us to be sure?"

He dismissed my question, saying, "Right now it's better not to think about this."

It was noisy and festive in the airplane. Jokes and laughter relieved the tension of four stressful days.

Babakin's group had remained at the Yevpatoriya center controlling the *Venera-5* spacecraft launched on 5 January and the *Venera-6* vehicle that had lifted off on 10 January. For the time being, everything was going just fine for them. I would say even more than just fine. Sometimes things just line up so well! In the interval between the launches of these two Veneras, on 8 January, the Central Committee and USSR Council of Ministers issued the resolution "On the Plan for Researching the Moon, Venus, and Mars Using Automatic Stations."

From the author's archives.

Boris Chertok (left) and Georgiy Babakin.

---

1. Mishin turned 52 in 1969.

Babakin had developed this resolution with Keldysh's very active participation and support. The next five years for Babakin's staff and the many scientists associated with them had been concisely mapped out. The automatic spacecraft "baton," which Korolev had passed to Babakin, had fallen into the hands of enthusiasts who could not conceal their joy both from their first successes and from the prospects that had opened up for them. Associating with Babakin and his comrades, I noted with chagrin that a similar optimistic *joie de vivre* had faded away among the TsKBEM staff. And this was not just the result of the disarray and vacillation in connection with the program of piloted flights and the Americans' successes.

On 22 January the entire TsKBEM management did practically no work—first they got ready and then set out for the Kremlin for the latest red carpet reception for four new cosmonauts all at once. Even Ivan the Terrible held feasts in the Kremlin for a reason.[2] A lavish table relieves stress for a while. Despite the abundance of the best sorts of alcoholic beverages and superb Kremlin *hors d'oeuvres* for every taste, at our "designer" table, conversations turned again and again to the latest UR-500K failure and the upcoming N-1 launch.

The latest 7K-L1 launch failure during the 501st second of the powered flight segment wedged itself between the safe return to Earth of four cosmonauts and their festive reception at the Kremlin.[3] The launch vehicle's safety system issued the command to the emergency rescue system (SAS) to save the spacecraft. For the umpteenth time we had seen for ourselves how reliable the SAS was! But the circumlunar flight had once again been stymied. At the festive table in the Kremlin, State Commission Chairman Georgiy Tyulin was clearly envious of State Commission Chairman Kerim Kerimov.[4]

On the morning of 23 January, Mishin called around to all his deputies to report that [MOM Minister] Sergey Afanasyev had decided to check on how we all felt after the banquet; he had hinted that it wouldn't be a bad idea if in the next few days we convened a small meeting of the Council of Chiefs regarding the upcoming N-1 launch and chat about the lunar landing expedition program in general.

We arranged to hold the council on 27 January. This council, which, as I understood it, had been convened at the insistence of Afanasyev and Keldysh, was unusual. The chief designers did not report on the readiness of their systems

---

2. Ivan IV (better known as Ivan the Terrible) (1530–1584) ruled Russia at a critical time when Russia was evolving from a medieval state to a more powerful and expansive empire.

3. The launch had taken place on 20 January 1969.

4. Tyulin and Kerimov presided over two different state commissions, the former directing the 7K-L1 circumlunar missions and the latter overseeing Earth-orbital Soyuz flights.

for the first launch. These reports were postponed until the large gathering at the firing range. Mishin began with a report about appropriations for the N1-L3 program. He argued rather emotionally that the program would not be fulfilled. For 1969, the plan budget retained production funding at the existing level, but no funding was stipulated for the construction of the experimental facilities that we needed.

"*Gosplan* considers experimental facilities to be capital investments," said Afanasyev, "You do know that that money is different."

"Let it be different," retorted Mishin, "But ultimately we must have facilities for ground developmental testing."

Then Ivan Serbin jumped in: "They released a lot of funds to the ministry to build Chelomey's experimental facilities in Reutov.[5] Why can't you use those facilities?"

"We're working on that," explained Afanasyev.

Judging by the course of the discussion, no one was prepared to come forward with any new proposals…except Keldysh. At first he was dozing. In the thick of the ruckus over experimental facilities he took the floor and said what neither Mishin, the minister, nor any of us could bring ourselves to say: "The status of operations on the N1-L3, in my opinion, is such that we need to postpone the date for the Moon landing to 1972 and make a decision in this regard as soon as possible."

Serbin showed his alertness: "And who gave you the right to cancel dates signed by the Central Committee?"

Keldysh remained very calm; Serbin's attack did not stop him.

"The assignment was decreed, it was written in a government resolution, no one is canceling it, but we need to take a sober look at things. Resolutions must be such that they don't discourage the working teams. One must not underestimate the prestigious role of our successes in space. We still don't know which has had the greater importance for our nation's defense—the intercontinental ballistic missile or the first satellite. Let's be honest, do we all really believe that landing a single human being on the Moon will be a priority? Can we surpass the Americans in this, or, perhaps we should be thinking today about Mars? Automatic spacecraft on the Moon and even lunar rovers will show up even without the N-1. Meanwhile, Barmin is designing the

---

5. Ivan Dmitriyevich Serbin (1910–1981) was the chief of the defense industries department of the Central Committee of the Communist Party. As such, he exercised strict ideological control over the personnel appointments in the Soviet space program.

lunar base.[6] They even told me that it has already been named 'Barmingrad.' What for? Is a base-station needed on the Moon? Perhaps it would be more beneficial to have a base in the form of a satellite station circling the Moon? Or circling the Earth? Who has analyzed this? It is difficult to anticipate how people's psychology will change tomorrow. They will simply speculate that Soviet scientists couldn't get ahead of the Americans. Especially since our program is classified, while the Americans put out an hour-by-hour schedule a year in advance. I brought up the matter of greater openness in the Central Committee, but I wasn't able to convince them. We need to proceed from this and think about other priority programs. That is what, it seems to me, we should have a serious discussion about."

Only Keldysh could have given such seditious speeches with Serbin present.

Tyulin gave a reply from his seat: "We are doomed to continue the N1-L3 program, but this work does not guarantee us priority, we understand that."

Keldysh continued: "The Americans have developed a program for 10 years. The American people believed in this program. It was publicized and the president reported on it. Now they are going to land a man on the Moon, they will celebrate, and it isn't even clear to them what they will do next. In my opinion, they will be thinking about this for another three years. Perhaps, we can take advantage of this confusion. I am not convinced that we need to update N1-L3 for the sake of the Moon, although, in principle, I am in favor of hydrogen.[7] But we need to have a goal. I am concerned that we don't have such a clear goal. Today we have two missions: a lunar landing and a flight to Mars. Aside from these two missions for the sake of science and priority, no one is naming others. The Americans will accomplish the first mission either this year or next year. This is clear. What's next? I am for Mars. We can't make a complex [launch] vehicle like the N-1 for the sake of the vehicle itself and then look around for a purpose for it. The year 1973 will be good for the unpiloted flight of a heavy spacecraft to Mars. We have faith in the N-1 launch vehicle. I'm not sure about 95 tons, but we'll certainly have 90. The latest Soyuz flights proved that we have docking down pat. In 1975, we can launch a piloted Mars satellite using two N-1 launch vehicles with a docking in orbit. If we were the first to find out whether there is life on Mars, this would be the greatest

---

6. In the late 1960s, Chief Designer Vladimir Barmin's design bureau, KB Obshchego mashinostroyeniye (Design Bureau for General Machine Building) began drawing up plans for long-term lunar bases as part of a future plan for settling the Moon. The organization's main line of work was designing launch complexes for Soviet missiles and launch vehicles.

7. This is a reference to the possibility of using high-energy propellants, particularly the combination of liquid hydrogen and liquid oxygen, on upper stages of the N-1.

scientific sensation. From a scientific point of view, Mars is more important than the Moon."

Given Keldysh's speech, there was the danger that there would be opposition despite directives from the highest levels. Afanasyev understood this. Considering it extremely undesirable to hold this discussion in front of Serbin, he [Afanasyev] came forward with a proposal that everyone give these matters a lot of thought, and since Mstislav Vsevolodovich [Keldysh] was in favor of the N-1 for any program, he asked Mishin to have a look at everything one more time before the first launch and ensure that all the chiefs and responsible parties have a timely departure for the firing range. The meeting did not progress any farther than this action. For us—developers of the N1-L3 program—Keldysh's behavior at this council meeting was a signal, a sort of request, for more active and concerted support for a new strategy in the policy of big space. In 1969 it was still not too late. The history of our cosmonautics could go differently if we would be more courageous. Ah, this is when our history really missed Korolev! Yes, he had dreamed about Mars more than about the Moon. An open-minded and far-thinking government leader could make a decisive change in course. But we were not destined to have such a leader.

Rereading my notes of Keldysh's speech a little less than 40 years later, I believe that it is even more relevant today. The role of personality in the history of cosmonautics has been great. It depends to a great extent on the personalities of state leaders. History simply did not bestow such talented commanders as Korolev and Keldysh, either in science or in politics, on the Soviet Union or on Russia, which inherited the USSR's space projects after its collapse. The only consolation, small as it may be, is that other nations also lack great, standout individuals. Incidentally, China might not have the talent of great commanders, but it exhibits Eastern wisdom capable of making an enormous nation into a great world power.

AND NOW, ONCE AGAIN WE RETURN TO THE FIRING RANGE. I settled in on the second floor of hotel No. 1. This hotel had permanent rooms assigned to Samokhin, Shabarov, Dorofeyev, Klyucharev, and Kozlov.[8] Mishin was

---

8. These were all senior management at TsKBEM involved in the N-1 program. Yevgeniy Vasilyevich Shabarov (1922–2003) was a deputy chief designer at TsKBEM in charge of flight-testing all new vehicles. Boris Arkadyevich Dorofeyev (1927–1999) was Shabarov's main aide and would later, from 1972 to 1974, serve as chief designer of the N-1 rocket. Dmitriy Ilyich Kozlov (1919–2009) was chief of the Kuybyshev Branch of TsKBEM and in charge of manufacturing the N-1 at the Progress Factory. Viktor Mikhaylovich Klyucharev (1917–1990) was director of the experimental production facility at TsKBEM.

Leading specialists from TsKBEM are shown here at the K. E. Tsiolkovskiy State Museum of the History of Cosmonautics in Kaluga. From left to right (standing) are Yu. P. Antonov, B. Ye. Chertok, M. S. Khomyakov, unknown, E. B. Brodskiy, Ye. V. Levashev, M. V. Melnikov, R. F. Appazov, V. F. Gladkiy, L. B. Vilnitskiy, A. S. Kasho, Z. F. Dorofeyeva, V. M. Arsentyev, V. N. Korzhenevskaya, E. I. Korzhenevskiy, B. A. Dorofeyev, and unknown. Dorofeyev served as the chief designer of the N-1 rocket from 1972 to 1974.

left to stay in a cottage. The hotels gradually filled up as the date of the N-1 launch approached. More and more people arrived from all over the country to participate, observe, monitor, and report. The brass preferred to live at Site No. 2. It was primarily the "working class" that populated the new residential development—Site No. 113.

Any first launch of a new rocket is an event. But for a rocket like the N-1, it was an exceptional event. Despite the fact that a good 4 kilometers separated the MIK of Site No. 2 and the enormous buildings of the N-1 assembly factory, the psychological tension that was generated around the gigantic rocket reached everyone, even those who had nothing to do with it. And people whom you knew well and were formerly cheerful, jocular, and prone to laughter now arrived at Site No. 2 at the "Luxe" dining hall or simply to meet with friends looking haggard from lack of sleep and ground down by the crush of responsibility.

Afanasyev, who headed the State Commission on the N-1, was also appointed chairman of the Lunar Council by government decision. The atmosphere in the crowded sessions of the State Commission on the N-1, which

From the author's archives.

The leadership of TsKBEM stands in front of an N1–L3 stack at the assembly and testing building at Site No. 112 at Tyuratam. From left to right are Ya. P. Kolyako, V. V. Kosyakov, G. N. Degtyarenko, V. A. Kalashnikov, O. I. Malyugin, I. A. Zubkov, V. F. Gladkiy, A. N. Voltsifer, K. K. Pantin, Yu. P. Ilin, V. V. Simakin, P. I. Meleshin, G. A. Fadeyev, D. I. Kozlov, P. F. Shulgin, A. P. Abramov, I. S. Prudnikov, A. P. Tishkin, K. M. Khomyakov, V. K. Bezverbyy, F. I. Ryabov, M. I. Samokhin, P. A. Yershov, K. D. Bushuyev, S. S. Kryukov, V. Ya. Litvinov, N. N. Ganin, V. M. Klyucharev, V. P. Mishin, I. A. Mordvinov, M. S. Khomyakov, B. G. Penzin, Yu. P. Antonov, and A. N. Ivannikov.

were conducted by the minister, was much more tense than in ordinary commissions on piloted launches.

The scale of operations on the N-1 required the creation of a special directorate at the military installation at the firing range, which coordinated all the preparation for tests and acceptance of the launch facilities, and the test fueling and launching equipment.[9] A new tribe of testers appeared, whose careers had spanned the R-7, UR-500K, and combat missiles, and of quite young ones, whose careers were just beginning with the N-1. The constituent parts of this army were still getting broken in and learning to work with one another.

The State Commission met for the first time in this enlarged form in the conference hall of the manufacturing plant building at Site No. 112. All you had to do was put on a white lab coat, descend to the first floor, present a pass to the Progress Factory security detail at the entrance, and you entered a realm of fantastic dimensions. In the bays stood rigs on which the lobes of the spherical tanks were welded. A first-time visitor couldn't help but notice

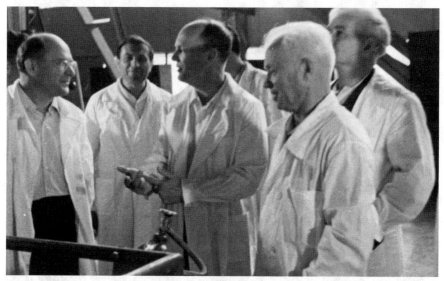

From the author's archives.

Senior designers discussing the assembly of the N-1 rocket at the assembly and testing building. From left to right, Dmitriy Kozlov, unknown, Boris Paton, and Sergey Okhapkin. Paton was a prominent full member of the Academy of Sciences and an expert in welding.

---

9. This was the Sixth Testing Directorate at Tyuratam (also known as Military Unit 96630) headed by Colonel Yevgeniy Georgiyevich Moiseyev from 1967 to 1974. The directorate had seven departments for ground equipment, engines, fueling, guidance systems, telemetry systems, and payload operations.

the assembled first, second, and third stages laid out there according to some mysterious principle. Tiny assemblers in off-white coveralls and engineer technicians in white lab coats were scurrying around on the openwork rigs. The bays were filled so tightly by the rocket stages in various degrees of readiness that it was impossible for someone at the front of the bay to make out where it ended. This made the hall seem even longer.

At the old MIK at Site No. 2 I knew and understood every piece equipment, stand, console, rocket block, and spacecraft. At the N-1 MIK, everything was new, unfamiliar, and had overwhelming dimensions. The fundamental distinction of the new building was that the rocket was manufactured here, and its testing was the last technical operation. The majority of the people moving unhurried through the bays were not firing range testers, but workers who were making the rocket here. Each person was involved with his or her own work. The curious superiors descending from the upper floors just got in the way.

Nominal, assembled, and launch-ready, launch vehicle N-1 No. 3L had undergone a cycle of factory horizontal tests and was awaiting the decision of the State Commission. Checking out the mating of the launch complex with

an engineering model of the rocket was a dress rehearsal. This rocket was a complete structural, electrical, pneumatic, and hydraulic analog. All of the prelaunch operations except for the actual firing of the engines had been worked out on it for several months. During this trial run process numerous glitches occurred in the interaction of systems, but the primary outcome was the interaction of personnel and systems.

THE STATE COMMISSION SESSION ON 9 FEBRUARY 1969 had the primary objective of making a decision regarding the N-1 launch. All the chief designers flew in. Commander-in-Chief of the Strategic Rocket Forces Marshal Nikolay Krylov himself came to the State Commission meeting.[10] For this reason the "jackets," as civil-

The N-1 in a ground-up shot.

From the author's archives.

10. Marshal Nikolay Ivanovich Krylov (1903–1972) served as Commander-in-Chief of the Strategic Rocket Forces from 1963 to 1972.

ians were referred to, got lost in a throng of officers and generals, who had hurried to take their places in the new meeting hall. There were many unfamiliar faces. Not only chief designers, but also deputy ministers, directors, and chief engineers of the main factories were invited to this historic meeting.

Despite the large confluence of people, Afanasyev took his time as he conducted the State Commission session and analyzed the readiness of each system in detail. Each chief designer had to report about the readiness of his system to begin flight-development tests, and the testers gave summary reports about the glitches that had occurred.

Two ministers who had flown in for the State Commission session—Petr Dementyev and Valeriy Kalmykov—also listened patiently to all the reports. Dementyev's arrival was understandable—his Ministry of the Aviation Industry was half responsible for the fate of the N-1. He oversaw Nikolay Kuznetsov's design bureau and the series-production engine factory in Kuybyshev.

During a break in the proceedings, after catching sight of me, Kalmykov greeted me very warmly and with genuine admiration said: "I have heard a lot about N-1 in the VPK, but now, after seeing it with my own eyes, I am simply amazed what a huge operation you managed to conduct during those three years while I wasn't here. I think that no matter what Afanasyev and Krylov decide concerning the first launch, groundwork has already been laid here for what would ensure us success not only for today's situation, but for many decades in the future. When Korolev first came with you to visit me at NII-10, God bless me, I can still recall, about 20 years ago, even science fiction writers had not dreamed of such scales."[11]

Of all the ministers with whom I used to meet back then, Kalmykov seemed the most capable of romantic flights of fancy from the prosaic managerial routine. We were able to indulge in reminiscing during the long break in the State Commission meeting, which Afanasyev had announced due to the fact that the chief of the firing range, General Kurushin, had come out with objections against the launch of N-1 No. 3L.[12] Based on the test results, the rocket and the ground equipment had many glitches, which they had not yet managed to eliminate. During the break, Afanasyev and Mishin worked on Krylov to get him to remove Kurushin's objections. Ultimately, Kurushin had to give in after assurances that all the glitches would be eliminated before the launch.

---

11. NII-10, which developed gyroscope systems for Soviet ballistic missiles, was headed by Kalmykov in the late 1940s. See Chertok, *Rockets and People, Vol. II*, p. 5.

12. Lieutenant-General Aleksandr Aleksandrovich Kurushin (1922–) was commander of the Tyuratam firing range (known as NIIP-5) from 1965 to 1973.

The individual delivering the main report at the State Commission was Mishin, chief designer of the head enterprise, TsKBEM. He reported about the work that had been conducted over the past year in accordance with the recommendations of the expert commission to increase the N-1's reliability and payload capacity. Unlike the [original] draft plan for the first stage, six additional NK-15 engines were installed [on the flight model]. Twenty-four engines arranged around the outer circumference of the bottom part of the first stage had variable thrust to control and stabilize the rocket. The six engines of the inner ring were not involved in control. Eight of these same NK-15V engines with high-altitude nozzles were installed on the second stage, and on the third stage—four NK-19 engines with high-altitude nozzles. The power margin in terms of thrust would enable the launch vehicle to fulfill its mission even if four first-stage engines failed in flight.

The launch path inclination was changed from 65 to 52 degrees. Another measure to increase the payload mass was to reduce the orbital altitude from 300 to 220 kilometers. On subsequent launch vehicles, the following changes would be implemented: placing inserts in the equatorial portion of the tanks to increase the working fuel margin; maintaining thermostatic control of the fuel's temperature to −15 to −20 degrees [°C or 5 to −4°F] and supercooling of the oxygen to −191 degrees [°C or −311.8°F]; and augmenting the thrust of the propulsion systems of all three stages by 2 percent.

While performing strength development tests of the rocket on a model, glitches occurred that required that the exterior panels of the hull be significantly reinforced.

The developmental testing of the rocket blocks (or stages) was conducted at NII-229 on special rigs. There, Blocks B, V, G, and D underwent both cold tests and firing tests. There were three firing stand tests on unit EU-16, simulating a full-scale Block V, and one firing stand test on unit EU-15, which had a full-scale model of Block B with eight engines producing a total 1,200 tons of thrust. Comments made about glitches during the integrated firing tests were taken into account and implemented on N-1 No. 3L using the electrically, hydraulically, and structurally similar 1M mockup of the rocket.[13] Developmental testing of the mating of the rocket with the ground transportation, erecting, fueling, and launch equipment was completed.

For the first launch they used a simplified L3 system upper stage with an unpiloted 7K-L1S vehicle instead of the LOK and LK. The emergency rescue

---

13. "Comments" (*zamechaniya*) in Russian technical parlance is comparable to the common technical phrase "anomalies noted" in English.

system was standard on the first launch. Liftoff was proposed to take place on 18 February 1969.

Boris Dorofeyev and Boris Filin reported on the results of the tests on the launch vehicle and upper stage. The majority of system chief designers gave brief reports recommending clearance for launch. Barmin gave a more detailed report than other chief systems' suppliers. He concluded that all the fueling equipment and all the launch systems should be cleared for the installation of the first flight rocket and, upon readiness, it should be cleared for the first launch.

Only the State Commission could make the decision to roll out the first N-1 No. 3L flight rocket to the launch site and prepare it for launch. However, long before this decisive meeting, rocket No. 3L had already been at the launch site and had undergone a cycle of electrical tests there, including a launch simulation. This wasn't done because we had "an abundance of resources," but for the simple reason that a full electrical equivalent—an integrated test stand—was not yet ready. Integrated developmental testing of all the electrical systems was supposed to have been conducted on a test stand in Pilyugin's department at NIIAP.

In keeping with longstanding practice, instruments, cables, and all the other production accessories were delivered first of all for the flight vehicles and then—much later, after the developers had howled hysterically—for the experimental test units and rigs on which the developmental tests for these very instruments were supposed to be performed. Everyone considered this procedure to be faulty, but no one could change it. The dates for the deliveries of the standard instruments for the flight rockets were under the strict control of the entire administrative staff. All other deliveries were almost considered to be the developers' whims.

The assembly of rocket N-1 No. 3L was completed before integrated electrical developmental testing on the stand. Therefore a daring decision was made: to roll out the rocket to the launch site and conduct all the necessary checkout procedures there jointly with all the ground equipment, after which the rocket would need to return to the engineering facility at the big MIK for electrical developmental testing. In addition, numerous other modifications had to be performed at the MIK according to the results of the strength tests.

THE YEAR 1968 PROVED TO BE UNUSUALLY DIFFICULT for Sergey Okhapkin and the design, strength, and materials departments that he supervised. The strength department at TsNIImash conducted structural strength tests on models. When Korolev was still alive, a decision was made to build at NII-88 a modern facility for researching the strength of rocket designs. After Korolev's death, Okhapkin and NII-88 scientists Viktor Panferov and Aleksandr Karmishin showed initiative and perseverance; as a result, in accordance with the N-1 resolution, a laboratory was built and fitted out with one-of-a-kind equipment for all manner of static-dynamic tests on full-scale assemblies, parts, and rocket models as a whole. The tests proceeded simultaneously with the production process. It was necessary to really hurry so that the factories did not make too many rejects.

Completely exasperated by the glitches he'd encountered during these tests, Okhapkin persuaded me to commiserate with him and drop by NII-88 to have a look at the equipment for strength testing. For me, a person unversed in the newest strength test methods, the scales of these operations and the laboratory equipment made quite an impression.

At the Progress Factory in Kuybyshev and at the big MIK at the firing range, they were wrapping up manufacturing the first No. 3L flight rocket, and production of the next two flight models was under way at full speed. At that time, the staff at the NII-88 "strength" building were performing round-the-clock testing that destroyed the main structural elements.

The destruction of the main load-bearing structural ring of the first stage—a ring with a diameter of 14 meters—delivered a most crushing blow for the strength engineers. The tests had begun back in 1967, and at first it seemed that they would be able to avoid major modifications.

"But look what happened after reaching design conditions," said Okhapkin, pointing to a jumbled heap of amorphous pieces of metal.

It was a depressing sight. In many cases, the load-bearing capacity of the panels of the exterior load-bearing hull also proved lower than required. Karmishin explained that, in the opinion of his specialists, our designers' calculations had not taken into consideration the impact of "marginal effects"—structural weakening on sharp corners and edges. On the R-7, R-9, and other "old" rockets, more ductile alloys were used and the "marginal effect" could be disregarded. New materials were selected for the N-1 with a view toward reducing its mass. These materials proved to be more brittle.

After the destruction of the load-bearing ring at NII-88, Mishin ordered that the lead TsKBEM specialists for strength and structural analysis be reprimanded. Modifications needed to be made to the "marginal effect" areas on the already manufactured rocket compartments in Kuybyshev and at the firing range, new parts needed to be manufactured, and sometimes it was necessary to return to old tried-and-true materials. But this meant time, time, and once again an increase in the mass!

The long-suffering assembly of the Block A (first stage) load-bearing structure was modified and underwent strength testing 10 times. Ten load applications resulted in premature destructions, and only after this did we manage to receive a satisfactory result. Production could not wait that long.

They decided to launch first one or even two flight rockets in light-duty mode and not make all the modifications to them.

But the designers' troubles did not end here. Two years after the beginning of production at the Progress Factory, highly unusual phenomena started to occur. Cracks were discovered under the rivets in riveted structural parts. Their appearance was first thought to be incidental. However, cracks were found not only at the factory in Kuybyshev, but also on a massive scale on the assembled units at the MIK. They immediately replaced impact riveting with pressure molding. Cracked parts were to be replaced with new ones. Where this was not possible, they attached special fastening plates. But that wasn't all. On the finished assembly they discovered a broken steel fastening bolt. An examination confirmed that the failure of the fastener, which was made of a new grade of steel, was not an isolated occurrence. The failure of bolts and screws subjected to loads began to take on a large-scale pattern. All of the fasteners made of the new grade of steel had to be removed and replaced.

All told, it took almost a year to resolve all of these problems and to modify the first two flight vehicles. However, this was not the main reason for the delay in the start of flight testing. It took so much time to complete the construction and acceptance of all the launch site systems and to set up and begin tests with a mockup spacecraft at the engineering facility and launch sites that the strength and miscellaneous modifications going on at the same time did not ultimately determine the completion time [of preparations for launch].

The N-1 No. 3L rocket was modified in response to all possible comments by the time of the January session of the State Commission. All that remained were deviations permitted by the technical management. On the second stage (Block B), contrary to the design, Kuznetsov's main engines did not have high-altitude nozzles. The control system's on-board digital computer, developed at NIIAP in 1969, produced so many malfunctions and such errors that it was impossible to clear it for flight. Deviating from the design, they made the decision to begin flight testing on an analog control system, which did not require an on-board digital computer. This impaired the parameters of the control system and of the rocket as a whole, but it was not possible to wait any longer for the on-board computer to be ready. The main concern was, would the three stages be tested out?

Barmin did not follow the American procedure of transporting the rocket to the launch site in a vertical position. He remained true to our tradition—the rocket was moved from the engineering facility to the launch site in a horizontal position on a transporter-erector, which moved in keeping with the erstwhile principle "cannons travel to battle backwards." True, this "backside" had a diameter of 17 meters. Four motor locomotives moved the erector along two parallel railroad tracks. Laying the rocket on the erector, securing it, and preparing it for rollout took several days, as did the commission's arguments before and after. Finally, 9 February was announced to everyone as the day of departure to the launch site, Site No. 110.

During the days commemorating Korolev's 90th birthday [in January 1997], I had the opportunity to refresh my memory and reexperience this ceremonial process reproduced in the frames of a documentary film. The cameraman had selected a good angle. The gigantic rocket was comfortably bedded down on the platform of the erector as if that was its rightful place. Under the roof of the MIK, the rocket and erector seemed monolithic and grandiose. The entire bottom portion of the first stage filled the lens of the movie camera. With its 30 nozzles it was looking at dozens of people thronging below in white lab coats. They were not working; they had gathered for the ceremonial rollout process. Most were smiling lightheartedly. The image of a laughing Mishin flashed by. Afanasyev's usually worried face lit up when a bottle of champagne was smashed against the erector. Shards of green glass were immediately snatched up as precious souvenirs. The N-1 did not abandon the traditions that Korolev established during the time of the first *Semyorka*. Operations at the engineering facility ended with a ritual gathering of those who contributed to the rocket all that they could. Then in a couple of hours, four motor locomotives would deliver the first flight model from the bright, warm MIK to the launch site where it would undergo several days of tests and begin launch preparation in a burning, frosty wind.

The launch was scheduled for 20 February. The day before, the weather service forecast low cloud cover hampering visual monitoring during the first-stage operation flight segment. The launch was postponed to 21 February. In keeping with the principle "God helps those who help themselves," the population at large was evacuated from Sites Nos. 112 and 113. The launch control "guest" hall, which out of habit we called the "bunker," was jam-packed with those involved with launch preparation, VIPs, and various representatives of similar status. Television screens made it possible to observe liftoff from here without using periscopes.

Chief of the firing range's Sixth Directorate Colonel Yevgeniy Moiseyev, Deputy Chief of the firing range General Anatoliy Kirillov, and N-1 Deputy Chief Designer Boris Dorofeyev occupied their places at the periscopes in the launch control hall. State Commission Chairman Sergey Afanasyev and technical manager Vasiliy Mishin were also here. At 12 hours 18 minutes 07 seconds, the rocket shuddered and began to lift off. The roar penetrated underground through several meters of concrete. The report of telemetry operators followed for the first seconds of flight announcing the shutdown of 2 of the 30 engines. Observers, who, notwithstanding the high security, managed to track the flight

From the author's archives.

Launch of the first N-1 vehicle on 21 February 1969.

from the ground, said that the plume seemed unusually rigid, "it didn't flap," and it was three or four times longer than the body of the rocket.

After around 10 seconds the thunder of the engines faded in the distance. The hall was completely silent. The second minute of flight had begun. And suddenly—the plume extinguished.... It was the 69th second of flight. The fiery rocket drifted away without a plume from its engines. At a slight angle to the horizon, it was still moving upward; then it tilted over, and, leaving a smoky trail, without breaking up, it began to fall.

It isn't alarm and it isn't dismay; it's more a certain complex mixture of intense inner pain and a feeling of absolute powerlessness that you experience while watching a crashing rocket approach the ground. Dying before your eyes is a creation with which you have become so intertwined over a period of several years that it sometimes seemed that this inanimate "article" had a soul. Even now it seems to me that each lost rocket has a soul made up of the feelings and experiences of the hundreds of creators of that "article."

The first flight rocket fell along the flight route 52 kilometers from the launch site. A distant flash confirmed: it's all over! The strained, stressed, tightly wound string is broken. The last stage of work on the rocket begins. It's time to look for what happened and why. The immediate start of the search is a sedative that always brings relief. Barmin attempted to offer the first consolation: "Don't feel bad, the launch site is unharmed."

On 15 May 1957, Barmin had breathed the same sigh of relief when he learned that the first *Semyorka*, which crashed in the 100th second of flight, did not damage the launch site. Back then, all of us, not just Barmin's team, had not been too upset: after all, reaching 100 seconds the first time—that's already an achievement. Now there are a lot more people, but far fewer people who can offer calming words and can crack a joke. The N-1 is indeed a very great rocket to be lost so easily and quickly after five years spent creating it.

From the author's archives.

Senior management shown prior to the launch of the first N-1. From left to right, Anatoliy Kirillov, Vasiliy Mishin, Sergey Afanasyev, Boris Dorofeyev, and V. I. Snegirev.

Mishin was too impatient to wait for investigations lasting many days. Turning to Iosifyan, he said right there in the bunker that the turbogenerator was the culprit for everything. Only its failure could have caused the simultaneous shutdown of all 28 engines. Minister Sergey Afanasyev— also chairman of the State Commission— appointed Mishin chairman of the accident investigation commission before he left the bunker. Iosifyan and Sheremetyevskiy were unusually insistent and proposed searching the impact area immediately and delivering the turbogenerators for verification.

The search team hunted for the turbogenerators. Surprisingly, they turned out to be whole and suitable for "repeat use." They were immediately transported to the test rig at the Istrinskiy facility, and after minor repair they started up! Telemetry also confirmed that the turbogenerators had operated up until the moment of impact with the ground. Who then shut down all 28 engines at once, and what was the offense of the two engines—No. 12 and diametrically opposed No. 24—that switched off during liftoff from the ground? What kind of devil had made short work of all 30 engines?

All the telemetry recordings were sent to Site No. 10.[14] The analysis bureau began its feverish round-the-clock deciphering. Scarcely 24 hours had passed when the first information emerged. At first it traveled like a rumor, then it began to be written up in reports, and finally it could be put out at the level of an accident investigation commission and then the State Commission.

At the end of this unusually long launch day I already knew that the shutdown of the first 2 engines during liftoff and of the remaining 28 during the 69th second of flight were prompted by a KORD system command. That night KORD system specialists, looking haggard from all the calamities that had come down on them, gathered in my hotel room. We wanted to have a talk without any outsiders eager for the latest news so that we could be the first to report to the higher-ups.

We had worked on the KORD system for three years! We could assuage our guilt for the failure only after a thorough study of the true causes. We would "brainstorm" all the possible scenarios. By morning we had drawn up a main list of experiments that needed to be conducted on the next flight model N-1 No. 5L in Podlipki on the equipment and at NIIAP on the integrated stand.

Mishin, after making arrangements with the minister, made the decision to create a special commission to analyze the KORD system's operation. "We don't need a lot of people," said Mishin. "Chertok will be the chairman."

It wasn't until early March, after arguments and calculations, and following repeated microanalysis of the telemetry films, that we began to establish a logical connection between all the events on board the rocket that had resulted in the tragic end. Analysis of such failures is truly a creative process and somewhat like the work of a criminal investigator getting to the bottom of a crime. However, the logic of cunning analysis available to lone geniuses such as Sherlock Holmes will not save you in these situations. A single human being is not capable of digesting all the multisystem and contradictory information, analyzing it after rejecting instructions from management and the hunches from people on the sidelines, and writing up incontrovertible findings. Dozens of people thought, pored over films, and argued.

After spending three sleepless days, the telemetry specialists provided unequivocal information: all of the engine shutdowns were prompted by KORD system commands. On 7 March there was a meeting of the technical management in which I felt myself to be the main culprit in the demise

---

14. Site 10 was the other name of the city center at Leninsk, the major town built next to the launch range at Tyuratam.

of the rocket. In keeping with the established tradition, the chairman of the investigation commission appoints each "suspect" to be his own investigator. My commission had the following membership: Vladilen Finogeyev—control system; Nikolay Sheremetyevskiy—electric power; Ivan Utkin—KORD system sensors; and Aleksandr Cherkasov—engines.[15] By the time the commission had been created, the KORD system specialists and I had already pieced together a picture of the system's behavior. Now we needed to explain it to all the other commission members, concisely write up our objective findings, and present them to the State Commission. "He who honestly seeks will always find" is a true statement for this sort of investigation.

I shall remind the reader that to monitor the operation of all the engines of Blocks A, B, and V, the KORD system used four control channels: pressure in the combustion chambers; pressure pulsations in the gas generator; revolutions per minute, i.e., rotation speed of the turbopump assembly; and temperature of the gas generator. No deviations from normal operation were detected in the pressure and temperature channels. The channel monitoring the rotations per minute (rpm) of the Block A turbopump assembly activated upon receiving the command "ignition" and functioned normally until receiving the command "main." Then, 0.34 seconds after the "liftoff" contact actuated, the control system shut down engine No. 12 after receiving a KORD system signal. The KORD system ostensibly reacted to the sharp increase in the rotation speed of the turbopump assembly. We determined that the command was false. The control system executed it and, in accordance with the logic, shut down engine No. 24.

Studies conducted in KORD system laboratories and at NIIAP showed that the KORD system unit of engine No. 12 responded to external interference, which occurred in the form of a spike of damped vibrations of voltage between the KORD system power buses and the hull; this spike occurred at the moment of detonation of the explosive cartridges opening the valves feeding propellant components to the engines upon receiving the command "main." The frequency and amplitude of the electrical vibrations that occurred when the pyrocartridges detonated simulated the emergency mode—"racing" of the turbopump assembly. The KORD system did not tolerate this.

---

15. Ivan Ivanovich Utkin (1910–1985) was chief designer at NII IT—*Nauchno-issledovatelskiy institut izmeritelnyy tekhniki* (Scientific-Research Institute for Measurement Technology)—responsible for developing various telemetry systems for Soviet missiles, launch vehicles, and spacecraft. This institute had been spun out of the larger NII-88. Aleksandr Vladimirovich Cherkasov was a deputy to Chief Designer Nikolay Kuznetsov at the Trud Design Bureau (KB Trud), which developed the engines for the N-1.

A spike of similar damping vibrations usually occurs in an electrical loop containing capacitance, inductance, and resistance if a sharp change in current strength "strikes" it. This strike was the impulse that activated dozens of pyro-cartridges. The capacitance and inductance of the cable network determined the vibration frequency. The cable network, in addition to performing its main task, simulated a sort of "ringing loop."

But why did this "ringing" cause only engine No. 12 to shut down? We performed an experiment on the integrated stand at NIIAP with a real cable network and real KORD system instruments. The investigative experiment confirmed the hunch that the parameters of the long lines of the cable net-work in the area of engine No. 12 were the most critical. The culpability of the KORD system in shutting down this engine with a false command was proven unequivocally. At the discretion of the layout designers, the subsequent assembly and length of the cables for the other engines could also prove "criti-cal." In these "presumed" instances, in the very first second, so many engines could shut down that the rocket would not take off. In this horrible scenario the destruction of the launch pad was inevitable. However, the remaining 28 engines held up until the 69th second. "Like the 28 Panfilovtsy heroes out-side Moscow in 1941," joked Kirillov grimly.[16] And all of them to a man fell simultaneously. Why?

What other "ringing" occurred there? The answer came from other inves-tigating groups. Rigorous analysis showed that during the 6th second of flight, elevated vibrations caused the sample probe sensor tube measuring the gas pressure downstream from the turbine to break off. Twenty-five seconds into the flight, the fuel pressure sensor tube upstream from the gas generator broke off. "Acid" gas at a temperature of 340°C [644°F] spewed out through the ruptured tube and mixed with kerosene gushing out of the other broken tube. A cloud of fuel mixture formed and burst into flame 55 seconds into the flight. The fire engulfed a large portion of the aft section of Block A. Sixty-eight seconds into the flight, the flame that was raging in the aft section burned through the insulation of the cable network, including the alternating current

---

16. This is a reference to an event early in World War II, on 18 November 1941, when 28 soldiers of the 1075th rifle regiment under the command of Major General Ivan Panfilov were said to have held off an advance of German tanks; all but three soldiers were killed. Their actions were immortalized in later Soviet accounts of the war. Anatoliy Semenovich Kirillov (1924–1987) was, at the time, the deputy chief of the Tyuratam range (NIIP-5). He was one of the oldest "testers" in the Soviet space program, having been responsible for launch operations for a generation of Soviet ballistic missiles and then space launch vehicles.

1,000-Hertz power cables. These cables and the cables of the KORD system's sensitive channels were bound in common bundles.

The 1,000-Hertz current of the power system of the functional turbogenerator found its way to the KORD system's sensitive inputs, which perceived it as inadmissible pulsations in the gas generators. Twenty-five volts of interference (given a maximum permissible value of 15 volts) penetrating through the fire-damaged insulation bypassed all the filters and shut down all 28 engines virtually simultaneously. Moreover, this interference also passed upward to the KORD system units of Blocks B and V.

The causes for the demise of the first N-1 flight rocker were unequivocally identified. Mishin's main commission and my commission on the KORD system developed measures that would be introduced immediately on the next N-1 No. 5 flight model. The cable bundles were made separate. They reinforced the thermal insulation around the engines wrapping them with an asbestos blanket. For the KORD system units themselves, they devised a protective system for the power circuits. And working according to the principle of "God helps those who help themselves," despite the objections of Kuznetsov's organization, they decided to disconnect the pulsation monitoring channel from the execution of the emergency shutdown command and keep it just for telemetry. After analyzing everything that had happened and approving anti-fire and anti-interference measures, the State Commission made the decision to launch N-1 No. 5L in June 1969.

When it came down to signing the certificate of findings, I recalled the dispute between Voskresenskiy and Korolev concerning the integrated stand for the development testing of Block A, the first stage. What had happened with No. 3L was not a random occurrence, but the logical result of our economizing on the development of a stand for ground testing. Subsequent events completely confirmed this truth.

Having returned from the firing range after such a painful failure, I arranged with my deputies and department chiefs to hold a wide-ranging discussion of our mistakes and the lessons that each developer should take away from this event. We held a conference of sorts in this regard at the very end of February. I had reckoned on celebrating my birthday on 1 March.[17] Feeling not the least bit festive, I announced that I had no plans to mark the event and asked that nothing interfere with work.

Nevertheless, without asking for my consent, Nikolay Golunskiy led a group of telemetry specialists—none of whom were officially subordinate to

---

17. Chertok turned 57 in 1969.

me—and burst into my office with a bottle of cognac. After brief speeches listing my shortcomings and my achievements blown out of all proportion, Golunskiy grabbed his guitar and strummed our old firing range song of unknown authorship. The words made us nostalgic because this song appeared soon after our space triumphs of the early 1960s.

I shall take the risk of reproducing the lyrics in their entirety. As for the tune, each performer selected one according to his or her own fancy.

The rocket is filled, of course, not with water,
And it's high time to push the launch button.
Come on, friend, let's get out of the way,
If only it would fly away, God forbid we should have to drain it.
   REFRAIN:
   I know, my dear friends, many years will pass by,
   And the world will forget our all our pains,
   But in the wreckage of many a rocket
   The mark we made always remains.
Let us be stumbling drunk tomorrow,
The rocket flew away; pour another glass.
We finished the job, and now it's time to hit the road,
Now let Comrade Levitan talk himself hoarse.
REFRAIN
Rockets are flying to points unknown,
Cosmonaut heroes—too many to count,
Space maps fill the plotting boards,
And they've given us our travel orders again.
REFRAIN
Hotels with bedbugs and dusty roads—
All of this, old pal, we had to endure.
Let the newspapers write that we live like gods.
Let's crumple the newspaper and go…for a stroll.
REFRAIN.

Chapter 11

After the Failure of N–1s No. 3 and No. 5

We were not capable—not at the highest levels of political leadership, not at the ministerial level, and especially not within our rocket space engineering community—of concentrating our efforts on a single mission of "crucial national importance": a lunar landing expedition. Having realized that it was impossible to catch up with the U.S. in the execution of a piloted circumlunar flight and an expedition to the lunar surface, we continued to expend our resources on a number of disparate goals: on an unpiloted circumlunar flight using L1 vehicles; on the automatic delivery of lunar soil; on accelerating the piloted flight program using 7K-OK model Soyuz vehicles; and on designing new, more advanced vehicles—modifications of the Soyuzes.

In March 1969, the accident investigation commissions and groups concluded their investigation into the causes of the failure of the first launch and

Система Н1-Л3 установлена вертикально на пусковое устройство. Транспортно-установочное устройство не отведено

Установка системы Н1-Л3 на пусковое устройство

From the author's archives.

These two images show the N-1 being erected on its pad at Site No. 110.

developed the latest batch of measures to increase the reliability of the N-1 rocket. The technical management gave the "green light" to prepare for the launch of rocket N-1 No. 5L. Why not N-1 No. 4L? For planning reasons, rocket N-1 No. 4L had been set aside "in reserve" so that a whole series of modifications, which they had not managed to implement for N-1 No. 3L and N-1 No. 5L, could later be performed on it.

Система Н1-Л3 в пути на стартовый комплекс

Система Н1-Л3 около пускового устройства стартового комплекса

Космическая система Н1-Л3 на транспортно-установочном агрегате в монтажно-испытательном корпусе, готовая к вывозу на старт

From the author's archives.

These three images show the N1–L3 stack being prepared (lower inset) in the MIK and then being transported to the launch pad.

From 3 through 13 March, the U.S. successfully conducted the experimental flight of the entire *Apollo 9* space complex in Earth orbit.[1] After this the Americans announced the program for the next two flights, having confirmed that a lunar landing expedition was planned for July of that year.

The TsKBEM staff headed by Mishin bore primary responsibility for compensating for the psychological damage inflicted on domestic and world public opinion, which had sincerely believed in the absolute priority of the socialist world in space. I cannot say that feelings of dismay or despondency reigned among my comrades on our staff. On the contrary, we were so busy with other programs under way at the same time that we simply did not have time to be demoralized. In conversations among ourselves we agreed that it was impossible to achieve victory advancing over a whole broad front. We needed to stop and concentrate our efforts on a single area, or perhaps two areas, as the Americans had done.

On one of these working evenings Pilyugin called me up on the "Kremlin line" and reported with indignation: "Aside from the fact that Chelomey is once again proposing his UR-700 in place of the N-1, he is now planning to adapt this design for a flight to Mars. I've been informed that Afanasyev is preparing an order in this regard. I will not take part in this risky venture."

I knew about Chelomey's work at OKB-52 (renamed TsKBM) in Reutov and at his branch in Fili on a design for the super-heavy UR-700 launch vehicle and the LK-700 lunar vehicle. All of my friends and I were miffed by this blatant redundancy.

When I started up a conversation about this with Tyulin, he said: "I objected, but as you know, my relationship with the minister is very complicated. If you and Mishin mess up with the N-1, he needs other proposals, even if only in the form of a draft plan."

Much later, by the time that our N1-L3 program had been shut down and the UR-700/LK-700 design had been placed in the archives, we established completely normal relations with Chelomey. At one of the regular meetings of our Academy department, after inviting me to the canteen for a "glass of tea and cookies," Chelomey asked an unexpected question: "Admit it, if 10 or 12 years ago they had accepted my proposal for the UR-700, we would now have a launch vehicle for both lunar and Mars expeditions that no one would

---

1. During the *Apollo 9* mission, astronauts James A. McDivitt, David R. Scott, and Russell L. Schweickart performed a complex set of maneuvers in Earth orbit involving the Command and Service Module (*Gumdrop*) and the Lunar Module (*Spider*).

be able to shut down. Three UR-700 stages have completed the debugging stage, and now everyone needs them."[2]

I had to admit that the UR-700 launch vehicle had its advantages. The design of the new rocket was based on the three-stage UR-500K, which had already been in service. The UR-500 was installed as the second stage [of the UR-700], whose first stage was undergoing development. The latter consisted of nine blocks with a single RD-270 engine in each of them. The total thrust of the first-stage engines near the ground was 5,760 tons. This made it possible to insert into orbit a payload with a mass up to 140 tons.

"We would have a launch vehicle that was just as good as the Saturn V, but with the advantage that the three upper stages would always be in series production, regardless of the lunar program," said Chelomey.

In this sense he was right. For the Mars expedition, Chelomey proposed a new version of the launch vehicle: the UR-900. The very same UR-500 comprised the second, third, and fourth stages of this launch vehicle. Unlike the UR-700, the first stage had 15 RD-270 engines. According to the design, the UR-700 had six RD-270 engines. This made it possible [for the UR-900] to insert a mass of up to 240 tons into a near-Earth reference orbit.

At one time Glushko had proposed RD-270 engines with a thrust of 640 tons to Korolev for the N-1. They were developed for use with high boiling components—*geptil* (unsymmetrical dimethylhydrazine) and nitrogen tetroxide.

"Can you imagine, Vladimir Nikolayevich, what would have happened if a rocket such as the UR-700 or, God forbid, the UR-900 came crashing down near the launch site? All of our pads and all the facilities would be turned into a dead zone for 15 to 20 years."

"Well, first of all, they wouldn't come crashing down because now the engines of your general designer Valentin Petrovich Glushko are failsafe. And second, the *Pyatisotka* [UR-500] flies without a hitch using these propellant components and hundreds of combat missiles have been standing on duty in silos and at sea on submarines for years. The fear of these components is quite exaggerated."

But in 2007, I realized that I had been right. Many years ago I had posed a somewhat provocative question to Vladimir Chelomey. By the beginning of the 21st century the Proton rocket had proven itself to be completely reliable. The Proton launch vehicle did not let us down during the construction of the *Mir* station and the Russian segment of the International Space Station. The

---

2. Chelomey is alluding to the notion that the upper stages of the UR-700 were derived from the UR-500K (Proton) and therefore already developed and tested.

leaders of friendly Kazakhstan grumbled about ecological troubles that resulted from first stages falling onto the steppe after exhausting their fuel, but they tolerated them. However on 6 September 2007, a Proton came down en route after 140.7 seconds of flight. Wreckage fell 50 kilometers to the southwest of Dzhezkazgan, poisoning a large area of formerly pristine steppe with the toxic propellant components of the second stage.[3] Launches were temporarily halted. Russia promised to pay Kazakhstan a large sum for the economic damages inflicted....

IN 1969, RESHETNEV, KOZLOV, AND BABAKIN provided consolation with the successful launches of *Molniya-1*, Kosmos reconnaissance satellites, and the Venera automatic interplanetary stations. Two dozen various Kosmos spacecraft were launched during the first six months of 1969. Our newspapers, which observed a ban on information about the American lunar successes, finally had the opportunity to fill their front pages with flights of enthusiasm over the successful arrival of Soviet automatic interplanetary stations *Venera-5* (16 May) and *Venera-6* (17 May) on Venus. A pennant bearing an image of Lenin in bas-relief and the emblem of the Soviet Union was delivered to the surface of Venus. On 19 May 1969, the front pages of all of our newspapers were filled with salutes from the Central Committee, Supreme Soviet, and Council of Ministers to the scientists, designers, engineers, technicians, workers, and all the staffs and organizations, thanks to which "our Soviet motherland had secured one more outstanding victory in space exploration."

Correspondingly, in the same order, "scientists, designers, engineers, technicians, and workers" who had been involved in the development, launch, and flight support of the interplanetary stations, and also in receiving and processing scientific information, reported to the Central Committee, Supreme Soviet, and Council of Ministers about the successful execution of the program: "We dedicate this achievement of Soviet science and technology to the 100th anniversary of the birth of the organizer of the Communist party, founder of the Soviet state, and standard-bearer of workers all over the world Vladimir Ilyich Lenin."[4]

The evening before, 18 May, we were watching television coverage of the *Apollo 10* liftoff and flight to the Moon, and the next morning, 19 May, we attempted to find information in the newspapers about the Americans' piloted

---

3. The launch was operated by International Launch Services (ILS) to carry *JCSAT-11*, a satellite owned by the private Japanese satellite operator JSAT Corporation. Because of a failure in the second stage, the satellite failed to reach Earth orbit.

4. Pravda, 19 May 1969. Lenin's 100th birthday was celebrated on 22 April 1970.

flight.[5] It proved anything but simple to track down more than a modest report on this event, even in the very back pages.

After meeting with Babakin, I congratulated him warmly and tried to joke about the fact that the latest "Venusian" successes were thanks to the January resolution "On the Plan of Work for Research on the Moon, Mars, and Venus using Automatic Stations." Babakin beamed, but swore good-naturedly and complained that excessive attention from the "brass" was already beginning to grate on his nerves and distract him from his work. These achievements to a certain degree compensated for the failure of the "lunar excavator," the Ye-8-5.[6]

"We timed our landing on Venus specially so as to muffle the Apollo liftoff," Babakin laughed it off.

In Yevpatoriya and at the firing range we often met with television correspondent Yuriy Valeryanovich Fokin.[7] He was firmly entrenched in our rocket-space community, and we all treated him with great respect, understanding how difficult it was for him to water down information about cosmonautics, leaving only the ceremonial window dressing. So, we heard from him, or perhaps it was from some other representative of the press, that before the Apollo launches newspaper, radio, and television journalists fly out to Cape Canaveral from every nation except the Soviet Union. And it wasn't the American authorities who prohibited this, but our own Soviet governmental agencies. International rules of etiquette require reciprocity. If our correspondents accepted an invitation and visited Cape Canaveral, then we would be obliged to invite Americans to our firing range for some launch. In those days even thinking such a thought could not be tolerated.

At the press conferences devoted to *Venera-5* and *-6*, in response to foreign journalists' cautious questions about our plans regarding the Moon, Keldysh gave vague explanations: that we had no intentions of being the first to send a human being to the Moon, or that we believed that a great deal could be learned using automatic stations before the need arose to risk landing a human being.

It is very difficult, from the standpoint of common sense, to explain the total blackout of space information where no state secrets were concerned. During a discussion of this problem within our "inner circle," we concluded

---

5. The *Apollo 10* mission, lasting from 18 to 26 May 1969, was the final dress rehearsal of the first piloted lunar landing. During the mission, astronauts Thomas P. Stafford, John W. Young, and Eugene A. Cernan performed a complex series of maneuvers in lunar orbit in their CSM (*Charlie Brown*) and LM (*Snoopy*).

6. The Ye-8-5 was the design designation of the lunar sample collector developed under Babakin. It was created using the basic design of Babakin's lunar rover, the Ye-8.

7. Yuriy Valeryanovich Fokin (1924–2009) was a famous Soviet TV journalist of the 1960s and the host of the popular news program *Estafeta novostey* [*Relay News*].

that the reason was the obtuseness or stupidity of the Central Committee staff. However, among the Party officials we mixed with and who sponsored us, I never met anyone who was either stupid or obtuse. When asked point-blank why there were information bans, they could not give any clearly defined answer. It made Academy of Sciences President Keldysh look foolish.

On 29 and 30 May, the technical management and State Commission convened at the firing range to officially "close" all the incidents regarding the launch of N-1 No. 3L and to make the decision to launch N-1 No. 5L. At a conference in Litvinov's office, the *Minobshchemash* section rehearsed its presentation for the next day's State Commission meeting.[8] For the umpteenth time I repeated my account of the KORD system's behavior on N-1 No. 3L and gave assurances that all necessary measures had been implemented on N-1 No. 5 and testing had confirmed their effectiveness.

"We are powerless to predict the behavior of the system if the cable networks are damaged by fire," I said. "The most unpredictable connections can occur when cable insulation breaks down."

"It's best not to mention that in the State Commission," advised Litvinov.

Barmin disrupted the peaceful dialogue at this meeting.

"The failure of N-1 No. 3L could also have occurred 50 seconds sooner. Who can guarantee that this will not happen? If the rocket isn't immediately diverted farther away, we are putting all the launch facilities at risk. I propose to let the control specialists completely inhibit the ability for the engines to shut down for the first 15 to 20 seconds and during that time the rocket will move a safe distance away."

Because of his proposal, we started to argue, as a result of which Barmin agreed not to bring this up in the State Commission, while Dorofeyev, Finogeyev, and I promised to give it some thought and work it out. We obviously did not have time to come up with these measures in time for No. 5L.

In the State Commission meeting on 30 May in the conference hall of the big MIK, Mishin gave the report on the failure of N-1 No. 3L and proposals for N-1 No. 5L. Afanasyev still insisted that I give a more detailed account of why the KORD system shut down operational engines when there was a fire in the aft section. Barmin reported on the readiness of all the ground fueling and launching systems. He kept his promise not to raise the issue of preventive engine shutdown inhibits. As for the rest, the commission proceeded rather

---

8. *Minobshchemash* was shorthand for the Ministry of General Machine Building (*Ministerstvo obshchego mashinostroyeniya*).

amicably until it came to the matter of verifying the status of the upcoming N-1 No. 6L rocket. The commission got "hung up" on this problem because, beginning with the N-1 No. 6L, Mishin promised to insert the Lunar Orbital Vehicle (LOK) capable of flying around the Moon as part of the "payload" rather than mockup L3S-type vehicles.[9]

Lidorenko asked whether anyone had investigated using a test procedure on the electrochemical generators (EKhG) at the monitoring and test facility. Electrochemical generators require liquid hydrogen and liquid oxygen. How does one work with such an explosive mixture if there are dozens of testers right around the corner? Finogeyev tried to calm everyone down, announcing that they were optimizing the procedure beforehand on a rig at their NIIAP facility in order to have a reliable EKhG equivalent and that the fueling process would take place only at the launch site. Ovchinnikov assured Afanasyev and the military officers, who had begun to pose difficult questions, that everything had been thought through. The EKhG would not be fueled with hydrogen until it was on the launch pad and the safety of the operation had been verified many times.

One was not supposed to close sensitive issues in State Commissions without a good explanation. Afanasyev proposed, "Set up a commission to review this problem under the leadership of Comrade Lidorenko and appoint Comrade Finogeyev as his deputy. And who shall we have from TsKBEM?" I suggested, "Ovchinnikov, Penek, Kupriyanchik, and Sosnovik. And put some military

From the author's archives.

types on the commission, subject to approval."

"I'll ask those who guarantee the safety of hydrogen on board to sign in blood," stated Afanasyev.

Similar commissions, as a rule, were set up when issues requiring additional tests and time arose during

A panoramic view of two N-1 vehicles on their respective launch pads at Site No. 110 at Tyuratam.

---

9. "L3S" was the combined designation of the L-1S circumlunar vehicle and a dummy LK (as was launched on the first N-1 rocket in February 1969).

State Commission sessions. The protocol usually noted, "Make a joint reasoned decision on such-and-such a date, and have it approved by the technical manager."[10] Per Mishin's proposal, a State Commission decision set a deadline of 3 July for the launch readiness of N-1 No. 5.

Hundreds of testers, designers, engineers, technicians, and workers faced stressful work in the fierce heat that had set in. For the first time they had gotten an air conditioning system in the new big MIK and the atmosphere was quite tolerable. But at the launch site there was no reprieve from the direct rays of the sun. No. 3L was prepared in January and February when the temperature was −25°C [−13°F]. Back then, people who had run to the heated sheds to warm their frozen hands and rub their frost-bitten noses said that the summer heat was better. Now, when guzzling liters of water that couldn't quench their thirst, those same testers recalled, "And when it was freezing cold you didn't feel thirsty at all."

On 1 June, I parted for a while from my comrades who were staying behind to work on No. 5L; packed my travel bag with a pile of letters, papers with instructions, and "off-the-record" comments; and hurried to the airfield

From the author's archives.
Another view, this from an aerial perspective, of two N-1s on the pad in 1969.

---

10. The "technical manager" was the person on the State Commission (usually a senior designer or a chief designer from the design bureau) responsible for the overall technical aspects of the spacecraft itself. The "technical manager" headed the "technical management," a subgroup of members of the State Commission responsible for particular subsystems of the spacecraft.

to depart for Moscow with Afanasyev and Mishin. On the airplane Afanasyev tipped us off that the previous evening Smirnov had telephoned him and, on behalf of Ustinov, asked us—TsKBEM management—to gather to discuss the program of upcoming N-1 launch vehicle launches.

On the morning of 3 June in Mishin's office—formerly Korolev's "big office"—a select company of chiefs gathered. We jokingly referred to similar gatherings as meetings of a "tight circle of limited people." Keldysh, whom we told about this aphorism, was quite amused. In attendance were Serbin, Smirnov, Keldysh, Afanasyev, Tyulin, Litvinov, Kerimov, Pashkov, Tsarev, Pilyugin, Ryazanskiy, Barmin, Iosifyan, Mozzhorin, and Galin.[11] From our side Mishin, Okhapkin, Bushuyev, Tregub, Abramov, Kryukov, and I attended.

Smirnov warned, "This meeting is very important—the Central Committee is very concerned about the status of the N1-L3 and about the state of affairs in general at TsKBEM. In view of the Americans' successes," added Smirnov, "the administration finds our failures particularly troubling. They would like to hear an objective report about the true status."

Mishin had not prepared himself very thoroughly for such an imposing meeting. He briefly reported about the results of the accident investigation of the flight of N-1 No. 3L and about the status of the preparation of N-1 No. 5L. He announced the launch date: "Exactly one month from now—on 3 July."

With an optimism that was natural for a chief designer, Mishin said that, despite its failure, the N-1 No. 3L launch had provided very important experimental material. We had learned the bitter lessons of using the KORD system, had protected it from interference, and therefore, in the upcoming N-1 No. 5L launch, we could boldly go on with the circumlunar flight program. Without having consulted with his deputies, Mishin then promised to launch N-1 No. 6L in its full standard configuration for the execution of a circumlunar flight and return to Earth in unpiloted mode.

"All of our systems and instruments are fully equipped; the matter is in the subcontractors' hands."

Looking at the briefing sheet prepared for him earlier, Smirnov asked, "Is this really so? According to our information, there is still a very large amount of missing equipment."

---

11. These people were Party officials (I. D. Serbin), defense industry bureaucrats (L. V. Smirnov, S. A. Afanasyev, G. A. Tyulin, V. Ya. Litvinov, K. A. Kerimov, G. N. Pashkov, A. I. Tsarev, and Yu. A. Mozzhorin), scientists (M. V. Keldysh), and engineers and designers (N. A. Pilyugin, M. S. Ryazanskiy, V. P. Barmin, A. G. Iosifyan, and Ye. N. Galin).

Igor Bobyrev had most likely prepared the briefing paper for Smirnov.[12] The other deputies and I often associated with him in the Kremlin offices of the VPK, not passing up the opportunity to ask for help to cover the deficit in equipment shipments, especially when we were dealing with outside ministries. Bobyrev himself traveled around to the organizations and knew about the actual state of affairs better than the other Kremlin officials of the VPK offices.

As was proper in such cases, I was supposed to come to Mishin's aid. "It is feasible to complete the manufacture and delivery of all the missing instruments for N1-L3 No. 6L this year," I reported. "But after we receive them they will need to undergo a cycle of testing—a test run of all the systems in the complex." Next I listed the most critical systems for this testing: the EKhG automatics, the NIIAP computer and its interface with the other systems, and Geofizika's optical sensors.

Keldysh interrupted my wordy response and asked whether it would be possible to provide N-1 No. 6L and N-1 No. 7L in two versions. If the N-1 No. 5L launch were to show insufficient reliability, N-1 No. 6L and N-1 No. 7L could be equipped just with mockups and the launch vehicle itself could be tested out.

"Ultimately," he said, "today we are arguing about instruments for lunar vehicles, without having a launch vehicle on which to send them to the Moon. It seems to me that we need to give people the opportunity to calmly prepare and test out the LOK and LK—that's where there are still so many unresolved problems, and independent of that, we need to speed up launch vehicle launches. Your L3S vehicle is, after all, not the LOK, but its 'ersatz.' By specifying a circumlunar flight at any cost, we once again tie our own hands. To this day we have been unable to reliably execute a circumlunar flight and return to the Earth using the special L1 vehicle. Where is the guarantee that the L3S will perform this mission better? In the coming year our task will be to optimize the launch vehicle."

Tyulin supported Keldysh. He went further and said that we needed to think through backup plans for launches even with a dummy model instead of a vehicle. Mishin fervently objected. He promised to have N-1 No. 7L in full flight configuration enabling the LOK not only to be inserted into lunar orbit, but also to ensure the automatic landing of the LK on the lunar surface.

"We don't need to make a mistake here," broke in Bushuyev. "The N-1 No. 6L launch is possible this year only in a simplified L3S version; we can't

---

12. Igor Timofeyevich Bobyrev was the deputy chief of a department within the Military-Industrial Commission (VPK).

guarantee any circumlunar flight. We need to plan an insertion into Earth orbit or a highly elliptical orbit that does not involve the Moon."

Serbin could not tolerate this hint at revising the Central Committee decision on the circumlunar flight, which he detected in the words of Keldysh, Tyulin, and Bushuyev.

"We have no right to abandon the circumlunar flight. If you pose a question like that, then you need to report to the Central Committee about it," he declared. Smirnov nodded his head in agreement; Afanasyev quickly jotted something down on his notepad. Everyone else kept quiet. The discussion ended with an instruction to the minister to look into the matter and give an additional report to the Central Committee.

THEY THEN TALKED ABOUT THE N-11 MODEL and a Mars landing expedition project.[13] These discussions proceeded with breaks for tea and sandwiches, which Kosyakov provided in abundance. Okhapkin gave a passionate speech in defense of the N-11 rocket. Mishin rather tactlessly quipped that neither Keldysh nor Afanasyev had given the proper support to the so-obvious advantages of this proposal.

Taking advantage of the fact that my tea-drinking neighbor was Pashkov, I asked, "And actually, Georgiy Nikolayevich, if we had begun with the N-11, as Korolev proposed, wouldn't we already have a launch vehicle every bit as good as the UR-500, but safe, with the two upper stages of the N-1 already tested out? That was the way the Americans operated, first developing the Saturn IB. If you became acquainted with Chelomey's UR-700 design, you'd see he came out with the very same idea: its upper stages were the already-tested-out UR-500."

"Now is not the time. The military is completely against the entire program. We already have to fight to tear hundreds of millions away from purely military missions every year."

Pashkov was right in the sense that the chiefs who had come out to this gathering with us today had their heads crammed with more than just lunar, let alone Mars, missions. The famous "little civil war" had flared up between the camps of Yangel and Chelomey. The selection of either of the two models

---

13. The N-11 was intended as a medium-lift capacity launch vehicle that would use elements of the larger N-1. Its first two stages were supposed to be modified versions of the N-1's second and third stages (Blocks B and V), while its third stage would be a new stage (Block S_M) using a high-energy liquid hydrogen–liquid oxygen engine.

of strategic missiles ran into several billion rubles.[14] Competing for scales of expenditures with the land-based strategic nuclear missile forces, the navy and atomic scientists had also proposed their own doctrine of "nuclear retaliation."

Socializing with Isanin and Makeyev at the latest Academy meeting, I already knew that work of unprecedented proportions was under way to rearm the fleet with ballistic missile submarines, each of which was equipped with 16 of Makeyev's missiles.[15] In the next five years there were plans to build more than a dozen strategic missile submarine cruisers. The conversation with Makeyev took place in a festive mood—the two of us had just been elected to the Academy of Sciences.[16]

"You must excuse me," said Makeyev, "as you know, I don't like to brag, but the atomic submarine cruiser with our 16 missiles is as expensive as the

From the author's archives.

Shown here are Chief Designer Viktor Makeyev (center) and Ye. N. Rabinovich congratulating Chertok (left) on his 60th birthday in 1972.

---

14. Chertok is referring here to the "little civil war," an acrimonious dispute between the two giants of the Soviet missile industry, Chelomey and Yangel, over the development of third-generation ICBMs for the Strategic Rocket Forces. Unable to decide between two very expensive options, Brezhnev and the Soviet Defense Council opted to develop systems proposed by both designers. See Chertok, *Rockets and People, Vol. III*, pp. 148–154.

15. As chief designer of TsKB-16 from 1946 to 1970, Nikolay Nikitich Isanin (1904–1990) headed the development of several generations of Soviet military naval ships, including nuclear submarines.

16. Both Chertok and Makeyev were elected Corresponding Members of the Academy of Sciences in November 1968.

N-1, and perhaps, as complex. We are constantly working on new designs. In two or three years, at a maximum, along with ships, we are going to deliver cruisers with intercontinental ballistic missiles. Find the time to come over and see for yourself."

I am very sorry that I didn't find the time and didn't make the trip out to Miass to see Makeyev. I found out about the tough problems with the submarine missile control system after visiting Semikhatov in Sverdlovsk.[17] Five years later, shipbuilders put the manufacture of atomic submarine cruisers on line. Missiles literally had to be made "like sausages" in order to arm them. In modern terminology this was sleek and high technology.

Ustinov was also absorbed in a new undertaking: Nadiradze's mobile missile complexes. Afanasyev opposed the development of such missile systems outside his ministry. With that stance he spoiled good relations with Ustinov. All of these problems addled the minds of our bosses far more than the prospects of the Moon and Mars.

Nevertheless, at this meeting Keldysh came out in support of Mars expedition studies that we had begun back when Korolev was still with us. He asked Mishin to briefly report on the status of the project. The Mars expedition project called for the preliminary assembly of an interplanetary expedition complex in Earth orbit. The main modules of the complex were an interplanetary orbital vehicle, a Mars landing vehicle, a module for the return trip to Earth, and a nuclear reactor–based power plant. The power plant supported the operation of electric rocket engines in interplanetary orbit en route to Mars and the return of the expedition to Earth orbit. The expedition would take two to three years. The use of artificial gravity was assumed. At that time the medical community did not believe that human beings would be able to maintain their health and performance under conditions of weightlessness for more than two or three months.

Work on the Mars expedition project was enthralling. But it distracted our main gurus from current problems that couldn't tolerate delays. Mishin's Mars report was received very unenthusiastically. On the contrary, the chiefs who had gathered let it be known that it was a total waste of our time. Only Keldysh spoke out in favor of continuing operations, "but not to the detriment of the L3."

---

17. From 1953 to 1992, Nikolay Aleksandrovich Semikhatov (1918–2002) served as chief designer of SKB-626, the primary supplier of guidance and control systems for Soviet naval ballistic missiles. In 1992, he became a full member of the Academy of Sciences. SKB-626 is currently known as N. A. Semikhatov NPO Avtomatiki.

"At OPM we've also looked into such possibilities.[18] I must say," declared Keldysh, "that if the N-1 launch vehicle flies reliably and if it's modified, making the third stage operate on [liquid] hydrogen, then the dual-launch scenario might prove sufficient for a piloted flight to Mars. I am not in favor of diverting efforts to the N-11 now. We already have the UR-500 with the same capabilities. We need to quickly test out the N-1."

Mishin assured everyone that we were working on the Mars project without diverting people from the L3, but had not abandoned the hydrogen block for the fourth stage, and in a year we would have it ready for rig testing.[19]

At the very end of the conversations, after glancing at his papers, Smirnov asked Mishin, "You promised the flight of three Soyuzes before the October Revolution anniversary. Can I convene a commission to make a decision and report to the Central Committee?" Coming to Mishin's aid, Bushuyev and I attested that preparation was under way for the program, which entailed the docking of two Soyuzes, while a third one would fly around them and provide television coverage. Litvinov supported us saying that the only things holding us up for the time being were technical bugs with *Igla*.

At the mention of *Igla*, Afanasyev looked at me and said, "These launches are extremely important for us. Let Chertok stay here and resolve all the issues with his friend Mnatsakanyan and look after the docking assembly. Disgracing ourselves with the piloted Soyuzes is the last thing we need right now. They're all we have for the time being." This instruction was one of the reasons why I was not at the firing range on the day of the launch of No. 5L.

At the mention of docking assemblies, Klyucharev came to my aid and chimed in, "Docking assemblies are being manufactured. They are very complex mechanisms, but we have mastered them. Machine tool builders and the Azov Optical-Mechanical Factory have helped us a lot."

On that note, the high-ranking guests who had been in conference with us for almost 4 hours went their separate ways after first agreeing that in late June, when prompted by State Commission chairman Afanasyev, they would gather at the firing range for the launch of N-1 No. 5L.

---

18. The OPM—*Otdeleniya prikladnoy matematiki* (Department of Applied Mathematics)— provided significant mathematical modeling support for the Soviet missile and space programs. It was originally established as part of the V. A. Steklov Mathematics Institute of the Academy of Sciences (MIAN) in 1953 but spun off as an independent Academy body, the Institute of Applied Mathematics (IPM) in 1966. It is known today as the M. V. Keldysh Institute of Applied Mathematics.

19. This "hydrogen block" was known as Block S_R and was equipped with two 11D56 engines developed by KB Khimmash headed by Chief Designer Aleksey Isayev.

However, the minister did not turn a deaf ear to the "Martian" conversations. On 30 June [1969], Afanasyev issued an order obligating Chelomey, over the course of a year, to develop a design for a Mars complex comprising the UR-700M (or UR-900) launch vehicle and the MK-700M Mars vehicle. After learning about this and having been officially relieved of my duty to fly out to the firing range to take part in the launch of N-1 No. 5L, I found the time to discuss proposals for the Mars expedition control system....

In August 1997, Igor Gansvindt dropped by to see me. In the 1960s he was the lead planner of the piloted vehicle's landing control system for both the Mars landing and its touchdown on Earth after returning from the expedition. At that time, he handed over a sketch of the vehicle, which he had received with the baseline data for designing the landing control system, and handwritten notes of my report. Gansvindt recalled that in the summer of 1969 I had convened a large technical conference with all the subcontractors concerned and delivered an audience-inspiring report about the makeup and structure of the Mars expedition control system. If it hadn't been for my inimitable handwriting, I might have questioned the authorship of the "Martian" manuscript. But I confess that a quarter century later I read this document with as much interest as I had read Aleksey Tolstoy's famous *Aelita* 75 years before.[20]

But my modern-day "Martian" activity didn't end there. A week after my conversation with Gansvindt, a BBC team that had flown in from London descended on me to make a television documentary about the history of Mars explorations. I told them about the incidents described in my third book, *Rockets and People: Hot Days of the Cold War*, in the chapter "The Cuban Missile Crisis...and Mars."

"We hadn't even dreamed of such success—finding a living participant of the first Mars rocket launch during the 1962 Cuban Missile Crisis! The world stood on the brink of an exchange of nuclear missile strikes across the Atlantic, and you were preparing for a launch to Mars!"

The young British woman leading the team peppered me with questions. She was very well versed in the history of all of mankind's attempts to send automatic interplanetary stations to explore Mars and promised that British television viewers would be receptive. In December that same year I received a videocassette from the BBC in which I discovered my own "talking head." However, Academician Sagdeyev, the former director of the USSR Academy

---

20. *Aelita* (1923) was one of the earliest and most famous space fiction novels of the Soviet era. Written by Aleksey Nikolayevich Tolstoy (1883–1945), it was made into an equally famous motion picture in 1924.

of Sciences' Institute of Space Research (IKI), who moved to the U.S. after his marriage to the granddaughter of President Eisenhower, proved to be in the forefront and unrivaled in the documentary....[21]

THE FAILURE OF N-1 NO. 3L WAS A PAINFUL BUT INSTRUCTIVE EXAMPLE of what happens when new methods for testing the reliability of complex rocket-space systems are disregarded. Catastrophic failures that developed during the first launch should have occurred earlier during integrated firing rig tests on the flight-ready first stage. Now we were paying for the fact that Korolev had resigned himself to the draft plan's lack of requirements for the construction of a rig for such tests. With the exception of the deceased Leonid Voskresenskiy, we all had humbly consented to this. We in Korolev's camp sympathized with the rebel Voskresenskiy, but no one dared side with him publicly.

The history of our aviation and the first years of atomic and rocket technology are rich with examples of the successful borrowing from outside experience in order to catch up. After World War II, our science, technology, and industry quite successfully, rapidly, and efficiently duplicated German V-2 missiles, which we called R-1, and the American B-29 Flying Fortress, which we called the Tu-4. Such duplication (right down to exact reproduction) was not only permitted, but it received the status of governmental decrees. Yet, the reliability-testing methods that the Americans used during the development of Saturn V proved to be unattainable in our rocket industry's economy. In rocket technology the "maybe it will work" method didn't work. We had not yet conducted a radical restructuring.

MISHIN GOT DRAWN INTO ARGUMENTS WITH KAMANIN over the list of candidates for the lunar expedition crews. This irritated Bushuyev and me; it seemed premature to us. It was presumed that, by virtue of their positions, Bushuyev and Mishin would champion our interests. After the list was finally approved at the most recent meeting on that issue, Mishin announced that we would complete an expedition to the Moon before the end of 1970. Corporate solidarity and years of discipline would not permit the exercise of active rebellion or disobedience.

---

21. The IKI—*Institut kosmicheskikh issledovaniy*—was the primary space science research institution within the Academy of Sciences. It was established in 1965. Roald Zinnurovich Sagdeyev (1932–) served as director of IKI from 1973 to 1988. He emigrated to the U.S. in 1990 and currently is Distinguished University Professor in the Department of Physics at the University of Maryland in College Park, MD.

MISHIN MADE THE DECISION TO LAUNCH N-I No. 5L for a circumlunar flight. Therefore, together with NIIAP, we assembled a hybrid complex (retaining the L3S designation) from the systems of the 7K-L1, new developments of the future LOK, flight-worthy Blocks G and D, and also the Lunar Vehicle (LK) cargo mockup. Instruments installed in the L1 Descent Module were supposed to control Blocks G and D according to the circumlunar flight program, after which all three N-1 stages would actuate normally. Only the SAS equipment on the L3S was completely standard.

Since the times of Korolev, our ballistics specialists had been considered the most critical thinkers on our staff. But an order is an order, and hoping for a safe circumlunar flight, the ballistics specialists had calculated the launch time for 3 July, 2318 hours. And what if such a miracle actually happened?

I was among the enthusiasts who had gathered, as usual, in Podlipki, in the large office of the chief—the running commentary from the bunker came here. Rather than relying on my own impressions, I am forced to describe everything that happened during the second launch based on information received from participants and eyewitnesses, and using documentary evidence.

The launch of N-1 No. 5L proceeded precisely according to the calculated time. As the engines of Block A were building up for operation 0.25 seconds before liftoff from the launch pad, peripheral engine No. 8 exploded. The remaining engines operated for a certain period of time, and the rocket lifted off. It managed to lift off vertically for 200 meters, and then the engines

From the author's archives.

The catastrophic night launch of the second N-1 rocket (vehicle No. 5L). The image shows the moment when the Emergency Rescue System began to operate.

began to shut down. In 12 seconds all of the engines had shut down except for one—No. 18. The only operating engine began to turn the rocket about its transverse axis. Fifteen seconds into the flight, the solid-propellant engines of the emergency recovery system actuated, the fairing segments opened—and the Descent Module [of the L1], which had broken away from the launch vehicle, flew off into the darkness. Twenty-three seconds into the flight the rocket fell flat on the launch site. A series of violent explosions followed.

In a white flame, 2,500 tons of kerosene and liquid oxygen burned, illuminating the steppe under the night sky for dozens of kilometers. The inhabitants of the town of Leninsk, 35 kilometers from the launch site, observed a bright glow, shuddering at the terrible thoughts. Their family and friends were there at the launch site. The blast waves blew out the windows not only in the buildings close to the launch site, but also in the residential areas of Site No. 113 and even at Site No. 2—6 kilometers from the launch site.

The firing range chief did not grant permission for Afanasyev, Dorofeyev, Kirillov, and Moiseyev to exit the bunker and go to the surface until a half hour later.[22] "When we emerged," recounted Dorofeyev, "an unusual mist was still drizzling down. Drops of kerosene, which had not managed to burn, were falling to the ground. They had been lifted high into the sky by the blast waves and were now precipitating out in the form of rain." The safety measures that the firing range command had taken proved to be effective. All reports about destruction ended with the reassuring words, "no one was harmed."

"Wrong!" exclaimed Barmin in a fit of temper, shaken by what had happened. "There are many hundreds of people who were harmed—all of us who built the launch site. Now we have to rebuild it. We are the ones actually harmed."

Barmin was in charge of the commission concerned with "ground destruction." He assessed damage not in rubles, which were of little interest to anybody, but in deadlines—rebuilding would take at least a year, even with the most intensive all-hands effort. It seemed amazing that the second launch position—the left launch pad located just 3 kilometers from the one that exploded—was practically unharmed.

"Flight testing can continue," joked (with very bad timing) someone from the accident investigation commission that had just been created.

"Impossible," objected Barmin. "I will not give my consent now for a launch until the rocket is modified so that the engines won't shut down right over the launch site. Take it out into the steppe and blow it up there! You can

22. The chief of NIIP-5, as the Tyuratam firing range was officially known, was Aleksandr Aleksandrovich Kurushin (1922–).

slap together a couple dozen rockets if you want, but we only have one launch site, and even that one still needs to be modified."

First thing in the morning, they began a cursory and then a rigorous study of the telemetry recordings. There were no particular differences of opinion about the source of the explosion. Everyone concluded that it had begun in engine No. 8. The investigators of the accident investigation commission painstakingly gathered the remains of the engine assemblies that had been strewn over a 1-kilometer radius from the launch site. Unlike the other 29 assemblies, which had retained their external shape, the turbopump assembly of engine No. 8 was melted and mangled by the internal explosion.

The rocket could not survive after such an explosion. The lines in the adjacent engines were broken and damaged. A fire broke out, and with a snowballing effect the lower section of Block A [first stage] began to disintegrate. With its last breath, the KORD system managed to identify permissible limits violations for pressure and rpms in engines No. 7, 19, 20, and 21 and issue commands to shut them down. Telemetry did not determine how the other engines shut down. In the midst of the general chaos, engine No. 18 continued to operate right up until the crash—at least, that is what the telemetry experts reported. For inexplicable reasons, this fact sparked keen interest during spur-of-the-moment debates, although it was obvious that it had nothing to do with the root cause of the accident.

N–1 rocket engine designer Nikolay Kuznetsov (left) and senior space forces official Andrey Karas (right).

From the author's archives.

The main heated arguments that flared up among the engineers were about the root cause. Kuznetsov and his entire team stood solidly behind the hypothesis of a "foreign object" in the pump. In their opinion, the steel diaphragm of the pressure pulsation sensor ended up in the oxidizer pump. They could not imagine any other foreign objects that could have become dislodged and then sucked into the oxygen pump. A study of the pressure sensor and experiments involving the forced breakaway of the steel diaphragm in question from its place did not clarify the situation. It was difficult to convince skeptics that the sensor was at fault. The assumption that the pump had exploded on its own, without a "foreign object," had dangerous implications. If the pumps exploded spontaneously, it meant that flight tests must not be continued. Kuznetsov's staff categorically rejected any scenarios other than the foreign metallic object one.

Raykov dared to tell his hypothesis only to Mishin: "A 'foreign object' has nothing to do with it. Most likely an axial shift of the rotor occurred. The clearances in the pump are negligible. A very small bit of play in the bearings, combined with extreme tolerances and deformations, could result in the rotor striking the stator. Local heating of hundreds of degrees would occur in the liquid oxygen medium and an explosion is inevitable."

Mishin wasn't about to blame Kuznetsov. Together they had made the decision to clear the engines for flight, relying on the findings of the interdepartmental commission, which in late 1967 had confirmed that the engines were fit for flight-development tests. Mentioning, even in the mildest of terms, that the explosion of the oxidizer pump could have been caused by design or process shortcomings meant the suspension of N-1 flight tests due to faulty engine technology. It was natural that Kuznetsov, all of his specialists, and even the military representatives argued that the explosion could only have been caused by the interference of a "foreign object."

JUST WHEN MEETINGS AND HEATED DEBATES of the accident investigation commissions were in full swing and we were working out schedules for rebuilding the launch site, we received news of the *Apollo 11* Moon launch.[23] The next eight days of the Americans' flight, the stunning stroll on the Moon, and the delivery to Earth of 25 kilograms of lunar soil samples might make high-ranking officials reconsider the N1-L3 program.[24]

We watched the *Apollo 11* flight on the television at TsNIImash. After the happy conclusion of the lunar expedition, Tyulin proposed stopping by the director's office. There, over a glass of cognac, he said: "This is all Chertok's fault. In 1945 he came up with a scheme to snatch von Braun from the Americans and didn't manage to pull it off."

"And it's a very good thing that Vasya Kharchev and I failed in that undertaking.[25] Von Braun would have sat for some time in our country uselessly on an island, and then he would have been sent to the GDR, where as a former

---

23. *Apollo 11* was launched on 16 July 1969 with astronauts Neil A. Armstrong, Edwin E. "Buzz" Aldrin, Jr., and Michael Collins.
24. The take on *Apollo 11* was closer to 22 kilograms.
25. See Chertok, *Rockets and People, Vol. I*, Chapter 21.

Nazi he wouldn't have been cleared to work anywhere.[26] And so with the help of the Americans, he fulfilled not only his own dream, but also that of all mankind," I replied bitterly.

Two N-1 failures due solely to the low reliability of the first stage should have been enough to halt flight tests, enact a thorough review of the strategy for testing reliability, and develop and propose a new project for an expedition to the Moon. Neither Mishin nor we, his deputies, dared to come out with such proposals. Neither the chairman of the expert commission—Academy of Sciences President Keldysh—nor Chairman of the State Commission and "Lunar Council," Minister Afanasyev, nor Central Committee Secretary Ustinov, nor the Politburo standing over all of them told us to stop. Ustinov invited Glushko to a private conversation under some appropriate pretext. Actually, Ustinov wanted to hear the opinion of the nation's most authoritative engine specialist about Kuznetsov's engines. Glushko told Ustinov that he didn't believe there was an evil spirit that tossed foreign objects into the pumps....

The larger the project being implemented by a nation's resources and its people, the more clearly the features of an epoch stand out in its history. The sanctity of the Central Committee decisions was above criticism, and we all were tied to this dogma. Cosmonautics should have abandoned the dogmatism of artillery and missile technology. A fundamentally different approach was needed. A large rocket-space system must fulfill its primary mission on the very first attempt. To do this, everything imaginable needed to be tested on the ground and tested out before the first dedicated flight. Preliminary experimental flights are needed to test out only those systems and processes that basically cannot be simulated under ground-based conditions. The Americans surpassed us in the practical implementation of this principle, and this enabled them, beginning in 1969, to take the position of the leading power in space exploration.

The first people who dared criticize our work methods were not scientists on expert commissions, but the military. Back when Korolev was still alive, they had prepared a démarche concerning the large number of failed Moon, Mars, and Venus launches. In 1965, I was present when Kirillov alerted Korolev that he had received the command assignment to prepare material incriminating the chief designers and industry in a large number of failures as a result

---

26. Here, Chertok is alluding to the Germans who *did* end up going to the Soviet Union, who were all eventually housed in facilities on the remote island of Gorodomlya. See Chertok, *Rockets and People, Vol. II*, Chapter 3.

of erroneous testing procedures. Subsequent triumphs, however, subdued the military's aggression toward cosmonautics.

But four years later, in response to the failures of two N-1s, failures in the circumlunar flight program using the 7K-L1, and the failed launches of Babakin's "Lunar excavators," the Commander-in-Chief of the Strategic Rocket Forces, Marshal Nikolay Krylov, was finally persuaded to sign a letter addressed to Afanasyev containing constructive criticism directed at us.[27] The letter said:

> *The results of the analysis of the two failed launches of the N1-L3 complex, as well as the statistics from the launches of other sophisticated rocket-space complexes show that the existing procedure for developmental testing of rocket-space complexes does not ensure that they have a high degree of reliability when they are released for [developmental flight testing]. The existing procedure of ground developmental testing of [rocket-space complexes] is basically analogous to the developmental testing procedure for missiles, which, as a rule, are significantly simpler than a [rocket-space complex] like the N1-L3. At the same time, during the process of [developmental flight testing] of missiles, several dozen articles (from 20 to 60) are expended for their optimization to the required level of reliability. When conducting [developmental flight testing] on heavy [rocket-space complexes] it is not possible to perform [such] prolonged troubleshooting during flight when it involves the consumption of a large number of launch vehicles. In view of this, it seems expedient to change the customary scope and nature of ground testing of these complexes before they are released for [developmental flight testing]. In our opinion, new methods for ground testing of heavy [rocket-space complexes] must be set up so that they are reusable, so that their component systems and assemblies have large service-life reserves, and so that engines and rocket blocks are tested without subsequent reassembly in order to expose production defects and [thus] undergo a breaking-in period.[28]*

We were aware of the main thrust of Krylov's letter long before its official distribution. When a copy of the letter with the minister's resolution reached

---

27. The "lunar excavators" were the Ye-8-5 sample return probes. Four had failed in 1969 (launches in June, July, September, and October 1969).

28. In the original text, Krylov uses the common Russian abbreviations for "developmental flight testing" (LKI) and "rocket-space complex" (RKK).

us in Mishin's absence, Okhapkin in his capacity as first deputy assembled a meeting of his inner circle to discuss the wording of the response to the Commander-in-Chief's démarche. Melnikov and I announced that we were in full agreement with Krylov's proposals. As a matter of fact, we had proposed the same thing a long time ago; and the Americans operate the same way. Our response needed to be that we accept the proposal of the Minister of Defense and to that end we consider the following necessary: to develop a reusable modification of Kuznetsov's engines; to design and build a rig for technological firing tests (OTI) on Block A; and to perform the assembly of subsequent rockets only after each of the Blocks A, B, V, and G have undergone firing rig tests.

Some reacted to our stance with sarcastic remarks, although we were all of the same mind, all part of the same staff, and had passed through Korolev's school. People argued with all earnestness. Okhapkin attempted to find an accommodating compromise. Summing up the results, he said essentially what we all anticipated and prepared in advance.

He noted that we had to propose a list of actions that we would introduce for the upcoming launches. We needed to show that measures were being taken in response to all probable causes for the failures, precluding the possibility of repeating them, and substantially increasing reliability. Specifically:

- Increasing the stringency of the system for accepting the engines;
- Modifying the oxidizer pumps at OKB-276, reducing the load on the bearings, and increasing the clearances;
- Installing filters upstream from the pumps to protect against the intrusion of foreign objects;
- Filling the aft compartment with nitrogen before launch and performing an in-flight nitrogen purge;
- Introducing a Freon fire-extinguishing system;
- Providing additional protection of instruments, cables, and the most critical structural elements against high temperature;
- Relocating instruments, moving them to safer areas; and
- Introducing inhibits to completely preclude the possibility of engine shutdown for the first 50 seconds of flight.

Arguments broke out over this last item.

"But what if the turbogenerators malfunction during the first seconds and all of the systems lose power?"

Petr Shulgin, Emil Brodskiy, and Sofya Lobanova—Iosifyan's curators specializing in the pneumatic system feeding compressed helium to the turbogenerator—helped me defend the honor of the autonomous turbogenerator. It had come to the point where the development of a sophisticated and heavy emergency power supply system using storage batteries might be required.

Almost all the actions were approved after heated debates during the work of the accident investigation commission that analyzed the causes of the N-1 No. 5L disaster. They increased the rocket's reliability but did not guarantee that the launch facilities would remain intact in the event of a failure during the first seconds after liftoff. If an emergency situation occurred during the first seconds, it was imperative to divert the rocket further into the steppe. Such a requirement seemed completely unconventional: since the times of the V-2 all short-range, medium-range, and any other range and size of ballistic missiles had launched vertically. It would be only 5 to 6 seconds after launch that they would be at a relatively safe distance from the launch site. Before the failure of N-1 No. 5L, no one had dared violate this 25-year tradition.

A collective and intense use of intellect, with the participation of individuals who are truly creative, rather than obedient, almost always brings success. Here is a list of the authors in alphabetical order: Degtyarenko, Dorofeyev, Gasparyan, Shutenko, Vilnitskiy, Voropayev, and Zelvinskiy. These are the men who came up with the "method" and the "device" for which an inventor's certificate was later issued. The invention guaranteed that the rocket would clear the area even if the electric power supply system of all the control surface actuators shut down, provided that the main engines were operating. Springs in the mechanisms of the control surface actuators, pre-armed for actuation in the event of an accident, set all the thrust control throttles of the first-stage engines in the proper position to divert the rocket "further into the steppe." This invention found application not only on subsequent N-1 rockets, but also in an appropriately altered form 15 years later on the Energiya rocket.

From the author's archives.

Shown here are senior specialists on the dynamics of rocket control at OKB-1: G. N. Degtyarenko, Ye. F. Lebedev, O. N. Voropayev, G. S. Vetrov, and L. I. Alekseyev.

Iosifyan considered the failure of the autonomous turbogenerator impossible, and when discussing ideas for diverting the rocket he did not miss the opportunity to comment: "There will always be Eskimos who will try to teach Africans how to avoid heatstroke."

WHEN ALL THE ACTIONS HAD BEEN EVALUATED in terms of labor intensity and deadlines, we came up with a disappointing picture. After gathering one more time in Okhapkin's office before the final approval, we realized that it would take at least a year to implement all the proposals along with the additional experiments. Our engine specialists Melnikov, Sokolov, and Raykov, who had achieved success in their own developments of the multiple-firing engines for Block D and who had seen enough of the experience of Kuznetsov's OKB-276, announced that they were developing new design specifications. In their opinion, it was completely feasible to develop reusable main engines. This

would make it possible to radically increase the engines' reliability. But these engines would not be available before 1972. Echoes of similar conversations and attitudes made their way to ministry offices, the VPK, and the Central Committee.

B. A. Sokolov (left) was a leading engine specialist at TsKBEM who worked on the N1-L3 program while G. N. Degtyarenko (right) worked on spacecraft and rocket control.

From the author's archives.

Yet another day of celebration was drawing nigh—the 100th anniversary of the birthday of V. I. Lenin. In the Politburo, Afanasyev, Smirnov, and Ustinov would inevitably be asked, "What's going on with our lunar program? You promised by the 100th anniversary to land a cosmonaut on the Moon, who would plant a Soviet flag and place a bust of Lenin beside it. Then you decided to argue that we don't want to take that risk and we would first send an automatic spacecraft that would drill, collect lunar soil, and deliver at least 100 grams to the Earth. But that's not working out, either!"

During the last seven years of his administration, Khrushchev secured indisputable precedence for the Soviet Union in space exploration and put to shame the most powerful nation in the capitalist world—the U.S. But after overthrowing Khrushchev, Brezhnev's cohorts eroded these achievements, and in the most important arena of space, America had now surpassed the Soviet Union.

The highest-ranking political leadership viewed success in space as an effective factor of ideological influence on its people and the peoples of the Warsaw Pact nations. Brezhnev could not invite foreign guests to a lunar launch of Soviet cosmonauts like the Americans could. Nevertheless, in late 1969 he dared to fly with a Czech delegation to the firing range and drove out with them to the left-hand N-1 launch site, which had remained intact.[29] An impenetrable fence surrounded the launch site to the right, which was "under repairs." Traces of the recent fire and explosions weren't visible. An N-1 engineering mockup stood on the left-hand launch site.[30]

"This rocket will enable us to go beyond the limits of the solar system"; that, according to the accounts of members of his entourage, was how Brezhnev ad libbed, showcasing the miracle of Soviet rocket technology.

IN CRITICAL CIRCUMSTANCES, the mind often works more intensely and the search for new ideas produces greater results than during periods of relaxation after a victory. Everyone jumped at the idea of immediately organizing a group flight of three piloted Soyuzes as a proposal that would partially restore our cosmonautics program. After the docking of *Soyuz-4* and *Soyuz-5* in January 1969 came the announcement that "the world's first orbital station was Soviet." We needed to solidify this important triumph in space by performing another docking and broadening the program of experiments. In particular, working with the Ye. O. Paton Institute of Electric Welding in Kiev, we began to study the possibility of performing a welding experiment under conditions of weightlessness in a vacuum. Future President of the Ukrainian Academy of Science Boris Paton assured us that they would be able to create the experimental conditions for these purposes by the required deadline.[31]

Meanwhile, all we had on hand were Soyuzes, and we were rushing to squeeze out of them everything that they were capable of giving us. In April

---

29. This was officially known as Site No. 110L.

30. This visit to Tyuratam that Chertok describes was code-named Operation Palma-3 and took place on 23–24 October 1969. The visiting delegation included Czech President Ludwig Svoboda. The hosts included Leonid Brezhnev, Aleksey Kosygin, Marshal Andrey Grechko, and Marshal Nikolay Krylov. During the trip, the Czech visitors were shown launches of UR-100 and R-36 ICBMs.

31. Boris Yevgenyevich Paton (1918–) is a well-known Ukrainian scholar of metallurgy and the technology of metals. Besides serving as the President of the Ukrainian Academy of Sciences from 1958, Paton also headed the Ye. O. Paton Institute of Electrical Welding, named after his famous father.

we still did not have a clear program of subsequent piloted Soyuz flights. May passed under the impression of the successful landing on Venus of *Venera-5* and *Venera-6* and of the lunar orbital flight of *Apollo 10*. On 14 June, the liftoff to the Moon of Babakin's Ye-8-5 fell through for the second time. Thus, our hope to surpass the Americans in delivering samples of lunar soil to Earth melted away.

Our third Ye-8-5 "Lunar excavator," announced as *Luna-15*, lifted off on 13 July, flew to the Moon, and entered lunar orbit. But its soft landing failed—for inexplicable reasons the spacecraft crashed into the surface of the Moon. They decided to launch the next "Lunar excavator" in September. Accident investigation commission sessions continued through July 1969. During breaks we discussed the *Apollo 11* flight, which had flown to the Moon on 16 July. We had not had the occasion to experience such a conjunction of personal defeat and foreign triumphs since wartime.

We had a small celebration in August in connection with the successful flight of 7K-L1 No. 11, called *Zond-7*. On 8 August, L1 No. 11 lifted off; on 11 August, it executed a pass around the Moon, and on 14 August, after plunging twice into Earth's atmosphere, it executed a soft landing [on Earth]. On 22 August, *Pravda* published black-and-white images of Earth delivered by the station before it dropped behind the rim of the Moon. Spectacular color photos appeared in magazines. These color shots became very popular as gifts for space-related anniversaries.

The last two 7K-L1 programs—*Zond-7* and *Zond-8*—owe a great deal to the energy of lead designer Yuriy Semyonov. It was up to him to keep in check the centrifugal forces of four leading organizations—TsKBEM, NIIAP, TsKBM, and ZIKh.[32] In any case, Chairman of the State Commission for the L1 Tyulin said that he resolved many issues with Semyonov more quickly and simply than with Mishin.

In August, the program for the group flight of three Soyuzes finally materialized. Two Soyuzes would dock and form an orbital station with a mass of 13 tons. A third Soyuz, maneuvering around this station, would confirm via television that the station actually existed. Preparation for the flight, which involved three vehicles and seven cosmonauts, took place in a very tense atmosphere. The process of fitting out the vehicles caused continuously missed deadlines, so tests at the monitoring and testing station (KIS) had to be hurried up to

---

32. These were the four principal organizations responsible for the Zond/L-1 project: TsKBEM was the lead developer of the L-1 spacecraft and the Block D stage, NIIAP developed control systems for the L-1, TsKBM (and its Fili Branch) designed the Proton-K rocket, and ZIKh manufactured the Protons.

accommodate the readiness deadlines of the systems, frustrating previously approved plans. Once again part of the problems carried over for followup work at the firing range.

It wasn't until 18 September that Smirnov conducted a session of the VPK, which made its final decision concerning the group flight of three Soyuzes in the first half of October. I was at that session, and in keeping with tradition, after the reports of Mishin and the other chief designers, I confirmed the readiness of the control systems of all three vehicles to execute the program. Cosmonauts Georgiy Shonin and Valeriy Kubasov (*Soyuz-6*); Anatoliy Filipchenko, Vladislav Volkov, and Viktor Gorbatko (*Soyuz-7*); and Vladimir Shatalov and Aleksey Yeliseyev (*Soyuz-8*) reported their readiness to execute their mission with enviable pride and optimism. Everyone was in high spirits and shared the hope that we would emerge from a streak of back-to-back failures. The color photographs of Earth and the Moon marked the beginning of an upswing in our mood and a strengthening of faith in our efforts.

On 19 September, Tyulin convened the State Commission on the L1, which after two successful circumlunar flights suddenly found empowerment, and Mishin even hinted about a possible piloted circumlunar flight on the L1 in 1970.

"Now if we can finally get the Ye-8-5 to the Moon and back five days from now," fantasized Tyulin.

On 23 September, the first three stages of the UR-500 operated normally, but the Block D failed to work through to the second firing, and the entire lunar complex stayed in Earth orbit, receiving the name *Kosmos-300*.

Our nation possessed enormous capabilities. However, during this period in history, there was no one at the helm of power capable of soberly analyzing the course of events, of displaying farsightedness, and of altering the official political course without regard for the established dogmas. In space politics, the Politburo under Brezhnev lacked the boldness of Khrushchev's time.

NASA management, inspired by its historic triumph, sent a report to the President of the United States' special committee on space in September 1969.[33] The document summarized the first results of the Americans' work in the field of the "peaceful" use of space and contained proposals concerning the program of operations for the next few decades. The military aspects, which the Pentagon managed, were not considered in the report. Throwing aside all my work, I read

---

33. Here, Chertok probably means the NASA Space Task Group, which issued a report in September 1969 entitled "The Post-Apollo Space Program: Directions for the Future." The recommendations from the report were heavily influential in informing the Nixon administration's policies for the post-Apollo era. See *http://www.hq.nasa.gov/office/pao/History/taskgrp.html.*

this 130-page document as if it were an absorbing novel. After reading any novel, it can be set aside and forgotten. Even now, after almost 40 years, this report serves as an object lesson in the advantages of a centralized government technocratic planning system [i.e., NASA] in developing large-scale systems. The most capitalistic country in the world, despite Marxist teaching about the anarchy of production, despite the infamous democratic principles of the free market and private initiative, created the most powerful state organization in the world, which develops nonmilitary space programs and coordinates and monitors the activity of all the nation's organizations in the field of space exploration. NASA management considered highly qualified experienced personnel to be a primary national asset. NASA had close ties with industrial firms and universities. This relationship increased NASA's capabilities many times over.

In 1969, NASA had a staff of 31,745. Of this number, 13,700 were scientists and engineers. The total number of personnel at that time who worked on NASA programs reached 218,345. In terms of numbers of personnel, we had just as many as the Americans, and even surpassed them. Without exception, all scientists and engineers worked only in government organizations, and as subsequent association with the Americans has shown, they were just as qualified and experienced.

What, then, was their advantage? The U.S. had a single unified government organization, which was endowed with the exclusive rights to develop nonmilitary space programs and received funding from the federal budget to finance them. In the USSR, each head, chief, or general designer came forward with his own concept for the development of cosmonautics based on his own capabilities and personal, subjective views. Rare enthusiasts attempted to occupy themselves with the development of an integrated long-range plan for decades into the future. The plans proposed by the head government organizations were reviewed in five places: in the head ministry, MOM; in the General Staff [of the armed forces]; in the Central Directorate for Space Assets (TsUKOS), which was subordinate to the Commander-in-Chief of the Strategic Rocket Forces; in the Central Committee; and in the *apparat* of the Council of Ministers, the VPK. Next, they were coordinated with dozens of ministries and, if they managed to make their way through, they were approved by a decision of the Politburo and the Council of Ministers. Each project participant received separate funding from the state budget according to these plans. Even in the offices of the VPK and in the Kremlin our cosmonautics management system was sometimes called "state feudalism."

And one more important feature distinguished the American organization of work from the Soviet. NASA management, its administration, and thousands of scientists and engineers bore no responsibility for arming the Army and Navy with nuclear missiles. Their time, intellect, and enthusiasm were devoted solely to the lunar landing expedition and to the problems of blazing a trail into space for humankind and for automatic stations.

Our head ministry, which was responsible for implementing each space program, bore even greater responsibility for producing combat missiles. The head organizations, their chief designers and leading specialists, who developed the nuclear missile shield, were "soldiers of the Cold War" and at the same time labored on a second front—space.

NASA's report began on what was for us an unexpected downbeat note:

> *At the moment of our space program's greatest triumph, the U.S. is going through a critical period. The decisions made this year will determine the nature of operations in space for several decades to come. At stake is the leading role of the U.S. in scientific and technical progress, the faith of 200 million Americans in their country, its achievements, and the practical advantages, which the broad program provides for the people, whose money in the form of taxes makes it possible....*

However, further on came several unexpected proposals:

> *One of the main elements of the recommended program for the development of non-military projects in space is the creation of a long-duration habitable station in near-Earth orbit to accumulate experience in long-duration human space flight, to obtain practical benefit from observation of the Earth and near-Earth space, and also for the performance of scientific experiments.*[34]

They proposed building the first habitable station in near-Earth orbit no later than 1977. Between 1980 and 1984, base-stations were supposed to appear in near-Earth orbit with a crew of 50 persons, and by 1989 their number would increase to 100. Truly "dreams, dreams, where is your sweetness!"[35]

Now, the U.S. together with Russia, Western European nations, and Japan are building the International Space Station (ISS), which, according to plan,

---

34. It is possible that Chertok is quoting from a source other than the Space Task Group's September 1969 report since there is little match between what he reproduces here and the original text of the Space Task Group's report.

35. These lines are from *Yevgeniy Onegin* (more commonly known in English as *Eugene Onegin*), the famous 1830s-era novel written entirely in verse by Aleksandr Sergeyevich Pushkin (1799–1837).

should have a crew of just six persons by 2009, with an active service life of 15 years. At first, it was assumed that by 2002 it would have a total of 8 to 10 crewmembers. Actually, in the first decade of operation (up until 2008), most of the time there was a crew of just three on the ISS. The crew numbers 10 members only during "visiting expeditions," which the Space Shuttle delivers to the Station.[36]

Later, the 1969 report describes missions that must have staggered the imagination not only of "average Americans," but also seasoned congressmen:

> *The continuation of flights to the nearest planets—Mars and Venus, and then to Jupiter and other distant planets of the Solar System— Saturn, Uranus, Neptune, and Pluto.*

The primary scientific mission of these flights was to search for extraterrestrial life. An expedition to Mars could take place as early as 1981! As far as the further use of vehicles from the Apollo program was concerned, it was assumed that eight more expeditions to the Moon would be carried out from 1970 through 1972. From 1978 to 1980, the Americans were preparing to build a habitable station in near-Earth orbit, and from 1980 through 1983 they were on the verge of beginning construction of a habitable base station on the Moon.

What a historical paradox! In the USSR, our lunar program crisis was a result of failures and disasters. The Americans' crisis—at the moment of their greatest triumph—was because they hadn't yet decided what to do next. And there was one more paradox: neither the Americans' triumph, nor our failures, nor subsequent joint efforts helped implement the plans of 1969!

---

36. Chertok wrote these words in 2008. In more recent times, beginning with Expedition 20 in 2009, there have been missions consisting of six astronauts/cosmonauts, some of whom arrive on the Station on different flights.

Chapter 12
Long–Duration Space Stations Instead of the Moon

The highest-ranking bosses weren't just simply tormented by thoughts that we absolutely had to come up with something to compensate for our N-1 failures; these thoughts literally just "hung in the air." For us, the employees of Korolev's firm, there was one more factor that motivated us to conduct an intensive search for new priority achievements. In 1967, OKB-52, which had been renamed TsKBM, started to develop its own version of an orbital station. Vladimir Chelomey understood that the only way to "win away" lunar conquest projects from Korolev's firm and the Americans would be to create a new launch vehicle that was more reliable and could carry a greater payload than the N-1 and was every bit as good as the Saturn V. The most optimistic calculations showed that it would take at least six or seven years to solve this problem. And it would require so much more effort!

Five years later, in a private conversation with Bushuyev and me, Chelomey confessed that he had not been assertive in implementing the design of the UR-700—the launch vehicle for the lunar expedition—because this work could have swallowed up all the other projects, and anyway the Americans already had the upper hand. The UR-500, a.k.a. the already-flying *Proton*, was capable of inserting a spacecraft with a mass of 20 tons into Earth orbit. An orbital station with that mass could thus be inserted in a single launch, and that was a lot better than launching two Soyuzes at 6.5 tons each.

Chelomey's new orbital station design was called Almaz. In 1968, mock-ups of the Almaz orbital station had appeared in Reutov, and in Fili on the territory of my old Factory No. 22, now the M. V. Khrunichev Factory (ZIKh for short), the manufacture of station hulls was under way at full speed.[1] For Myasishchev's great design team—the former OKB-23, which had become a

---

1. The factory was named after Mikhail Vasilyevich Khrunichev (1901–1961), one of the most powerful defense industry administrators in the Soviet Union in the 1950s. Reutov was the location of Chelomey's "head" OKB-52.

branch of Chelomey's OKB-52—the development of large orbital space station hulls was not a very difficult task. In any event, the designers together with the process engineers and workers of ZIKh came to grips with it quicker than the designers at our TsKBEM and ZEM could have.[2] In this sense, Fili had a clear advantage over Podlipki. The experience, traditions, and manufacturing process of aircraft builders played their roles.

Officially, the Almaz was developed per Ministry of Defense specifications. It consisted of an Orbital Piloted Station (OPS), a Return Vehicle (VA) for the crew's descent from orbit to Earth, and a large-capacity Transport-Supply Vehicle (TKS).[3]

It was assumed that the Almaz OPS would be a more state-of-the-art space reconnaissance vehicle than the *Zenit* automatic unpiloted photoreconnaissance satellites. The Almaz's large camera only used up film to photograph ground-based objects at the cosmonauts' discretion. They could examine Earth in the visible or infrared spectrum through powerful "space binoculars," and if they saw something suspicious, they gave the command for a series of snapshots. The films were developed on board under the crew's control. Fragments of images deserving the attention of military intelligence were transmitted to the ground over a television channel. These and any other sections of the planet could also be scanned using side-scan radar. Reconnaissance conditions required that the OPS be continuously oriented to Earth while the camera could be turned and aimed at various objects. These conditions required that the station's control system provide a high degree of precision in maintaining three-axis orientation for an extended period, rotation about the longitudinal axis at specified angles, and orientation of the solar arrays on the Sun. At the same time, [limiting] working fluid consumption enabled the spacecraft to actively operate for at least three to four months.

Following our example, Chelomey organized his own team responsible for developing the entire control system complex. The absolute philosophical priority of Chelomey's control specialists was the installation of the electro-mechanical stabilization system developed at VNIIEM, which used a spherical rotor and ring flywheel with great kinetic momentum. The spherical rotor

---

2. ZEM—*Zavod eksperimentalnogo mashinostroyeniya* (Factory of Experimental Machine Building)—was the main production facility for TsKBEM. It was formerly known as Factory No. 88.

3. OPS—*Orbitalnaya pilotiruyemaya stantsiya*; VA—*Vozvrashchayemyy apparat*; TKS—*Transportnyy korabl snabzheniya*. For a detailed history of the Almaz, see Asif A. Siddiqi, "The Almaz Space Station Complex: A History, 1964–1992," *Journal of the British Interplanetary Society* 54 (2001): 389–416 and 55 (2002): 35–67.

suspended in an electromagnetic field was an original development in which Sheremetyevskiy took great pride.

Many years later, speaking at an election gathering of my Academy department in support of Sheremetyevskiy's candidacy, I praised this development: "Nikolay Nikolayevich managed to create an electromagnetic field in near-Earth orbit that could support a 20-metric-ton station." During a break in the meeting Pospelov rebuked me, "What nonsense! It's a sphere scarcely larger than a soccer ball that hovers in the electromagnetic field, not an orbital station."[4]

I objected: "According to the theory of relativity, an observer located on the surface of a sphere is justified in asserting that his own field keeps the metallic 'sky' surrounding him, i.e. the station, from falling. Remember the debates of our student days in philosophy seminars on the theory of relativity."

Nikolay Sheremetyevskiy was later elected corresponding member of the USSR Academy of Sciences, and the Almaz played no small role in this event.[5]

Another innovation that was exotic for those times was the use of *Argon-16* on-board digital computers to control the surveillance equipment. I mention these because the developer—the Scientific Research Center of Electronic Computer Technology (NITsEVT)—soon refined these Argons for a new Soyuz modification, and 15 years later they were installed on the *Mir* station, where (in a very updated version, of course) they crossed over from the 20th century into the 21st![6]

The development and manufacture of all the components of the sophisticated control complex for the Almaz and its special-purpose photo-television and radio equipment required significantly more time than Chelomey had assumed. Over the course of 1969, ZIKh manufactured the station's hull, but meanwhile there was nothing to fill it with. Thanks to good relations with colleagues involved with control systems at subcontracting organizations, I

---

4. Germogen Sergeyevich Pospelov (1914–), a specialist in automatic control, was elected a full member of the Academy of Sciences in 1984.

5. Sheremetyevskiy became a Corresponding Member of the Academy in March 1979.

6. The NITsEVT was established in March 1968 to develop computer technology for various applications. The institute was established by combining two older institutions, the Institute of Precision Mechanics and Computer Technology (ITMiVT) and the Scientific-Research Institute of Calculating Machines (NIISchetmash). An earlier Soviet design bureau, SKB-245, had been the primary developer of Soviet computers during the Cold War, and it was eventually attached to NITsEVT to support the new center's work. NITsEVT developed the first Soviet digital computer for space applications, the *Argon-11S*, used on the 7K-L1 circumlunar spaceships. Later, the institute developed the *Argon-12A* and *Argon-12S* for the Almaz space station complex. The first piloted Soyuz spacecraft with a digital computer was *Soyuz T-2*, which launched in 1980 and used the *Argon-16*. The *Mir* space station used a variety of different computers, including the *Argon-16*, the *Salyut-4*, and the *Salyut-5* computers.

had a more comprehensive idea of the prospects for the Almaz as an orbital station than other managers and specialists at TsKBEM.

Back in Korolev's day at OKB-1, the idea of a Multipurpose Space Base/Station (MKBS) had come up.[7] After becoming chief designer, Mishin assigned planner and ballistics specialist Vitaliy Bezverbyy to manage this project. The MKBS was supposed to serve as a spaceport, where other spacecraft, primarily reconnaissance vehicles, would dock to hand over their photographic materials, reload them, refuel, and perform maintenance and repairs. A well-trained crew on the MKBS was supposed to perform this servicing. The presence of a base station of this sort in near-Earth orbit would make it possible to prolong the service life of spacecraft, which even in the present day, once they exhausted their resources or in the event of a failure, we are currently forced to descend to Earth or scuttle in the ocean.

It was intended that the Multipurpose Space Base/Station would be outfitted with various types of missile-defense and space-defense weapons, including particle-beam weapons. In this regard, Academician Gersh Budker from Novosibirsk gave us a lecture on the possibility of developing accelerators for particle-beam weapons using uncharged particles.[8] There were enthusiasts who immediately began studying this problem. Besides these exotic (for those times) ideas, it was intended that all sorts of reconnaissance photographic and radio systems be installed on the MKBS. The plan was to use the N-1 launch vehicle to insert the base/station into space. Thus, until there was an N-1, there could be no MKBS. On the other hand, the Almaz did not require a new launch vehicle. The UR-500 had already gotten through its period of "childhood diseases."

While we at TsKBEM were experiencing a period of disarray and vacillation, the combined forces of Reutov and Fili were able to create a real orbital station for the Ministry of Defense. I told Bushuyev, Okhapkin, and Tregub about my thoughts on the possibility of our joining forces with Chelomey. But they just laughed at me and said that Chelomey and Mishin would never agree with each other. Tsybin took my idea more seriously: "If our 'godfather' [Stalin] were alive, he would settle all these differences himself in about 20 minutes or he'd hand it over to Lavrentiy Pavlovich to sort it out. Comrade Beriya, in such cases, didn't meddle in differences between chief designers. If Stalin instructed him to sort it out, he'd call in both parties and say: 'If two

---

7. MKBS—*Mnogotselevaya kosmicheskaya baza-stantsiya.*
8. Gersh Itskovich Budker (1918–1977) was a well-known Soviet nuclear physicist who served as the founding director of the Institute of Nuclear Physics at Akademgorodok. He became an Academician of the Academy of Sciences in 1964.

communists can't come to an agreement with one another, it means one of them is the enemy. I don't have time to figure out which one of you is the enemy. I'll give you 20 minutes. You decide for yourselves'."[9]

"I assure you," continued Tsybin, "that after such action, Chelomey and I would work like the best of friends. However, one must take into consideration that certain powers of today will not see our friendly association with Chelomey favorably. We could become too powerful and independent a corporation, and the Central Committee and ministry need humble and obedient staffs."

ONE DAY IN AUGUST 1969, AFTER A HEATED DISCUSSION of the program for the flight of three Soyuzes, Rauschenbach, Legostayev, and Bashkin stayed behind in my office. They asked me to listen to their proposal to develop an orbital station within a mind-bogglingly short period of time, enabling us to beat out the Almaz. The idea entailed taking any *Semyorka* tank, filling it with Soyuz systems, adding on more powerful solar arrays and of course a new docking assembly with internal transfer, and the station would be ready! We just needed to come in at 18 tons in order to use the UR-500. We could build such a station in a year.

At first I tried to resist: "The thermal control and life-support systems of the Soyuz are completely unsuited for this tank."

"No problem! We already discussed this with Oleg Surguchev and Ilya Lavrov. It wasn't we who convinced them, but they who convinced us that it was completely feasible to produce the new systems within a year using tried-and-true Soyuz pumps, assemblies, and fittings. Piping and cables are no problem."

"That's not all," I resisted, "a new correction engine and attitude-control engine system will also be needed. Although…."

Right then and there I telephoned Isayev on the Kremlin line.

"Aleksey! How much time do you need to adapt your correction engine from the Soyuz to a new vehicle, after tripling the volume of the propellant tanks and increasing the time spent in space from two weeks to three to four months?"

"You know," answered Isayev, "we already solved that problem for the Almaz. Maybe it will work for you too. Take a look."[10]

What a tip! Combine already existing tried-and-true systems of an operating Soyuz with the Almaz production stock—this thought quickly got a strong

---

9. Lavrentiy Pavlovich Beriya (1899–1953) was the feared manager of the Soviet security services. Between 1938 and 1945, he headed the NKVD, the predecessor to the KGB.

10. Isayev's design bureau developed the 11D442 (or KRD-442) main engines for the Transport-Supply Ship (TKS), part of the complete Almaz space station complex.

hold on our minds. "Theory itself becomes a material force when it has seized the masses," as Karl Marx once wrote.[11]

I am not capable now of reconstructing in detail who first voiced this proposal, which radically affected the future of cosmonautics in our country. Moreover, now one can assert that the 21st century program for the creation of the International Space Station originates from the ideas discussed in the autumn of 1969 among a relatively small circle of people. Konstantin Feoktistov joined this circle and seized the initiative. A group of "conspirators" of sorts formed. I cannot reliably name the author of the most seditious and aggressive portion of the proposals developed. Such enlightenment descends all at once on a group of individuals the way that great ideas dawn simultaneously on inventors in different countries. Someone first merely mentioned it, and then all the "conspirators" enthusiastically snatched it up: why mess with tanks at all? In Fili, there were ready-made hulls for the Almaz orbital station lying around. We needed to use them filled with Soyuz systems adapted for great new purposes—this was so much easier!

Presenting a half-formed idea to somebody higher up the chain of command is dangerous. Especially since right away it would encounter the fierce resistance of Chelomey, from whom we had suddenly decided to take ready-made Almaz hulls. The Almaz military customers would also be bound to object. Nor could we count on the approval of our own chief—Mishin. He would be against it because this proposal would harm work on the MKBS. Minister Afanasyev and his deputy Tyulin would not support us directly, either: they might be accused of thwarting the resolution on the development of the Almaz. It meant that we needed to "skip over" everyone and take this proposal straight to the Central Committee, to a person who was capable of understanding its advantages. The only one there that fit that description was Ustinov. And he, Ustinov, in particular really needed new proposals to present to the Politburo.

It was time for us to fly our separate ways for the launch of the three Soyuzes: some of us went to the launch site, others to Yevpatoriya. Not putting things off, Feoktistov organized the development of proposals in one of his design groups and flew off to the cosmodrome with Bushuyev. Rauschenbach, Bashkin, and I departed for Yevpatoriya having left instructions to render Feoktistov's designers whatever assistance might be needed.

---

11. Here, Chertok is quoting from *Contribution to the Critique of Hegel's Philosophy of Right* (1843). The complete quote is "Material force can only be overthrown by material force, but theory itself becomes a material force when it has seized the masses."

On 11 October 1969, *Soyuz-6*, carrying [Lieutenant-Colonel] Georgiy Shonin and Valeriy Kubasov, successfully went into orbit. On 12 October, *Soyuz-7* lifted off into space with [Lieutenant-Colonel] Anatoliy Filipchenko, Vladislav Volkov, and [Lieutenant-Colonel] Viktor Gorbatko on board. On 13 October, *Soyuz-8* went into orbit carrying Colonel Vladimir Shatalov, the commander of the space fleet, and flight engineer Aleksey Yeliseyev.

We hoped that in Yevpatoriya, the group of "conspirators" would be able to refine its tactics for promoting the design of the new orbital station using the Soyuz and Almaz. But this was not to be.

According to the program, the docking of *Soyuz-8* with *Soyuz-7* was supposed to take place on 14 October. After orbital corrections, *Soyuz-7* began the rendezvous process from a distance of 250 kilometers. The vehicles approached to a range of 1 kilometer, but the *Igla* equipment simply could not establish intercommunications between the active and passive vehicles: the "capture" command did not go through. Consequently, the active *Soyuz-8* did not have the relative motion parameters required for further rendezvous control. The crews reported that they could see each other, and Shatalov requested permission for manual rendezvous control. After consulting with us, Mishin gave his permission. But while we were arguing and weighing our options, the spacecraft drifted more than 3 kilometers apart. Shatalov, the active one, had no means to achieve reliable mutual orientation, and he didn't risk consuming precious fuel supplies.

The situation in Yevpatoriya at the command post, in the workrooms, in hotels, and even in the dining halls was red hot, despite the cool autumn weather. Minister Afanasyev and Kerimov interrogated Mnatsakanyan with the faint hope that he would resurrect the failed *Igla*. Mishin consulted with Tregub, Agadzhanov, Rauschenbach, Feoktistov, the ballistics specialists, and me trying to prepare instructions. On 15 October, after a series of maneuvers, the spacecraft converged to within 17 kilometers of one another. Shatalov fired the docking and attitude-control engines four times, but without the ability to measure the rate of approach and line-of-sight rate he was unable to generate a burn of the necessary magnitude and direction. Naturally the crews were nervous. The on-duty medical officer reported that the heart rates of all the cosmonauts exceeded 100 beats per minute. At the command post, nobody took our pulse, but most likely it was just as high. It wasn't the *Igla*'s failure that had us worked up so much as our powerlessness to perform rendezvous working together with the crews of the space vehicles.

Flight director Pavel Agadzhanov was under extreme stress. He commanded the entire network of ground- and sea-based tracking stations and was supposed to be able to task each of them to issue real-time commands at the strictly specified time determined by the coverage zones. But in order to do this, he first had to receive the decision of the technical management, which continued to shout and argue until the very beginning of the brief communication session. Usually, the shorter the time before communication with the crews, the more alternative proposals and recommendations appeared. Given the primitive data-processing and display technology that we had back then, and given the need to continuously report about all of our actions to the chairman of the State Commission, to the minister, and sometimes to Moscow as well, Vladimir Pravetskiy hypothesized that the adrenaline levels in the bloodstreams of the chiefs at the command post were higher than those of the spacecraft crewmembers.[12]

For us, the developers of the control system, the failure to execute rendezvous and docking was a harsh and painful lesson. In two years' time we had not figured out how to provide the spacecraft with basic instruments measuring mutual parameters in order to perform manual rendezvous. I could not pass up the opportunity to reproach Rauschenbach, Bashkin, and Zvorykin, who at one time had accused Beregovoy of performing an unsuccessful manual docking: "If Shatalov and Yeliseyev, well-trained cosmonauts with previous flight experience, could not manage to make it to the berthing phase with our constant prompting, it means that we are to blame, not the *Igla*. Electronics can fail, but we simply did not come up with a simplified system for manual control."

On 16 October 1969, the *Soyuz-6* crew returned to Earth safe and sound. On 18 October, the flight of the entire Soyuz space group ended. The eight days of flight of the three Soyuzes provided such a wealth of experience that right away we agreed to immediately modify the systems, something that we had not even dreamed of earlier. After that kind of stress there were more than enough proposals. As soon as he learned that the rendezvous program had failed because of the *Igla*, Minister Afanasyev arranged with Kerimov and Mishin to name me chairman of the commission to investigate the causes for the failure. I requested Yevgeniy Panchenko as one of my deputies. He served as department chief at the Main Directorate of Space Assets (GUKOS), and we had become friends in Kapustin Yar back in 1955 during the testing of R-2R.[13]

---

12. Vladimir Nikolayevich Pravetskiy (1921–1980), a veteran biomedicine specialist from the early nuclear tests in the 1950s, had served in the 1960s as the chief of the Third Main Directorate of the Ministry of Health, i.e., the subdivision in that ministry responsible for aviation and space medicine.

13. GUKOS was the agency within the Soviet Strategic Rocket Forces responsible for space operations between 1970 and 1981. It is the predecessor of the current-day Space Forces of the Russian Federation. The R-2R was an experimental missile developed to test radio control systems for the R-7 ICBM. It was flight-tested in 1955. Yevgeniy Ivanovich Panchenko (1927–) rose up to be first deputy chief of the space forces in the late 1980s before retiring.

After his time at Kapustin Yar, Panchenko had quickly risen through the military ranks. His fundamental radio engineering training combined with his innate erudition encompassed an entire complex of sophisticated spacecraft control problems. As a military officer, Panchenko was officially supposed to play the role of the exacting customer, who wasn't obliged to delve into the systems developers' problems. However, he was happy to immerse himself in the process of studying the systems, especially when investigating numerous off-nominal situations. His suggestions were sometimes quite useful. Together we got to know the *Igla* rendezvous system during the process of its frequent failures.

Yevgeniy Panchenko was a leading official in the Soviet space forces who helped investigate the docking failure of *Soyuz-7* and *Soyuz-8*.

From the author's archives.

As often happens in such situations, the immediate developers of a system guess the true causes of a failure before the high commission tracks them down. This time we quickly concurred that capture had not taken place due to a discrepancy between the frequencies of the transmitters and receivers, which were stabilized by special quartz resonators. The piezoquartz crystals were supposed to be in thermostats at a strictly constant temperature. A thermostat malfunction caused the failure to create the second piloted orbital station.[14] The low degree of reliability of our electronics elements caused off-nominal situations in rocket-space technology time after time.

On 19 October 1969, everyone departed from the Crimea, convinced that there would be reprisals for the flubbed program or at least notification of reprimands and strict warnings in the ministry collegium. However, Moscow received us with such delighted greetings from the Central Committee, Presidium of the Supreme Soviet, and Council of Ministers, which were published in all the mass media, that it simply would have been a shame after that to impose some sort of punishment. Then, on 22 October came decrees about awards for the crews, who were celebrated in a manner befitting them at a Kremlin banquet. A week later the

---

14. The Soviet press had announced the docking of *Soyuz-4* and *Soyuz-5* as the "world's first piloted orbital station."

traditional press conference took place, at which Keldysh in his opening speech mentioned that "in January of this year a spacecraft docking was performed and the world's first experimental orbital space station was created." Without having uttered a single word about the intentions to create another orbital station, he announced that "the multiday group flight of three Soyuz spacecraft successfully worked out cutting-edge problems pertaining to the creation of piloted orbital space systems and the testing of the vehicles' interaction while they performed wide-ranging maneuvers in Earth orbit."

Cosmonauts Shatalov, Kubasov, Shonin, Filipchenko, Gorbatko, Volkov, and Yeliseyev spoke at the press conference describing their work in space. They shared their observations, which were very interesting for specialists, but not one of them dared hint that the program's main mission had not been accomplished. And no one recalled that this had happened because of an ordinary quartz-stabilizer thermostat.

Very few knew about one other off-nominal incident on *Soyuz-6*. Kubasov had performed an in-flight plasma arc welding experiment. While welding, he almost burned through the hull of the vehicle's Living Compartment, which in the absence of spacesuits could have resulted in a catastrophic situation. At the press conference and in the press there was talk of a unique experiment that had been performed with complete success.

From the author's archives.

"We can't allow the thought to even occur to our people about our having mishaps in space. We have our own path, our own road, and if the Americans also achieve success, then it is somewhere to the side of our general line." This is more or less the directive that the Central Committee issued not only to all the mass media, but even to the president of the Academy of Sciences, all the cosmonauts, and the publicly known scientists working on space issues.

Cosmonauts (left to right) Georgiy Shonin, Valeriy Kubasov, Vladimir Shatalov, and Aleksey Yeliseyev are shown during the parade in Moscow following the *Soyuz-6/7/8* mission in October 1969.

AFTER THE FIRST DAYS OF EUPHORIA, which we endured with mixed feelings of pride for what we had accomplished and disappointment over the actual failure (unbeknownst to the world) of the program, our group of "conspirators" gathered in Bushuyev's office to develop a plan of further actions to enlist Ustinov into our "conspiracy." Bushuyev, being discreet, proposed that we wait until Mishin left on vacation.

"We can't just approach the Central Committee secretary without having informed our own chief designer."

Everyone agreed with this, and each of us pledged, if Ustinov would receive us, to prepare a presentation arguing the feasibility and necessity of creating an orbital station within a timeframe that was inconceivable for everyone except for us.

"We need to take advantage of the buzz that the group flight is still generating. And as deputy chief designer for piloted flights, Bushuyev should call Ustinov on the Kremlin line." That was my proposal. Bushuyev didn't like it. Feoktistov summoned up his courage and offered to make the call himself. But we questioned whether this would be proper: why should non–Party member Feoktistov appeal directly to the secretary of the Communist Party Central Committee while Party members vacillated in doing this?

I hesitate after the passage of almost 40 years to come up with an explanation as to why Ustinov decided to invite Okhapkin, Bushuyev, Feoktistov, Rauschenbach, and me to his office right after Mishin departed for Kislovodsk.[15] Officially, we did not ask for the meeting and we didn't know what to think. Each of us received a phone call from the Central Committee, and no one dared refuse. Not even non–Party member Feoktistov.

When we entered the office on Kuybyshev Street, we saw Keldysh, Afanasyev, Tyulin, and Serbin, who had probably already come to an agreement on something. Sitting there were three Central Committee defense department staffers—Boris Strogonov, Vyacheslav Krasavtsev, and Viktor Popov. All three were from Podlipki. We had no doubt about their goodwill and active participation in organizing this event.

While we were coping with the three Soyuzes, Krasavtsev, who looked out for our TsKBEM in the Central Committee bureaucracy, had received information from Bushuyev's designers about our underground operations on a new orbital station. Information was properly checked and reported to Ustinov. He was informed about the disastrous state of the Almaz. Independent of us,

---

15. Kislovodsk, located in southern Russia between the Black and Caspian Seas, was a popular holiday destination during Soviet times.

the Central Committee understood that in the best case it would be two years before the Almaz could become an orbital station. But even if this happened, then we couldn't make a fuss for the whole world: the Almaz must remain a secret military spacecraft. If possible, we needed to have a nonsecret station and demonstrate to the whole world that we offer international cooperation in the interests of science and economics. We needed to do all of this quickly, before the Americans hit upon the idea of taking an astronaut from some European country with them to the Moon. An unexpected report from NASA to the president (which I mentioned in Chapter 11) also hinted at the idea of accelerating operations on a nonmilitary orbital station.

At the meeting, as we had expected according to our script, Feoktistov was called upon to speak first. Konstantin Petrovich talked very convincingly about the advantages of our proposal and assured them that, given the proper monitoring and assistance, a Long-Duration Orbital Station could be inserted into space within a year. I, in turn, assured them that I foresaw no serious problems for the control system because everything that we needed had already been tested in space on the Soyuzes. However, there would be a new element—a docking assembly with internal transfer. It was currently being manufactured and would undergo a cycle of development tests, but we would manage to do that within a year.

After the pertinent presentations of Bushuyev and Okhapkin, Keldysh asked an unexpected question: "So, you all say that this can be done in a year if you get help setting up the operations and have no days off and even work practically around the clock. But how is all of this going to affect your work on the N1-L3?"

Okhapkin answered for all of us: "A whole different group of people should work on the Long-Duration Orbital Stations (DOS). In our shop a permanent contingent is working on the N-1, and we, God forbid, won't bother anyone there." Sergey Osipovich kept silent about the fact that if all the brass were to start managing the DOS "storm," this would inevitably affect all the other operations, and the N1-L3 first and foremost.

We were already headed in the direction in which the "hand of Fate" was pointing: we should be in charge of developing an orbital station. It seemed to me that something dawned on all of the participants of this momentous meeting. Evidently our proposal came at the best possible time.

The meeting ended with an instruction to immediately prepare a ministerial order, a decision, and a VPK timetable, and to issue a Central Committee and Council of Ministers resolution concerning the development of an orbital station no later than January.

Certain of Ustinov's support, after arriving at work the day after the meeting in the Central Committee, we announced the dawning of a new era: in a year's time we must develop a heavy-duty orbital station. It is most astounding that this new project was perceived among the majority of staffs as very timely. What's more, one heard choruses of voices asking: "And where were you before? It's about time we merge with ZIKh and develop a real station instead of having our heads in the clouds with whimsical projects." Taking advantage of the situation, many specialists who were needed for the lunar program crossed over from L3 developments to the DOS. Bushuyev openly expressed his apprehensions for the fate of the L3 program.

Once they had gotten wind of the conference in the Central Committee, staffs subordinate to me started to celebrate. Three or four days later this gave way to lawful requirements concerning the "legalization" of projects via the appropriate timetables, introducing them into monthly schedules, and reviewing other projects benefiting the DOS. Rauschenbach, after banding together the main "troublemakers" (as he referred to them)—Legostayev, Bashkin, Karpov, Sosnovik, Knyazev, and Babkov—appeared with this noisy delegation in my office and delivered an ultimatum: "Immediately give us a timetable for coordinating projects with the draft designers and the designers from Fili, shift dates for lunar vehicles, and speed up preparation of the order about the new project and its 'legalization.' This project can't be conducted on enthusiasm alone."

It was unacceptable to hold off on organizational decisions any longer. But how could an order be issued in the absence of the chief designer, being fully aware of his negative attitude? We urgently needed both a ministerial decree and a VPK timetable for the subcontracting organizations.

IN THE INTERVALS BETWEEN OUR NOISY SHOUTING MATCHES, I found the time to look into the state of affairs with the new docking assembly [allowing internal transfer]. Kalashnikov, Vilnitskiy, Syromyatnikov, and Utkin were full of designers' optimism. The original electromechanical assembly, despite its apparent complexity, looked pretty good. The main thing was that we needed to believe in it. The team of designers that was working on the drawings was made up of realists, who understood what was required and what the capabilities of our technology were. Now it was a matter of production. That was our general opinion.

The day after the meeting in the Central Committee, we familiarized factory director Klyucharev with the upcoming work. A day later, Klyucharev and chief engineer Khazanov discussed with us in detail the problems of manufacturing and performing experimental development testing on the new docking assembly. We agreed to have a special team sent on an urgent mission to the Azov Optical-Mechanical Factory—the primary manufacturer of the docking assembly mechanisms. Kalashnikov and I found the time to visit the

Mashinoapparat Factory in Moscow, which had been tasked with producing the electric motors and damping devices. We had enjoyed excellent relations with this factory and its chief designer, Georgiy Katkov, for 20 years now, since the time when the first control surface actuators were mastered.

Okhapkin, Bushuyev, and I decided that we needed to take the risk and appoint a lead designer to coordinate operations, prepare the ministerial decrees and the government decisions, and maintain constant contact with OKB-52 and its branch.[16] Naturally, he needed to be freed from all other concerns.

"In my opinion," said Okhapkin, "operations on the L1 are wrapping up today. Well, perhaps there will be another one or two launches. It doesn't matter what Mishin promised the 'brass,' no one dares conduct a piloted circumlunar flight. And who needs it now? How about if we transfer Semyonov from the L1 and make him lead designer on the DOS?"

I agreed with Okhapkin: "After all, he is the only one of the potential candidates who has dealt with Fili, and if something happens, he won't be cowed by Chelomey."

I proposed that he [Okhapkin] issue a directive. But he said that, first of all, he would consult with the Party committee; second, he would telephone Mishin; and third, he would contact the minister as well.

"I have a feeling, " continued Okhapkin, "that this place is going to be very hot, and I don't want to catch hell for untimely independent action."

But the fat was in the fire. The candidacy of Yuriy Semyonov passed through the entire hierarchy. This determined his subsequent fate. In late 1969, we who had promoted Semyonov as a candidate for the lead designer for the DOS, and Semyonov himself couldn't and didn't even attempt to predict the subsequent development of events based on what seemed such an ordinary decision. But the future, over which we had no command, took charge in its own way: 20 years later Semyonov occupied that historic office from which Academician Korolev departed forever in January 1966.[17]

People working in a group that seethes with creative impulses are completely immersed in internal problems and not always capable of properly assessing external circumstances. The idea of drawing up a six- or seven-year plan for the development of domestic cosmonautics and reporting to the Politburo came to fruition under such critical circumstances for our

---

16. The title of "lead designer" was actually a formal position in the design bureau hierarchy, lower than deputy chief designer but ultimately responsible for a particular product.

17. Yuriy Pavlovich Semyonov (1935–) became the fourth person to head Korolev's design bureau (after Korolev, Mishin, and Glushko) when he was appointed General Designer of NPO Energiya in 1989. He served in that position until retirement in 2005.

rocket leadership. Feverish preparation of the latest resolutions began in December 1969.

On Saturday, 6 December, Minister Afanasyev came out to see us at TsKBEM for a managerial conference. At his request, Pilyugin, Ryazanskiy, Viktor Kuznetsov, and Chelomey's deputy—Arkadiy Eydis— also came.[18] Afanasyev announced that he had received instructions to consult with us and work out additional proposals for the six-year plan and objectives for the next two years for the Central Committee and the Politburo to discuss.

"How can we fix things so that the 100th anniversary of Lenin's birthday and Twenty-fourth Party Congress might be properly celebrated?" With that question Afanasyev began his long speech.[19] "We have a proposal to update piloted 7K-OK vehicles and execute a flight of record-setting duration in recognition of the 100th anniversary. Things are still going badly with the orbital stations. Chelomey is way behind on the Almaz. You hinted at how to correct the situation: take an Almaz hull and place a passive *Igla* unit and a passive docking assembly on it and provide life support for the station using the active 7K-OK vehicle. There are objections to the 7K-S.[20] We need to decide what to do with this vehicle. The military needs it very much. This does not mean that we intend to abandon the Almaz. We need to think of a way to set up joint projects.

"When it came to the L1, the majority [of Central Committee members] spoke out against the piloted circumlunar flight. We need to use the available vehicle production stock for scientific purposes, after installing additional equipment. We should design the orbital station more thoughtfully and put together a phase-by-phase developmental testing plan. Would it be worth it to make a piloted L1 vehicle using the *Pyatisotka* [UR-500]? Everyone is complaining that very strict weight limits have been imposed on the N1-L3. They say that the LK has just 20 seconds to maneuver before landing. That's ridiculous! If things keep going like that, we'll only be able to land half a man on the Moon. Some people propose removing the backup systems. This is a risk that reduces reliability. You need to guarantee that at least one man can safely land on the Moon! The designers' attitude is unclear. There is no certainty when it comes

---

18. Arkadiy Ionovich Eydis (1913–2004) was deputy general designer at TsKBM from 1965 to 1973.

19. The Twenty-fourth Party Congress was held in March and April 1971. Lenin's birthday was on 22 April.

20. The 7K-S was an improved military variant of the original 7K-OK Soyuz. It was originally proposed as a crew delivery vehicle for the small (and later, abandoned) Soyuz-VI space station. Improvements to the vehicle included updated avionics, communications, and safety systems.

to [liquid]-hydrogen Blocks S and R and the two-launch scenario—N1-L3M.[21] We've already come up with a name, but the work isn't organized!

"If this configuration provides weight advantages, I promise you: we will get the ministry enterprises involved and we will do everything as soon as possible.

"I ask that you thoroughly work out and present a plan for N1-L3. We have Mars proposals. We do not want to retrace the Americans' path. We must have forward-looking plans.

"Squeezing all the proposals for equipment weights, the TsKBEM designers put the subcontractors in an extremely difficult position. Why did the Americans have an engine chamber pressure of 50 atmospheres on the Saturn, while Kuznetsov had 150?[22] You chased after super parameters and you reduced reliability. I heard that the initiative is coming not from Kuznetsov, but that Mishin and Melnikov demanded these parameters from him so that the engine would be the best in the world. It really is the 'best'—in terms of explosion hazard.

"We need to radically revise the organization of operations. To eliminate noncompliance with program cycles. Stop biting off more than you can chew. For example, Mishin has one control system and Chelomey has another. Why? Perhaps, transfer all the operations to Pilyugin? Let him decide the tasks for everyone."

After a brief pause, Afanasyev explained what he wanted from us: "Very soon we will be granted a hearing in the Central Committee and Politburo. We must explain what is going on and provide specific plans and tangible commitments. These matters are very serious. I ask that you speak candidly, from the heart, without looking to your neighbor."

After the minister's long, emotionally charged speech, there was a brief pause. Pilyugin was the first to take the floor.

"We need to break all the tasks into groups and think about how to tackle them. We can't prepare for a flight to Mars without careful consideration. We'll get into hot water like we did with the L1. We need to decide and not draw things out with this program. As for the L3, I sense that we are going to end up in the same situation as we did with the L1. They pushed me out of the

---

21. The Block S and the Block R were upper stages equipped with liquid-hydrogen engines designed to replace the Block G and Block D stages, respectively, of the N1-L3. Block S used Lyulka's 11D57 engine while Block R used Isayev's 11D56 engine. The L3M plan involved a two-launch scenario using uprated N-1 rockets to launch a heavy piloted spacecraft to the surface of the Moon. See Asif A. Siddiqi, *Challenge to Apollo: The Soviet Union and the Space Race, 1945–1974* (Washington, DC: NASA, 2000), pp. 757–766.

22. The chamber pressure in the H-1 engine (used on the Saturn I and Saturn IB) was about 43 atmospheres. The value for the F-1 engine (used on the Saturn V) was about 70 atmospheres.

way and I'm standing on the sidelines unable to make decisions.[23] At OKB-1 (Pilyugin used our old name; he didn't like the new abbreviation TsKBEM) the assignments are supposed to be worked out and coordinated with the subcontracting organizations. The organization of the L3M project is inept. We need to admit this without hesitation. It is difficult to speak calmly with Mishin. Let's organize the work ourselves. We won't wait for the 'brass' to do it for us."

Bushuyev spoke out in favor of preparing for a long-duration flight, saying that this mission could be accomplished very soon. Bashkin made two specific proposals: execute a flight of record-setting duration with a single 7K-OK vehicle for the 100th anniversary of Lenin's birthday and launch a prototype of the heavy orbital station for the Twenty-fourth Party Congress. He expressed confidence that these two missions could absolutely be accomplished in the time remaining. Kryukov also proposed preparing for a long-duration flight of the 7K-OK for the Twenty-fourth Party Congress. He reminded us that we had wanted to perform a circumlunar flight with the L1 in 1967 for the 50th anniversary of Soviet rule.

"I am attending the third such meeting, " said Kryukov, "and I am convinced that many comrades are approaching the matter casually, making promises that are not technically sound. We are not prepared today to take on commitments for an orbital station in time for the Twenty-fourth Party Congress. Moreover, even given all of our failures, the L1 was not a useless project. It has provided great results. The Ye-8 and Mars-N designs have come into being and Block D has already been tested out. We mustn't consider a circumlunar flight unnecessary. We had to go through it."

Kryukov sighed and continued, "The N1-L3 is a very complex and difficult matter. We will achieve the weights that were promised today, but this is minor, very minor. We have to admit that we underestimated the difficulties we have encountered. The most important thing is that we need to combine our efforts. We are working with different approaches in different organizations on the same missions. Why?"

Feoktistov took the floor. "I am going to speak only about my personal vision of our missions. I am not going to hide the fact that my position is quite different from the others. The 7K-OK needs to be launched for a 16-day mission—this is a leap that we must make. The orbital station can be created using the load-bearing structure of the Almaz. Konstantin Davidovich [Bushuyev] estimated the time necessary for that at a year and a half; Yevgeniy

---

23. This is a reference to the fact that TsKBEM chose to do much of the control and guidance for the N1-L3 instead of handing it over to Pilyugin's institute, as would have been typical.

Aleksandrovich [Frolov] said one year.[24] There are difficulties, and big ones at that. As an engineer, I believe that it can be done in less than a year if TsKBEM is given the assignment and if specialists from the TsKBM branch provide assistance.[25] If we all make a concerted effort we will do it. But I have to tell you straight that this work will delay the N1-L3, and especially the L3M. We're all leaving 'for the front,' for the station, and we won't have anything left for the Moon. This is an enormous experimental project, and there is no doubt that the N1-L3 will suffer.

"It's a shame to abandon the L1. We need to use the hardware as long as we have it. We need to go into the Zond orbits and try to use the L1 production stock for the sake of science, for example, for radio interferometry. The astrophysicists have ideas like this. If the Central Committee wants an orbital station to be developed, the N1-L3 program needs to be reconsidered, and it needs to be shifted two or three years."

Looking over the rough drafts of our speeches at this conference recently, I could not recall whether we had stated everything that we had prepared. It turned out that I spoke for 25 to 30 minutes. By the way, this time the minister did not interrupt anyone. He diligently jotted down notes on his notepad.

I attempted to impart to my presentation a sense of program and history.

"During the development of the R-7, we got way ahead of the Americans because the demands of the atomic scientists forced us to design a very far-sighted configuration. Twelve years have passed since the first launch, but the capabilities of the launch vehicle have yet to be depleted and there is no end in sight to the upgrades.

"We were ahead of the Americans for many years despite our weak economy. During the R-7 phase, we really managed to combine 'Russian revolutionary sweep with American efficiency.'[26] During the development of N1-L3 the scope was not revolutionary; in many cases efficiency contributed to a reduction in the volume and scale of experimental operations.

---

24. Yevgeniy Aleksandrovich Frolov (1927–2003) was a senior designer at TsKBEM. He had served as "lead designer" for the Vostok and Voskhod spacecraft and was a senior designer in charge of testing the DOS space stations.

25. The TsKBM branch (also known as TsKBM's Branch No. 1) was located at Fili and responsible for designing the *Proton* launch vehicle.

26. This famous quote from Stalin recalls the enthusiastic adoption of American management practices (particularly Ford's mass-production techniques and Taylor's scientific management) in the Soviet Union in the 1920s. Stalin's full quote was: "American efficiency is that indomitable force which neither knows nor recognizes obstacles; which continues on a task once started until it is finished, even if it is a minor task; and without which serious constructive work is impossible.... The combination of Russian revolutionary sweep with American efficiency is the essence of Leninism."

"Today we are struggling for a mass in Earth orbit of 95 tons, while the Americans have achieved more than 130. The difference is so palpable that we cannot be silent about it! We didn't have [liquid] hydrogen—it was just a wish. The experimental hydrogen Blocks S and R are appearing on the scene only now. One of the reasons for our falling behind is that after Korolev's death there wasn't an organ like the Council of Chief Designers that could organize, conduct business, and provide guidance. Neither ministerial nor VPK directives could replace the Council of Chiefs. Once we had come to grips with this situation, we did not find the courage to review the decisions made during Korolev's time on the expedition concept, and planned a glaring shortfall of 30 to 40 tons of mass inserted into Earth orbit. This triggered a series of crucial subsequent decisions. I shall cite several of them.

"The expedition has two persons, rather than three, and only one of them lands on the Moon. This is not just a foreign policy failure, but also a loss of reliability. It would be frightening for a single cosmonaut on the Moon: if he were to stumble in his heavy spacesuit, no one could lift him up or drag him away. The weight restrictions compel us to do away with automatic backup of manual control on the LOK in the piloted version, which reduces reliability. For this same reason, we did away with the docking assembly configuration with internal transfer between vehicles. The fatigued cosmonaut must execute a circus act of questionable safety: making his way from the LK to the LOK in an external transfer. Now a docking assembly with internal transfer is being urgently developed for 7K-S, for 7K-T, and for the future DOS.[27] Unfortunately this can't be achieved for the lunar vehicles as there are no weight reserves.

"We left a ridiculously small amount of time for 'hovering' over the surface of the Moon while selecting a site for landing: just 15 to 20 seconds. The Americans had 2 minutes, and still they consider this very little, even though there are two astronauts looking and controlling, and they have a good view.

"We did away with television en route there and back, even black-and-white, while Apollo had color television along the entire route.

"We are taking a step backwards in autonomous navigation even compared with the L1. On the L1 we regularly conduct orientation sessions to determine navigational parameters. On the L3 we have the equipment, but not enough fuel for these measurement sessions.

"The time margin for the LK to function autonomously is very small—just 12 to 16 hours. If an error occurs again, then it will be all over for the

---

27. The 7K-T was a modified version of the original 7K-OK Soyuz designed only to deliver crews to DOS.

cosmonaut in the LK. The Americans have 48 hours, and if docking does not take place right after liftoff from the Moon, then they can make one more attempt, with some risk."

"We have done away with a backup automatic descent control system during return to Earth. This is one more step backward compared with L1.

"Apollo's gyrostabilized platform activates while still on the ground, before liftoff, and corrects itself once every 24 hours using the stars. A similar system that we have was tested out for Lavochkin's Burya and underwent testing in 1959.[28] But the Americans have advanced even further thanks to television star trackers. They developed a sextant that automatically scans and enters data into a computer. We have not managed to place an order for such a star tracker.

"We have pitiful ground-based flight control facilities. As yet no center has been set up in Moscow like the one in Houston, and automatic processing and real-time display facilities are primitive.

"All of this has a bearing on N1-L3. Hence the following proposals:

1. A long-duration flight up to 16 to 18 days on 7K-OK for the 100th anniversary of Lenin's birthday can be executed. This is a problem only for the life-support systems. The control systems can cope with this mission.

2. Create a reliable Long-Duration Orbital Station through the joint efforts of the two head organizations, ours and Chelomey's, together with the Fili branch and ZIKh.

"During the first phase for the DOS we will use 7K-OK systems, which have been standardized both for the vehicles and for the station itself. We'll be in a position to realize this phase in 14 to 15 months and to insert the station into space in the spring of 1971.

"Having gained experience operating piloted DOSes with 7K-OK vehicles, we can move on to the second phase—the creation of an orbital station using more state-of-the-art control equipment. We can use Almaz production stock, but our 7K-OKs will still be the piloted transport vehicles. During the final phase, we'll create a transport vehicle with a control system using an on-board digital computer and an orbital station that meets all the requirements of the Ministry of Defense.

"Over the next 12 to 18 months, our primary resources need to be aimed at the creation and developmental testing of a complex of orbital stations. Therefore, the N1-L3 project plans should be reviewed. The main task for

---

28. Burya was an intercontinental cruise missile developed between 1954 and 1960 by NII-1 and OKB-301 (the Lavochkin design bureau). See Chertok, *Rockets and People, Vol. II,* Chapter 12.

the upcoming year is to increase the reliability of the [*Proton*] launch vehicle. We should not distract specialists involved with the N-1 launch vehicle with work on DOSes. In this case, the process of perfecting the launch vehicle will not suffer. In actual fact, if we want to have orbital stations in 1971, work on lunar vehicles will stop of its own accord. And perhaps this is for the best.

"During that time we need to redesign the L3—transition to a dual-launch L3M configuration. We will be able to land at least two cosmonauts on the Moon in 1975. We need five years to develop and produce a new design that will enable us to surpass the Americans' lunar successes. Over the course of those five years we will produce orbital stations, we'll secure superiority in that field, and at the same time we'll have the opportunity to work on the lunar vehicles with no rush."

During my long speech I kept an eye on Afanasyev's reaction. When I listed the shortcomings of N1-L3, he took elaborate notes all the while contritely shaking his head. When I moved on to proposals, his face brightened, and as he took notes, he nodded his head in agreement. But when I mentioned the date for the expedition to the Moon—1975—tearing himself away from his notes, he looked at me with reproach and remarked: "Keep this in mind: God help you if you ever mention these dates."

Our proposal to Ustinov and the Central Committee to develop an orbital station did not envision Pilyugin's participation in these operations. He wasn't even invited to take part in the discussion. Chelomey designed Almaz without Pilyugin, too. At the same time, the control systems of the entire N1-L3 complex were developed primarily by Pilyugin's NIIAP. In my program-oriented speech, Pilyugin sensed the danger of the lunar operations being phased out in favor of orbital stations and he took the floor for a second time.

"If that's the way we're going to treat the L3, then before too long we'll end up the same way on this project as we did with the L1. We need to get to the bottom of what's going on with the launch vehicle as soon as possible. In order to work confidently, we need a launch vehicle. And let's be honest—we don't have one yet. But we don't have lunar vehicles either. Mishin, Bushuyev, and Feoktistov keep demanding that we reduce the weights. But we have a job to do besides reducing the weight! We don't have any weight left at all for scientific and military missions. Then what are we flying into space for?

"Chertok and Feoktistov are trying to make you afraid that they're going to stop work on the lunar vehicles for the sake of the orbital stations. I think this is a mistake. If things don't pan out for you, honestly admit this and correct your old mistakes instead of throwing yourselves into a new project. We're prepared to help salvage the N-1. If we can pull off the project for the launch of three cosmonauts using a dual-launch scenario, we need to revamp the vehicles right away. We are prepared to modify our systems: our organization will take care of everything.

Using what we already have, we are prepared for reconfigurations. We already have a new on-board computer for the launch vehicle.[29] People are working very enthusiastically. There's no need to draw it out any further with decision making. We are not participating in projects involving orbital stations, therefore our L3 projects are not going to suffer, but make a decision! Don't dawdle!"

Keldysh also took up this appeal of "Don't dawdle!" and ran with it.

"The situation with the weights is really very tense. I think that if we can guarantee the landing of one cosmonaut on the Moon, we need to do this as soon as possible, and then we can make the complex more sophisticated and move to a dual-launch scenario or one that is even more complicated. But if there are no guarantees, and we get ourselves tied up with already existing plans and developments, then this is unacceptable. It is better to say it now, rather than a year and a half from now, that the weights won't work. The 20 seconds already mentioned here serve as an example. I am announcing that I will not give my consent for selecting a lunar landing site within just 20 seconds. It will be a tragedy for all of us if before liftoff it turns out that we can't launch. We need to stop obscuring the issue here and now and tell the truth and nothing but the truth. I am sorry that Vasiliy Pavlovich [Mishin] isn't here today. I have the impression that our comrades on the expert commission are being deliberately obscure and are not laying out all the difficulties they've been having with weights. This is unacceptable.

"I propose that we assign a group comprising Mishin, Okhapkin, Bushuyev, Chertok, Kuznetsov, Likhushin, and Ryazanskiy to review the program, and if there is no guarantee for landing two cosmonauts, we switch over to a dual-launch scenario.[30] But only if there are no 'ifs'.

"One particular issue that worries me very much is the reliability of the engines on the N-1. I have the impression that the investigations into the causes of the latest failure were not very objective. It seems to me that this matter needs further examination. I want to speak with Dementyev about this.

"We can't make a decision on the N1-L3M configuration without a thorough reliability analysis. We should work out the dual-launch scenario using reusable engines. If we don't attain reliable engines, they need to be changed."

Viktor Kuznetsov brought up an objection to Keldysh: "Even given a high degree of reliability in the program for landing one cosmonaut on the Moon, we need to review it and come up with a new strategy. Today we need to plan a lunar

---

29. This was the S-530 computer.
30. Valentin Yakovlevich Likhushin (1918–1992) was director of the Scientific-Research Institute of Thermal Processes (formerly known as NII-1).

landing of not one cosmonaut, but two or three. We must have two full-fledged launches. We can't work without a backup. This will ensure the reliability of the dual-launch scenario. Chertok's observations are very serious, but where were you before? Does the expert commission know about them? We need to seriously examine what automatic systems can do. I do not agree that they supposedly can do everything. A cosmonaut in the LOK is both a backup and a controller of the automatic systems. During phase one we need to launch the N-1 and the LOK carrying a cosmonaut without landing on the Moon. We will gain experience, which we don't yet have right now. The safe return of a human being after a circumlunar flight is also a phase that we need to pass through before landing on the Moon."

Ryazanskiy took the floor next: "Switching to a fully automatic vehicle for a lunar landing and liftoff should be well argued not only from the standpoint of weight. Krayushkin's antenna experts have developed a good antenna array. But the instruments for switching the arrays have no backup—Bushuyev isn't setting aside weight for that. This puts us in a stupid position. We're expected to provide a full guarantee of reliability, but then the head design bureau [TsKBEM] refuses the several kilograms needed for it. If you want to set a record of lunar conquest with the lightest weight, then don't demand guarantees.

"We have been approaching the 'man or machine' problem in several stages. The main trend must be switching to machine. It will be a while before the dual-launch scenario appears. Chertok estimates it will take five years. We need to find the courage and say that we're going to give up landing on the Moon during this phase. Orbital stations must serve as compensation. I agree with the proposition that the first station can be produced rapidly using the fabricated stock that we all have."

Afanasyev had invited Chelomey to this conference, but the latter sent his first deputy, Eydis, instead. He took the floor, defending the Almaz program and proposed a compromise.

"We are proceeding from the premise that the Almaz program will continue. We have begun developing Dmitriy Fedorovich's and Sergey Aleksandrovich's assignment calling for the docking of our station with 7K-OK. We will finish the study by 1 January. We are having difficulties with life support for Almaz—this is now the most crucial issue. I disagree with Boris Yevseyevich's proposal for the control system. You want to take an empty Almaz hull and fill it with a completely different system. Such a large undertaking requires the involvement of many organizations. You can disregard us or dash us to pieces, but there will be no benefit from that because we can't influence the Ministry of the Aviation Industry [MAP] and the Ministry of the Defense Industry [MOP]. These projects require a body vested with the authority that will be able to handle everything. This is a decisive issue. Almaz is standing there without its main military "innards" and without life-support systems.

"Let me remind you that we have been working on Almaz since 1965 and all of our ideas were coordinated with the Ministry of Defense. The military needs an orbital station to conduct comprehensive surveillance. Together with the Central Directorate of Space Assets [TsUKOS] and the Main Intelligence Directorate [GRU], we have done a thorough study of the state-of-the-art capabilities. Accordingly, government decisions have placed orders for systems making it possible to conduct surveillance in the infrared and visible ranges at high resolution. For the first time, surveillance footage will be transmitted via television channel.

"The participation of our branch and of ZIKh in the manufacture of DOSes will disrupt operations on Almaz. We agree to combine our efforts with TsKBEM to produce a transport system using the 7K-OK spacecraft. Help us get it fitted out and there will be an orbital station."

The minister thanked everybody for their comments. Exercising caution, he neither praised nor criticized anyone. He alerted us that in the near future many of us would take part in a conference with Ustinov. Afanasyev was in the most difficult situation. He answered to the Politburo for the entire area of endeavor. Ultimately he would have to "make a decision and report." But what?

On 26 December 1969, Ustinov convened a conference at his office on Kuybyshev Street. Okhapkin, Chertok, Bushuyev, Rauschenbach, and Feoktistov represented TsKBEM. Mishin was still on vacation in Kislovodsk. Neither Chelomey nor his deputies had been invited. Once again, the chief designers of the old council attended—Pilyugin, Kuznetsov, Ryazanskiy, and Barmin. As I understood it, Glushko had not been invited so that he would not alienate us with his fiercely negative attitude toward the reliability of Kuznetsov's engines.

Keldysh did not bring with him anyone representing "pure science." In addition to us, cosmonautics' highest ranks of leadership were represented by Smirnov, Serbin, Afanasyev, Tyulin, Mozzhorin, Kerimov, and Karas. In 1964, Kerimov became the head of the recently created Ministry of Defense GUKOS, but by March 1965 he had transferred to MOM as Chief of the Main Directorate for Space.[31] Karas was appointed chief of TsUKOS.[32] Officially, he alone represented the Ministry of Defense at meetings.

Chelomey's absence made the discussion of problems concerning orbital stations one-sided. We had already received preliminary information to the effect

---

31. This directorate was officially known as the Third Main Directorate.

32. The Central Directorate of Space Assets (TsUKOS) was established in October 1964. It was renamed the Main Directorate of Space Assets (GUKOS) in March 1970 and Directorate of the Chief of Space Assets (UNKS) in November 1986.

that Ustinov was not the only one in the Central Committee who supported our proposal for the production of a DOS and that in the very near future we would be "turning ourselves inside out" to pay for our initiative. Chelomey vigorously objected and asked the military for help. But the prospect of building a space station in a year and a half—something the Americans didn't have yet—on the eve of the report to the Twenty-fourth Party Convention was so tempting that all the objections were swept away.

During the time between the two meetings, we conducted an intense study of the scenario using Almaz hulls to build our orbital station. Without waiting for Mishin's return, at the request of Okhapkin and Bushuyev, Yuriy Semyonov as acting lead designer took on the coordination of organizational issues and the preparation of ministry orders and of the governmental resolution concerning DOSes. While working on the L1, Semyonov had established good contacts with the design bureau and with the production plant in Fili. Their assistance was decisive. Unlike Chelomey, his deputy in Fili—branch chief Bugayskiy—didn't object to the use of Almaz stock, and he also supported our proposal with unconcealed enthusiasm.[33]

At the very beginning of the meeting, we understood that this gathering at the office of the Central Committee Secretary was not intended as a forum to discuss problems and work out certain program decisions, but was primarily a motivational lecture. Each of us, this time very briefly, gave assurances that, working with the TsKBM Fili branch and with the active participation of ZIKh, we could produce a DOS in one and a half years. It should be mentioned that we had agreed in advance to whenever possible avoid conversations concerning N1-L3, since we knew that we would be "lectured," and with such a preponderance of forces in favor of the topmost leadership, any resistance was not only futile, but also dangerous. Therefore, our speeches were short.

As we had anticipated, Ustinov summed things up with a lecture.

"We have conducted a sensible, serious conversation. I want you not only to understand what is troubling the Central Committee, but I also want you to follow up this understanding with actions. What we discussed today is a course. Get set on this course and scrupulously fulfill this line. God forbid you should stop thinking about landing a man on the Moon. That's a shallow and irresponsible attitude. You all are being shown the greatest trust, you're spending enormous state resources, you're praised throughout the world, and

---

33. Viktor Nikiforovich Bugayskiy (1912–1994) served as chief of TsKBM's Branch No. 1 (or Fili Branch) from 1960 to 1973. He was an experienced engineer who had previously served under the famed Soviet aviation designer Sergey Vladimirovich Ilyushin.

suddenly you've questioned the mission that the Party assigned. Keep in mind that the Central Committee's patience will soon come to an end, too.

"Now we have our only chance to correct the situation. We need to use the DOS not to disrupt operations on the N1-L3 project, but to fix the situation. For the time being the Americans have gotten ahead of us in one very important area. But, after all, we have the Molniya, the Meteor, spy satellites, and Soyuzes. We are first everywhere, except the Moon. Above all, we must prove it to ourselves: we will have our revenge. We need to work on that, and I repeat, God forbid that you should doubt that we can land our man on the Moon. Stop all your doubting. Communists need to be in charge of the operations. The number one task should be concern about reliability. Spare no one and nothing to get this work organized. If someone doubts, let him yield his place to someone else. I've been told that Mishin has a tendency to dig in his heels. He is often wrong. MOM must have a heavy hand. I gave instructions to prepare a decree regarding the DOS. A month has passed and there is still no draft. What is the minister doing? In such a critical situation, we must intensify our insistence on high standards, not let up on it.

"We won't see each other again before the new year. Accept my best wishes, stay healthy, and I hope for new success in the new year."

We left in high spirits. The working groups involved in the creation of the DOS felt enthusiasm that was neither affected nor perfunctory, but sincere. We didn't need any meetings or slogans calling for acceptance of socialist obligations.

DURING THIS PERIOD (late 1969 and essentially all of 1970), new problems cropped up like mushrooms after a summer rain. Over the course of the workday, the attention and energy of each manager was spread out in many directions. A five-, six-, or seven-year integrated plan for the development of cosmonautics was never even approved by a government decree. But the spectrum of operations remained exceptionally broad.

After the Americans' successes, a lunar expedition gradually ceased to be perceived as a "critical" mission as the old decrees had demanded. Throughout 1970, the Soviet Union inserted 88 different spacecraft into space. Kosmos spacecraft alone accounted for 72 of these. Twenty-nine of those 72 Kosmoses were various models of Zenits developed at the TsKBEM Kuybyshev branch and manufactured at the Progress Factory in Kuybyshev.[34]

---

34. These various Zenit models included the Zenit-2, Zenit-2M, Zenit-4, Zenit-4M, and Zenit-4MK.

I should remind the reader that the Progress and ZIKh Factories, former giants of the aviation industry, at that moment determined the industrial potential of Soviet cosmonautics. The Progress Factory worked on OKB-1 projects, i.e., those of Korolev, then Mishin, and Chief Designer Kozlov, who soon thereafter became independent. The Progress director was responsible for manufacturing R-9 missiles, space reconnaissance satellites, all modifications of the R-7 launch vehicle for all piloted and unpiloted vehicles that it could insert into space, and the N-1 super rockets in Kuybyshev and at its branch at the launch site. The ZIKh director first and foremost facilitated the production and servicing of *Sotka* (UR-100) missiles, the most common intercontinental missiles. He also rolled out *Pyatisotka* rockets (Protons), and now he would be manufacturing the Almaz and DOS.

Also among the Kosmoses was the experimental lunar vehicle, the LK of the L3 complex. It is amazing, but the flight-developmental testing of the lunar landing vehicle—the LK (11F94)—was ahead of the developmental testing of the main lunar orbital vehicle—the LOK (11F93). The spacecraft for the L3 program (LOK and LK), all models of 7K spacecraft, and booster Blocks D for the N-1 and UR-500 launch vehicles were small-scale production. It was the domain of our ZEM. I say "our" because the director of ZEM was subordinate to Chief Designer Mishin, and the directors of Progress and ZIKh were immediately subordinate to the ministry. The planners of Feoktistov's department were responsible for the LOK. Having been responsible for the piloted Soyuz flights, many of them switched over to the DOS project.

The LK was set apart for independent development. Contributing to a speedup of the operations was the fact that Yangel, who absolutely demanded near-Earth flight development, was developing Block Ye, which was part of the landing and liftoff propulsion system. The first flight of the LK, referred to as T2K (*Kosmos-379*), took place on 24 November 1970 without significant glitches and involved the multiple firings of Block Ye. To a great extent, this was the result of the self-sacrificing efforts of Department No. 222 Chief Ivan Prudnikov; his deputy, Yevgeniy Ryazanov; Sector Chief Yuriy Frumkin; and also Yuriy Labutin and Vyacheslav Filin. In all, there were three launches.[35]

The Central Committee, VPK, the Academy of Sciences, the Ministry of General Machine Building, and the Ministry of Defense nevertheless agreed to prepare a five-year space plan. The primary motivator of this development was our Ministry of General Machine Building. Afanasyev understood that

---

35. The remaining two T2K launches were on 26 February 1971 (*Kosmos-398*) and 12 August 1971 (*Kosmos-434*).

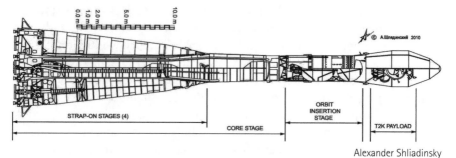

Alexander Shliadinsky

The launches of the T2K (an Earth-orbital version of the lunar lander) used a unique version of the Soyuz launch vehicle known as the 11A511L that used a special payload shroud.

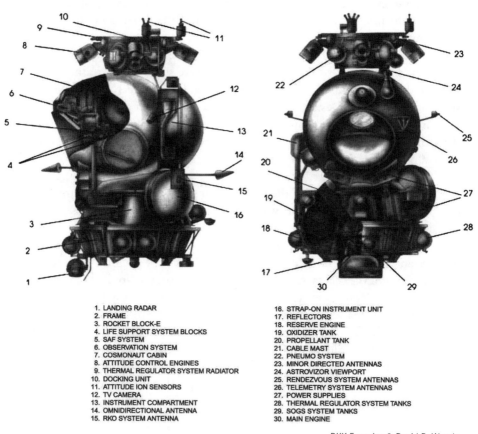

1. LANDING RADAR	16. STRAP-ON INSTRUMENT UNIT
2. FRAME	17. REFLECTORS
3. ROCKET BLOCK-E	18. RESERVE ENGINE
4. LIFE SUPPORT SYSTEM BLOCKS	19. OXIDIZER TANK
5. SAF SYSTEM	20. PROPELLANT TANK
6. OBSERVATION SYSTEM	21. CABLE MAST
7. COSMONAUT CABIN	22. PNEUMO SYSTEM
8. ATTITUDE CONTROL ENGINES	23. MINOR DIRECTED ANTENNAS
9. THERMAL REGULATOR SYSTEM RADIATOR	24. ASTROVIZOR VIEWPORT
10. DOCKING UNIT	25. RENDEZVOUS SYSTEM ANTENNAS
11. ATTITUDE ION SENSORS	26. TELEMETRY SYSTEM ANTENNAS
12. TV CAMERA	27. POWER SUPPLIES
13. INSTRUMENT COMPARTMENT	28. THERMAL REGULATOR SYSTEM TANKS
14. OMNIDIRECTIONAL ANTENNA	29. SOGS SYSTEM TANKS
15. RKO SYSTEM ANTENNA	30. MAIN ENGINE

RKK Energiya & David R. Woods

This cutaway shows the special Earth-orbital version of the LK. The test version was flown three times in Earth orbit in 1970 and 1971.

he bore the main responsibility for developing the plan. All the head design bureaus and scientific-research institutes had submitted their proposals in March [1970]. We had a certain clarity, if not for five years, then at least for the next three years about the following programs: the near-Earth piloted programs (Soyuz, DOS, and Almaz); the Meteor, Molniya, and Zenit programs; the lunar, Venus, and Mars launch programs; and miscellaneous odds and ends, as the N1-L3 and orbital station builders put it.

The decree on the development of Long-Duration Orbital Stations came out in the version that we needed on 9 February 1970. In this regard, after summoning 3 of my deputies and 11 department chiefs subordinate to me and their deputies, I began my speech as follows: "Mikhail Zoshchenko wrote that some people will find their way into a bathhouse accidentally, others—under pressure from those around them.[36] Up until now, we have had accidental elemental plans coming from below. Now 'under pressure from those around us' we must take a steam bath in an organized fashion in accordance with a multiyear—most likely, five-year—plan, but the first Long-Duration Orbital Station must fly in a year."

How close these various people were to me! They were all already scorched by the launch site sun, they had been through numerous rush production jobs, had also had reprimands and rewards, but had not lost their sense of humor, optimism, and faith in their own strength. I could trust my life to any of these people.

On 5 May 1970, Afanasyev, Litvinov, and Kerimov once again came out to consult with us at TsKBEM. After some tongue-in-cheek comments regarding the five-year plans, at the end of the meeting we announced: "We'll make DOSes too!" But the minister decided to speak his mind on the lunar program.

"The situation with the N1-L3 has become extremely complicated," Afanasyev said. "I talked long and in detail with Keldysh. He believes that landing a single cosmonaut on the Moon is uninteresting from the standpoint of large-scale science. It is a matter of technology and engineering, but we won't obtain any fundamental results. I tried to object and argued that any lunar expedition *is* large-scale science. Unfortunately, neither of us changed our opinion. A platoon of cosmonauts isn't necessary to plant a flag and collect some soil. We need to determine how many men we are going to land on the Moon.

---

36. Mikhail Mikhailovich Zoshchenko (1895–1958) was a Soviet author and satirist who attained great popularity in the 1920s.

"I went over to consult with Ryabikov.[37] I posed the question: 'Maybe we shouldn't come out with a proposal to land one cosmonaut on the Moon?' He answered that no one in the Politburo would understand giving up on landing on the Moon. A Soviet cosmonaut needed to set foot on the Moon. This was now a matter of Big Politics rather than science. In his opinion, this operation needed to be fulfilled in the interests of testing out the launch vehicle. As you see, everything boils down to the fact that the N1-L3 must not be abandoned. What worries me most of all is how we are going to guarantee the reliability of this whole operation. The Americans, even with their *Apollo 13* failure, pulled the rug out from under us.[38] Ustinov has ordered that we report on the reliability of the N1-L3 project proceeding from the *Apollo 13* experience. TsNIImash confirms that, given a similar situation, we would not be able to return our people to Earth. So, just order somebody to report to Ustinov?

"After the explosion of N-1 No. 5L, Politburo members reacted in different ways. Brezhnev asked: 'Is everybody alive? Well, thank God! Although you have told us little to be glad about, think about what needs to be done next!' Kosygin rebuked us: 'So, without having studied the situation, you once again took such a risk? Why? Who is it that decides things over there? Look through the stage-by-stage development testing process one more time.' I realize that Kosygin doesn't determine these issues, but he needs to be reckoned with. The other Politburo members said nothing. Understand this, each one has his own adviser there too.

"The N1-L3M stirs up various opinions. If one insists on [liquid] hydrogen, then the issue of its storage needs to be resolved. We risk losing 1 cubic meter to evaporation every 24 hours. When I mentioned constructing two more launch sites for the L3M program, this made the people at *Gosplan* and the Ministry of Finance grin: 'So you want to blow up two more launch sites?' In my opinion, all one can stipulate in the five-year plan for the L3M is a draft plan. Is a new hydrogen-engine launch vehicle necessary? You must set a goal and explain why.

"My opinion: we need to plan for a landing in 1973—that gives us three to three-and-a-half years. Keldysh is demanding that the five-year plan include

---

37. Vasiliy Mikhaylovich Ryabikov (1907–1974) served as the 1st Deputy Chairman of *Gosplan*, the state economic planning commission, from 1965 to 1974. Prior to this, Ryabikov had had a long and illustrious career as a manager in the Soviet defense industry.

38. *Apollo 13*, the third attempted piloted lunar landing, had to be aborted due to an explosion in the Service Module. The crew of James A. Lovell, John L. Swigert, and Fred W. Haise successfully returned to Earth by using the resources of the Lunar Module. The mission lasted six days, from 11 to 17 April 1970.

N-1 flights to Mars and the development of new power-generation trends. Nuclear engines, high-capacity systems for using solar energy—this is very enticing, but where are we going to find the resources for all this?

"We have examined the problems of orbital stations once again. The DOS and Almaz are very similar stations in terms of design and purpose. If one listens to you, we need to include a multipurpose station on the basis of the N-1 in the plan.

"You yourself have brought forward the decision on the MOK-N1.[39] This is a 70- to 80-ton orbital station for new space weaponry. What should we do with it? If we are to plan a launch, then in what year should it take place?

"There's a VPK decision regarding that, and it's already two years old. Before we start up a war in space, we need to catch up with the Americans on Earth. We still lag way behind in terms of the number of missiles in silos and on submarines. That's where our main resources are going now. *Gosplan* and the Ministry of Finance will budget enormous amounts of funding for the next five-year plan to ensure the state's military and technical power. They're allocating 9.4 billion rubles for research and development activities plus 3.3 billion just for major construction work, of which 2.1 billion rubles is just for experimental facilities. And this doesn't even count the expenditures of the Ministry of Medium Machine Building. The atomic scientists have their own account, but nobody is aware of it.

"And now, according to our information, the U.S. will have a satellite just for television broadcasting by 1975.[40] Why aren't we working on this? You need to sort things out with orbital vehicles more quickly. I feel like we will soon be in a mess—7K-OK, 7K-VI, 7K-S, 7K-T—and what else is Vasiliy Pavlovich proposing for us?"[41] Afanasyev paused, studying his notes. He found the sorest spot for the N-1: "Keldysh has once again reminded me about the firing tests. He has been informed that the Americans' engines for the Saturn undergo firing tests three times, and after the burns in the stage, they go into flight without reassembly. And you and Kuznetsov don't allow a single one. How do you want

---

39. MOK—*Mnogotselevoy orbitalnyy kompleks* (Multipurpose Orbital Complex).

40. The world's first (experimental) direct broadcasting satellite for television services was *ATS-6* (Applications Technology Satellite-6), which was launched on 30 May 1974. During its mission, the NASA satellite also contributed to a joint U.S.-Indian program to beam educational TV programs to rural areas in India.

41. The 7K-VI was a military version of the basic 7K-OK Soyuz proposed in the mid 1960s. It was developed by TsKBEM's Kuybyshev Branch headed by D. I. Kozlov and was designed to be part of a larger space station named Zvezda. It was superseded by several other piloted military programs, including Chelomey's Almaz and Mishin's Soyuz-VI (or Orbital Research Station). See Siddiqi, *Challenge to Apollo*, pp. 596–599.

me to respond to that? Dementyev promised me that Kuznetsov would also start to develop reusable engines. So, maybe we should wait? Should we not hurry with the N-1, go to the 'brass' and repent and request that we postpone the flight to the Moon? I'm just afraid that after that they will shut down the N-1 project completely. Mark my words."

This calm conversation was one more way to contemplate the situation. At OKB-276, in July 1970, Kuznetsov had just begun developing reusable engines for the N-1 with a long service life. The work had been downplayed to avoid the question of what exactly are they going to do now.

In early 1970 it was still not too late to halt flight testing on the N-1 with the old engines. Three years later, new engines really did appear that were so reliable that a quarter century later the Americans were delighted with them and wanted to get some to install on their own launch vehicles.[42] However, back then it seemed inconceivable that the N-1 flight tests with the new engines could be started up again before the end of 1973.

Neither Keldysh, nor Afanasyev, nor Mishin, nor Kuznetsov dared take a three-and-a-half-year break in flight testing. Only their joint action, coordinated with the military, brought about by the need to use new engines and promising proposals for the new L3M system, was able to stop the N-1 from creeping towards its ultimate demise. A certain herd instinct came over everyone. Everyone—from the assembler at the big MIK to the minister—took off like a stampede of horses, in which the ones at the back inevitably push those at the front into the abyss.

The people who created cosmonautics made up a very thin layer of Soviet society. If those people, scattered among various design bureaus and factories, main directorates and ministries, launch sites and even Central Committee departments, had gained some general understanding of the situation, an idea about the reality—if a general solidarity had formed that removed the psychological pressure from the higher political leadership—then the history of cosmonautics could have been different. The ideology of struggle "for the plan" permeated all forms of social life. Decrees of the Central Committee and Council of Ministers were not subject to criticism. Incidentally, this affected more than just cosmonautics. After the removal of censorship restrictions on publications on the history of missile technology and cosmonautics, when describing one development or another, they began to refer to the date and

---

42. In the mid 1990s, the former Kuznetsov design bureau sold 36 of these engines to Aerojet General. Currently, Orbital Sciences is planning to use these engines on its new Taurus II launch vehicle.

number of the appropriate Central Committee and government decree. During the era of Stalin, a few days, or even hours, were spent on issuing decrees on the beginning of new projects. Stalin made a decision personally in his office after the individuals summoned there had made their report. If he approved, modified, added to, or rejected the document, it was, without exception, a final decision, which in a matter of hours was duplicated and distributed to those responsible for its execution.

The post-Stalinist state *apparat* [Party bureaucracy] gradually began to acquire certain traits of democratization. Khrushchev allowed significantly more free discussion. The fear that had muzzled it before disappeared. But a final decision could not be made without Khrushchev's approval. As with Stalin, the state *apparat* did not risk passing off to him the necessary paper for his signature. Discussions ended only with his personal participation.

During the post-Khrushchev era, the bureaucratization of the *apparat* intensified, and sometimes it took months for the text of a decree to be approved and for the necessary authorizations to be gathered. The issuance of each new decree was all the more significant an event.

Finally, it became clear that there was a need to produce a single decree and doctrine plan for the future development of cosmonautics. Confusion with the distribution of the priorities in the preceding decrees, disruption of deadlines for many of them, and the successes of the U.S. space program gave rise to the inevitability of developing a single policy defining the main goals and missions and precisely drawing up the priorities. Each chief designer had his own ideas, biases, and supporters in the Party and state *apparat*.

Decisions were drawn up not only in the calm of offices, but also at the launch sites, and matured in the intense discussions of expert commissions and in the councils of chief designers. Ultimately, however, a decree was implemented only after a report to the Politburo and after approval by the Central Committee *apparat*. Among the many routine minor and even erroneous decisions were those that defined the fate of space technology for many years.

The initiative for the issuance of one decree or another for the development of a new rocket-space system could originate "at the top" and descend "below" as a directive. In this case, ministries and chief designers transformed this initiative into a form suitable for execution, the bureaucracy imparted the necessary formalization to the text, and the latest law obligating everyone appeared. Such were the decrees obligating Korolev as chief designer to develop the intercontinental delivery vehicle for the hydrogen bomb in 1954, and the decree of 1964, which named him chief designer of the system for landing a Soviet cosmonaut on the Moon.

But, after Stalin's time, an initiative "from below" could also be the source of decrees. A chief designer could propose developing something extremely unconventional and effective that would guarantee the superiority of our science and technology, but only under the condition that a special decree of the Central Committee and Council of Ministers be issued. This was necessary for funding, for receiving various benefits, for enlisting the cooperation of factories, etc. General Designer Chelomey was the record holder for issuing proposals for an initiative "from below." He was ordered to develop the UR-100 intercontinental ballistic missile and the heavy UR-500 only after he himself proposed them and prepared the draft decree. Next he submitted the IS satellite fighter [antisatellite system] and Almaz piloted orbital station for space reconnaissance.

All of these proposals "from below" gave rise to decrees, from the texts of which it was impossible for an uninformed individual to know whether an all-seeing, all-understanding, wise [Communist Party] General Secretary himself had realized that this needed to be done or a general designer had "enticed" the nation's top political leadership to assign this development project to him.

The competition between the schools of Korolev, Yangel, Chelomey, and Nadiradze existed under the conditions of a totalitarian state and in the absence of the notorious market economy. Subcontractors—the developers of systems for the top chiefs—also competed among themselves. The government encouraged such a rivalry within a scientific and technical context; it yielded positive results.

Not just our experience, but that of China, market-based U.S., Japan, Great Britain, and France shows the indispensable need for competent, firm government leadership and tight control over the development of large-scale, high-technology defense systems or systems of large-scale economic importance.

The activities of a chief designer's deputies also included unofficial technical policy discussions of the most urgent problems in the offices of the Kremlin, Central Committee, and ministries. To begin with, one could count on hearing a litany of criticisms: how bad we all were, how many deadlines we had missed, that our minds were not focused, that our plans were obscure, that our designs lacked perspective and a sense of purpose, that our testing lacked discipline, that we didn't insist on high enough standards from our subcontractors, and that all of our work, in general, was a mess.

If there weren't any bystanders in their office, *apparat* workers allowed themselves to say what they really thought about the behavior of Chief Designer Mishin or General Designer Chelomey. Sometimes they hinted that they marveled at our long suffering with regard to the animosity between Mishin and Glushko. When these conversations were irritating, I played the fool and retorted: "Why do you criticize them behind their backs? You're the authority; tell somebody higher up to set things right if you know everything."

They explained to me and, as I understood, to other deputies, that "You should set things right in your own house on your own. We can only help. The building superintendent makes sure that the garbage chute is working, but the mistress of the house is supposed to clean up the apartment."

On the one hand, visiting the offices of high-ranking bureaucrats gratifies one's sense of vanity—"I am among a small group of people who are invited here"—but on the other hand, you experience a certain discomfort from the awareness of your own second-class standing compared with the elite who sit here. The *apparat* recognizes your talent and high academic and other titles but lets you know, even during the most cordial meeting, that it, the *apparat*, nevertheless stands over you.

Chapter 13
Preparing for the Launch of DOS

The new year of 1971 brought a profusion of conferences where the topic of discussion was how to develop cosmonautics. A conference was prepared in the Central Committee on the prospects for orbital stations and the status of operations on the N-1. We gathered preliminarily in Mishin's office to work out the platform from which we should proceed. During the "rehearsal" I attempted to articulate some ideas, which had taken about 30 minutes, when Mishin interrupted me: "You're saying a lot of valid things, but this is for students. It's pointless to tell Ustinov these truths. Uncle Mitya isn't the same now as he was before."

What did I manage to say?

Here is what I have saved in a notebook:

> *For more than a year we have been working on developing the first Long-Duration Orbital Stations. DOS-1 will soon be delivered to the launch site; DOS-2 will arrive at the KIS [monitoring and test facility] to undergo factory tests. More than a year of work experience makes it possible to make a series of important conclusions and proposals. After completing work on DOS No. 1 and No. 2, we must concentrate our efforts on the next, more advanced generation of stations. In collaboration with the TsKBM branch [at Fili], Iosifyan's institute, NITsEVT, the microelectronics center in Zelenograd, academic science, military institutes, and all the other cooperative networks, we must develop a station that can carry out the primary missions of the Almaz and, at the same time, perform operations in the interests of fundamental science and the national economy. The first requirement: performance capability in space for at least one year, low propellant consumption with precise orientation—5 to 10 angular minutes in the orbital system and 1 to 2 angular seconds when performing a precise celestial orientation.*
>
> *Thanks to its non-gimbaled precise orientation system and super-precise stabilization of scientific instrumentation, this station will*

279

be able to perform a broad range of scientific missions. If we create such a station [sometime] in 1973 or 1974, it will be used to test out the main systems of the future MKBS in space.

The MKBS should be planned for a 1975 to 1976 [timeframe]. Over the course of 1971, we must figure out what we want from the MKBS. DOS No. 1, No. 2, and then No. 3 will provide a wealth of experience. A cardinal issue will be the problem of artificial gravity. For the time being, it can be asserted that if a human being maintains his or her ability to perform in weightlessness for 20 to 30 days, then this is sufficient to ensure the station's performance capability. We need to introduce crew turnover. With good training on Earth, 90 percent of the tasks can be performed automatically or semiautomatically. I do not see defense missions that require the permanent presence of a human being in orbit.

Science missions are another matter. The insertion into space of a large, well-equipped laboratory with highly skilled research scientists could lead to fundamental discoveries that will ensure the superiority of our science and, possibly, lead to far-reaching ramifications for the use of space. It is difficult in our time to be a prophet of scientific discoveries. However, the experience of the history of science teaches that underestimating the potential for the rapid practical use of the results of fundamental research can have tragic consequences.

In 1933, the father of nuclear physics, Ernest Rutherford, ridiculed the idea of the practical use of nuclear energy.[1] This dampened the enthusiasm of many scientists. But just seven years later in his famous letter to Roosevelt, Einstein demanded that practical research begin immediately on a broad scale to develop an atomic bomb. The world was saved only because scientists who had experimentally proven the potential for the occurrence of a chain reaction had escaped from fascist Germany, Italy, and Hungary.

The argument about the role or advantages of a human being versus a machine in space is often of a subjective or scholastic nature. It is much less expensive to deliver machines on lunar rovers to the Moon. But even Luna-16, successfully repeated three times, was not capable of providing that information and producing those

---

1. Ernest Rutherford (1871–1937) was the New Zealand–born British chemist and physicist often known as the father of modern nuclear physics. Among Rutherford's many important contributions were his postulations on the planetary structure of atoms and the first splitting of the atom.

observations that enriched humankind after six astronauts returned from the Moon.[2]

The high-priority political factor is also very great. A human being must become acclimated and learn to exist in space, in an environment that is new. No machines could replace people on the first North Pole 1 station in 1937.[3] *After the Great Patriotic War there were no more skeptics regarding Arctic exploration. Now we are proud of our achievements in this field.*

We also need to solve the problem of artificial gravity. It is much more beneficial to take advantage of a natural satellite—the Moon and its natural gravity. It makes more sense to conduct long-term studies there over a broad range of military and scientific problems rather than wracking our brains over artificial gravity designs on the MKBS. We have accumulated our own wealth of experience, but we must not ignore the Americans' experience either. It is time to return to ideas of long-duration lunar bases. This mission was assigned back during Korolev's time and written in decrees by the Central Committee and Council of Ministers.

Researchers can be sent to a lunar base for two or three months, and perhaps even for a half year. This idea is completely realistic for the state-of-the-art level of technology. The main difficulty, most likely, is not in the development of the base itself, but in the transport system and, first and foremost, a reliable launch vehicle.

But what should we do on the Moon before that?

As early as 1972 we need to combine the L3 program with the Lunokhod programs and create a "Lunar Orbital Station–Lunar Vehicle–Lunokhods" project. To do this, it will be necessary to overcome a psychological barrier and combine various programs [and] various chiefs, as we did when we combined the DOS, Almaz, and Soyuz programs.

We can begin with unpiloted programs. This is even simpler and less expensive than landing a single cosmonaut on the Moon for 5 or 6 hours, as some are demanding, citing the old Central Committee decree.

---

2. *Luna-16* was the first automated spacecraft to return soil samples from the Moon. It was launched on 12 September 1970.

3. In the 1930s, the Soviets pioneered the use of crewed drifting stations to explore the Arctic. In 1937, Soviet scientists deployed the first successful arctic drifting station, North Pole 1 (*Severnyy polyus-1*), approximately 20 kilometers from the North Pole.

Do we need to rush to land a cosmonaut on the Moon? If we fail it will be a political fiasco. The technology for that is already obsolete; we will need to invest a lot more energy into this operation. There is one more argument against blindly continuing this program. The people at the various enterprises have lost their sense of purpose. We didn't have clearly formulated goals and missions for the Moon. The DOS was developed within the shortest timeframe ever—not because of economic incentive, but because of the enthusiasm and sense of purpose among the individuals involved. We were able to show goals and missions to its hundreds, perhaps thousands, of creators that were worthy of their creative work, goals and missions for which it was worth taking a justified risk and working with the enthusiasm and unity that we achieved while working on the stations.

Why was the DOS created within this inconceivably short period of time? It wasn't simply because we used systems that had been tried out on 7K vehicles. Did you see how the people worked? It wasn't a matter of economic incentives, nor one of administrative pressure. They worked with great enthusiasm as they had during wartime, as they did during the days of the Vostoks. We swept away bureaucratic walls. It would be unforgivable to lose this remarkable experience! With respect to funding we won: reducing the time is always an economic gain, so long as it does not come at the expense of ground experimental operations. We can't make people work like that for the sake of an old program, such as landing a single cosmonaut on the Moon for 5 or 6 hours, because economic or moral incentives won't work.

As far as prestige is concerned, all preceding flights, first of all ours, and now the Americans' too, show that the world is delighted if a new, daring goal is achieved using new, reliable means. Could we fly across the ocean in a single-engine, single-seat airplane? Yes, but Lindbergh already did this in 1927. So why do it again if we now have modern, comfortable airliners? For the sake of a few lines in the newspapers?

We need to critically utilize the experience of the Apollo flights to the full extent. And we have already lost at least a year, having rejected a more efficient scenario—an expedition aimed at creating a base.

WHEN I REREAD MY SPEECH OUT LOUD, I understood that in the best case, even if I read it as fast as I possibly could, it would take me 40 minutes. This was completely unrealistic. Nevertheless, I wasn't going to redo it and shorten it. I decided to play it by ear. I didn't manage to say everything; my full load for the program speech simply went unused.

Ustinov once again called a conference in his office in the Central Committee building on 15 February [1971]. The office was filled to capacity. Ustinov announced that we had gathered to review the status of operations on the DOS and lunar landing expedition. He had determined in advance that he would give the floor for the report to the minister, rather than to the chief designer of the DOS (for the time being officially there was none), to avoid jealousy between Mishin and Chelomey, so as not to preordain which of them would be the chief designer.

Afanasyev reported in a calm and serious tone: "Work at the factory on the first DOS has been completed. We are shipping it to the launch site, but there are still a number of issues. First, the quality is not completely satisfactory. Second, experimental work has not been completed. To date, the life-support system has not been completely debugged and vibration testing has not been completed on the effectors system and thermal systems. At the end of March, upon completion of the experiments, we have the opportunity to launch station No. 121. Station No. 122 will be transferred to the KIS in Podlipki. The documentation for DOSes No. 3 and No. 4 will come out in February—this is according to schedule, but actually we expect it in April or May. I must say that DOSes No. 3 and No. 4 are not updated stations as the designers had explained to us earlier, but new ones. No. 5 and No. 6 are already in the design process. These are absolutely brand-new stations."

After mentioning the brand-new stations, Afanasyev shifted the course of the conference to the chief designers.

Here Ustinov said: "The briefing paper prepared for our conference mentions dates from the decree of 9 February 1970. For No. 1 and No. 2 this is the fourth quarter of 1970, and for No. 3 and No. 4 it's the third quarter of 1971. During the period from 1971 through 1975, it proposes that two stations be launched each year. In my opinion, the state of affairs is out-and-out bad, out-and-out abnormal. I thought that we would settle on one single model of station and would duplicate it. But you want to rework and change the documentation so that it's always in a state of developmental testing. When will it be time to fly and carry out missions? Don't forget that aside from the DOSes we really don't have anything else up our sleeves. Until the N1-L3 and MKBS, we have to tide ourselves over with just the DOS program."

Mishin couldn't stand it. He could not conceal the fact that he didn't support all of this "DOS monkey business."

"Work on DOSes No. 2, No. 3, and No. 4 is really going badly. ZIKh cannot carry on this many new, sophisticated spacecraft projects simultaneously, and then Almaz to boot. We shouldn't pretend that we don't understand this.

We still don't have VPK documents regulating the deliveries for DOSes No. 3 and No. 4. ZIKh is occupied with Almaz, too. But the concept of the Almaz project as such is risky. We need to combine the DOS and Almaz missions and make a DOS-A."[4]

Mishin's speech provoked quite a stir. Ustinov, trying to calm the crowd, proposed: "Let's define our position, and you, here in attendance, tell us what to do after DOSes No. 1 and No. 2. Perhaps DOS-A right off the bat? Or the Multipurpose Space Base/Station (MKBS), and maybe continue a series of continuously modifiable DOSes? Precisely define your stands. Mishin, what do you propose?"

"DOS-A plus the MKBS."

"Chertok?"

"DOS-A, and then give it some more thought."

"Bushuyev?"

"Also DOS-A and then decide."

"Feoktistov?"

"DOS-A isn't necessary. The MKBS straight away."

"Bugayskiy?"

"DOS-A. I don't know what the MKBS is."[5]

Keldysh and Smirnov both said that they didn't know why DOS-A was necessary. It was better to build the MKBS.

When it was his turn, Mozzhorin responded as was befitting the director of a head institute: "We aren't going to decide an issue like this by voting. This requires serious studies. We are involved with that now."

ZIKh Director Ryzhikh evaded a direct answer but said that DOSes No. 3 and No. 4 were 95 percent new vehicles and very significant in terms of

---

4. The rather confusing series of pronouncements from various luminaries at this meeting dealt with three broad programs: DOS, Almaz, and MOK. Originally, the DOS program entailed the launch of four stations, DOSes No. 1, 2, 3, and 4. The first two were to be ready by late 1970 and the second two by late 1971. The program was, however, delayed by at least a year. There were future plans for much-improved DOSes (Nos. 5 and 6 and DOS-A), but these were indefinite at best. Also on the agenda was Chelomey's Almaz military space station project, which was planned to proceed in two phases. In early 1971, the Almaz project was at least two years behind schedule. The MOK was a very large-scale space station project that included the MKBS, scheduled for the mid-1970s. The massive elements of the MOK could only be launched by the N-1. This rocket's development was, of course, intimately connected with the now-stalled piloted lunar landing program, which had been a very high priority for Mishin through the late 1960s.

5. Bugayskiy had no knowledge of MKBS because he headed the Fili Branch of Chelomey's TsKBM. The MKBS proposal had emerged from Mishin's TsKBEM.

technology.[6] No more than 40 percent of the hull parts would be retained, and 10 percent of the internal gear.

"Nevertheless, if I were given drawings for DOS No. 3," he declared, "we would make the vehicle this year. We need to consult and determine where we stand with the Almaz and the Transport Supply Vehicle. It's difficult to digest the DOS and Almaz documentation together at workstations. The factory is in a very difficult position, but we are trying to do both jobs. However, this combination does not bode well."

Here, Barmin broke in: "We need to modify the launch facility for DOS No. 4. This means 3.5 million rubles for cryogenic technology. We need to resolve issues taking into consideration the actual situation. The Almaz will appear before DOS-A. The preferred scenario is DOSes No. 1, No. 2, No. 3, No. 4, DOS-A, and then the MKBS. Konstantin Petrovich Feoktistov, like a snipe away from his own bog, has delivered a verdict on the Almaz in advance. But at Site No. 92 we are already completing the construction of a luxurious three-story bunker for the Almaz. Not even Hitler had one like this. If DOS-A is more promising than Almaz, then we have an issue and it needs to be examined seriously. Almaz consists of two vehicles.[7] We need to compare two conceptual chains: one consisting only of DOSes, the other of DOSes and Almazes."

"I am not a snipe," Feoktistov said indignantly, "and you forget that all the Almaz missions can be entrusted to the MKBS."

"And what does the Ministry of Defense think about this?" asked Ustinov.

Karas answered, "I report that the KIK and launch site are ready to work with DOS. However, one needs to take into consideration that we are constantly refitting the launch sites at the request of the designers. We don't have any materials for DOS-A and we can't give an assessment. It is clear that Almaz and DOS-A cannot be pulled off at the same time. In terms of timeframes, certainly the Almaz will appear earlier. We need to concentrate all our efforts on the MKBS—take the bull by the horns right away. Until we have the MKBS, the Almaz should fly: it has everything conceived for our military requirements. The MKBS is good for wartime, but we need the Almaz before that. Everything must be explored and researched. We will test the role of a human being on the Almaz. This role cannot be downplayed. A direct report

---

6. Mikhail Ivanovich Ryzhikh (1910–1982) served as director of the M. V. Khrunichev Factory (ZIKh) from 1961 to 1975.

7. These two vehicles were the Orbital Piloted Station (OPS) and the Transport-Supply Vehicle (TKS).

from space, having screened out superfluous information, an assessment of the situation—that is work for a human being."

Tsarev from the VPK administration also spoke out against DOS-A: "We're getting proposals for five modifications in a single Almaz hull—five control systems![8] That's outrageous! Our general line must be the MKBS."

Tyulin said, "DOSes No. 3 and No. 4 need to be completed—there is surplus production stock—otherwise, it will be a fiasco. As for DOSes No. 5 and No. 6 or DOS-A, this matter has not been studied sufficiently. The materials won't be ready until May, and the MKBS hasn't been studied in depth at all. There's a lot of science fiction surrounding that. I think that when we have materials to compare, then we will decide the matter in favor of the MKBS. In the American materials, the issue of the MKBS is disputed. Above all, we need to delineate a set of missions and see how to get them resolved. We must study the matter of transport vehicles. To date, no one is doing anything on reusable transport vehicles. We need to quickly organize research activities under the leadership of TsNIImash and make TsAGI and NIIAP work.[9] We won't solve this problem without the MAP."

Keldysh listened to everyone without interrupting and seemed to be dozing. Finally he decided that it was time to put an end to the arguments, and he spoke so long and in such detail that it became clear: when he was "half asleep" he was listening, remembering, and processing all the speeches.

"We're in a critical situation with the orbital stations. They 'loaded' the Almaz about five years ago. Then they demanded that it be split into phase one and phase two. Today we have six different orbital stations—phase-one Almaz, phase-two Almaz, DOSes No. 1 and No. 2, No. 3 and No. 4, DOS-A, and the MKBS. It is unrealistic to let such a number of different stations pass through development, factory, and flight tests. DOS-A appeared unexpectedly. We arranged with [VPK Chairman] Leonid Vasilyevich [Smirnov] not to make DOSes No. 5 and No. 6 at all. Now this matter is up for review again. DOSes No. 3 and No. 4 are sufficient for us in 1973.

"Why is DOS-A necessary? If you want to replace the Almaz, then go ahead and make DOS-A.

"Our life is full of contradictions. It was said that the MKBS would appear in 1973. But the control system can't be finished within that timeframe. Now they claim that supposedly it can be. They say that DOS-A has the very same

---

8. Aleksandr Ivanovich Tsarev served as deputy chairman of the Military-Industrial Commission (VPK) from 1965 to 1989.

9. TsAGI—*Tsentralnyy aerogidrodinamicheskiy institut* (Central Aerohydrodynamics Institute)—has long been one of the leading aeronautics research institutions in Russia.

system. The deadlines for DOS-A and MKBS are very close. We imagine the MKBS as an experimental station. Chertok told me that he wanted to test out its systems on the DOS-A. Our positions must be clearly delineated."

"The Americans are developing automatic systems for all of the service systems. An orbital station is an experimental laboratory. In this sense, it must be very flexible and large. We can focus on the MKBS if it will be ready in 1973. Let's go for it. But it seems to me that it's unrealistic. I am not repudiating Almaz, but the two Almaz phases don't make sense to me. If the military thinks that they need the Almaz as an intelligence-gathering tool, then why is some half-hearted system necessary? We need to make one habitable intelligence-gathering station. We are not coordinating the work of the designers, and each one does his or her own thing, wants only to push through his or her own work at any cost. This beats us up terribly. I don't want to make the final decision. I don't hide the fact that I am inclined toward Feoktistov's point of view: DOSes No. 1 and No. 2, No. 3 and No. 4, and right away the MKBS. But don't think that we can work miracles with the MKBS. We need to draw up a joint Central Committee and VPK report on habitable stations, otherwise every two weeks new viewpoints will emerge."

After Ustinov and Keldysh had the floor, it was difficult to expect anything different from Leonid Smirnov's turn. Officially, the VPK was the organization primarily responsible for formulating the nation's space plans. Smirnov said, "I can't understand why we are having these arguments. We defined the line we would follow when we put together the five-year plan. Operations on DOSes No. 1 and No. 2, No. 3 and No. 4 must be carried out without any wavering or doubt and in full force. The five-year plan calls for two DOSes per year. Series production is supposed to be set up on the basis of DOSes No. 3 and No. 4. Let's carry out this clear-cut line for the DOSes to the end.

"In my opinion, this MKBS is a completely new matter. Is it worth it to make a draft plan? Someone said earlier that the MKBS is the main line of the five-year plan. Now we are revising that. DOS-A should not be made either instead of or as a substitute. Which path to the MKBS is shorter? The path through DOS-A to MKBS is a long way off. For the time being, let's firmly resolve to make DOSes No. 1 and No. 2, No. 3 and No. 4. Perhaps at mid-year, when we gain experience from the flight of DOS No. 1, the situation will become clearer. Then we will be able to meet again and, if necessary, we will reconsider the decisions."

Serbin had the opportunity to break his silence. An ardent supporter of the Almaz, he hadn't wanted to speak at such a blatantly pro-DOS meeting. Nevertheless, he did, although, aside from the usual criticism regarding the failure to fulfill the previous Central Committee decisions, he said nothing new.

"We need to finally bring order into this mishmash. We have a Central Committee decision, but the MOM allows willfulness. OKB-1 and Comrade

287

Mishin are involved in all sorts of hodgepodge to cover up their own inactivity. A totally half-baked, totally unprepared issue is passed on to the level of the Central Committee in order to explain why the deadlines have been missed for DOSes No. 3 and No. 4. Such a method is unacceptable. New ideas were hatched over two or three days and rushed over here to wreak havoc. This is inflicting a great deal of damage on our work. We need to seriously sort things out with Almaz. Are two phases necessary there? For the DOSes they're proposing that we have three phases—No. 1 and No. 2, then No. 3 and No. 4, and DOS-A as a special treat. All of this is being dumped on ZIKh. When will the minister sort out the mess with the workload at ZIKh? Almaz and DOS will interfere with each other there. To date there are no proposals from the MOM. A small amount of time needs to be set aside to sort out the mess and report to the Central Committee. We need to demand documents from Mishin, not his word."

It was no picnic for Mishin to speak after being accused of inactivity and "all sorts of hodgepodge." Especially since the majority of participants knew about his negative attitude toward our DOS initiative.

"I disagree with the accusation of inactivity. Actually, the first orbital station was produced within an exceptionally short period of time. This is a highly sophisticated spacecraft with 980 instruments installed on it, with more than 1,000 cables running through it, which are connected among themselves and with instruments using 4,000 connectors. If you were to stretch out all the wires in a single strand the total length would exceed 350 kilometers. The on-board cable network alone weighs 1,300 kilograms. It is an incredibly difficult task to manufacture, assemble, debug, and test all of this within the timeframe known to all of you. But the people have been working and continue to work with exceptional enthusiasm, and you mustn't make any claims against them. Developing spacecraft of this degree of complexity within such a timeframe is also an exceptional task because their reliability needs to be ensured. That is why I don't think the two-series Almaz and DOS stream should be developed simultaneously. We should limit the number of DOSes to the first four and then curtail their further production. All the missions that we are assigning to the DOSes should be entrusted to the Almaz. It should perform both military and economic missions. For our part, we are ready to provide 7K-T transport vehicles for the Almaz and then replace them with the 7K-S, which are being developed per the military operational requirements of the Ministry of Defense.

"For us at TsKBEM, the main mission should be MOK—the Multipurpose Orbital Complex—and its main component, the MKBS. The launch vehicle for the MKBS and for the lunar mission is where we need to concentrate our efforts. We mustn't forget that the lunar vehicles are a much more crucial project than the DOSes. We have this summer ahead of us to conduct the third N-1 launch. If all goes well, then we'll throw all our efforts at the Moon. Please keep that in mind."

After Mishin's speech the discussion threatened to go into a second round. Ustinov decided that it was time to move along to issuing position papers and ending the haphazard conversations.

"We mustn't rely on good intentions, but rather proceed from the situation and prospects that have developed. The Almazes are already two years behind schedule. This is very bad. However much we have criticized the developers, the DOS is a go. The DOS is on its way! That's clear to everybody. Four DOSes are scheduled; we need to schedule more, two per year. These DOSes can provide a lot. We have no right to treat them like routine work. Rather than a phaseout plan, we need to draw up a plan for the development and support of these operations. The work is complicated, I agree, but we must not completely ignore the deadlines; also unacceptable is the superficial attitude toward the developmental testing of systems and subsystems. I believe that we have an obligation to produce DOSes, and the Almaz, and the MKBS.

"It will be necessary to bring in other organizations, new forces, but under no circumstances should we change the old teams. Don't forget that there is one more very complex problem: a reusable spacecraft. We must not view it as some additional burden. Meanwhile, we have a very limited number of people working on these vehicles. But, after all, a problem like this won't be solved in one or two years. Then we might lose our priority status. Meanwhile, we are still talking, and the Americans are already acting. Our design bureaus are concealing their projects from one another more stringently than they would from foreign spies. We need to organize an active exchange of information and experience on a 'you scratch my back, I'll scratch yours' basis. If we all believe that the MKBS is necessary, then why are we dragging our feet?

"Immediately prepare a decree in which everything is spelled out in hard and fast specifics. This same decree should also cover the reusable shuttle spacecraft. But you need to show the prospects for the MKBS.

"It seems to me that you talk about it a lot, but you still haven't thought everything through yet. Before you try to sell us on it, you yourself must have an appreciation for its prospects. It's time to stop arguing and assess the role of a human being. We have to stop swinging from one extreme to the other: either a human being decides everything or a machine decides everything. We need to take advantage of the capabilities of both a human being and a machine to the maximum extent. A human being isn't needed to compete with a machine when it comes to pushing buttons, but for research and discoveries, where his heuristic capabilities and mental reserves are needed. We are not yet using these reserves in space.

"We are going to launch the first DOS in March. We need to get under way with the second right away and breathe life into the third and fourth. This is clear, and there will be no more discussions on this matter. We're going to ask a lot of tough questions regarding the disruption of deadlines.

"Now, regarding the N-1. Today we have no more time for a thorough discussion. In addition to the lunar expedition, we also intend to insert the MKBS on this launch vehicle. I have gotten the impression that we're arguing and raising a ruckus here, and the N-1 is floating along, all by itself. The situation with the N-1 couldn't be worse, couldn't be more difficult. But instead of dealing with the N-1 to the full extent of our power, we're creating a sort of a vacuum around it. Keep in mind: you need to immediately prepare a decree describing the prospects for the DOSes and MKBS, and for the N-1 we will soon begin to mete out severe punishment for the complete collapse of not just the lunar program, but also of all of the projects associated with this launch vehicle.

"I thank you all. I hope that our next meetings will be more productive."

The meeting had lasted 4 hours. We stepped out onto *Staraya ploshchad* (Old Square), which was now bathed in twilight, and hunted for the cars waiting for us. Bushuyev, Okhapkin, and I were about to get into our car, when Mishin came up to us and said: "It's all your fault! Mixing everything together in one pile. But just you wait, soon we'll unscramble it all!"

RUMORS ABOUT THE HISTORIC MEETING (for DOSes) in the Central Committee quickly spread throughout all the design bureaus and factories, MOM, and related ministries. According to the law of "conservation of attention," midlevel administrators had now weakened their attention with regard to N1-L3.

On our staff, almost all the leading specialists knew about Mishin's negative attitude toward the DOS project. Nevertheless, the wave of enthusiasm for the development of the first DOSes did not decline. The main focus of work—preparing our first orbital station for launch—shifted in March from ZIKh and ZEM to the engineering facility at Site No. 2 in Baykonur, which we all stubbornly continued to refer to as the firing range. We were preparing the DOS and the piloted transport vehicle 7K-T No. 31, or *Soyuz-10*, at the same time. A VPK meeting approved the first crew of the orbital station—Vladimir Shatalov, Aleksey Yeliseyev, and Nikolay Rukavishnikov. None of us doubted their competence in the least.

Testing of DOS No. 1 began at Site No. 2 in the new assembly and testing building, which, unlike the old facility, was called the Assembly and Testing Building for Spacecraft (MIK KO).[10] As before, launch vehicles and transport vehicles were prepared in the old MIK.

---

10. MIK KO—*Montazhno-ispytatelnyy korpus kosmicheskikh obyektov.*

From the author's archives.

Leading managers of TsKBEM are shown here during the annual May Day parade at Kaliningrad. From left to right are B. Ye. Chertok, A. P. Abramov, V. D. Vachnadze, A. A. Zuyev, V. P. Mishin, G. V. Sovkov, V. M. Klyucharev, A. P. Tishkin, and I. B. Khazanov.

Yuriy Semyonov, lead designer for the DOSes, set up strict control to eliminate all the glitches that had occurred during tests on DOS No. 1 and that had begun once again to appear at the KIS, where DOS No. 2 had been delivered. At operational meetings, when the conversation drifted to shortages and delays in deliveries, he insisted on precise record keeping and accountability for any minutiae "down to the last nail!" Even when there were hundreds of such "nails," it was necessary to deal with each one individually. On Bugayskiy's side, the lead designer was Vladimir Pallo.[11] Usually, for the sake of brevity, among ourselves we referred to an organization using the chief's last name or its location. Thus, a specific jargon developed:

TsKBEM was called Podlipki or Mishin;

TsKBM was called Reutov or Chelomey;

---

11. Vladimir Vladimirovich Pallo (1923–1994) was the leading designer responsible for the DOS program at TsKBM's Fili Branch. In 1979, he became chief designer for DOS stations on behalf of the Fili Branch. He was the brother of Arvid Vladimirovich Pallo who for many years worked with Sergey Korolev.

The TsKBM branch was called Fili or Bugayskiy;

M. V. Khrunichev Factory was called ZIKh, Fili, or Ryzhikh;

ZEM was called Podlipki or Klyucharev.

In conversations one of the possible names was used, while in correspondence the enterprises were usually concealed behind a "post box" number. Thus, for example, TsKBEM was called p/ya V-2572.[12]

AFTER THE MEETING IN THE CENTRAL COMMITTEE I found some time and assembled my comrades. Despite the fact that it wasn't proper to talk openly about such meetings "at the very top," I felt that my comrades at work should receive their information from a primary source rather than have to resort to rumors. When I had finished my 1-hour story about the 4-hour meeting, Yurasov commented: "The steeds, the men all disassembled."[13]

"And what's Lermontov's next line?" asked someone.

"And cannon volleys' sound resembled / a moaning o'er the land...."

"That's it—that's what I was trying to remember. Only we're going to be the ones moaning," quipped the usually circumspect Sosnovik.

None of those gathered could have been accused of skepticism or indifference. They greeted success with unconcealed joy, and they never gave up when faced with failure. Wrapping things up, I said, "Each of us needs to distribute his efforts carefully in order to ensure failure-free operation at the firing range while preparing the first DOS, and we must not allow work to be disrupted at the factories on the second DOS and subsequent spacecraft."

"But why aren't you saying anything about N1-L3?" asked Zverev. "Did the Central Committee decide not to fret any more after *Apollo 14*?"[14] "We're running at full speed to upgrade the KORD system series of instruments at the instrumentation factory of an outsider ministry. These aren't toys." The department provided documentation and supervised the production of KORD system instruments for the N-1 at the Zagorsk Optical Mechanical Factory (ZOMZ). ZOMZ supplied 50 sophisticated electronic instruments for each N-1 and the backup. The Ministry of the Defense Industry, which was in charge of ZOMZ, in order to give tit for tat, approved a plan for it until the end of 1971. This plan provided N-1 launch vehicles up to and including

---

12. p/ya—*pochtovyy yashchik* (post box).

13. This is from a poem by Mikhail Yuryevich Lermontov (1814–1841) entitled "Borodino" (1837) about the Battle of Borodino during Napoleon's invasion of Russia in 1812.

14. *Apollo 14* was the third piloted lunar landing mission, performed between 31 January and 9 February 1971. The crew consisted of Alan B. Shepard, Jr., Stuart A. Roosa, and Edgar M. Mitchell.

No. 10 with these instruments. Similar fabricated stock was also available at other series-production factories.

Chizhikov, who had similar troubles at the Ufa and Kiev instrument-building factories, chimed in to support Zverev by noting, "Series production factories don't understand our jokes." He added, "Bashkin and Zvorykin are changing their rendezvous-control, angular rate sensor, and docking and orientation engine ignitions again. We've already lost count of the changes. Let them go over to the factories themselves; otherwise they leave for the firing range, while we don't know how to look the workers in the eye. We're modifying and resoldering a single instrument 20 times, so that the military rep refuses to accept it. They're continuously resoldering in Karpov's electrical 'boxes' too. When is this going to end?"

Similar instances of "score settling," sometimes very contentious ones, broke out when concept developers and designers, who converted an idea into an electrical circuit in a working diagram for production, gathered together in my office. After heated conversations, we usually made decisions regarding the modification methods; we were careful in the wording of the reasons for the changes so that "dirty laundry" from our instrument department would not be aired in front of the "powers that be," especially the Party committees.

These are just a few episodes from a succession of events, which to a great extent determined the path that our cosmonautics would take from this point onward.

ON THE CLEAR, WARM MORNING OF 5 APRIL 1971, at 0730 hours, Bushuyev and I left Academician Korolev Street and drove to our company airport, Vnukovo-3. By a florist shop on Prospekt Mira we picked up Yevgeniy Yurevich, who had just arrived from Leningrad. He dragged a green box filled with spare instruments for the emergency x-ray system (ARS) over to our car from the taxi.[15] This brand new x-ray system was supposed to assist the cosmonauts with controlling the active vehicle during manual rendezvous. In this case, the x rays were not analytical tools, but rather they served to measure the relative position parameters during the final approach segment.

Almost all the chiefs who were supposed to attend the State Commission meeting had gathered at the airfield service building. Our Il-18 took off at 0910 hours. Kerimov, Bushuyev, Shcheulov, Bugayskiy, Severin, and I were

---

15. ARS—*Avariynaya rentgenovskaya sistema.*

sitting in the forward cabin.[16] Yurevich settled into the main cabin so that he could "catch up on his sleep away from the bosses." Now one could relax and enjoy the view of the ground from a cloudless sky. Below was a typical April scene—black fields with white patches of snow that hadn't melted yet running off into the hollows and ravines. Dirty snow could be seen between the bare trees of the black forest. For some reason there was a lot more snow in the steppes beyond the Urals than in the area surrounding Moscow.

Squadron Commander Khvastunov had instituted a mandatory ritual for the passengers in the forward cabin: tea and cookies. After 3 hours of flight everyone had their noses pressed up against the windows to admire the Aral Sea. The glare from the bright sun on the white ice in the inlets was blinding. The ice had already vanished from the middle of the sea. The bright azure surface of the open water was calm. Murky streams flowed into this pure blueness in the delta of the Syrdarya River.

From the author's archives.

I tore my fellow travelers away from their gazing at the Aral, which was then still alive and filled with water, in order to show them the TASS alert about the American large orbital station project.[17] The Americans had been conducting design work for more than two years, having drawn many private companies into it in addition to NASA's Centers, but they weren't rushing to implement it. They felt that the idea needed to undergo comprehensive scientific and design evaluation before a decision would

Soyuz-18 cosmonaut Vitaliy Sevastyanov signed this photo on board the *Salyut-4* station as a gift to Chertok in 1975.

---

16. Viktor Ivanovich Shcheulov (1922–) was the 1st deputy chief of the Main Directorate of Space Assets (GUKOS). Gay Ilich Severin (1926–) was chief designer at the Zvezda Factory, i.e., the prime contractor for Soviet spacesuits.

17. This is probably a reference to the Apollo Applications Project (AAP), which involved the use of a "dry workshop" derived from the S-IVB upper stage of a Saturn V booster. The project was renamed Skylab in February 1970.

be made to build the station. According to the comments of American scientists, all the submitted designs required very large financial investments and there was still much about them that remained unclear. Neither the military, nor the scientists, nor the economists were able to make convincing arguments proving the necessity for creating the large station.

Severin commented on my report: "We got ahead of the Americans because they are always unclear about something. Essentially, everything should be clear to us. But if it isn't, we receive explanatory instructions right away."

Everyone smiled knowingly.

In Tyuratam our airplane very softly "brushed" the surface of the landing strip. At the airfield I recalled Leonid Voskresenskiy's words; when the two of us used to land at the firing range he would usually say, "We're home." I had not been here, "home," since the times of preparing *Soyuz-9* for the record-setting flight of Andriyan Nikolayev and Vitaliy Sevastyanov.[18]

Yevgeniy Shabarov was one of Korolev's (and later, Mishin's) leading deputies. He was responsible for flight-testing various rockets and spacecraft designed by TsKBEM.

From the author's archives.

On 6 April, a meeting of the technical management was held to discuss the results of preparing DOS No. 1, which was officially called 17K No. 121, and vehicles 11F615A8 Nos. 31 and 32, or, using their other designation, 7K-T No. 31 and 7K-T No. 32; for open publications, they were called *Soyuz-10* and *Soyuz-11*. Shabarov opened and conducted the meeting. Lead designers Yuriy Semyonov (from Podlipki) and Vladimir Pallo (from Fili) reported on the progress of the preparation of all three vehicles. The deputy chief of the First Directorate, Colonel Vladimir Bululukov, commented on behalf of the military installation.

---

18. Cosmonauts Nikolayev and Sevastyanov flew a record 18-day solo mission between 1 and 19 June 1970 on board *Soyuz-9*.

At the firing range, Anatoliy Kirillov had been in charge of the First (Korolevian) Directorate for nine years after the death of Yevgeniy Ostashev. In 1967, he was transferred to Site No. 10 as the deputy to firing range chief Aleksandr Kurushin, and soon thereafter he was promoted to the rank of major general. Kirillov's former deputy, Colonel Vladimir Patrushev, became chief of the First Directorate, and Colonel Vladimir Bululukov became his deputy. In 1975, Patrushev was transferred to GUKOS and Bululukov became chief of the First Directorate.

They had already investigated 182 glitches in the DOS. Of those, 10 were allowed, 20 were still in the process of being eliminated, and the rest were dealt with through modifications or the replacement of instruments. By and large, everything was more or less satisfactory. In 24 hours the DOS could be cleared for fueling. Allowing for its transport to the second engineering facility for integration with the launch vehicle, we could draw up a schedule of subsequent operations aiming for launch on 19 April 1971. Soyuz vehicles No. 31 and No. 32 were in good condition. No. 31 could be handed over to be fueled so that on the DOS launch day it would be mated with the launch vehicle and ready for launch on 22 April.

Yuriy Semyonov and Vladimir Pallo had a bone to pick with the subcontractors, who were dragging out the release of the final reports. Even until the early 1990s, drawing up the reports in a timely manner before the launch of any spacecraft remained an extremely acute problem. The lead designers of the head organizations "pried out" flight clearance reports from each program participant literally as if they were nails. If this "nail" produced a glitch during the preparation process at the factory or at the firing range, the corresponding chief designer and the manufacturing plant had to jointly submit a new finding coordinated with the military representatives—for the nth time confirming clearance for flight and explaining the reasons for the glitch and describing the actions taken to eliminate it.[19]

After the official portion of the meeting we spent a long time deciding which of the glitches warranted a report to the State Commission.

On 9 April 1971, Kerim Kerimov opened a session of the State Commission. Bululukov took the floor first to report about the test results on station 17K. Based on the number of glitches, our orientation and motion control system

---

19. It was customary for the relevant military service to have a representative at every design bureau that built military systems. These representatives were responsible for the final "signoff" to experimental test flight.

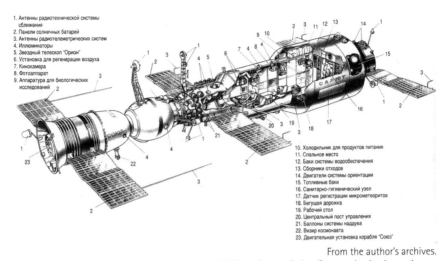

1. Антенны радиотехнической системы
   сближения
2. Панели солнечных батарей
3. Антенны радиотелеметрических систем
4. Иллюминаторы
5. Звездный телескоп "Орион"
6. Установка для регенерации воздуха
7. Кинокамера
8. Фотоаппарат
9. Аппаратура для биологических
   исследований

10. Холодильник для продуктов питания
11. Спальное место
12. Баки системы водообеспечения
13. Сборники отходов
14. Двигатели системы ориентации
15. Топливные баки
16. Санитарно-гигиенический узел
17. Датчик регистрации микрометеоритов
18. Бегущая дорожка
19. Рабочий стол
20. Центральный пост управления
21. Баллоны системы наддува
22. Визир космонавта
23. Двигательная установка корабля "Союз"

From the author's archives.

A cutout of the DOS-1 station with the 7K-T variant of the Soyuz docked on the left. The legend is 1) Antennas of the radar approach system, 2) Solar panels, 3) Antennas of the radio-telemetry system, 4) Cosmonauts' sight, 5) *Orion* solar telescope, 6) Movie camera, 7) Oxygen regeneration unit, 8) Camera, 9) Equipment for biological research, 10) Refrigerator for food, 11) Sleeping station, 12) Tanks for water support system, 13) Waste collections, 14) Attitude-control system engines, 15) Propellant tanks, 16) Hygiene-sanitation station, 17) Micrometeoroid sensor, 18) Treadmill, 19) Work table, and 20) Central control station.

(SOUD) had taken the lead.[20] The remote radio communications system (DRS) was in second place.[21]

The entire cycle at Site No. 2 took 36 days. The first instrument to be replaced was the *Salyut* computer, which was supposed to be used for experiments on navigation. In all, 205 glitches were tallied up, of which 27 were related to ground testing equipment, 145 were corrected, and the rest were allowed. After Bululukov's report, in which he dwelled in detail on previously reconciled glitches, the representatives responsible for developers' systems began to give their presentations. Bashkin was the first to speak. He was responsible for the SOUD. Breaking into a smile, Mnatsakanyan reported that this time there were no glitches associated with the *Igla* system.

"Impossible!" shouted someone from his seat, which set the room laughing.

Georgiy Geondzhan accounted for the instruments of Viktor Kuznetsov's company. For some reason the solar sensor was interfering with the string

---

20. SOUD—*Sistema orientatsii i upravleniya dvizheniyem.*
21. DRS—*Sistema dalney radiosvyazi.*

accelerometer. They decided not to activate them at the same time and "to find the cause and eliminate it" beginning with DOS No. 2. Anatoliy Azarov cheerfully reported that all the optical sensors had been cleared without any anomalies observed.

"And if they give somebody trouble, then it's your fault that you didn't develop elementary protection against interference."

Yevgeniy Yurevich attempted to speak about the work done to increase the reliability of the *Kaktus* (Cactus) gamma-ray altimeter for soft landing and about the prospects of the ARS, but Kerimov interrupted him.

"Any glitches?"

"No."

"Thank you, you may sit down."

"I request that Comrade Sheminov give us his remarks about the current converters."

"They've been cleared, no anomalies."

"Primary current sources—batteries. Who's reporting?"

"Institute of Current Sources, Tenkovtsev. No anomalies."

The chairman addressed the chief designers quite differently.

"Vladislav Nikolayevich Bogomolov, on the correction engine unit system."[22]

"No anomalies. Cleared for flight."

"Ivan Ivanovich Kartukov, you have everything in order as usual?"[23]

"The SAS and soft landing solid-propellant engines are cleared."

"Comrade Galin."

"The on-board radio complex had glitches, which were allowed, and instruments have been replaced due to failures, and findings have been released. The DRS is cleared for flight."

"*Zarya* system—Vladimir Isaakovich Meshcheryakov."

"No anomalies, it's cleared."

"Comrade Solodov from OKB MEI."

"The radio range-finding equipment has been cleared, no anomalies."

"Petr Fedorovich Bratslavets."[24]

"No glitches in the *Krechet* [Gyrfalcon] television system. It's cleared."

"Gay Ilyich, what do you have to tell us?"

---

22. Vladislav Nikolayevich Bogomolov (1919–1997) was the 1st deputy chief designer at KB Khimmash (the Isayev design bureau). He later succeeded Isayev.

23. Ivan Ivanovich Kartukov (1904–1991) was chief designer of KB-2 at Factory No. 81, responsible for low-thrust solid-propellant rockets for a variety of applications.

24. Petr Fedorovich Bratslavets (1925–1999) was a department chief at NII Televideniya, responsible for TV-imaging systems for Soviet spacecraft.

Smiling, Severin listed all the developments: "Sanitation systems, chairs, survival kit, *Kolos* [Spike] regenerator, and cosmonauts' suits have all been cleared!"

"Cosmonauts consoles—Sergey Grigoryevich Darevskiy."[25]

"Cleared, no anomalies."

"Who is giving the final report on the science equipment?" asked Kerimov, not finding the surname on the list in front of him. "Oh, here it is—Comrade Novikov, Yulian Vasilyevich."

"It's cleared for flight," came the boilerplate response.

After the individual reports came the recapping ones. I reported about the entire on-board control complex, electrical equipment, power supply system, new docking assembly, and antenna feeder unit (AFU), having attested that everything had been verified, signed off on, and cleared for flight-developmental testing.[26] Bushuyev did the same thing for the spacecraft's life-support and thermal control systems and its design. Viktor Nikiforovich Bugayskiy cleared the DOS design. The representative of our Kuybyshev branch, Mikhail Fedorovich Shum, reported on the clearance of the 11A511U launch vehicle. This was the designation of the distinguished and often modified three-stage *Semyorka*. Regional Engineer Colonel Aleksandr Vaganovich Isaakyan—chief of main military acceptance—spoke next. Chelomey's deputy, Dmitriy Alekseyevich Polukhin, reported on the readiness of the UR-500K launch vehicle, which was referred to as 8K82K No. 254 in official documents.[27]

In all, 130 people had gathered for the State Commission meeting. Thirty-five of them reported on the readiness of the Soyuz spacecraft and DOS. Next came reports about the readiness of the Command and Measurement Complex, launch sites, medical service, and radiation safety service. Shabarov took the floor with a proposal to permit the fueling of the DOS and spacecraft 7K-T No. 31. Colonel Patrushev, chief of the firing range's First Directorate, announced the schedule of operations, which determined the launch of the first orbital station on 19 April and the piloted spacecraft on 23 April 1971, "if there are no contraindications on board the DOS (article 17K)."

Kerimov scheduled the next State Commission session at Site No. 92, Chelomey's launch area, to make the decision to roll out the launch vehicle with station 17K attached.

---

25. Sergey Grigoryevich Darevskiy (1920–2001) was chief designer of SOKB LII, the design bureau in charge of cockpit control panels for Soviet piloted spacecraft.

26. AFU—*Antenno-fidernoye ustroystvo.*

27. Dmitriy Alekseyevich Polukhin (1927–1993) was a senior designer at TsKBM's Branch No. 1 in Fili responsible for the development of the UR-500K Proton launch vehicle. He later headed the branch from 1973 to 1993.

Despite the cheerful report, my notebook was overflowing with a list of errors and "half-baked ideas," and I swore to myself that the guilty parties' "heads would roll" when I returned to Moscow. The main glitches had to do with interference between the systems. There was no time or experience to test out electromagnetic compatibility. Vilnitskiy and the factory process engineers, having performed heroic work to create a new docking assembly, had not thought about protecting it against dust, dirt, and possible damage during the spacecraft's ground preparation. There was no safety equipment and no "anti-bonehead" protection!

"Where is the guarantee that the pristine mirrored surfaces, which are supposed to form the pressurized tunnel after docking, won't be damaged when the fairing is put on—or even worse, when it is ejected during the powered flight segment? And God only knows what kind of scraps will fly into the docking port!" I shouted at Vilnitskiy over the high-frequency communications line. Vilnitskiy humbly heard me out and then requested that his representatives keep an eye on things day and night to see that the docking surfaces were immaculately clean and that the rubber seals were intact.

Over dinner I met with Boris Dorofeyev, who had arrived from the big MIK, where testing had finally begun on N-1 No. 6L.

"You've completely forgotten us," he complained. "Come and take a look at Block A on the inside. You won't recognize it. We've rerun the cable conduits and wrapped them so that no fire would pose a threat to them now. We moved the instruments around where we could, a bit further away from the explosion-hazardous turbopump assemblies. The top brass isn't rushing us now. By all accounts, we'll be ready for launch in July. We'll start to work from the left launch site. The right site is still under repairs."[28]

"And as for us," I boasted, "in the State Commission even the *Igla* had no glitches—knock on wood!" And I knocked on the table, which was covered with a white tablecloth. In such cases you're supposed to knock on wood, and this table, I later learned, had a plastic veneer.

Late that evening, I had just managed to fall asleep when the telephone awakened me. Sosnovik was calling.

"Bashkin and I need to make an emergency report about an incident."

"Where's the incident?"

"On vehicle No. 31."

---

28. The N-1 launch area at Site No. 110 was divided into two areas, Site No. 110L ("L" for *levyy* or left) and Site No. 110P ("P" for *pravyy* or right), each containing a separate launch pad.

"Like we don't have enough troubles. Come on over."

For 30 minutes in my hotel room we studied the incident, which supposedly had happened back at the factory, but the danger wasn't recognized until today, and that was by accident.

The electrical circuit of the descent control system has a remote switch (DP).[29] It has two windings: "activate" and "cancel. " When power is fed to the "activate" winding, the main contacts close, supplying power to the "ballistic descent" circuit. When this happens, the circuit supplying the "activate" winding is simultaneously broken to avoid overheating. Upon receiving the "cancel" command, the contacts open the emergency ballistic descent circuits and restore the guided descent circuit. During normal flight, "guided descent" is always selected. Therefore, the remote switch is not engaged. But when the "SAS" (emergency rescue system) command is issued, the "ballistic descent" mode is selected and the emergency rescue system sends a command to the "activate" winding. This command comes from the launch vehicle simulator during ground tests. During tests at the factory and at the engineering facility this command was issued again and again. However, based on the logic of subsequent work, when simulating spacecraft separation from the launch vehicle, the "cancel" command is issued for guided descent. Other commands got tangled in this seemingly simple logic, so that during testing both DP windings were simultaneously supplied with power for a long period of time. The specifications for the DP categorically forbid this. According to the information that came from the developers at the Mashinoapparat Factory, where Katkov was the chief designer, after 5 seconds the DP windings overheat to the point that they start smoking, and after 10 seconds—they burn out.

"But, you know, this DP worked glitch-free during tests, and no one reported anything about smoke," I tried to object.

Usually the testers smell the smoke before something burns. Perhaps, smoke appeared back at the factory. At the KIS the windings burned a little, and in flight or during tests at the launch site they would finish burning, and the remote switch would get stuck in a "neither here nor there" position.

"Which descent will be selected?" I asked.

"The devil only knows. It's just the luck of the draw. In the best case, the Descent Module will return to Earth," answered Bashkin.

"So, here's the thing," I proposed. "Tally up how many times both windings of this DP ended up being supplied power simultaneously through the fault of our testing methods, and the maximum number of seconds that the windings

---

29. DP—*Distantsionnyy pereklyuchatel.*

could be in that state. We'll multiply those numbers by three and perform the experiment on the same DP. If it malfunctions under these conditions, then we'll have to report to the chairman of the State Commission, immediately call for an instrument from Podlipki that hasn't undergone testing, and repeat all the tests on 7K-T No. 31. This will mean an additional five or six days. All the schedules, both for the DOS and for spacecraft launches, have already been sent to Moscow, perhaps even to the Politburo. Everyone is waiting for the orbital station, and then we come out with burned-out remote switch windings. That's a nice little present you've come up with."

For half the night, the SOUD laboratory conducted experiments on the viability of the remote switch. They ran it 20 times in the prohibited mode for 5 seconds, each time with 1-minute breaks in between. The remote switch heated up to 120°C [248°F], but it didn't give up and produce smoke. According to the calculations, this mode was four times more demanding than during all possible errors while conducting previous tests. In the end, they confirmed that actual smoke appeared just 25 seconds after power was supplied simultaneously to the windings. After 30 seconds the remote switch stopped responding to commands. We unanimously decided that this could never happen. Therefore, we weren't about to report anything to anyone.

"The designers at Mashinoapparat have been piling up reserves that they've been concealing from us. Tell them thanks if everything works out. Forget about the all-nighter, and correct the test documentation right away. In the morning send a radiogram to Rauschenbach and Karpov telling them to immediately insert inhibits to prevent such situations," I said, drawing the line.

On Cosmonauts' Day, 12 April, they finished the retesting of 7K-T No. 31 because of another holiday gift—the replacement of the telemetry memory unit. This enabled us once more to "quietly" confirm that the ill-fated remote switch was okay.

During all the round-the-clock vigils in connection with dismantling 7K-T No. 31 and the replacement of instruments, the assemblers and fitters of our shop No. 444 worked heroically and without complaint. Having served in 1948 as a "catwalk" soldier on R-1 rockets in Kapustin Yar, Kostya Gorbatenko, now deputy chief of the shop, managed to come up with a way for his "working class" to perform all the work twice as fast as we had planned.

A participant in the launch of Yuriy Gagarin, Major Vladimir Yaropolov, who had been in charge of the testing of spacecraft 7K-T No. 31, reported at the technical management's operational meeting that by the end of 18 April the launch vehicle and spacecraft would be ready for rollout to the launch site, and on 19 April it would be possible to begin work at Site No. 1 [i.e., the launch pad] according to the program for the first launch day. Now the

DOS could be delivered to the fueling station. Somewhere someone decided that the first Soviet orbital station should be called "Zarya" (Dawn) rather than DOS, and certainly not 17K. This word was painted on her hull in red against a white background.

It took all night to fill the DOS with propellant components and gases for the correction engines and attitude-control thrusters. When I stopped by the fueling station in the morning, I met Anatoliy Abramov, who had been on duty there since the evening before.[30] Abramov reminded me what cunning it had taken to get Korolev to agree to the construction of this spacecraft fueling station. Korolev tried very hard to save money on the construction and kicked Abramov out several times when the latter brought him the fueling station plans for his signature. Then Abramov arranged for an architectural scale-model of the fueling station to be made. A month later he brought the model into the reception area and asked Korolev to step out of his office for a minute. When S. P. returned he saw the model and swore: "Are you trying to get your way again? You can't calm down! But, I suppose you're right. Do it!"

All this time S. P. didn't forget about the ground specialists' proposal and tested himself against their stubbornness.

"Now it is funny to recall," said Abramov, "what we were saving money on. Those were such crumbs compared with the grandiose 'construction project of the century' for the N-1. At Site No. 2 alone there are 1,200 people who have flown in on temporary assignment for the DOS and two spacecraft, and that's not counting the military and civilians working here permanently."

To transport the *Zarya* via the railroad to Chelomey's Site No. 92, it was loaded onto a platform and covered with a protective cover. Like an honor guard, there were two submachine gunners standing at the front of the platform and three at the rear. This is how the first DOS was rolled out from the fueling station.

ON THE MORNING OF 14 APRIL, Yurevich, Nevzorov, and I climbed onto the vertical test stand of the 7K spacecraft in the old MIK, where we indulged in speculation about the rendezvous systems "on location." The emergency x-ray system developed by Yurevich for the final approach segment was the reason we were there. We had agreed that far approach was, of course, the prerogative of the radio engineers, while a simple x-ray system with cosmonaut

---

30. Anatoliy Petrovich Abramov (1919–1998) was one of Mishin's most senior deputies and in charge of ground systems. He served as deputy chief designer from 1966 to 1980.

participation would be good for the near segment. A laser could also be used instead of an x-ray unit.

"We could have done everything a lot more simply and reliably than *Igla* and *Kontakt*, but now it's a little late to start from scratch," said Nevzorov.

By a strange coincidence, Legostayev called me from Podlipki over the high-frequency communications line. He reported that once again the expert commission had begun working "like crazy" on the N1-L3. The chairman of the control section, Academician Bunkin, insisted on the criticism that *Kontakt* had no backup on the L3.[31]

"One failure after lifting off from the Moon to dock with the LOK, and the cosmonaut will stay in near-lunar orbit forever," Bunkin argued his position. "At least back up *Kontakt* with a simple laser system."

"That's a valid comment," I answered. "There's nothing I can say to that—agreed."

"So are you going to give me the weight for a second *Kontakt*? Perhaps you and Bushuyev will also arrange this."

"Don't worry and don't argue with the commission. If only we could wait until the first successful flight of the N-1 and then sort out the situation with the vehicles."

"Okay," responded Legostayev. "We need to accept all of Bunkin's proposals. And also, Vasiliy Pavlovich [Mishin] has flown out to see you."

Over lunch we agreed that Bushuyev and I would drive out to meet Mishin, and Shabarov would "mind the store." To our surprise, none of the cosmonauts, who had already spent several days under Kamanin's leadership at Site No. 17, had come to the airfield [to greet Mishin]. Only the firing range deputy chief of staff represented the military authorities. After descending the airplane's stairway, in response to our greeting, Mishin brusquely, unconstrained by his surroundings, tore into me and Bushuyev: "And why are you here? There's nothing else for you to do?"

After seeing the bewildered faces of the onlookers, he greeted us eventually. We couldn't help but recall the times when we had met Korolev here when *he* flew in. Usually Korolev made whoever picked him up—Voskresenskiy, Shabarov, or me—take a seat in his car and, the whole way to his cottage, questioned him about things at the firing range and shared the latest news from Moscow.

---

31. Boris Vasilyevich Bunkin (1922–) was one of the leading designers in charge of the development of Soviet antiballistic missile systems. He served as general designer of MKB Strela (later TsKB Almaz) from 1968 to 1998. *Kontakt* was the rendezvous radar system designed to bring together the LOK and LK in lunar orbit.

At 1800 hours Shabarov suddenly convened a meeting of the technical management. Two glitches had been discovered on the DOS, which had already "departed" for Site No. 92. One of the planners, after consulting with the optics specialists, determined that when the cover of the x-ray telescope opens, it falls within the field of vision of the infrared vertical [sensors]. This threatens the loss of attitude control using Earth—since the telescope cover is "hotter" than Earth, the infrared vertical will "latch" onto it. Therefore, it was proposed that the cover be opened manually from a special console rather than in automatic mode, if after thorough analysis the "ground" would grant permission for that. And that was the end of that.

The second glitch proved to be not so "refined." Belikov, our specialist on electric power supply systems, discovered at the last minute that the tiny battery of the instrument measuring the solar constant had been installed in such a way that during the powered flight segment, when exposed to g-loads, electrolyte would leak out of it. Shabarov proposed granting permission for access to the inside of the already sealed DOS. This meant they would need to release the internal air pressurization from the entire station, open the hatch, and very cautiously lower a man in there, who could either take out the battery altogether or reposition it. Then they would have to pull the man out, close the hatch, repressurize the station, recheck the pressure integrity, and....

Mishin didn't let Shabarov finish and with a scowl asked: "Who? Tell me his name."

Shabarov asked for permission to finish his report. Mishin didn't want to hear it and once again demanded: "Tell me his name; who did this?"

Shabarov didn't quite understand whose name Mishin was asking for, and gave an unfortunate response: "Well, Belikov. But, you know, that's not the issue here."

"You cover up for everyone. It's all the planners' fault! Just you wait, I'll get to you," threatened Mishin and, turning to Feoktistov, he added: "Soon we are going to impose stringent order."

"This little battery," said Feoktistov, "was installed using Bugayskiy's drawings rather than ours."

Mishin evidently realized that he'd gone too far: "Don't remove anything and don't do anything without consulting me! I forbid everything!"

Shabarov wanted to object but gave up and fell silent. In a few minutes the atmosphere of good teamwork and trouble-free, self-sacrificing mutual assistance that had developed between our staffs had been destroyed. The tension in the technical management room suddenly broke when Kerimov dropped by.

"As chairman of the State Commission I have received a serious warning notice from Moscow. We informed the Central Committee that we had named the orbital station *Zarya*. This might offend the Chinese, who supposedly have already announced that they are preparing for the launch of their new rocket, which they named "Dawn" before we did. What are we going to do? Repaint it?"

"Why repaint it? No one is going to photograph our DOS in space, and we can come up with a new name for the TASS announcement," I proposed.

But what name? Someone suggested "Salyut" (Salute). Everyone liked it. Thus, a series of orbital stations emerged under the general name "Salyut."

After dinner Shabarov said to me: "I'm sending Mishin on vacation, and you and I need to hear out the alarmist Bashkin. He has dug something up in the SUS (descent control system) of spacecraft No. 31 and No. 32."[32]

Bashkin had begun to suspect a problem in the operation of the descent control system even before the State Commission meeting. But despite calling in specialists, he was unable to understand and clarify the cause. He consulted with our comrades in Podlipki over the high-frequency communication line. They hatched a plan (without filling out paperwork for the trip) to find a seat for Anatoliy Shchukin on the Il-18 that Mishin flew out on.

Shchukin related: "On Cosmonauts' Day at 11 p.m. a car arrives at my house to pick me up. They take me to the design bureau and put me on the high-frequency telephone. I hear horrible things from Bashkin from the firing range. Well, that's all there is to it, I think: the liftoff needs to be canceled. I find out that the Il-18 is flying out in the morning. Nobody will fill out the paperwork for an official trip at night. They take me to Vnukovo-3 and shove me onto the plane with no documents and without being on the manifest. All my people are here at the firing range. Shabarov helped. They let me through all the checkpoints. I toss my suitcase somewhere and go straight to the MIK. We worked all night long. It's a good thing that the military helped, especially Yaropolov. We performed five individual programs. We simulated everything, understood everything. The culprit for everything was a defective ground. We can close the comment on the SUS in the logbook with a clear conscience."

"Our people are infallible," I thought, as I "signed off" on these very glitches.

LATE IN THE EVENING ON 14 APRIL, the desk attendant called me to the high-frequency communications telephone. This time Rauschenbach had phoned. He told me about Keldysh's expert commission, which had convened the previous day from 1600 to 2200 hours. Keldysh had absolutely insisted that several items be inserted in the commission's findings. First and foremost, the external transfer from the LK to the LOK needs to be replaced with an

---

32. SUS—*Sistema upravleniya spuskom.*

internal transfer, similar to the way that cosmonauts will transfer from the 7K-T to the 17K. Moreover, he added the following:

- provide for firing tests for each block (or stage) of the N-1 launch vehicle,
- provide a backup for *Kontakt* or put in a second system for reliable rendezvous,
- develop a principle for the piloted lunar expedition's interaction with Babakin's automatic probes, and
- exclude an ocean touchdown from the program.

"And a lot of other odds and ends," added Rauschenbach. "This time Keldysh was very angry. I haven't seen him like this for a long time. He let it be known that if we don't agree to these modifications, then he is abandoning support for the N1-L3 program."

I asked Rauschenbach if Mishin knew about Keldysh's stance.

"Most likely he does. Keldysh said that before yesterday's meeting he had already talked with Mishin and warned him about the majority of the most serious claims."

The following day over lunch, Mishin spoke with us on this subject. Khottabych (as we sometimes amiably referred to Okhapkin) had managed to telephone him in this regard.[33] In Mishin's opinion, the commission had no serious concerns.

"According to Rauschenbach, there are issues that will require the radical redesigning of the vehicles. And we don't have weight capabilities for that," I said.

Bushuyev backed me up.

"Admit it, Vasiliy Pavlovich, you do not like to keep us, your deputies, informed about things that are at odds with your optimism."

This time Mishin was amicably disposed, and he did not lash out at Bushuyev. He calmly responded: "But really, whom are you criticizing? We began the entire project as a team, along with Korolev. It's our job to sort things out, and none of us can walk away from this. And we also need to decide together what to do next. This commission, like all commissions, will give recommendations; all of its members will run off and attend to their own business, and we will be left behind. There's no running away from the N1-L3."

---

33. Khottabych is the title character of the 1937 book *Starik Khottabych* (*Old Man Khottabych*), the best-known work of Soviet satirist and children's author Lazar Iosifovich Lagin (1903–1979), the pen name of Lazar Ginzburg. It is the tale of a genie freed from captivity by a Soviet schoolboy and the difficulties he encounters adjusting to his new Communist lifestyle. The story was made into a film in 1956.

Mishin was right about this. There was no running away from the N1-L3 for him; for us, his deputies; and especially for Bushuyev, Okhapkin, and me.

At 1700 hours, after making a 45-kilometer dash, we arrived at Chelomey's Site No. 81. Here the UR-500K was being prepared. The State Commission was supposed to make the final decision clearing the launch vehicle for mating with the DOS and subsequent rollout to the launch site. Kerimov, Mishin, Karas, Shcheulov, and Kurushin had taken their places in the presidium. Polukhin was reporting on the readiness of the launch vehicle. Mishin asked whether Chelomey's report clearing the launch vehicle for liftoff was available. Polukhin announced that he was authorized to sign the report. "I demand the general designer's own report," insisted Mishin. As State Commission chairman, Kerimov announced that he had already assigned this difficult mission specifically to Polukhin. Chelomey had sent a radiogram confirming Polukhin's right to sign the report. And that was the end of the incident.

After the State Commission session, for the first time I carefully checked out the *Pyatisotka* [UR-500K], which had been prepared for mating with the DOS. Despite our "hue and cry" regarding its ecological hazard, outwardly it was a sight to behold. It wasn't painted at all. The cleanness of the welding and riveting was clearly visible against the bare metal. "We saved 300 kilograms on the paint," said the ZIKh representative standing next to the *Pyatisotka* beauty.

One could sense the high degree of aviation technology culture in the cleanness of the fittings of all the structural curves and transitions. All the electrical and pneumatic lines connecting with the ground equipment terminated at the aft end. This provided a substantial advantage—you could do without the cable tower and the tense anticipation: would it pull away or not?

While the *Pyatisotka* was being mated with the DOS, Bashkin stood on the tall service platform and made sure that the fragile "ionic tubes" were not damaged. Everything worked out.

It seemed that all the troubles were over; the coast was clear for the first orbital station. But all the while I had a nagging feeling that there was something very important that was still unresolved, something that lacked the finishing touches. It wasn't until I was on my way back to Site No. 2, when I caught sight of the big MIK glistening with lights, that I realized that this oppressive feeling was caused by deep-seated anxiety and fear over the N-1. We ourselves had not rejected anything that the expert commission had proposed in its findings. I even think that certain of our colleagues suggested something or other to the experts, naturally, with the best of intentions.

At the hotel, Bushuyev and I debated for a long time regarding the possible scenario of how events would unfold for the N1-L3 program. I insisted that he, as the chief designer's deputy responsible for the LOK and LK, support the expert commission's proposals as they related to vehicles.

"Admit it, Konstantin Davidovich," I said, "it was you, Feoktistov, and I who came up with the plan for the cosmonaut to crawl over from the LOK to the LK and back through space in lunar orbit, not Mishin. Why this potentially lethal stunt if a docking assembly with internal transfer has already been manufactured and will be tested in space in a week? You and Feoktistov stubbornly claim that there isn't weight. What you should say is that we made a mistake. We really need to change the program and modify the vehicles. We also should support the proposals calling for the introduction of firing tests (OTI) for the engines or the stages as a whole. Based on the Americans' positive experience and our negative experience, we simply cannot just reject OTI. At a minimum it will take Kuznetsov another three years to introduce them, that is, switch to reusable engines. Over that period, we might have time to revamp the vehicles and upstage the Americans. But...but...we need to convince Mishin, and then Keldysh, then Afanasyev, and finally Ustinov. We need to act as quickly as possible. We're losing time, not making a realistic decision about the dual-launch scenario."

Agreeing with me, Bushuyev took exception to immediate appeals through that chain of command.

"They will all rub our nose in the launch vehicle failure and say that now there is no time to redo the design unless we prove that we have a launch vehicle."

"It's a vicious circle," I replied. "We will check the launch vehicle's reliability without OTI. And we won't institute OTI because to do this will take three years that they won't give us. For those three years factories will produce launch vehicles and vehicles that invariably will not fulfill the mission."

Having resolved nothing, we went to bed.

On 15 April the duty attendant woke us up at 5 a.m. At 6 a.m. we drove out to Site No. 92 in order to be there for the traditional rollout of the first UR-500K rocket-space complex—the DOS—to the launch site. The launch vehicle and first orbital station mated together were slightly longer than 50 meters in length. This was, of course, half the size of the future MKBS on the N-1, but still an impressive beginning for this new field. Yuriy Semyonov, Vladimir Pallo, and Viktor Bugayskiy were engaged in a heated argument over something with the military men. The rollout was delayed by 20 minutes.

Kerimov began to grumble: "You're disrupting the schedule!"

"Twenty minutes isn't a disruption," a colonel whom I didn't know remarked rather sarcastically. "We lose years because of ungainly equipment and design errors. And there's no need to be in a rush in the final phase."

Rollout to the launch site is less exciting than liftoff, but it's still a magnificent sight. On the way back we looked around the construction of the new MIK building for the Almaz. I couldn't help but think of the questions that firing range chief Kurushin had already asked out loud time and again. Why construct independent factories in the steppe for work that involved identical procedures just because the chief designers and ministry administration want it that way? Is it really not possible to concentrate the preparation of DOSes, Almazes, Soyuzes, and other spacecraft at a single assembly and testing factory at the firing range? And perhaps build it a bit closer to the city so that we don't have to build each chief designer his own autonomous residential village? Imagine how many resources we could save if instead of feudalistic fiefdoms—the firms of Korolev, Chelomey, Yangel, Kozlov, and Reshetnev—the firing range had a single technical facility, a factory in the immediate vicinity of the town of Leninsk so that the workers could walk to it, or at the very least, make their way there on a bicycle!

The launch sites were separated from one another by 40 to 50 kilometers in the hope of preserving them in the event of a nuclear attack. But who would need space launches in the event of a nuclear missile war? After all, these weren't missile silos that were actually needed for a retaliatory strike. We could have saved billions of rubles on roads and electrical, rail, heating, and communication lines alone—enough to build a single space technology center. This was no longer a mistake, but a "my-home-is-my-castle" mindset.

As a counter to this peculiar feudalism, where each chief secludes himself from his colleagues behind a wall of secrecy, we, acting of course on instructions from the Central Committee, had begun talks with the U.S. concerning cooperation in piloted flights. Babkov told us over the high-frequency communication line about the results of the negotiations in the U.S. that he had participated in. According to him, the Americans had received the idea of cooperation very enthusiastically.[34]

After lunch Shabarov and I once again departed for Site No. 81. Unlike our launch site, it was forbidden to enter this site without a gas mask. This was the difference between our genteel oxygen and kerosene and Chelomey's nitrogen tetroxide and unsymmetric dimethylhydrazine.

The *Pyatisotka* and DOS stack were already standing in the gantry of the right-hand launch site. Launch control was being conducted from the bunker, which was referred to as "Site No. 83." In this bunker we caught up with the indignant Mishin. He was walking out of one of the underground halls into another one accompanied by Volkov and Khomyakov. When he

---

34. By March 1971, the Soviet and U.S. sides had already had two significant meetings (in October 1970 and January 1971) about a potential joint space mission in Earth orbit. The Soviet delegations had been led by Academicians Boris Petrov and Mstislav Keldysh, respectively.

caught sight of Shabarov and me, he began, evidently for the second time around, to rant and rail.

"Well, just look at this underground palace! A year ago it wasn't here. They didn't provide money for a building for demothballing the N-1, but here they've turned out a facility like this in a year's time."

They really had built the two-story bunker on a large scale. Here they had provided everything needed for a long period of independent subsistence, including its own diesel electric station and life-support system for all the bunker personnel.

"Just look what's going on here! And our idealist planners are insisting that they don't need anything for the MKBS. Don't you see, they're happy with spartan conditions and are ready to control a launch from a hole in the ground."

Khomyakov tried to calm down the infuriated Mishin as best he could. When we reached "our" room in the bunker, from whence control of the DOS preparation process was supposed to be conducted, we found ourselves in the dark, to which we had become accustomed since 1947. They had squeezed our indispensable station 11N6110 and the rack for the remote radio communications system in here for the DOS tests. On the way home Abramov couldn't help teasing Bushuyev and Feoktistov.

"And Mishin was right to let you idealists have it. Chelomey has shown what kind of scale you need—not just for rockets and spacecraft, but also the 'ground' for them. And you all thought that us ground specialists were second-class people."

"Don't badmouth us, Anatoliy, or we won't bring you home for a friendly dinner," said Bushuyev in a conciliatory tone.

Darevskiy really did invite us to his cottage for a friendly dinner. I must say that each firm involved in our cooperative network built cottages for its own employees at Site No. 2, kept house, and didn't need the services of hotels. As a rule, these cottages had a kitchen and dining room, which their own people took care of, rather than "housekeepers" provided by the military. Therefore, room and board was homestyle. The cottage that belonged to OKB Geofizika even had a rather ferocious dog.

Hot-smoked asp-fish was considered to be the company's official dish. Local angling specialists managed to fish enormous asp-fish from the shallow, muddy waters of the Syrdarya River. The smoking process had been developed as far back as the time of the trailblazers of 1957, and it made this fish an exquisite delicacy.

The star attraction of an evening at Darevskiy's cottage was Sergey Anokhin.[35] Usually taciturn, shy, and reserved, after the first few shots of vodka he became a most interesting conversationalist and ingenuous storyteller of the most extraordinary flight incidents. Anokhin related his stories with amazing simplicity, in a straightforward manner and without any theatrics. An unsuspecting listener who didn't know Anokhin would get the impression that the work of a test pilot was a simple affair, far from heroic, and it would be quite baffling why test pilots would die in peacetime. This time Anokhin was telling about the tragic death of a test pilot who had been famous since World War II: two-time Hero of the Soviet Union Amet-Khan Sultan.[36] He perished in the crash of a Tu-16 flying laboratory. The airplane's wing flaps failed. The landing speed was catastrophic. Anokhin himself had also lived through an

From the author's archives.

Famous Soviet aviator Sergey Anokhin (left), shown here with cosmonauts Gennadiy Strekalov and Aleksandr Ivanchenkov. Anokhin headed the civilian cosmonaut detachment at OKB-1 (and later NPO Energiya) for many years.

---

35. Sergey Nikolayevich Anokhin (1910–1986) was a famous Soviet test pilot who in his later life joined the Korolev design bureau to supervise the training of civilian cosmonaut trainees from TsKBEM.

36. Amet-Khan Sultan (1920–1971) was one of the most well-known Soviet wartime pilots; he was awarded the Hero of the Soviet Union award twice during the war for his daring exploits. In his later life, he served as a test pilot for a variety of military systems.

extraordinary hair-raising experience on a Tu-16. Before our next liftoff to Venus, the ability to start up the engine of Block L needed to be checked out in tests that included the simulation of weightlessness.[37] Block L didn't start up, but it did catch fire.

Anokhin ordered the crew to abandon the airplane, since a crash was inevitable. For some reason the cockpit canopies didn't open in the standard places. The crew dashed to the tail and jumped from the tail point. Anokhin attempted to save the burning airplane but, after realizing that this was impossible, managed to fly it "a lot further" and also bailed out. They searched for him for several days. They already considered him dead, if not from injuries sustained in the crash, then from the –30°C [–22°F] cold.

But Sergey didn't freeze to death. In the forest he found a little hut where a forest ranger was spending the winter. The latter had large supplies of alcoholic beverages. Anokhin spent several days in this little hut. Once he had relaxed and caught up on his sleep, he said goodbye to his hospitable drinking buddy, made his way to a large road, and returned "from the land of the dead" to his permanent duty station.

Anokhin was also acquainted with the Polish pilot Levanevskiy, the brother of our Sigizmund Levanevskiy, and with Wiley Post, who died in Alaska during his attempt to fly around the world.[38] "And he flew with one eye—he was one-eyed just like me," said Anokhin, who had lost an eye in a plane crash.

ON THE MORNING OF 16 APRIL, cosmonauts Vladimir Shatalov, Aleksey Yeliseyev, and Nikolay Rukavishnikov were doing their "sit-in" in vehicle 7K-T No. 31 (the future *Soyuz-10*). They were supposed to give their final comments after all the modifications were introduced into the standard equipment and layout. When I asked the unflappable Rukavishnikov how he felt, he replied that their regimen was too lax. They weren't under any pressure at all; they just run a lot in the morning.

"I'm even fed up," he said.

Yeliseyev seemed more anxious.

---

37. Block L was the transplanetary (or translunar) injection stage of the four-stage Molniya (or 8K78M) launch vehicle. It was the first Soviet upper stage designed specifically for firing in weightlessness.

38. Sigizmund Aleksandrovich Levanevskiy (1902–1937) was a famous Soviet aviator, often known as the "Soviet Lindbergh." He was killed in 1937 during a record-breaking flight over the North Pole from Moscow to the United States. See Chertok, *Rockets and People, Vol. I*, Chapter 7. Wiley Hardeman Post (1898–1935) was an American pilot who gained fame for being the first pilot to fly around the world solo, a feat he accomplished in 1931. He was killed in an air crash in 1935.

"Why are they reporting in the VPK that the engines of the actuator system have a service life of 4,000 activations, while according to my calculations they'll need more than 20,000. Is there a guarantee that there will be a reliable ignition of the propellant components in space at low temperature?"

Yeliseyev was pondering and trying to predict the off-nominal behavior of the vehicle's systems in flight.

The film, television, and photo journalists showed up. Under the blinding light of the floodlights the cosmonauts climbed into the spacecraft. After another telephone call from Shabarov, who had beseeched Mishin to attend the "sit-in" ceremony, the latter appeared and said: "Go on without me. I'm rushing over to the airfield to meet the minister."

Vladimir Shatalov's crew sat in the vehicle for 2 hours. After airing out the vehicle with fans, the second (or backup) crew climbed in, Aleksey Leonov, Valeriy Kubasov, and Petr Kolodin.

At 1800 hours, all Party members assembled in the small dispatch room for a Party meeting. Shabarov briefly and concisely reported about the work performed to prepare the first orbital station and first transport vehicle for liftoff. He didn't go into technical details, but emphasized the people's self-sacrificing work. In particular, when the failure of a memory unit was discovered in the remote radio communication (DRS) system of vehicle 7K-T No. 31, it was necessary to disassemble and separate the compartments to replace it. Seven to 10 days were needed for the subsequent retesting cycle for this operation! But in actuality, the factory brigade of shop No. 444 under the leadership of Gorbatenko managed to pull this off in three days.

After the meeting, Mishin solemnly presented Bushuyev, Shabarov, and me with certificates and commemorative medals in honor of the 10th anniversary of the flight of Yu. A. Gagarin.

That evening, when I entered the dining hall to have dinner, all the seats at the table were already occupied. The only empty chair was next to the newly arrived minister. I greeted him and moved along to sit down at the other end of the long mess hall table, around which about 20 people were sitting.

"So, you don't want to sit next to the brass?" asked Afanasyev mockingly.

I sat down next to him.

"Incidentally, in similar cases I try to sit a little farther away, too," said Afanasyev to put me at ease.

I had to laugh it off. On the whole, the minister was simple and approachable in everyday interaction. He seemed menacing and instilled fear only at Miusskaya Square, when he led meetings of the collegium.

WORK DIDN'T SLOW DOWN EVEN FOR A MINUTE. I spent half the night at the MIK. When I approached the fairing with which they were about to cover the vehicle after it had been mated with the launch vehicle, I caught sight of a perturbed Yuriy Semyonov. Earlier he had assigned the task of cleaning dust and any sort of debris off the fairing before the mating process, ordering that this be done using alcohol to wipe it down. Having used the alcohol for another purpose, workmen from Progress were now trying to mate the fairing, having limited themselves to a "dry" wipe-down. Semyonov made a last-ditch effort, announcing that he would not allow the mating process until he made sure of the surgical cleanliness of the interior surface of the fairing. It was not an easy job introducing a culture of cleanliness at the firing range. During dust storms sand finds tiny holes and penetrates into the halls of the assembly building, and the air is simply heavy with suspended particles. The fans drawing in the dust move it around, and that's all.

On the morning of 17 April, I went to the MIK again to check the cleanliness of the fairing. The likelihood of foreign particles getting onto the clean surfaces of the docking assemblies was very worrisome. If something were to hinder their snug engagement, pressure integrity would not be ensured and crew transfer from the spacecraft to the DOS would be ruled out.

Semyonov couldn't sleep all night because of the fairing.

"Today's Saturday and there's a Communist volunteer cleanup going on all over the country. And we're also spending the day cleaning up the fairing. But we can't delay the assembly process any longer," he said. "They went over everything with a vacuum cleaner, then they wiped it down with rags moistened with alcohol."

I ran a clean handkerchief over the surface of the mating ring and showed it to the Progress Factory foreman.

"You're going to have to wash your handkerchief," he said, "but there's nothing more we can do. That is the film from a layer of dust. Alcohol will only dissolve it. We need to change the manufacturing process."

At 1000 hours Bushuyev, Shabarov, and I drove over to the big MIK. In the chief designer's spacious office, Mishin decided to discuss the proposals for the prospects of a new scenario for the L3M lunar expedition and the upgrading of the orbital station. Sadovskiy and Bezverbyy had flown in specifically to report on these matters.[39]

I had already seen these materials and had even signed them about two months before. Now, after looking them over with a fresh eye, I realized the

---

39. Igor Nikolayevich Sadovskiy (1919–1993) was a deputy chief designer at TsKBM, primarily responsible for the development of solid-propellant ICBMs. Vitaliy Konstantinovich Bezverbyy was a senior designer at TsKBM responsible for new projects.

weaknesses and shortcomings in them. Many assertions about the effectiveness of the antispacecraft beam weaponry and the deadlines for its development seemed naïve. After all, we had proposed developing a design for a new DOS with "death rays" in all but two years' time! Infrared sensors would scan all the underlying terrain. Once they detected the plume of a launched missile in their field of vision, radar antennas would be directed at it, measuring its trajectory parameters, and would guide antiballistic missiles to destroy it during its powered flight segment before separation of the warheads from the delivery vehicle.

The American designs for a missile defense system, which appeared 10 years later during the Ronald Reagan presidency under the infamous SDI program, hardly differed from our pipe dreams of that time.[40]

After lunch, Mishin invited Generals Karas, Kostin, and Shcheulov to discuss these materials, but at the old MIK.[41] The generals' objections annoyed Mishin. He countered the criticism, arguing that "there are organizations that understand this better than we do."

Viktor Shcheulov was first deputy chief of TsUKOS; because of this, he had been awarded the rank of major-general-engineer.[42] I had become very well acquainted with him at Kapustin Yar back in 1949. We liked each other and had been on friendly "*ty*" terms since that time.[43] Despite his military ranking, from time to time he was unhesitatingly quite critical of the military leadership. This time he did not spare my leadership.

"Pray tell, Boris Yevseyevich, why your dear Vasiliy Pavlovich considers us to be such dimwits? Karas and I were entrusted with the management of the Central Directorate for Space Assets. Kostin is in charge of space-based reconnaissance and even more. To a great extent, decisions for the prospective military space program depend on us, and Mishin makes it sound like we are just bothering him."

"Don't take offense, Viktor Ivanovich," I reassured Shcheulov. "When Mishin gets carried away, he really does not tolerate objections, but then he'll quickly recover and everything will be normal."

---

40. See Chertok, *Rockets and People, Vol. III*, Chapter 11.

41. Petr Timofeyevich Kostin was chief of the space intelligence directorate of the Main Intelligence Directorate (GRU) and, as such, was responsible for the receipt and processing of space-based intelligence gathered by Soviet satellites. He served in that position from 1961 to 1973.

42. The TsUKOS (Central Directorate for Space Assets) abbreviation had been superseded in 1970 by GUKOS (Main Directorate of Space Assets).

43. Russian has two forms of the word "you": *ty* for close or informal relationships and *vy* for formal relationships.

TEN YEARS AFTER THE FLIGHT OF YURIY GAGARIN we hoped once again to astonish the world. The days and hours that remained before the DOS launch—the first real Long-Duration Orbital Station—passed relatively placidly. On our so-called "reserve day," 18 April, the large contingent that had gathered at the firing range was not engaged in its ongoing blistering-paced business, but, splitting up "by interests" in hotels and departmental cottages, discussed prospects and space policy, and picked apart the chief designers, who simply couldn't come to an agreement about actually uniting efforts.

I decided to pay Pilyugin a visit. Recently diabetes had begun to torment him. It wasn't easy for him to fly to the firing range. But this time he flew in to see for himself what was going on with the N1-L3 and at the same time to please the high-ranking leaders who had demanded that the chief designers be present "in person" at the launch of the DOS. Factories in Kharkov had performed the main operations to manufacture the instruments for the *Semyorka* launch vehicle and UR-500K control systems. But Pilyugin was still the chief designer.

When I dropped into Pilyugin's cottage, he was with Vladilen Finogeyev and Georgiy Priss discussing a list of glitches that had managed to appear at the very beginning of the tests performed on N-1 No. 6L. Pilyugin moved a stack of documents aside. He was beginning to grow weary of the multitude of minor problems.

"It's all trivial matters. You sort it out yourselves. Boris, it's a good thing you stopped by. I want to teach Vasiliy so he'll finally understand: if he doesn't get seriously involved with N-1 then your organization is going to become useless. We're finishing up the development tests on the digital control system for N1-L3. We've got the computer and we need to quickly prepare N-1 No. 7L with the new system. You've gotten mixed up with the DOSes, you've pulled the rug out from under Chelomey's Almaz, you're being drawn into negotiations with the Americans, and if one examines the situation carefully, you've got a complete fiasco on your hands when it comes to the N-1 and lunar vehicles. The Kuybyshev [factories] have moved into action with all their might—they're riveting the hull; here at the big MIK they're welding the tanks, and soon we're going to have all the bays chock-full of metal. But you know, speaking frankly, with the weights you've got a real mess.

"I've told Mishin this again and again. After all, the proposal for the dual-launch scenario had been around for a long time. We need to decide, not drag our feet. You and Rauschenbach have started your control systems developments. Go ahead, I don't object, but you won't make lunar vehicles without us, you know. But my guys are already tired of reporting that Bushuyev and Feoktistov have run into size and weight limits, and basically they don't want to talk. Do you think Keldysh doesn't understand this? He even complained to me that we're just hearing wishful thinking from Mishin. If the N-1 doesn't pan out, then we're going to have a rough time, too. We have put so much effort into the work.

"Yangel has loaded me down again. We're conducting a large project with him now. Chelomey wasn't able to smother Yangel with his *Sotkas* [UR-100 missiles]. If you'd just let Chelomey make his Almaz in peace. What, you don't have enough work? I'm over my head in work. Uncle Mitya [Ustinov], without asking our minister, talked me into working with Nadiradze. The job is very interesting. But you keep in mind, if they overload us with military stuff, and you get carried away with DOSes and the Americans, N-1 will completely wither away."

I was unable to come up with any convincing arguments in response to Pilyugin's monologue. The situation with N-1 really was such that the more progress we made the more confidence we lost in the certainty of fulfilling the final objective.

How could I contradict Pilyugin? I was part of the group that had approached the Central Committee with the proposal for the development of the DOS without having asked Mishin for his consent. The initiative for cooperation with the Americans and setting up a joint Soyuz-Apollo flight came from Bushuyev, and at the Academy of Sciences Keldysh and Boris Petrov backed it.[44] Keldysh reported to the government, the Americans had put out a high-level counterproposal, and work had come to a boil, pulling in more and more leading specialists. And one could not accuse Mishin of having come up with this very crucial work.

As far as the N1-L3 weight problems were concerned, there was only one way for a comprehensive solution—switching over to a dual-launch scenario. We needed to make a decision immediately and designate new deadlines. But who would go before the Politburo to explain this or at least go see Leonid Ilyich [Brezhnev] in person? Nobody was brave enough.

The nation's top political leadership had devoted a great deal of attention to the production of strategic missile armaments, attempting to work out an integrated concept. However, even for this problem of utmost national importance they were unable to adopt such a concept. The chief designers defended their ideas before the Council of Defense with enviable courage. Pilyugin

---

44. Boris Nikolayevich Petrov (1913–1980) was a prominent control systems scientist who was also chairman of Interkosmos, the socialist bloc space cooperative organization, from 1966 to 1980. During the Apollo-Soyuz Test Project (ASTP), due to secrecy restrictions on actual designers working at TsKBEM, Petrov served as the public face of the Soviet side of the project.

participated actively in this so-called "little civil war."[45] I took advantage of the opportunity and reminded him: "So you're taking part in the 'civil war.' You there in the commissions and on the Council of Defense argue, laying each of your scenarios out on the table or depicting them on posters. Chelomey has an artistic presence; Yangel seems more unassuming but is also convincing. They have fundamentally different concepts for the construction of our strategic missile systems. And what's the result? Brezhnev listened carefully to everything and made a decision, with which everyone agreed: do both, that one and the other one, and a third. For national defense and to intimidate the Americans, perhaps, it was worth it to act in that way. But to tackle everything that's been conceived is simply impossible. Not just because we'll leave the whole country in rags, but also because we're not capable of getting all this through our own heads. If not the Defense Council, then we need someone else to finally develop an integrated national cosmonautics development program for 10 years. Until they understand this 'at the top,' we'll be rushing about between dozens of assignments of 'critical national importance.' Kosygin proposed reforms in the economy based on common sense. Everyone there "at the top" seemed to agree with him and applauded them. But what happened? Goberman—chief of Moscow motor pools and someone from among the directors in the textile industry—started to do something and then everything fizzled out."

"Now, hold your horses," Pilyugin stopped me. "Did you hear the story about the old woman who came to the Party district committee to complain about a leaky roof? While she was complaining about the collective farm chairman and even about the regional officers, they listened to her attentively. But when she started to ask what the ministers and Brezhnev himself were doing, they cautioned her: 'Granny!' They shook their fingers at her, but ordered that her roof be repaired."

---

45. For the "little civil war," see Chertok, *Rockets and People, Vol. III*, pp. 147–157.

Chapter 14
Launching *Salyut*

On 19 April 1971, all the participants and distinguished guests convened for the launch of the *Pyatisotka* carrying the first DOS. The UR-500K *Proton* standing on the launch pad, with the DOS invisible beneath the fairing, was that bundle of metal and electronics which embodied the creative energy of dozens of chief designers and therefore, for the time being, reconciled all their differences.

At T minus 15 minutes, the State Commission and all the guests left the stuffy service rooms and climbed up on the stands of the observation center. On such a spring night you enjoy breathing in the air lush with the aromas of the steppe. It seems bizarre, why each of us has a bag containing a gas mask slung over his shoulder. Certainly no one wants to think about the possibility of the off-nominal situation that might occur if the nocturnal beauty standing on the launch pad decides not to fly off to a safe distance.

The *Pyatisotka* really is beautiful under the floodlights when it is standing on the launch pad, liberated from the service towers and prelaunch commotion on the ground.

T minus 1 minute!

All at once the conversations cease. I feel the inner tension of everyone standing at the observation post. For a few seconds, blinding light floods the nocturnal steppe and a deafening roar bears down on us. The *Pyatisotka* lifts off easily, outdazzling the stars with its own bright plume. The first DOS is on its way to space.

By the time we had dashed over to Site No. 2, reports had already come in from Yevpatoriya and Moscow that *Salyut*, or, as we referred to it, DOS No. 1 or 17K No. 121, had entered its intended orbit. The solar arrays and all the structural elements, including the *Igla* antenna boom, were deployed. At that time we still did not realize and could not foresee that this launch had opened the age of orbital space stations. Our sole concern was the events of the next few hours and days.

In our jargon, the first and subsequent Long-Duration Orbital Stations were referred to simply as DOSes. In production documentation all the DOSes had the index 17K and were given ordinal numbers: No. 121, No. 122, etc.

For the mass media—for the public—the first DOS was called *Salyut* with no number. It was followed by *Salyut-2, -3, -4, -5, -6, -7,* etc. TASS reports also referred to the piloted Almazes as Salyuts. The former were never called DOSes in our departmental terminology.[1]

After separation from the launch vehicle, the attitude-control system dampened the oscillations of the DOS, and program tests began under Yevpatoriya's command. At the firing range all the attention switched to *Soyuz-10*. If the tests on the DOS did not turn up any contraindications, then Vladimir Shatalov, Aleksey Yeliseyev, and Nikolay Rukavishnikov would lift off into space from the first Gagarin launch site on 22 April 1971.

The weather had drastically deteriorated. Even those of us who considered ourselves Tyuratam old-timers couldn't recall an autumnal cold rain falling in late April. A glitch in the form of a failure of the pull-off plug to eject from Block I—the third stage of the *Semyorka*—was chalked up to this rain on launch day. All the systems were brought into their initial state. The launch was called off.

"Shatalov simply can't lift off on his first try," they joked in the bunker.[2] They decided not to take a risk, to sort out the problem with the pull-off plug, evacuate the crew, and postpone the launch by 24 hours.

On 23 April, the launch proceeded normally. The first crew reports from orbit were also optimistic. The technical management and the State Commission flew out to Yevpatoriya. At the naval aviation airfield in Saki, so many passengers streamed out of the Il-18 that we barely managed to squeeze into the automobiles sent for us. Once again we were in the blossoming Crimea. Everyone who had just arrived, displaying genuine eagerness, dropped their suitcases at the hotel and rushed over to the control center, despite the hospitable invitation to dinner. Agadzhanov, Tregub, and Rauschenbach, who in the absence of the State Commission were in charge of the Main Operations Control Group (GOGU), were ready to report.

Agadzhanov delivered the report: "Everything is normal on board the *Salyut* and Soyuz vehicles. The DOS is now in its 79th orbit. At the recommendation of the ballistics experts, we must conduct the orbital correction of both vehicles during the 81st orbit. For the *Salyut*, this will be performed automatically; for the Soyuz, manually. To do this, during the 80th orbit we will mark the settings. On the *Salyut* the settings will be performed via command radio link;

---

1. *Author's note*: Almazes were given the Salyut numbers 2, 3, and 5.
2. This is a reference to the many attempts to launch *Soyuz-4* (carrying Shatalov) in January 1969.

on the Soyuz we will perform them by voice transmission via *Zarya*, and the crew will input the data required for correction from the console. As a result of the corrections, the long-range ballistic rendezvous process will begin on the 82nd orbit. According to the ballistics experts' calculations, the vehicles will approach one another to a distance of up to 11 to 12 kilometers at around 0400 hours. The subsequent rendezvous will take place in automatic mode per commands from *Igla*. According to our calculations, rendezvous and docking should be completed within the period from 0536 hours until 0552 hours. According to the flight program, transfer from the vehicle to the DOS will be performed during orbit No. 84, the cosmonauts will unpack during orbits Nos. 85 and 86, and the crew should already be sleeping during orbit No. 87."

They had just managed to sort out the list of operations for the two vehicles and the allocation of responsibility for them in the control and analysis group when two instructions came in from Moscow: first—prepare the crew for a conversation with Brezhnev; and second—transmit on board the text of a greeting from the Communist Party of Bulgaria. Then suddenly the report came in that during the fifth orbit of *Soyuz-10* the first correction failed. Afanasyev was reporting the situation to Ustinov at that time and requested that the crew not be distracted by conversations with Brezhnev and greetings to the Bulgarians. Mishin demanded that Rauschenbach explain the causes for the failed correction.

So many people were crammed into the control room that there was no place for the bosses to sit. And it was quite difficult to consult with one another, talk, and command the various services over the dozens of telephones. Pavel Agadzhanov, who had been giving voice commands over the only conference line at the Command and Measurement Complex (KIK), had to aurally receive all the information pouring in over the intercom and telephone and the guidelines of the State Commission that had just flown in. It wasn't easy for Pavel Popovich either.[3] He was in direct communication with the crew. His assignment, among other things, also included psychological support for the crew.

But what were they to do? Minister Afanasyev, Mishin, Kerimov, Strogonov, Komissarov, Karas, Popov, Tsarev, and Spitsa were people with whom one could not raise one's voice; one couldn't tell them: "Don't disrupt my work!" Maintaining his enviable unflappability, Rauschenbach was reviewing the task for the upcoming corrections with Bashkin and the ballistics experts and

---

3. Pavel Romanovich Popovich (1930–2009) was one of the original group of cosmonauts chosen in 1960. He flew the *Vostok-4* mission in 1963 and was, at the time of *Soyuz-10*, head of the 1st Directorate at the Cosmonaut Training Center.

explaining—in rather unintelligible terms—to the chiefs gathered around them the causes for the preceding failure.

"The correction time," he said, "changes depending on the calculations of the ballistics experts, who adjust the orbits based on the measurements taken during each orbit. The cosmonauts received the data for the beginning of the correction very late, and when they pressed the key on the console, the ionic orientation system's readiness for orientation was reset."

During his explanation a report came over the loudspeaker: "*Soyuz-10* correction designated for 0134 hours, engine operation time 17 seconds."

Yeliseyev reported that orientation had been executed and they were ready for correction. No. 35 (NIP-15) confirmed that the settings had been input into the DOS for the corrective acceleration at 0254 hours.[4] I requested that a command be issued to the DOS to switch on the television cameras for an orientation check. Mishin was arguing about something with Kerimov, and suddenly they both demanded reports about backup scenarios in the event that *Igla* were to fail.

At that time *Soyuz-10* was in our tracking stations' coverage zone, but we couldn't properly conduct conversations with the crew. Mishin and Kerimov repeatedly interrupted flight management demanding continuous reports. At that time, to make matters worse, information came through about some glitch in the *Saturn* system for monitoring the stations' orbits.[5] Usually such glitches are not reported. Kerimov and Mishin broke out in a furor at the ballistics experts and at Bogomolov. Reports from the loudspeaker cut into the general uproar:

"Rendezvous is in progress. Soyuz is 2 seconds ahead of *Salyut*."

"Why are you giving it to us in seconds? Give it to us in kilometers!"

"*Granit* is reporting: radio lock-on has occurred, *Igla* is operating."[6]

Agadzhanov couldn't stand it, and, despite the presence of his direct superiors—Generals Karas and Spitsa—he yelled into the microphones feeding out to the general conference line and communication with the crew: "I read you, range 10 kilometers. Don't disrupt my work!"

---

4. NIP-15 was located at Galenki (a village near Ussuriysk) in the Primorskiy Kray on the eastern seaboard of the Russian landmass.

5. Chertok is referring to the *Saturn-MS* and *Saturn-MSD* systems developed and installed at various NIPs to support tracking of lunar and interplanetary probes in the 1960s. In 1971, a *Saturn-MSD* system was installed at NIP-15. The complex included a P-400 parabolic dish with a mirror diameter of 32 meters.

6. *Granit* (Granite) was the call sign of the *Soyuz-10* crew.

Evidently, the last statement caused bewilderment on board. The cosmonauts were offended: "We're reporting on the rendezvous progress according to the readings on the console."

Over the general uproar and conversations, I was trying not to miss any reports from the analysis group or crew about an off-nominal situation.

"If I don't have a stroke after this work, it will be a miracle," Ivan Meshcheryakov managed to mutter, as he gave the latest instructions via high-frequency communications to the computer center in Bolshevo.[7]

"Why aren't you reporting about the completion of the orbit?" asked Kerimov.

Agadzhanov, barely managing to control his temper (he was conducting talks with *Granit*), reported loudly: "*Igla* is operating, I read you, this is for *Granit*. Range 11 kilometers—that's for the guests."

"What's going on with you—first 10, then 11 kilometers? Who's the culprit?" asked Mishin.

The minister behaved more calmly than anyone.

Agadzhanov continued: "We have shutdown of the propulsion system on DOS! *Granit* is reporting about the operation of its engine. The program for orbit No. 81 has been completed. The engine on DOS operated for 60 seconds. This is 12.[8] *Granit*, during orbit No. 82, we're awaiting the most crucial reports from you about the operation of *Igla* and automatic rendezvous mode."

"Why so many unnecessary words?" fumed Mishin.

"Well, he's giving information for communication with the crew, playing the role of commentator for the State Commission, and giving orders throughout the entire Command and Measurement Complex," I said, trying to defend Agadzhanov.

"Orbit No. 82, search in progress."

"All of the KIK systems are operating. *Granit* is reporting: DPO nozzles are winking."

"What do you mean, the nozzles are 'winking,' what kind of nonsense are you talking?"

"Don't get distracted," I say to Agadzhanov, "they can wait!"

"NIP-16 is receiving via the *Saturn* system. DPOs are operating 20 seconds, 25 seconds, 30 seconds, 35 seconds, 40 seconds, 45 seconds...."

"Why don't they shut down on their own?" someone sobbed hysterically.

---

7. This center was located at NII-4.

8. Agadzhanov used the code name "12" during ground-to-crew transmissions. Since the launch of Gagarin in 1961, each contact person on the ground was typically associated with a specific number.

"Approach rate 8 meters per second, stable radio lock-on…."

"We see a bright dot in the periscope. Range—15 kilometers, rate—24."

"Quiet in the control room!"

"But who will explain what is going on, why was it 11 and suddenly the range is 15? Chertok, Mnatsakanyan, Rauschenbach, why are you sitting and doing nothing?"

"*Igla* is doing it for us," answers Mnatsakanyan.

"If you were sitting in the spacecraft, perhaps you would be doing something, but now you need to listen and not interfere," I was the one losing my temper now.

"What a madhouse," says Rauschenbach quietly. "I hope *Igla* doesn't go crazy."

Despite our squabbling, the automatic rendezvous process continued. Over the conference line the telemetry experts, the crew, and NIPs conducted their reports, which the chiefs, eager for action, jumped on. Any person who had not mastered all of our acronyms and in-house jargon would really think that data transmission and flight control were "sheer chaos" and it was high time to punish the out-of-hand GOGU members.

Despite the fact that it was 0400 hours, no one was snoozing in the control room. Reports were coming from space and from the NIPs, and local commentaries were in such abundance that even I didn't always figure out the source of the information. The most reliable information, of course, was the telemetry being processed in real time and the *Granit* reports on *Zarya*. They were coming almost simultaneously. The communications baton was passed seamlessly from NIP to NIP.

"Range 11, rate 26 point 5."

I couldn't restrain myself and said to Agadzhanov sitting next to me at the microphone: "How about that Colonel Voronov—well done! It's just chaotic here in the control room, but communication in the KIK is excellent today all the way to Kamchatka."

"Yes, we're lucky to have Boris Anatolyevich," Agadzhanov just managed to respond.

He was right. Hundreds of KIK officers and soldiers at the NIPs, communications centers, and radio stations invisible and unknown to the top chiefs were doing their jobs calmly and selflessly. Colonel Voronov was in charge of creating and then operating all the KIK communications structures for all of the space programs. He was the KIK deputy chief, but he had a very modest manner and tried not come to the attention of the high-ranking guests.

"Range 8, rate 27 point 5; range 6, rate 27. DPO nozzles are burning. They've begun turning the spacecraft."

"They can't approach at that rate," fretted Mishin. "Why aren't you doing anything? Tell the crew what to do!"

"We don't need to do anything; deceleration will begin now," Rauschenbach reassured Mishin.

"The turn was completed. SKD has executed a deceleration burn; engine is operating—5 seconds, 10 seconds, 13 seconds."

"Range 4, rate 11. DPO nozzles are burning; turn is in progress."

"Range 3 point 5, rate 10. SKDs have fired again. Ten seconds, 15 seconds, 20 seconds, 25 seconds, 30 seconds, 33 seconds—shutdown. Range 2 point 7, rate 8."

"We see the target against the background of Earth, the spacecraft lights are flickering, range 2 point 5, rate 8. We see the target in the periscope…."

Oh, how time seems to stand still! The fear persists that suddenly something inexplicable will happen. It's already 0500 hours! Do these on-board automatic control systems really understand better than we do what to do and when, and they won't slip up? Sitting here in the control room on the seashore, nothing threatens us. But what do they feel, these *Granits*, hurtling through space around the planet for a rendezvous with the DOS?

In response to my unspoken question, Nikolay Gurovskiy hands a note to Tregub. He reads it and holds it out to me: "According to telemetry, Shatalov and Yeliseyev have a pulse rate of over 100 and Rukavishnikov's is 90!"

"They've started another turn. Range 1,600, rate 8. Engine operating—7 seconds. Range 1,200, rate 4, turning again. Range 950, rate 2. Engine firing again—5 seconds. Turn, DPO nozzles flickering."

"We see the object; turning again, SKD firing for 4 seconds; range 800, rate 4."

"This is *Granit*; I have a good, clear view of the target."

This is the last report from the spacecraft before it leaves the coverage zone. Bashkin goes up to Rauschenbach and whispers something.

"Bashkin, Rauschenbach, don't keep secrets, tell us why rendezvous is going so slowly. This is your logic. According to the calculations that were given to me, they should have made contact while they were still in the coverage zone," says Mishin.

"We checked the reserves," answered Rauschenbach. "They had fuel reserves on board for rendezvous for just 13 meters per second for the SKD and 20 kilograms for the DPO. If they enter our coverage zone now, without having docked, we need to make the decision to call it off. We can't risk the fuel reserves for descent."

I reassure the minister: "They understand everything very well there. We talked over such a situation with Yeliseyev. He won't risk it. With Shatalov, I'm convinced they'll make the right decision."

The 30-minute break in the coverage zone was agonizingly long.

"Attention! We're about to begin the communication session of orbit No. 83; readiness 5 minutes!"

"*Granit*, this is 36. I'm giving the count: one, two, three, four...."

"This is *Granit*; I hear you fine! At 0447 hours we executed manual final approach. We had contact and mechanical capture. Retraction began. But in the 9th minute the docking and internal transfer system (SSVP) mode halted; retraction wasn't completed.[9] Docking isn't working. We don't know why. Look at the telemetry. Can you suggest what to do?"

"Where are the docking experts?"

Zhivoglotov, Vakulin, and Syromyatnikov appeared. They were pale and uneasy. They simply had not expected that of all the possible hypothetical failures, the one that would occur bore no resemblance to anything that had happened during ground testing.

Stammering from agitation, Zhivoglotov explained to the hushed control room: "The rod, which is the probe of the active docking assembly, was extended in front of the docking surface. The entire distance for complete retraction using the ball screw is 390 millimeters. Retraction began normally on a signal from the automatics. There was a retraction of 300 millimeters and then it stopped. The retracting mechanism was working and trying to draw in, but the gap between the surfaces of the active and passive assemblies didn't decrease. It is 90 millimeters. The possible causes are very preliminary:

- there was an error in the installation of the centering pins by 180 degrees;
- there was a manufacturing error when aligning the axes, which is highly unlikely;
- the hydraulic connectors have gotten hung up on each other, although this is 50 millimeters rather than 90;
- there was an error with the electrical connectors, if their housings have gotten hung up, which gives just 30 millimeters;
- the assembly has gotten hung up on supplemental reinforcing brackets; we call them balconies, but this was checked very thoroughly at the factory;
- it is possible that there is dirt on the screw—true, it would take lot of dirt to stop the screw dead;
- ice formed upon insertion into space—but there was no rain during liftoff, and the ice would have melted under the pressure of the screw; and
- finally, it is possible that the side levers broke—there was a very intense rolling motion right after capture."

---

9. SSVP—*Sistema stykovki i vnutrennego perekhoda.*

"Why rolling? Where were the dynamics? Rauschenbach! Why were there oscillations?" Mishin demanded an answer.

An unpleasant thought tore through me. I asked Pavel Popovich, who was communicating with *Granit* at that moment: "Ask *Granit* to describe the oscillations during retraction."

"There's no need to ask. Yeliseyev reported that after capture the DPO nozzles indicator lit up and blinked for about 30 seconds. During that time the vehicle rocked intensely."

I understood that further questioning of the docking specialists would be futile, and after consulting with Rauschenbach and Tregub, I laid out for Mishin and Kerimov my version of what had happened: "Most likely a mechanical failure occurred due to the large lateral oscillations. We didn't shut down the control system. Right off the bat, as soon as contact was made, disturbance occurred, which the angular rate sensors monitored. The control system tried to compensate for the angular deviation, but capture had already taken place, so instead of settling down, rocking began, but rather than about the center of mass, it was on the rod that was engaged with the DOS in the receiving drogue. We broke something. It's useless to continue docking attempts. We need to make the decision to undock."

However, it turned out that it wasn't so easy to give the command to undock; that is, the command could be given, but that didn't mean that the spacecraft would undock from the station. According to the electrical diagram, which Zhivoglotov and Vakulin were bent over while Tregub and I tried to elbow our way between them, it turned out that we needed to "go back to square one" for undocking. Undocking would proceed if the electrical connectors were mated beforehand and the SSVP mode was executed in its entirety.

The system had been developed in a purely automatic version, and no provisions for human intervention were included in the process of executing intermediate operations. The logic of the automatics was technically correct. After the tip of the active assembly's probe entered the receiving well of the passive assembly's cone, the latches captured it and issued the "capture" signal. This signal initiated the retraction of the active and passive parts. The ball screw pulled the rod into the active assembly. Retraction continued until the electrical and hydraulic connectors were mated. After the mating of the connectors, special hooks, which emerged from the active assembly and pulled the passive assembly toward it, performed final retraction ensuring the pressure integrity and strength of the interface between the two spacecraft. Only after this did the latches holding the head of the probe in the cone's receiving drogue open. The rod retracted completely into the active assembly.

The "undock" command could be issued over the command radio link from Earth or from the Soyuz console. Upon receiving this command, the retracting hooks are retracted and the vehicle is released from its mechanical connection with the DOS. The DPO executes a back-out burn, and the spacecraft separate. In this long chain of operations there was no provision for the possibility of undocking if the entire docking cycle had not been executed. The "undock" command wasn't capable of freeing a probe that was firmly held by the latches of the passive part of the docking assembly. It is true that an emergency undocking provision had been made for such an off-nominal event. Upon receiving an emergency command, an explosive cartridge jettisons the probe from the active part. But in so doing, it would remain in the passive cone, and redocking with the other vehicle is now impossible.

"Well, way to go, you guys. You dreamed up an assembly in which 'mama' won't let go of 'papa'," Andrey Karas needled us.

"We have a reliable emergency alternative—jettisoning the docking assembly. True, in this case we free the vehicle, but the probe and levers will stay on the DOS 'with mama'."

"This amputation is no good. Do you want to lose the first orbital station, or what? Find a way to deceive your super intelligent system," said the minister.

An incredibly tragic situation had developed. We couldn't separate the vehicle from the DOS so that another vehicle could make a second attempt at docking.

"There's an alternative," said Zhivoglotov timidly. "We need to get to our instrument in the vehicle's Habitation Compartment, find connector Sh28/201, and on the instrument side place a jumper on plug pins No. 30 and No. 34. Then from the console issue a docking command and remove the jumper. The command will pass through the circuit, removing the stops that the rod is getting held up on in the receiving well of the cone. We'll sort of unlatch the door from the other side."

"Brilliant idea, but who on board the spacecraft will be able to perform such an operation?"

"Rukavishnikov performed harder tricks as an electrical engineer before he became a cosmonaut. Of course, never in space," I said.

For about an hour and a half we composed detailed instructions and transmitted them on board.

"We read you," responded the *Granits*, albeit without any enthusiasm.

And suddenly one of the docking specialists recalled that there was one more alternative. Supposedly, it was possible to issue a command to the DOS rather than to the vehicle, and this command would release the latches and thus free the rod.

"That's all well and good, but now the entire mass of the vehicle is hanging from these latches and the drive simply does not have enough force to open this lock."

"We'll give it a try. Perhaps, over the time needed for the command to take effect, the vehicle will rock and the amount of force on the latches will turn out to be small."

We grasped at this straw. During the 84th orbit, this unprecedented (at that time) operation was executed, and during the 85th orbit at 0844 hours, the undock command was received.

"Undocking occurred, DPO executed a back-out burn," reports came in simultaneously from on board and from the analysis group.

The *Soyuz-10* spacecraft and *Salyut* orbital station had flown for just under 5 hours in a mated state. Hardly anyone had believed in our gamble with a successful undocking. For that reason, reports about the undocking caused considerably greater elation than during a normal docking. When the first dust settled, a group of docking specialists approached me and with obvious embarrassment reported "in confidence" that they didn't understand why the undocking operation had worked. It shouldn't have!

Next came preparations for descent and landing. Agadzhanov and Tregub could manage just fine without Rauschenbach and me. The State Commission was preoccupied with the crew's return to Earth. Rauschenbach and I got on the high-frequency communication line with Kalashnikov, Vilnitskiy, and Legostayev, who had also been up all night in Podlipki, and fired them up about the unacceptable oscillations and the need to immediately set up experiments in shop No. 439 to simulate what had happened that night.

When we were back in Star City after landing on 26 April, we heard from the cosmonauts. Spacecraft commander Shatalov reported first: "The vehicle has good maneuverability, it responds very well during manual control. All the dynamic operations were performed without any glitches. It is true, when *Igla* took over rendezvous control I was somewhat ill at ease from the frequent turns and SKD burns. At a range of 140 meters I took over control for the final approach process. Manual final approach proceeded right away, without incident. It was easier for me than on *Soyuz-4* and *-5*. Contact was soft; there was no rattling or grating. As soon as capture occurred, the vehicle rolled to the right as much as 30 degrees, then swung back to the left. The oscillation period was 7 seconds. We were afraid we would lose the docking assembly altogether. Then the oscillations subsided. What happened during retraction, we couldn't imagine. Undocking proceeded smoothly. Visually, the station's condition looks good. It's too bad, of course, that we weren't able to get inside. Landing took place in complete darkness. We did a somersault."

Before they landed, Yeliseyev realized the fundamental error that they had committed in the dynamics of docking control. He told his story with more emotion than Shatalov.

"Everything was going normally, and on the whole the vehicle systems also were functioning normally. But why did the 'DPO Nozzles' indicator light up after contact and why did we flail from side to side? It shouldn't have lit up. They were the reason we were rocking so. I am amazed we didn't completely break the docking assembly. I attempted to perform a background correction of the ARS emergency range meter developed in Leningrad. The marker wandered between two and two and a half kilometers. We need to develop a method for tuning the ARS. With their instructions, the 'ground' left us very little time to prepare for correction."

Rukavishnikov complained: "With the temperature in the spacecraft set at 20°C [68°F], it's very cold to sleep in a flight suit. We slept just 2 or 3 hours. Instead of sleeping you sit and shiver. We need sleeping bags. Communication in the coverage zone is good. But when we left the zone, we were left with no communication—that's bad. When the big oscillations began, we wanted to switch on manual control and manually compensate for these disturbances, but we were afraid to."

Shatalov interrupted Rukavishnikov: "We approached with virtually zero misalignment between the vehicle and station axes. That's why we simply didn't expect that such oscillations would begin. The probe entered the receiving drogue softly, without any impact. And suddenly something started that we absolutely did not expect. Before docking, the pressure in the DPO tanks was 220 atmospheres, and afterwards it was just 140. We used up an incredibly large amount on this turbulence."

After these frank conversations with us, the crew met with correspondents hungry for space news. Everything was presented to them as if there had been no intention of performing a transfer into the station. This was just a rehearsal, and it demonstrated the reliability of all the systems.

The official report stated: "On 24 April, cosmonauts V. A. Shatalov, A. S. Yeliseyev, N. N. Rukavishnikov on *Soyuz-10* conducted a series of experiments in joint flight with the *Salyut* station. These included the testing of new docking mechanisms." The *Kosmonavtika: Entsiklopediya* (*Cosmonautics: An Encyclopedia*) states that the goal of the flight was to perform a "trial run of the improved docking system of the *Soyuz-10* spacecraft with the *Salyut* orbital station."[10]

---

10. In the 1985 edition of this book, the editors note that "docking and joint flight of the [*Salyut*] station with the *Soyuz-10* [spacecraft] was performed in the first stage [of the station's mission]. Systems were verified which ensured search, approach, and docking of the [spacecraft] with the station. Due to a malfunction in the docking equipment of the *Soyuz-10* [spaceship], the transfer of the crew into [*Salyut*] did not take place." See V. P. Glushko, ed., *Kosmonavtika: entsiklopediya* (Moscow: Sovetskaya entsiklopediya, 1985), p. 342.

When we returned from Star City to Podlipki, we gave free rein to self-criticism.

"What a bunch of jerks we are!" fumed Rauschenbach. "Nobody foresaw that immediately upon contact we needed to shut down the control system, and certainly shut down the DPO, and on and on."

By the end of the day we had discussed a list of modifications with Lev Vilnitskiy, Viktor Kuzmin, Vladimir Syromyatnikov, and Vsevolod Zhivoglotov. The probe should begin to retract only after the vehicle's oscillations subside. We needed to have the capability to control the rod manually: pulling in and backing out. All the automatics needed to have manual control backup! The dynamics specialists needed to reduce the impact velocity to 0.2 meter per second. We needed to install a special console on the Soyuz for manual docking control capability. But most importantly, God helps those who help themselves—in addition to the alignment levers around the rod, we decided to engineer a sort of "jabot," just not a lacy one, but a good steel collar that would take up the load during oscillations.

"Everyone get started right away! When will the documentation for the modifications come out?" the usual question was asked.

"Allowing for night work, we'll have the memorandum and clean copy for you by tomorrow evening," answered Vilnitskiy.

"Good, let's call Khazanov."

Khazanov straight away ordered that the shop process engineers team up with the designers.

"The shops have no more than a week to modify the assemblies and instruments," he ordered.

I reported our proposals to Mishin over the telephone. He approved and warned us:

"Tomorrow Ustinov and Serbin are coming to shop No. 439. They want to have a look at the docking assemblies and docking process. Prepare posters, rehearse docking, explain everything, and show the measures we're taking."

"Pipe all hands on deck! We're moving over to shop No. 439!" I commanded Kalashnikov and Vilnitskiy.

After the unsuccessful docking of *Soyuz-10* with *Salyut*, demonstrating the process to Central Committee Secretary Ustinov and Central Committee Defense Department Chief Serbin was an extremely critical matter. They had promised the top political leaders that the piloted orbital station would reduce the impact that the four U.S. lunar expeditions had made on our populace.[11]

---

11. By this time, three American crews had landed on the Moon, on *Apollo 11* (in July 1969), *12* (in November 1969), and *14* (in January–February 1971). The next mission, *Apollo 15*, was scheduled for July 1971.

Ustinov and the Central Committee *apparat*, and ultimately Serbin as well, had backed the initiative of the enthusiasts—Bushuyev, Okhapkin, Chertok, Rauschenbach, and Feoktistov—and with the considerable efforts of Minister Afanasyev, at the expense of Chelomey's operations, in just a little over a year and a half had helped build and insert into space a real orbital station.

They notified the whole world about this. And suddenly the transport vehicle crew, after brilliantly executing approach and docking, couldn't enter the station. How do you explain that to the "people upstairs?" Brezhnev would still understand. Kosygin would say that this was slovenliness again and that enormous sums of money were being wasted. But the others simply wouldn't understand what's what. The Central Committee and VPK took our failure very badly.

It had been two and a half years since Beregovoy's unsuccessful docking.[12] Over that time, Shatalov had flown twice. The first time he achieved a successful docking.[13] The second time, the docking process failed, supposedly through the fault of the radio system.[14] Now finally Shatalov docked, but he couldn't get through to the station. "Who is organizing all of this over there? Who's checking?" These are the questions that Kosygin asked.

After Mishin had explained and shown the high-ranking guests what could break down and interfere with retraction, Serbin asked, "And which one of your people made that? Show me the designer."

Lev Vilnitskiy wasn't about to wait until he was pushed forward out of the crowd of administrators gathered there, and emerging into the "line of fire," he decided to seize the initiative from the "attacker."

"Department Chief Vilnitskiy. Request permission to report," the former captain introduced himself military-style. "This docking assembly has been radically remodeled compared with the ones that have already been tested three times in flight. It has been integrated with an internal transfer structure. We must not only join the vehicle with the DOS, but also provide a pressurized transfer tunnel. We calculated the strength of all the mechanisms using our experience in terms of impact velocity, lateral velocities, and possible angles of deviation, which were obtained during the three preceding dockings. A whole series of dockings were conducted preliminarily on this unit. After the experiments, many parts were modified. Docking began normally. But during

---

12. In October 1968, during the *Soyuz-3* mission, Beregovoy failed to dock with the automated *Soyuz-2*.

13. Shatalov successfully conducted a docking during the *Soyuz-4/5* joint mission in January 1969.

14. This was a reference to the failed docking attempt of *Soyuz-7/8* in October 1969.

retraction, the Soyuz rocked vis-à-vis the DOS at substantially larger angles than we expected. Here, on this unit, we have reproduced an analogous mode and found the weak point. We understand everything, and in a week a newly modified assembly will arrive for testing."

"So, you order that a TASS report be issued saying that Comrade Vilnitskiy made a mistake? In a week he'll make amends, and the next crew will make their way through the hatch to the *Salyut*."

"For me, it's an honor to be in a TASS report, but the next docking will proceed normally, I give you my word."

"You all know how to give your word, and then you miss deadlines, hoping for full impunity."

Vilnitskiy didn't have time to respond. Ustinov broke in: "The minister can sort out whom to punish and how to punish without us, but you show us what hatch the crew needs to crawl through from the spacecraft to the DOS."

Now Isaak Khazanov, coming to Vilnitskiy's rescue, quickly climbed up onto the service ladder in order to show how the hatch covers open in the docking assembly. I'm probably not the only one who breathed a sign of relief. After catching sight of Khazanov, Ustinov brightened. Perhaps he was remembering Boris Abramovich Khazanov—a major general, though at the beginning of the war, he was a military engineer first class, "specially commissioned by the people's commissar of armament of the USSR [i.e., Ustinov] in support of missions of the State Committee of Defense."

During the war, Ustinov threw Boris Khazanov into the most difficult artillery arms production sites. Khazanov Senior never let you down. He devoted all of his professional knowledge, moral courage, and physical strength to his work. In 1942 he was named director of the artillery factory in Krasnoyarsk. Under extremely difficult conditions, he pulled the factory out of a deep failure. Back then he had a bitter clash with the Central Committee's authorized representative, Serbin. But Ustinov did not allow reprisals against Khazanov.

And now, a quarter century later, Khazanov's son was showing Ustinov a spacecraft docking assembly. After seeing for the first time the hole that a cosmonaut was supposed to crawl through, Ustinov was amazed: "Who in the world can squeeze through that tunnel? Even in weightlessness I couldn't do it."

We had argued with the planners a great deal about the diameter of the hatch. Ustinov had hit a raw nerve. During the design process I had fought for a hatch diameter of one meter, as the Apollo had. Feoktistov, enjoying the authority of chief planner and the experience of a former cosmonaut, "squeezed" the designers down to a diameter of 800 millimeters. Bushuyev backed him up. Now he needed to come to Vilnitskiy's rescue, and I gave Bushuyev a hard nudge.

"And we won't let you, Dmitriy Fedorovich," said Bushuyev, after quickly pushing Vilnitskiy aside. "The Americans have a bigger diameter on the Apollo—almost a meter.[15] When we told [the Americans] that ours was 800 millimeters, they were undaunted and believed that that's enough."

Now factory director Klyucharev joined in the argument that was flaring up.

"Dmitriy Fedorovich, I must report to you that for docking with the Americans the designers are designing a completely new docking assembly. We are going to have to do a trial run all over again."

"What, you do all this work and then start everything from the beginning again?" fumed Ustinov.

"Yes, we've begun negotiations, in which we've arrived at the idea of an androgynous assembly. So that neither side will be offended, we're going to make completely identical halves on each vehicle."

"And why do you call it androgynous? What does that mean?"

Now Vilnitskiy came to Bushuyev's aid: "It's a 'hermaphrodite' assembly. Unlike our current system, where the active rod goes into the passive cone, here the structures on the active and passive sides are identical. Hermaphroditus, as the ancient Greeks believed, was the son of Hermes and Aphrodite. He was so handsome that the gods made him bisexual. We considered it improper to introduce the term 'hermaphrodite' into technical documentation. Therefore, we used terminology used in botany for bisexual plants—'androgynes'."

"Yes, there's never a dull moment with you," concluded Ustinov.

"Everything's ready; we request permission to begin," Khazanov addressed Ustinov, anticipating the danger of a debate on the subject of new development.

The attention of the brass switched to the mockup of the active vehicle, which with its extended probe was driving toward the passive cone on the weight equivalent of the DOS. Low-impact dynamic parameters were selected on the experimental unit to demonstrate docking to the brass. The impact of the probe against the inner surface of the cone, its capture by the receiving drogue, the subsequent rocking of the vehicle mockup, and the entire retraction process had a pacifying effect on the high-ranking guests.

When the high-ranking Party leaders had departed and we were comparing notes with one another, the relieved Khazanov confided: "We wanted to begin right away with the docking show, but the dirty rotten 'visit effect' kicked in. Zhivoglotov had some sort of problem on the console. While Serbin was hearing Vilnitskiy's confession and then Ustinov was hearing Bushuyev's, we

---

15. The Unified Crew Hatch on the Apollo Command Module had a diameter of 74 centimeters. The forward docking hatch had a diameter of 76 centimeters.

336

found the glitch. When I worked under Vasiliy Gavrilovich Grabin, he taught us: 'If you want to convince irate superiors of something, there's no point in arguing and annoying them with verbosity. You need to quickly demonstrate it "for real" at the firing range or in the shop. The brass will become familiar with your ideas, they'll calm down, and there will be no reprimands.' "

"The example of Grabin suggests otherwise," I retorted to Khazanov. "Stalin was never in the shops, much less at the firing range, but he always backed Grabin, while Ustinov, who saw everything, was his enemy."

These events marked the beginning of a rush job to perform modifications and all manner of tests on the "rod-cone" docking assembly. Vilnitskiy, Syromyatnikov, Utkin, Zhivoglotov, Bobkov, Rozenberg, Vakulin, Chizhikov—I could go on and on with the list of people who were involved. In two shifts they conducted a series of tests with production workers, checking the structural strength and the logic of the new automatics. The assembly was subjected to various static loads, to the point of failure. They varied the rates and angles of approach from nominal values to the maximum possible emergency situation values.

The automatic and manual docking control structures and logic optimized in 1971, with small improvements as statistics were accumulated, have now been operating failure-free for 37 years. They were used on the *Mir* orbital station for 15 years and have been in service on the Russian segment of the International Space Station for eight years now.[16]

As for the androgynous assembly, in 1975 it supported the docking and meeting of the *Soyuz-19* and *Apollo* crews. After this, it was used in our domestic programs only one more time, during the docking of *Soyuz TM-16* with one of the *Mir* station modules.[17] An objective comparison of our versions and American versions of docking assemblies gives preference to ours without much hairsplitting. Few people are aware that in 1971 engineer Vladimir Syromyatnikov took on the responsibility for the development of docking assemblies for the reusable U.S. Space Shuttle and International Space Station. The Americans declined to compete. Thus, Syromyatnikov's teams, ZEM and the Azov Optical Mechanical Factory, which were small by today's standards, monopolized the field of spacecraft docking design and technology. It is astonishing, but in the 21st century, RKK Energiya continues to hold on

---

16. Chertok wrote this in 2006.

17. *Soyuz TM-16*, with cosmonauts Gennadiy Manakov and Aleksandr Poleshchuk, was launched on 24 January 1993. It docked with *Mir*'s *Kristall* module two days later using the APAS-89 androgynous docking system.

to its monopoly for the delivery of docking assemblies to the U.S. for Space Shuttles and for the new European transport vehicle.[18]

---

18. The European transport vehicle that Chertok mentions here is the ATV (Automated Transfer Vehicle).

Chapter 15
Sun City

After the first unsuccessful "appointment" with the *Soyuz-10* spacecraft launched on 19 April 1971, the DOS continued to fly in unpiloted mode. The program of science experiments that were supposed to be conducted suffered due to the fact that the cover of the infrared telescope had not been jettisoned. This greatly reduced the value of the science program. TASS reports said nothing about the failure of the cover to open or the incomplete docking process. At press conferences the crew made no mention of the docking node's breakdown. Everything supposedly had gone according to the program—period.

We needed to rehabilitate the piloted orbital station flight program as soon as possible. For that reason, work was under way 24 hours a day to prepare *Soyuz-11*.

Shabarov performed the duties of technical chief at the firing range. According to his reports, preparations were going according to schedule and liftoff could take place on 6 June. Mishin had also put Shabarov in charge of technical management of the preparation of Block D at Site No. 31. This time the fourth stage of Chelomey's UR-500K launch vehicle—our Block D—was being tasked with sending interplanetary stations *Mars-2* and *Mars-3* to Mars. The launches of these stations were tied hard and fast to the astronomical deadlines of 19 and 28 May. These new spacecraft differed substantially from our *Mars-1*, which we launched during the days of the Cuban Missile Crisis in 1962. Each of them had an orbital compartment and a descent module. Babakin's team had done an enormous amount of work to ensure the reliability of these interplanetary stations. We were also in a rush because the launch of N-1 No. 6L was scheduled for June.

On 24 May on Miusskaya Square, the State Commission convened in the hall of the ministerial collegium, where I thought my report about the results of all the work conducted on docking dynamics would finally be the last one. A group comprising Okhotsimskiy, Legostayev, Voropayev, and Lebedev had done an excellent job preparing the materials. Right off the bat, Dmitriy

Okhotsimskiy had discovered our weak spot.[1] Voropayev's department was responsible for the rocket flight dynamics, Legostayev's department for spacecraft control dynamics, and Vilnitskiy's department for loads on the docking assembly after docking. But the dynamics of the process from the moment of contact until retraction were ownerless.

Vilnitskiy's report about the measures taken to protect the docking assembly structure against the dynamic environment, which he illustrated with good posters, convinced the collegium that the theoreticians were the culprits rather than the designers. The members of the collegium weren't about to penetrate into the depths of dynamics, and discussion ended at this ministerial level.

On 25 May, a month after Ustinov and Serbin visited shop No. 439, we reported at the Kremlin to the VPK about the launch readiness of the *Soyuz-11* spacecraft for docking with the DOS. Mishin made the traditional general report about the work performed and readiness for launch. Using posters, I gave a very brief report (as the VPK staffers had requested of me beforehand, having arranged it with [VPK Chairman] Smirnov) about what had caused the docking node on *Soyuz-10* to fail and the actions we had taken. To my astonishment, not one of the VPK members asked a single question.

After my speech, Keldysh deemed it necessary to say that, at the request of Minister Afanasyev, specialists of his institute had participated in a study of the dynamics of the docking process and in the development of measures guaranteeing its reliability.[2]

Next, the primary and backup crews were introduced. The primary crew was made up of Aleksey Leonov, Valeriy Kubasov, and Petr Kolodin. Georgiy Dobrovolskiy, Vladislav Volkov, and Viktor Patsayev formed the backup crew. [State Commission chairman] Kerimov reported that the launch was scheduled for 6 June 1971 and, considering its particularly critical nature, asked the chief designers to be there "in person." This call to action, which had become standard by now, did not elicit any emotions. "Tomorrow morning the State Commission will fly out," concluded Kerimov.

May in Moscow was unusually rainy and cold. At the airfield, as we were walking to our airplane, an icy north wind cut through us. Our group—Kerimov, Severin, Darevskiy, Yurevich, and Pravetskiy—gladly warmed up with the hot tea that Khvastunov arranged for them soon after takeoff. Over

---

1. Dmitriy Yevgenyevich Okhotsimskiy (1921–2005) was one of the leading Soviet applied mathematicians involved in the Soviet space program. He was employed as a scientist at the Institute of Applied Mathematics of the Academy of Sciences.

2. The institute in question was the Institute of Applied Mathematics of the Academy of Sciences.

tea, Khvastunov—a Hero of the Soviet Union, combat pilot, and the current chief of our flight squadron—astonished doctor of medical sciences Pravetskiy.

I was conversing with avid downhill skier Gay Severin about his latest accomplishments. He complained about acute pains in his legs and about space technology, which were both interfering with his ski jumps and falls.

"I can give you some advice regarding your legs," Khvastunov broke into our conversation. "After the war I flew a lot as an instructor, and suddenly my legs 'gave out.' I couldn't walk at all. They dragged me to hospital after hospital—nothing helped. It was terrible: they were going to write me off into retirement. But my dear old mother cured me. She put me to bed at her house in the village and covered my legs with raw potatoes. Three days later I stood up. And, as you can see, I'm flying."

"And you had no relapses?" asked Pravetskiy.

"None. As if nothing had ever been wrong."

After a little more than three hours' flight from cold Moscow, we found ourselves in hot Tyuratam at Dalniy airfield, formerly Lastochka. Later, for some reason, they renamed it Krayniy.[3]

Shabarov, who met us, dumbfounded me: "It's 36 degrees [96°F] here now, but for you it's going to be even hotter. There's a serious glitch in the docking system in the latest tests."

After arriving at Site No. 2, I dashed into the hotel to toss off my warm jacket. And without grabbing some lunch, I set off on foot under the scorching Sun to the MIK. I was itching to find out what the docking and internal transfer system had in store for us now.

Oh, this path from the hotel to the MIK! I have been walking it since the spring of 1957. It used to be a dusty dirt trail from the special train, then from the barracks to the MIK standing all by itself on the steppe. Now, shady poplar trees along the asphalt protect the pedestrian from the scorching sun. After the checkpoint, where a soldier scrutinized my pass, I was in the "garden." A group of control specialists and engine experts, who were heatedly arguing with one another, greeted me from a cozy gazebo.

In the testing hall our specialists and military testers were crowded around the manual control console for the docking mechanism, arguing. They explained to me that the previous day, during the performance of a test operation to extend the probe three times, they decided to make sure that in the retraction process, no erroneous cosmonaut actions would lead to the firing of the DPO nozzles, which caused the breakdown of the node on *Soyuz-10*. For this,

---

3. The Russian word *dalniy* means "far," while *krayniy* means "farthest."

Bashkin demanded that new commands be written into the test instructions. During the tests, in their haste, something got messed up, and the passage of the "undock" command lit up on the console at the wrong time.

Boris Vakulin, Boris Chizhikov, and Yevgeniy Panin—the developers of the docking electrical and mechanical systems—discovered this defect the day before at 4 a.m. It had been two days now that they'd gone without sleep looking for what caused the mysterious signal behavior. First off, I asked them to head over to the hotel and get some sleep. And in the morning after they had rested, they should be back here to search for the cause of the glitch in the individual programs. I explained the situation to Kerimov over the telephone and asked him to postpone the State Commission meeting from that evening to 27 May, no earlier than 1700 hours. He grumbled but agreed.

The next morning they ran five individual programs. And immediately everything became clear to everyone. In the circuit of the test console they discovered an "extra" relay, supposedly protecting the overload coupling against possible operator error. The circuit in which this relay was located did not participate in operations at the KIS or at the engineering facility. It was only needed during the testing process of the docking assembly when it was being assembled and handed over at the factory in shop No. 444. This relay failed, and the circuit, which wasn't necessary for tests at the engineering facility, turned out to be hooked up and displayed false commands.

The overnight "cerebral eclipse" resulted in the discovery of the failure, which had nothing at all to do with an on-board system. Repeated checks confirmed that the on-board portion of the SSVP was in perfect order.

When everything had been ascertained, signed over, signed off on, and reported to the chairman of the State Commission, I walked out of the stuffy MIK with a light heart, sat down in the cozy gazebo, and lit up a cigarette with great pleasure. Pravetskiy and Severin dropped by the gazebo for a "puff." They had their own problems with the cosmonauts' spacesuits and life-support equipment.

"From your blissful expression I gather that you've caught the *bobik* that disrupted the State Commission for us," said the always upbeat Severin, squinting cheerfully.[4]

I told them what the situation was.

---

4. Beginning with the first and only ground-firing test in 1947 from Kapustin Yar, testers often used the words *bob* or *bobik* to describe a technical glitch requiring hours to identify and eliminate.

"In medicine this is called a 'paired incident', " said Pravetskiy. "If a patient is brought in with an inexplicable diagnosis, don't hurry. Wait. A second patient will certainly appear, and he will help form the diagnosis of the first."

As a result of such a seemingly stupid mistake in the testing procedure, we lost a day. But losses of time and rattling of nerves did not end there. An installer from our factory brigade, who was referred to as an "old hand," was standing next to the open hatch of the instrumentation compartment during a leak test on the [Soyuz] spacecraft's thermal control system.

"Suddenly," he said, "I heard a 'pshh' and saw a 'cloudlet' that smelled like a hot iron."

He called over a testing officer, and he supposedly also saw the "cloudlet."

If "pshh" and a "cloudlet" were signs of a loss of pressure integrity in the thermal control system (STR), then this meant a no-go for the launch.[5] They started retesting. They raised and then released the pressure in the system several times. Then they called for a delay of 12 hours. There were no signs of leaks and no more "pshh." On the night of 28 May, the haggard STR testers guaranteed pressure integrity and approval for handing over the vehicle for the irreversible fueling operations.

But right then and there the issue arose: how were they to write out "pshh" and "cloudlet" in the logbook? What was this? And what if the STR didn't come into play here at all? Perhaps it was some other instrument that went "pshh," and the cloudlet was smoke from it? What if the nature of the "pshh" was electrical rather than pneumatic?

Lead designer Yuriy Semyonov called for lead tester Boris Zelenshchikov to write a full explanation in the logbook of what had actually happened and what they spent time on. Zelenshchikov asked for a timeout to consult with lead military tester Vladimir Yaropolov. After a 30-minute private discussion, both testers announced: "If you demand guarantees from us disavowing the 'pshh' and 'cloudlet', we ask permission to repeat integrated test No. 1 in its entirety, which will take 12 hours."

If the integrated tests were repeated to this extent, then rollout to the launch site would be postponed from 3 June to 4 or 5 June and it would be impossible to launch on 6 June. Postponing the launch date would be a disaster! What's more, we had just reported at the Kremlin that we were ready for launch on 6 June! Yet Semyonov, Feoktistov, and I convened a small review team at which we all voted in favor of repeating the integrated tests.

---

5. STR—*Sistema termoregulirovaniya.*

Now we needed to quickly seek out Shabarov, who had driven out to Chelomey's Site No. 81, where that day, 28 May, the launch of Babakin's interplanetary automatic station *Mars-3* was supposed to take place. Then we needed to find Kerimov. He was supposed to make the decision in the State Commission to postpone the launch.

We decided to drive with Semyonov and Patrushev to Site No. 81. The Mars launch was scheduled for 2028 hours. We still had time; they had only just announced T minus 2 hours there. We needed to race 50 kilometers. In order to go through the checkpoint, we were supposed to get a gas mask. That was the fundamental difference between Chelomey's and Korolev's launch sites.[6]

In the office of the "Martian" State Commission, old acquaintances— Glushko's deputy, Viktor Radutnyy; Pilyugin's deputy for flight tests, Georgiy Kirilyuk; Yuriy Trufanov from the ministry; firing range Chief Aleksandr Kurushin; and State Commission Chairman Aleksandr Maksimov (behind his back everyone called him "San Sanych")—were busy with amicable prelaunch conversations.[7] Sergey Kryukov, our former chief planner, was now Babakin's first deputy. (He didn't work well with Mishin, but Babakin and Kryukov were very happy with one another).[8]

We called Shabarov into another office and began to try to persuade him. He agreed to rerun the integrated tests, but we still needed to track down Kerimov. Kurushin wouldn't let us go, and before the launch he invited our entire crew for a "soldier's pilaf" on the occasion of his birthday.[9] I don't know whether it was really soldier's pilaf, but that particular evening we considered it magnificent.

We admired the launch of the UR-500K from the observation post. The red disk of the Sun was just touching the horizon and dramatically illuminated the rocket as it lifted off with a roar. Separation of the stages took place like a color animation display against the background of the darkened sky. Without waiting for the report about the flight's progress toward Mars, we dashed off to the airfield in pursuit of Kerimov. Both cosmonaut crews were arriving

---

6. The gas masks were needed because the Proton used toxic storable propellants, while Korolev's rockets used nontoxic cryogenic propellants.

7. "San Sanych" is an informal shortening of the first name and patronymic "Aleksandr Aleksandrovich."

8. Sergey Sergeyevich Kryukov (1918–2005), one of Korolev's most senior deputies, was demoted in 1966 by Korolev's successor, Vasiliy Mishin. In March 1970, disgruntled with the nature of work at TsKBEM, Kryukov left and joined the design bureau at the Lavochkin Factory as a deputy to Georgiy Babakin. After Babakin died in August 1971, Kryukov succeeded him as chief designer.

9. Kurushin had turned 49 on 14 March 1971.

there, and we guessed that Kerimov would have to meet them. As we raced through the dark town, our headlights blinding people strolling after the heat of the day, we arrived at the airfield checkpoint (KPP) and found out that the cosmonauts had already driven out to their quarters at Site No. 17.[10]

We turned around and, slamming on the brakes at the intersections, rushed to find Kerimov at the cosmonauts' base. The cosmonauts had just arrived and were happily talking amongst themselves while unloading their baggage with the trainers and physicians. After we had greeted one another they invited us to dinner, but we had to turn them down. Having telephoned around to all the attendants on duty, we determined that Kerimov had left to find us at Site No. 2. In the service building next to the MIK there was a communications room where flight progress reports poured in. We tore over to Site No. 2 in complete darkness, completing a trip of 170 kilometers. On the way, at the KPP of the "third ascent," we ducked into the line of vehicles and, taking advantage of the delay, got out of the car.[11] Of all things, what a coincidence! A spark flared up in the dark sky, and moving rapidly against the background of stars toward the east, it extinguished before it reached the horizon.

After looking at the time, I guessed: "We just saw the second firing of Block D. By the time we get back, in Yevpatoriya they'll determine how much of an error Block D gave *Mars-3*."

The communications room was crammed full of "Martians" who had come here for communications. The first reports about that beginning of the seven-month flight to Mars had already arrived here from the Yevpatoriya and Moscow ballistics centers. According to the preliminary data, the deviation error was 1,250,000 kilometers, instead of the calculated figure of no more than 250,000 kilometers.

"It's a long trip, you'll be able to correct it," I reassured Kryukov.

"To correct an error like that we'll have to use up precious fuel," fretted Kryukov.[12]

We finally caught up with a disconcerted Kerimov in Patrushev's office and began to explain the situation with the "pshh" and our proposal to rerun the integrated tests and postpone the *Soyuz-11* launch for 24 hours.

---

10. KPP—*Komandnyy punkt polka.*

11. The "third ascent" was one of several observation points at the firing range.

12. *Mars-3*, launched at 1926 hours 30 seconds Moscow Time on 28 May 1971, became the first spacecraft to perform a soft landing on the surface of Mars when it landed on 2 December 1971. Unfortunately, transmissions from the lander ceased only seconds after it began transmitting its first image.

"I can't decide a matter like this at my own discretion. In the morning we will convene the State Commission. This evening, I mean, yesterday," said Kerimov, after glancing at the clock, "I reported to Smirnov that we are confirming the launch for 6 June. And you want me to go find him this morning, on a Saturday, at his home or at his dacha, apologize, and say that I was misled: launch on 6 June is impossible. After this, what kind of confidence can we have in the competence and reliability of our tests?"

There was a long pause. Our spirits hit rock bottom, lost in the contemplation of our own inadequacy. And suddenly! Such miracles really do happen! During this tragic pause Boris Zelenshchikov burst into the office. Usually very calm, he explained with a slight stammer: "The 'pshh' happened again. We can reproduce it."

We rushed downstairs into the testing room. Despite the fact that it was 4 a.m., a large crowd of "well-wishers" huddled around the spacecraft vertical test stand. Sure enough! The "pshh" threatened to ruin the military testers' Sunday, a day that their wives and children looked forward to perhaps even more than they themselves.

Oleg Surguchev, one of the chief developers of the STR, stuttering slightly, explained: " 'Pshh' is the sound of the compensator actuating, if excess pressure gets into it. This shouldn't happen. But our operator made a mistake. We can repeat this mistake and reproduce the 'pshh.' We guarantee that everything is just fine and there is no need for any retesting."

Yaropolov commanded: "Integrated tests for the 'pshh' incident are canceled. Send the spacecraft for fueling. Those who want to can go get some sleep. We'll review the testers' actions at the briefing."

[Chief of the firing range] Kurushin, who had approached us, invited Semyonov, Shabarov, and me to a symposium, which was being held for the first time at the firing range.

"At eleven o'clock in Building Zero. I really hope you'll be there. You still have time to get a little sleep."

It wasn't until 5 a.m. that we finally managed to get to bed. But by 10 a.m., after grabbing a quick breakfast, Shabarov, Feoktistov, Semyonov, and I drove out to the symposium "On the Prospects for the Development of Space Technology and Missions of the Firing Range." TsUKOS Deputy Chief Aleksandr Maksimov delivered a good introductory report.[13]

---

13. TsUKOS had been renamed GUKOS in 1970.

I talked about the prospects for the modular construction of orbital stations with respect to the three dimensions of launch vehicles: 7K-S transport vehicles inserted on R-7s, DOSes on the UR-500K, and the MKBS on the N-1. Sergey Kryukov, who had broken away from talks with Yevpatoriya regarding *Mars-3*, gave a report on plans for the exploration of the Moon, Venus, and Mars using automatic stations. Yevgeniy Vorobyev, chief of the Third Main Directorate of the Ministry of Health and the State Commission member concerned with piloted launches, talked about the biological problems of the human body during long-duration flights.

Aleksandr Kurushin interrupted the discussion that was under way and invited everyone to lunch in honor of his promotion to the rank of lieutenant general. And that is where, between toasts, a real discussion about the fate of the firing range started.

"They call us military installation No. such-and-such," said Kurushin, "and actually, we are the nation's central cosmodrome, where we don't just conduct launches, we also perform large-scale scientific work. State-of-the-art information processing methods and test procedures are being developed; very valuable experience is being focused on ensuring the reliability and safety of rocket-space technology."

Aleksandr Maksimov, somewhat fired up by the preceding toasts, spoke out for the first time regarding the historical mistakes that were made during the design and construction of the firing range.

"In order to be referred to as a cosmodrome rather than a firing range, it needs to have a large centralized base. Now there are many scattered engineering facilities. The firing range was constructed based on old ideas about the inevitability of a nuclear attack, and therefore, the sites are spread out 50 kilometers or more from one another. The entire main engineering and technical staff live with their families in a modern town, but every day they need to drive as much as 100 kilometers to work. This is a waste of precious time, and nothing justifies wastefulness now. Only the launch pads need to be spread out in the interests of safety. There should be a single base for the preparation of all the spacecraft and piloted vehicles. Zenit, Soyuz, DOS, Almaz, Venera, Mars, and Molniya, and perhaps the future MKBS, need to be tested and readied for launch at a single factory base. Such a factory should be located close to town. This will create conditions for recruiting and retaining a workforce. The town still needs to be improved so that people will want to live here. They created a genuine garden city in the middle of the desert in Uzbekistan called Navoi.[14] Are they better than us?"

---

14. Navoi is a town in southwestern Uzbekistan founded in 1958.

No one contradicted Maksimov, and we raised our glasses to the construction in Kazakhstan of a "Space Navoi," which they called Leninsk. Someone began to wax lyrical and in conclusion proposed a toast to "Sun City" [*Gorod solntsa*], about which the utopians of the past century had dreamed.

I proposed to my comrades from Site No. 2: "Kerimov has flown off to Kuybyshev to hand out awards to the Progress Factory and Kozlov. There's no pressing business. No one will be looking for us, let's spend the evening in town as if we were visiting it for the first time."

"Actually, we've only ever seen it from automobiles. We've never had a chance to take a nice stroll," said Pravetskiy.

Everyone accepted the proposal. Semyonov, Feoktistov, Pravetskiy, and I went out to the city of Leninsk—formerly Site No. 10. We didn't have any particular plans, and we decided to start with a movie. The new Saturn Theater was a credit to any in Moscow. It had 1,100 comfortable seats with an excellent view, a large screen, and good acoustics. We were virtually the only grown men in the movie theater. Most of the movie-viewers were young women with children and teenagers. The French film *La Grand Vadrouille* [*The Great Stroll*], with famous stars of the French cinema Bourvil and Louis de Funès, was by no means a children's film.[15] All around us was noise, laughter, and even howling children.

A woman sitting near us explained that there was no one to leave children with at home. On their day off all the husbands go fishing, hunting, or to distant garden plots. These are young families, and there are no grandmothers and grandfathers in the town. We realized this one more time when we went out for a "great stroll" around the town. Among the public decked out in their Sunday best we encountered officers that we knew, who had changed into civilian clothes. Many were with their wives and pushing baby carriages.

"The only other place you might find such a concentration of beautiful, young, tanned women is at a southern resort," noted Pravetskiy.

"Yesterday at the symposium Vorobyev said that Leninsk had moved into first place in the nation in terms of birth rate per thousand inhabitants. The local doctors complain that the superb hospital needs to be rebuilt as a birthing center."

The Palace of the Pioneers was located next to the movie theater in the midst of a young and vivid green space, while closer to the Syrdarya River was a large sports stadium. In this same green area they had built an enclosed

---

15. *La Grande Vadrouille* (1966) was released in the English-speaking world under the title *Don't Look Now... We're Being Shot At!*

swimming pool with 50-meter lanes. Enjoying the rare opportunity to stroll unhurried, we went down to the bank of the Syrdarya. I tried to show my comrades the spot where we had gone swimming during the hot summer of 1957. Back then the Syrdarya was still deep and treacherous in places.

"Over there, where that kid is standing up to his waist, there was a deep hole with a whirlpool. I pulled a targeting system specialist from the Arsenal Factory in Kiev out of there."

"What? He didn't know how to swim?"

"The thing is, it wasn't a he, but a she. The person I saved was then a senior representative of Arsenal. During preparation for the first launch she dared to show up at the launch pad in trousers and calmly puttered around with the ground targeting instruments. When Korolev saw such irregularities, he ordered Voskresenskiy: 'Get that broad off the launch site!' Voskresenskiy retorted unflappably: 'This young woman is the official representative of Arsenal. Without her we might mess something up with the targeting. Not long ago, Chertok risked his life pulling her out of the deep whirlpool, and you are order-ing me to run this specialist off of the launch pad. It's an awkward situation.' "

" 'Oh, God, you guys still find time to go swimming with girls! Well, good for you!' "

"Voskresenskiy took advantage of the mood shift, and catching sight of me, shouted: 'Chertok! You saved her in the Syrdarya, now save her here, introduce her to the Chief.' Korolev had absolutely nothing against making the acquaintance of an attractive woman, and the incident was patched up."

My story amused my companions. Now on the site of the historic event there was a dock, and next to it a landscaped beach spread out. Despite the fact that the Syrdarya River had grown considerably shallower since the days of heroic 1957, 150 private boats were assigned to the dock.

"And this is the Gagarin gazebo," I showed my companions. "We had lunch here with the first corps of cosmonauts two days before Gagarin's launch."

Behind the Gagarin gazebo in the shady park we could see the hotels and cottages for the visiting marshals, generals, and "various and sundry State Commission chairmen." In May 1957, we couldn't have guessed that a socialist Sun City would sprout up in place of the dusty, truck-battered roads, mud huts, and barracks on the bare steppe. The population of one hundred thousand in the closed city, in which there were no power outages, and no heating outages in the winter chill, and no problems with the supply of any necessities, labored solely for the sake of the Soviet Union's rocket-space technology. In the years that followed, the city continued to improve, develop, and grow prettier.

A terrible blow to my rosy remembrances of this town was something I saw 24 years later [in 1995] and then heard repeatedly from comrades who have visited it regularly in the past few years. The modern-day destroyers of the closed flourishing towns didn't kill anyone or set anything on fire, like the Vandals who destroyed ancient Rome. The once flourishing town of Leninsk and the immense economy of the firing range at the end of the 20th century perished without the use of any weapons.[16]

In order to destroy a modern town all it takes is to deprive it of electricity, fuel, and municipal authorities. Radical reforms condemned the community in which powerful production forces and cutting-edge science and culture were created simply because it was called "socialist."

Twenty-four years later, on just such a sunny, bright day, I once again was strolling around "Sun City." But now, rather than being involved in preparation for the latest launch and burdened by the work-related worries, I was a distinguished guest. The Il-18 loaded with Moscow guests arrived at the Krayniy Airport on the occasion of the 40th anniversary of NIIP-5—the rocket firing range known to the entire world as the Baykonur Cosmodrome.

From the airfield we were taken to the hotel at our former home, Site No. 2. There was a rather brief official celebration time at the soldiers' club right there at Site No. 2. There were many warm meetings between veterans who had flown in from various towns and with those still living here, in the "near

From the author's archives.

This picture was taken outside of Korolev's former home. From left to right are B. Ye. Chertok, A. G. Reshetin, N. S. Koroleva (Korolev's daughter), I. S. Prudnikov, and A. V. Lukyashko.

---

16. Leninsk was renamed Baykonur in December 1995.

abroad" of the former Soviet Union. The next day we had a minibus at our disposal to tour the various monuments. By "we" I mean the family of Nataliya Sergeyevna Koroleva, the daughter of Sergey Pavlovich, and myself. Nataliya Sergeyevna was accompanied by her children Masha, Andrey, and Sergey, already grown and on their own, the grandchildren of the legendary Korolev. Nataliya Sergeyevna Koroleva already had her own grandchildren—Sergey Pavlovich's great grandchildren. By force of habit I continue to call Nataliya Sergeyevna Koroleva, who is a doctor of medical sciences and a surgeon, by the nickname "Natasha."

In the first volume of *Rockets and People* I talked about the work of Soviet specialists who lived and worked in Germany from 1945 to 1946, restoring rocket technology together with the Germans after World War II. The Germans perceived us, the victors—officers and soldiers of the Soviet Army—as occupiers. Therefore, the wives and children who arrived from the Soviet Union to be with us in the spring of 1946 comprised a certain clan of victors. This isolated our families from the German populace more than the language barrier. When interacting, the local residents emphatically assigned the husbands' ranks to their wives. [My wife] Katya was indignant that the German women who worked in our villa, the chauffeur, and even the wives of German specialists addressed her not by name or surname, but as "Frau Major." They called [Pilyugin's wife] Antonina Konstantinovna Pilyugina "Frau Oberst." Our children, who didn't know the language, didn't understand this, especially since the German children shunned them.

From the author's archives.
Chertok's wife, Yekaterina "Katya" Golubkina.

In late May 1946, Korolev's first wife—Kseniya Maksimilianovna Vintsentini—arrived in Bleicherode from Moscow with their 11-year-old daughter Natasha. That summer a close friendship developed between our families. Nikolay Pilyugin's wife Tonya was glad that her daughter Nadya now had a Russian friend. My wife Katya hoped these demure young girls might be able to keep an eye on our seven-year-old son Valentin while out on walks and splashing in the municipal pool and, if necessary, protect him against unnecessarily close association with German boys of his age. Since that time, the daughters of Korolev and Pilyugin, even after they became grandmothers, remained "Natasha" and "Nadya" to our families.

Korolev's wife and daughter left Germany soon thereafter. The chief surgeon of the famous S. P. Botkin Hospital in Moscow, Kseniya Vintsentini, rushed back to her patients, and Natasha had to get back in time for school.

From the author's archives.

The sculptor Z. M. Vilenskiy designed and built a bust of Korolev that now resides in Natasha Koroleva's residence. From left to right are Ye. V. Shabarov, P. V. Tsybin, Koroleva, S. S. Kryukov, Vilenskiy, and B. Ye. Chertok.

From the author's archives.

Chertok at the Gagarin Pavilion on the banks of the Syrdarya River at Baykonur in June 1995.

After our return from Germany, changes took place in Korolev's personal life.[17] This in no way affected our warm relationship with Kseniya Maksimilianovna and the adult Natasha. After the death of her great father, then her grandmother and mother, Natasha exhibited truly Korolevian character. She raised her sons, Andrey and Sergey, and her daughter, Masha, and obtained academic degrees, titles, and a State prize. In addition to all that, she created a one-of-a-kind private museum dedicated to the memory of Sergey Pavlovich Korolev.

The airplane in which I flew with Natasha from Moscow to the celebration of the 40th anniversary of NIIP-5—present-day Baykonur—served as a fantastic time machine for us. The "time machine" had carried Natasha and me from the German city of Bleicherode in the green forests of Thuringia in 1946 to the "Sun City" of rockets—Leninsk in 1995.

This land became a second home, to borrow Voskresenskiy's phrase, not only for the permanent residents of Site No. 10, but also for those of us who flew in every year beginning in 1956 for temporary assignments lasting many months. After the terrible war ended, we spent many years restoring, building, and creating. Over the years that have passed since the war we became accustomed to thinking that only earthquakes could destroy the city. It was painful and horrible to see how the once flourishing "Sun City" was now dying without a single shot fired, without earthquakes or other natural disasters.

In 1995, a French journalist and entrepreneur, who had studied the history of cosmonautics in general and our history in particular, visited Baykonur. After this he did several interviews, including one with me. He did not conceal

his admiration and indignation: "I was stunned by the grandeur of what I saw in Baykonur. I visited all the launch facilities. Regardless of the plans of Russia and Kazakhstan, this needs to be preserved for generations to come like the Egyptian

Boris Chertok shown here on a visit to Baykonur in June 1995. He is standing at Site No. 2 outside the MIK. The writing in the background says "Road to the Stars."

From the author's archives.

---

17. Korolev and his first wife, Kseniya Maksimilianovna Vintsentini (1907–1991), divorced in August 1949.

pyramids. If everything is abandoned like this, the desert will eventually swallow up these testaments to the achievements of your cosmonautics. The town leaves a particularly painful impression. How can you endure the fact that a process of such barbaric destruction is going on? You have surrendered. You need your own General de Gaulle." I agreed with him with regard to de Gaulle.

In the last few years so much has been said and written on this subject that I won't torment the reader further and shall return to my recollections of the last days of May 1971.

AFTER OUR "BIG STROLL" IT CAME TIME TO RETURN to the "provinces," to Site No. 2. Along the way we stopped in at Site No. 17—the cosmonauts' residence—in order to wish Aleksey Leonov a happy birthday. He was 37. He was proud of the fact that he had been named commander of *Soyuz-11* for the upcoming flight to the DOS. "We will enter that haunted station," Leonov assured us. We toasted Leonov with Narzan mineral water and promised to drink to his health with something stronger when we got home: a strict dry law was in effect here at the cosmonauts' residence.

After autographing the mock newspaper posted on the wall, which had been published in honor of Leonov's birthday, we went out to stroll around the garden. Here, especially thick greenery had grown up and already achieved its deep, summertime coloring. Thickets of shrubbery that reminded me of our acacia were in bloom giving off a delicate fragrance. That evening the air here was particularly delightful, somehow reminiscent of the atmosphere of gardens in Central Russia. At the entrance to the hotel real roses were in bloom. A rose garden instead of camel thorn! The Kazakhstani steppe was blooming with more than just its famous April tulips.

On the way home we once again discussed how the firing range had grown and improved. The steel latticework of a television tower adorned the right side of the road leading out of the city. Spread out on the left side of the concrete road was a distribution substation with masts and transformer pillars crowding each other, looking from the side like a tangled skein of wires. High-voltage transmission lines were running in various directions.

On the hill of the "third ascent" before the traditional checkpoint established here back in 1956, two new 32-meter parabolas had sprouted up among the dozens of small antenna dishes. This was NIP-23 of the Command and Measurement Complex.[18]

---

18. According to other data, NIP-23 was established in 1986 at Khorol in Ukraine and decommissioned in 1995.

From here it was 30 kilometers to the N-1 launch sites. It was easy to determine the direction to them by the bright glow on the horizon. Work there was humming along 24 hours a day.

On Monday, 31 May 1971, the *Soyuz-11* returned from the fueling station and was installed in the vertical stand. They were awaiting the arrival of the cosmonauts for their fit check "sit in." Out of hygienic considerations, the entire stand structure was thoroughly wiped down with alcohol at the request of the medical staff.

"What are you doing?" I asked them. "The smell alone will make the cosmonauts dizzy, and we need sober comments on the spacecraft."

"We are hoping that you and the others in your entourage will take the opportunity to breathe in the rubbing alcohol fumes before they arrive. There won't be any left for the cosmonauts," they joked. The main crew sat in the spacecraft for more than the routine hour. There were many questions and disputes, but no serious modifications were required. The backup crew also sat in the spacecraft for around 20 minutes.

Chapter 16
The Hot Summer of 1971

On Monday, 31 May 1971, Bushuyev telephoned me at Site No. 2 over the high-frequency line from Podlipki and said that Keldysh had gathered the "inner circle" of the members of the expert commission on N1-L3 in his office. Keldysh announced that it was time to decide the fate of N1-L3. Then he enumerated the anomalies that were already known, which, if one took an objective approach, were difficult to dispute. According to Bushuyev, Keldysh was very amicably disposed. However, he firmly stated that he considered the approved version of a lunar expedition in 1973 to be unrealistic, and he proposed to Mishin, without conflicting with the expert commission, to find mutually acceptable solutions that together they could bring before the VPK, and then even higher.

Mishin showed a complete lack of self-restraint and objected to Keldysh on each point: "We'll clarify everything and show that everything will work out."

"I was forced to listen and keep my mouth shut," said Bushuyev, "so that I wouldn't put my boss in an awkward position. You and Feoktistov were lucky that you were at the firing range and weren't involved in this spectacle."

When I told Feoktistov about my conversation with Bushuyev, he had the following take on the situation: "It's difficult to come to an agreement when one side is extremely resolute while lacking any sort of circumspection and the other side is cautious while having no right to make a decision."

"Well, Konstantin Petrovich," I objected, "when it comes to radical decisions you're also a master. On your advice they did away with spacesuits on the Voskhod; you then talked Korolev into reducing the diameter of the Soyuz Descent Module by 200 millimeters, as on the Voskhod, but we still lost, weight-wise: we had to put lead in for compensation. You squeezed us control specialists so much on the L3 that I lost faith in the system's reliability. This year we are testing out the Soyuz-DOS docking assembly with internal transfer, but on the L3 until very recently the weight reports still have a transfer through open space."

"We're not going to pour salt in the wounds," suggested Feoktistov. "The L3 is already obsolete. The experience that we will gain on the DOS will help a lot, and I don't think it will be difficult for us to convince the top brass that the L3 needs to be redesigned."

"I agree. Now the main thing is to manage to get into the DOS."

MISHIN, WHO FLEW IN A DAY LATER, did not consider it necessary to tell us about the results of the N1-L3 discussion at the expert commission in Keldysh's office. Mishin looked chipper, although he reported that he had spent three days in the hospital, after which he had flown to Perm on electoral business as a deputy of the Supreme Soviet of the RSFSR.[1]

Yeliseyev arrived with Mishin. After the flight on *Soyuz-10* he was named Tregub's deputy for flight control.[2] Yeliseyev insisted on inserting precise instructions into the crew procedures about the time limitation on firing the rendezvous and correction engine (SKD) during rendezvous in the event that the limits designated in the so-called phase-plane diagram were exceeded.[3] This diagram depicted a corridor of permissible closing velocities depending on the distances between objects. The SKD fired to accelerate or brake when zigzags on the diagram leaned toward one of the walls of this corridor.

The instruments controlling rendezvous were adjusted using the graph that our theoreticians had designed. In order to write down a specific number in the procedures, on 2 June, I summoned Rauschenbach and Legostayev over the high-frequency line. They promised to give it some thought. The morning of 3 June, evidently under pressure from Shmyglevskiy, our chief theoretician on approach, they announced that *Igla* and the rendezvous control unit (BUS) could sort out how many seconds the engine needed to operate in each specific case better than a cosmonaut could.[4]

Feoktistov and I tried to convince Yeliseyev. But he persistently argued, "You can't give a cosmonaut a diagram indicating the maximum closing velocities and at the same time not tell him what he's supposed to do when the motion parameters exceed these limits. If he doesn't do anything, then later we'll accuse

---

1. RSFSR—Russian Soviet Federated Socialist Republic. All of the Soviet republics had their own legislative bodies, called Supreme Soviets, which were modeled after the national Supreme Soviet. On paper, the Supreme Soviet was the highest organ of state power, but the delegates "elected" to serve on the body were largely determined by patronage systems, and elections were always unopposed. The Supreme Soviet had little de facto power in state governance, which was exercised by the Council of Ministers.

2. Yakov Isayevich Tregub (1918–2007) was a deputy chief designer at TsKBEM who also served as the flight director representing the design bureau on the Main Operations Control Group (GOGU), or the flight control team. He was appointed to this position in 1968.

3. SKD—*Sblizhayushche-korrektiruyushchiy dvigatel.*

4. BUS—*Blok upravleniya sblizheniyem.*

the crew of botching the rendezvous. I want to eliminate accusations against the crew of incorrect actions in the event the BUS fails to shut down the engine."

Bashkin broke in, having taken offense over the BUS.

"But a failure can occur during a burn, too. In this case it's simply dangerous to give the cosmonaut instructions."

Feoktistov backed up Bashkin.

"I understand why the theoreticians don't want to saddle the cosmonaut with the responsibility for making decisions, because an algorithm can be very complicated and one can't foresee the combinations of all the input data that one will need to take into consideration."

I connected Yeliseyev with Legostayev over the high-frequency line and proposed that they continue their debate as two of "Rauschenbach's best students."

AFTER LUNCH, A LARGE MEETING, referred to as a State Commission session, took place in the MIK hall. Usually as many as a hundred participants and "enthusiasts" came to such prelaunch landmark sessions, although there were hardly more than 10 real members of the State Commission confirmed by decision of the Central Committee. Opening the meeting, Kerimov said that he had received information about a Politburo meeting at which the matter of the upcoming *Soyuz-11* flight was discussed.

"Minister Afanasyev informed me that he, Keldysh, Smirnov, and Bushuyev were summoned to the Politburo. They attested that everything to support the flight and docking had been provided for, the necessary modifications had been confirmed by experimental tests, the crew was well trained, and everything would be in order. Leonid Ilyich Brezhnev asked that everything be checked one more time so that docking and transfer would be executed this time. Comrade Brezhnev asked us to convey the message that this is very important. He is entrusting everything to us and hopes that we will execute the mission. Afanasyev reported to the Politburo about the makeup of the crews. Kosygin asked whether they were all well trained. Smirnov assured him that yes, the crews had reported before the VPK about their readiness. Brezhnev announced that the French government had made an inquiry about when we intended to perform manned flights, in view of the fact that France was getting ready to conduct an atmospheric nuclear test in the next few days.[5] After consulting with comrade Keldysh, Smirnov and Bushuyev answered that a nuclear explosion would not interfere—that's what comrade Afanasyev said."

---

5. The French conducted eight nuclear tests in 1970: three in May, one in June, two in July, and two in August. The test in June took place on 24 June and was known as *Eridan*.

It was up to Shabarov to report briefly about all the test results, and he took the opportunity to mention the "pshh" as well. Aleksandr Soldatenkov, Kozlov's deputy, presented the report about the launch vehicle.[6] Safety problems in the event of solar flares—and consequently, any other radiation hazard— were Yevgeniy Vorobyev's sphere of responsibility. The decision allowing the flight during a nuclear test had been made "at the top" without asking him. Vorobyev said nothing, but Severin voiced his opinion: "We need to instruct the cosmonauts to look to see what a nuclear explosion looks like from space."

"What for?"

"So that they themselves can decide whether it is worth it to return to the ground if a nuclear shoot-out begins."

This bit of improvisation made everyone laugh.

The State Commission set the dates: rollout to the launch site on 4 June and launch on 6 June 1971.

From the author's archives.

Spacesuit Chief Designer Gay Severin (left) and Boris Chertok.

ONE HOUR REMAINED BEFORE DINNER, AND I DECIDED to spend it in a peaceful, horizontal position. But Mikhail Samokhin dropped by to share ideas on peopling new hotels and financing new construction.

On the way to the mess hall a very agitated Gay Severin stopped me.

"They called me from Site No. 17. The doctors have rejected Kubasov because of some sort of symptom and have made the decision to replace the entire crew. This means that I have to replace all the seat liners and medical belts, prepare the spacesuits, and other things, and the spacecraft is already integrated with the launch vehicle and is under the fairing."

I was dumbfounded. We stopped in at the mess hall. Shabarov was calmly dining.

"Have you heard the news about the replacement of the crew?"

"This is the first I've heard of it."

---

6. Aleksandr Mikhaylovich Soldatenkov (1927–) was Kozlov's most senior deputy responsible for the development of R-7-derived launch vehicles. He served as the first deputy chief designer at TsKBEM's Kuybyshev Branch (later TsSKB) from 1961 to 2006.

"You mean your boss didn't think it was necessary to consult with you on such a fundamental issue?" asked an astonished Severin. Replacing the crew two days before a launch—this had never happened either in our experience or that of the Americans.[7] Once again we were conducting a "world's first" experiment.

We began a heated discussion of this sensational event in the mess hall. Mishin telephoned Shabarov and ordered him to assemble management in the MIK at 11 p.m.

"An order is an order," said Shabarov and turned to Feoktistov: "Do we need to recalculate the center of gravity? After all, the cosmonauts' weights are different."

"We'll get on it right away. Since that's the case, I'll go find our theoreticians."

At the nighttime meeting in the MIK, Vorobyev said that an x ray done on Kubasov that morning during a standard medical examination had shown a dark spot on his right lung. The dark spot was the size of a chicken egg. Pravetskiy, Vorobyev's predecessor in management of the Ministry of Health Third Main Directorate, was the first to become outraged.

"Why is this being discovered two days before the launch? This kind of process can't develop in a week's time."

"It's well known that the Air Force Medical Monitoring Service looks after the cosmonauts. Ask them," replied Vorobyev.

"After they overlooked Belyayev's ulcer, nothing surprises me," Pravetskiy continued to rant. "You know that Belyayev had hemorrhages, but he managed to avoid being examined for two years; he was afraid that he would be selected out of the corps of cosmonauts. In our time, to let a cosmonaut die in the hospital in Moscow from hemorrhaging is really not that easy! A team of surgeons headed by Vishnevskiy couldn't save him. So that's what the statements of medical ignoramuses about constant monitoring are worth."[8]

"Well, Belyayev is not the issue now," said Vorobyev in a conciliatory tone.

At the midnight meeting we came to an agreement that regardless of the "spot on the lungs," the launch vehicle and spacecraft would roll out to the launch site at 6 a.m. This was the only possible decision. Semyonov, Severin, and Konstantin Gorbatenko, the head of all the machinists and installers,

---

7. In a similar situation, NASA replaced a single crewmember instead of the entire crew. In April 1970, just three days before launch, original *Apollo 13* Command Module Pilot (CMP) Thomas K. Mattingly II was taken off the crew because of suspicion that he was not immune to German measles. Instead of replacing the entire crew, NASA management replaced Mattingly with John L. "Jack" Swigert, the original backup CMP.

8. Belyayev died on 10 January 1970 as a result of complications from purulent peritonitis.

estimated the amount of work at 4 or 5 hours. Work would begin right after the launch vehicle was erected. But the replacement of the crew was the prerogative of the State Commission.

In the morning, after accompanying the rocket train to the launch site, the State Commission convened. Opening such an unusual meeting at 7 a.m., Kerimov said: "The doctors have informed us that Kubasov cannot be cleared for flight. This is a total surprise for all of us. Just yesterday we reported the crew makeup to the Politburo, got the green light—and suddenly we have this snafu. Let Yevgeniy Ivanovich Vorobyev explain why this became possible."

"The cosmonauts underwent the standard preflight examination. When Kubasov was x-rayed, they noticed a dark spot. They performed a sectional x ray. They determined that the mass was located at a depth of 9 centimeters and was the size of a five-kopeck piece.[9] They assessed the process as acute and active."

"Oh, come on," Kerimov flared up, "cosmonauts are under continuous observation. After all, this isn't an upset stomach. Where were you earlier?"

"The last time we performed an x ray on him was in February. Everything was in order, and all this time Kubasov has felt fine."

"To the best of my medical knowledge, this is an acute tubercular process. Were we really not able to find anything suspicious in the blood work?"

"They have now detected an elevated eosinophil count; other indices are normal."

"This is all just words, but do you have a written medical finding? Who signed it?"

Vorobyev assured them that there was such a paper.

Kerimov turned to Kamanin: "What shall we propose, Nikolay Petrovich?"

"We believe that engineer-tester Volkov should take the place of engineer-tester Kubasov in the primary crew.[10] Leonov has already been in space; he even performed a spacewalk. Volkov has already flown on a Soyuz.[11] Such an engineer can cope with the mission."

Mishin's objection came as a surprise to everyone.

"We object. I consulted with our comrades. We have a document signed by the Air Force stating that in such cases the entire three-man crew must be replaced. The backup threesome underwent training with a good evaluation.

---

9. A Soviet five-kopeck coin was 2.5 centimeters in diameter.

10. At the time, the three members of the station crews were defined as commander, engineer-tester (*inzhener-ispytatel*), and engineer-researcher (*inzhener-issledovatel*). Later on, after 1971, the second member of the crew was known as flight engineer (*bortinzhener*).

11. Volkov flew his first space mission on *Soyuz-7* in October 1969.

A new crew that hasn't worked together will be worse than the backup crew. We absolutely insist on replacing the entire crew."

Air Force Chief Engineer and Deputy Commander-in-Chief Ponomarev stood behind Mishin rather than with Kamanin.[12] The others weren't about to get involved in the argument, reasoning, "What difference does it make to me who flies?"

The State Commission decreed that the entire crew be replaced—the entire trio. Kamanin was tasked with informing the crew of the decision. Bashkin, who had participated in cosmonaut training and had graded their exams, took the crew replacement as a personal tragedy.

"My comrades and I spent so much time on the primary crew that we were completely at ease about them. But we simply did not have enough time for the backup crew. And they themselves didn't think they'd be flying. In our history we have never changed a crew approved by the VPK. Frankly speaking, for some reason I was very confident in Kubasov; he's practically an expert. And suddenly he gets an infiltration and lets us down."

From the author's archives.

The new *Soyuz-11* prime crew of Georgiy Dobrovolskiy, Vladislav Volkov, and Viktor Patsayev is shown here with the crew they replaced, Aleksey Leonov, Valeriy Kubasov, and Petr Kolodin. The image is from the State Commission meeting a few days before their launch.

---

12. Aleksandr Nikolayevich Ponomarev (1903–2002) was a well-known Air Force scientist and academic who, since 1953, had served as a Deputy Commander-in-Chief of the Soviet Air Force. He was the author of many famous books on the history of Soviet aviation.

"Comrade Chairman," Shabarov spoke up, "Severin, Feoktistov, and I need to be at the launch site to make adjustments to the vehicle for the new crew, and we haven't shaved or had breakfast yet. Request permission to leave!"

"The technical management's proposal has been accepted. I hereby close the meeting," announced Kerimov.

We hurried off to our morning grooming and breakfast, not suspecting that a decision had just been made to divide the crews into the living and the dead.

A DIFFICULT DAY STOOD BEFORE US. It would be nice after a shower and breakfast to catch a quick nap. It was only 7 a.m. Moscow time. But this wasn't to be: I slept sweetly for no more than 10 minutes. The telephone woke me. The high-frequency line operator on duty informed me, "You have an urgent call from Bushuyev and [Viktor] Innelaur in Podlipki. Hurry, I already have a long queue."

As I walked over to the high-frequency communications center, I ran through scenarios of possible problems that they might be reporting from Podlipki. Most likely, during tests at the monitoring and testing station (KIS) on the next [Soyuz] vehicle No. 33, they discovered something that required changes on vehicle No. 32, which was already standing on the launch pad. As if we hadn't had enough problems!

It turned out that everything was much more cheerful. Innelaur said that last night they had completed the factory tests on spacecraft No. 33 with one glitch in the long-range radio communications system (DRS). They're "signing away" the glitches and disconnecting the unit. But they called me to warn me.

"At 7 a.m. Moscow time the minister is flying out to you," said Bushuyev. "Yesterday I was with him at the Politburo. Tsarev is flying with the minister. He knows the details. But I can tell you that the situation was calm and amicable. Vilnitskiy, Syromyatnikov, and I looked through all the materials on the docking assembly tests again and decided that if you don't break anything during preparation, then everything should be fine."

I informed Bushuyev about the State Commission's decision to replace the crew. He was furious: "How can you make decisions there without having consulted with Moscow? We reported to the Politburo that Leonov's crew would be flying. We assured them how well they were trained, and you replaced everybody just because of Kubasov. What kind of a position have you put Afanasyev, Smirnov, and Ustinov in? Now they have to give an emergency rebriefing. The minister is going to arrive there in 3 hours and he's not going to say thank you. I called you to the telephone to put your mind at ease. Vilnitskiy and Syromyatnikov are completely confident in the reliability of the docking assembly. But be prepared: Afanasyev is going to be worked up and he's going to interrogate you for the details."

In order to prepare, I went to the MIK, after first summoning the rested docking specialists there. Yevgeniy Bobrov, Boris Chizhikov, and I tried once again to run through possible troubles during the last millimeters of retraction. They both put my mind at ease. We had lived with the Chizhikov family at the Villa Frank in Bleicherode, Germany, in 1946. My two sons and three-year-old Borya Chizhikov comprised the Villa Frank "kindergarten," to which Semyon Chizhikov and I paid almost no attention. Only on Sundays did we drive out for picnics and strolls in the forested countryside, of which Thuringia had such a wealth. Now 28-year-old engineer Boris Chizhikov argued: "We monitored the pressure integrity of the interface very carefully. We were afraid that due to lack of vigilance a lock wire, a piece of multilayer insulation, or some sort of rag would get onto the surface of the mating ring after the fairing was put on. The installers of shop No. 444 and Gorbatenko himself were very careful. They ordered 16 liters of alcohol just for wiping down the surfaces!"

"You put my mind at ease. Sixteen liters for the docking assembly—that's not bad. For all I know, it will begin to sway."

"Everything will be all right!"

THAT DAY AT THE LAUNCH SITE, general testing of the launch vehicle was under way. The weather was perfect. It had rained recently, accompanied by an unusually cold wind for that time of year. As one might expect, the Tyuratam old-timers tried to convince us that they couldn't recall such a pleasant early June.

Afanasyev arrived at the launch pad. Kerimov had already informed him about the decisions that had been made. Strolling around the launch pad, the enormous Afanasyev stooped to hear the reassuring explanations about how preparation was proceeding normally. Aleksandr Tsarev, who had flown in with Afanasyev, recounted the details of the events the day before in Moscow. The fact that Keldysh, Smirnov, Afanasyev, and Mishin were summoned before the Politburo regarding the upcoming flight was unexpected. Mishin was at the firing range, and Afanasyev had received permission to bring Bushuyev along instead. That morning Bushuyev had briefed the minister on proposals for the upcoming negotiations with the Americans.[13] Bushuyev had just left the ministry before the subsequent summons to the Politburo. He took with him the documents and posters describing the flight program and new docking assembly.

"Find Bushuyev and return immediately," ordered the minister.

He wasn't at work, nor at home, nor with Boris Petrov at the Academy of Sciences; wherever he was going, they couldn't find Bushuyev. Time was

---

13. This is a reference to planning for the Apollo-Soyuz Test Project (ASTP).

marching on, they needed to go to the Kremlin, and there were no posters and no documents for the report. Afanasyev arrived at the Kremlin, found Smirnov, and explained the situation. Smirnov made an unusual decision: telephone Minister of Internal Affairs Shchelokov.[14]

"Help us find Konstantin Bushuyev and bring him to the Kremlin immediately."

Afanasyev and Smirnov appeared without Bushuyev at the appointed hour in Brezhnev's reception room. Fortunately, the Politburo, discussing the preceding issue, had violated the time limit by about 30 minutes, which saved the day. Shchelokov gave the command to all State Automobile Inspectorate (GAI) posts in Moscow to find Bushuyev's car.[15] They detained it on Yaroslavskiy Highway between the Exhibition of Achievements of the National Economy (VDNKh) and the ring road.[16] They delivered Bushuyev to the Kremlin 5 minutes before they were called into the Politburo meeting.

Afanasyev made the report about the upcoming launch. Andrey Kirilenko asked how confident they were about the crew's training. Nikolay Podgornyy asked why they had decided to perform final approach manually rather than entrusting it to automatic controls. Brezhnev himself answered, "This is, after all, a very complicated affair. Often, even here on the ground, not everything works out for us. Here our comrades have properly divided the responsibilities. Furthermore, we remember spacecraft commander Leonov. He performed bravely during his spacewalk and then he and Belyayev pulled off an unusual landing. Don't you think?"

"Quite so, Leonid Ilyich," confirmed Afanasyev. "The automatic system failed and the cosmonauts availed themselves of manual control."

"And what does Mstislav Vsevolodovich say?" asked Brezhnev, addressing Keldysh.

"I did not sign the letter to the Central Committee concerning continuation of operations and launch documents until I personally looked into the causes of the previous failure. I tasked qualified scientists with verifying the

---

14. Nikolay Anisimovich Shchelokov (1910–1984) was head of the Ministry of Internal Affairs (MVD) from 1968 to 1982.

15. GAI—*Gosudarstvennaya avtomobilnaya inspektsiya.*

16. The VDNKh—*Vystavka dostizheniy narodnogo khozyaystva*—opened in 1954 to showcase notable achievements of the Soviet economy (including scientific and technical accomplishments). One of the most popular sections of the VDNKh was the Kosmos Pavilion where many mockups and models of Soviet rockets and spacecraft were put on display. The "ring roads" in Moscow are concentric roads that circle Moscow and crisscross the spoke roads that emanate from the center of the city. The outermost ring road, the Moscow Automobile Ring Road (MKAD), which opened in 1961, served as the administrative boundary of Moscow until the 1980s.

reliability of the actions taken. Over that period of time a great deal of work has been performed to increase docking reliability. I believe that everything reasonable that was proposed has been done, and the docking will occur."

I asked Tsarev whether Bushuyev had spoken at this Politburo meeting. Tsarev said that after the Politburo meeting when Bushuyev stopped in at his office (in an adjacent building where the VPK offices were located) to catch his breath he looked pretty bad.

"His unexpected seizure and delivery to the Kremlin by GAI had scared him so much that he didn't even remember who was at the Politburo meeting and what assurances he had given after Keldysh's speech."

THE GENERAL TESTS WERE COMPLETED WITHOUT ANY GLITCHES. Without time to even grab a bite of lunch, Shabarov and I drove straight from the launch site to Site No. 17—the cosmonauts' residence. It was poor form to be late for the "ceremonial" State Commission meeting. We met Mishin in the garden.

"Oh, God, what a difficult conversation I just had with Leonov and Kolodin!" he told us. "Leonov accused me of supposedly deliberately refusing to replace Kubasov with Volynov so that we could get Volkov into space one more time.[17] Kolodin said that up until the last day he could just feel that they weren't going to launch him into space under any pretext: 'I'm the black sheep in their midst. They are all pilots, and I am a rocket engineer.' "[18]

At the State Commission meeting I ended up sitting next to Kolodin. He sat there with his head hanging, nervously clenching and unclenching his hands, the muscles in his jaw twitching. He wasn't the only one who was nervous. Both crews were feeling rather low. The first was stunned from being removed from the flight, the second from the abrupt change of fate. After the flight, amidst fanfare, the second crew would climb the marble stairs of the Kremlin Palace and receive Heroes' stars while the music of Glinka played in the background. But there was no joy on their faces. A chest x ray, which hadn't been performed at all before the preceding flights, had altered the fate of the six men!

The State Commission meeting under the glare of movie floodlights and popping flashbulbs lasted 20 minutes. Dobrovolskiy assured everyone that the crew was ready and the mission would be accomplished. Instead of assurances,

---

17. Chertok may be in error here with reference to Volynov. It is worth noting, however, that cosmonaut B. V. Volynov was briefly considered for one of the DOS crews in April 1970 but had not been involved in DOS training in 1970 or 1971, having begun training for Almaz in 1971.

18. Unlike most of the military cosmonauts who were from the Air Force, Lieutenant Colonel Kolodin had an artillery background, having served at both Plesetsk (Mirnyy) and Baykonur (Tyuratam), as an officer of the Strategic Rocket Forces.

Leonov gave a wave of his hand as if to say, "It's a shame that things turned out like this."

When the meeting started to break up, I found myself next to Valeriy Kubasov. With a guilty smile he sort of apologized: "I just caught a little cold. In a week everything will clear up and the x ray won't show anything."

No one tried to cheer him up. But he, rather than the doctors, turned out to be right. And to this day Kubasov is alive and healthy. He did not have any sort of acute tubercular process.

When we returned to Site No. 2, Pravetskiy stopped by my place to let off steam. The two of us sat together late into the night, polishing off some bottles of cognac that had somehow gone unfinished. Pravetskiy was a remarkable storyteller. He was a witness to and participant in more than 60 surface and underground nuclear tests and spoke glowingly of Zavenyagin, Malyshev, Kurchatov, Sakharov, and Khariton.[19]

"We're worried about the life of several cosmonauts, while at the Semipalatinsk firing range we feared for the life and health of thousands of testers. One incident with a 3-megaton bomb will take quite a toll! An airplane carrying this bomb took off to test the effectiveness of a high-altitude burst before it touched the ground. The pilot got cold feet. He didn't drop the bomb. He didn't make a second approach. What was one to do? Kurchatov took the responsibility on himself, calmed everyone down, and assured them that nothing would happen with the bomb when the plane landed. The landing went fine. But what we went through before we transported the bomb away from the airfield is difficult to convey. Incidentally, this kind of stress has aftereffects. I'm convinced that the fatal heart attacks of Malyshev and Kurchatov were a vestige of that very event."[20]

At 5 a.m., before the heat of the day had set in, hundreds of people were striding along the paved road from Site No. 2 to Site No. 1. At the request of the firing range political department, it was not just military testers who were on their way to the meeting. There were many civilians in the stream of people, including women who had arrived by motor locomotive from Site No. 10. Everyone arriving at the launch site encountered a cordon set up to

---

19. Avraamiy Pavlovich Zavenyagin (1901–1956) and Vyacheslav Aleksandrovich Malyshev (1902–1957) were senior managers of the nuclear weapons program. Igor Vasilyevich Kurchatov (1903–1960), Andrey Dmitriyevich Sakharov (1921–1989), and Yuliy Borisovich Khariton (1904–1996) were high-level physicists.

20. Malyshev died of cancer, probably caused by his visit to a landfill left from the testing of the first Soviet thermonuclear device in 1953.

distribute people around the perimeter, leaving an empty square in the middle of the zero mark.

The deputy commander for political affairs opened the meeting. Lead military tester Vladimir Yaropolov spoke first: "Few are aware of our difficult work. Here, at the launch site, we hand over the spacecraft to you," he said, addressing the crew standing at attention. "We feel certain that you will sense the responsibility because millions of people on Earth will be following each of your actions."

Next to speak were a sergeant from the military installation and the industry representative, Armen Mnatsakanyan. When it was Dobrovolskiy's turn to give his response speech, it was evident that he was quite uneasy. Actually, never before had there been such a mass sendoff into space. Usually the meetings were limited to those directly involved in the preparation of the launch vehicle and spacecraft. And here it looked like at least three thousand people were gathered.

On the way here I prepared a speech," said Dobrovolskiy. "But now, after seeing your smiles and friendly gazes, I will simply tell you: dear comrades and friends, thank you so much for your selfless labor. We will spare no effort, we will do everything in order to fulfill our mission."

From the author's archives.

This image shows the ill-fated *Soyuz-11* crew of Dobrovolskiy, Volkov, and Patsayev on the eve of their launch near the pad area. Behind them from left to right are senior official in the Ministry of General Machine Building Anatoliy Kirillov (saluting in hat), Chief Designer Vasiliy Mishin (in sunglasses), Minister of General Machine Building Sergey Afanasyev (the tall man in a suit and tie), and Chairman of the State Commission Kerim Kerimov (saluting). In sunglasses on the right of the picture is Boris Chertok.

The crew did the traditional lap of honor around the square and another one around the rocket. The meeting broke up and the people ambled back in an elated, festive mood.

"Let's celebrate the good weather," proposed Shabarov. We walked down from the launch pad to the obelisk in honor of the launch of the world's first satellite, which was standing in the shade of some trees. Shabarov, Semyonov, Gorbatenko, and I took photographs of each other standing next to this historic obelisk, which had the following words engraved on it:

> *Here, thanks to the genius of Soviet people the daring assault on space began / 1957 /.*

These were the last hours of the day when one could relax and live in an unstructured manner. Tomorrow, 6 June, at 0300 hours Moscow time, we would get up; the prelaunch State Commission clearing the crew to take their places in the spacecraft would take place at 0500 hours; and at 0757 hours—liftoff.

During the fourth orbit the first correction would need to be performed to boost the vehicle's orbit to the orbit of the DOS based on the results of the first measurements. At 1600 hours the commission would depart for Yevpatoriya. Using the secure communications line (ZAS), I told Agadzhanov and Tregub in Yevpatoriya that everything was in order with us and warned them to get ready to meet a large crowd of guests.[21]

On the launch pad, before vehicle commander Georgiy Dobrovolskiy took his seat in the spacecraft, he clearly recited his report to State Commission Chairman Kerim Kerimov. Vladislav Volkov was animated and cheerful. Viktor Patsayev seemed very uneasy. Afanasyev and Marshal Krylov, who had flown in the day before, arrived for the launch. Both went down in to the bunker. All of the operations proceeded precisely, calmly, without any slipups.

"Off you go, sweetie!" said someone, who had heard the telemetry experts' reports about the normal start up of stage three—Block I.

Our Il-18 didn't leave Tyuratam for the Crimea until 1700 hours. We weren't able to admire the panorama of the Caucasus this time: we slept through it. We came to only when we had arrived in the Crimea and landed in Saki. Incidentally, everyone on the plane slept; after all, our workday had begun at 3 a.m.

After dropping off our overnight bags at the hotel, all of those who had just arrived walked over to the control room without stopping in at the hospitable dining hall. Agadzhanov reported, "Both spacecraft have departed the coverage

---

21. ZAS—*Zakrytyy (zashchishchenniy) apparat svyazi.*

zone and are out of communication. Everything on board both vehicles was normal. The crew had been granted permission to rest. According to the medical staff's findings, Volkov has adapted best of all to weightlessness. The coverage zone of the first daylight orbit will begin at 0725 hours over Kamchatka and will end in Ussuriysk at 0748 hours. If all goes well, at the end of the coverage zone we should receive a report from Ussuriysk via circular about the beginning of the final approach phase. According to the ballistics experts' calculations, conditions for rendezvous after orbital correction turned out to be ideal. At 0725 hours the range should not exceed 2 kilometers at a closing rate of up to 5 meters per second. GOGU recommends that everyone who just arrived go grab some dinner, get some sleep, and meet here at 6 a.m. We will receive the report about the nocturnal orbits."

At 6 a.m. the small control room began to rapidly fill up. Through the open windows a refreshing breeze blew in from the sea. In addition to the five main GOGU members—Agadzhanov, Tregub, Chertok, Rauschenbach, and Yeliseyev—the control room work required another five or so people representing the analysis group, KIK, the communication service, telemetry, and medical services. More than 50 people were crammed into the room.

At 0726 hours Yeliseyev called up the crew: "This is *Zarya. Yantar*, do you read me? Come in!"[22]

The response was slow.

"This is *Yantar*. Everything is okay here. We're working according to program. We have radio lock-on. Automatic rendezvous is in progress. At 0727 hours, range 4; rate 14."

"We read you. Everything is normal; continue your report."

"At 0731 hours, SKD fired for 10 seconds, range 2.3; rate 8."

Judging by the voice, it wasn't vehicle commander Dobrovolskiy reporting, but Volkov. The multiple relay and amplification couldn't muffle the agitation in his voice before his words reached the loudspeakers in the room. We could all feel his tension.

"Rate is decreasing. In the VSK we see a bright glowing spot. Range 1400, rate 4...."[23]

"0737 hours, range 700, rate 2.5. We've turned away—we only see Earth. We've got lock-on again!..."

---

22. These call signs mean "Dawn" and "Amber," respectively.

23. The VSK—*Vizir spetsialnyy kosmonavta* (cosmonaut's special visor)—was the cosmonaut's optical sight.

"According to the telemetry data from NIP-13," another voice announced, "final approach mode has occurred—range 300; rate 2 recorded."

In the room there is not just silence, but a growing tension. The pause that has set in is alarming. Perhaps everything is fine, but right now only Ussuriysk is receiving information from space, and it is being relayed to us via ground-based channels known only to the communications operators at KIK. How easy it would be for somebody with a power shovel to unwittingly break this thin, 8,000-kilometer-long thread!

"*Yantar*, this is *Zarya*, I don't read you."

Volkov's cheerful voice interrupts the seconds of silence: "Range 300; rate 2. I have an excellent view of the station in the VSK. Adjusting roll. Cone and trap are very clearly visible. Roll adjustment complete—range 105; rate 0.7. We are switching on manual final approach."

"*Yantar*, at short range carefully inspect the docking node," instructed Yeliseyev.

"We read you. Range 50. Rate 0.28. DPO nozzles are operating. Receiving cone looks clean. Very clearly visible…. Range 20; rate 0.2. Vehicle is behaving stably. We are going for docking!"

And at that moment the coverage zone ends. Like the line in the famous joke, "again this damned uncertainty!"[24]

"Communication during next pass will be at 0856 hours."

Oh, how the time drags on! Between communications sessions even non-smokers leave the building for some air, for a smoke break reducing the nervous tension. Will the spacecraft and the orbital station draw together, or will there once again remain a gap of a few millimeters? The room is already crammed full of as many as a hundred agonizing people. Each one is no mere spectator or fan, but a participant in the event, bearing a small part of the responsibility. This small part in the whole chain might turn out to be fatal. Each one of the hundred waiting people is now helpless. There is nothing anyone can do. Just wait.

The silence is broken by *Zarya*'s typical background noise. Without waiting for them to make radio contact from space, Yeliseyev calls them: "*Yantars*, this is *Zarya*, come in!"

No answer. He repeats the call several times.

"We have television!"—exclaims Bratslavets. "Docking occurred! The picture is excellent."

---

24. This refers to a joke about a man who can't decide whether his wife is having an affair, even though he's followed her to her lover's house, because at the crucial moment, they turn out the lights.

"*Yantars*, come in, this is my fifth call. Why are you silent?"

"*Zarya*, we're reporting: docking occurred without oscillations, retraction is complete. Mode executed! We are checking the pressure integrity of the interface. Now equalizing the pressure. We'll continue to work per the program. Now opening the hatch from the Descent Module to the Habitation Compartment. Now transferring into the Habitation Compartment. Everything is normal."

The noise in the room crescendoed. Someone decided to applaud, but we almost strangled him.

"Wait until they transfer into the DOS or we'll jinx it."

"The docking analysis group is reporting. Everything went according to the program. The spacecraft hooks reinforced retraction. The DOS hooks were not activated. The process is fully completed. Now the 796th DOS orbit has begun, or the [Soyuz] vehicle's 19th orbit, and its 3rd daylight orbit. According to the program, pressure equalization should be completed, allowing the transfer hatch to open. Transfer into the DOS will proceed only when clearance is received from Earth."

"Attention! Quiet! We are beginning the communication session!" shouts Agadzhanov.

And just then, without waiting for Yeliseyev's call, Volkov's cheerful voice rings out: "*Zarya*! Everything is normal here. We are still sitting in the Descent Module. All pressures are normal. We're equalizing per the table. No glitches to report. Request permission to open the transfer hatch from the Descent Module to the Habitation Compartment."

Yeliseyev turns to us. Tregub searches for someone in the crowd. Then he makes the decision himself and nods his head.

"Permission granted to open hatch!"

"*Zarya*! Command issued to open transfer hatch at 10:32:30. The 'closed' display light went out. If it doesn't open, we'll use a crowbar."

"*Yantars*, everything is going fine. You guys are great. Don't get excited. Work calmly."

"*Zarya*! The opening process has been executed. But the display light isn't illuminated. Evidently, we didn't hit the limit switch. We're not going to wait. *Yantar-3* waved and went over!"[25]

Again there is a pause. Silence. We sense that there in space the first man is now floating into the first DOS. He's in *Salyut*! Volkov took the opportunity to joke, "We're flying past the fifth floor, everything is okay!"

---

25. The three-man crew used numbers to differentiate themselves during communications sessions, using *Yantar-1* (Dobrovolskiy), *Yantar-2* (Volkov), and *Yantar-3* (Patsayev).

"*Yantars*, attention! You are now going to have a conversation with 'No. 1'." This is Moscow stepping in already. There, they are also nervously waiting and decided, without taking into consideration the complexity of the situation, to break in at the most strained moment of the transfer for the crew to communicate with Brezhnev.

"*Zarya*, wait. No. 3 is in *Salyut*. Don't interfere until…. *Zarya*, No. 3 came back. There's a strong odor in *Salyut*. He's donning a mask; he's going again."

Afanasyev is talking with Moscow. He's trying to postpone communication with "No. 1" until the next orbit.

Mishin steps in: "That's enough unauthorized activity! All conversations and instructions to the spacecraft are only through me."

Now, the mated *Salyut*-Soyuz begins leaving the coverage zone.

AT 1202 HOURS THE FOURTH DAYLIGHT ORBIT WAS UNDER WAY. During that time the Central Committee was informed that the docking had proceeded normally. Moscow was even shown a nonbroadcast television image of the crew reading a report to the Central Committee at the entrance to DOS. Finally the cosmonauts tore themselves away from their previously prepared texts and reported: "In seconds we'll be able to jump into the *Salyut*. When we opened the hatch, we looked in and it seemed like there was no end to this station. After our tight quarters, there's so much room!"

"*Yantars*, switch on the regenerators in *Salyut*. Communication is ending. We'll wait for you during the next orbit in *Salyut*. Here, we're all just as happy as you are. Congratulations!"

The silence in the room gives way to unimaginable noise. Mishin asks the medical staff for findings about the odors. Does it pose a danger for the cosmonauts? But what can they say without having smelled it?

Pravetskiy recommends: "Switch on the regenerators! They'll get used to the smell and everything will be normal."

Ilya Lavrov frets. He is in charge of life-support systems at TsKBEM. Odor falls within his field. He tries to reassure the others.

"Vasiliy Pavlovich! We don't need to give any instructions now. When you go into a new apartment there's always an unfamiliar smell! I'll tell you another story from the time of the Civil War. It's freezing cold winter and a member of the intelligentsia squeezes into a train car jam-packed with small-time traders and their bags. He breathes in some air, reels, holds his nose, and jumps back out, gasping for breath! Next a worker enters: 'Whoa, guys, what farts you've let off! I'm going to look for another car.' A peasant crawls in with a bag, breathes in, and sighs, 'Warmth!' and he climbs into the top bunk."

"Attention, 1335 hours. We are beginning the communication session of the fifth orbit of the day."

Before *Zarya* established contact, we saw Volkov and Patsayev clearly on the television screen for the first time. For the first time, the cosmonauts were in the DOS. They were having an animated discussion about something. At that point it was impossible to restrain ourselves. We broke out in a thunderous applause.

"They heard our ovation!"

Actually, both cosmonauts looked in the camera, at us, and waved.

"They breathed for a bit and got used to the smell," commented Lavrov.

We did it! We have a real piloted orbital station!

"*Yantars*, this is *Zarya*! The State Commission and GOGU congratulate you from the bottom of our hearts. You are the first Earthlings on a Long-Duration Orbital Station. Permission granted to have some dinner and rest, and tomorrow first thing in the morning we'll begin work according to the program."

An hour later the State Commission listened (not very attentively) to the reports of the medical staff and life-support-systems analysis service. No glitches had occurred that would require "ground" intervention. After three o'clock in the afternoon the control room emptied. The dining halls began to "hum," and then the hotels. A festive mood swept away departmental, corporate, service, and company barriers. People broke up into "interest" groups. The most active ones headed to the beach with swimming masks and nets to catch crabs. Others, after procuring transportation, set out for Yevpatoriya. But by evening the majority had lain down and fallen asleep in their hotel rooms. I had assembled a group to wander off to the seaside for a stroll. I persuaded Ryazanskiy, Bogomolov, Mnatsakanyan, and Pravetskiy.

"Only one condition," I demanded. "Today no arguments about *Igla* and *Kontakt*."

As we were leaving the compound we ran into Babakin. He was in charge of the "Martian" team.

"We have a communications session with *Mars-3* in an hour."

Ryazanskiy hesitated: "If you don't mind, I'm going to stay. I'd like to have a look at how communication is going with Mars."

"What new things have they discovered on the way to Mars?"

"We can report one discovery already," answered Babakin. "In Korolev's time it was thought that for any spacecraft the weight of the science equipment must not exceed 5 kilograms. This was a universal constant. Like a speed of 300,000 kilometers per second that not a single body is capable of exceeding. And here we exceeded the 'science' mass by almost double. That's why the ballistics experts are convinced that we won't get to Mars."

"We have the lead when it comes to the amount of deviation from the universal constant of mass. On the DOS we installed a heavy infrared telescope that weighs almost 100 kilograms," I responded.

"As a result, God has punished us—the telescope cover didn't open. Don't violate covenants."

The red disk of the Sun sank into the sea. On the horizon a steamer crossed a sea-lane, blinding from the Sun's glare. The inimitable fragrances of the Crimean seashore wafted through the clear air.

"There are no regenerators with aromatic additives that can reproduce the freshness of the air that the Lord God created for the Crimea," I uttered some banality heard long ago.

"You're probably right, and in future space settlements mankind will not create a model of the Black Sea coast," agreed Pravetskiy.

"But, you know," said Bogomolov, "in such rare hours of our lives as these, it grieves me that Sergey Pavlovich isn't here with us. Imagine what he would feel now, being here, admiring this delightful sunset and knowing that the orbital station that he had dreamed of was making its latest orbit, that an automatic interplanetary station was on its way to Mars, and that news about all of this was being broadcast from Moscow to the Far East via a Molniya communications satellite. And he conceived and began all of this. No one, except for him, dared yell at me, 'You insolent child!' Perhaps that's why I miss him so."[26]

THE NEXT DAY TURNED OUT TO BE BUSINESSLIKE AND BUSTLING. At the State Commission meeting Mishin proposed leaving a small group of specialists headed by Tregub and Yeliseyev at NIP-16 in Yevpatoriya to control the flight and monitor program execution. The rest would update documentation and in the morning depart for our "permanent places of work." Whoever might be needed in the course of affairs could be called up if necessary, since the exchange of real-time information had been arranged. The State Commission would return here one day before the landing.

We departed from the Crimea after agreeing that Dobrovolskiy's crew should set a new record for time spent in space. A preliminary landing date of 30 June was set. In this case, the previous record set by Nikolayev and Sevastyanov would be broken by five days.[27]

"Before the Soyuz lands we'll have to launch N-1 No. 6L," Mishin reminded us at an informal State Commission meeting.

---

26. For the incident that Bogomolov is referring to, see Chertok, *Rockets and People, Vol. III*, pp. 236–238.

27. The *Soyuz-9* mission had lasted 17 days, 16 hours, and 59 minutes.

"Yes, and this mission, I must tell you, is perhaps no less complicated," said the minister somewhat sadly. "As soon as we get back, we'll have to gather together once again, but in Tyuratam rather than Yevpatoriya."

Having turned toward State Commission Secretary Vladimir Khodakov, the minister continued: "As soon as we arrive, draw up a list of whom to invite to the State Commission and when. Most likely, at first we'll gather in my office, and then we'll convene the prelaunch commission at the firing range. I've consulted with Dorofeyev and Moiseyev. They've put together a schedule figuring on the launch of N-1 No. 6 on 27 June."

OVER THE COURSE OF THE FIRST WEEK of piloted flight of the first DOS, the crew became familiar with the station.

"Judging by conversations with Earth, the guys are still dealing with the 'where are we?' problem," they reported from Yevpatoriya. For the ground services and GOGU, mastering the techniques of control and the real-time processing of data arriving from DOS were also new matters. Misunderstandings, glitches in the instructions, and errors in telemetry processing occurred every day.

Having taken advantage of the fact that in the break between launches and landings the majority of the leading figures were in Moscow, Keldysh convened the presidium of Academy of Sciences on 15 June [1971] to discuss issues of fundamental scientific research in space.

"The first full-fledged orbital station has been in space for nine days now. A three-man crew is working on it. This is certainly a great achievement for our cosmonautics. However, if one examines how this flight will enrich science with fundamental research, then quite frankly, we have nothing to boast about. I have asked several of our leading scientists to give their proposals for primary fields of study in connection with the opportunities that are presenting themselves thanks to orbital stations. These materials have been assembled at the Institute of Space Research (IKI). I ask the director of IKI, Georgiy Ivanovich Petrov, to report the main results to us."[28]

Petrov reported that astrophysicists would like to have a 2.6-ton science equipment complex on orbital stations during the first phase and, during the second phase, a 20-meter-diameter parabolic antenna as well.

"They request that 5.6 tons be reserved for the study of Earth's natural resources, including 0.4 tons for spectrozonal photography. In all, by our

---

28. Georgiy Ivanovich Petrov (1912–1987) served as the founding director of IKI from 1965 to 1973. He became a full member of the Academy of Sciences in 1960.

calculations, the total weight of the science equipment will be around 10 tons," concluded Petrov.

"And could you please tell us what year these tons will be converted into equipment and instruments suitable for failsafe operation in space?" asked Keldysh.

"There is some disagreement among us on that point, but for the time being no one will promise anything before 1973."

IKI Chief Engineer Khodarev and Academician Vernov tried to provide details for Petrov's multi-ton concept.[29]

I asked when we could receive the dimensional-installation drawings and main requirements for the attitude-control and stabilizations systems, not even asking for the "real, live" instruments for installation on board.

"First, will you tell us what kind of perturbations will be caused by the cosmonauts 'running around' inside the station?"

"If the cosmonauts are going to bother you, they can go into the vehicle and undock it from the station during the science sessions."

"And who then will adjust the equipment and observe?"

"For that you include one research scientist in the crew, running the risk of leaving him in isolation for a long time."

The discussion had taken on a nature that was far from academic. Keldysh took the proposed programs as a starting point and instructed Petrov to coordinate specific proposals with TsKBEM within a month.

On 16 June, a serious incident occurred in space. That morning Mishin called me unexpectedly. Bushuyev, Feoktistov, Semyonov, and Tregub, who had arrived from Yevpatoriya, were already in his office.

"Yeliseyev just reported over the high-frequency line that there was a fire on DOS. The crew is getting ready for an emergency landing. We need to report to Kamanin so that they can bring the search and rescue service into readiness. Tregub and the ballistics experts need to figure out during which orbit the vehicle should separate from DOS so that the landing is guaranteed to take place on our territory.

---

29. Yuliy Konstantinovich Khodarev was a deputy director of IKI, responsible for technical and engineering development at the institute. Sergey Nikolayevich Vernov (1910–1982) was, at the time, director of the Scientific-Research Institute of Nuclear Physics at the Moscow State University. Vernov (who became an Academician in 1968) was closely involved in developing space science instruments for Soviet spacecraft.

"I somehow sensed," Mishin turned to Tregub, "that you should have stayed in Yevpatoriya. Yeliseyev is alone there and might panic. I'm going to give Khvastunov the order now to quickly prepare the airplane for takeoff to Saki."

"With all the driving, the flight will take 5 hours. In that time the landing might even take place. It's better to stay here in communication," I said.

Tregub was busy talking over the high-frequency line, and gradually the situation began to become clearer. On 16 June, the odor of burned insulation and smoke started coming from the science equipment control console (PUNA).[30]

"We have a 'curtain' on board," Volkov transmitted to the ground.

In code, "curtain" meant either smoke or fire. On the ground they had forgotten about the code and began to ask again what kind of "curtain." Instead of the crew commander, Volkov was conducting the talks with the ground. He lost his composure, and after cursing, he said in plain language: "We have a fire! We're evacuating into the vehicle now."

Then he said that they couldn't find the instructions for an emergency evacuation and descent and requested that ground dictate to them what they needed to do and in what sequence. In Podlipki we managed to arrange to back up the conversations between the DOS crew and NIP-16.

"Tell us the information for an emergency undocking," demanded Volkov in a very agitated voice.

After a long period of searching, the ground responded: "Read the actions to take in the event of an emergency evacuation on pages 110 to 120. These pages contain the actions to take for transfer to the Descent Module. After transfer, reactivate vehicle per instructions on 7K-T, pages 98a and 98b. Nominal undocking. Prepare pages 133 to 136. Land only on instructions from the ground. Don't hurry. The console is switched off and the smoke should stop. If you evacuate the station, then leave the harmful contaminant absorber activated. Take headache tablets. According to telemetry data, CO_2 and O_2 are normal. The commander makes the decision to transfer and undock."

Dobrovolskiy understood that it was time for him to take over communication with the ground: "*Zarya*, this is *Yantar*. We've made the decision not to hurry. PUNA is switched off. For the time being, two will be on duty, one is resting. Don't worry, we are geared up to keep working."

"*Yantar-1*, this is *Zarya*. We are analyzing the state of the on-board systems and believe that the actions taken guarantee normal operation. We hope that you continue to work per the flight program. The odors will pass. We recommend a day of rest for you on 17 June; then go into mode. Keep in mind that

---

30. PUNA—*Pult upravleniya nauchnoy apparaturoy.*

after leaving the NIP coverage zone, tracking ship *Akademik Sergey Korolev* [*Academician Sergey Korolev*] will read you well."

From these remote conversations we understood that Dobrovolskiy and Patsayev were downplaying Volkov's emotions and had sent him to rest. After a couple of orbits, tracking ship *Akademik Sergey Korolev* transmitted that everything was okay on board the spacecraft. *Yantar-1* and *-3* were having dinner and *Yantar-2* was resting. When everything calmed down a little, Mishin assembled everyone who had experienced the unexpected incident and instructed Tregub to return to NIP-16 in Yevpatoriya to restore order. Rauschenbach and I were supposed to fly out there with the necessary specialists in five days. Mishin himself planned to fly out to the firing range with the minister on 20 June for the preparation and launch of N-1 No. 6L.

"The launch is scheduled for 27 June. We'll spend a day analyzing glitches. It means the minister and I will arrive in Yevpatoriya to join you on 29 June. If they don't have any more fires up there, prepare all the materials for a nominal landing on 30 June."

The commotion surrounding the code word "curtain" passed through all the levels of our hierarchy all the way to the chairman of the VPK. Subsequent reassuring reports from the control center in Yevpatoriya and from space eased Yuriy Mozzhorin's situation. He had been instructed to prepare the text of a TASS report about the incident on the orbital station and, in connection with this, about the safe but premature return of the crew. Now there was no need for such a TASS report, and he could calmly sign off on standard reports about the flight of the station, the cosmonauts' work, and how well they felt.[31]

ON 20 JUNE, MISHIN DEPARTED FOR THE FIRING RANGE, bringing along Okhapkin, Simakin, and a whole "complement" of representatives from the services and enterprises involved in the preparation and launch of the N-1. After the departure of the expedition headed by Mishin, a brief lull set in. I decided to take advantage of it in order to reduce my "debts" on upcoming projects. That evening the duty attendant brought me a pile of mail from the first department.[32] I began by reviewing directives and letters from subcontracting organizations. My study of the documents and redirecting of assignments moved quickly until I discovered a transcript of Ustinov's speech about creating orbital stations. I had never properly secured these four sheets of paper—instead I had shuffled them together with

---

31. Mozzhorin headed the group at TsNIImash responsible for producing and vetting press communiqués on the Soviet space program.

32. During Soviet times, the "first department" at any workplace was the division concerned with security and secrecy. It controlled the access of all documents at that particular enterprise.

unclassified documents in a folder, and therefore I still had the memo. It was dated 4 September 1970. In the document, Ustinov is carrying on a conversation with the chiefs of TsKBEM in Podlipki, having already visited ZIKh in Fili.

Rereading this transcript 28 years later [in 1998], it occurred to me that the modern achievements in the orbital station programs, including *Mir* and the International Space Station, are to a great extent the result of the firm position that Ustinov took in 1970 and subsequent years. Meanwhile, Ustinov would have been justified not only in withholding support for our initiative, but even in shutting it down. As it happened, the people responsible for the failure of the N1-L3 program, instead of concentrating all their efforts on saving this program, came out with proposals to create DOSes. I believe that it is better to be late than never than to never cite some excerpts from Ustinov's statements in order to objectively assess his role in the history of the emergence of orbital stations.

> *The way that we set out to create DOSes is absolutely correct. Your proposals contain a great deal of what is needed to elevate the space program as a whole. From the very beginning I viewed this proposal not as a temporary rescue, but as a crucial independent field of endeavor. I now have an even greater appreciation for Long-Duration Orbital Stations than I did before.*
>
> *All of your statements, concerns, anxieties, and proposals have convinced me that we have set out on the right path. I am profoundly convinced of this. However, I would like to caution against draw-ing conclusions that are too hasty and extravagant. Perhaps, from the standpoint of tactics and politics, you sometimes make mistakes and preach to the choir. Now the important thing isn't arguing, but fulfilling this grandiose task that you have taken on.*
>
> *The first and second DOSes—this isn't exactly what we would have liked. I understand that it simply isn't possible to do more in that period of time. But I'm not going to cave in. Pay attention to the third and fourth, and prepare very seriously for the fifth and sixth DOSes. These orbital systems must be tested out to the maximum. Under no circumstances should we be involved now with setting systems against one another. At this stage, no good will come of this. We need to map out the sequence for the implementation of engineering solutions and rigidly adhere to it, making adjustments as we gain experience. In terms of creativity, it is difficult to help you. If you view the DOSes as many years of work rather than the latest "makeshift" project, then show it. If DOSes solve the overwhelming majority of problems, then we can postpone Almaz and review our programs. This is the natural*

course of events. However, we also need to listen to the other side and determine our position without excessive emotion.

There's a lot of dissatisfaction in the Central Committee with the general progress of work on the space programs. They're saying there are too many project themes. We need to study all the themes and perhaps review our previous thinking and decisions.

We were all energetic, positive, and enthusiastic in 1969 when we got down to work promising to launch the first station in 1970—before the Party congress. The congress was postponed three months or more, and a certain cooling off began in your work too.[33] This doesn't look very pretty.

The orbital station needs to begin to fly as soon as possible! Flights will show us our weak points; they'll help us make the necessary corrections. You have a tremendous amount of work that is truly creative—essentially you are solving a problem for the whole future of orbital station development. We have a struggle between schools of thought ahead of us—concerning the role of a human being on an orbital station. A person should be given the opportunity to use his reason. He should know how to get out of any difficult situation. You must show that you will take on all of Almaz's problems and solve them at a higher level.

After receiving our support, you made a truly revolutionary step toward creating orbital stations. At the same time, you are losing perspective on the N1-L3 program. The N-1 failures are annoying, but they shouldn't dispirit you. Think how you can speed up work on the N1-L3 using the experience of working on the DOSes.

Is there no possibility of sending a two-man expedition to the Moon? The experience of working on the DOSes shows that our staffs have enormous reserves. We need to train crews for the orbital stations so that we will have competent space navigators, intelligence officers, and researchers. You must not compare the capabilities of a human being to a machine, but use the advantages of both to the greatest extent possible. The near-Earth space programs in effect now—Almaz, DOS, Soyuz 7K-T, Soyuz 7K-S, Yantar, and others—need to be reviewed with an eye to economizing effort and resources by harmonizing the programs, having them complement each other, and eliminating redundancy.

Looking forward, your goal must be to create a standardized multipurpose orbital complex for military, economic, scientific, and

---

33. The Twenty-fourth Party Congress was ultimately held from 30 March to 9 April 1971.

political missions in near-Earth space. You should already be thinking about the fact that the DOSes will be modules of a future MOK. The N-1 is needed for the MOK. The Central Committee has yet to see any of your proposals about the prospects for the N-1, except for the old plan calling for the landing of one cosmonaut on the lunar surface. This is causing the most profound concern in the Central Committee. You don't have the same creative force on the N-1 as you put together for the DOSes. Perhaps we could give it some thought and create a branch organization that will deal only with the prospects for using the N-1? You also don't have a real struggle for the RT-2 [solid-propellant ICBM], for this system's place in the general concept of strategic missile forces. You aren't really fighting for this. To date, these missiles have not been placed on combat duty.[34] *Your organization is at fault. We in the Central Committee do not feel the will of Chief Designer Mishin in resolving these crucial matters.*

Look at how passionately Chelomey and Yangel defend their concepts for combat missiles and see them through to realization. With regard to the RT-2, we will have to have a special conversation.

THAT EVENING, AFTER SETTING ASIDE THE NEVER-CLASSIFIED PAGES containing the transcript of Ustinov's speech, I began to edit the key points concerning the program for the creation of a standardized Multipurpose Orbital Complex. This material contained interesting ideas that had been developed in my departments, too. Many of them strayed from the directive proposals of the design departments. A hard line needed to be adopted for standardizing the service systems of the transport vehicles and the different modules. I prepared a memo with a list of proposals for standardization of the following items:

- the motion control and navigation systems of particularly sensitive elements, as well as Sun and star trackers;
- the control moment gyrostabilization system;
- the life-support system assemblies;
- the thermal control system equipment;
- the integrated power supply system equipment;
- the final approach, docking, and airlocking assemblies and automatic systems;
- the rendezvous control radio systems;
- the radio telemetry systems for monitoring all on-board systems;

---

34. The RT-2 was officially declared operational on 28 December 1972.

- the integrated radio systems for transmitting, receiving, and processing data, including commands, voice, television, and orbital-monitoring data;
- the on-board digital computers, communication devices, and analog-to-digital conversion devices; and
- the correcting braking engines (KTDU) and their fittings.

Was it possible in principle to standardize the KTDU for spacecraft with different masses and orbital lifetimes? I had a conversation with Isayev on this topic on one of my days off.

One weekend, instead of taking a day to go canoeing, Katya and I accepted an invitation from Isayev and drove to Pirogovo to have a look at how our many gardening friends lived.[35] Might we too switch over to a sedentary form of recreation? Isayev showed us his garden cabin, unable to conceal his pride at having designed it. Laws at the time restricted the area of a cabin to 25 square meters. In order to get around this limit, he himself had designed the cabin tilting the walls outward so that the interior volume was considerably greater than prescribed, but the area of the foundation did not exceed the permitted size.

Isayev's wife, Alevtina Dmitriyevna, an avid participant in canoe trips, argued that keeping a garden on the shore of a magnificent reservoir could be completely compatible with paddling around in a canoe. Isayev recounted, "Alevtina and I got married after the canoe trips, which our visitors used to arrange. But when our daughter Katya came into this world, we realized that sun, fresh air, and water weren't just necessary during holidays. And that's when we got this 'bungalow'. If you could manage to get 600 square meters here, it would be more than enough in terms of workload to replace canoe trips lasting several days."

From the author's archives.

Chertok and his wife Yekaterina "Katya" at their dacha.

That day we visited "gardeners" Chizhikov, Raykov, Melnikov, and Stepan—they all unanimously tried to persuade us to abandon our "paradise in a hut" on the Pyalovskoye Reservoir and become "landowners." They proudly showed us young apple trees, currant bushes, and radish sprouts on their own garden plots.

"And as far as standardizing the KTDU is concerned," said Isayev, when we were already about to say our good-byes, "I don't see any

---

35. Pirogovo is a suburban area located about 70 kilometers west of the Moscow city center.

From the author's archives.

Retired veterans of the Soviet space program, from left to right: A. G. Reshetin, B. Ye. Chertok, V. V. Vorshev, and V. F. Skvortsov at Chertok's dacha in 2006.

problems there. We just need to make sure your planners don't put on airs, and we'll always come to terms."

That evening Rauschenbach and Chizhikov interrupted my late-night pursuits.

"It's time to get ready to go home," said Chizhikov. "We're here to bum a ride off of you. Today neither of us has a car."

I glanced at my watch. It really was time. After scooping all the classified materials into the file, I telephoned the first department.

"Yesterday at Pirogovo we had an incident. I wanted to drop by and see you first thing in the morning, but instead I ended up in the shop and I got all tied up," said Chizhikov.

"What happened?"

"An ambulance took Aleksey Isayev straight from his garden plot to the hospital."

"He got a Czech *Jawa* motorcycle quite recently. Don't tell me he crashed."

"No, that's not it at all. It seems he had bad chest pains."

"That's worse. Wait. Let's find out what's going on."

I dialed Isayev's number on the Kremlin line. His first deputy—Vladislav Nikolayevich Bogomolov—answered. He was also the owner of a garden plot in Pirogovo. Bogomolov confirmed that Isayev had started to have intense pains

385

near his heart. They called an ambulance from Mytishchi.[36] At the Mytishchi hospital the diagnosis was that he'd had a heart attack. Consequently, they put him on strict bed rest on his back, IV line, and shots. He, Bogomolov, immediately informed the ministry of this calamity. There they had a fit: "What do you mean, he's in Mytishchi? Get him to the *kremlevka* immediately!"[37] An ambulance rushed from the *kremlevka* to Mytishchi with a request to release the patient. The Mytishchi doctors objected. In their opinion it was risky to transport the patient in such a condition.

After examining Isayev, the *kremlevka* medical staff supposedly said that there was absolutely no danger and that it wasn't a heart attack at all, but pains from intercostal neuralgia.[38] They took Isayev to the *kremlevka*. For the time being Bogomolov couldn't say whether Isayev had had a heart attack or neuralgia. And I had been on the verge of inviting Aleksey Isayev to fly with me to Yevpatoriya for the landing of Dobrovolskiy's crew. I had dreamed of talking him into making a trip with me to Koktebel after the landing and spending the day there reminiscing about our prewar croquet tournaments and strolls to Kara-Dag.

I reminded Chizhikov: "Remember what a fantastic time we had with Isayev in Koktebel—it's been 31 years! Those were the good old days. Koktebel is quite close, but apparently it's not in the cards any more for us to get there."

What should we do now? We couldn't possibly drive home. I called Yevgeniy Vorobyev on the Kremlin line. Despite the late hour he was on the job.

"I'll try to find out. But keep in mind that at the *kremlevka* they don't like it when we interfere." Five minutes later Vorobyev telephoned.

"I managed to find out that the situation is serious. Of course, they told me that they're doing everything they can and they don't need our help...."

On 25 June 1971, Aleksey Isayev died. The staff at the Khimmash Design Bureau was stunned.[39] Isayev not only enjoyed the authority of a chief, but also the sincere love of his staff, which rarely comes to a boss from his subordinates. Rarely did a spacecraft get along without Isayev's orbital correction engines. Air-defense, missile-defense, and submarine-launched missiles flew using Isayev's engines.

---

36. Mytishchi is a city on the northeastern limits of Moscow.

37. *Kremlevka* was the nickname of the Kremlin hospital where high-ranking officials were treated.

38. Intercostal neuralgia describes severe pains due to rib muscles contracting during inhalation.

39. In 1967, Isayev's OKB-2 had been renamed *Konstruktorskoye byuro khimicheskogo mashinostroyeniya* (Design Bureau of Chemical Machine Building) or KB Khimmash.

Isayev didn't have many people who were jealous of him, and he had no enemies. I had known him for 35 years. All that time it seemed that not only his brain, but also his heart, burned with the flame of engineering creativity. He belonged to a rare breed of creator/manager who could arrive at work in the morning, assemble his colleagues, and say, "Everything that we thought up yesterday needs to be tossed into the trash can and forgotten. We slipped up."

Isayev was not afraid to admit his own mistakes and bravely contested popular opinion. His behavior sometimes caused outrage in the ministries when deadlines were missed because Isayev demanded that a large amount of production stock be "thrown out" like potato peelings. Simplicity, approachability, and unselfishness set Isayev apart from his peers.

Mishin telephoned me from the firing range.

"Tomorrow we have a launch. I won't be able to fly back for Aleksey's funeral. As an old comrade and representative of our organization, you go support the Isayevites."

It wasn't difficult to arrange support at funerals. First Deputy Minister Tyulin headed the Funeral Commission. He explained: "There's just one day for the funeral. On 27 June there is the N-1 launch. On 30 June there is the landing of the *Soyuz-11* crew. A day later all the managers, including those from Isayev's firm, must fly out to Yevpatoriya. That means the funeral has to take place on 28 June. The Central Committee gave instructions to have the burial at Novodevichye Cemetery. We need to quickly select the site. I've been told that his relatives insist on the old section of Novodevichye. It's very difficult to find a plot there. But all the commands have been given. You in the city prepare the Palace of Culture for him to lie in state. You know the drill. The ministry will absorb all the expenses. Don't forget about transportation. If we don't have enough buses, rent municipal ones. Help Bogomolov if problems arise. I will come straight to the Palace first thing in the morning."

The launch of N-1 No. 6L wedged itself into our ritual schedule as a funeral salute. Liftoff took place overnight from 26 to 27 June 1971 at 2:15:52 Moscow time. Beginning in the evening, communication was established with the firing range via the high-frequency line, but we weren't able to set up real-time transmission of telemetry parameters. We received information about what happened after liftoff in the form of not very distinct oral reports from the bunker, and then from the firing range computer center, where the telemetry systems' information was processed in real time.

All 30 first-stage engines transitioned to mode. The rocket lifted off normally. Five seconds after liftoff the telemetry operators began their running commentary: "Pitch and yaw normal; roll angle is increasing."

From the first seconds, the rocket began to spin about its longitudinal axis. After 14 seconds of flight, the roll angle exceeded 8°. The gyro platform issued the AVD (emergency engine shutdown) command. The command failed to pass. It was inhibited until 50 seconds into the flight. This inhibit had been introduced after the crash of No. 5L for the safety of the launch facilities. By the 50th second of flight, the rocket had spun 60°. As soon as the inhibit was removed, all 30 engines of the first stage shut down at once. The rocket fell to the ground 20 kilometers away. If it hadn't been for the safety inhibit of the AVD command, the rocket would have crashed a kilometer from the launch site. The blast wave, equivalent to 500 tons of TNT, would have destroyed the launch facilities for a second time.

In 1948, during the testing of R-1 missiles in Kapustin Yar, Pilyugin had dared to assert to the State Commission that failures provide us with experience that we don't gain during normal launches. Recalling this, addressing Pilyugin and me at one of the accident investigation commission sessions, Barmin said with bitter satisfaction: "You have experimentally confirmed the fulfillment of my requirement for defective rockets to fall a safe distance from the launch site."

What forces spun the rocket? It seemed the answer lay on the surface—a false command from the roll-control system. This scenario has been declared the most likely in similar cases. During that very difficult, sleepless night, even I gave in to the hypnosis of that very simple explanation—that it was a failure in the roll command transmission circuit. But the more likely scenario was that the command polarity was mixed up. "The same thing happened on our first Soyuz. They could also have gotten it mixed up on a rocket," said those taking part in the all-nighter in Podlipki, having no credible information from the firing range. Proponents of the mixed-up polarity tried to calculate the angular rate of spin. In this case, instead of the stabilization automatic control unit providing negative feedback, the control unit provided positive feedback. Rather than responding to the roll angle error with counteracting torque from the rotation control nozzles, the automatic control unit would add to and intensify the torque.

By 10 a.m., according to reports from the firing range, the scenarios pointing to the culpability of the control system and also the likelihood of mixed polarity had been rejected. Georgiy Degtyarenko explained via the high-frequency communication line that the control system had fought honorably for the rocket's life. From the very first seconds of flight, the engines' control nozzles attempted to stop the rotation but quickly reached their stops, and the spinning continued. Perturbation torque about the longitudinal axis, which came from who-knows-where, proved to be much greater than the torque of the control nozzles.

That day they telephoned us relentlessly from the offices of the Central Committee, VPK, and various ministries and related organizations, convinced that the secret of the N-1 crash had already been discovered, but that we were intentionally keeping them in the dark and hiding something. Khitrik was one of the first that day to come out with a scenario, which was later proved true.

"Using the reports of our comrades from the firing range, we have tried to reproduce the process on our models. The control system acts that way only when perturbation torque is five times greater than the value you noted in the baseline data. I have already informed Pilyugin of that, and he informed Mishin. Before they arrive I advise that we call together all the aero- and gas-dynamics specialists and let them try to find where this perturbation is coming from, given that we didn't have it during the exact same seconds during the first launch."

All that I managed to do on that chaotic and difficult day was to pass on Khitrik's doubts to the chief of the aerodynamics department, Vladimir Roshchin. "We couldn't have committed such a large error," he said. "Perhaps during modifications of the aft end they deformed the structure. Tell Khitrik to look for the problem in his own shop." Alas, it all turned out to be considerably more complicated. This became clear after prolonged studies and labor-intensive experimental work.

It wasn't until late that evening, at home, that I was able to reminisce about Isayev. Katya and I sorted through memories of our meetings with him beginning in 1935: in Fili, Khimki, Koktebel, the Urals, Podlipki; strolls together through Leningrad; the commotion of children on the meadows in Pirogovo; the exclamations of "well, blow my brains out" on the occasion of both success and failure.

Daniil Khrabrovitskiy—the screenwriter of the film *Ukroshcheniye ognya* [*Taming the Fire*]—was shaken when I called to inform him of Isayev's death.[40]

"His stories, his dedication, his real help with the launches of rockets enriched the film much more than I had anticipated," said Khrabrovitskiy. "Despite your objections, after getting to know Isayev, I sent Bashkirtsev to the construction of Magnitogorsk.[41] I didn't make up the scene with the black caviar in the cold barracks. Isayev told me about that."

---

40. Daniil Yakovlevich Khrabrovitskiy (1923–1980) was a well-known Soviet director who directed *Taming the Fire*, the first Soviet-era fictionalization about the space program put to film. Chertok has much to say about this film in the final chapter of this volume.

41. Andrey Bashkirtsev was the lead character in *Taming the Fire*, representing a fictionalized version of Sergey Korolev.

On the day of Isayev's funeral, according to the established tradition, he lay in state at the Palace of Culture. However, it wasn't long before such a throng (several thousand people) had gathered at the entrance to the building that it became clear: it would not be possible to allow everyone to pass through the hall. The Commission made an unusual decision—the casket would be carried out to the central square of Kaliningrad. The employees of Isayev's design bureau very efficiently reorganized the previously written protocol.

Isayev lay in an open casket in the town's central square under the hot June sun. Fresh-cut flowers carefully placed by the casket by the hundreds of people who had come to pay their last respects were added to the many dozens of wreaths from organizations. The Hero of Socialist Labor gold medal, four Orders of Lenin, the Lenin and State Prize laureate badges of honor, the Order of the October Revolution, and a multitude of medals sparkled on red pillows. I never saw Isayev decked out in with all of these government awards when he was alive.

That day *Pravda* came out with an obituary and picture of Isayev. After Korolev's obituary in 1966, this was the second posthumous declassification.

> *Aleksey Mikhaylovich Isayev was among the first creators of rocket engines and the head of a design staff that created a whole series of engines for missile and space technology. The engines created under the leadership of A. M. Isayev were installed on Vostok, Voskhod, and Soyuz piloted spacecraft and on automatic interplanetary stations.... Aleksey Mikhaylovich was one of the designers of an airplane that performed the world's first flight using a reactive engine on 15 May 1942. In 1944, A. M. Isayev became the head of a leading engine building design organization....*

Below the obituary were the signatures of Brezhnev, Podgornyy, Kosygin, other members of the Politburo, ministers, and also Tabakov, Tyulin, Glushko, Grushin, Lyulka, and Kuznetsov. It is inexplicable why the Central Committee dared place the signature of Grushin—a developer of air-defense and missile-defense missiles—under the obituary and drew the line at publishing the surnames of the main consumers of Isayev's engines—Makeyev and Mishin.[42]

---

42. Petr Dmitriyevich Grushin (1906–1993) was one of the most powerful and famous chief designers in the Soviet defense industry. He headed OKB-2 (later known as MKB Fakel) from 1953 until his death; this organization designed many important air-defense and antiballistic missiles in the Soviet military arsenal.

Tyulin opened the funeral ceremony. His speech repeated the text of the obituary printed in *Pravda*. Before my speech I was handed a note: "Don't mention anything about projects for Makeyev or missiles." I couldn't find the speech that I'd written and so I spoke extemporaneously. Later I was told that my speech was "from the heart." The only words I remembered were that "Isayev was a real human being and a great engineer."

Makeyev was deprived of the right in his eulogy to mention Isayev's decisive role in the strategic missiles that Makeyev had developed for submarines.[43] He got out of that difficulty by emphasizing Isayev's human qualities.

According to established tradition, a second funeral ceremony took place at Novodevichye Cemetery. Other orators spoke more briefly. Not everyone got to throw a handful of earth into the grave. In the old section of Novodevichye with thousands in attendance, it was anything but easy. After filling the grave, the gravediggers with their professional knack erected a hill of wreaths and fresh-cut flowers. I had arranged with [my wife] Katya, who had dozens of acquaintances here, that if we were to lose one another in the multitude of people at the cemetery, we would meet up in the parking area. I wanted to walk through to the graves of Boguslavskiy and Voskresenskiy.[44] For me this was a visceral need. That day, two true comrades of mine had been joined by a third, perhaps my closest.

While I was standing at Voskresenskiy's grave an unfamiliar woman approached me.

"You don't recognize me?"

I looked at the no-longer-young, somehow imperceptibly familiar face under the mop of frizzy gray hair and confessed that I didn't recognize her.

"It's me, Mira, have you forgotten?"

After embracing, I asked: "But where's Oleg?"[45]

"Oleg has been gone for a long time. He just couldn't deal with the tranquil life. I have a candidate of sciences degree. It's interesting work, right near here on Pirogovskaya Street. I have two children. There's no time to be bored. I saw the obituary in the newspaper and came to say goodbye to Isayev. I remembered him as a gallant knight, although back then he didn't have a single medal."

"He really was a gallant knight," I said. "But unlike Don Quixote, he possessed the talent of an engineer and he performed real feats. He didn't do

---

43. Isayev's organization designed engines for several Makeyev rockets, including the R-17, R-27, R-27M, R-27K, R-27U, R-29, R-29M, R-29R, R-29RM, and R-39.

44. Leonid Voskresenskiy and Yevgeniy Boguslavskiy had died in 1965 and 1969, respectively.

45. *Author's note*: I wrote about Oleg Bedarev and his wartime girlfriend Mira in Volume I of my memoirs (pp. 314–315).

battle with windmills. But he worked on fantastic designs without losing his common sense."

Mira opened her bag, pulled out an envelope, and handed it to me.

"What's this?"

"You'll see."

"Let's walk to my car, Katya is waiting there, we'll drive to the funeral reception."

"No. Soon everyone will be leaving; I want to be here alone for a while."

It wasn't until I got home that I opened the envelope. It contained a photograph from the summer of 1945: Oleg Bedarev and I. We were both in military uniform. Printed on a sheet of onionskin paper were poignant lines of poetry. Oleg had performed them while he played his guitar at our last "fireside" get-together.

> *A somber yellow field and grove.*
> *The wind flutters like a captive dove.*
> *The autumn whirlwind stirs dead leaves—*
> *No more their beauty will we see.*
> *Winds tear them up, drive them away,*
> *Laughing and moaning as they play...*
> *The bitter moan of words unsaid,*
> *The anguish of dreams that are left for dead.*
> *The pain of a strange and unknown dream...*
> *The autumn whirlwind stirs dead leaves.*
> *Life's tumult ended.... And in the mist*
> *They hug the ground, reduced to dust.*
> *Hear their prayer, life's truth, O Earth.*
> *Receive them in peace, you who gave them their birth.*

THE NEXT MORNING, 29 JUNE 1971, I flew to Yevpatoriya with Kerimov and a group of Isayev's coworkers who had stayed on for the funeral. There everyone had already prepared for the communication sessions for undocking, subsequent spacecraft orientation, deorbit, and landing. Minister Afanasyev and Mishin were supposed to fly in from the firing range. However, the failure of N-1 No. 6L had not yet been explained, and they did not feel that they could depart for Yevpatoriya.

Tregub reported to the State Commission that the crew, having spent around 23 days in space, had set a record. They had conducted experiments with the military's OD-4 optical sight/range finder, with the *Orion* ultraviolet-range observation system, and with the secret *Svinets* (Lead) radar system. They had photographed Earth, performed spectrographic studies of the horizon, and conducted experiments on gamma flux intensity and on a procedure for manual orientation of the station. Tentatively, this very intense program of scientific, military, medical, and technical experiments should be considered fulfilled. The final report would be done after the materials that the cosmonauts delivered to the ground were processed.

The crew spent the last two days deactivating the orbital station, packing up materials, and activating and preparing the spacecraft. The undocking command was supposed to be issued on 29 June at 2125 hours. After separation from the station, two orbits were allocated for preparation for descent. The crew would perform manual orientation outside our coverage zone and would transfer control to the gyro instruments. NIP-16 would issue the command to activate the descent cycle; NIP-15 would stand by in reserve. An SKTDU deboost burn would take place at 0147 hours on 30 June.[46]

Vorobyev confirmed that, according to the physicians' findings, the condition of the cosmonauts during the last few days was good. No one expected anything sensational at the traditional nocturnal meeting in the cramped control room of NIP-16. All commands to the vehicle were routed without a glitch. The crew reported the execution of all operations on time, without causing any aggravation on the ground. Everything was proceeding calmly and according to schedule. The ship-based tracking stations received information from the spacecraft as it passed over them and reported in real time that the engine had executed the deboost burn at the calculated time and the integrator had shut it down. The Command and Measurement Complex and GOGU accumulated good experience monitoring the spacecraft during the landing orbit.

After engine shutdown, the spacecraft left the coverage zone of the ship-based tracking stations located in the Atlantic. Separation took place over Africa—the Habitation Compartment and Instrument-Systems Compartment were jettisoned from the Descent Module. The Descent Module did not have a radio telemetry system. We had hoped to hear about what had happened after separation in the cosmonauts' oral report before entry into the atmosphere when the hot plasma would shut down the *Zarya* system's slot antenna. A *Mir* multichannel automatic recording unit had been installed to record the processes in the Descent Module. After the death of Komarov, two Olegs—Sulimov and Komissarov—and their comrades at the Institute of Measurements perfected this stand-alone recorder, increasing its thermal protection and mechanical strength.[47]

---

46. SKTDU—*Sblizhayushche-korrektiruyushchaya tormozhnaya dvigatelnaya ustanovka* (Approach and Correction Braking Engine Unit).
47. This was the Scientific-Research Institute of Measurement Technology (NII IT), which had spun off from TsNIImash in July 1966. NII IT was responsible for developing data sensors and recording devices for various Soviet spacecraft.

"We asked Dobrovolskiy the whole time to give us a running commentary as soon as the Descent Module enters our coverage zone, but he hasn't said a word," complained Yeliseyev. "It's strange that Volkov is quiet. During the last session he was very talkative."

"When you and Shatalov descended," I affirmed, "we saw how effective the slot antenna was. Shatalov's running commentary replaced telemetry for us."

"Before undocking, the 'hatch closed' indicator for the hatch between the Descent Module and the Habitation Compartment didn't light up. Volkov was clearly nervous, but he quickly figured it out and stuck some bandage tape under the limit switch that registers hatch closure. Then they were quite wordy in their running commentary," said Tregub.

"They're still doing great," I said, sticking up for them. "They're the first crew of a Long-Duration Orbital Station. They've withstood an unscheduled flight and for one thing, let's tell it straight, they performed a very intense program."

A report came over the loudspeaker: "The space monitoring service tracking the Descent Module per prognosis."

Finally, the long-awaited report arrived: "General Kutasin's service reports that airplanes have spotted the Descent Module.[48] Parachute descent is in progress. Per prognosis the overshoot is around 10 kilometers, no more, relative to the calculated touchdown point. Helicopters are flying out to the landing site."

After about 20 minutes we began to get nervous. No more reports were coming in from the landing area. The officer in contact with the search and rescue service felt guilty. We pelted him with a flurry of rebukes, but he was unable to tell us anything. State Commission Chairman Kerimov had the duty of being the first to report to Moscow—to Smirnov and Ustinov—about the successful completion of the mission. But he found himself cut off from communication with the landing area.

"It's not General Kutasin's fault! Most likely, Commander-in-Chief of the Air Force Aviation Marshal Kutakhov has taken over communication and has ordered Kutasin not to report without his knowledge," was the explanation that an experienced communications operator gave.[49]

Around 30 minutes after the calculated landing time, Kerimov decided to complain to Ustinov about the behavior of Air Force Commander-in-Chief Kutakhov. It took another 10 minutes to connect with Ustinov. The room fell silent. Finally Kerimov gave the sign: "Quiet!" But this time we heard

---

48. Major-General Aleksandr Ivanovich Kutasin (1903–1978) headed the Air Force's search and rescue service for the Soviet human spaceflight program.

49. Marshal Pavel Stepanovich Kutakhov (1914–1984) served as Commander-in-Chief of the Soviet Air Force from 1969 to 1984.

no complaints about Kutakhov. Kerimov said nothing. He hung up. With a changed expression on his face, Kerimov began to recount what he had heard from Ustinov.

"Two minutes after landing, a rescue crew from a helicopter ran up to the Descent Module. It was lying on its side. Externally there was no damage at all. They knocked on the side. No one answered. They quickly opened the hatch. All three were sitting in their seats in tranquil poses. There were dark blue spots on their faces. Blood was running from the nose and ears. They pulled them out of the Descent Module. Dobrovolskiy was still warm. Doctors continued to perform artificial resuscitation. According to their reports from the landing site, death was the result of asphyxiation. No foreign odors were detected in the Descent Module. Measures were taken to evacuate the bodies to Moscow for examination. Specialists from Podlipki and the Cosmonauts Training Center flew out to the landing site for an investigation."

In the total silence someone said: "It was depressurization."

The horrible news stunned everyone. No one delighted in the clear blue sky or in the vast expanse of the mirror-smooth sea from whence the sweet, fresh morning air wafted through the wide-flung windows.

At 11:30, the State Commission and everyone who could fit onto the airplane departed from the Saki airfield for Moscow. A small group stayed on in Yevpatoriya to monitor the flight of DOS No. 1, which went down in the history of cosmonautics as *Salyut 1*. The orbital corrections prepared and performed for its missions supported the station's flight until October. But now this no longer mattered. According to the disaster investigation results, so many measures would have to be taken that, in the best-case scenario, the next piloted Soyuz would not be able to fly until early 1972. For the N-1, the break in flight-development testing, regardless of what the other commission found, would also drag on for at least another six months. These were the thoughts running through our heads on the airplane. (In fact, considerably more time was needed for all the modifications. Test flights of unpiloted Soyuzes didn't start up again until June 1972.[50])

After arriving at the site where the Descent Module had touched down, the group of specialists headed by cosmonaut Aleksey Leonov and Descent Module developers Andrey Reshetin and Vladimir Timchenko looked over the module and checked it for leaks. They were not able to detect any off-nominal loss of pressure integrity. They removed the magnetic tape from the *Mir* recorder and

---

50. This was the *Kosmos-496* mission, flown from 26 June to 2 July 1972.

quickly dispatched it. Everyone was confident that after it was processed the cosmonauts' cause of death would immediately become apparent.

Moscow met us with such a heat wave that the Crimea seemed cool by comparison. Just a week before, I had stood in the honor guard by Isayev's casket in Kaliningrad. Now they were preparing the Red Banner Hall of the Central Building of the Soviet Army for a funeral ceremony of three cosmonauts at one time. All three were posthumously awarded the title of Hero of the Soviet Union. It was the second time for Volkov. From the Central Building of the Soviet Army, through a vast throng of people, the funeral procession headed to Red Square. The urns containing the cosmonauts' ashes were immured in the Kremlin Wall.

From the author's archives.

Shown at the funeral of the *Soyuz-11* crew in early August 1971 at Red Square are (left to right) Boris Chertok, Yuriy Semyonov, and Vakhtang Vachnadze.

Over the five days from 25 through 30 June 1971, fate had dealt us three blows: on the 25th, the death of Isayev; on the 27th, the failure of N-1 No. 6L; and on the 30th, the death of the *Soyuz-11* crew. There was no doubt that throughout July and August our staff would be given a shaking by at least two independent commissions: one for the N-1 and the other for the Soyuz. After a brief hesitation, the Politburo added to Keldysh's concerns. They made him chairman of the government commission investigating the causes of the death of the *Soyuz-11* crew. They appointed Georgiy Babakin deputy chairman. Members of the commission were Afanasyev, Glushko, Kazakov, Mishuk, Grushin, Shcheulov, Frolov, Burnazyan, Shatalov, and Tsarev (commission secretary).[51]

Keldysh convened the first commission meeting on 7 July. Opening the meeting, Keldysh announced that in addition to the members of the commission appointed by the administration, from TsKBEM he had invited Mishin, Bushuyev, Chertok, Tregub, Shabarov, and Feoktistov, and—at the request of the Ministry of Defense—Karas.

"We are obliged to submit a report to the Central Committee and Council of Ministers within two weeks," said Keldysh.

He went on to say that that morning he had been invited to the Politburo along with Smirnov and ministers Afanasyev and Dementyev.

"After expressing his sorrow over what had happened," continued Keldysh, "Leonid Ilyich asked that I tell you that under no circumstances has this given rise to any mindset for curtailing operations. We need to figure out as quickly as possible what caused this and continue the program of flights using long-duration space stations. Over the past few days various groups created to assist our commission have performed a great deal of work, and therefore, we shall begin by listening to what these working groups managed to find out."

Mishin was the first to report. He spoke in detail about the modifications and how the *Soyuz-11* 7K-T vehicle differed from its predecessors. Since November 1966 a total of 19 vehicles had been launched. Of these, 17 were 7K-OK models and two were 7K-Ts. The last one, 7K-T No. 32, differed from the previous one [*Soyuz-10*] only in terms of its modified docking assembly. Before descent, no in-flight off-nominal situations were recorded on vehicle No. 32. All operations for descent proceeded normally until the moment of separation. According to the data from the *Mir* recorder, at the moment of separation the pressure began to drop in the Descent Module. Over a period of 130 seconds the pressure dropped from 915 to 100 millimeters of mercury.

Keldysh interrupted Mishin: "The Commission needs to know by all means about all abnormalities, not only on the vehicle but also on the station. We need to prepare a list of all, I repeat, all glitches without exception. The entire prehistory needs to be clear to us. In particular, explain: why did we begin flights into space in spacesuits and then do away with them so quickly?"

---

51. These men represented various branches of the Soviet space program including industry (S. A. Afanasyev, V. A. Kazakov, A. I. Burnazyan, and A. I. Tsarev), designers (V. P. Glushko and P. D. Grushin), the Air Force (M. N. Mishuk and S. G. Frolov), the Rocket Forces (V. I. Shcheulov), and cosmonauts (V. A. Shatalov).

Mishin made a show of instructing Tregub and Feoktistov to prepare posters with a list of all glitches by tomorrow morning. He must have been very uncomfortable. First, because the guilty party in the tragedy, the news of which had spread throughout the world, was TsKBEM, and consequently, he, its boss and chief designer. Second, this disaster came on top of the N-1 failure, for which TsKBEM was ultimately also at fault. Each accident had specific responsible parties. The blame for each of them might be different. The fact that everyone collectively didn't know, didn't foresee, didn't understand something served as a general excuse. That's the very learning process that Korolev used to talk about. These arguments come in handy for a lawyer if a case were to go to trial. But this was a trial where each person was his own investigator, prosecutor, judge, and lawyer. Even the aim of the members of the Commission was not to look for the guilty party, but to understand what caused the disaster. Each of them had his own failure. And each understood full well that there were no evildoers or slovenly individuals here. There were flaws or unexplored spots in a large system. They needed to be hunted out.

It was difficult for Mishin to answer Keldysh's question about why we had done away with spacesuits. Korolev had made that decision personally before the launch of *Voskhod* [in 1964]. It was also impossible to fit three men in spacesuits in the Soyuz Descent Module. When Korolev was alive only Kamanin had come out strongly in favor of spacesuits. But chief planner of piloted vehicles Feoktistov had himself flown without a spacesuit with Komarov and Yegorov. He actively supported Korolev's initiative. Mishin had nothing directly to do with abandoning spacesuits. No problems had arisen with maintaining pressure integrity during a single one of the Vostok, Voskhod, and unpiloted and piloted Soyuz flights. Somehow demands to reinstate flights in spacesuits were of their own accord forgotten.

Mishin set forth some scenarios, supporting them with posters that Feoktistov put up.

"After landing, the Descent Module was checked out and no damage was found. Depressurization could have occurred due to two causes. The first is the premature actuation of a breathing vent valve. In this case the pressure should fall according to the upper curve. The second possible cause is an improper hatch seal. The curve of the calculated pressure drop when the valve is opened precisely coincides with the recording of the actual pressure drop after separation. In addition to the coincidence of the calculated and actual drop curves, we have evidence from the descent control system (SUS). The recording of the SUS behavior shows the presence of off-nominal disturbance. Judging by the magnitude and character, this disturbance coincides with the calculated value for the egress of air from the opening formed when a breathing valve is opened."

Grushin interrupted Mishin, trying to understand why this breathing vent was necessary in the first place.

"Is the valve closed on the launch pad? It's closed. Is it closed throughout the entire flight? It's closed. Is it closed during descent? It's closed. And you only open it at an altitude of 2 or 3 kilometers above Earth. You open up the hatches anyway right after landing. You've outsmarted yourself here somehow."

Unintelligible explanations began as to why this valve was necessary. To be perfectly frank, they were very unconvincing and contradictory. The discussion that had started became even more complicated after it was determined that in addition to this [breathing] valve, which is opened automatically by an explosive cartridge, there is also a manual butterfly valve. It was provided in the event of a water touchdown. By turning the handle of this valve, it is possible to block off the opening formed by the ill-fated breathing vent valve so that water doesn't get into the Descent Module.

Mishuk asked how the electrical scenario had been analyzed and why no one was talking about it. I answered that both the telemetry recordings and the autonomous recorder data had been thoroughly examined. There were no indications that a false premature command had been issued to the explosive cartridge opening the valve. An analysis of the *Mir* recordings showed that pressure integrity was lost at the moment of separation of the Descent Module from the Habitation Compartment. The pressure drop curve corresponded to a hole size equal to the cross section of a single valve. In fact there were two valves: one was a feed valve and the other a suction valve. If a false command had passed, then both valves would have opened right away: electrically, they were in the same circuit. The command to open two valves passed nominally, as it was supposed to at a safe altitude. According to the findings of specialists from the Scientific-Research Institute for the Operation and Repair of Aviation Technology (NIIERAT) (that's the clever title worn by the Air Force institute that holds a monopoly in the investigation of all aviation disasters), the explosive cartridges were not actuated in a vacuum, but at an altitude corresponding in time to the issuance of a nominal command.[52] But by this time one valve had already opened *without* the electrical command.

"In your opinion, what kind of evil spirit could have opened it at an altitude of 150 kilometers?" asked Kazakov.

"Let's not get carried away prematurely with one scenario," intervened Keldysh; "we need to discuss all of them on equal terms. I propose that we listen to Shabarov and medical science."

---

52. NIIERAT—*Nauchno-issledovatelskiy institut ekspluatatsii i remonta aviatsionnoy tekhniki.*

Shabarov reported on the results of the analysis of the data from the *Mir* recorder, which for us performed tasks similar to a "black box." In aviation disasters recovery crews hunt for the "black box" among the charred remains of the airplane, and we removed it safe and sound from a Descent Module that had executed a normal landing.

"The separation process lasted just 0.06 seconds," reported Shabarov. "At 0147 hours 26.5 seconds, a pressure of 915 millimeters of mercury was recorded in the Descent Module. One hundred fifteen seconds later it had dropped to 50 millimeters and continued to fall. During entry into the dense layers of the atmosphere the operation of the SUS was recorded. G-loads reached 3.3 units and then decreased. But the pressure in the Descent Module began to slowly increase: there was an inflow of air from the external atmosphere through the open breathing vent. Here on the chart is the command to open the valve. We see that the intensity of the inflow has increased. This corresponded to the opening of the second vent on command. Analysis of the *Mir* recordings confirmed the scenario of the opening of one of the two vents at the moment the vehicle modules separated. The temperature on the Descent Module's structural ring, not far from the hatch rim, reached 122.5°C [252.5°F]. But this was due to the general heating upon entry into the atmosphere."

"Before we go any further, let's hear the results of the medical investigations," proposed Keldysh.

Burnazyan made the report.

"During the last days of the flight the physical condition of the cosmonauts was good. They had been taking invigorants. They did three hours of general physical conditioning exercises every day. Dobrovolskiy had a resting pulse rate of 78 to 85. His blood pressure was normal. Volkov was more emotional. His pulse was high, in general; before separation of the vehicle modules his pulse reached 120. Patsayev's pulse was from 92 to 106. Based on the experience of other cosmonauts, pulse rates reached as high as 120 during peak periods, and Tereshkova's even went up to 160. During the first second after separation, Dobrovolskiy's pulse rate increased immediately to 114, and Volkov's to 180. Fifty seconds after separation, Patsayev's respiration rate was 42 per minute, which is characteristic for acute oxygen deprivation. Dobrovolskiy's pulse quickly dropped and his breathing stopped at about that time. This was the initial period of death. At the 110-second mark, no pulse and no breathing is recorded in all three of them. We believe that death occurred 120 seconds after separation. They were conscious for no more than 50 to 60 seconds after separation. During that time, evidently, Dobrovolskiy wanted to take some sort of action, judging by the fact that he had thrown off his safety belts.

"Seventeen top specialists were called in for the autopsy. Subcutaneous hemorrhaging was found in all three cosmonauts. Air bubbles, like fine sand, had gotten into their vessels. All of them had hemorrhaging in their middle ear and ruptured eardrums. Stomachs and intestines were bloated. Gases—nitrogen, oxygen, and CO_2—dissolved in the blood—seethed under the acute low pressure. The gases dissolved in the blood, after being transformed into bubbles, occluded the vessels. When the pericardium was opened, gas escaped: there had been air plugs in the heart. The vessels in the brain looked like strings of beads. They were also clogged with air plugs. Also indicative of the enormous emotional stress and acute oxygen deprivation is the amount of lactic acid in the blood—it was 10 times higher than normal.

"A minute and a half after touchdown, resuscitation attempts began. They continued for more than an hour. It is obvious that given this degree of injury no resuscitation methods could save them. In the history of medicine, and very likely not just medicine, there are no comparable examples known, and nowhere have experiments been conducted, not even on animals, to determine the body's reaction to such a regime of pressure reduction—from normal atmospheric pressure to virtually zero within dozens of seconds. There have been cases of depressurization of flight suits at altitudes in excess of 10 kilometers. In these cases the pilot lost consciousness from lack of oxygen, but when the airplane descended he regained consciousness. In this case, irreversible processes occurred over the course of dozens of seconds."

Burnazyan's calm report made a harrowing impression. Mentally placing themselves into the Descent Module, everyone tried to imagine how the cosmonauts felt during those first seconds. The excruciating pain throughout their bodies prevented them from thinking and comprehending. Certainly they heard the whistle of escaping air, but their eardrums quickly burst and silence set in. Judging by the speed of the drop in pressure, they were able to actively move and attempt to do something for perhaps the first 15 to 20 seconds.

THE GOVERNMENT COMMISSION FOR THE INVESTIGATION of the causes of death of the *Soyuz-11* crew broke into groups according to scenario and areas of expertise. Three days later another plenary session of Keldysh's commission took place. This time the leaders of the investigative groups had already reported. With regard to Mishin's comment that the cosmonauts "could have figured out by the sound to plug the opening with their finger," Yevgeniy Vorobyev officially declared that given that rate of pressure drop they would have lost consciousness in 20 seconds.

"To figure out what had happened, unfasten the safety belts, and find the hole beneath the interior paneling within 20 seconds is unrealistic," Vorobyev said. "They would have had to have been trained to do that beforehand. We tested the ability to close the breathing vent using the manual drive, which is done in the event of a touchdown in water. This operation takes 35 to 40 seconds under calm circumstances. So they had no chance of saving themselves. Clinical death occurred 90 to 100 seconds later simultaneously in all of them.

"Meanwhile we affirm that 23 days in space could not have caused their condition to deteriorate. We affirm that subsequently we will give our approval for cosmonauts to stay on the station for 30 days."

"There can be no discussion of how many days until we establish the cause of this incident and completely eliminate the probability of it happening again," concluded Keldysh, closing the meeting.

THE ROOT CAUSE OF THE DEPRESSURIZATION of the Descent Module was not immediately apparent, and the fierce arguments continued. Now it was difficult to find the individual who was the first to come out with the scenario that became the leading hypothesis during all subsequent investigations conducted per the commission's decisions.

The two compartments—the Descent Module and the Habitation Compartment—were firmly linked together. The surfaces of the Descent Module and Habitation Compartment docking rings were held together with eight pyrobolts. During assembly the installers tightened the compartments together using special torque wrenches. The operation was critical and was monitored not visually, but in a special pressure chamber. The interface must be airtight. According to another requirement, the Habitation Compartment and Descent Module must instantaneously separate along this interface before landing.

How was this done without unscrewing the tightening bolts? Very simply. The bolts needed to be pulled apart by an explosion. Each bolt had a powder charge, which was detonated using explosive cartridges triggered by an electrical command from the sequencer. All the pyrobolts were detonated simultaneously. In a vacuum, a shock wave can only spread through metal. Its impact is so strong that a valve mounted in the same structural ring as the explosive bolts could spontaneously open. That's such a simple scenario.

We began performing experiments at our factory and at NIIERAT. Valves were subjected to stability tests under exposure to large impact loads. The Politburo-imposed two-week deadline for the commission's work passed, but dozens of experiments did not bring the proof that was so indispensable. The valves had not opened due to explosive shock.

At Mishuk's suggestion, several valves that had intentional manufacturing defects were assembled at the factory. From a quality control standpoint, they were obvious scrap parts. But even they wouldn't yield to explosive shock. Out of frustration, Keldysh, who almost every day reported to Ustinov about the progress of the work and once a week to Brezhnev, proposed that the Descent Module and Habitation Compartment separation process be simulated in the large pressure chamber. It was assumed that during the simultaneous detonation of all the pyrobolts in a vacuum, the shock wave spreading only through metal would be more powerful than at normal atmospheric pressure. "We'll delay the report a week, but we'll have a clear conscience: we did everything that we could," Keldysh said.

One of the organizers of this very difficult experiment was Reshetin—at that time chief of the design department that had been responsible for developing the Descent Module. Today, Andrey Reshetin, a doctor of technical sciences, professor, and my colleague in the core department of the Moscow Physical Technical Institute, recalls, "We conducted this complicated experiment in the large pressure chamber at the Cosmonauts Training Center in Star City. The Descent Module and Habitation Compartment mockups were held together with standard pyrobolts. The breathing vents were intentionally installed with manufacturing defects, which supposedly could have taken place during their production. The pyrobolts were detonated simultaneously according to the configuration used in flight. The experiment was conducted twice. The valves did not open. The true cause of the opening of the breathing vent during separation of the *Soyuz-11* Descent Module and Habitation Compartment remained a secret."

Instead of the two weeks set aside for the commission and everyone participating on it, a month passed. Over the course of this month they prepared radical proposals guaranteeing the cosmonauts' safety in the event of Descent Module depressurization.

Gay Severin, who was in charge of the Zvezda Factory, made use of his considerable aviation experience and quickly developed the new *Sokol* (Falcon) spacesuits. The number of crewmembers would have to be reduced from three to two. A life-saving oxygen unit occupied the place of the third cosmonaut. In the event of the Descent Module's depressurization an automatic control was triggered, starting the flow of oxygen from the tanks. This unit would allow the crew to survive for the amount of time required for descent even without spacesuits.

To Ilya Lavrov, the most emotional of our life-support systems developers, the cosmonauts' deaths were a profound personal tragedy.

"I'm tearing myself up over the fact that I went along with Feoktistov and Korolev to do away with spacesuits. I wasn't able to persuade them to install simple oxygen units with masks, which were widely used in aviation. Of course, given such a vacuum, a mask wouldn't have saved anyone, but it would have prolonged their lives by 2 or 3 minutes. Perhaps, that time would have been enough to close the opened breathing vent using the manual valve."

Lavrov and Boris Penek's electrical engineers spent six months developing an emergency oxygen system. In addition to all sorts of other measures, they introduced a quick-closing manual drive for the breathing vents.

"And as far as the final wording of the causes is concerned," said Keldysh at the commission's final meeting, "we will consider that the opening of the valve was the result of a shock wave spreading over the metal of the structure. This is a probabilistic phenomenon. In order to achieve it under real conditions it would be necessary to conduct dozens or hundreds of experiments. After those measures, which will be implemented at the recommendation of our commission, evidently, it will no longer make sense to continue these costly pyrobolt firings in pressure chambers."

And that was that. However, when we had estimated how much weight it would take for all the projected measures, we wept. In order to maintain the Soyuz spacecraft's weight limit, the planners persuaded Mishin to take off the solar arrays. The argument was simple: from now on the Soyuz would be just a transport vehicle for delivering a crew to the orbital station and returning it to Earth. Soyuzes were no longer needed for independent long-duration flights. After docking with the DOS, the Soyuz's chemical batteries would be charged from the DOS power system before returning to Earth.

MODIFICATION, HOWEVER, DRAGGED ON. It wasn't until 26 July 1972 that a Soyuz under the name *Kosmos-496* executed an unpiloted flight. After a series of failures with orbital stations, one more unpiloted Soyuz was tested on 15 July 1973, under the name *Kosmos-573*. Only after this did a piloted flight of the new spacecraft take place. In the press it was referred to as the transport Soyuz. Vasiliy Lazarev and Oleg Makarov were the first cosmonauts to test out this Soyuz after the death of Georgiy Dobrovolskiy's crew. They did not fly until September 1973 on *Soyuz-12*. Soyuzes continued to be operated with a two-man crew until 1981.[53] Over that period of time 18 piloted flights took place.

From the author's archives.

Energiya cosmonaut Oleg Makarov in a signed picture given to Chertok.

---

53. The first three-person crew to fly a Soyuz after the *Soyuz-11* disaster was the *Soyuz T-3* crew (L. D. Kizim, O. G. Makarov, and G. M. Strekalov), who flew in November–December 1980.

THE HOT SUMMER OF 1971 ENDED with the decision to scuttle the first Long-Duration Orbital Station. Initially, the flight of the *Salyut* orbital station had been designed to last three months. After being in space for more than six months, the station proved to be completely functional. However, our hope to resume piloted expeditions to the first orbital station was gone. We had no transport vehicles. We could have continued operating the station to test out the reliability of on-board systems and to train ground services. However, after estimating the fuel reserves, the ballistics experts and planners came up with another proposal. In the event of excessive fuel consumption or the failure of the control system or power supply, the station would become uncontrollable. Gradually losing altitude, it would enter the dense layers of the atmosphere, and everything that didn't burn up would end up who knows where. International complications might arise. Georgiy Degtyarenko, who was in charge of a group of analysis and computation departments, approached Mishin with a memorandum. He proposed that while *Salyut* was still controllable and there was enough fuel to issue a command for a retroburn, we should arrange for the station's safe descent into the Pacific Ocean. Mishin consented. The proposal met no objections in the ministry or in the VPK.

On 10 October 1971, commands were issued from Yevpatoriya to orient the station in orbital mode. When telemetry confirmed the stable operation of the control system at the calculated time, the propulsion system fired a retroburn. On 11 October 1971, the *Salyut* station, launched into space on 19 April, entered the dense layers of the atmosphere and plunged into the Pacific Ocean as a gleaming meteorite.

The experience of scuttling the *Salyut* came in handy as a conflict-free way to end the operation of all subsequent Salyuts until it came to *Salyut-7*. DOS *Salyut-7* was inserted into orbit on 19 April 1982. This is the only station in the history of cosmonautics that experienced "freezing" and subsequent reanimation in space.[54] *Salyut-7* remained a fully operational station after the appearance in space of the *Mir* orbital station.[55] It is very difficult to control two stations at the same time in piloted mode. However, after four years of operation it was possible to prolong the station's existence in unpiloted mode and obtain invaluable experience in terms of the service life of various systems. The *Salyut-7* station was transferred to elevated orbit in August 1986. According to the prognosis, it could have continued to exist for another 10

---

54. Chertok is referring to the loss of control of *Salyut-7* in early 1985 and the subsequent rescue mission of *Soyuz T-13*.

55. The *Mir* core module was launched on 19 February 1986.

years, but the Sun interfered with the ballistics experts' calculations. Its activity increased the density of the upper layers of the atmosphere, and the station began to rapidly descend in uncontrolled mode. By late 1990 there were no longer any fuel and electric power reserves for a concerted scuttling operation. According to data received from the space monitoring services, the remains of the station were supposed to collide with Earth's surface in early 1991. In this regard, the foreign mass media whipped up passions, denouncing the raining down of red-hot fragments of the station on heavily populated areas of Earth.

On 7 February 1991, *Salyut-7* entered the dense layers of the atmosphere. Unburned remains reached Earth in the mountainous terrain of Chile. To the great disappointment of fans of space spectaculars, there was no news of destruction or victims from the impact site. Fans searching for the station's remains, hoping to obtain unique souvenirs, came away empty-handed.

The *Mir* orbital complex, which owes its birth to the first *Salyut*, was also scuttled in the ocean after working in orbit for more than 15 years.[56] For the developers of the station and for all those who controlled its flight for years, this was collective *hara-kiri*. There were no technical justifications to sink in the ocean such a unique space facility as *Mir*. But the Russian budget at the end of the 20th century could not sustain the expenditures to maintain the performance capacity of a piloted orbital station launched by the Soviet Union in 1986.

A group of American scientists, who banded together to form the Space Frontier Foundation, addressed an open letter to Russian President Boris N. Yeltsin with an appeal not to scuttle the *Mir* station, but to transfer it to a more elevated orbit, to wait there until Russia experienced better times and then continue its active life.[57]

"In and of itself, the pressurized volume of the station is of enormous value. Salyut-class space stations (very similar to *Mir*) often executed flight in automatic mode...."[58]

Mir was a unique science complex that made it possible to conduct research in the fields of astrophysics, biotechnology, space medicine, ecology, geophysics, and materials science. The construction in space of the *Mir* multimodule orbital station lasted 10 years. In February 1986, the first module—the core module—was inserted into space. The *Mir* complex comprised seven modules,

---

56. The full *Mir* complex reentered on 23 March 2001.

57. The Space Frontier Foundation was established in 1988. In February 1998 it called on then–Russian President Boris Yeltsin to reverse plans to destroy the *Mir* space station as part of its "Keep Mir Alive" campaign.

58. *Izvestiya*, No. 53 (24 March 1998); "Tsentr MAKS," *Vestnik* no. 8 (1998). See also *http://www.spaceref.com/news/viewpr.html?pid=4204* (last accessed 11 August 2011).

which housed 11.5 tons of science equipment produced in 27 countries.[59] Each expedition to *Mir* brought new experience and new information on the construction of space structures, the control of large space facilities, and the optimization of the reliability of numerous systems.

More than 3 billion U.S. dollars were spent on the creation and operation of *Mir*. According to the assessments of cosmonauts and the developers of the different systems, the station's service life was far from exhausted. The International Space Station's operational capabilities reached *Mir*'s level in terms of its operational capabilities by 2003. So was it necessary to scuttle the *Mir*? There were more people in favor of scuttling the station in Russia than in the U.S. Russian supporters of scuttling the station justified their position by the fact that the cost of operating *Mir* was 220 to 240 million dollars per year. The Russian budget didn't provide for such expenditures. During the time of the so-called "reforms," the once-mighty rocket-space power was subjected to such an economic defeat that against the background of the across-the-board impoverishment of the people, expenditures on space science and technology seemed an intolerable luxury. The historical paradox is that during the first decades after the profoundly grueling World War II, the Soviet Union allocated 100 times more resources annually for the development of rocket-space technology than Russia does today.

In October 1998, I visited Germany with a group of Russian and European cosmonauts. My meetings with people involved with the European space programs and representatives from the mass media showed me that the European space community did not understand why we needed to scuttle *Mir*. At that time the struggle to save *Mir* had only just begun. They said that after *Mir* was scuttled, Russia would cease to be the leader in human spaceflight, thousands of jobs for highly skilled specialists would be lost, Russia would sustain a grievous loss of scientific and technical potential, and the country would experience yet another political defeat. The fully operational, unique *Mir* station was scuttled in the Pacific Ocean on 23 March 2001.

BUT LET'S RETURN TO 1971. In addition to the rush jobs to modify the Soyuz, during the second half of 1971, design work was started up on three spacecraft modifications: one for servicing the Almaz orbital station (7K-TA), one for the Soyuz-VI military-use complex (7K-S), and one for docking with the U.S. Apollo (7K-TM, or Soyuz-M).

---

59. These six other modules were *Kvant* (launched in 1987), *Kvant-2* (1989), *Kristall* (1990), *Spektr* (1995), the *Docking Module* (1995), and *Priroda* (1996).

The designs of each of these vehicles differed substantially from the Soyuz already flying. A lot of new technology was packed into the Soyuz (7K-TM) for rendezvous and docking with the Apollo. For the first time, the 7K-S spacecraft called for a computer-aided control system. This was a qualitative leap for which we had been preparing for 10 years. If you add to these projects the changes that we introduced into the subsequent DOS designs, then today it is easier to understand that past in which we "forgot" about the Moon race. Our immersion in DOSes and Soyuz modifications drastically reduced the pace of work on the lunar vehicles of the L3 complex. Even Keldysh, absorbed for a month with investigations into the causes of the *Soyuz-11* and N-1 No. 6L disasters, stopped pestering us about L3 lunar vehicle problems. Studies of the causes of the N-1 No. 6L failure required serious gas dynamics experiments. The hot summer of 1971 ended with such a [long] list of modifications for the N-1 launch vehicle that, according to the most optimistic schedules, it would be a year before the next launch of N-1 No. 7L.

Chapter 17
The Last N-1 Launch

In July 1972, a ministerial order authorized the restructuring of Korolev's OKB-1, which had been called the Central Design Bureau of Experimental Machine Building (TsKBEM) since 1966. The bravest subcontractors poked fun at us with regard to this abbreviation: "As before, we will give preference in our work to Mishin's organization. It used to be that everything was clear: Korolev's organization was called OKB-1, and Chelomey's was OKB-52. Any fool could see that OKB-1 was many times more important. Now under Mishin they're calling you TsKBEM, and Chelomey's organization is simply TsKBM. For your previous services you've been granted a one-letter advantage. But on the other hand, Chelomey is a general designer, and Mishin is simply a chief designer."[1]

The fundamental difference in the new TsKBEM structure was that chief designer [Mishin] had chief designers of specific rocket and space complexes

From the author's archives.

subordinate to him. Boris Arkadyevich Dorofeyev was named chief designer of the N-1 launch vehicle. Vladimir Andreyevich Borisov became the chief designer of the main payload for the N-1, i.e., the system that comprised

N-1 Chief Designer Boris Dorofeyev shown at the periscope during a launch.

---

1. In December 1956, the aviation industry introduced the rank of "general designer" to denote a rank higher than the usual "chief designer." Other sectors of the Soviet defense industry did not adopt this higher rank until the early 1970s. In the 1960s, for example, Korolev and Mishin were chief designers while Chelomey was a general designer.

the lunar vehicles: LOK, LK, and booster Blocks G and D. Yuriy Pavlovich Semyonov was in charge of the entire complex of orbital stations, i.e., DOS-7K. Igor Nikolayevich Sadovskiy was named chief designer of the updated 8K98P [or RT-2P] solid-propellant rocket complex. Bushuyev obtained the position of chief designer of the Soyuz-Apollo project and, consequently, of the 7K-TM vehicle (or Soyuz-M) for docking with Apollo. In addition, by government decree, Bushuyev became director of the Soviet portion of the Soyuz-Apollo program. Shabarov was in charge of work on the military 7K-S vehicle.

In the early 1970s, the small book *Fiziki shutyat* [*The Physicists Are Joking*] was very popular in scientific-technical circles.[2] By analogy with the fun-loving physicists, the smart alecks in our organization proposed issuing the secret publication *Raketchiki shutyat* [*The Rocket Scientists Are Joking*]. Among other witticisms, one was asked to answer the question, "How many chief designers need to be appointed at TsKBEM (former OKB-1) in place of one S. P. Korolev in order to confuse American intelligence officers in the field once and for all?"

The 7K-OK Soyuzes that were already flying, the multipurpose orbital complex project, *Mars-75*, and nuclear propulsion systems remained officially without chief designers.

Mishin was directly in charge of ongoing piloted flights and all prospective areas of endeavor. Each of Chief Designer Mishin's deputies was responsible for the group of related departments organizationally united in complexes. They made me a deputy chief of the enterprise and the chief of Complex No. 3, which contained 11 departments for motion control systems, electrical and radio engineering, antenna feeder systems, electromechanical devices, and actuators. The 11 departments entrusted to me were divided into three clusters, each of which was supervised by my deputies—Rauschenbach, Kalashnikov, and Yurasov.

Sergey Okhapkin was appointed as Mishin's first deputy. Main design Complex No. 2, which Deputy Chief Designer Viktor Simakin managed, and material engineering Complex No. 8, where Anatoliy Severov was in charge, remained under his authority. Mishin retained control over design computational analysis Complex No. 1, including the computer center. Engine-related matters and nuclear power topics were combined in Complex No. 5, which deputy chief designer Mikhail Melnikov managed. Mishin also retained control over Melnikov's activity.

---

2. This work was a collection of science-related humor compiled by Yu. Konobeyev, V. Pavlinchuk, N. Rabotnov, and V. Turchin and published in 1966 by the Mir publishing house, Moscow. Subsequent collections were *The Physicists Continue To Joke* [*Fiziki prodolzhayut shutit*] and *The Physicists Are Still Joking* [*Fiziki vsye yeshche shutyat*].

Isaak Khazanov, the chief engineer of the experimental factory colocated with TsKBEM.

From the author's archives.

There was no Complex No. 4. This number was supposed to be left for the production portion of TsKBEM. However, our Factory of Experimental Machine Building (ZEM) was so big and independent that it never occurred to anyone to equate it with a complex.[3] After Roman Turkov, Viktor Klyucharev became the factory's director and Isaak Khazanov became its chief engineer. In addition, Klyucharev had the status of first deputy chief of TsKBEM. The factory was an independent administrative entity, which had its own "post box," its own accounting department, and its own bank account. We shared the same territory, Party committee, professional committee, Komsomol committee, and various social organizations, as well as a health resort in Kislovodsk, recreation facilities, and pioneer camps.[4]

The aforementioned reorganization of TsKBEM took place a little over six years after the death of Korolev. Nevertheless, Korolev's people remained in all the key posts of complex chiefs, their deputies, and chiefs of the main departments and production facilities. A journalist wrote that those in Korolev's entourage were not just people, but personalities! Each one! I agree. They were not very obedient, but they were intelligent, unique individuals who loved their work and couldn't think of life without it. Not one of them, as the result of their many years of righteous labor, acquired a stone mansion or made a fortune that could compare in any way to what the bosses of Russia today acquired in the 1990s.

The majority of chiefs of complexes and departments came from families of simple workers and intelligentsia. All of them carved out their own way to rockets. We didn't belong to the stratum of the "creative intelligentsia." For

---

3. The ZEM was formerly known as Factory No. 88 where the original NII-88 had been established in 1946.

4. The Komsomol was officially known as the All-Union Leninist Communist Union of Youth (*Vsesoyuznyy leninskiy kommunisticheskiy soyuz molodezhi*—VLKSM). This nationwide organization was the youth wing of the Communist Party, organized to inculcate the values of an ideal socialist society.

some reason humanities experts, and after them, the various news media, do not classify physicists and other representatives of the exact sciences, much less engineers, among the so-called "creative intelligentsia." Yes, we were technocrats. We didn't have time to jealously keep up with belles-lettres, we rarely went to the theater, and we didn't always manage to see new films. We were not righteous men in the Christian sense. But I cannot recall examples of turpitude, underhanded schemes, or treachery. We worked and enjoyed the companionship of people just like us, subcontractors. Each of us felt a responsibility to the nation and to history. We were more like clear-eyed devotees than blind fanatics. With rare exceptions, each person in a managerial post was a member of the Communist Party. However, it wasn't a utopian idea of building Communism and destroying parasitic Western imperialism that united us. We had captured an advanced foothold in worldwide scientific and technical progress and understood that we would not be able to hold onto this foothold, much less expand it, without the help of the entire industrial sphere and all branches of the nation's science and economy. For that reason, each of us was touched by the words of the song:

> *…Our work is simple,*
> *Our concern is this:*
> *That our homeland will live—*
> *That's all that there is—*

Identifying ourselves with triumphs in space, our attitude toward the unlimited praise for achievements in other areas of science and economics was not without irony.

A wicked anecdote came out in the 1970s: "What is Soviet authority plus electrification of the entire nation? It's when everybody is burnt out."[5] We weren't burnt out about anything. For the majority of us, years of working with Korolev were like a school that had no written rules of conduct. This school selected people of action. For them, the daily struggle with problems and difficulties became a customary way of life. Here, each one proved him- or herself, striving for self-expression, like an artist creating a painting. No one attempted to shirk responsibility, no matter what happened. Therefore, to act rather than talk, to take risks, to influence the course of events as decisively as possible—this was our working style. Those who burned out were quickly

---

5. This is a play on Lenin's famous rallying call that "Communism is Soviet power plus electrification of the whole country."

weeded out. It is possible that many in our midst lacked refinement, etiquette, tact, and good breeding. But we all shared an appreciation for a sense of humor, showed consideration for a comrade's work, and tried, if needed, to come to their aid.

Criticism of national economic policy was not at all prohibited. Sometimes it was conducted openly and officially on what were referred to as "political instruction days." Once, I received a warning from the TsKBEM economic planning department that, according to financial figures, by year-end the complex entrusted to me would violate the plan. Antonina Otreshko, the chief of the economic planning department, explained to me: "You failed to fulfill the plan in terms of volume by an entire 10 million rubles."

At that time, that was a very sizeable amount. They had begun an audit. I argued, "Antonina Pavlovna, you are quite familiar with how our work goes, you've seen for yourself that all the work assigned to our complex has actually not only been fulfilled, but we have even saved these same 10 million rubles for the enterprise. Instead of handing them over to a subcontractor, we have done the work ourselves for our own salary."

"Now that is an unforgivable sin," objected Otreshko. "It's time to get used to our perverse planning system. If we planned to allocate 'x' amount of rubles for you, then you must spend them or at least show that they were spent. If you can't, that means the plan was not fulfilled. Instead of a bonus for saving money, you're going to receive a reprimand, and your whole staff will lose bonuses."

We were obliged to comply with this system. We had to write off large sums of money, in no way raising our salary. In nondefense industries, getting carried away with the amount of money hampered the solution of many problems. Echoes of the battle with so-called "cosmopolitanism" also made themselves known.[6] In nondefense industries, in one stroke they would reject foreign experience just because it was foreign. At the same time, they passed up opportunities that came to light through their own experience, the results of scientific research, since realizing them would involve strenuous work and risk and might disrupt the tranquil life of a staff accustomed to constant smoke breaks.

On the way toward the improvement of automobiles, combines, bathroom fixtures, footwear, industrial goods, household appliances, and many,

---

6. "Cosmopolitanism" was a code word to broadly denote excessive "subservience" to Western ideas but had distinct anti-Semitic overtones in the late 1940s and early 1950s during the late-Stalinist era.

many other things; on the way toward high quality and a sharp increase in the range of products, stood a habit that had been nurtured for years—to value quantity more than anything: units, tons, meters, and liters, rather than the quality of the articles. Increasing quantity under the slogan "Catch up and overtake…" is historically quite understandable.[7] But the times had changed, and the volume-quantitative practices in planning and reporting remained. The human being proved to be the most conservative link in scientific-technical and economic progress. The scales of the economy grew tremendously, while the customary standards, which at one time had been quite reasonable, proved to be extremely harmful once the times had changed. At the individual levels of the economy, quantity simply turned into a genuine fetish. The fierce battle for the quantity of shells, cannons, tanks, and airplanes had been quite necessary for victory during World War II. During the last years of the Cold War, the quantity of these essential military commodities sharply declined, but instead the range of items expanded due to the emergence of numerous types of rockets and nuclear warheads. The fight for new kinds of weaponry resumed. This continuous fight for a plan based on quantity entered our consciousness like a religion, like worshipping an all-powerful Moloch.

Vasiliy Ryabikov came to see us at TsKBEM in early 1971. My contact with him had begun back in Germany. I wrote about this in my first book.[8] I recall that People's Commissar for Armaments Ustinov had sent his first deputy, Vasiliy Ryabikov, to find out about the V-2 and rocket technology and what was going on in Bleicherode. He was the first of the managers from the Ministry of Armaments to decide that this was what the ministry needed to be involved in after or even instead of cannons, and, of course, at the expense of the number of cannons.

In the early 1950s, Ryabikov was in charge of the special committee for the creation of air defense systems.[9] In 1957, he was chairman of the State Commission for launches of the first R-7 rocket. Ryabikov came to see us in 1971 as first deputy chairman of *Gosplan* to find out what we were involved with.[10] He did not conceal his satisfaction about what he saw and heard.

---

7. "Catch up and overtake" was a prominent slogan of the Stalin years, coined in reference to the Western industrialized nations.

8. See Chertok, *Rockets and People, Vol. I*, p. 323.

9. Between February 1951 and June 1953, Ryabikov was chief of the Third Main Directorate (subordinate to Beriya's Special Committee), which was responsible for the development of the Moscow air defense system.

10. From 1965 to 1974, Ryabikov was the first deputy chairman of *Gosplan*.

Over lunch we were having what had become a habitual conversation about the delay and even stagnation in other branches of the economy. Ryabikov said, "Yes, there are latent processes that our economists are unable to properly explain. In our society the amount and rate of development mean the same thing. But now this is a political error, which is not so easily corrected. Here's a typical example for you. Our machine-tool industry in due course mastered the production of pretty good general-purpose machines, and their production continued to increase. The machine-tool builders ended up with very high labor productivity performance indices in series production. But on the whole, the economy loses from this because we need new specialized machines of considerably higher quality. The machines, of which we produce record numbers, lag behind the world standard by 10 years. And so for you we are forced in each decree to insert a clause allocating hard currency for the importation of modern machine tools, instruments, and laboratory equipment. I assure you that what we acquire abroad is technically not as sophisticated as your technology. But we need serious economic reforms in order to master the production of similar equipment in our other branches of industry. Until we have decided what needs to be done to make industry itself vitally interested in renewal, then let it be at the expense of quantity. You achieved this, but at what price! For you [rocket scientists], for the atomic scientists, for those who ensure our parity in strategic armaments with America, we are creating the necessary conditions but at a very high price. You deserve this. But for all the others, who, by the way, feed you, we cannot create these conditions."

Ryabikov was right; to achieve political and strategic parity for the military-industrial complex and for the science supporting it, conditions were created—at the expense of the whole nation's resources—that other branches of industry could not even dream of. They weren't envious of us; they believed in us and relied on us. We didn't always live up to these expectations. However, decades later the world realized that the output of our military-industrial complex surpassed similar articles from the leading capitalist nations, not only in terms of quantity, but also in terms of quality.

THE LAST (FOURTH) LAUNCH OF N1-L3 No. 7L took place on 24 November 1972, but to this day arguments continue as to whether it was necessary to conduct it. Did we do the right thing? For me and for the majority of those who participated in the ambitious rocket epic, everything that happened back then with the N-1 was a personal tragedy.

On 15 August 1972, Mishin held a meeting of the N-1 Council of Chief Designers. All the chiefs gave positive reports on their systems and gave their unanimous support for launch preparation. On 21 August, the State Commission concurred with the proposals of the Council of Chiefs and approved the schedule of operations. A week later, Mishin fell ill.

But I should relate this in the order it happened. Mishin was admitted to the *kremlevka* (hospital for dignitaries) in Kuntsevo.[11] His first deputy, Okhapkin, began to perform his chief designer duties. He tried to delve into each unresolved matter. Not having mastered the art of passing the buck, Okhapkin was literally smothered by the plethora of problems, for which he was personally responsible, and by the burden of the cares that had befallen him.

One Sunday he nevertheless managed to break away to relax at his dacha in Zagoryanka.[12] As his wife Klavdiya Alekseyevna later recounted, Sergey Osipovich came home from a stroll in the forest (he was an avid mushroom hunter) with an unusual gait. The doctors were later amazed that he managed to get home at all: he was having a stroke. Through the efforts of our patrons, Okhapkin also ended up in the hospital in Kuntsevo. The minister gave factory director Klyucharev the responsibilities of chief of enterprise [i.e., TsKBEM] and those of chief designer to me.

Now I began to suffocate. After the death of the *Soyuz-11* crew in June 1971, a long period of spacecraft systems modifications had begun. During this period we did not have any piloted flights. To a certain extent this eased my situation. From July 1971 through April 1972, the Americans had carried out two more expeditions to the Moon.[13] Their lunar successes had applied considerably more pressure to our psyches than the secret information concerning the latest upgrading of hundreds of Minuteman missiles and their placement on duty. In terms of the total number of strategic nuclear assets and, above all, of intercontinental ballistic missiles, we were steadily catching up with the U.S. None of us believed in the real possibility of a nuclear missile shootout, but this didn't reassure anyone.

At the very beginning of September 1972, Minister Afanasyev summoned me. Anatoliy Kirillov was in his office.

"Something has happened at the firing range again." I had a sinking feeling inside.

Until June 1969, Kirillov had been deputy chief of NIIP-5, known today as Baykonur.[14] Without retiring from active military service, he transferred to work in the offices of the Ministry of General Machine Building. Officially, Kirillov performed the duties of deputy chief of the Third Main Directorate,

---

11. Kuntsevo is a district on the western outskirts of Moscow.

12. Zagoryanka is a village of dachas northeast of Moscow, in Shchelkovo Rayon.

13. These were the *Apollo 15* and *Apollo 16* missions, respectively.

14. NIIP—*Nauchno-issledovatelskiy i ispytatelnyy polygon* (Scientific-Research and Testing Range).

but actually he was one of the minister's closest advisers on the flight testing of space systems.[15]

"Do you see what we have ahead of us at the firing range this next month?" began Afanasyev, addressing me from afar. "I hope that we complete preparation of N-1 No. 7L. It's getting to the point that the launch is possible at the end of October. But we have a crisis on our hands with the technical management: Mishin and his first deputy, Okhapkin, are in the hospital. I have inquired about their condition, and the answers I got were not encouraging. Neither one of them will be able in the near future to go out to the firing range and take part in the work of the State Commission. They promise to restore Mishin's health and release him no sooner than the end of the year, and Okhapkin had a real stroke. We don't need doctors to know what that means. We've had consultations here, including with Keldysh, and have decided: until Mishin gets back, you are being appointed acting technical manager of the State Commission for the launch of N1-L3 No. 7L."

Such a twist of fate came as a complete surprise to me, and I fervently protested.

"But, Sergey Aleksandrovich, Boris Dorofeyev was appointed chief designer of the N-1 by your order. He's already been living at the firing rang for a long time and isn't involved with anything but the N-1. He knows and feels this vehicle better than any of us. His deputy, Georgiy Degtyarenko, complements Dorofeyev beautifully in terms of all the design and theoretical problems. This pair is completely competent. And as for me, I'll be involved anyway in the preparation of those systems for the development of which I am personally responsible. Just recently, you lambasted me in Ustinov's presence for making a mess of things with the transport vehicles' control systems and all manner of other things."

"You don't need to repeat all this to us. This launch might determine the fate of the N-1. It needs triple monitoring or even more. We must make decisions very responsibly. We are certainly not releasing Dorofeyev from his chief designer duties. But in the absence of Mishin, either his first deputy must be in charge of engineering for the complex as a whole, or the next one in line, and Okhapkin is ill. So we have decided that this will be Chertok. Incidentally, the technical management is made up of chief designers from related organizations, with whom you have worked

---

15. The Third Main Directorate was one of several main directorates in the Ministry of General Machine Building. Each main directorate was responsible for a single thematic area dealing with the development of missiles and spacecraft.

for many years. Matters of prestige are important for them. It's easier for us to deal with them if the technical manager is a member of the Academy of Sciences.[16] You will always find common ground quickly with Pilyugin, Ryazanskiy, Iosifyan, Bogomolov, Lidorenko, and Shishkin.[17] And I give you my word; I will help with Barmin and Nikolay Kuznetsov. Dementyev promised me personally to check on the status of affairs with Kuznetsov's engines and to confirm whether a decision about their clearance for launch will be necessary."

Before departing from the ministry, I stopped in to see Gleb Tabakov. He had recently been relieved of his job as chief of NII-229 and appointed deputy minister.[18] He was in charge of engine topics for the ministry and subcontractors.

Regarding my meeting with the minister, he said, "I have complete information on the status of affairs at OKB-276. Despite the more or less successful testing of individual engines on EU-15 and EU-16 in Zagorsk, I am not confident about Block A [the first stage].[19] Say what you will, but of the three failures, two occurred due to the engine systems. Kuznetsov understands this and his shop is working at full speed on the reusable engine. I reported to the minister and even advised that we wait for the new engines. Don't rush with the launch! But he doesn't yet know how to do this."

Tabakov was unable to say anything more encouraging.

Thus I became a direct participant in the launch preparation of N1-L3 No. 7L and the subsequent analysis of the last flight. Do I now regret this confluence of circumstances? I suppose not. What happened in the flight was already predestined, lurking in the propulsion system long before the rocket was prepared at the firing range. No matter who had served as technical manager, he could not have prevented what happened in flight. The failure of N-1 No. 7L could have been avoided only if the decision had been made to cancel the flight, to stop flight tests. But we'll discuss this below.

---

16. Chertok had become a corresponding member of the Academy in 1968.

17. Oleg Nikolayevich Shishkin (1934–) was the director of NII izmeritelnoy tekhniki (Scientific-Research Institute of Measurement Technology).

18. Tabakov had been appointed deputy minister of general machine building in March 1965.

19. EU-15 and EU-16 were the names of two static test stands located at the premises of NII-229 in Zagorsk. EU-15 was designed to test the Block B second stage, and EU-16 was designed to test the Block V third stage. Individual engines of the Block A first stage were tested on the EU-87 static test stand.

In September 1972, I arrived at the firing range in this new capacity. Dorofeyev, Degtyarenko, Simakin, Gutskov, and all the other old hands of the big MIK gave me a warm reception. From the first day, we established a relationship of trust and working rapport. Dorofeyev, who had been managing N-1 testing for some years now, made sure that rapport was excellent both with the military leadership of the firing range and with the engineering staff of the Sixth Directorate's military testers.

Emil Brodskiy and Boris Filin, who had supervised the testing and numerous modifications of the L3, did not pass up the opportunity to tease me: "So, Boris Yevseyevich, they dragged you away from the Podlipki dacha and spa resort? Instead, here you have no days off. There's only a few papers, but you have daily briefings. They won't let you get bored."

They had already rolled the rocket out to the launch site, and there, on 30 August, the first preliminary tests began to work out the ground-to-spacecraft communications. The telemetry recordings of the tests served up one headache after another. At one of the meetings of the technical management, Aleksandr Mrykin delivered a report in which he recapitulated the results of the previous three N-1 flight tests.[20] "We have only just begun testing on N-1 No. 7L, and we already have 17 serious anomalies for 17 control system instruments and over 100 for telemetry measurement systems," he announced. "Given these statistics, we should think more conscientiously about the advisability of the launch."

In addition to the official heavily attended meetings of the technical management, our inner circle gathered in a hotel room in order to calmly discuss the progress of preparation and to determine the main tasks of each chief for the next few days. At one such meeting Anatoliy Kirillov, who had arrived with me, described the "general disposition" like this:

"As everyone knows, Earth is held up on three whales. Science has proven that even without these three whales, Earth will stay put in its orbit. And here for us, three whales isn't enough. With our N-1 rocket we are capable of holding on only with four. The first whale is the head organization, TsKBEM. Sergey Pavlovich's best students represent it here. The second whale is the military testers and all the services of the firing range. This whale has accumulated such experience that we can easily rely on it. The military supports the most daring proposals of the technical management. All of the officers associated with N-1 have been dreaming for a long time of coming up from the ranks like

---

20. Until April 1965, Lieutenant General Mrykin was the first deputy chief of the Ministry of Defense's Main Directorate of Missile Armaments (GURVO). At retirement age, he transferred to TsNIImash to the position of deputy director of the institute without retiring from active military service.

the one who is launching the piloted vehicles and DOSes. The third whale is production, and above all, the Progress Factory in Kuybyshev. The people there are first-rate and flawless. But we need to put things right when it comes to checking out all the modifications. In my opinion, there isn't always complete clarity between the first and third whales. I hope that Dmitriy Ilyich Kozlov will help us in this matter. He's flying in tomorrow. Well, and the fourth whale is the most unreliable—our subcontractors. In my opinion, our new technical manager [i.e., Chertok] needs to pay particular attention to this whale. For the first time the N-1 has two on-board computers, and for the first time the N-1 is equipped with standard Blocks G and D and with a LOK that is not exactly standard. We've had so many problems with the subcontractors that without the personal intervention of the technical manager we will be threatened with constant breakdown of the preparation schedule."

"You forgot about the fifth whale," I added. "Engines."

"No, I didn't forget. I am afraid that engines are not one of those whales that hold us up. Ministers Afanasyev and Dementyev have agreed that they will personally provide the flight clearance certificate for those batches of engines that were selected for the LKI [flight-developmental tests] of No. 7L. For the whole package, not counting the lunar vehicle, the N-1 has 48 engines, including the control thrusters. At the launch site, if necessary, we can replace any instrument. But if we have to replace any engine, this means the N-1 returns to the MIK. Then the launch will be postponed by a month, and perhaps even more."

The replacement of any instrument during the process of testing at the engineering facility is, in fact, routine. Replacement at the launch site is an unpleasant event, but permissible. Replacing engines was a complicated operation that required factory conditions.

At one of these meetings I asked Dorofeyev and Degtyarenko once again to give a run-down of all the ways that rocket No. 7L differed from the preceding ones. Although all the modifications were described in engineering reports and I had kept track of them to the extent possible over the course of the year, when we added everything up in a calm conversation, we realized that essentially we were beginning the flight testing of a new rocket with this fourth launch.

All three previous launches of rockets No. 3L, No. 5L, and No. 6L were failures. The first two launches were actually firing tests of the 30 first-stage engine assemblies. It wasn't until the third launch of N-1 No. 6L that we were able to test out the control dynamics for the first time with all the first-stage engines functioning properly. And then we ran into the roll instability. Fourteen seconds into its flight the rocket began to spin, and after 50 seconds it was gone. This failure was the fault, above all, of the gas dynamics specialists and the TsNIImash and TsAGI scientists consulting with them.

From the author's archives.

The N-1 rocket on the pad.

The fiery streams from 30 engines joined in a common fiery plume so that perturbation torque, which the theoreticians had not foreseen and no calculations had predicted, was generated about the rocket's longitudinal axis. The controls were unable to cope with this disturbance, and rocket No. 6L lost stability. When asked, "Why didn't rocket No. 3L lose roll stability before it broke up due to an explosion in the aft section 50 seconds in to its flight," the gas dynamics specialists replied, "Because the rocket lifted off with two engines shut down. The perturbation torque was within the limits of the controls' ability to compensate for it."

They managed to simulate genuine perturbation torque about the longitudinal axis using computers. In this case, the data from telemetry measurements received in actual flight were programmed in as the baseline data rather than the calculations of the gas dynamics specialists. Georgiy Degtyarenko, Leonid Alekseyev, and Oleg Voropayev, who were in charge of this urgent work at Vladimir Stepanov's computer center, showed that the actual perturbation torque was several times greater than the maximum possible roll control moment that the control nozzles generated at their worst-case deviation.

To correct this fundamental shortcoming of the rocket, beginning with No. 7L, four control engines were installed to control roll (about the longitudinal axis). This was a large modification requiring an all-hands rush job. The engine specialists of Melnikov, Sokolov, and Raykov performed the design task of selecting the engines and developing the circuits to fire and swivel them and connect to the main lines of the primary propulsion systems to supply propellant components. The control-surface actuator specialists of Vilnitskiy and Shutenko developed the actuators for swiveling the engines.

For the first stage, one more propulsion system consisting of four movable engines was practically redeveloped. Rather than using liquid oxygen as the oxidizer, the original special feature of this new propulsion system was its use of "acid" generator gas, tapped from the gas generators of the main engines. This simplified the problem of ignition.

The engine assembly production facility of our factory coped brilliantly with the manufacture of these special engines, swiveling assemblies, and sophisticated fittings. Vakhtang Vachnadze had been in charge there for a long time and subsequently became director of NPO Energiya; after him, Aleksey Borisenko, who later became the director of ZEM, was responsible for this task.

The three previous rockets had not had this fundamentally new system of actuators. The experience gained on the steering chambers of the *Semyorka* and during the development of engine 11D58 for Block D (article 11S854) helped our engine specialists and production facility. But the N-1 control specialists had to break in this channel for the first time.

But this wasn't the only reason why the entire control system of rocket No. 7L was considered fundamentally new. The *Biser* (Beads) on-board computer system appeared five years after the deadlines stated in the first directives. Mikhail Khitrik, chief theoretician at Pilyugin's firm, and our chief rocket dynamics specialists, who issued the baseline data for it, elected not to use a rigid flight control program, where all the parameters—fuel consumption, engine thrust, the coordinates for their shutdown in space—had strict time schedules. Such control systems had operated on all first-generation rockets until the emergence of on-board computers.

"There was no 'free will'," I explained to students at lectures. All the parameters were assigned for each second of flight. There could be no deviation from the firing table. With the emergence of the on-board computer system came the opportunity to "liberate" the rocket, using what are referred to as terminal control principles. In simplified form this means that the rocket is permitted to fly with deviations within a broad corridor: fly as you wish, as long as you get the payload to the target with a minimum expenditure of fuel and minimum deviations from the target point.

Terminal control made it possible to gain an advantage in payload mass. In order to control motion, all the information from the gyrostabilized platforms and accelerometers mounted on them was sent to the on-board digital computer for all three axes. This was no longer "automatic stabilization control" in the previous sense, but an inertial navigation system. The emergence of the on-board digital computer made it possible to simplify the relay automatics for the control of all the rocket's systems, having shifted the solution of complicated logic problems to microelectronic integrated circuits. Using the on-board digital computer in the process of preflight ground testing and in flight, it became possible to perform diagnostics and replace a failed instrument or segment of a circuit with backup units.

The N1-L3 No. 7L complex contained two on-board digital computer sets—one in Block V, the third stage of the launch vehicle, and another on the LOK. The first on-board digital computer controlled the three stages of the launch vehicle for insertion into an initial Earth orbit. The second (LOK) computer was supposed to control exit from near-Earth orbit to the Moon, flight to the Moon, circumlunar flight, and return to Earth. The on-board digital computers were developed using *Tropa* (Trail) series-produced integrated microcircuits manufactured domestically by factories of the Ministry of the Electronics Industry.

The new control system required the use of new testing equipment to test the rocket and, consequently, new instructions and retraining of the testers. During ground testing of the rocket, they didn't always manage to determine what had caused a program execution anomaly or a failure. These anomalies often occurred not because of a computer failure, but as a result of tester error in the process of man-machine interaction.

In the "precomputer age," a human being sitting at a console felt completely in charge of the testing process. Now he had to take into consideration the fact that the spacecraft had something on board capable of making decisions at the discretion of the on-board digital computer developers. Those who had created the electronic computer, loaded the software into it, and quickly found a common language with it forgot that at the firing range new people would be dealing with it, people who had not yet mastered all the nuances of electronic "etiquette." The "man vs. machine" problem was new and took up a lot of time during the No. 7L preparation process.

A new Freon fire-extinguishing system had been installed on No. 7L and also a small "emergency" telemetry system that was developed at OKB MEI. Aleksey Bogomolov was very proud of this system. It enabled OKB MEI to get back the telemetric glory that it had temporarily relinquished to NII-885. All in all, the N1-L3 No. 7L telemetry systems received information from 13,000 sensors.

From the author's archives.

Senior space program veterans attend Chief Designer Aleksey Bogomolov's 75th birthday celebration in Moscow in 1988. From left to right are cosmonaut N. N. Rukavishnikov, K. P. Semagin, K. K. Morozov, B. Ye. Chertok, A. F. Bogomolov, N. P. Galunskiy, B. A. Dorofeyev, and G. K. Sosulin.

In May 1972, I was sitting in the big MIK at a meeting of the State Commission that Afanasyev was conducting. Mozzhorin presented a briefing paper about the three previous N-1 launches. I reported for the umpteenth time about the faults of the KORD system and the measures taken to protect it against any interference. At this time various modifications of Blocks A, B, and V were still continuing, preceding final assembly into an integrated super-heavy rocket.

"It's better to see something once than hear about it one hundred times." On the strength of this old aphorism, I changed into a pair of off-white coveralls, and after checking to see that there were no foreign objects in the pockets, I climbed into the rocket's aft section—Block A.

The total height of the rocket was 105 meters. Block A took up 30 meters of that. It was in the shape of a truncated cone. The diameter of the upper periphery was 10.5 meters, while that of the lower base was 15.8 meters. Finding myself inside this truncated cone under the spherical oxygen tank, I felt no claustrophobia and found a comfortable spot by the turbopump assembly of one of the 30 engines. Looking at the aft section of the rocket from the outside, it is difficult to imagine that everything you see inside could fit within a diameter of just 15.8 meters. Fear of fire compelled us to introduce firewalls, increase the thermal protection of the bottom plate, wrap the cable bundles with asbestos fabric, and "dress" the instruments in thermal protective "coats." I tried to imagine what would happen here when all 30 engines started up. Maybe one of these engineering creations is hiding a land mine, a concealed technological defect that would cut short the flight of the gigantic rocket.

I recalled Germany of April 1945. On the walls of the buildings suitable to house command staffs and rear services, in addition to signs such as "Colonel Fomenko's unit," there was "Verified, no mines" scrawled in large uneven letters along with the signature of the chief combat engineer. The only way to check for technological mines in Block A was its preliminary firing test or, in the worst case scenario, a firing test of each of the 30 engines with their subsequent installation without overhaul. That's what the Americans did with the Saturn V. My deceased comrade Voskresenskiy had called for this, and our common (and also deceased) chief Korolev had elected not to do this. Each N-1 flight for us was like going out in a minefield without a minesweeper.

Over the intervening years nothing fundamentally new has been done to absolutely prevent a disaster like the one that happened with No. 5L. It's impossible to prevent the possibility of an earthquake in an earthquake zone. All one can do is take measures to minimize destruction. That's what we try to do, too. It is difficult to figure out what else will be destroyed if this turbopump assembly, next to which I was so comfortably ensconced, were to explode. Hundreds of telemetry sensors installed in all the critical places will give their account of vibration overloads and acoustical noise thousands of times greater than what a human being can endure. The sensors will translate the pressure in each combustion chamber and the turbine revolutions, temperatures, and pressure in the gas generators into electrical language; will record the opening and closing of each of hundreds of valves; and will show what angles the motor drives are turning to, thereby changing the thrust of the peripheral engines for angular stabilization, affecting the electrical drives of the rate control system, and synchronously changing the thrust of all the engines. Affixed to the interior surfaces of the hull are temperature sensors—the most credible witnesses of a possible fire in the aft section. These were the sensors that helped to establish the true cause of the crash of the first flight model N-1 No. 3L in 1969. One more radical innovation was developed to suppress similar fires—tanks, valves, pipes, and injection nozzles, which under great pressure will begin to blow fire-extinguishing Freon gas into the aft section.

A worker from the Progress Factory who glanced into the hatch and saw an outsider boss sitting there pondering couldn't help himself and said, "That place is poorly suited for resting. It's the most labor-intensive compartment in the whole spacecraft and the most difficult to monitor. Very many changes have been made." How many little pipes of all possible calibers and high-capacity pipelines there were, connected by thousands of pipe connectors to various types of fittings and to each other!

I attempted to add up how many connections there were on a single engine and the area surrounding it. When I got to a hundred, I gave up. So, it's more than 3,000. All it takes is for one to lose its pressure integrity—leak hot "acid" gas, kerosene, or oxygen—and a fire is inevitable. And then Freon is supposed to save the day—that's if a fire has started. And what about the KORD system that my comrades and I spent so much effort on? Over the course of five years of stand and flight operation, all the KORD system equipment had finally achieved a high degree of reliability. All the experts agreed with this. But Kuznetsov's engine specialists and other specialists didn't react to the announcement by the developers of the KORD system and of the engines' automatic electric control system that the KORD system was not capable of saving the rocket if processes developed that destroyed the turbopump assembly in hundredths of a second.

Something alien, extraterrestrial, unintelligibly complex—that was the impression that N-1 interiors would have on an uninitiated engineer who wasn't privy to our technology if he were "caught" and blindfolded so that he couldn't guess where he was going, taken to the firing range, and shoved into the aft section. And it is quite difficult to believe that this entire macro-complex is controlled in flight by microelectronic circuits the size of a kopeck. Micro- and macro-technology were harmoniously combined to blaze the trail to other planets for humankind.

All 30 engines—consolidated on the first stage of the rocket into a complex that was very complicated in terms of structure, dynamics, electrical circuitry, and operating logic, with a power capacity of 50 million horsepower—would be fully tested during one flight alone on which we pinned so many hopes. This Block A had been manufactured, assembled, modified, and remodeled for three years now. And it was expected to operate for only the first 112 seconds, if the flight were normal. Then it would drop off the rocket, after passing on the baton to Block B, and fall to the steppe, having been transformed into a shapeless heap of metal. And then it would become the concern of a special team whose duty it was to turn the engines and large parts into small fragments and then bury all of it in the ground to maintain secrecy. Such was the bitter fate of nonreusable launch vehicles. That is why it costs many thousands of dollars to insert each kilogram of payload into space.

Not far from me, an installer from the Progress Factory was showing an inspector that according to some last-minute notification, such-and-such a cable had been run along a safer route in case the turbopump assembly exploded. They came to an agreement on a statement: if the oxygen pump exploded again, no insulation or rerouting of a cable would save the day.

Tearing me away from reflections that had lasted way too long, the worker said, "I've got a couple of boys here, school-age, who asked me in confidence to explain to them what's what in this 'room,' with respect to a future flight to the Moon. I told them, fools, all this stuff is going to drop off and fall to the ground right near here. It's all going to be flat as a pancake. They were almost in tears: it was a pity that such work had been done—and just for a little over 100 seconds. And incidentally, it will be many years yet before these kids have a chance at an apartment in Kuybyshev. They'll live year after year in a dormitory. And here this single Block A is worth a whole street of multi-unit apartment buildings."

This simple down-to-earth notion tore me away from my reflections regarding the greatness of our engineering minds. At the same time, work was going on in the big MIK on the three stages of the launch vehicle; work was also proceeding in the spacecraft MIK at Site No. 2B, where they were modifying Blocks G and D and the LOK—which as a whole we referred to as the L3. Here, deputy director of ZEM Yuriy Lygin was in charge. He had been at the firing range without a break for months supporting the production and engineering part of ZEM's activity, which had been moved from Podlipki to Baykonur. Despite the multitude of problems associated with the production of space technology under firing-range conditions, Lygin invariably radiated confidence and optimism. This time, however, when he met me he said, "We are expending so much effort on preparing this payload, but honestly, none of us believes that the N-1 will carry it into space."

Horizontal tests of the stack—all three Blocks A, B, and V interconnected with one another—began a month after my "little getaway" in Block A described above. Right away anomalies cropped up involving interference in the systems and the unstable operation of the on-board digital computer. Searching for and correcting the errors dragged out the testing process. On 24 August, N-1 No. 7L with its payload—the L3 upper stage—was rolled out to the launch site.

I AM NOW RETURNING TO THE EVENTS OF SEPTEMBER 1972. Afanasyev, who had flown in to the firing range, demanded a detailed report from Vladimir Lapygin (who was standing in for Pilyugin) about the causes of the on-board digital computer's unstable operation. Pilyugin's computer experts argued that the on-board digital computer was right: it had detected a false electrical connection with the circuit activating the Freon fire-suppression system. They resoldered the cables. Three days later they repeated the tests and the on-board digital computer suddenly began to operate according to a strange program. Multiple rechecks confirmed that there was a defect. The testers from Pilyugin's company had no time to sleep. I knew almost all of Pilyugin's testers from previous projects. Now I focused my attention on Vladimir Morozov. I had been told that he lived next to the rocket rather than at a hotel. At any time of the day, he really could be found at the test consoles puzzling out the latest rebus that the computer had come up with.

At the request of the developers, Dorofeyev permitted the first flight model of the on-board digital computer to be removed from the rocket standing on the launch pad. It was taken away to the input control laboratory, where they confirmed that there was a defect. Overnight at the lab, they pulled the electronic assemblies out of the housings, removed suspicious buses, and soldered in new ones removed from the same sort of computer on the LOK.[21] They urgently requested that another on-board digital computer be sent from Moscow for the LOK. During retesting, the on-board digital computer produced another couple of anomalies.

Among other problems, they discovered a breakdown in the device converting computer commands into control signals for the actuators. The device was called VP53. There were a total of 42 of them on board. The Kommunar Factory in Kharkov conducted the design development and manufacture of the device at Pilyugin's request. The defective device was transported via Moscow to Kharkov. Three days later a report arrived from Kharkov: a break had been discovered in the transformer winding. They decided to check the other VP53 devices in reserve at the firing range. They also discovered a break in one of them.

"Report to the State Commission," demanded Afanasyev, who had just arrived at the firing range. At the State Commission meeting, Afanasyev asked Lapygin a question not so much for himself (he had heard the answer more than once already when he was at NIIAP) as for the enlightenment of the large number of military and civilian specialists gathered there: "Tell us, please, why, after four years of developmental testing of the system on three flight vehicles, was it necessary to throw everything out for the sake of an on-board digital computer? Now, when the rocket has already been rolled out to the launch site, do we need to begin developmental testing from scratch? And how many integrated tests do we need to perform in order to get all the defects out of the on-board digital computer?"

Lapygin calmly reported that the control system had been designed from the very beginning for the use of two on-board computers: one to service the three stages of the launch vehicle, and the other on the LOK for the entire payload. For the first N-1 flight models, No. 3L, No. 5L, and No. 6L, it was necessary to do without the on-board digital computers because the electronics industry had fallen way behind in testing out the *Tropa* microcircuits. The

---

21. This was the S-530 digital computer.

latest defects were clearly random. The failure took place in the on-board digital computer, which until then had run through its entire cycle in bay No. 4 of the assembly building and had an accrued on-board running time of 110 hours. The first stand-alone tests had begun back on 20 July! Twenty-five integrated tests had been conducted on it and 39 full cycles equivalent to a flight. As for the VP53 instruments, one needed to ask Kharkov. During the investigation of the defect at the Kommunar Factory they discovered a strange green coloration on the transformer windings. The defect in the second instrument was similar. The specialists in Kharkov contended that a chemical process was taking place, causing the copper wire of the winding to deteriorate.

At that, Mikhail Khitrik hopped out of his seat.

"Allow me to add something. The on-board computer enabled us to logically integrate all the rocket's systems requiring control into a single processing center. We gained the capability to optimize the trajectory, to allow the system to self-adjust and adapt in the event of off-design external jet flows in the upper layers of the atmosphere, partial engine failures, and other events. As telemetry information passes through the computer, we compress it, process it, and send it to the ground so that it will be easier to make reliable diagnoses (in particular, to make decisions for the use of backup instruments). This is in the event of a flight to the Moon, when there will be time. For the first three stages there won't be time, and the on-board digital computer will have to make all the decisions on its own, without intervention from Earth. On the LOK during the flight to the Moon, circumlunar flight, and return to Earth, it will be impossible to solve problems at all without the on-board digital computer. It will help execute navigation, solving celestial mechanics equations on board."

"You've done a good job refreshing my memory concerning celestial mechanics," Afanasyev interrupted Khitrik. "We are making the decision to remove all VP53 devices from on board and we're flying to Kharkov early tomorrow morning. There we'll sort out the green discoloration in the transformer on-site, we'll obtain the findings, and we'll decide what to do next. A commission with the following members will fly out: Chertok, Kozlov, Iosifyan, Priss, and Ryazanskiy. Mikhail Ivanovich Samokhin will arrange for the airplane so that it can land at the factory airfield.[22] You'll have a day to put together the findings, fly back without spending the night, and then discuss the plan for subsequent operations in a meeting of the technical management. Specialists

---

22. Mikhail Ivanovich Samokhin (1902–1998) was a famous Soviet war hero who was tapped by Korolev to head OKB-1's (and later TsKBEM's) air transport service. He was promoted to colonel general in the Air Force in 1944 and was awarded the Hero of the Soviet Union award in 1945.

on coil-winding wire and insulation materials will fly from Moscow to meet you in Kharkov. All the commands have already been given. Thank you!"

After such a radical decision by the minister, all 42 instruments were removed from on board [the rocket] in 40 minutes, and 3 hours later they had been packed up and delivered to the airplane. When the meeting broke up, Samokhin walked up to me in the full uniform of a colonel general with service ribbons and all.

"To be on the safe side I'm going to fly with you so that there won't be any delays in Kharkov through the fault of aviation."

We departed early in the morning on 12 September, having counted on arriving at the factory at the very beginning of the workday. After takeoff, of all those who hadn't gotten a good night's sleep, Iosifyan was the first to come to his senses: "Can you tell me why we're flying? Two corresponding members of the USSR Academy of Sciences, a chief designer from Kuybyshev, I'm vice president of the Armenian Academy of Sciences, Mikhail Ivanovich Samokhin is a colonel general and Hero of the Soviet Union, and we've left a 100-meter colossus standing on the launch pad and racing off thousands of kilometers in an airplane just because someone saw green speckles on the winding wire of a transformer. Let's say that this really is mold from dampness or God knows what. So what? What year was the transformer manufactured?"

"The vehicle was manufactured in 1971, and the transformer in 1970," answered Priss.

"And now we're taking these unfortunate transformers to Kharkov, and there they're going to check them to see that they conform to their documentation and all the specifications. I have no doubt that everything will be in order. What are we going to do then?"

"Then," I proposed, "we will demand that this 'green stuff' be analyzed and that we be given a certificate clearing the instruments for a flight towards the Moon."

"If I were the factory director that we're flying out to see," retorted Iosifyan, "I would give each of us a glass of cognac and send us back to Tyuratam. By the way, Mikhail Ivanovich, couldn't you treat us to a drink now?"

"I'd be happy to," answered Samokhin, "but I have strict instructions to look after your political and moral welfare. So you'll have to wait until the return trip."

In Kharkov a vehicle was already waiting for us at the airfield. The deputy factory director who met us, before taking us to the director's office, took us through mass production shops where new color televisions were being made. At the end of a long conveyer there were vast storerooms packed solid with ready-made television sets. It looked like there were many hundreds of them there.

"Why aren't you selling them?" I asked. "Even in Moscow people are standing in line for your televisions, and here you've got them all packed in from floor to ceiling."

"You won't believe it," answered the deputy director. "We were forced to shut down the conveyer because they won't give us railroad cars."

"What kind of railroad cars?"

"Ordinary freight cars to load and off-load televisions. We've already given every railroad official a television set, but there still aren't enough railroad cars. They imposed a plan for televisions on us without taking into account the railroad's capabilities."

After a brief meeting in the director's office, we split up among the production shops and laboratories. We checked out the transformers' unsophisticated production process as painstakingly as possible. The instruments that we had brought with us were subjected to voltage-withstand tests, insulation resistance tests, and vibration tests and then tested once again for all electrical parameters. Testing continued throughout the night. By morning we had found several more breaks in the transformer windings coated with the mysterious green mold.

A brigade of cable specialists that flew in the following day presented a theory, according to which mysterious "green stuff" appeared on a widely used PELSHO (enamel-, lacquer- and silk-coated winding wire) brand of winding wire, which had been washed after the lacquering using a new process involving some new, poorly tested emulsion.[23] To be on the safe side, it would be a good idea to hunt down a supply of old wire, manufacture all the transformers again, and replace them in every single one of the instruments. After our report to the minister at the firing range, then to Moscow, to the VPK, and even to the Central Committee, we were detained in Kharkov to draw up a schedule for the modifications and delivery of all the instruments.

Thus, preparation of the rocket was temporarily halted. Round-the-clock work to modify the instruments began on the night leading to 14 September, after which we received Afanasyev's permission to fly back. When we arrived at the airfield Samokhin boasted, "If it weren't for me, you would have spent another night in Kharkov. It's not easy getting the Air Force to let you make a night landing in Tyuratam."

That morning, before we'd even had breakfast, we reported as a whole commission to the minister about our mission in Kharkov. After breakfast Afanasyev asked Kirillov, Dorofeyev, Degtyarenko, and me to stop by his office. When we appeared, he seemed very concerned.

---

23. PELSHO—*Provod emalirovannyy lakirovannyy shelkovoy obmotki.*

"While you were on the plane, I had several conversations with Moscow. And I have to tell you, the attitude there toward the N-1 is pretty bad. You are doing everything possible to prepare the vehicle. You're changing the computers right there on the launch pad; you've switched out dozens of instruments; in the time you've been gone they've told me about two telemetry transmitters—in a word, you're crawling on your belly toward the 'Launch' button. If only you could launch. But do you understand that if there is one more failure, they might shut down the project altogether? Perhaps, after amassing all the anomalies, we should recommend postponing this launch?"

"Well, let's suppose the technical management takes such an initiative, and the State Commission makes the decision to postpone the launch; then what?" I asked.

"Well, that's the whole thing. I'll say it again, you are crawling on your belly toward the 'Launch' button, without pondering the possible consequences."

"If I pose a question about postponing the launch to the technical management," I said, "I need to cite serious reasons. After receiving a new computer from Moscow and new instruments form Kharkov, we're going to check out the control system for two days and get a certificate of clearance. Personally, the engines are the only thing I am afraid of. Each chief designer will declare that his system has been thoroughly tested and debugged, and he and the military representative will give a certificate of clearance for flight. I cannot officially make a claim against a single developer. None of them will say, 'Wait, in a month or two I'll give you a new, more reliable system.' And I really am confident today that everything possible has been done on each system. Except for the engines. Everyone knows that OKB-276 is working on developing new high-quality reusable engines that can be used three times after firing tests. They'll be delivered to the rocket without reassembly. It means Kuznetsov isn't confident in the ones we have now. We're going to deliver the new engines for No. 8L. But Kuznetsov isn't about to remove the guarantee from the old single-use engines. If Kuznetsov took the initiative and said, 'Let's wait, we already have the new reusable engines, we need to put them on No. 8L, and I request that No. 7L return from the launch pad to be modified for the new engines because they are fundamentally more reliable,' then it would be a different thing. But Kuznetsov will never do that. We have an approved decision that the new engines will not be used until No. 8L. I have talked with Raykov and Yershov. They are aware of the status of the engines, not from documents and not from hearsay, but from direct participation in testing at OKB-276. Raykov said without hesitation that there would be complete confidence only after the new reusable engines are produced. Work is under way day and night in Kuybyshev.

"None of the representatives here from Kuybyshev talk about this, but they have modified a gas generator for the reusable engines and have completely redone the turbopump assembly. Rig testing has already begun, and the first ignitions went smoothly. The factory has begun to prepare for manufacturing the first production batch. Raykov predicts it will go into the assembly of No. 8L in six months. No matter how much you plan, with new engines it will be at least a year and a half before a launch vehicle will fly. It turns out that this year-and-a-half delay will be Kuznetsov's fault; in other words, MAP's fault. If Minister Dementyev issues the recommendation to wait until we have the new engines, then the technical management certainly isn't going to object. But without such a move we don't have any official grounds for backing out of the launch."

"No, forget it: Kuznetsov and Dementyev are never going to take the initiative for such a delay of flight tests," said Afanasyev bitterly.

By all indications, he had already spoken with Dementyev.

"But where is the guarantee that we won't destroy the launch site again?" asked Afanasyev.

"We are confident," answered Degtyarenko. "The presence of the on-board digital computers has enabled Pilyugin and me to develop a new program for the first 30 seconds. Immediately after the rocket lifts off the launch table it doesn't just go upward, but also to the side of the launch facilities. The control system has an inhibit that won't allow a single engine to shut down regardless of what KORD demands. Even if one of the engines or its turbopump assembly explodes, the remaining engines will still manage to pull the rocket a bit farther away and the launch site will not be harmed. We have already tested this inhibit in flight during the previous launch."

I laid out the last argument in favor of the launch for the minister: "Even if we consider No. 7L unreliable and come out with a proposal to postpone the launch, we'll be asked: what are you going to do with this rocket? Are you going to return it and modify it with new engines? That's going to cost a lot more. There are already five new rockets in the process of being built. We need to launch this one for their sake. We will gain experience from the separation of the stages, we will check out the new control systems and roll control circuit, and also the idea for getting the rocket away from the launch site, and finally, if we're lucky, we'll check out Blocks G, D, and the LOK in flight. And they have so many problems of their own! Politics aside, for the program as a whole, it is more advantageous to launch this rocket than to remove it and wait another six months until No. 8L comes out."

We left it at that and went our separate ways to pursue our duties. But an internal voice tormented each of us: maybe we really should stop the race. Since the very first years of the rocket age, our psychology was set up so that if a rocket was standing on the launch pad, it was a one-way trip for her.

BECAUSE OF THE BREAK IN TESTING, Afanasyev flew back to Moscow and allowed Dorofeyev and me to leave the firing range. Meanwhile the round-the-clock rush job in Kharkov ended. On 20 September, the modified instruments arrived at the firing range. All the different electrical tests were run again to the fullest extent, and on 14 October, Dorofeyev and I returned to the firing range.

On 18 October, Afanasyev and Komissarov flew in. We presented the schedules for subsequent operations. The following day at the N-1 launch site, we fearfully tracked the movement of a dirty, rust-colored cloud of toxic gases that had formed during the failed launch of one of Chelomey's rockets. Nevertheless, we were lucky. The wind blew in such a direction that the cloud didn't affect a single site at the firing range.

On the evening of 27 October, Kirillov and I departed from the launch site for Site No. 2. Our mood was not the best. The inconsistent results of the integrated tests with the on-board digital computers had disrupted the schedules we had put together. Without stopping by the hotel, we drove up to the deluxe dining room. The regular customers were dining there. Here, as a rule, a strict "dry law" was observed. Of the beverages, Borzhomi mineral water was the most popular.

Out of the blue, Kirillov announced, "Today Chertok and I are allowed to violate the 'dry law.' We are celebrating the 10th anniversary of the salvation of the human race."

Everyone looked in bewilderment at me. I was at a loss and could not recall playing a role in saving the human race.

"You all sure have a short memory," Kirillov grinned. "Exactly 10 years ago I received the order to install an R-7A missile carrying a warhead at launch Site No. 1 and to prepare for launch on a command, which might come from Moscow. But in order to deliver the combat missile, another rocket, which had been prepared for a Mars launch, had to be removed from the launch site. And this is how Chertok's and my interests became intertwined. He wanted to launch the rocket to Mars, and I had been ordered to prepare a launch on America. Thank God, Khrushchev and Kennedy came to an agreement. At that time, we had a glorious celebration of the event. Now it would be good to remember it."[24]

Meanwhile, computer anomalies had once again occurred during the latest round of tests. And once again the computer had to be replaced. There was a hard rain during the night from 8 to 9 November. Water accumulated on the bottom plate in Block A, and the insulation resistance was below normal. We

---

24. See Chertok, *Rockets and People, Vol. III*, Chapter 4.

dried everything out, the air temperature dropped below zero, and the weather service promised the rain was over.

On 16 November, after lunch, an expanded technical management meeting was convened with the participation of Minister Afanasyev and firing range chief Kurushin. Dorofeyev gave a general report about the work conducted over the last 10 days.

"In all, testing during these days has identified three failures in the on-board digital computer: two in the arithmetic units and one in the memory unit. After eliminating all the anomalies, two fully integrated control tests were conducted. One issue remained unresolved: should we fill the electric power plant (EU) running on electrochemical generators (EKhG) with hydrogen? The issue was fundamental from a flight program standpoint. If they weren't filled, we wouldn't fly to the Moon: there was only enough electric power on the LOK from the battery to start up Block G, and then the control system would have no power—and TASS would have to announce the flight of one of the latest Kosmos spacecraft.[25]

I asked, "Does anyone have doubts about the hydrogen?"

Dorofeyev stopped short. Only the minister had doubts. Nobody else objected to filling the EU tank with 20 kilograms of hydrogen.

Understanding that this was a ticklish situation, I announced, "We're not going to hold up everyone with this problem. Whoever needs to—stay after the technical management meeting."

Colonel Moiseyev, chief of the Sixth Directorate of the firing range, spoke after Dorofeyev: "Everything is ready. The entire staff is confident."

Istomin confirmed that all the launch systems were ready. The general reliability of the ground launch complex was 93 percent. This number created a stir in the room.

Lapygin reported in detail about the state of affairs with the on-board digital computer. The most probable causes of the failures that had occurred were the *Tropa* microcircuits. There were more than 1,500 such microcircuits in each on-board digital computer. Now both on-board digital computers—the launch vehicle's and the LOK's—had been rechecked and had been through a trial run during integrated testing. There were no contraindications to launch.

Then the minister interrupted, "How many integrated trial runs are necessary in order to get all the defects out of the on-board digital computers? Take

---

25. In those days, the convention was to disguise failed launches under the catchall designation of "Kosmos."

an example from the ground specialists: they named numbers—almost 100 percent confidence."

Next came the standard reports of the chief designers of the systems. Hoping to amuse the audience, in the conclusion of his report about the turbogenerator, Iosifyan said, "According to experimental data, the reliability of the turbogenerator is greater than 100 percent. After the failure during the first launch, all the systems were destroyed, but both turbogenerators proved to be functional after they were delivered from the crash site. After separation from stage three of the launch vehicle, the primary source of electric power for the payload (L3) should be the EU with the EKhG, which are installed in the Lunar Orbital Vehicle. The EU has never been checked out in flight."

Afanasyev recommended that Iosifyan, Lidorenko, Ovchinnikov, Dorofeyev, Moiseyev, Abramov, Degtyarenko, and I stop by his office to discuss the controversial issue. In this inner circle I recalled what the EKhG was. The EKhG obtains electric power when hydrogen is combined with oxygen. Back in middle school an experiment demonstrated this: the chemistry teacher blew a soap bubble with hydrogen and when it floated away he held a match to it. To the delight of everyone, the bubble exploded in such a way that the girls screamed, and the boys began discussing the process for obtaining the explosive gas under nonlaboratory conditions.

When hydrogen is combined with oxygen in a special generator, one can avoid the explosion. The energy released in this process is removed from the generator's electrodes as electric current. The reaction produces pure water, which is used in the spacecraft life-support system.

According to the flight program of No. 7L, the EU and EKhG, developed specially for the lunar expedition, comprised the main source of electrical power for the payload. For the flight from Earth to the Moon, around the Moon, and from the Moon to Earth, the tanks of the EU and EKhG needed to be filled with 20 kilograms of liquid hydrogen.

WHILE EDITING THE SECOND EDITION OF THIS FOURTH VOLUME, I made some additions, taking into consideration the comments of hydrogen power engineering enthusiast Sergey Khudyakov, who at that time was chief of the design and testing sector dealing with the EU and EKhG and was responsible for preparing it for launch as part of the LOK.[26] He later became deputy program

---

26. Chertok originally published his four-volume memoirs between 1994 and 1999. He revised and added significantly new information for a second edition, which was published in 1999. This English version is based on the revised 1999 edition.

director for power plants using EKhGs. I agreed to add the history of the EU because, despite the tragic fate of the N1-L3 rocket complex, the broad use of hydrogen to directly obtain electrical power is inevitable in the near future.

The EU and EKhG designed for use in space on the basis of fuel cells first appeared on the U.S. piloted Gemini vehicles and then were the main sources of electric power and drinking water on all the Apollo lunar vehicles.[27] We trailed behind the Americans in terms of production dates, but in the Soviet Union we were the first. I maintain that in Russian cosmonautics in the next decade of the 21st century, only the specialists of RKK Energiya and their partners from the Ural Electrochemical Works (developer of the EKhG) will be capable of creating powerful and reliable power-generating systems for future piloted spacecraft using just two of the most noble elements from Mendeleev's periodic table—hydrogen and oxygen.

Fuel cells differ from conventional galvanic cells in that the components—fuel (hydrogen) and oxidizer (oxygen)—are continuously fed into the reaction zone. The reaction product (water) is also continuously removed from the reaction zone. Unlike various batteries, which store electric power from an external source, fuel cells are generators—the primary source of electric power.

The voltage in an individual fuel cell does not exceed 1.1 volts. To raise the voltage in rocket-space systems to a specific value, fuel cells are connected in sequence in batteries, and to obtain a specific power output the batteries are connected in parallel. The necessary number of fuel cells joined into a single structure with gas distribution elements and autonomous thermal control is called an electrochemical generator (EKhG). Depending on the power demand, the necessary number of EKhGs are combined into a [single] power plant, which includes devices for storing and feeding components, a thermal control system, a reaction products (water) removal system, a power distribution and switching system, an automatic protection and control system, pneumohydraulic lines, and a cable network.

In the Soviet Union and later in Russia, Korolev's organization certainly ranked at the top in the practical use of EUs with EKhGs. During his tenure as chief designer, Vasiliy Mishin assigned the development of a power plant using EKhGs to Mikhail Melnikov—chief of the complex; at that time, Viktor Ovchinnikov was his deputy. He was responsible for the manufacture and testing of the EU and was confident in its reliability. Subsequently, under his management, the EU and EKhGs for the Buran reusable space transportation

---

27. An operational fuel cell was first used on a piloted spacecraft on *Gemini 5* in August 1965. Russians typically use the abbreviation TE—*Toplivnyy element* (literally, fuel element)—to denote what Westerners refer to as "fuel cells."

system (MKTS) were developed.[28] A surviving group of enthusiasts continues to fan the flame of the "hydrogen fire" to this day.

American developments, and after them our developments as well, showed substantial advantages of EUs with EKhGs over other chemical current sources. Let's list the main ones:

- direct conversion of chemical energy into electrical power is highly efficient (efficiency coefficient ≈ 65%);
- unbeatable ecological cleanliness (the reaction product is super-pure water);
- stable output voltage over a large range of loads;
- can be connected with the spacecraft life-support system;
- high specific efficiency (ratio of watt-hours to kilograms of weight of the power plant) compared with batteries.

In 1967, TsKBEM set up a competition between several organizations that were vying for the leading role in the production of EKhGs. The development by the Ural Electrochemical Works under the Ministry of Medium Machine Building showed the best results in terms of the totality of the main parameters of the design specifications. The atomic scientists managed to produce the EKhG faster than the specialized electrochemical organizations. The development, manufacture, and developmental testing of all the units and assemblies of the EU for the LOK weren't completed until 1970. By mid-1972, the entire system had undergone a whole cycle of ground tests, including tests at the engineering facility in Baykonur, and was among the systems that received clearance to be rolled out to the launch site. EUs were placed in two compartments of the LOK. The main EU assemblies were located in the cone-shaped Transfer Compartment, also called the power compartment. These included three EKhGs (with an output of 1 kilowatt each), two hydrogen cryostats (10 kilograms of hydrogen in each), two oxygen cryostats (100 kilograms of oxygen in each), assemblies of the working fluids (hydrogen and oxygen) storage and delivery system, the thermal mode control system, and others. Automatic control, monitoring, and electric power switching instruments were installed in the LOK's pressurized Instrumentation Compartment.

At the launch site the EU was waiting to be filled with hydrogen (20 kilograms) and oxygen (200 kilograms) from the next-to-last location on the service tower specially designed for this purpose at a height of 88 meters from the ground. Preparatory operations began on 14 November. On 16 November, a discussion arose among the chiefs regarding the safety of the hydrogen filling process. On the morning of 18 November, the minister himself looked into this problem yet another time.

---

28. MKTS—*Mnogorazovaya kosmicheskaya transportnaya sistema.*

"For the first time there will be hydrogen at the launch site. We don't have any experience working with it. Special safety measures will be required. If we forgo the hydrogen filling this will simplify the situation at the launch site and will shorten the preparation cycle by one and a half or two days. Under the freezing conditions that the meteorologists are promising, this is extremely important. Working for the first time with the EU, there might be all kinds of eventualities peculiar to such complex systems. Our main task is to check out the launch vehicle—Blocks A, B, and V. We don't need the EU to do that. In any event, it doesn't decide the fate of the N-1. If all three N-1 Blocks operate, we'll go into circular orbit and send off Blocks G and D, and that will be more than enough. Each of you can have a monument erected in your honor," reasoned Afanasyev.

Ovchinnikov, with whom Dorofeyev, Abramov, and I had already discussed all the "pros" and "cons" more than once, came up with counterarguments.

"We need to test out a promising electric power source for space technology under real conditions. We have to gain experience and assure ourselves that our five years of work with the atomic scientists haven't been in vain. If we don't fill the system with hydrogen we'll need to change the flight program, which has been approved at all levels. Without electric power the LOK won't be able to go into high elliptical orbit and then return to Earth. And so, we'll be giving up on the program to return to Earth at reentry velocity and test out the landing system."

Abramov was responsible for the hydrogen filling process. He assured the minister that all the operations had been tested out, he personally had verified everything, and he would be present at all times during filling process. Moiseyev confirmed that the military detail was confident in the safe outcome of the filling process.

"So what, then, are we going to decide by taking a poll of everyone? You understand the cost of a mistake," said Afanasyev.

Dorofeyev, Abramov, Degtyarenko, Ovchinnikov, Moiseyev, Iosifyan, and I spoke out in favor of hydrogen. Lidorenko and Kirillov abstained.

"Have it your way, but you'll sign off for the reliability of this operation in blood," recapitulated the minister.

Cheered by the results of the vote, Ovchinnikov addressed Afanasyev: "If I may ask, where are you going to draw the blood that we'll be using to sign off?"

"We'll send a nurse to you, and the two of you can figure out the best place to draw blood."

Cheered up by our determination, we agreed that in the State Commission we would finally approve the preparation and launch schedules.

I got in touch with Bushuyev via the high-frequency communications line from the big MIK in order to find out about attitudes in Moscow. Recently he had been a frequent visitor to the Kremlin in connection with the negotiations that had begun between the Soviets and Americans.[29] Bushuyev said, "Your train is on the tracks and under steam. You can only go straight, not to the right, not to the left."

"But what about backward?"

"No one here will understand that. Only forward!"

Forward, then, forward.

THE STATE COMMISSION ASSEMBLED ON 21 NOVEMBER. Everything in working order had already been mentioned. Primary attention was devoted to the action timeline and preparation schedule. However, the minister decided to "tickle" Lapygin one more time regarding the on-board digital computers and the abundance of anomalies involving the control system.

"Actually, here at the launch site we conducted a clean trial run of the control system," reported Lapygin. "We performed stand-alone tests in their entirety six times and all sorts of integrated tests 41 times. All the anomalies were looked into, corrected, and written up. We are confident in the control system. It is cleared for flight."

Moiseyev reported the timeline of events at the launch site minute by minute.

On 22 November at 1600 hours, the launch team formed up, and Shumilin and Dorofeyev gave reports. At 1700 hours, the 12th day of launch preparation began. At 1830 hours, the cooldown of all the feed lines began. At 2000 hours, oxygen fueling began. At 2340 hours, oxygen filling ended. Preparation and fueling with kerosene took place from 2340 hours until 0130 hours on 24 November. From 0000 hours to 0500 hours, the filling of the EU with hydrogen and oxygen took place. From 0400 hours to 0500 hours, the fuelling of Blocks G and D took place. From 0500 to 0615 hours, the thermostatic control of Blocks G and D took place. From 0645 hours until 0755 hours, the preparation and removal of all the fueling lines and ground cable connections took place. At 0815 hours, they began to pull away the service tower.

The launch took place on 23 November at 0900 hours Moscow time.

The State Commission put Dorofeyev and Moiseyev in charge of managing all the preparations. Kurushin reported on the readiness of all the firing range services and put special emphasis on safety measures.

"Everyone not involved in preparation, except for security, communication, power, and medical services, must be evacuated from all launch sites, including

---

29. This was in relation to the Apollo-Soyuz Test Project (ASTP), which to the Soviets was known as the Experimental Apollo-Soyuz Flight (*Eksperimentalnyy polet Apollon-Soyuz* or EPAS). Bushuyev was the director of the Soviet side of the mission, which was scheduled for July 1975.

from No. 2 and No. 113. We are arranging for all evacuees to stay in heated facilities in the city. Traffic on all roads will be restricted."

After the mention of the State Commission meeting, I couldn't find a single word in my notebooks about the last hours of preparation and the actual launch of No. 7L. The general emotional stress and heavy burden of responsibility on each of us is no excuse. I should have shown more discipline and found just 15 or 20 minutes to jot something down. I cannot forgive myself for this gap in my notes. Decades after the fact, a few illegible lines will help drag details of events from the depths of one's memory that a future historian won't find in any archives.

The overwhelming majority of people who have become participants in great historical events, at the moment they occur, are not aware of how much their descendants need their testimony. I reconstructed the events with the help and prompting of Boris Dorofeyev and Georgiy Priss, who had held onto the scraps of their records. Even the three of us, who were direct participants in this N-1 launch and made routine notes, when we compared them we argued about dates and various episodes. In this regard, I am amazed by the fanatical confidence with which historians describe the details of events back then when there wasn't even a written record.

Except for the firing crew located in the bunker, no one really saw the launch. The thunder of the firing did not penetrate underground. Those who were far away in the steppe said that the morning was clear and sunny with a light frost. The white beauty of a rocket could be seen in the thin mist awaiting its first and last flight.

The reports from IP-1 were clearly heard: "Fifty seconds! Pitch, yaw, and roll normal. Flight normal."

"Ninety-five seconds! Center engines are shut down. Flight normal."

"One hundred seconds! Flight normal."

That's how it should be. According to the program, 94.5 seconds into the flight the six central engines of Block A shut down. Did it really make it? For the umpteenth time I glanced down at my crib sheet where the times of the main flight stages were listed. I tensed up in expectation of the report about the separation and ignition of Block B. This was supposed to take place 113 seconds into the flight.

"One hundred ten seconds…an anomaly! An information anomaly. Loss of information over all channels!"

After the anomaly report, information from on board simply couldn't be restored. It was already clear. It didn't make it! The failure was in the first stage. This time it was just a few seconds before the firing of the engines of Block B and separation.

My memory and notes return to the events of 24 November. At around 1500 hours the technical management and State Commission—all sullen, having had no sleep that night and stunned with general grief, gathered in town in the hall of the firing range computer center. The telemetry information had been routed here during the flight. The *Lotos* (Lotus) automatic system, which the Scientific-Research Institute for Measurement Technology developed, had already performed the first express processing of it. We were waiting for the information. The lieutenant colonel of the computer center made the very first, preliminary report. He and his comrades had gone without sleep for over 24 hours.

"Up until 106.94 seconds into the flight, the propulsion systems of Block A had functioned normally. During liftoff all the engines had built up to the main stage per design. At 94.5 seconds into the flight, a control system command shut down the six central engines. The program stipulated this. At 106.94 seconds into the flight, nothing abnormal was detected in any of the 24 peripheral engines. The behavior of the new control thrusters was also normal.

"No commands were sent to the propulsion system of Block B for the ignition of the second stage. After 106.9 seconds, we were able to record an abrupt drop in pressure in the oxidizer and fuel tanks.

"During flight, the stabilization controller supported stable flight. The roll and yaw angles were negligible.

"After the 107th second of flight, there was no information at all on Block A. Pronounced deviations, as high as 18 degrees, were recorded on the upper gyro platform for all three axes before communication broke off at 110 seconds into the flight. After 110 seconds, the on-board digital computer recorded an emergency situation.

"The KORD system issued no emergency signals to shut down the engines before 106.7 seconds into the flight. This once again confirms the normal operation of the propulsion system. It is still not clear whether an SAS command passed. It seems as though there was a change of level in the anomalies—we need to do some additional checking.

"The structural sensors recorded a G-load surge on the load-bearing ring at 106.95 seconds. The greatest loads were in the second plane. There was an information cutoff 0.05 seconds after the load surge for all channels."

Aleksey Bogomolov interrupted: "Except for our microwave line. The transmitter is on Block B, and it continued to operate until the 282nd second on a falling and burning rocket! The microwaves passed through the plasma!"

"That's right," confirmed the lieutenant colonel, and he continued, "the telemetry system of Block B failed at exactly 107.28 seconds, in other words, 0.33 seconds after the telemetry unit of Block A.

"The preliminary conclusion is that up until 106.95 seconds into the flight, all the rocket's on-board systems were operating normally. There were no anomalies reported in the operation of systems and assemblies. More precisely, at 106.97 seconds an impact effect occurred in the area between the second and third planes of the load-bearing ring of Block A. Immediately after this, there were failures in all channels and then there was a total breakdown of communications for all radio systems. We could no longer decipher the microwave line."

After the report, which everyone listened to in silence, as if it were a grave-side speech, the shocked silence lasted several minutes. Gradually, discussion began throughout the room, here and there developing into arguments.

After consulting with the minister, I announced, "From the report it is clear that the cause of the failure has still not surfaced. We need time for each service to conduct a thorough microanalysis of all the information concerning its system. All those who haven't had any sleep, go rest for a couple of hours so that tomorrow, 25 November, at 1500 hours, we'll gather right here and listen to the following reports:

- Degtyarenko—general analysis;
- Churkin—on the operation of the RTS-9 telemetry systems of Block A; there are 28 local switches in various zones;
- Bogomolov—on the operation of the *Orbita* telemetry systems;
- Komissarov—on the operation of the BRS-4 telemetry system;
- Tanayev—on the operation of all the engines;
- Priss—control system analysis; and
- Nikitin—general analysis of the operation of the radio systems."

I asked the most impartial and objective Valentin Yakovlevich Likhushin, director of the Scientific-Research Institute of Thermal Processes (the former NII-1 in Likhobory), to conduct an independent expert evaluation. Actually, my request proved to be unnecessary; he had already received the same instructions from the minister. Raykov took me aside from all the arguing, and, agitated, he said, "I managed to look through what I needed to with our guys, and I am convinced that the oxygen pump on engine four exploded."

At my request, Ryazanskiy assigned Anatoliy Churkin to match up the telemetry information of the various systems with a unified time system. This was performed with a guaranteed accuracy of down to 0.1 microseconds.

At the second plenary session of the accident investigation commission, reports were delivered about the place and size of the space where an explosion might occur. Now no one had any doubt that an explosion had occurred on board. The swift development of the loss of radio communication was very convincing evidence in this regard. Therefore, I asked Boris Nikitin—chief of our radio department—to speak first.

"We consider it proven that at 106.9 seconds, a process began that caused the formation of a dense layer of plasma, which rapidly enveloped the entire rocket and became an impenetrable shield for radio communications between the on-board antennas and ground tracking stations. The anomaly in radio communications over all ranges took place within tenths of seconds. We're dealing with a more intense explosion than in 1969 on No. 3L. In that case, the process of communications loss also developed like an avalanche, but more slowly. The break in power feed connections between the electrical systems of Blocks A and B is another indicator of the explosive nature of the process. These connections are made using strong, heavy-gauge cable rather than fine wires. As you know, this cable had additional thermal insulation. The cable didn't overheat, but instantly broke. This was pinpointed at a point between 107.45 and 107.5 seconds."

In all, the behavior of 5,500 parameters was examined! And throughout, a picture describing an explosion took shape.

"Why are you assuming the responsibility of speaking about an explosion without acknowledging the possibility of structural failure due to an off-nominal regime? Consequently the pipelines were damaged and then there was a fire," Nikolay Kuznetsov asked. He and his deputies had been searching for proof of the absolute innocence of the engines since the very beginning. Since the very first years of the development of rocket technology, the turbopump assembly and combustion chamber had been considered to be explosion hazards. It meant that the chief designer of the engines was directly to blame for the demise of a rocket. In order to refute this scenario, it was necessary to propose another one, but it must also be an "explosion" scenario. I had already been warned that Kuznetsov's people would come out with their own scenario.

"Before opening the floor to discussion, let's listen to other reporters," I proposed.

Degtyarenko explained how they tried to determine the site "where everything started" based on the G-load sensors and other parameters. This sort of analysis required singling out thousandths of seconds, rather than hundredths, on "fast telemetry." Everyone who was involved in this search came to the conclusion that the "first dynamic effect" (so as not to use the term "explosion" prematurely, as Degtyarenko said) began in the area of the load-bearing ring of Block A between engines No. 3 and No. 5. Thus, the source of the explosion was engine No. 4.

Degtyarenko displayed a diagram that showed that during the time interval from 106.95 seconds to 107.1 seconds, in other words over a period of 0.15 seconds, three shocks occurred and were pinpointed by the load sensors along the longitudinal axis.

Subsequent reports confirmed that up until 107.1 seconds, all of the engines operated anomaly-free, except for engine No. 4. The revolutions-per-minute sensor and other indicators for engine No. 4 provided evidence of an interruption in the circuit at the same time that information still continued to come in on the other engines. This meant that first, an interruption occurred in the circuits to the turbopump assembly of engine No. 4, and after that, the cloud of plasma and breaks in cables during the disintegration deprived us of information.

Very thorough microanalysis managed to establish the guilt of engine No. 4. The revolutions per minute of the turbopump assembly on engine No. 4 had stopped suddenly 0.022 seconds before adjacent engines No. 5 and No. 6. The first failure in telemetry was pinpointed by local switch No. 13 at 106.848 seconds, and the loss of all telemetry, according to general consensus, took place at 107.210 seconds. Consequently, 0.362 seconds remained for all the groups to analyze. And so all investigative efforts needed to be concentrated on this slice of time.

At the end of the day, four subcommissions were formed. Heading them were [the following chief designers]: Kuznetsov—propulsion systems; Kozlov—rocket structure; Lapygin—control system; and Dorofeyev—the entire complex and summation of results.

The next day, 26 November, we began to have heated arguments concerning the hypothesis that Kuznetsov had advanced. He demanded that the strength and stability of the structure of Block A be examined. One of the causes for the structural failure, in his opinion, might have been the simultaneous shutdown of the six central engines. This scenario prompted a dramatic negative reaction from Dmitriy Kozlov.

"Once again I declare that the margins of strength are completely sufficient. I gave instructions in Kuybyshev to immediately check all the calculations and test results, and to perform any experiment necessary on the hardware available at the factory. If we erred, then tell us, please: why did the breakup take place during the flight segment with the simplest mode?"

"But will you also take into consideration the fact," objected Kuznetsov's supporters, "that the Freon ran out several seconds before these events. Why did everything start after the Freon was used up? You had a component leak somewhere. Until then, Freon hadn't provided the opportunity to ignite the mixture of kerosene and liquid oxygen, which violently vaporized when it leaked in and accumulated. As soon as the Freon was used up, some stimulator actuated and this whole mixture blew up!"

Dorofeyev, Degtyarenko, and Kozlov—all experienced fighting men in such situations—could scarcely restrain themselves. As technical manager I was forced to maintain the appearance of neutrality, although the bias of Kuznetsov's position disturbed me.

While we were in the midst of heated arguments, someone from among the military employees of the computer center wrote the following on the chalkboard:

No. 4   106.932 (+0.000),
No. 3   106.936 (+0.004),
No. 2   0106.948 (+0.016),
No. 22   106.962 (+0.030).

That's when, having forgotten about neutrality, I said, "Very obvious! Look how the shock from engine No. 4 spread through the structure. It takes three-hundredths of a second to knock engine No. 22, located opposite No. 4, out of action. And they're separated by 28 meters along a semicircle and by 14 meters along a straight line. Isn't it clear that we are dealing with an explosion that began with No. 4?"

The arguments began to take on such an intransigent nature that the official meeting had to be adjourned, and it was announced that the next day, on 27 November, Valentin Likhushin would make a report. Likhushin had gained the reputation of a benevolent but strict and objective judge in the disputes of chief designers over engine problems. And this time he made a calm, convincing report. Understandably, I am citing just the main thrust of his report.

"The spread of the strong shock at precisely 106.932 seconds proceeds from the area where engine No. 4 is mounted. This fact can be considered unequivocally established. Shock was detected throughout other engines too, but this was the result of the main shock. The whole process of the shock disturbance spread to all the peripheral engines in 0.04 seconds, the speed of sound through metal. The readings from the turbopump assembly rpm sensors confirm this. The main question is, what was the nature of this shock? What is it, an external explosion or a failure inside an engine in a liquid-propellant rocket engine chamber? Here, there can be various points of view. It is less likely that something happened in the engine itself, in its combustion chamber. The most thorough analysis fails to confirm that some sort of kerosene or oxygen leak occurred before the shock. Freon was fed just to the central engines for a long time. We tried to reproduce—down to the hundredths and thousandths of a second—the sequence of the disintegration of the manifolds of the oxidizing gas feeding the turbines and compared this with the actual structure and layout. For the time being, for me, the most probable scenario seems to be the explosion of the turbopump assembly rather than the combustion chamber. As far as we know, similar phenomena occurred on the test stand, and we finally arrived at this conclusion, analyzing the failure of rocket No. 5L."

Priss, who spoke after Likhushin, presenting an analysis of the control system, and Kunavin, who reported on the KORD system, argued that all systems, even the on-board digital computer, were operating anomaly-free before the "shock." Moreover, after the "shock," at 110.847 seconds, a command in Block V—"emergency shutdown of engines"—was pinpointed. That meant the control system had been working, because this command is sent from the on-board digital computer if the rocket loses control, which clearly happened 3 seconds after the explosion.

After one more day of fierce debates, Afanasyev advised, "There's nowhere to rush to now. The subcommissions and working groups must appoint individuals to be personally responsible for the thorough processing of all the materials and their delivery to Moscow. There we will listen to the first results in a panel and we'll prepare an order for the development of a report."

The telemetry processing confirmed that the power plant (EU) and electrochemical generator (EKhG), filled with hydrogen and oxygen, had operated normally the entire flight up until the moment of impact with the ground. But now this was only interesting to their creators.

After long debates, the final text of the report had an unequivocal conclusion: "The rocket had an anomaly-free flight for 106.93 seconds, but 7 seconds before the calculated time for the separation of stages one and two, the oxidizer pump of engine No. 4 experienced a virtually instantaneous disintegration, which resulted in the rocket's destruction."

At the firing range throughout the following year of 1973, work to prepare rocket N-1 No. 8L with new engines continued, but the disarray and confusion surrounding the lunar program itself intensified at all levels from the Politburo to those involved in its practical implementation.

Chapter 18
People in the Control Loop

Originally I set out to write this chapter out of a desire to inform the reader about the role and place of the human being in the control of actual rocket-space systems. Back in the "hazy youth" of my engineering career, I was interested in the man vs. machine issue. I wasn't able to come up with any new theories in this field. For the most part, the printed works and numerous dissertations on this subject, with which I became acquainted, could not serve as a guide for specialists who bore personal responsibility for the reliability of a specific system.

Human involvement in the control process is one of the factors determining the reliability and effectiveness of spaceflights. This problem was solved radically for launch vehicles. Human involvement in the flight control of a ballistic missile or launch vehicle ends on the ground with the keying in of commands that set up ignition.

During all flight segments from the actuation of the "lift-off contact" until engine shutdown on the last stage, there is no human involvement in flight control of the rocket from the ground or from on board the spacecraft being inserted by this rocket. The only exception is the radio transmission from the ground to the spacecraft of commands to shut down engines and to actuate the emergency rescue system, if observers on the ground consider this to be necessary.

The full set of equations describing the behavior of the launch vehicle, taking into account the liquid it is carrying, its structural flexibility, and various other qualities, is referred to as the mathematical model. Differential equations also describe the behavior of the rocket's flight control system. The developers of this system have the opportunity to update the mathematical description by simulation using the actual spacecraft, and finally, they conclusively verify the reliability of the design calculations through flight testing. The flight testing of ballistic missiles usually takes several dozen launches.

Such a testing method is economically wasteful for a spacecraft. It is too expensive and one-of-a-kind and must fulfill its mission on the very first launch.

The motion control and navigation system of any contemporary spacecraft consists of two complexes interconnected by radio links: a ground control complex and an on-board control complex. Depending on the distribution of tasks between the ground and on-board complexes, and also on the structure and reliability of the on-board complex control equipment, three control methods can be used:

- autonomous and automatic, using programs previously loaded into the on-board equipment. On contemporary spacecraft, these programs are loaded into the memory of the on-board digital computer in the form of algorithms;
- commands and programs transmitted on board the spacecraft from ground complex control posts; and
- manual control performed by the crew.

Unpiloted spacecraft combine the first two methods. Piloted spacecraft use all three. In this case, the control system creators can give priority to any of the three versions during various flight phases. The selection of an optimal combination is one of the tasks that control system creators solve. Beginning with the flight of Gagarin and continuing until recent times, we have had heated arguments about the priority and degree of responsibility of the crew in the motion control of a spacecraft. The flight programs for Vostoks and Voskhods did not call for the inclusion of a cosmonaut in the control loop. They were permitted to take control only for a trial or in a desperate emergency situation. The use of manual control saved the lives of the *Voskhod-2* crew.[1]

To avoid turning my memoirs into a boring scientific treatise, I am trying to show the dialectic and dynamics of the development of all three methods in specific examples of emergency and off-nominal situations from the history of piloted programs in which I was directly involved. Here, I am limiting myself to the most interesting examples from the history of motion control, orientation, stabilization, and navigation.

Working on these memoirs, I realized the validity of asserting that catastrophic, emergency, and off-nominal situations are some of the strongest incentives for speeding up progress in space technology. Pilyugin first expressed a similar seditious (in the opinion of any high-ranking manager) thought in Kapustin Yar at a meeting of the State Commission on the flight testing of the experimental R-2 rocket in 1949. The very first launch proved to be a failure. Based on the results of the analysis of this failure, decisions were made for a fundamental modification of the rocket's control system and structure.[2]

---

1. See Chertok, *Rockets and People, Vol. III*, Chapter 9.
2. See Chertok, *Rockets and People, Vol. II*, pp. 183–186.

"A single failed launch teaches us more about a system and about how to operate it than 10 trouble-free launches," Pilyugin declared.

This declaration outraged the State Commission's Ministry of Defense representative Colonel Aleksandr Mrykin: "So you're actually proposing that we launch rockets 'beyond the hills' just to satisfy your professional curiosity?"

Several years later some aphorisms composed by American rocket technology specialists reached us, and among them was "Murphy's law": "If it seems to you that everything is going well, it means that you've overlooked something."

IN OCTOBER 1998, the Presidium of the Academy of Navigation and Motion Control awarded me the N. N. Ostryakov honorary prize "[f]or outstanding scientific achievements in the development and study of gyroscopes and autonomous navigation systems."[3] President of the Academy Vladimir Peshekhonov warned me that after he handed me the prizewinner's certificate at the general assembly of the academy, I would have to make a scientific report. In my report, among the incentives contributing to the progress of motion control systems, I mentioned "Pilyugin's law," which he expressed for the first time in 1949. None of the very competent scientists who were members of the Academy voiced any challenges in this regard. "Pilyugin's law," which he formulated long before the Space Age, is also valid for space systems.

In publications on the history of Soviet and Russian cosmonautics there is very little mention of the numerous off-nominal situations, which were caused not by hardware failures, but by the actions of people participating in the control loop on the ground or by crew actions on board the spacecraft. Analysis of the specific circumstances in such instances, as a rule, was the destiny of special commissions; their conclusions and recommendations resulted in changes not only in technology, but also in the organization of flight control operations. Time and again I had the occasion to be the chairman or a member of accident investigation commissions and also to act as defendant before other commissions or high-ranking managers.

I'LL RECAP THE HISTORY OF THE DEVELOPMENT of spacecraft control systems. Ballistic missiles and launch vehicles underwent developmental testing together with their control systems. Once debugged, these systems remained almost unchanged in series production. This was one of the conditions for

---

3. The International Public Association of the Academy of Navigation and Motion Control was established in February 1995.

achieving a high degree of reliability in a rocket complex. Missiles put into military service were updated following new flight tests of modified missiles.

Unlike missiles, each spacecraft of the first decades of the Space Age was unique in and of itself. Even among present-day spacecraft it is difficult to find two completely identical ones. Each spaceflight brings new experience, which entails the introduction of changes to the design, circuitry, and control methods. Identical launch vehicles insert spacecraft into space that vary widely in terms of the purposes of their missions and, consequently, in terms of their structure. Each of them requires the production of equipment, a power supply, a motion control system, telemetry, an on-board control complex, and special test equipment developed specifically for those missions—and, with the appearance of on-board computers, its very own software.

In the late 1950s, the scales of operations on spacecraft hardware and control systems turned into a problem that required radical and swift solutions. It didn't take long for me to convince Korolev that we needed to set up our own facility for the development of control systems and production of spacecraft instrumentation. Furthermore, as soon as Korolev recognized the need to create such an organization within his own OKB-1, he sometimes very roundly criticized me for being slow to organize developments of spacecraft control systems.

Over a short period of time, specialized departments and laboratories were formed. Shops were created at the factory to implement their design developments and were combined for specialized instrumentation production. We were not able to develop and implement all of our ideas at our own facility at OKB-1. Gyroscopic and optical instruments, radio engineering systems, current sources, electric motors, relays, remote switches, and electronics parts were made according to our specifications at dozens of specialized design bureaus and factories.

Having first of all created our own research, design, and production facility supporting the development of spacecraft control systems, we became the initiators for the creation in the Soviet Union of a unified infrastructure of design bureaus and factories working in the field of cosmonautics. In 1966, the year of Korolev's death, there were already more than 50 independent enterprises and laboratories in NIIs and at institutes of higher learning that were loaded down with our assignments.

We took on the developments that were most crucial and those that no amount of effort could assign to subcontractors. In late 1966, the total list of instruments that we had developed and that were in space or were involved in ground testing consisted of close to 1,000 types of units.

Essential decisions by the Commission on Military-Industrial Issues under the USSR Council of Ministers supported our active efforts for the development of spacecraft control technology.[4] In those days the so-called civil service by no means hindered the solution of our problems, but assisted with them. Civil servants working in the Kremlin and in the Central Committee Party *apparat* on Old Square assisted us in overcoming interdepartmental and inter-republic barriers.

During the first decade of the rocket age (1947–1957) we created the basis for the infrastructure of a powerful rocket industry. During the second decade (1957–1967) the formation of the rocket infrastructure was completed and the construction of the space infrastructure began in parallel. This process went far beyond the limits of the capabilities of our OKB-1. The new Ministry of General Machine Building (MOM), Minister Sergey Afanasyev, and his deputies showed initiative, perseverance, and boldness uncharacteristic for government officials in the integrated organization of the rocket-space instrumentation industry. At MOM, specialized main directorates for gyroscopic technology, radio systems, and system-wide technology were created.[5] Finding themselves at the epicenter of these processes, the staffs that were combined under my management at Korolev's OKB-1 became our country's first and foremost creators of control systems for spacecraft for a wide variety of missions. The capacities of our own production facilities were quickly depleted, but we found good assistants in our nation. With the assistance of the Central Committee *apparat* and the VPK, we recruited factories to collaborate with us. They became our main production base, which worked using the documentation of OKB-1 control departments, and continue this work to this day.

One of the first was the Plastik Factory in Moscow, whose primary output consisted of electric fuses. Nevertheless, it quickly mastered the production of on-board sequencers and electronic amplifier converters for attitude-control systems. The Ufa Instrumentation Factory, which until that time had produced autopilots, set up special shops where they manufactured switching instruments for on-board complex control and integrated electric power systems. The Azov Optical-Mechanical Factory set up the series production of ground testing stations, known under the index 11N6110. More than 200 of these stations served until the 1990s as the basic means for testing spacecraft at factory monitoring and testing stations and at cosmodrome engineering facilities and launch sites. This same factory took on the burden of manufacturing complex electromechanical spacecraft docking assemblies.

---

4. This was the formal name of the Military-Industrial Commission (VPK).

5. At the time of its formation in 1965, MOM was established with the following main directorates: First (military rockets), Second (engines and naval rockets), Third (spacecraft and launch vehicles), Fourth (ground systems and launch pads), Fifth (radio systems and on-board instruments), and Sixth (gyroscopes and control systems).

Korolev, Khazanov, and I flew to Kiev in 1963 to incorporate the instrument builders of Ukraine into our space sphere. For several days we haunted the doorways of the Ukrainian authorities. We went to Ukrainian Communist Party Central Committee Secretary Shelest.[6] He avoided resolving the issue after giving us a lecture on the very difficult situation in the ferrous metallurgy industry. Korolev muscled his way in to see Ukrainian Communist Party Central Committee First Secretary Podgornyy. After an hour-long conversation, during which Korolev, according to his story, improvised as never before on the subject of prospects, we "received" the Kievpribor Factory. This factory served as the main supplier of on-board complex instruments for Soyuz and Progress spacecraft.

The instrument production facility of our ZEM, together with all the other factories loaded down with our projects, became a powerful production base without which our successes in space would have been impossible. Many of our developments (we realized this many years later) turned out to be firsts. The Iron Curtain prevented us from associating with American specialists. In Europe, even if there had been such a possibility, we couldn't have borrowed anything. Everything that was required to control spacecraft we and our component suppliers thought up, developed, and manufactured at new production facilities on our own. We really were genuine trailblazers. Four decades later, much in the history of control systems from the 1960s and 1970s can seem naïve. Once again calling to mind this period, filled with the joys of triumphs and tragic failures, I can say with a clear conscience that we have something to be proud of. It's only worth being sorry that in our time we couldn't tell the world what we had really done and what efforts this took. The timid attempts of open publications or speeches at international forums ran up against a thick wall with the inscription "don't let anything through!" After gaining worldwide fame, as they traveled around the world and gave numerous interviews and speeches, the cosmonauts did not mention the name of Chief Designer S. P. Korolev and the other actual creators of the rocket-space systems that had carried the heroes into space.

In this regard, in his own circle of confidants, Korolev said with bitterness, "The biggest secret in our space program is the names of the chief designers."

When it nevertheless did come to publications, Korolev was called "Prof. Sergeyev" and Mishin "Prof. Vasilyev." In one of my first articles, "Man or

---

6. Petr Yefimovich Shelest (1908–1996) was a member of the Politburo (from 1964 to 1973) and First Secretary of the Central Committee of the Ukrainian Communist Party from 1963 to 1972. In that capacity, he was the highest serving Party official in Ukraine.

Machine," my identity was concealed under the pseudonym "Prof. Yevseyev."[7] During those action-packed years, such circumstances amused us and even filled us with pride: look how valuable we were to the state!

Our obvious achievements and successes did not protect us from the "childhood diseases" of rapid growth. The primary causes of failures were our enthusiastic idealization of our subject matter, an overestimation of our own strengths, and a frantic race against time.

Our staff did not have a chief designer of control systems because at our OKB-1 there was only one Chief—Korolev. When Mishin replaced him, this detail of the situation remained unchanged. Rauschenbach, Yurasov, Kalashnikov, and I were completely satisfied with our title of "deputy chief designer." Sometimes our subordinates grumbled or teased us: "In our sub-contractors, a developer who is providing us with a somewhat insignificant system is called a 'chief designer,' while the person responsible for the entire big system, containing dozens of subsystems and hundreds of instruments from all sorts of 'chiefs' is still called a 'deputy chief designer'." The damage to one's pride was compensated by the fascinating work, where each person had the rare opportunity to demonstrate all of his or her capabilities and be involved in realizing designs, which quite recently had seemed fantastic.

Each government decree about the development of a new type of missile or launch vehicle mentioned not just the general designer of the rocket complex, but also without fail the surnames of the chief designers of the engines, the ground-based launch equipment, and the control system. The decrees for the creation of the spacecraft of Chief Designer Korolev (and after him Mishin), General Designer Chelomey, and Chief Designers Kozlov and Reshetnev made no mention of the names of the chief designers of the spacecraft control systems. That's the way it had been since Korolev's time. The decrees for the N1-L3 and Buran were exceptions to this rule.

I am making an attempt to correct a historical injustice and am naming the names of my comrades at OKB-1, each of whom by rights could have been called "chief designer of such-and-such a system," or at the very least "scientific chief." At the top of this list is the patriarch of attitude-control and navigation systems, world-renowned scientist Boris Rauschenbach. Without naming their academic degrees and ranks, I shall list the others in alphabetical order: Leonid Alekseyev, Oleg Babkov, Yevgeniy Bashkin, Vladimir Branets, Ernest Gaushus, Yuriy

---

7. Chertok is probably referring here to an essay published as B. Yevseyev, "Chelovek ili avtomat?" in *Shagi k zvezdam* [*Footsteps to the Stars*], ed. M. Vasilyev (Moscow: Molodaya gvardiya, 1972), pp. 281–287.

Karpov, Viktor Kalashnikov, Larisa Komarova, Mikhail Krayushkin, Viktor Kuzmin, Petr Kupriyanchik, Viktor Legostayev, Boris Nikitin, German Noskin, Boris Penek, Boris Savchenko, Igor Shmyglevskiy, Boris Skotnikov, Vladimir Syromyatnikov, Yevgeniy Tokar, Lev Vilnitskiy, Oleg Voropayev, and Igor Yurasov.

From the author's archives.

Shown here at a function are G. V. Noskin, B. Ye. Chertok, and V. P. Khorunov. Noskin was a key developer of control and navigation systems.

None of the individuals listed above ever complained about the small number of medals or other governmental awards and prizes. The scientists in our school of control enjoy celebrity and are deservedly respected not only in our own country, but also among the specialists of many foreign firms, with whom it became possible to associate after the fall of the Iron Curtain. The size of my book and my own limited capabilities prevent me from speaking about the character and contribution of each person listed.

We triggered a snowballing process in the development of the space industry and science. Decades later we still held a monopoly in the field of piloted flight control. The supplier organizations that worked on our assignments formed their own scientific schools, going far beyond the jurisdiction of the three control specialist chief designers: Pilyugin, Ryazanskiy, and Kuznetsov, who were members of the legendary sextet of the first Council of Chief Designers. The new organizations for space control, radio electronics, and electrical engineering soon had their own Academy of Sciences members, individuals with doctoral and candidate degrees, and professors: Aleksey Bogomolov, Gennadiy Guskov, Yuriy Bykov, Andronik Iosifyan, Nikolay Sheremetyevskiy, Nikolay Lidorenko, Armen Mnatsakanyan, Aleksey Kalinin, Vladimir Khrustalev, Sergey Krutovskikh, and Vyacheslav Arefyev.[8] Rather than being abstract theoreticians, each one was the creator of systems that were really essential to cosmonautics.

---

8. These men were all chief designers at their respective enterprises, as opposed to Chertok and his associates (such as Rauschenbach, Yurasov, Kalashnikov, and others), who, despite their prominent contributions to spacecraft and launch vehicle control system design, were either deputy chief designers or lower-ranked designers at TsKBEM.

INTERPLANETARY TRAVELS WERE THE MAIN SUBJECT OF SCIENCE FICTION, which stirred up people's imaginations long before it became possible to realize this dream. Now, when the realization of the future was in our hands, we were eager to move closer to it. In the early 1960s we lived and worked in a risk-loving atmosphere of constant racing. Races were going on simultaneously in four areas of endeavor:

- securing absolute superiority in nuclear missile armaments;
- achieving all "firsts" in piloted spaceflight;
- sending automatic interplanetary space stations to the Moon, Venus, and Mars; and
- creating space communications systems.

Beginning with the first satellites, we considered it the norm that reports about success in space, introduced by the characteristic chime of the Moscow call sign, were broadcast by what had become the very dear voice of Levitan: "This is Moscow speaking! All the radio stations of the Soviet Union are operating!"[9] For understandable reasons no mention was made over the airwaves of the fifth field of endeavor—military space systems.

Analyzing my work, the work of my comrades, and of the many people and organizations associated with us from a distance of a little more than three decades, I marvel at our collective faith in our strengths and our naïve tendency to "embrace the unembraceable" within inconceivably short deadlines. Now even science-fiction buffs have come to terms with the harsh necessity of considering the life cycle for the creation of sophisticated space systems with a high degree of reliability. It takes 8 to 12 years from the beginning of their development until their practical implementation. We couldn't tolerate that. If in 1959 some futurologist had predicted that we wouldn't execute the first soft landing on the Moon until 1966 after using up 12 four-stage launch vehicles, that it would be 1967 before we would transmit fragmentary telemetry data to Earth from a spacecraft that had penetrated Venus's atmosphere, and that we would deliver a pennant of the Soviet Union to Mars in 1971, we would have considered him to be an incompetent pessimist or a spiteful critic.

Errors at the beginning of our difficult path to the creation of complex technical systems also had their good side. They unified teams of people, made them have a more critical attitude toward their work the more experience they gained, and made them seek out more reliable designs and organizational

---

9. Yuriy Borisovich Levitan (1914–1983) was undoubtedly the most famous Soviet radio announcer; he first gained fame during World War II when millions of Soviet citizens first heard major events of the war, including the fall of Berlin, through his announcements.

forms of interaction. The organizational structure that we worked out and our placement of specialists in departments and laboratories proved successful. Certainly luck was on our side in terms of having talented and untiring, hard-working people.

The present-day structure of operations for the creation of a complex of systems at NPO Energiya and other organizations that have put our experience to use is evidence of this. The departments have grown, split, and combined into new complexes. But the leading specialists, who determined the fate of each field of endeavor, stayed with their own work. Natural biological attrition has occurred over the course of 30 years, and a small number of people have left for other fields, but a surprisingly consistent framework of control specialists, which took shape in the 1960s, until very recently defined the state of the art in our country for spacecraft control.

After several events, including our union with Grabin's TsNII-58 in 1959, the transfer of Rauschenbach's team from NII-1 to OKB-1 in 1960, and several reshufflings of people in the space field, Korolev appointed me his "second first" deputy, placing me in charge of all design and research departments located at the second production site. He named German Semyonov, who had returned from Dnepropetrovsk, to be manager of the factory portion of the second production site. Deputy chief engineer Isaak Khazanov received the assignment to start up construction of an instrumentation facility at our second territory and, as the new buildings were put into operation, to wind down production at the factory of the first territory. Thus, by 1965 I had officially combined not only the departments of the instrumentation-control complex, but also the planning and design departments of all the space-related projects at OKB-1. This reorganization substantially expanded my authority, duties, and responsibility.

Despite the structural configurations, the creatively robust staffs of Konstantin Bushuyev, Mikhail Tikhonravov, Pavel Tsybin, and Konstantin Feoktistov remained in direct creative subordination to Korolev. The following chief planners worked under their supervision: Yevgeniy Ryazanov, Gleb Maksimov, Yuriy Denisov, Yuriy Frumkin, Vyacheslav Dudnikov, Andrey Reshetin, and other specialists brimming with enthusiasm.[10]

From the very beginning I asked Korolev to relieve me of responsibility for planning work over all space projects so that I could concentrate on a completely new area of endeavor—the development of spacecraft control systems. He agreed in principle, under the condition that, being his first deputy after

---

10. These were the people directly responsible for conceptual design, as opposed to engineering or production tasks.

Mishin, I had to "watch over and keep track of" everything that Bushuyev, Tikhonravov, and Tsybin were doing. "Considering the fact that they let their imaginations get away with them a lot, the planners' assignments need to go through you on their way to Boldyrev's design department." And that was that. I quickly made arrangements with Bushuyev and the other managers who oversaw the planners and hit it off very well because their work to a great extent was determined by the ideas and successful work of the control specialists.

By Korolev's way of thinking, Mishin was supposed to concentrate his energy and experience on the development of the new R-9 and the global GR-1 missiles, on rocket engines, and on the development of a future strategy, including the future N-1 heavy launch vehicle for a lunar expedition. During all the reorganizations that Korolev undertook beginning in 1947, Mishin always remained his "first" first deputy not only concerning engineering matters, but also administrative ones.

The very multifaceted work for the creation of new spacecraft control systems got under way at the same time as my subdivisions were retaining developments of steering systems and internal tank systems and supervising the development of control systems for missiles and launch vehicles. I shall list only the main areas of our work:

- motion control (orientation, navigation, rocket, and spacecraft dynamics);
- systemic integration of on-board equipment control using the ground-to-spacecraft system, electric equipment, special stand-alone systems, radio engineering systems, and antenna-feeder units; and
- design work, electromechanical and electro-hydraulic systems, and instrument testing.

It would take too much time and space to list everything that the control and instrumentation teams were involved with. Especially since any one of our projects was linked with supplier organizations, and telling about them deserves a special treatise.

Below I shall dwell only on those projects of ours that were appreciated in scientific circles, made an epochal contribution to the development of cosmonautics, were realized or begun during the second decade of the Space Age, and also those that were the most interesting from the standpoint of the science of human behavior in the control loop.

The first two Soviet satellites, as is generally known, flew into space without any motion or attitude control in orbit. The laws of celestial mechanics controlled them. As we used to say, they answered only to our ballistics experts.

Unlike its predecessors, the third satellite, launched on 15 May 1958, now had the first command radio link that we had ever put into practice. I developed the design specifications for the command radio link (KRL) together with our radio engineers Shustov, Shcherbakov, and Krayushkin, and with our first "space" electrical engineers, the developers of the control logic, Karpov, Shevelev, and Sosnovik.[11] On 22 August 1956, I received Korolev's signature of approval on the design specifications. The decision about the first very simple satellite had not yet been made, and we believed that secret Object D—the future third satellite—was going to be the first spacecraft.[12] Controlling the activation and modes of the science equipment via command radio link at that time seemed to us to be a qualitative leap compared with the radio control systems of ballistic missiles. Director and Scientific Chief at NII-648 Nikolay Belov was in charge of developing the on-board and ground equipment of the first space command radio link. It took a year and a half to create the first command radio link. It supported the transmission on board of 20 immediate-execution one-time commands. This command radio link served as the basis for the development of more advanced versions for the piloted programs.

Motion control of future spacecraft was to be the next step. It turned out that for the specialists developing the automatic motion control systems for rockets, the creation of spacecraft motion control systems required overcoming a psychological barrier. This barrier was successfully overcome when Boris Rauschenbach arrived on the staff at OKB-1. Beginning with *Luna-3*, all of our spacecraft had systems making it possible to correct near-Earth and interplanetary trajectories. The essence of the correction process consisted in the fact that the parameters of the actual orbit or flight trajectory were measured beforehand using ground-based Command and Measurement Complex facilities. Next, the deviation of the trajectory from the design value was determined, and depending on the magnitude of the error, the required correcting pulse was calculated. At a specific point in the trajectory, at a specific time, the engine of the on-board orbital correction system fired and set up a new orbit.

In order to execute this operation, the spacecraft had to know how to orient itself in space, turning at any angles assigned by the settings transmitted via command radio link from Earth; maintain the given orientation while the

---

11. KRL—*Komandnaya radioliniya*.

12. When the first satellite project was approved in January 1956, the Object D scientific observatory was slated to be the first Soviet satellite. By late 1956, it was clear that development of Object D would be delayed. As such, Korolev, Tikhonravov, and others proposed a smaller and simpler satellite, PS-1, to be launched on an R-7 as the first satellite. It was this satellite that eventually became the first *Sputnik* on October 1957. See Asif A. Siddiqi, *The Red Rockets' Glare: Spaceflight and the Soviet Imagination, 1857–1957* (New York: Cambridge University Press, 2010), Chapters 8 and 9.

correcting engine was operating; and control the engine system itself, ensuring the required magnitude of the correcting pulse.

Attitude control was one of the most crucial motion control modes. During this process the spacecraft had to hold the necessary angular position relative to known reference points by turning about its center of mass. Spacecraft attitude-control systems were crucial during the execution of the braking burn that was necessary for return to Earth. In the event of an error, the spacecraft might not return to Earth at all if the burn executed by the engine raised the orbit rather than lowering it. Attitude control in space was necessary not just for orbital correction, but also for scientific observations, photography, and setting up the pencil-beam antennas and solar arrays in the required direction.

Since 1960, Rauschenbach's team, which was originally called Department 27, had been responsible for solving spacecraft attitude and stabilization control problems. The abundance of programs in this field required a sharp increase in the size of Department 27 and then its division into three departments: Viktor Legostayev's theoretical department of motion dynamics; Yevgeniy Bashkin's circuit and equipment development department; and Dmitriy Knyazev's orientation effectors—correcting microengines—department. The powerful radio electronics department of Anatoliy Shustov (who had successfully developed sequencers—the predecessors of the modern on-board computers); Semyon Chizhikov's design department, which issued the working drawings for any instruments to be manufactured at the factory; and the developments of supplier organizations assisted these three departments.

Working from our design specifications, Vladimir Khrustalev, the chief designer of optical electronics instruments at the Geofizika Design Bureau, developed sensors for orientation on Earth, the Sun, and stars. Chief rocket gyroscope specialist Viktor Kuznetsov also developed gyroscopic instruments according to our design specifications. At VNIIEM under Andronik Iosifyan, Sheremetyevskiy created a heavy-duty flywheel to control the orientation of the Molniya satellite. The Electron Microscope Factory in Suma manufactured sensors for the ionic attitude-control system that we had invented.

Each space project required its own attitude-control systems developed specially for a given specific spacecraft. Something they all had in common was the requirement to ensure triaxial orientation at the appropriate time; in other words, to have the capability to locate the spacecraft in space either having fixed its three mutually perpendicular imaginary axes rigidly in relation to stars or Earth's surface and a velocity vector or maneuvering them according to a specific program or commands. Legostayev entrusted the conceptual development of triaxial orientation of a satellite on Earth to one of the first graduates of the

Moscow Physics and Technology Institute (MFTI), Yevgeniy Tokar.[13] Tokar had begun working on such a system back at NII-1 with Rauschenbach under Keldysh's guidance. In 1957 he issued a report titled "On an active stabilization system for an artificial Earth satellite."[14]

Tokar was the first to propose a system that became classic for all Vostoks, Voskhods, and Zenits and existed until the dawn of the epoch of "platformless" systems. To orient one of the axes of a satellite on a local terrestrial vertical (i.e., pointed toward the center of Earth), he proposed using an instrument sensitive to the infrared radiation of the planet's surface. Rauschenbach had come out with the idea of scanning the boundary between the disk of Earth visible from the spacecraft and outer space. Yevgeniy Bashkin and Stanislav Savchenko played significant roles in developing the layout and theoretical underpinnings of the instrument. Vladimir Khrustalev and Boris Medvedev at TsKB Geofizika created the first actual infrared vertical (IKV) sensor. Currently, not a single near-Earth satellite can get along without an infrared vertical sensor—a local vertical plotter. Since those long-ago days, TsKB Geofizika has brought the reliability, accuracy, and mass of the infrared vertical sensor to scales that we had not even dreamed of during those first years.

In addition to orienting two axes along the angles of pitch and roll, which the infrared vertical sensor provided, the satellite's free rotation about the vertical axis pointed at Earth had to be stopped, i.e., we had to learn how to orient it relative to its heading plane, or, as the rocketeers put it, in terms of the yaw angle.

To this end Tokar proposed a gyroscopic orienting instrument, later called a gyro-orbitant. It was used on virtually all domestic automatic and piloted spacecraft that required orbital orientation. The theory behind the gyro-orbitant was the basis for Tokar's candidate of sciences dissertation, which he defended in 1959. We were not able to manufacture the gyro-orbitant using our own resources. This required high-precision specialized production facilities. Naturally, we turned to Viktor Kuznetsov, who held a monopoly in the field of rocket gyroscopes at the time. His first reaction was quite negative. Kuznetsov didn't want to manufacture an instrument in his shop if the idea for it had come from somewhere on the outside. Moreover, Kuznetsov questioned

---

13. MFTI—*Moskovskiy fiziko-tekhnicheskiy institut.*

14. This document cited by Chertok has been reproduced in the following source: V. S. Avduyevskiy and T. M. Eneyev, eds., *M.V. Keldysh: izbrannyye trudy: raketnaya tekhnika i kosmonavtika* [*M. V. Keldysh: Selected Works: Rocket Technology and Cosmonautics*] (Moscow: Nauka, 1988), 198–234.

the very idea of the gyro-orbitant, which was, as he told me, "the principle of a marine gyrocompass, corrupted for use in space."

But in those days Kuznetsov couldn't brush us off; otherwise, he might have to explain himself to Korolev, and the latter, for all anyone knew, might say: "Well, Vitya, if you refuse to help me, I'll look for others." "Vitya" asked Aleksandr Ishlinskiy to conduct a detailed review of the theory at the Mathematics Institute in Kiev, where he had been appointed the director back in 1948.[15] Oskar Raykhman, one of his leading specialists, carried out an independent experimental review of the principle at Kuznetsov's request. Not being a great theoretician, but rather a good organizer and gyroscope specialist, Raykhman quickly built a test stand, on which he confirmed the instrument's functionality. Ishlinskiy's and Raykhman's great service was the fact that they convinced Kuznetsov independently of one another. He believed them and gave the "green light" for the manufacture of the first series. Kuznetsov's instruments, with the designations KI-008, KI-009, etc., were on the first spacecraft: Vostoks, Zenits, subsequent reconnaissance spacecraft, and Chelomey's Almazes.

On Salyut orbital stations we made an attempt to replace the gyro-orbitant with so-called "ionic orientation" using heading and pitch. One of the reasons for this replacement was the duration of the original "setting" period of the gyro-orbitant after insertion on orbit. Triaxial orientation of a satellite using an infrared vertical sensor and gyro-orbitant took almost an entire orbit. Orientation using the ionic system using pitch and heading took around 10 minutes. However, the use of such a tempting orientation system (in terms of time) without first thoroughly testing it resulted in the loss of DOS No. 3. I will tell about this tragedy below.

Tokar worked with Gordeyev and Farmakovskiy, marine gyroscope specialists from the Elektropribor Factory in Leningrad, to develop and implement the idea of a more accurate block of gyro instruments that would provide orientation based on heading and filter the fluctuation of the optical infrared vertical sensor. In the design bureau of this factory they conducted an extremely conscientious study of the layout and developed the design of a two-rotor orbital gyroscopic complex for the new Zenit-4 reconnaissance satellite. This complex

---

15. Aleksandr Yulevich Ishlinskiy (1913–2003) was a very prominent Soviet scientist who specialized in the science behind gyroscopes and inertial navigation systems. He authored a number of major works on the theory of elasticity, plasticity, the theory of vibrations, and gyroscopes. From 1948 to 1955, he served as director of the Mathematics Institute of the Ukrainian Academy of Sciences and from 1964 was the director of the Institute of Problems of Mechanics of the Soviet Academy of Sciences. He was one of the top scientists involved in the Soviet space program and served on many State Commissions in the 1960s.

included a gyroscopic vertical sensor corrected using signals from the infrared vertical sensor and the gyro-orbitant proper. Due to the Leningraders' attention to detail, the system's accuracy was 10 times greater than that of the Zenit-2! To conserve the working fluid, for the first time a system of electric motors and flywheels developed at VNIIEM was provided. On the whole, Zenit-4's system of attitude-control instruments manufactured by all the suppliers was a noticeable qualitative leap in the technology of control in space.

Larisa Komarova was one of the leading specialists of the new system for Zenit-4. She brilliantly defended her candidate's dissertation on this subject. Unfortunately, the Zenit-4 control system did not fly into space in this configuration. More and more launches of the already mastered Zenit-2 were needed. However, much later, Chelomey (OKB-52) implemented the ideas developed during those turbulent years on the Almaz, and Kozlov implemented them on new photoreconnaissance spacecraft.

For missiles, aircraft, and ships, the gyroscope companies developed increasingly complex instruments, which were poised on the brink of what was possible, manufacturing-wise. The rocket control specialists on Pilyugin's, Kuznetsov's, and Arefyev's teams sought to create a high-precision inertial control system, the foundation of which was the precision gyroscopic platform. This field of endeavor also dominated the Americans' efforts.

The aspiration to have attitude control in space so that a spacecraft could execute any turns and maneuvers was limited by the design of the gyroscopes' gimbal mount. As soon as the angle permitted by the design of the gyro-orbitant or gyro platform was exceeded, the gyroscopes "hit the stop" and a glitch occurred—loss of attitude control. The gyroscopic systems of missiles had no fear of this phenomenon because the possible angles determined by the program of the powered flight segment were deliberately less than those permitted by the gyro systems.

Somewhere within Legostayev's theoretical department the idea cropped up to do away with the classic gimbal mount because the very task of controlling the orientation of an artificial satellite, due to the requirements for unlimited angular evolutions (programmed turns, change of attitude-control modes, docking maneuvers), suggested the need to do away with mechanical restraint. Spacecraft systems should have no maneuverability-arresting devices! That's how the problem was formulated.

Theoretically, platformless systems, or, as they are now referred to, strapdown inertial navigation systems (BINS), had been well known for a long time.[16] There

---

16. BINS—*Beskardannaya inertsialnaya navigatsionnaya sistema.*

were even dissertations available on that score. But the most prominent rocket control specialists, Kuznetsov and Pilyugin, believed that this was an amusement for the theoreticians, sort of the latest version of perpetual motion. Nevertheless the theoreticians confirmed that, in principle, one could create a platformless attitude-control and navigation system if one mastered the numerical integration of systems of kinematical equations and conversions of coordinate systems. The system of angles contained in the equations describing the movement of a solid body, in principle, can simulate a gimbal mount for gyroscopes. If there is a good computer receiving information, it can replace the sophisticated design of gyro platforms.

The practical solution of such a problem exceeds the abilities of a pure mathematician. This situation requires an engineer's view on the classical theory of the angular motion of a solid body. In this case it was necessary to find a practicable method for replacing complicated mechanics with complicated mathematics that have no "arresting devices" or metal weighing many dozens of kilograms. How could this be done?

The history of science and technology shows that serious discoveries are made by individuals or very small teams of two or three people. And when the discovery has been made, then its implementation requires courageous managers who will take a risk, pull a large staff onto this project, and find the necessary resources. A proposal from two young MFTI graduates who came to OKB-1 along with Rauschenbach should be considered the beginning of the epoch of domestic platformless systems. In 1963, 27-year-old Vladimir Branets and 30-year-old Igor Shmyglevskiy turned to the works of [Irish] mathematician Sir William Rowan Hamilton, who was the first to come up with the theory of quaternions in 1843, striving to find a convenient device for studying spatial geometry.

In 1973, 130 years after Hamilton's discovery, already battle-tested at the rocket firing range, Branets and Shmyglevskiy published the work *Application of Quaternions in Solid Body Orientation Problems.*[17] The Nauka publishing house released the book two years after receiving the manuscript, which was the result of many years of research. The work is considered to be classic and has even been translated into Chinese. A grave illness prematurely took the life of Shmyglevskiy, and he was unable to admire his own work rendered in Chinese characters. Chinese scientists presented such a souvenir to Branets when he went to Beijing on official business.

---

17. V. N. Branets and I. P. Shmyglevskiy, *Primeneniye kvaternionov v zadachakh orientatsii tverdogo tela* (Moscow: Nauka, 1973).

The methods of numerical integration of kinematical equations using quaternions that Branets and Shmyglevskiy proposed for use in attitude-control tasks of any flying vehicle, which mathematicians call a "solid body," also solved problems of optimal control, i.e., maneuvers and attitude control with minimal power losses, and of stability of the process. However, even a gimballess system with the most brilliant mathematics must "begin at the beginning." The "beginning" was the optical and even ionic sensors, which had already been mastered and were flying. If these sensors were supplemented with very simple angular velocity meters for each of the three orientation axes, then the control system would have the requisite set of baseline information.

I already mentioned that producing a coherent formulation of the problem for subcontracting chief designers required not only one's wishes, but also one's own specialists, who knew the actual capabilities of the subcontractor. After a subcontractor accepted an order for development, these specialists performed engineering supervision, protecting our interests and resolving the discrepancies that inevitably arose between what we demanded and what we actually got. These specialists were called curators, thereby emphasizing how they differed from pure developers. This division always seemed unjust to me. A specialist standing between two chiefs is, if he is a creative individual, capable of making contributions to the process of creating a new system that neither the customer nor the contractor came up with on their own.

We had such creative curators: for optical instruments—Stanislav Savchenko, whom I have already mentioned; for rendezvous radio systems—Boris Nevzorov and Nina Sapozhnikova; and for gyroscopic instruments—Yuriy Bazhanov. Together with Lev Zvorykin, Bashkin's deputy, Bazhanov took me out to an aviation design bureau that was able to manufacture lightweight, simple, and reliable angular rate sensors (DUS) per our requirements.[18] My old acquaintance from prewar times—former Aviapribor Factory Chief Designer Yevgeniy Antipov—turned out to be the chief of the needed organization. The meeting gave us the opportunity to reminisce about our work during the hazy youth of the aviation industry. As fate had it, we had not seen each other a single time since 1934. After 30 years we very quickly came to terms with all the issues, and before long Antipov had signed off on the VPK's draft decision, making him responsible for developing angular rate sensors according to the specification requirements of Korolev's OKB-1.

For this revolutionary leap in control systems technology, the most difficult question for those times remained to be answered: where would we get

---

18. DUS—*Datchik uglovykh skorostey.*

a good on-board computer? The history of the creation of on-board computers is fascinating and instructive. But its telling requires a special place and a separate chapter. In recent years on-board computers have blended into the structure of spacecraft control systems so organically that a young specialist beginning to work in our field simply cannot imagine how we could have flown without them.

When creating the Soyuz spacecraft, of all the motion-control problems, descent from orbit to Earth of the axially symmetric Descent Module with poor aerodynamics and low design overload required special treatment. A slight shifting of its center of mass in relation to its axis of symmetry created the lift of such a spacecraft. It was necessary to develop a very reliable structure, algorithms, and range and stabilization control instruments for the Descent Module, minimizing the area of the possible landing zone for a rapid search and crew evacuation. The descent control system should calm down the Descent Module so as to guarantee the initial conditions for a reliable introduction of the parachute system, which is controlled by an autonomous landing system. To ensure the reliability of the descent and landing control systems, they selected the simplest algorithms and used redundancy, and sometimes triple redundancy, of instruments and assemblies, the failure of which could have catastrophic consequences. For the first time, it was necessary to create not just new control technology, but also a new developmental organization, in which the baton of responsibility for motion control was passed from department to department, from the staff responsible for control of orbital flight to the descent control specialists, and from them to the landing system developers. In addition to their standard tasks, descent and landing control systems had to perform functions as part of the emergency rescue system during the insertion phase.

We created the three systems—descent control, landing control, and emergency rescue—in the form of automatic units, calling for no human intervention. Over a period of 30 years, in hundreds of launches, not a single one of these systems let us down. Both we and the Americans had catastrophes and off-nominal situations occur during the descent and landing phases for reasons attributable to *other* systems.

THE HISTORY OF THE DEVELOPMENT OF SPACECRAFT CONTROL SYSTEMS is part of the history of cosmonautics. Not wanting to thrust on the reader my own conception about the degree of responsibility of a human involved in the control loop, I shall move on to a description of actual events. I remind the reader that after the death of Vladimir Komarov on the first piloted 7K-OK spacecraft called Soyuz, there was a prolonged break in the flights of these vehicles so that the parachute portion of the landing system could undergo substantial modification. For the flight testing of the modified vehicles and, at the same time, to test out the rendezvous and docking systems, we embarked upon launches of unpiloted 7K-OK vehicles under the name Kosmos.

Kosmos-186 and *Kosmos-188* approached one another, docked, separated, and returned to Earth during the period from 27 October through 2 November 1967. *Kosmos-212* and *Kosmos-213* executed a program of automatic rendezvous, docking, and safe landing from 14 through 20 April 1968. As the saying goes, "God helps those who help themselves," and to be absolutely sure, on 28 August 1968 a single 7K-OK vehicle, or *Kosmos-238*, was launched and safely returned to Earth.

To this day it is difficult to explain why the unpiloted 7K-OK vehicles were classified as anonymous, secret Kosmos vehicles. With a human being on board, the same vehicle was called a Soyuz. I dared to pose this question to the KGB officer assigned to us back then.[19] He smiled and answered, "Our organization has nothing to do with this game of hide-and-seek. What to announce in TASS reports and how is the concern of political bureaucrats. They are convinced that the best way to keep state secrets is this inane, overly cautious approach and confusion in the open press. Such methods don't increase the standing of our nation."

Five successful flights of the 7K-OK, despite the fact that they were called Kosmoses, convinced not just us, the creators, but also all the skeptics from the Air Force, TsUKOS, and the VPK that it was time to switch to piloted launches. A governmental commission headed by the chief of LII of the Ministry of the Aviation Industry, Viktor Utkin, summarized the results of the work performed after the tragic death of Komarov and gave the clearance for piloted flights of 7K-OK vehicles.[20] There was much arguing about the program for the first flight. We insisted on a complete repetition of automatic rendezvous and docking, but with a cosmonaut on board. Under pressure from the cosmonauts, Kamanin demanded maximum human involvement in rendezvous and docking control. They decided that from a distance of 150 to 200 meters the cosmonaut of the active vehicle would control the final approach process.

"To begin with, it's not worth the risk," said Keldysh at the next discussion. "Let the passive vehicle remain unpiloted and the active vehicle be piloted. This is already impressive. A vehicle carrying a cosmonaut approaches an unpiloted vehicle and docks with it."

---

19. KGB—*Komitet gosudarstvennoy bezopasnosti* (Committee for State Security).

20. The M. M. Gromov Flight-Research Institute (*Letno-issledovatelskiy institut imeni M. M. Gromova*, or LII), based in the Moscow suburb of Zhukovskiy, was the Soviet Union's primary aviation testing facility.

Everyone agreed.

"But now we have to call both vehicles Soyuzes," said one of the critically thinking members of the State Commission.

Together with the ballistics experts and control specialists, the planners began to schedule the program hour by hour and minute by minute. Mishin, with the support of Kamanin and Karas, insisted on landing both vehicles during the first half of the day. In late October, the days in our latitudes were already short. According to the program, the passive vehicle was inserted first. A day was set aside to thoroughly check it out in flight and, if necessary, perform an orbital correction so that a day later it would fly over the firing range, from which the piloted active vehicle would lift off to meet it at the calculated rendezvous point. Radio lock-on would take place immediately after orbital insertion. During the first orbit the vehicles would approach one another and dock. It was agreed that far approach should take place in automatic mode using the *Igla* radio system measuring relative motion parameters, and when the vehicle reached a distance of 200 meters, the cosmonaut of the active vehicle would switch off *Igla* from controlling the vehicle and perform berthing manually. The *Igla* on the unpiloted vehicle would remain activated and control it so that the funnel of the docking assembly cone was facing the probe of the active vehicle.

"If we show that we are capable of docking with our own vehicle right after liftoff, it means we are capable of going right up, if necessary, to an enemy satellite and destroying it."

This argument was provided in favor of a liftoff with docking during the very first orbit, especially since the method had already been tried out in the two previous unpiloted dockings.

At one of the regular meetings on the flight program, which Bushuyev conducted, Zoya Degtyarenko, who represented the ballistics experts, pointed out that the most crucial berthing and docking segment was going to take place in the dark portion of the orbit.

"Why have you planned it like that?" Bushuyev fumed. "Set the launch time so that docking takes place in the sunlight portion."

But then it would be necessary to abandon a guaranteed landing during the first half of the day, and we couldn't let Rauschenbach and Bashkin scare us with "ionic holes."

"No, these restrictions are absolutely necessary."

"Why argue?" intervened Feoktistov. "Docking at night using lights is even more reliable than during the day when the Sun might fall in the field of vision of the optical sight."

And so it was decided. The cosmonaut would have to learn to manually control the spacecraft using lights, which we would install on the passive vehicle.

469

Rauschenbach tasked Bashkin, Skotnikov, and Savchenko to develop the procedure for manual control using lights. The cosmonaut was supposed to observe the lights through a periscope sight (VSK) installed in the Descent Module.[21] Two "upper" lights were constantly illuminated; two "lower" ones blinked. Using manual control, the cosmonaut was supposed to fire the approach and attitude-control engines so that the lights located in the angles of an imaginary trapezoid lined up in a straight line.

It all seemed very simple. The State Commission tasked Sergey Darevskiy with quickly devising a simplified simulator so that the process of orientation using lights could be understood not only by the creators of the manual control procedure, but by the cosmonauts as well. Kamanin, guarding the interests of the cosmonauts who had familiarized themselves with the control procedure using lights, was satisfied.

During these very hectic days of program development, I was occupied filling out flight readiness certificates and certificates for each of the systems. I

From the author's archives.

Boris Chertok is shown here signing copies of the first Russian edition of his memoirs *Rakety i lyudi* (*Rockets and People*) for famed aviator Mark Gallay at Moscow's House of Journalists in 1995. Waiting in line is a former deputy to Korolev, A. P. Abramov.

---

21. VSK—*Vizir spetsialnyy kosmonavta* (special sight for cosmonaut).

had to look into dozens of glitches that had cropped up during testing of the two vehicles, first at the KIS and now during preparation at the firing range. On one of those days, dropping by Bushuyev's office, I bumped into Mark Gallay there. Despite the jealous attitude of Kamanin and all the Air Force training specialists involved with spaceflights, Gallay's thoughts about the human factor had been decisive for Korolev. Possessing the exceptionally great experience of a combat-seasoned test pilot and aviation engineer, Gallay, a man with an acute and critical intellect, who remained outside departmental interests, gave surprisingly interesting advice on controlling piloted vehicles.[22] He had become acquainted with Korolev back before the war and had also met up with him during the war at the *sharashka* in Kazan, when Korolev had tested airplanes with rocket boosters.[23] Not a member of any official commission, Gallay had the opportunity to personally tell Korolev his views, which he was not always able to express in public.

After Korolev's death, Gallay lost his main support at our OKB-1. Mishin didn't take him to his bosom. Gallay maintained good relations with Bushuyev, Rauschenbach, and me.

Turning to me, Bushuyev said, "Mark Lazarevich has his doubts about manual docking in the dark."

"I've had to land at night at unlit airfields," Gallay began to reassure us. "I have to say that even for an experienced pilot this is a big risk. But what are you going to do if, after an air battle, you've run out of gas, and like it or not, you return to the ground. I'm one with the airplane until it touches the ground. I myself am touching the ground, not the airplane. During each flight, from takeoff to landing, the airplane and I are a single organism. The relationships between a cosmonaut and a spacecraft are completely different. A cosmonaut is in flight for the first time in his life. Perhaps he is a fantastic pilot. But not once, you understand, not once has he experienced liftoff on a rocket and the state of complete weightlessness. You don't give him time to adapt and then you demand that, in the dark, looking through a sight with a very limited field of vision rather than through a big cockpit canopy, he take over control from a tried-and-true automatic system, and in its place begin to control a spacecraft

---

22. Mark Lazarevich Gallay (1914–1998) was one the most famous Soviet aviators and test-pilots of the Stalin era. From 1958 to 1975, Gallay worked at the M. M. Gromov Flight-Research Institute at Zhukovskiy and was simultaneously a consultant for Korolev's OKB-1, where he helped train the early group of cosmonauts. Later in his life, he turned to writing a series of memoirs and books on aviation.

23. *Sharashka* was the nickname of the special prison design bureaus organized in the late 1930s by the NKVD—(*Narodnyy kommissariat vnutrennikh del* [People's Commissariat of Internal Affairs])—to house imprisoned designers, engineers, and scientists.

for the first time in his life, and at the same time, in complete darkness, get the active probe into the passive cone. Now, why would you take the risk and place a cosmonaut in a dangerous situation? At least let him fly for 24 hours before docking and become acclimated. We on Earth will make sure that a cosmonaut knows how to control the spacecraft and won't do anything foolish."

"We don't have these 24 hours," objected Bushuyev, "because they will require additional fuel consumption for correction, and our life-support reserves are not very big. We're scrimping on every kilogram now."

"Well, look. When we launched Gagarin, then Titov, and others, I was more confident. Even the manual emergency orientation for landing with Belyayev and Leonov, in my opinion, was simpler than what you are undertaking now. And on top of that, Darevskiy simply isn't capable of making a simulator that reproduces the actual dynamics of the situation within these deadlines."

"If docking fails in the dark, the cosmonaut can hover, and after about 20 minutes he can make a second attempt in daylight without any lights."

"Let's hope so," agreed Gallay. "The Air Force has two candidates for this flight—Beregovoy and Shatalov. Both are test pilots. Beregovoy saw combat on fighter-bombers under Kamanin's command. I think that Kamanin will put him in the first slot."

That's what happened. Kamanin prudently coordinated the candidacy of Hero of the Soviet Union Georgiy Beregovoy with the Commander-in-Chief of the Air Force and with the Central Committee. The State Commission agreed with his proposal. According to the preparation schedule, the launch of the first unpiloted 7K-OK, which was referred to as *Soyuz-2*, was set for 25 October, while the piloted 7K-OK, or *Soyuz-3*, was set to lift off on 26 October 1968.

On Wednesday, 16 October, Bushuyev and I were called in to the minister's office. Afanasyev explained that he had been asked to report to the Politburo about piloted spaceflights. The unexpected summons had him very nervous and worried. I had never before seen Afanasyev like this, somewhat dismayed. They had warned him that he would have no more than 10 minutes for the report. Sergey Aleksandrovich asked us to "work a little" on the text of the 10-minute report with him and assist him with the responses to possible difficult questions. We "worked a little" and left the minister at 10 p.m. In parting, he thanked us and said that he would work another 3 hours or so on his own.

In the morning, Bushuyev and Rumyantsev did a final edit on the report at the ministry. At 3 p.m., Afanasyev appeared before the Politburo. However, contrary to his expectations, they did not give him the floor. Brezhnev, who was conducting the meeting, said that the minister did not need to be heard.

"I spoke with Mishin," declared Leonid Ilyich. "He assured me that everything was ready and we needed to launch a man into space. Who is against this?"

No one spoke out against it. Only Keldysh, who was present at the session, asked for the floor and for about 5 minutes talked about the work performed over the past year and the program for the upcoming flight. When Afanasyev returned to his office he telephoned me on the "Kremlin line" and said that his report would be left for history, but he thanked Bushuyev and me for our help at a crucial moment.

On the cold Moscow morning of Monday, 21 October, Shabarov and I arrived at our airport, Vnukovo-3. A piercing wind drove wet snow mixed with fine, stinging rain. We endured the unwritten boarding protocol—no one enters the plane until the brass show up. We waited for the arrival of Afanasyev and Keldysh. Only after them did we climb the stairs into the Tu-134.

In Tyuratam the Sun was shining. After the foul autumn weather in Moscow we were carried off to the sweet weather of the steppes cooling off from the summer heat. At Site No. 2, I settled into cottage No. 1 next to Korolev's cottage. Recently they had placed a memorial plaque there made of pink granite with a bas-relief of Korolev: "Here lived and worked Chief Designer and Academician Sergey Pavlovich Korolev. 1956–1965." The poplar trees that had grown up around the cottages in the stillness filled the air with an aroma that was unusual for the steppes. That evening, as part of a large retinue with the minister, we drove around the N-1 launch sites under construction.

The *Soyuz-3* launch was being prepared to take place from Site No. 31. The next morning Beregovoy had his "sit-in" and received an additional briefing. That evening in the MIK at Site No. 2, an imposing State Commission gathered.

"It's been a long time since we've had such a gathering," said Isayev, who was sitting next to me. Afanasyev's summons to the Politburo was not in vain. Glushko, Barmin, Pilyugin, Ryazanskiy, Konopatov, Iosifyan, Yurevich, Lobanov, Khrustalev, Severin, Darevskiy, and Bratslavets had flown in for the State Commission meeting.[24] Mishin, Karas, and Kurushin sat next to Kirillov in the presidium of the State Commission. The readiness check of all the services began with the launch vehicle. Aleksandr Soldatenkov was thoroughly prepared and confidently responded to questions concerning glitches that had occurred on all *Semyorkas* during launches over the past six months. After the reports about complete readiness, the State Commission made the decision to roll out the launch vehicle and unpiloted spacecraft 7K-OK No. 11 to launch Site No. 1.

---

24. These were all the principal chief designers involved in the Soviet human space program at this time.

On the evening of 23 October, at Site No. 17 in the cosmonauts' residence, a ceremonial session of the State Commission took place with the showing of movie and television footage. Afanasyev spoke at the meeting.

"Today we made a very important decision," he said. "There has been a prolonged break in piloted flights. We have suffered a heavy loss. But we have overcome this barrier. We have performed more than 70 test drops to check out the parachute systems and more than 700 tests of all kinds on individual elements. We have complete confidence in the success of the upcoming flight. With great satisfaction we accept the proposal for the flight of Georgiy Timofeyevich Beregovoy, Hero of the Soviet Union and distinguished test pilot.[25] We are confident that he will fulfill this crucial assignment.

Keldysh also spoke.

"I would like to wish comrade Beregovoy success in the fulfillment of this very important assignment. With his flight, Georgiy Timofeyevich will restore faith in the reliability of the piloted programs. All of us have been preparing for this flight for a long time. Hundreds of people have invested a great deal of heart and energy in order to ensure success, which is so essential after the compulsory break. Once again I wish comrade Beregovoy success in the fulfillment of his assignment."

Karas represented the Ministry of Defense.

"The personnel of the cosmodrome and of the military units participating in the work by order of the Commander-in-Chief of the Strategic Rocket Forces will ensure the fulfillment of all tasks assigned to them."

In an emotional response Beregovoy thanked everyone for their confidence and promised to make every effort to fulfill the assignment of the Party and government.

According to the staffing chart, I was GOGU deputy chief and was supposed to be at the control center in Yevpatoriya. On 24 October, after reporting before the commission, a group of comrades and I flew from Tyuratam to Saki on an An-24. With a stopover for refueling in Uralsk, the flight took more than 8 hours. By the time we landed it was 1900 hours. The Crimea, even in late October, is still the Crimea. After freshening up at the hotel, I enjoyed an excellent dinner in the hospitable officers' dining room. The table abounded with the bounty of Crimean nature. But it was the lively exchange of news and the stories full of good-natured humor about the latest "*bobiks*," which inevitably occur in large rocket-space systems on the ground before a launch, that truly delighted those who had just arrived and the local "aborigines."

---

25. Beregovoy received his first Hero of the Soviet Union award in 1944.

The intense work on flight control of *Soyuz-2* began on the morning of 25 October. Liftoff proceeded normally. The orbital parameters were unusually close to the design parameters.[26] For all the groups and services of the Command and Measurement Complex, the 24 hours of work on the unpiloted Soyuz was excellent training before the piloted launch.

Early in the morning on 26 October 1968, during brief time segments of coverage, the ballistics centers of NII-4, OPM, and TsKBEM were supposed to process the orbital measurements of the first orbits over our territory, calculate the precise time for the liftoff of the active vehicle, and transmit the data to the firing range 2 hours before the launch.

The beginning of the 13th orbit at 0500 hours was in the coverage zone of two Far East tracking stations. A 10-minute communication session was sufficient to determine that all the on-board systems of *Soyuz-2* were operating normally. By 0900 hours the ballistics centers had sent telegrams: "Launch time 1134 hours, 18.1 seconds. Permissible launch delay for beginning of near rendezvous no more than 1 second."

The idea was for the *Igla* radio system on the passive and active vehicles to warm up and switch on for mutual radio lock-on right after the insertion of the active vehicle into orbit. Radio lock-on would be ensured if, immediately after the orbital insertion of *Soyuz-2*, the distance to *Soyuz-3* did not exceed 20 kilometers. We issued a command to NIP-3 in Saryshagan to prepare to cancel the near rendezvous program loaded before the launch if liftoff were to be delayed by more than one second. In this case, GOGU would have to decide to issue a command to activate the far rendezvous mode from NIP-15 in Ussuriysk.

Very precise work was required of the ballistics centers and communications services so that we in Yevpatoriya could make decisions and transmit them to the NIPs in a matter of seconds. The actual liftoff time with errors of tenths of a second would have to be reported from Tyuratam to NIP-16 within 3 minutes.

AT 1125 HOURS THE T MINUS 5 MINUTES ANNOUNCEMENT IS MADE. For the time being, communication hasn't let us down. The usual, but always worrisome, reports are arriving in the control room: "Feed one," "purge," "T minus 1 minute," "pressurization," "feed two," "we have tower pullback!" "Liftoff!" There is an agonizing pause, and then: "Thirty seconds—flight is normal!"

---

26. According to official Soviet data, the orbital parameters of *Soyuz-2* were 185 × 224 kilometers with an orbital inclination of 51.66°.

And then Beregovoy's voice breaks through: "It's a go...it's a go! Slight shaking, mild shaking.... Nose wandering a bit.... G-load increasing no more than three.... We have separation of the strap-ons.... Fairing ejection...." Beregovoy continues to give a running report of his surface impressions.

"Attention!" a voice from the ballistics center interrupts. "We are reporting the precise time of liftoff: 1134 hours, 18.4 seconds."

The error in relation to the design value is just 0.3 seconds!

Agadzhanov looks at Tregub, then at me, we nod, and he picks up the microphone: "Now hear this! This is 12 speaking, informing 13 not to issue the cancel command![27] We are working using the primary program!"

NIP-3, which is referred to as 13 over communication lines, reports, "Cosmonaut's pulse is 104." And almost simultaneously reports come in from Saryshagan and Ussuriysk about telemetry data. Our experienced telemetry operators, who can give a running commentary directly from the tapes, had arrived ahead of time at these tracking stations.

"Shutdown from integrator.... We have separation!... All elements deployed.... *Igla* antennas and solar arrays deployed.... We have target presence signal!... Range 1,000 meters!"

There is a rapturous whisper in the control room.

"What a shot! Entering the zone with no more than a kilometer's deviation right after separation without any correction! Way to go, ballistics!"

The latter compliment is addressed to Zoya Degtyarenko and Vladimir Yastrebov, who modestly mumble that it wasn't they, but the ballistics centers that had calculated so precisely.

Yastrebov set the record straight: "According to our data, it was 10 kilometers before lock-on. The report of 1,000 meters was after approach with *Igla*'s assistance."

During the last seconds of the communication from Ussuriysk a report came from Beregovoy via *Zarya*: "Range—40."

AFTER *SOYUZ-3* LEFT THE COVERAGE ZONE, alarming telemetry data came in from Ussuriysk. As it approached *Soyuz-2*, the *Igla* antenna platform on *Soyuz-3* was drifting in some inexplicable way in the pitch angle. The consumption of working fluid from the DPO system during the last seconds of communication was higher than any norms.

The most agonizing minutes had set in. We waited for the appearance of two spacecraft at once in our zone. How would they arrive: mated or

---

27. Agadzhanov's call sign was 12.

asunder? The experience of the two previous dockings allowed us to hope that we would see rigidly docked spacecraft in our zone. It was an hour of excruciating anticipation. Just 40 meters separated the two vehicles before we lost communication. In any event, Bashkin and Kozhevnikova were instructed to prepare a correction maneuver program for a repeat approach. But that wasn't necessary. As soon as the two spacecraft appeared in the coverage zone, the reports that came from the telemetry operators and from Beregovoy himself immediately quashed hope of the possibility for another docking attempt.

Beregovoy reported, "At 12:25, as soon as the vehicle emerged from the shadow, I saw that the vehicle had rolled with an error of around 180°. I attempted to correct the roll using the DO-1 system for 3 minutes but realized that it was dangerous to continue approach. Pressure in the DPO system was 110 atmospheres, and per instructions I had to shut down the system if pressure fell to 135."

Cosmonaut Pavel Belyayev was conducting communication via *Zarya*. He asked, "How do you feel?"

"I feel great. My mood is lousy," responded Beregovoy.

One could understand how he felt. He had given up flying, trained for a long time, earned the right to perform a crucial spaceflight, and pledged to everyone that he would fulfill the assignment of the Party and government. How could he explain to his comrades that in the darkness he was unable to make heads or tails of the four lights and, after taking over control from the automatic system in the final approach zone, the vehicle had begun to roll with an error to the point where it was upside down? The conditions for automatic final approach and docking had been ideal. And with his intervention, he had not only messed everything up, but for some reason he had used up so much propellant that the ground wouldn't permit him to perform a repeat approach now. There was only enough working fluid for maneuvers to return to Earth. And after all, he was 47 years old! Would he have another opportunity to fly into space?

We convened a special on-the-spot technical management meeting. One after another, the team members gave their reports that all systems on both spacecraft were operating normally. Reproduction of the telemetry data showed that the cosmonaut had operated the controls very actively. There had been an excessive consumption of the working fluids due to the cosmonaut's inexplicable actions.

"During automatic approach of the vehicles, 30 kilograms of propellant were consumed, and after the cosmonaut took over control, consumption was more than 40 kilograms in 2 minutes," reported the analysis group.

"He was fighting with *Igla*," said Mnatsakanyan.

The cosmonaut's actions particularly outraged Bashkin and Feoktistov. I stood up for Beregovoy.

"We did some great things, too. We devised a program that makes a human being, who has just endured extremely strong g-loads and who is experiencing weightlessness for the first time in his life, without preliminary training, 10 minutes after liftoff, in the dark, search with a sight for four lights and move a control stick so that the shape of an imaginary trapezoid is changed in some incomprehensible way! We ourselves are at fault for agreeing to manual approach without any adaptation, and at night no less, and the ballistics experts didn't want to select liftoff times so that approach would take place in daylight."

"I don't accept this blame," objected Zoya Degtyarenko. "It's your comrades' fault that we were forced into a docking at night. They were afraid of ionic holes, and the brass demands landings, even off-nominal ones, during daylight only. Preference should have been given to approach and docking right after liftoff in daylight, and we would have done that. What's more, Feoktistov argued that the approach and rendezvous at night using lights was even easier than during the day."

Tempers flared, but we had no time for squabbling. We needed to quickly reorganize the program and prepare the assignments for landing. A report came in from Tyuratam that an Il-18 carrying Minister Afanasyev, Keldysh, Kerimov, Mishin, Kamanin, Karas, and all the chief designers—75 persons in all—was flying out to us.

"Now, not just Beregovoy but GOGU as well is going to start controlling with precision until everything is upside down. Because of a proliferation of management, we're going to confuse the piloted vehicle with the unpiloted one," hypothesized someone who still had a sense of humor.

"Stop joking!" announced Agadzhanov. "A report has come in that on the passive vehicle, where, thank God, there isn't a cosmonaut, the 45K Sun-star tracker messed up again during the orientation session. But it's impossible to figure out what happened. Through a blunder of the control group programmers, information was downlinked from the flight recorder to Saryshagan instead of to us. You see, they decided to free up our tracking station for the downlink of information about Beregovoy's actions."

Two "emergency rescue teams" were formed: one just for *Soyuz-2*, and the other to downlink Beregovoy's work and analyze his actions.

When the members of the recently arrived State Commission and their "entourage" filled our small control room, we tried to distract the attention of the brass with detailed reports about the results of the first day so that they wouldn't interfere with the ongoing operations. Beregovoy had been loaded down with experiments on constellation identification, photographing Earth's snow cover, studying the twilight background, observing luminous particles, and checking out the 45K Sun-star tracker.

"You're chasing me like a rabbit," complained Beregovoy, receiving one radiogram after another from Earth.

"You asked for it," retorted Shatalov, who was communicating with him via *Zarya*.

During the night leading up to 29 October, I was still the responsible duty officer for GOGU. My partner monitoring the actions and communicating with the cosmonaut was Pavel Belyayev. According to the schedule, Beregovoy was supposed to be sleeping, and we could calmly chat about what had caused his errors.

"All the same, that was very stressful," said Belyayev. "It's not at all like controlling an airplane. They trust a pilot with his first solo flight after many flights with an instructor. It used to be simple for us cosmonauts, because not only did they *not* require us to intervene in control, but they also forbade us from doing so. Automatics did everything for us. Before our flight with Leonov on Voskhod, I met Sergey Pavlovich in the dining hall when I was off duty and asked, 'Couldn't we try manual control in the upcoming flight?' He said, 'No, under no circumstances.' And despite the prohibition, we had to do it. The attitude-control system failed for the first time, and Korolev himself gave permission from the ground for manual orientation and to fire the SKDU for landing."[28]

From the author's archives.

Belyayev recounted very vividly how he and Leonov attempted manual orientation for the first time, leaning against one another, "so as not to float away in zero gravity."

"We did everything calmly. Only later did we realize that if

Cosmonaut Aleksey Leonov congratulates Boris Chertok on his 80th birthday in 1992.

28. See Chertok, *Rockets and People, Vol. III,* Chapter 9.

we had made a mistake, we might have remained in orbit. Before firing the engine I took a look at the globe and understood: if we rush we'll come down in the water. We need to fly over Europe. Thoughts flashed through my head very quickly. Leshka [i.e., Leonov] was also looking; he checked how the vehicle was oriented—for acceleration or braking. Before firing the engine we managed to seat ourselves so that the center of mass did not shift very much relative to the design value. We fired the braking engine—dust immediately shot downwards. That's it! That means we're braking! Next came rocking, separation, a cracking sound. There was no fear. We were going back to Earth! Closer to home.

"At any rate, there's no need to berate Beregovoy. At the launch site the tension grows even before you take your seat in the spacecraft. Then all these commands transmitted from the bunker. The powered flight segment. After all, it isn't like taking off in an airplane. A rocket is carrying you into space, but who's controlling it? Your automatics. A human being in a spacecraft is powerless to do anything during that time. Just wait: the spacecraft will either go into orbit or it won't. From his running commentary I felt that he was very excited. He spoke hurriedly, with unnecessary details. It was evident that he was very worried. And we could also tell by his pulse. G-loads and then, immediately, weightlessness. There is always a temporary mental fog. Even for such an experienced pilot. I remember it happened to me. But we were able to calmly come to our senses during the first hours, and right off the bat he had to use the optical sight to figure out what to do with those lights. A human being performs without making mistakes if he is well trained, like pilots landing during wartime. Wounded, on fire, but they still landed at their airfield: something in the subconscious mind switched on. To tell you the truth, I feel sorry for Beregovoy. It will be difficult for him to explain to you why it turned out the way it did."

On the evening of 29 October, 24 hours before the landing, the State Commission heard the preliminary reports about the reasons for the failure to fulfill the program. It was clear that the cosmonaut had committed irreversible control errors. However, Kamanin and the cosmonauts objected to this wording of the findings in which all the blame was placed on the cosmonaut. In the debate, Mishin's accusation, that the Cosmonaut Training Center had a frivolous attitude toward cosmonaut training, triggered anger.

"Here we don't need pilots. Our engineer could have executed such a simple operation. And we can get by without parachute jumps!"

Keldysh, Karas, and Kerimov, who inwardly agreed with Mishin, understood that they needed to smooth things over. Ultimately, the State Commission's secretariat was tasked with drafting wording that contained no direct accusations that singled out the cosmonaut.

"And all of this because we don't have a single strong-willed master of the flight program," said Karas during a calm discussion of the results of the day over dinner. "Korolev never would have agreed to manual docking at night after two splendid automatic ones."

Two days later we listened to Beregovoy's explanations on the ground.

"They gave us the flight program very late. We need to know everything that is to be done during the flight at least a month before the flight so that it can be run through and debated. It took me half a day to adapt to weightlessness. An antenna in the field of vision hampered observation through the VSK. There's a shiny object in front of your eyes the entire time, and it's difficult to adapt in the darkness. But I did see the lights. I was going after the trapezoid; I tried to line it up. The range to the passive vehicle was decreasing, and the trapezoid was getting bigger. I braked at a range of 30 meters. I didn't understand that I needed to turn over. I decided to go out into the light and figure it out there. When I was stationkeeping, the pressure in the DPO was 160. I wanted to get the camera. I was fumbling around in the bag with the camera and snagged the control stick. The spacecraft spun. The spacecraft was very sensitive, and I couldn't feel this through the control sticks. I couldn't find my place in the man-machine structure. The whole time I had the feeling that propellant consumption increased at the slightest movement of the stick. There was virtually no dead zone. This is good for an automatic system, but it generates unnecessary nervousness in a human being. An unpleasant feeling of nausea continued for 10 to 12 hours. Self-control is better than when you are continuously controlled from the ground. You feel like a powerless passenger or guest—this isn't my style. Contact between the human being and the spacecraft needs to change. You need to feel effort when you use the control sticks. Before stationkeeping in the darkness the pressure was 160. I lost around 30 atmospheres out of carelessness. I could have flipped over on the light side. But then there still wouldn't have been anything left for approach. A cosmonaut needs to be allowed to fly for at least 12 hours, and *then* load him with maneuvers so that there's no response lag. Adaptation is necessary. A spacecraft weighs 6 tons, and when you control it you can't feel any effort in the control stick. We pilots are not accustomed to this. The training procedure needs to be changed. Moreover, the simulator doesn't give a true idea of the possible situation. We learned how to take up slight roll error. But then it turned out that the passive vehicle had flipped 'upside down' by almost 180°. We weren't trained for this situation. Now they've just explained to me that you also need to look where the main antenna of *Igla* is located. This antenna isn't shown on the simulator at all...."

I have cited only the most interesting excerpts from Beregovoy's report. Despite his "lousy mood," Beregovoy made a lot of valuable comments aimed at improving the spacecraft's operation and increasing its degree of comfort. My colleagues, who were proponents of pure automatics, could have celebrated. In this case, the human being had not been able to cope with a task that automatic systems had executed two times before this. But no one was jubilant and no one gloated.

I have dwelled on the story of Beregovoy's flight in such detail because it was very instructive. The developers themselves—planners, automatics specialists, and ballistics experts—all of them in concert had placed a human being in conditions where he was the decisive yet least reliable link in the control loop. Not only had we assured ourselves, but we had also shown the whole world that we knew how to reliably dock spacecraft without human involvement. Why was it necessary during the first piloted flight after the death of Komarov to include a human being in the control loop?

This plan had its own logic. On a piloted spacecraft the person needs to be included in the control loop in case of a failure of the primary automatic loop. But this person needs to be provided with observation, control, and monitoring equipment. All conceivable failures of the automatic loop need to be rehearsed on the ground long before the flight, and the future cosmonaut must prove on the simulator, not in flight, that he is capable in an off-nominal and even in an emergency situation of substituting for the automatic systems.

ALL OF THE MASS MEDIA REPORTED about the latest triumph in space. There was not so much as a hint at the reception at the Kremlin Palace of Congresses, or at the press conferences, or in dozens of various articles that there had been any trouble whatsoever during the flight. Despite the warm congratulations of the Party and the government, we, the actual culprits of the "major victory in space," were demoralized. These were more or less the truths that I pronounced at the debriefing meetings among my control specialist colleagues when discussing the results of Beregovoy's flight. The road from the pronouncement of these obvious truths to their practical implementation proved difficult.

Just two months after Beregovoy's flight, the active *Soyuz-4* spacecraft, piloted by Vladimir Shatalov, was launched (on 14 January 1969), and two days later—the passive *Soyuz-5* spacecraft with Boris Volynov, Aleksey Yeliseyev, and Yevgeniy Khrunov on board (on 15 January 1969). This time no one demanded a docking immediately after liftoff. Shatalov was given time for adaptation. Twenty-four hours later he executed automatic approach and manual final approach in daylight. We did without the notorious trapezoid formed by the four lights. After the manual final approach operation performed by Shatalov, I didn't pass up the opportunity to tell my comrades in Yevpatoriya about the warning that Gallay had given Bushuyev and me a while back.

"And what's more, we didn't listen to your overly cautious colleagues regarding the ionic holes," said Zoya Degtyarenko. "The planners had to look for reserves for the extra day of flight before approach, while we ballistics experts found daylight time for two spacecraft to land."

"Yes, now one can admit that on our recommendation Beregovoy's flight program was risky. At least it is good that everything ended well," said Rauschenbach.

However, our chief spacecraft planner, cosmonaut Konstantin Feoktistov, and Rauschenbach's very close associate Yevgeniy Bashkin didn't agree with us and contended that we had lost a day of flight for no good reason just because Beregovoy made a mistake. If he had docked, then we would have undoubtedly approved this same program unanimously for a new crew as well.

Subsequent events showed that we had nevertheless put our minds at ease too quickly and had not learned all the lessons that we could have from Beregovoy's flight. In October of the same year of 1969, three spacecraft—*Soyuz-6*, *Soyuz-7*, and *Soyuz-8*—were launched one after another in a group flight. Two of them were supposed to approach one another in automatic mode. The crew comprising Vladimir Shatalov and Aleksey Yeliseyev, who already had experience in space, were tasked to perform final approach and docking in manual mode. This time there was a failure in the *Igla* system, which excluded the possibility of subsequent automatic approach.

The ground, i.e., the control center in Yevpatoriya, together with the ballistics centers measuring the orbital parameters, repeatedly gave the crews data for correction in the hope that they could approach to the extent necessary for Shatalov's experienced crew to be able to take over control and carry out manual final approach. The spacecraft did in fact manage to approach to the point of visual contact. However, there was no equipment on board to measure the relative range and velocity between the vehicles, and while maneuvering, the cosmonauts kept losing visual control.

During subsequent evaluations of this flight within my inner circle, we directed a lot of strong language at ourselves. There was nothing to blame the cosmonauts for. We had not provided them with fundamental autonomous navigation equipment for mutual approach.

The failure with rendezvous encouraged basic research and development of backup systems for *Igla* in the event of its failure. One such system, based on the use of x-ray radiation, was the ARS, proposed by Yevgeniy Yurevich, chief of the OKB of the Leningrad Polytechnic Institute. This system itself was not included in the automatic control loop. It was a measurement system and made it possible to perform manual control at short distances, receiving information about the range and velocity of approach.

The off-nominal situations described above are examples of the failure of cosmonauts engaged in the control loop to perform an assignment because of a combination of two factors: the fault of the systems developers hobbled by a lack of appropriate simulators of the real-world circumstances, and an overestimation of the capabilities of a human being when preparing a flight program.

IF A GROUND CREW IS RESPONSIBLE for the execution of a task rather than an on-board crew, the spacecraft might break down through the fault of the ground services. An instructive example of this is the tragedy of DOS No. 3. After the death of Dobrovolskiy's crew in June 1971, there was a prolonged break in piloted flights. Modifications of the Soyuz vehicles for an absolute guarantee of the crew's safety in the event of depressurization dragged on for more than a year. During this time a second orbital station was manufactured—DOS No. 2. It was prepared for launch in mid-1972. This station carried with it the hope to restore piloted flights, so necessary for the rehabilitation of our cosmonautics against the background of a series of American expeditions to the Moon.

But fate continued to pummel us. The "hot summer" of 1971 at Baykonur handed off the baton of failures to the hot summer of 1972. On 29 July 1972, the Proton launch vehicle flew "over the hill" and DOS No. 2 was transformed into formless fragments of metal strewn over the steppe.[29] Once again there was an all-hands mobilization to speed up preparation of DOS No. 3. This was a second-generation station. The staff of TsKBEM, KB Salyut, ZIKh, and dozens of subcontracting organizations began developing the station, taking into consideration the experience of the flight of the first *Salyut*. In December 1972, DOS No. 3, which had earlier been dubbed *Salyut-2*, was delivered to the engineering facility at Site No. 2. Preparations began the very first day in all-hands rush mode.

Slightly ahead of us at Chelomey's firing range launch sites, they were preparing for the launch of the first Almaz. Both the political and state leadership encouraged the competition between TsKBEM with Chief Designer Mishin and TsKBM, headed by General Designer Chelomey. Now, more than 30 years later, the Soviet Union's creation of two orbital stations at the same time seems an incredible waste. Twenty-five years later, the Russian budget was incapable of supporting the existence in space of the unique *Mir* orbital station, while in 1973 they were about to launch two stations: the Almaz for the Ministry of Defense and DOS No. 3 in the interests of science and politics.

---

29. During the launch, at T plus 162 seconds, the control system of the second stage of the Proton launch vehicle failed, preventing orbital insertion.

The Almaz lifted off on 3 April 1973. It was called *Salyut-2*. Right after it was inserted into orbit they detected a depressurization of the station.[30] *Salyut-2* ceased to exist on 28 May 1973. Now all hopes were pinned to DOS No. 3.

DOS No. 3 had been substantially modified compared with the first two. Three solar array panels were installed on the station, each one with autonomous orientation on the Sun. Rauschenbach's departments had developed the super-economical *Kaskad* (Cascade) attitude-control system to extend the station's service life. To generate control moment in the effectors, one could use the economical and rapid orientation mode. In the rapid, more efficient mode, three times as many rocket control nozzles were fired. The *Delta* on-board navigation system, which enabled the cosmonauts to independently determine and predict the orbital flight parameters, appeared for the first time. The water recovery system was also an innovation. Compared with the first Salyut, DOS No. 3 was packed with a rich assortment of scientific instruments. All of these improvements came at a price—power reserves had to be found.

The planners, having no real opportunity to reduce the station's mass, having no desire to deplete the program by "throwing out" science equipment, and without having received the approval of the launch vehicle's chief designer to increase the total mass that Proton would insert into orbit, made the decision to lower the orbital altitude. The lower the orbit, the greater the payload the launch vehicle was capable of inserting.

The aspiration to "drag" as large a payload as possible into space by lowering the altitude inevitably required a rapid raising of the orbit after separation from the launch vehicle using the DOS's own orbital correction engine. The computed initial orbit was fairly low, and taking into account the possible insertion error in the worst-case scenario, such a large spacecraft, in terms of ballistics, could not stay in that orbit for more than three or four days. The more time that elapsed after orbital insertion before raising the orbit using the station's own propellant, the more propellant it would have to consume. Delaying raising the orbit was also forbidden because the ballistics experts might miscalculate. If the atmosphere turned out to be "denser," the station might "bury itself in" on the second day. Then there would certainly not be enough propellant to save it.

---

30. Ground controllers lost contact with the station on 15 April 1973. See Asif A. Siddiqi, "The Almaz Space Station Complex: A History, 1964–1992, Part 1: 1964–1976," *Journal of the British Interplanetary Society* 54 (2001): 389–416.

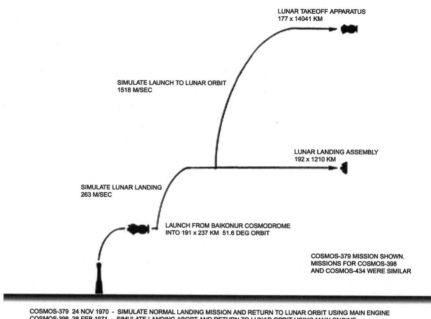

LUNAR TAKEOFF APPARATUS
177 x 14041 KM

SIMULATE LAUNCH TO LUNAR ORBIT
1518 M/SEC

LUNAR LANDING ASSEMBLY
192 x 1210 KM

SIMULATE LUNAR LANDING
263 M/SEC

LAUNCH FROM BAIKONUR COSMODROME
INTO 191 x 237 KM 51.6 DEG ORBIT

COSMOS-379 MISSION SHOWN.
MISSIONS FOR COSMOS-398
AND COSMOS-434 WERE SIMILAR

COSMOS-379 24 NOV 1970 - SIMULATE NORMAL LANDING MISSION AND RETURN TO LUNAR ORBIT USING MAIN ENGINE
COSMOS-398 28 FEB 1971 - SIMULATE LANDING ABORT AND RETURN TO LUNAR ORBIT USING MAIN ENGINE
COSMOS-434 12 AUG 1971 - SIMULATE NORMAL LANDING AND THEN RETURN TO LUNAR ORBIT USING BACKUP ENGINE

David R. Woods

The breakdown of the T2K mission profile shows the two major orbital changes used to test the main LK engine in Earth orbit. This profile shows the flight of *Kosmos-379*.

Based on the results of the flights of *Kosmos-398* in February 1971 and dozens of Soyuzes, the effect of the exhaust stream of attitude-control engines on the signals of ionic sensors was discovered.[31] But the engines had to be fired to dampen angular velocities and then to search for and orient using the oncoming ion flux. After the sensors locked on to the ion flux, firing the engines could markedly increase the level of interference and even block the legitimate signal altogether. In this case, stabilization using the maximum ion flux value was compromised. Large oscillations in the pitch and heading planes relative to the velocity vector are possible.

New ionic sensors were installed on DOS No. 3 for the first time. Instead of two separate pitch and heading sensors, they developed one that gave the

---

31. *Kosmos-398* was the cover name for the T2K (vehicle no. 2), a test version of the Soviet lunar lander designed for testing in Earth orbit. During the mission, ground controllers put the spaceship through two major maneuvers that simulated descent to the lunar surface and then subsequent liftoff from the Moon.

486

control system a signal for two axes. This sensor had one common input for the oncoming ion flux. If noise from the engines went to this input, then it gave rise to false signals now coming over two channels at once. Before the flights, the control system didn't undergo ground testing with an actual ion flux, much less with a simulation of exhaust interference. It was also noted that interference behaves differently depending on the geographic latitude and orientation relative to Earth's magnetic field. It would seem that, in view of this, it was absolutely necessary to exercise maximum caution with the new orbital station: activate the ionic system in Yevpatoriya's coverage zone only after settling down, after using the infrared vertical mode and low-thrust engines for this. But that takes time! Such a cautious control program required using up at least two and perhaps three orbits! Just setting up the station in terms of roll and pitch using the infrared vertical took almost an entire orbit.

Our telemetry and launch vehicle control specialists had learned to report in real time: "Thirty seconds, pitch, yaw, spin normal; pressure in chambers normal; flight normal...." Now we also wanted to achieve this degree of efficiency when controlling the DOSes. The most reliable maneuver control method should have been selected only after analyzing the tests. The waiving of control system tests was an error that the control system developers made.

TsKBEM management, the chief designer, and the heads of complexes and departments were so absorbed with testing DOS No. 3 at the engineering facility that they didn't devote the proper attention to developing the flight control program. The planners simply did not issue the main defining document—the ground rules for flight control. Consequently, the control service did not develop a detailed program signed off on by everyone (above all by the control system developers) with a minute-by-minute, hour-by-hour, day-by-day schedule of the control modes and each of the commands issued to the spacecraft. To a certain extent this was a reflection of the traditional guerilla manner in which we had worked controlling the first Soyuzes. But then the GOGU chiefs—Agadzhanov, myself, Tregub, and Rauschenbach—had actually constituted a think tank, which improvised in real time and drew up a program for each session over the course of the flight in the absence of approved flight programs. The program was discussed in the gap between communication sessions; sometimes changes were introduced during the actual session. This was possible thanks to the rapid processing of telemetry information, which systems specialists conducted virtually in real time sitting next to the telemetry operators.

On the day of the launch, in Yevpatoriya from the old GOGU lineup, there was Yakov Tregub, the flight director. His military deputy was Colonel Mikhail Pasternak. At the firing range on the day of the liftoff of DOS No. 3 were the State Commission, Mishin, Semyonov, Feoktistov, myself, and the main developers of all the systems. Just one of our specialists on the motion control system and just one telemetry information-processing specialist were sitting at NIP-15 in Ussuriysk. Two shifts of specialists on the attitude-control system (two men per shift) were working at NIP-16 in Yevpatoriya, which played the role of the mission control center (TsUP). But low staffing wasn't the main shortcoming of the ground control complex. Despite the experience that had already been gained in real-time telemetry processing and data transmission, during the flight of DOS No. 3 the people monitoring and controlling the flight acted slower than they needed to. This was certainly not because they were slovenly, but quite the contrary, because they sought to introduce rigid military order and discipline. Groups of telemetry, analysis, and systems specialists worked in isolation from one another, "in order not to disturb others," and the information made its way to the person who really could assess what was going on with the system only after passing through a long chain of people receiving, transmitting, and reporting. Information came from distant stations to NIP-16 in the form of telegrams, the content of which had been encoded, and upon receipt it had to be decoded followed by the mandatory registration of all the messages as was the procedure with the document control of classified material. Throughout all of this a chain of command was also observed: before information requiring an immediate decision reached the flight director, it passed consecutively through the NIP chief, the heads of the communications or telemetry groups, the information-security service, and the analysis group. NIP-16 was the first to try out an automatic telemetry information processing system called STI-90, which was developed at NII-885. The ground-based M-220 computer was used for the automatic processing. The military authorities at KIK in concert with NII-885 began to install this system at all NIPs that had telemetry stations. However, this new system had not been mastered to the extent that it could be entrusted to the "old hands" accustomed to manual telemetry processing.

For the sake of raising the orbit during the first orbit, at the request of the planners, we elected not to perform the preliminary tests on the control system. Having made the mistake that I mentioned earlier, we were obliged to set up a real-time flight control service. Even with that primitive technology, this was possible, a fact that we had learned from our experience with previous space launches.

One more fateful error in the tragic chain of events led to the loss of DOS No. 3. After its insertion into orbit, the State Commission received a report from NIP-3 (Saryshagan) that all of the structural elements and solar arrays had deployed.[32] Twelve minutes after liftoff, NIP-15 in Ussuriysk transmitted

---

32. DOS-3 was launched at 0320 hours Moscow Time on 11 May 1973. Once its failure was recognized, it was announced by TASS as *Kosmos-557*.

a command to the spacecraft to activate ionic orientation using the high-thrust engines in the effector system.

Subsequent investigation showed that the documentation on hand at NIP-15 called for issuing a command for orientation using the low-thrust engines [as opposed to the high-thrust engines]. A motion control theoretician from OKB-1 who had flown to Yevpatoriya discovered that the schedule of commands called for a low-thrust mode. Before his departure he and his boss had conducted a laboratory simulation of the orientation process in low- and maximum-thrust modes. For the simulation they had received the baseline data from the ionic system developers for the interference values that might occur during low and maximum thrusts. On the models, the process ran normally in both modes with the specified interference. However, orientation using low thrust took so much time that they might not have been able to correct [i.e., raise] the orbit during the second orbit.

This motion control theoretician sent his boss at OKB-1 a telegram with a proposal to begin the ionic orientation mode right away using the high-thrust engines. His boss was a top-notch specialist on the theory and dynamics of control. He trusted the baseline data that he had received from the ionic system developers and concurred with the proposal of his colleague. He sent his approval in a telegram to the control center in Yevpatoriya. After receiving the telegram, the author of the proposal approached the flight director. The latter accepted the proposal, and the change in the schedule of commands that were to be issued to the spacecraft during the first communication session was sent via telegraph to Ussuriysk. Ussuriysk had a radio coverage zone of around 10 minutes. This was completely adequate to assess the nature of the orientation process. However, the only specialist capable of doing this couldn't receive the information until the military telemetry operators, who were located in a different building, had processed it, recorded it, and reported to the brass. And only then was he allowed access to it. Right away he saw that instead of single engines in the effector system (SIO), they were working in groups of three, which contradicted the documentation that he had.[33] The station's angular spin rate was 10 times greater than the expected value! The process was reminiscent of a dog chasing its tail. But a dog spins in one plane, while the station was rocking about its center of mass in two planes at once! The triple thrust engines were heartily guzzling precious fuel.

---

33. SIO—*Sistema ispolnitelnykh organov.*

This needed to be reported immediately to the mission control center (TsUP). But instead of a simple telephone conversation, he had to send a telegram. First the text is written. The text goes to the tracking station chief for his signature. The telegram is encoded and goes to the communication group for transmission to Yevpatoriya. There it is received, typed, and the strip of paper containing the text is glued to a blank sheet of paper as is done at post offices. All of this took so much time that DOS No. 3 managed to fly around Earth and enter the NIP-16 radio coverage zone.

During the first communication session, TsUP was responsible for issuing a command to the spacecraft to initiate the program for the orbit-raising maneuver. At first everything went according to the timeline. STI-90 issued a report about a large consumption of propellant.

"We don't need to scare the brass," the analysis group decided. "Most likely this is an error in the program of the new telemetry processing system."

But there was a specialist of the SIO system who was not so gullible. Violating discipline, he ran into the telemetry building to look at the initial information tapes for himself. One of the control specialists also couldn't stand it. He also tore himself away from his workstation, and violating procedure, ran over to the telemetry operators.

Once he had seen the tape, he wanted to scream over the telephone to the flight director: "Shut down the engines!" But, as everyone knows, bread always falls buttered-side down. The telephone in this room wasn't working. And the specialist sprinted (as he later averred) out of the telemetry building to the other one where the control room was located on the second floor. The SIO specialist managed to beat him and was already reporting to management that they needed to immediately transmit a command to the spacecraft to shut down the attitude-control system.

One must also understand the flight director. Responsibility for the fate of the DOS had come crashing down on him. Instead of a command to raise the orbit, two junior engineers were demanding that the control system be shut down immediately and that the orientation process be halted. How many orbits would it be now before another attempt to raise the orbit could be made? And wouldn't the DOS "bury itself" in the atmosphere so that it would be impossible to drag it back out?

The chief designer, chairman of the State Commission, minister, and chief planner at the firing range got in their cars to drive to the airfield. It would take at least 6 hours for them to get to Yevpatoriya. Priceless seconds were slipping by. The DOS was now sweeping over Yevpatoriya, and they needed to transmit the order to Ussuriysk to issue an engine shutdown command to the spacecraft. Perhaps the radiation of their antenna might still manage to catch up with the DOS as it departed over the radio horizon.

Here, it is fitting to recall the words of a song from a famous film: "Don't take the seconds for granted…. They whiz by like bullets past your head…. Moments…moments…moments…."[34]

Finally the flight controller made the decision, "Shut down orientation mode."

"Too late!" his deputy told him. "The spacecraft left our Command and Measurement Complex coverage area 2 minutes ago."

Now we had minutes to deal with the first notification from Ussuriysk and with our own telemetry. It was obvious that the orientation process, as a result of the active influence of the engines, was running its course with rocking in the heading and pitch planes searching for the ion flux, which was blocked by powerful interference. The disastrous consumption of propellant corresponded to the commands that the control system issued to the high-thrust engines trying to find their rightful ion flux.

About 40 minutes later the DOS would once again appear in the coverage zone of NIP-16…but now with empty tanks. If they had shut down the attitude-control system right at the beginning of the NIP-16 coverage zone, then there would still be a chance during the next orbit to make an attempt to orient the spacecraft and raise its orbit using the "IKV plus IO" (infrared vertical plus ionic orientation) mode.

The minister, State Commission, and planners who created the erroneous program arrived in the Crimea and reached Yevpatoriya 8 hours after liftoff. While they were still in the air they found out about the large propellant consumption, but there was still a glimmer of hope that the station might be saved. On site it became clear that it was all over. TASS broadcast the announcement that the launch of the latest *Kosmos-557* had taken place. Without any further TASS announcements, on 22 May, DOS No. 3 entered the dense layers of the atmosphere on its own and sank in the ocean.

THREE ORBITAL STATIONS IN A ROW had perished ignominiously: DOS No. 2, Almaz, and DOS No. 3.[35] The patience of the Party and government leaders was exhausted. To investigate, they organized a government commission headed by Vyacheslav Kovtunenko, the chief designer of KB-3, which was part

---

34. This is a line from a song from the 1972 Soviet television miniseries *Semnadtsat mgnoveniy vesny* (*Seventeen Moments of Spring*) about the penetration of the German Reich in Berlin by a Soviet intelligence officer in the waning days of World War II. The hero of the film is Maksim Isayev, alias Max Otto von Stirlitz, played by Vyacheslav Tikhonov. Tatyana Mikhaylovna Lioznova (1924–) directed the series. Soviet poet Robert Ivanovich Rozhdestvenskiy (1932–1994) wrote the lyrics to the song.

35. These were DOS-2 (launched on 29 July 1972), Almaz OPS-1 (launched on 3 April 1973), and DOS-3 (launched on 11 May 1973).

of KB Yuzhnoye.[36] Members of the commission included Nikolay Pilyugin, Boris Bunkin, Boris Petrov, and other very competent control systems specialists.

At the same time the high commission was at work, the state security authorities began their own investigation. They conducted lengthy interviews with those directly involved in the incident and made them write explanatory notes. Most likely, if they really wanted to, historians could hunt down these explanations somewhere in the archives. The decision to initiate orientation using the high-thrust engines caught the attention of state security. Why did the control system engineer insist on changing the mode and persuade the flight director to change a command timeline that had already been transmitted to Ussuriysk? Not only did the KGB officers consider this decision to be the chief cause of the station's demise, but some of our colleagues did, too.

It would seem that the control system engineer and the flight director were the real culprits. But either the times were different, or the investigation had been entrusted to sensible people in the KGB. The KGB understood that it wasn't a matter of two specialists, but it was much more profound. The KGB did not find the elements of a crime, and they did not bring official charges against anyone. However, they made it known that our ministry should punish the guilty parties. If there were Party members among them, then let them bear Party responsibility, but not criminal responsibility.

The accident investigation commission gathered in a private conference. Above all, the scientists were interested in the very idea of using the ionosphere as a medium for orienting a spacecraft. It seemed very exotic.

"Experience has not yet been accumulated in this field, and consequently, anything worse than your worst nightmare might happen," said Kovtunenko.

On the first day of the investigation Pilyugin declared, "I have never been an executioner for my professional comrades and I'm not going to be."

Other members of the commission were also of the same mind.

Boris Petrov asked a naïve question, "So, who is officially the chief designer of the control system?"

I answered that we did not have such a position and we couldn't have one. There's a TsKBEM chief designer, there's a DOS chief designer, there are subcontracting chief designers, but we don't have a chief designer for just the control complex. If there were one, then he wouldn't have agreed to this program

---

36. Vyacheslav Mikhaylovich Kovtunenko (1921–1995) served as chief designer of KB-3, the division at KB Yuzhnoye responsible for spacecraft development, from 1965 to 1977. Kovtunenko later went on to serve as general designer of NPO Lavochkin.

of system activation without preliminary tests, which the chief designer had to approve at the recommendation of the enthusiastic planners.

"So that's one cause, if not the fundamental cause of what happened," said Pilyugin. "You gained the right to develop control systems yourselves and succeeded in this field back when Korolev was alive. But being the subordinates of a chief who is not very strong in control systems, you will never gain the proper perspective and time to test out its systems. I proposed to Sergey Pavlovich that he transfer all spacecraft control specialists to me. The idea even came up of creating an NIIAP space branch at our second production facility. But Chertok and Rauschenbach dreamed of independence—and this is the result."

This was the first I had heard that Pilyugin had proposed to Korolev to transfer development of spacecraft control systems to him at NIIAP. There really had been such an idea. Three years after Korolev's death, Pilyugin's deputies Finogeyev and Khitrik came to see me on N1-L3 matters. For the first time they had become interested not only in the technology, but also in the organization of our work on systems for the Soyuz. That's when a conversation about creating an NIIAP space branch on the basis of my complexes really did take place. After estimating the amount of electronics and control systems in the total volume of work, we reached the conclusion that it was too great to take it away from TsKBEM and hand it over to NIIAP.

"Then you have to change the chief designer. Without electronics and control devices your spacecraft is an empty barrel. And what's more, if we pick you up, that means we need to transfer flight control with all its headaches."

Since then, there has been no further discussion of this idea.

Based on the results of the accident investigation commission's work, organizational findings were later issued at the ministerial and Party-committee level. Tregub received the harshest punishment. He was removed from his post as deputy chief designer and told to look for other work. He went over to work for Iosifyan at VNIIEM as his deputy for flight testing. On 30 October 2007, in the ceremonial hall of the Ministry of Defense, located next to Burdenko Hospital, along with many other veterans I paid my last respects to former Major General Yakov Isayevich Tregub.[37] While waiting for the eulogy, I conversed with Rafail Vannikov. Beginning in 1946, he and Tregub had served in the first Special-purpose Missile Brigade, which General Aleksandr Tveretskiy commanded.[38] We both agreed that if it hadn't been for the failure of DOS No. 3, Tregub's life would have taken a very different turn.

---

37. Tregub had died three days previously.
38. See Chertok, *Rockets and People, Vol. I*, pp. 354–355.

Rauschenbach was relieved of his administrative duties as chief of the complex of departments and transferred to a consultant's position. Soon thereafter he retired of his own volition "in connection with a transfer to another job." This other job was staff professor and department head at the Moscow Institute of Physics and Technology. Legostayev was appointed director of Complex No. 3 in Rauschenbach's place. I received a reprimand by order of the minister and a reprimand by resolution of the Party committee of TsKBEM. An administrative order called for almost everyone who was involved in the production of the ionic system or who was at the control center in Yevpatoriya during the critical hours to be reprimanded and have their salaries temporarily reduced. Similar disciplinary sanctions were imposed on the flight control military staffs.

The reader might have noticed that when describing the circumstances surrounding the demise of DOS No. 3 I did not mention the surnames of many specialists who were directly involved in preparing the flight program, in control, in telemetry analysis at the center in Yevpatoriya and in Ussuriysk, and in the processes simulated in TsKBEM laboratories. For everyone who was involved in those operations, the loss of DOS No. 3 was so traumatic that even more than 30 years after the fact, they were unable to recall the events of those bitter days with indifference.

When things had calmed down, TsKBEM Party Committee Secretary Anatoliy Tishkin invited me to his office and asked whom I might recommend as director of the new crew training and flight control complex. Without hesitating I named [cosmonaut] Aleksey Yeliseyev. Tishkin agreed with my recommendation. After interviewing Yeliseyev, the Party committee recommended that Mishin prepare a ministerial order naming Yeliseyev deputy chief designer of TsKBEM. The present-day flight control service came into being the day the order was issued for Yeliseyev's appointment.[39]

IN THOSE YEARS ABOUT WHICH I AM NOW WRITING, triumphs and mistakes were put out for consideration at Party work meetings. Usually a chief who spoke at the meeting summed up the results of the past year, gave an evaluation of the work of the subdivisions, and spoke about the plans for the year ahead. In such reports it was considered good form to combine achievements and praise for those who were the most outstanding with relentless criticism for mistakes and shortcomings.

---

39. Chertok is referring to Yeliseyev's appointment to head TsKBEM's Complex No. 7, which was approved on 11 October 1973.

In January 1974, the traditional annual Party work meeting was held for the complexes assigned to Legostayev, Kalashnikov, Yurasov, and me, which comprised 15 departments. The total number of workers in the complexes was 1,300. Usually at these meetings everyone was concerned with the general tasks, and they certainly weren't there under duress. Inexplicably, the texts of my directive reports have been preserved. Similar documents have either been destroyed or relinquished to closed archives. After rereading them, I decided to extract quotations having to do with our work in 1973 and with the assessment of the failure of DOS No. 3. I am citing several of them in order to bring the reader closer to the atmosphere in which we worked in those days.

> *Yesterday on television we observed the stirring picture of an enormous meeting during which the people of Cuba met with Leonid Ilyich Brezhnev.*[40] *We have a right to be proud of the fact that the entire world and our whole nation were able to see and hear this grand historic demonstration of revolutionary solidarity in real time because the first Molniyas, which relayed the television broadcast through space, were developed here by our team. We are not just witnesses, but first-hand, vanguard participants in a science and technology revolution. The work to enable humankind to conquer and explore space began here with this team in our enterprise.*
>
> *At the same time we can't forget that over the course of 1973 we executed five space launches, including one—DOS No. 3—which ended in failure.*
>
> *This is an example of an instance when ill-considered decisions lead to tragic results. The highly qualified comrades of Rauschenbach's group risked using a new orientation system without the necessary critical analysis and thorough scrutiny under ground conditions, taking into consideration the experience of previous launches. At the same time, they did not take advantage of advice from specialists next door in another department. They had no time. They were in such a hurry that they gave up on science.*
>
> *Everyone knows the result. Disrupting the plan not only of our enterprise, but also of many enterprises throughout the entire country. It was a harsh lesson. Many, myself included, were severely punished.*

---

40. This is a reference to Brezhnev's historic first visit to Cuba in January and February 1974.

> *The loss of DOS No. 3 stunned our entire enterprise. We had displayed blatant carelessness and conceit in technology and science in one of the most vulnerable places—the orientation and control system. Such disregard for the analysis of previous experience and loss of vigilance and critical attitude toward one's own work are very dangerous.*
>
> *Not just those directly involved in the failed outcome, but also all who were involved in the creation and production, must learn from the events of May 1973.*

I gave this impassioned speech when the results of many of the investigations of the behavior of the ionic systems were already known. Specialists simulating the stability of the attitude-control system before the flight of DOS No. 3—using the baseline data from the developers of the ionic system—were solving an inverse problem. Having a real picture of the behavior of DOS No. 3 in flight, they were attempting to reproduce it on a model. They succeeded in doing this only after they fed interference into the system's input that was 10 times greater than what they had loaded, having settled on the high-thrust engine mode.

The loss of DOS No. 3 was a devastating tragedy for all the creators of orbital stations. Against the background of the Americans' successes in space, this event could have inflicted a very severe blow to the prestige of the first space power. However, all of the information concerning the flight of *Kosmos-557* was classified as secret so that neither the world nor Soviet society knew anything specific about it. Since there was no human loss of life, there was no need for funeral ceremonies, they reserved judgment on judging anyone, and back then representatives of the mass media displayed excessive curiosity only with permission from the "top." A real danger emerged that the Long-Duration Orbital Station program would be shut down. However, it became the main thrust of Soviet cosmonautics.

THE NEXT LONG-DURATION ORBITAL STATION, *Salyut-4* (DOS No. 4), which was analogous to DOS No. 3, but without the ionic system, went into orbit on 26 December 1974. For this station, they engineered a triaxial orientation system using an infrared vertical and performed preliminary development testing of it and carried out two maneuvers using gyros. It took a long time, but it proved to be very reliable.

While we were licking our wounds after the demise of DOS No. 3, at OKB-52 (TsKBM) and at ZIKh accelerated launch preparations were under way on the Almaz orbital station. It was inserted into space on 25 June 1974; the Almaz was called *Salyut-3*. Chelomey had to agree to the use of our Soyuz vehicles to deliver a crew to the Almaz. *Soyuz-14* delivered the first expedition to *Salyut-3*—cosmonauts Pavel Popovich and Yuriy Artyukhin—on

3 July 1974. Approach, final approach, and docking proceeded successfully in automatic mode.

And then the next expedition to *Salyut-3* experienced adventures that ended with the creation of another accident investigation commission. During the approach segment of the *Soyuz-15* spacecraft (launched on 26 August 1974) with the Almaz orbital station, the celebrated and, it seemed, well-examined *Igla* didn't simply fail—it issued false commands. *Igla* recognized the true range of 350 meters as a range of 20 kilometers. Based on these data, *Igla's* rendezvous control automatics turned the station and fired the engine to build up approach velocity corresponding to a range of 20 kilometers. The vehicle rushed toward the station at a relative velocity of 72 kilometers per hour.

We didn't even have time to figure out that the possible impact velocity exceeded the speed permitted by the State Automobile Inspectorate (GAI) in populated areas. Disaster was inevitable. The fact that the automatic rendezvous control algorithms called for lateral velocity beginning at a range of 20 kilometers saved the day. This enabled the spacecraft to shoot past the station at a distance of 40 meters. While flying past the station, *Igla* lost radio lock-on and stopped measuring relative motion parameters. The crew didn't know what was happening. The malfunctioning *Igla* made the vehicle repeat the approach sessions. The spacecraft executed the potentially lethal station flyby two more times until the ground intervened and issued a command to shut down automatic approach mode. After these acrobatic stunts, docking simply did not take place. There was only enough propellant left for descent.

"It is not possible to foresee all off-nominal situations, but it is the crew's duty to figure out from the information available on the console and from visual observation that the automatic approach mode needs to be shut down immediately"—such was the reasoning of the specialists who were responsible for the logic behind the automatic control mode that we had developed.

"But there is no such failure or any identifying flags in our list of off-nominal situations," objected the training specialists from the Cosmonauts Training Center.

Each side agreed to disagree; it was good that the crew—Gennadiy Sarafanov and Lev Demin—safely returned to Earth, and the culprit of the flight incident—the *Igla* system—was "caught red-handed" after processing the telemetry measurements. I was appointed chairman of the accident investigation commission. My traditional comrade-in-arms for accident situations, Colonel Yevgeniy Panchenko, was my deputy. Our commission quickly got to the bottom of the technical causes of the unusual failure. During the very first session of the commission, Chief Designer Armen Mnatsakanyan from the Scientific-Research Institute of Precision Instruments and *Igla* developers

Morgulev and Suslennikov explained that they understood everything and that they would introduce the necessary modifications to the next unit.

We did not limit ourselves to examining the causes for the hardware failure and proposed increasing the reliability of the human factor. Delivering a report before the ministry collegium, I said that the commission proposed creating a special operational group at TsUP to monitor the approach process and make instant decisions. The group should develop the approach control procedure for nominal flight and in off-nominal situations, analyze the approach process and issue recommendations to the director during the flight, and also perform the postflight analysis of the approach modes.

Such a group was created. Department Chief Yevgeniy Bashkin was appointed as its first chief. The group comprised "theoreticians" (Shmyglevskiy and Shiryayev), curators who had studied *Igla*'s radio electronic properties (Nevzorov and Kozhevnikova), manual mode developers (Skotnikov, Fruntz, and Nezdyur), and also systems specialist Borisenko. The most crucial role was set aside for the first-hand developers of the *Igla* radio equipment—Morgulev and Suslennikov. A year later, Oleg Babkov, who was calm and not inclined to unpredictable improvisation, replaced the emotional and impulsive Bashkin in the position of group chief. Soon thereafter, Boris Skotnikov, solid and professorial, occupied this hot seat.

From the author's archives.

V. N. Branets and E. V. Gaushus.

When digital computers for control appeared on board spacecraft, responsibility for the approach process fell to Vladimir Branets. From 1982 to the present, rendezvous professional Borisenko has been the group chief.

The creation of a specialized group, which included the main developers of the logic, theory, and hardware supporting the approach process, completely justified itself. The flight director gained the capability to make decisions in compressed real time, relying on the prompting and advice of the most competent specialists, who were completely aware of their moral and professional responsibility. The many years of experience of the rendezvous group is an example of the real increase in the reliability of a large system that includes a human being in the control structure. Nevertheless, rendezvous and dockings in space are the sources of off-nominal situations more often than not.

THE *SOYUZ-23* SPACECRAFT, which had lifted off on 14 October 1976 with a crew comprising Vyacheslav Zudov and Valeriy Rozhdestvenskiy, was on its way to rendezvous with the Almaz station (*Salyut-5*). The program called for automatic rendezvous and final approach. *Igla*'s radar had executed "lock-on," and the process of autonomous approach without human involvement began. The crew did not react to the spacecraft's clearly abnormal oscillations around its longitudinal axis and unacceptable propellant consumption. The ground-based group understood that *Igla* was behaving abnormally on the channel measuring the line-of-sight angular rate. The range made it impossible to switch to manual approach, especially since the fluctuation of *Igla*'s parameters might have resulted in erroneous actions on the part of the crew. The group made a difficult decision—abandon rendezvous.

Once again I found myself reporting before the ministry collegium about an emergency situation associated with the off-nominal behavior of *Igla*.

"Large fluctuations occurred in the radio channel measuring the line-of-sight angular rate. The control equipment perceived these fluctuations, and the attitude-control engines responded to them. As soon as the process was transmitted via telemetry to Earth in the coverage zone, mission control issued the command to shut down *Igla* and terminate the approach mode. The accident investigation commission is continuing its work."

"Why didn't they decide to make a second approach?" asked one of the members of the collegium.

"There was a great deal of temptation to make a second attempt. However, the risk of consuming too much propellant remained, and we are required to have a guaranteed supply to return to Earth."

"When you were preparing the vehicle on the ground, why didn't you pay attention to these very fluctuations?" asked Minister Afanasyev.

The question was legitimate, and the response was difficult.

"Unfortunately, we didn't standardize the range of fluctuations in a single document and there was no mention of monitoring this parameter. The testers had the official right not to pay them any attention."

The individual who bore primary responsibility for *Igla*'s behavior—Mnatsakanyan—stepped up to the podium. He tried to explain the physical nature of the fluctuations but was unable to answer intelligibly why they hadn't observed it earlier and why he, *Igla*'s chief designer, had not demanded that the range of the fluctuations be monitored during ground testing.

"Now you are going to establish the range of permissible fluctuations, and before the next launches you are going to personally report to me that you guarantee *Igla*'s reliability," said the minister.

Here Mnatsakanyan made a mistake. For three years now at his institute they had been developing the new, more advanced *Kurs* (Course) radio system for measuring relative motion parameters. *Kurs* was supposed to replace *Igla*. As usual, routine work on *Igla* diverted the main contingent of specialists away from future developments. Mnatsakanyan was interested in placing further limits on bringing in new specialists [for work on *Igla*].

He declared, "It's useless to set fluctuation norms for *Igla*—further use of *Igla* is tantamount to death. We need to introduce *Kurs* more quickly." The words "tantamount to death" stunned the audience. Glushko was the first to regain his senses.

"Sergey Aleksandrovich," he addressed the minister, "in connection with this statement from *Igla*'s chief designer, I request that you schedule a special investigation. We are also in favor of *Kurs*, but *Igla* is on the upcoming vehicles. Such an irresponsible statement jeopardizes government-approved programs for orbital stations."

It was dangerous to stir up a scandal in the collegium when high-ranking officials of the Central Committee, VPK, and Ministry of Defense were present.

"We shall thoroughly examine comrade Mnatsakanyan's irresponsible statement," declared the minister, "and we will take the appropriate actions."

Despite pressure "from above" to meet deadlines, the accident investigation commission produced an exceptionally extensive body of investigative work. According to one of the hypotheses put forward by Mnatsakanyan, elastic vibrations of the rod on which *Igla*'s gyrostabilized antenna was mounted caused the fluctuations. Eduard Korzhenevskiy, together with TsNIImash, set up strength and resonance testing for the rod. They had to reject the hypothesis. At that time we simply were unable to find the true source of the fluctuations, but we determined that they did not occur in the majority of the series-produced hardware sets or they were not strong enough to pose a hazard. The commission proposed a procedure for factory measurements of the fluctuations in order to sort out instruments that were suspicious based on these indices.

Without waiting for the commission's final report to appear, officials at MOM prepared a portentous order, which the collegium approved on 2 December 1976: "For insufficient ground testing and shoddy procedures for measuring the main parameters of equipment during all stages of its manufacture, testing, and operation, which resulted in the failure to fulfill the flight program of *Soyuz-23*, NIITP Director and Chief Designer Mnatsakanyan is given a severe reprimand and put on notice that if effective measures are not taken to rectify the situation, he will be relieved of his post."

On 9 December 1976, Mnatsakanyan and I flew out to the firing range for the preparation of the latest *Soyuz-24* spacecraft. We wanted to try one more time in the anechoic chamber to determine the nature of the fluctuations' occurrence. Late that evening Mnatsakanyan stopped by my hotel room to see me and showed me a radiogram that urgently summoned him to Moscow. On 10 December, the chief of the Main Directorate of the ministry recommended that he [Mnatsakanyan] submit a "voluntary" resignation notice. Mnatsakanyan refused. On 6 January 1977, the minister issued an order: "For failure to ensure proper supervision of operations at the institute, comrade A. S. Mnatsakanyan is relieved of his post as NIITP director and chief designer."

Armen Mnatsakanyan took it very hard. He was not permitted to continue working in another post at his home institute. He transferred to work for Andronik Iosifyan, who was not afraid to take in people who had been burned in other organizations.[41]

"We accept all 'insulted and humiliated' individuals," said Iosifyan's deputy Sheremetyevskiy, "under the condition that they are have character and talent."

Working at VNIIEM as laboratory chief, Mnatsakanyan continued to "demand his rights." He was even so bold as to make a request to the Presidium of the Twenty-sixth Congress of the Communist Party of the Soviet Union to appoint a commission to conduct an investigation of his work as NIITP director and of the persecution that he had endured in the Ministry of General Machine Building.[42] On 9 April 1981, an instructor from the general department of the Central Committee informed Mnatsakanyan over the telephone that "no action had been taken" on his letter.[43]

WHILE WE WERE PREPARING the latest *Soyuz-24* in February 1977, fluctuations were negligible. The crew of *Soyuz-24* (launched on 7 February 1977)—Viktor Gorbatko and Yuriy Glazkov—safely docked with *Salyut-5*. Gradually the fear of fluctuations disappeared.

On 29 September 1977, the latest orbital station, the *Salyut-6*, was inserted into space. On 9 October 1977, *Soyuz-25*, carrying cosmonauts Vladimir Kovalenok and Valeriy Ryumin, was sent up to meet *Salyut-6*. The process of approach with automatic control proceeded normally. According to the program, in the final approach zone at a range of 100 meters, the crew shut down *Igla* and switched to manual control. When they were just 1 meter away from the station, the cosmonauts allowed a 2° deviation of the spacecraft's longitudinal axis relative to the nominal position, which is

---

41. Other dismissed designers and scientists (such as Yakov Tregub) had also found refuge at Iosifyan's institute, the All-Union Scientific-Research Institute of Electromechanics (VNIIEM).

42. The Twenty-sixth Congress of the Communist Part of the Soviet Union was held between 23 February and 3 March 1981.

43. "Instructors" were apparatchiks who worked in the Central Committee as aides to the top-level secretaries of the Central Committee.

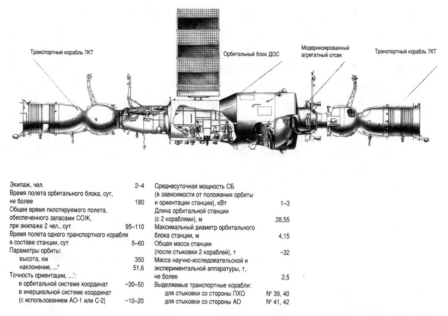

Транспортный корабль 7КТ	Орбитальный блок ДОС — Модернизированный агрегатный отсек — Транспортный корабль 7КТ

Экипаж, чел.	2–4	Среднесуточная мощность СБ	
Время полета орбитального блока, сут,		(в зависимости от положения орбиты	
не более	180	и ориентации станции), кВт	1–3
Общее время пилотируемого полета,		Длина орбитальной станции	
обеспеченного запасами СОЖ,		(с 2 кораблями), м	28,55
при экипаже 2 чел., сут	95–110	Максимальный диаметр орбитального	
Время полета одного транспортного корабля		блока станции, м	4,15
в составе станции, сут	5–60	Общая масса станции	
Параметры орбиты:		(после стыковки 2 кораблей), т	~32
высота, км	350	Масса научно-исследовательской и	
наклонение, ...°	51,6	экспериментальной аппаратуры, т,	
Точность ориентации, ...':		не более	2,5
в орбитальной системе координат	~30–50	Выделяемые транспортные корабли:	
в инерциальной системе координат		для стыковки со стороны ПХО	№ 39, 40
(с использованием АО-1 или С-2)	~10–20	для стыковки со стороны АО	№ 41, 42

From the author's archives.

This drawing shows a slightly unusual configuration of the third-generation DOS station, one with two docking ports. The first third-generation station was flown as *Salyut-6*, launched in late 1977. This image shows the basic station with one Soyuz 7K-T transport ship docked on each end. The spacecraft docked to the right is docked to an extra "Modernized Equipment Compartment" that was never used in the flight version. The legend below the drawing provides some basic statistics on the station. These included crew size (2–4), maximum flight time of the station (180 days), average stay of a two-person crew (95–110 days), time of stay of a transport ship at the station (5–60 days), and orbital parameters (350 kilometers at 51.6° inclination).

completely permissible. Based on simulation results, a deviation of up to 4° is permissible. However, at just 1 meter from the station, with all systems functioning completely normally, the cosmonauts' conditioned reflexes of ground training let them down. The simulator did not have an exact replica of the station's image in the optical sight's field of vision when the vehicle's axis deviated by more than 1°. The cosmonauts perceived the image that they saw at a range of 1 meter when there was a 2° deviation as the "station's belly"—they reported this to the ground, halted the final approach process, backed up from the station, and tried twice to perform docking manually, after shutting down *Igla*. Both docking attempts failed because the cosmonauts had not been able to adequately perceive the real situation. At TsUP they quickly realized that the fuel allocated for docking had been entirely consumed. There was only enough left for descent. It's true, they still had the "emergency supply" (NZ) in the so-called backup system—but that was the last chance in case the main system deorbit burn system failed.[44]

Flight director Yeliseyev made the decision to prepare the vehicle for landing. However, after three final manual approach attempts, the vehicle had not received the backout pulse stipulated in the logic of the shut-down automatic system. And over the course of three orbits, the Soyuz was dangerously close to the station. The threat of collision was quite real. A dynamic backout would require the consumption of fuel, reducing the guaranteed supply for return to Earth. Ultimately the upper atmosphere slowed down the station after all, and the vehicle backed out to a safe distance. The crew safely returned to Earth without having fulfilled its main mission.[45]

IN 1974, OPERATIONS BEGAN at the Mission Control Center (TsUP) on the outskirts of Moscow. It was built for the Apollo-Soyuz project. In the fall of 1977, a new station—*Salyut-6* (DOS No. 5)—was controlled from the new TsUP. Regular long-duration piloted flights began with this station. The flight control service was reorganized. Instead of a quasi-guerrilla mob similar to the Cossack army, made up of several hundred specialists "from various tribes" who came out to the Black Sea, a professional service emerged with an efficient structure of responsibility and a division of functions among stations, vehicles, and shifts.

With great enthusiasm, Aleksey Yeliseyev completed the creation of the professional flight control service, which Tregub had begun. Yeliseyev deserves the credit for developing the efficient structure on the basis of a single authority and strict responsibility during flight preparation and throughout the flight. The Main Operations Control Group (GOGU), as a temporary interdepartmental command organization, gradually evolved into a permanent and professional one. Since 1974, GOGU has been run by a flight director who was a cosmonaut and representative of TsKBEM (subsequently NPO Energiya). The first was Aleksey Yeliseyev. In 1986, Valeriy Ryumin replaced him in this post, and from 1988 until the present, Vladimir Solovyev has directed the service.[46]

The first generation of control specialists remembered the control center in Yevpatoriya as paradise lost. The Black Sea, kilometers of wild, sandy beaches,

---

44. NZ—*Neprikosnovennyy zapas.*

45. *Author's note*: A. S. Yeliseyev provides a detailed description of this event in his book *Zhizn kaplya v morye* [*Life Is a Drop in the Sea*] (Moscow: Aviatsiya i kosmonavtika, 1998).

46. These three men were all veteran civilian cosmonauts from the cosmonaut detachment of NPO Energiya. Valeriy Viktorovich Ryumin (1939–) was appointed to become flight director of *Salyut-7* operations on 1 January 1982. He became a deputy general designer at NPO Energiya on 5 June 1986 and simultaneously became flight director of *Salyut-7* and *Mir* operations. Vladimir Alekseyevich Solovyev (1946–) became flight director of *Mir* operations in April 1988.

the steppe covered with scarlet poppies in the spring, inexpensive dry wine, grapes, melons, fruits, the caressing sea breeze—all of this Crimean romanticism has faded into the past.

The powerful computers of the new TsUP in suburban Moscow processed telemetry virtually in real time during a communication session and delivered it in an intelligible form to the specialists' screens. On his own screen, the shift flight director could call up any parameter and any information having to do with navigational and ballistic flight support or the status of an on-board system.

The new mission control center was built in response to a special resolution of the Central Committee and USSR Council of Ministers. The state did not scrimp on the construction and outfitting of the facilities, which by the creators' design was supposed to surpass similar American centers in all aspects.

Ustinov personally supervised the construction of the new TsUP. The NIPs in Yevpatoriya and Simferopol were under the dominion of the Ministry of Defense. Originally, they intended to make TsUP in Podlipki an independent organization of the ministry, but eventually they put the director of TsNIImash in charge of it. Afanasyev, Tyulin, and Mozzhorin devoted exclusive attention to the creation of TsUP. We had grown accustomed to the rather shabby service facilities at the firing ranges and at the Ministry of Defense's control centers. The palatial splendor of the new TsUP, in particular the part that had been built especially for the Apollo-Soyuz project, astonished us because it was so different.

The marble steps covered with Kremlin-style carpet runners, colorful stained-glass windows; a mosaic wall bearing the likenesses of Tsiolkovskiy, Korolev, and Gagarin; numerous offices with upholstered furniture, televisions, and an abundance of telephones; an amphitheater with visitors' seating; a separate hall for the State Commission; the Blue Hall for meetings and press conferences; offices for the chief designer and flight director; lounges for the top brass; a separate grand entrance; a buffet bar for foreigners; maximum-security guards allowing admission according to a roster—at first all of this bore heavily on the psyches of the control specialists, who were accustomed to freewheeling Yevpatoriya.

The "Indian Shrine" was the term used to refer to that part of TsUP designed to impact the psyche of American guests.

"We didn't use as much marble as they did in the Taj Mahal, but in terms of the amount of plastic and aluminum oxidized to look like copper and gold, we surpassed it by far," boasted Mozzhorin.

It seemed that we were now armed, equipped, and organized so that we would be able to easily overcome any off-nominal situations. But a human being was still a human being. In the new spacecraft and station control loop built using state-of-the-art science, the human being, as one of the links in this loop, retained to right to make mistakes.

ON THE OCCASION OF THE 25TH ANNIVERSARY of the flight control service, *A Brief Course on the History of the Flight Control Service* was published. This document shows that the directors of the service had not lost their sense of humor, which is so essential to a modern human being.[47] The *Brief Course* says that before each regular expedition, public Party-Komsomol meetings were supposed to be held. Without these meetings it was considered generally dangerous to begin any serious business whatsoever. Vladimir Ivanovich Volkov, the Party Committee Secretary at the complex, giving instructions to prepare for such a meeting, said, "We will hold the usual Party-Komsomol prayer service asking that victory be bestowed on us...."

At these meetings the chiefs of all the groups solemnly promised to make every effort and not dishonor the control service. For example, usually when Arkadiy Sudachenko finished his speech he loudly pronounced, "The analysis group will fulfill its assignment!" and quietly added, "If there are no off-nominal situations."

The new magnificent TsUP didn't save us from off-nominal situations. On 19 April 1982, the *Salyut-7* orbital station (DOS No. 5-2) went into space. Seven expeditions visited it until 1985. Seven piloted vehicles approached and docked with *Salyut-7*, and 10 Progress cargo transport vehicles did so in purely automatic mode.[48]

Analyzing the causes of the off-nominal situations, we realized that an on-board computer could save us a lot of headaches. The simplest on-board computer could shut down

The *Salyut-7* was launched in 1982 and hosted seven long-term expeditions between 1982 and 1985.

From the author's archives.

---

47. The title of the publication (*Kratkiy kurs istorii sluzhby upravleniya poletami*) was a play on the infamous *A Brief Course on the History of the Communist Party of the Soviet Union (Bolsheviks)* published at the height of Stalinism in 1939.

48. The Progress spacecraft (7K-TG) was a cargo variant derived from the original ferry version of the Soyuz (7K-T). A total of 13 Progress vehicles visited *Salyut-7*. These were *Progress-13* (1982) through *Progress-24* (1985) plus *Kosmos-1669* (in 1985).

the system when there were manual control errors such as those that Beregovoy committed. Propellant would be preserved, and it would be possible to repeat the approach in a purely automatic mode.

In the off-nominal situation described above on *Soyuz-15*, an on-board computer could have recognized the target and issued *Igla*'s commands corresponding to the actual range or could have shut down the system and made it possible for the ground to decide what further actions to take.

Actually, an on-board computer supplementing an already well-mastered "computer-free" control system was inefficient. It was much more tempting to develop a fundamentally new system in which the on-board computer was not an appendage, but a main link making it possible to solve control problems on a qualitatively new basis; to create a system that was considerably more reliable. They decided to implement this idea on a modification of the Soyuz vehicle (factory index 7K-S, drawing number 11F732). The 7K-S transport vehicles, which were designed to deliver crews to orbital stations and were intended to replace the 7K-T (Soyuz), were assigned the index number 7K-ST. During their flight testing, which began in 1974, the first five unpiloted vehicles were called Kosmoses. The revolutionary leap in technology for controlling these vehicles made it possible to produce the strapdown inertial navigation system. The on-board digital computer was given the task of mathematically simulating the vehicle's orientation and motion. Position sensors—infrared verticals and Sun trackers—were retained for the preliminary "setting" and correction of the mathematical model. The main sensitive elements, the data from which underwent numerical integration, were digital angular rate sensors and accelerometers.

Branets, Shmyglevskiy, and the young enthusiastic MFTI graduates who joined them began developing the idea behind the system in Legostayev's department in 1968. MFTI graduate Mikhail Chertok was among them. The final decision to install a strapdown system, among other innovations on this modification of the Soyuz, wasn't made until 1972, when we were confident that we could series-produce an on-board digital computer. It took six years from the beginning of development until the first unpiloted flight of the new computer-controlled vehicle! The launch of the first 7K-S No. 1L spacecraft, called *Kosmos-670*, didn't take place until 6 August 1974. Flight testing of another four unpiloted Kosmoses—*Kosmos-772*, *Kosmos-869*, *Kosmos-1001*, and *Kosmos-1074*—lasted five years![49]

Finally, on 16 December 1979, 7K-ST No. 6L lifted off. It was referred to publicly as *Soyuz-T*. The unpiloted spacecraft in automatic mode approached

---

49. The first three (*Kosmos-670*, *Kosmos-772*, and *Kosmos-869*) were 7K-S variants. The final two (*Kosmos-1001* and *Kosmos-1074*) were 7K-ST variants.

and docked with the *Salyut-6* station, executed joint flight for 100 days, and safely returned to Earth.

However, the first attempt at automatic docking using the on-board digital computer misfired. It wasn't so much that the computer was capricious, but that it "threw a fit" as a result of the disregard that the "ground" showed for its character. They had loaded a regular self-check algorithm into the computer's program. It set up the test itself in order to "go to work" being confident that it was "spruced up" and ready to go. This test lasted just 5 seconds. TsUP began to enter the program assignment for approach right after switching on, during these very sacred 5 seconds. The next day, 19 December 1979, they took into account the computer's caprice, and the automatic docking of the unpiloted *Soyuz T* spacecraft with the *Salyut-6* station took place without incident.

In May 1980, cosmonaut No. 2, German Titov, as deputy chief of TsUKOS, issued a finding that cleared the 7K-ST vehicles for piloted flight.[50] The first flight-control computer thus received its ticket to space signed by Earth's second cosmonaut, General German Titov.

Finally, on 5 June 1980, 12 years after the beginning of development, 7K-ST No. 7L (*Soyuz T-2*) lifted off with cosmonauts Yuriy Malyshev and Vladimir Aksenov on board—the first testers of the new spacecraft. For reasons unknown, the unpiloted version successfully executed approach and docking, while more often than not in piloted flight during the final approach segment they ended up terminating automatic mode and requiring human intervention. At a range of around 200 meters from *Salyut-6*, the approach-monitoring program loaded into the on-board digital computer's memory generated an emergency message and switched off the digital control loop. TsUP gave the cosmonauts permission for manual control of final approach. A ground investigation of what

Борт
космического корабля „ Союз-22"
15-23 сентября 1976г.
From the author's archives.

NPO Energiya cosmonaut Vladimir Aksenov inscribed this picture of himself while he was in space during his *Soyuz-22* flight in 1976.

---

50. TsUKOS—*Tsentralnoye upravleniye kosmicheskikh stredstv* (Central Directorate of Space Assets)—was the official name of the Soviet "space forces."

took place showed that the computer was performing dynamic monitoring of the approach parameters and predicting their changes. The computer prognosis differed from the actual motion. Consequently, the computer decided that the process was abnormal, issued an "emergency" command, and shut down the automatic control system. The computer was not the culprit. It was a human error, this time committed by representatives of a new profession—programmers. The control algorithms required a greater rendezvous velocity than was actually the case.

It was mandatory that any changes in the drawings of a rocket, of a spacecraft, or in electrical circuits be documented in "change notices." Depending on the causes and consequences, these notices had to be signed by the authors, managers, lead designers, and—in acute situations—the chief designer, too.

Changes in the software, on the other hand, could lead to much more significant consequences than changes in the electrical circuitry or design. For the design and circuitry, there were sets of drawings and technical documentation, which were accounted for in accordance with all the stringency of state standards. The originals were stored in archives, and each change was strictly recorded in accordance with the rules of technical documentation management. Something intangible, unaccounted, incomprehensible—software—broke into this strict order, which had been in place practically since the times of the artillery of Peter I.

This prompted some heated conversations between Yeliseyev's and Legostayev's services.

"We must train the TsUP operators and cosmonauts using documents that are accounted for—drawings, diagrams, descriptions—which exist for all the vehicle's systems," Yeliseyev said. "But when it comes to motion control, they tell us that now we need to study algorithms and programs rather than instruments. We are prepared to do this, but show them [to us]. It turns out that in the best-case scenario they are in the developers' notebooks, and each one of these idea men is storing all the changes in his own memory. That's fine if the person isn't off on a business trip or on vacation, and without him no one can remember the 'patch'." These were more or less the completely valid grievances that Yeliseyev mentioned to me.

It took two years before some order was brought into this system. During the first years of on-board digital computers, the authors of algorithms and programs were themselves the record-keepers and executors of changes introduced into the computer memory. There were a lot of arguments, turmoil, and all sorts of incidents associated with this. Software was supposed to be updated, supplemented, and improved based on observations after each flight. *Soyuz T-3* and *Soyuz T-4* had been launched to *Salyut-6*, and *Soyuz T-5* launched to *Salyut-7*. The computer on *Soyuz T-6* once again decided to give notice that it was high time to bring strict order to the data that the whiz-kid programmers were using to try to "train" it. Cosmonauts Vladimir Dzhanibekov, Aleksandr Ivanchenkov, and Frenchman Jean-Loup Chrétien flew on the *Soyuz T-6* launched on 24 June 1982. Dozens of correspondents and foreign guests, including the French ambassador and his diplomatic entourage, filled the visitors' gallery at TsUP. There was no need to say anything about our brass. After all, the first Frenchman in the history of cosmonautics was being launched into space on a Soviet spacecraft.

I was at TsUP following the course of the approach process on the monitors with those directly participating in this crucial historic event. Groups of approach and docking specialists had moved their workstations out of the main control room into a separate room on the second floor so that they wouldn't disturb others and others wouldn't disturb them. The crew switched on the automatic approach mode during the 17th orbit after executing the two-burn maneuver prescribed by the ballistics experts for the vehicle to make a safe entry into *Igla*'s coverage zone.

At 2009 hours, the first information appeared on the monitors: "Target availability signal received; range 11.4 kilometers; approach velocity 18 meters per second." Ten minutes later the on-board digital computer requested crew permission to execute a braking burn. The crew gave permission from its console. After that the computer acted according to the algorithm loaded into its memory, in concert with the information received from *Igla*. Upon receiving its commands, the *Chayka* control system turned the spacecraft's pitch by 90° and fired the engine to reduce the line-of-sight angular rate to zero. Now it executed a reverse turn to put the spacecraft into the initial state and then to swing around to fire a second correcting burn.

At 2026 hours, at a range of 1.4 kilometers, they began the second turn in the yaw angle. Meanwhile, the lock-on mode strayed. The *Igla* antennas were unable to maintain lock-on at wide angles. But the on-board digital computer kept this in mind. Upon receiving the computer's command, the engine fired at a range of 960 meters. The approach velocity slowed to 3.3 meters per second. The computer did not "forget" to issue the command for a turnaround. In so doing, communication was restored via *Igla*.

"So that's how we rendezvous now!" someone standing behind us marveled, with bad timing. "Remember, in Yevpatoriya we only found out from the films that the SKD had fired 20 times for approach. And now all it takes is two burns."

"Quiet!" blurted out someone at an adjacent monitor, where *Igla* specialists were sitting.

While turning around, the spacecraft turned its "nose," i.e., its docking assembly, toward the station. During the turn, at 2028 hours, the telemetry struck the nerves of everyone sitting in hushed silence at the monitors: "The first block of DUSes is shut down! Backup activated…. Backup block of DUSes is shut down! *Chayka* digital circuit shut down. *Igla* shut down!"

"Look what comes from nostalgia for Yevpatoriya," I sighed, stunned by what had happened.

Twenty-five degrees were left until the turn was completed. The spacecraft's angular motion continued due to inertia. Flight management at TsUP was in shock for several seconds. But it was as if the crew had just expected this. Without any hesitation, Dzhanibekov switched on the backup analog manual control loop. Just 25 seconds passed after the "accident," which was displayed simultaneously on board the spacecraft and on the monitors in the TsUP control rooms. Dzhanibekov saw the DOS on the screen of his optical sight and calmly halted the spinning of the spacecraft. According to the radio coverage conditions, right at that time KIK lost communication with the vehicle for 10 minutes.

At the most tense moment a special messenger ran in: "They're asking for Yeliseyev to report to the State Commission!"

Yeliseyev gave Legostayev, Branets, and me a questioning look.

"*Igla* was operating normally according to all parameters all the way up until it shut down," Suslennikov managed to say.

I made the following recommendation: "In 3 minutes the vehicle will appear in the coverage zone. We'll go downstairs to the communications room and make a joint decision there. It's not right to summon a commander from the field of battle in a critical situation. Pass that on to the chairman of the State Commission."[51]

At 2036 hours, the spacecraft entered the coverage zone. It was just 100 meters away from the station. The crew very calmly reported that everything was fine and requested permission to perform manual docking. Permission was immediately granted. Docking proceeded without a hitch. During the following orbit the crew entered the DOS. There was thunderous applause from the guests in the balcony. Flashbulbs popped as the latest triumph of Soviet cosmonautics and the traditional friendship with the people of France was recorded for history. Our top brass didn't have time to realize what had actually happened. The French guests smiled happily.

While the large throng of brass and distinguished guests congratulated one another and those who had absolutely nothing to do with it, the true experts and culprits huddled around the consoles, not sharing the general jubilation,

---

51. The chairman of the State Commission was Kerim Kerimov.

trying to grasp what had happened. Vadim Kravets, who was in charge of the analysis group in Yevpatoriya, congratulated me for the brilliant docking and pointed to Mikhail Chertok, who had retreated into himself.

"I thought that I had done a good job learning the signs that are quick tip-offs to off-nominal situations in the behavior of *Chayka*. If Mikhail Chertok is silently scratching his beard it means that he understood everything. There were no failures. This is the latest mathematical discrepancy in the program."

Evidently, Branets also knew that pensive scratching of the beard is a sign of enlightenment. Mikhail began to explain to him in a deliberate manner and drew something on his notepad.

"Despite the happy ending, the State Commission demands my explanations," said Yeliseyev, who had joined us. "What shall I report?"

"Report that there were no failures in the system," advised Branets. "There was a glitch in terms of tolerances for runtime check. The crew was well trained; it executed manual approach perfectly. We're looking into the details on our test stand, and we'll report in the morning."

There was no need for prolonged investigations of the "French off-nominal situation."

After conducting an investigation according to the service hierarchy, Branets reported, "The program algorithm for the runtime check had values for angular rates for each of the three axes loaded into it. Rendezvous required two correction burns. In so doing, the vehicle is turned at angles that are optimal for propellant consumption. After issuing the command to fire the attitude-control engines for a turn, the computer monitors the vehicle's angular rotation rate relative to its center of mass. The angular rate depends on the operating time of the attitude-control engines and the moments of inertia relative to the corresponding axis. The computer knows the engine's operating time, and the ratio of the angular rate to the inertial moment is loaded into the algorithm."

In this case, the angular rates during the turns exceeded the tolerance. The computer interpreted this as a failure of the angular rate sensors and switched from the first set to the second. But the second set also showed rates that did not correspond to the design values. Then, according to the runtime check algorithm, the digital (i.e., computerized) control loop was shut down. This happened at a range of 800 meters.

Soyuz-T vehicles have a backup analog manual control loop. At the initiative of Dzhanibekov and our manual control specialists, the crew had preliminary training for approach using this loop at a range up to 1,500 meters. Therefore, as soon as the computerized loop "failed," Dzhanibekov switched on the backup, took over control—and docking took place at the calculated time.

As far as root causes were concerned, the computer was not to blame. The culprit was a telephone connection between the planners and our dynamics specialists. The actual moments of inertia of this specific spacecraft differ from those that our dynamics specialists used to calculate the angular rate values. Instead of having official, accounted-for documents, they received the information over the telephone.

After our circle of control specialists had pored over how much the values of the actual center-of-mass characteristics had deviated from the design values loaded into the runtime check program and received assurances that now everything would be corrected, I then had to brief the general designer on the causes of the incident. To my astonishment, instead of reacting to the incident with the anticipated and completely understandable outrage, Glushko dealt with it very calmly but was meticulously interested in the mathematical operations that the on-board digital computer received in order to predict the angular rates that depended on the duration of the attitude-control engines' burn. A calm conversation resulted in the following instructions: announce orders that stringently stipulate the requirement to issue, before each launch, an archived calculation, in which the center-of-mass coordinates and moments of inertia will correspond to the actual vehicles and crews, rather than to designs from three years before.

"It was quite difficult for us to establish a weight discipline," Glushko said, "and we even strictly monitor the cosmonauts' weight. But I didn't think that you had tasked the computer to monitor the moments of inertia. All the planners must understand what parameters are involved in the field of computer monitoring and bear responsibility for their authenticity."

The *Soyuz-T* crew proved that it was possible to perform docking using manual control from a range of around 1,000 meters. However, subsequently, the initial conditions did not always favor such a happy ending. *Soyuz T-8*, carrying cosmonauts Vladimir Titov, Gennadiy Strekalov, and Aleksandr Serebrov, lifted off on 20 April 1983. After insertion, the traditional all-systems test was performed, including the *Igla* rendezvous radio system. During this process, it was determined that *Igla*'s main gyrostabilized pencil-beam antenna was unable to assume the necessary position. All of the experts agreed that the antenna control mechanism had jammed. To avoid aborting the docking, TsUP formed a team that worked through the night and came up with an automatic rendezvous control procedure based on prediction without using *Igla* until the range was no more than 1 kilometer and then switching over to manual mode. After the completion of the automatic rendezvous using the scenario the team had developed, the range was 3 kilometers. Exercising discipline, the crew waited 30 minutes for instructions from TsUP. Finally, TsUP made its decision and granted permission for manual approach.

Fifteen minutes later, the spacecraft approached to a range of around 200 meters from the station. Precisely at that moment, the vehicle and station entered

Earth's shadow. In the darkness the crew managed to avoid collision, "diving" under the station. After emerging from the shadow, the *Soyuz T-8* once again was 3 kilometers from the station. Calculations showed that the remaining propellant reserves were insufficient for new attempts at approach. After being briefed, the State Commission made two decisions: to have *Soyuz T-8* return to Earth and to form the latest accident investigation commission to determine the causes for the failure of the *Igla*. Once again I found myself in the thankless role of chairman.

Our commission succeeded in reproducing the mechanical jamming of *Igla*'s gyrostabilized antenna, having resorted to a "foreign object" scenario. We supposed that a wayward nut or something of that ilk floating freely in weightlessness under the housing of the drive mechanisms had gotten into the works. In this connection we recalled Mnatsakanyan's sensational declaration at the collegium of ministers: "Flying with *Igla* is tantamount to death!" But we didn't have *Kurs* yet, and we had to fly. Until we had *Kurs*, our commission recommended to the ballistics and approach dynamics specialists that, "just in case," they develop an approach procedure in the event of a complete radio system failure, so that it wouldn't be necessary to improvise at the last minute. The recommendation was accepted for implementation.

The team of Legostayev, Branets, Degtyarenko, Borisenko, Bragazin, and Semyachkin, unique in terms of its concentration of intellectuals, acquired an inventor's certificate for a rendezvous method to be used in the event of the failure of the radio system that measures relative motion parameters. Special algorithms were introduced into the software of the on-board digital computer. In combination with the crew's actions, this made it possible to substantially increase the probability of rendezvous with the station in the event of the failure of the on-board radar.

"It bodes ill that you came up with this," someone at the next meeting of our accident investigation commission said to the inventors. "Now in addition to failures of *Igla* or *Kurs*, we'll have to figure out why your procedure failed."

A YEAR AND A HALF LATER THE NEW TECHNOLOGY came in handy to save the *Salyut-7* orbital station. The story of the "clinical death" and resuscitation of *Salyut-7* serves as a classic example, it would seem, of a small human error in the control loop and, subsequently, the truly heroic actions of people involved in another large control loop to eliminate the catastrophic consequences of this error.

On 2 October 1984, a crew made up of Leonid Kizim, Vladimir Solovyev, and Oleg Atkov departed the station.[52] Temporarily, the *Salyut-7* station

---

52. This was the *Soyuz T-10* crew.

remained in unpiloted mode and peacefully drifted in near-Earth space. The calm mode, which generated no interest in the press, the lack of a crew that might "do" something and require constant attention on the ground—all of this dulled the sense of vigilance of the personnel involved in the large control loop at TsUP. This sort of tranquility in space is deceptive.

On 11 February 1985, at the end of the watch of the latest shift at TsUP, telemetry reported that current protection in the on-board complex control system had been tripped, shutting down the first, primary radio transmitter of the long-range radio communication system. It was an unpleasant incident, but far from an emergency. Unit S-190, stuffed with long-range radio communication system (DRS) equipment, housed two identical transmitters. It also contained receivers and decoders receiving commands from Earth.

Once the radio system automatics had perceived the failure of the primary transmitter, it switched on the second—the backup. The shift that was on duty at TsUP was not surprised after discovering the automatic switch to the backup transmitter. It was well known that the set of radio instruments had exhausted its service life and had the moral right to one failure that would not lead to the failure of the whole system. A cargo transport vehicle had previously delivered the spare set that was on board. The crew of the upcoming expedition was supposed to replace the spent S-190 set with the new one.[53]

The shift recorded the unremarkable incident (compared with the scales of other space incidents) in the flight log with the recommendation to call in a specialist on the on-board complex control system (SUBK) from TsKBEM and the DRS specialist from the Scientific-Research Institute of Space Instrumentation Building (NIIKP) in Moscow so that they could analyze the situation together and prepare a report.[54] But meanwhile they decided to work using the second transmitter.

Flight control was conducted from TsUP in four shifts. Each one was on duty for 24 hours. I wasn't able to determine what information the members of that shift, who were hurrying off to get some rest after a sleepless night, passed on to their relief shift members. And that's really just a detail. All we know is that the director of the new shift did not summon or did not wait until the arrival of the specialists, i.e., the SUBK developers responsible for current

---

53. The original slated next crew for Salyut-7, the fourth primary expedition, included V. A. Vasyutin, V. P. Savinykh, and A. A. Volkov. Their backups were A. S. Viktorenko, A. P. Aleksandrov, and Ye. V. Saley.

54. SUBK—*Sistema upravleniya bortovogo kompleksa*; NIIKP—*Nauchno-issledovatelskiy institut kosmicheskogo priborostroyeniya*. The latter was formerly known as NII-885.

protection and the radio complex developers capable of making a diagnosis and giving a report about the shutdown of the primary transmitter.

Subsequent examination determined that in keeping with tradition and the existing procedure, it was the duty of the shift flight director to wait for the specialists (developers of the DRS and SUBK) to show up. After analyzing the telemetry information, having debated with one another, they were supposed to make recommendations as to how to work thereafter, having signed off on the corresponding conclusion in the logbook.

Evidently, the shift director decided "we didn't just fall off the turnip truck." Without waiting for those responsible for the systems, he gave the command to switch on the first DRS transmitter. And really, why not give the first set one more try? Perhaps an accidental actuation of the automatic protection had occurred. And if there really is a malfunction there, that's what the current protection is for—it will trip again. You can reason like that at home if you've blown a fuse. Even a housewife who has seen smoke coming from the television or vacuum cleaner will not count on the reliability of the fuses and risk switching it on again. At TsUP they didn't see whether smoke had appeared on board the DOS. But the actuation of the current protection in itself meant that the strength of the current exceeded the norm by three to five times.

The findings regarding this incident, approved by Oleg Shishkin (deputy minister [at MOM] at that time) and signed by me, Ryazanskiy, Vorshev, and two military representatives, said:

> . . . *3. Analysis of the circuit, design, and operational documenta-*
> *tion, and also the broad experience accumulated during the joint*
> *operation of the DRS and SUBK systems on spacecraft 11F615-A8,*
> *11F615-A12, 11F615-A15, and 17K, showed that the principle*
> *"any one failure in any of the systems must not lead to the failure*
> *of a system" has been fulfilled.*[55]
>
> *4. Failure of the first transmitter of the DRS system, identified*
> *on 02 November 1985 during orbit 16,252, was contained by*
> *the current protection of the SUBK system and did not result in a*
> *failure in the operation of any of the systems. Up until 1320 hours,*
> *51 seconds, all on-board systems were operating normally according*
> *to data from the analysis of telemetry information.*

---

55. These indices denote the following spacecraft: 11F615A8 (Soyuz ferry vehicle, 7K-T), 11F615A12 (Soyuz vehicle for the Apollo-Soyuz Test Project, 7K-TM), 11F615A15 (original Progress cargo vehicle, 7K-TG), and 17K (DOS-class stations).

5. Commands from the ground to reactivate the first transmitter, which came after the actuation of its current protection during orbit 16,252, resulted in the development of a failure process. During orbit 16,254, attempts to switch on the clearly malfunctioning transmitter using a command from the ground resulted in a snow-balling short-circuiting process, as a result of which the integrity of the power circuitry of both transmitters was irreversibly damaged and the operation of the decoders was shut down.

The failure of the decoders, which were installed in the same framework as the transmitters, deprived the station of the ability to receive any commands from Earth. The station went out of control. We were unable to reproduce the "snowballing process" under laboratory conditions with a short-circuiting current of 120 amperes passing through the transmitter because of the ambiguity and randomness of the phenomena. The findings contained the following modest statement: "The failures were confined to the S-190 framework of the DRS system and in the power circuits of the transmitters of instrument BKP of the SUBK system." The short-circuiting current in excess of 100 amperes rapidly discharged the buffer batteries. The voltage of the on-board network fell to the minimum level, at which point the automatic circuit breakers were tripped, shutting down the electric power consumers one after another.

After commands were issued from the ground to reactivate the malfunctioning transmitter, the strength of the current in the power circuit exceeded 100 amperes. Most likely the contacts of the radio transmitter power switch "burned out," the insulation melted, and possibly there was short-circuiting somewhere else "along the way" in the cable network.

There was a weak glimmer of hope that despite the loss of orientation, the station, while turning, would still receive enough energy from the Sun to support the thermal mode to the minimum extent necessary. However, this same "snowballing process" also resulted in the malfunctioning of the sequencer, which at least once per day issued a command to connect the solar arrays to the buffer battery charging circuit. The command to charge the batteries did not get through from the ground or from the on-board sequencer. The system orienting the solar arrays on the Sun ceased to operate. The single power supply system—the on-board electric power station—completely broke down. All the electrical systems, including the thermal mode control assemblies, ceased to function.

The station began to freeze. According to the calculations of the thermal mode specialists, the temperature inside the station would fall to –20°C [–4°F] in a week. The station became a big, useless, artificial satellite, which only the missile defense system's space monitoring facilities could track. *Salyut-7* fell into a state of anabiosis. No ingenious sets of commands sent on board from TsUP were capable of bringing it out of this state.

The station could only be saved by a human being, who after entering the station would disconnect the failed S-190 casing; replace it with a spare, which fortunately was on board the station; replace the cables damaged by the current surge with others brought from Earth; connect a warm storage battery that was also brought along; begin warming up the system; and restore orientation, thermal control, and everything else, including the life-support system.

This repair team would have a lot of work to do. And it was unusual work. But how would a human being get there if the station was silent and the *Igla* rendezvous radio system, among others, also remained without power? This was the full-scale manifestation of Pilyugin's law: "Emergency situations are the strongest impetus for new ideas and the improvement of systems." This was one more of my versions of this law. Against the background of the Americans' success, the loss of the *Salyut-7* orbital station could become one more powerful blow against the Soviet Union's prestige in space.[56] Moreover, there were many costly instruments and materials for science programs on the station. "Save the station no matter what" was the overriding mission that the teams of control specialists set for themselves.

Throughout February [1985] we assessed the degree of possible damage incurred in the station's electrical network and developed measures to reanimate the systems, which inevitably go out of order when exposed to prolonged freezing. Everything that was needed for the repairs and restoration was immediately put to work. The most important thing was still the question, who would fly to the station to revive it and how would they get there? After brief discussions they settled on the plan that Vladimir Dzhanibekov and Viktor Savinykh should be in the primary crew. Dzhanibekov already had experience in manual approach from great distances and was quite familiar with the station.[57] Engineer Savinykh from NPO Energiya was officially considered a specialist in optical sensors and manual orientation systems

---

56. Chertok is probably referring to the many successes of the early Space Shuttle program from 1981 to 1985.

57. Vladimir Aleksandrovich Dzhanibekov (1942–) had, by 1985, flown four orbital space missions, more than any other Soviet cosmonaut. These included *Soyuz-27* (1978), *Soyuz-39* (1981), *Soyuz T-6* (1982), and *Soyuz T-12* (1984). All of these missions had involved docking with Salyut space stations.

From the author's archives.

The *Soyuz T-4* crew of Vladimir Kovalenok and Viktor Savinykh are shown here discussing one of their scientific experiments with A. V. Leventsov.

but actually was highly capable at figuring out all kinds of motion control technology problems.[58]

Three months went into the training of the rescue expedition. During this time they developed the process for the interaction of TsUP with the Ministry of Defense Space Monitoring Service. With unique antenna systems and powerful computers at their disposal, the missile defense service and space monitoring service were able to determine the true orbit of *Salyut-7*. Unlike our space Command and Measurement Complex, they did not need an on-board responder for radio monitoring of the orbit. When we asked them not only to determine the station's orbit, but also to try to measure its angular rotation rate using their powerful resources, they gave a reassuring answer: "Your station is hardly rotating at all!"

Igor Gansvindt explained the theoretical underpinning of the station's seemingly strange behavior. He explained that once the station was deprived of its nominal control system, if it was rotating about its center of mass, it gradually settled down as a result of the effect of gravitational orientation. Thus,

---

58. Viktor Petrovich Savinykh (1940–) had flown aboard *Salyut-6* as part of the *Soyuz T-4* mission in 1981. He had graduated from the Moscow Institute of Engineers of Geodesy, Aerial Photography, and Mapping (MIIGAiK) with a specialization in optical electronic instruments in 1969. He obtained his Candidate of Technical Sciences degree in 1985 on the topic of "Problems of Orientation of Space Vehicles in Earth Orbit."

our ballistics experts had the opportunity to predict the orbital motion of the frozen station and provide the on-board digital computer of the *Soyuz T-13* spacecraft, which was being prepared for the rescue expedition, with baseline data for rendezvous. Algorithms making it possible to predict motion up to a range of 1.5 to 2 kilometers were loaded into the on-board digital computer software of this spacecraft. From a distance of around 5 kilometers the cosmonauts measured the actual range to the station using the LPR-1 manual laser range meter, specially manufactured for this unique flight. Using the LPR-1 measurements, the cosmonauts were supposed to switch to manual rendezvous and final approach from a distance of 1.5 to 2 kilometers.

The *Soyuz T-13* spacecraft lifted off on 6 June 1985. This flight can serve as a model of the excellent combination of the human being as the main link in a large control system with two large man-machine systems. Not only did Dzhanibekov and Savinykh execute approach and docking with the dead station brilliantly, but they also entered it and worked heroically to save it. They succeeded in this completely. Among all piloted flights from the time of Gagarin, this expedition deserves the highest marks for the heroism and professionalism of a human being in space. Radar quickly located the frozen orbital station. The rescue expedition successfully proceeded to the station thanks to a combination of the heroism of the rescuers and the achievements of radio electronics and spaceflight control technology.[59]

I HAVE DISCUSSED A VERY SMALL NUMBER OF OFF-NOMINAL SITUATIONS. It would be good, as a training manual for anyone who works on the problem of "the human being in a large system control loop," to compile a description of the main off-nominal situations in cosmonautics over the past 40 years! I am confident that an analysis of their causes and the methods for eliminating them would be much more useful than dozens of theoretical developments on the subjects of reliability and safety.

Until very recently, striving to "keep in shape," I would show up at Mission Control Center at least an hour before the next docking session of a piloted vehicle or cargo vehicle with the orbital station. They even reserved a seat for me

---

59. Having repaired and resuscitated the station, the crew returned to Earth separately. Dzhanibekov returned to Earth on 26 September 1985 with cosmonaut G. M. Grechko after a 112-day, 3-hour, 12-minute, and 7-second mission. Savinykh remained on board for nearly two more months and returned to Earth with cosmonauts V. A. Vasyutin and A. A. Volkov after a 168-day, 3-hour, 51-minute, and 9-second mission. Vasyutin, Grechko, and Volkov had arrived on board the station in September 1985 in *Soyuz T-14* as part of a "handover" from *T-13* to *T-14*, the first of its kind in the Soviet space program.

in front of a monitor where all the information about the rendezvous process is displayed. Rendezvous and docking continue to be the most complex and crucial process of flight control technology. The availability of reliable on-board computer systems on the station and on spacecraft makes it possible to fully automate this process.

The role of observers and high-level supervisors has been assigned to the multitude of personnel at the Mission Control Center. The ballistics and navigation service of the Mission Control Center calculates all the events of the rendezvous process the day before, and they are loaded into the memory of the on-board computers via radio links in the form of settings. When, as an idle veteran-observer, I occupy the seat prepared for me in the control room, I can compare the design data with the actual data coming in via television and telemetry channels with the help of a geostationary communications satellite with accuracy down to the second.[60] All that's left to do is to anxiously await the "Contact" signal. After the "Contact" signal, Academician Viktor Legostayev, also according to tradition, loudly announces "One less reprimand!" from his seat next to me.[61]

Radio electronic technology has made a qualitative leap. And the people in the control loop have grown much wiser. Now it wouldn't occur to anyone to propose the approach and docking scenario that we saddled Beregovoy with in 1968. And nevertheless, even with the most trouble-free approach process, a vexing feeling will crop up. Russia—the first space power—is unable to transmit information from the spacecraft to TsUP during "silent" orbits just because we don't have a relay satellite like Altair or Molniya. Sometimes we use American geostationary satellites. And all because people in the government control "loop" are not performing their direct functions.

---

60. In its later years, the *Mir* space station complex used the *Altair* (or *Luch*) data relay satellite systems in geosynchronous orbit to relay communications. The system degraded in the 1990s and was no longer in use by 2010, although there are plans to launch two new *Luch* satellites in 2011.

61. Viktor Pavlovich Legostayev (1931–) is a Soviet pioneer of spacecraft control system design. He began his active work career at NII-1 in 1955 working for the famous Boris Rauschenbach and transferred to Korolev's OKB-1 in 1960 when Rauschenbach's whole team moved. Legostayev succeeded Rauschenbach at the design bureau, and until 1989, Legostayev headed the complex in charge of control systems at NPO Energiya. He became a Corresponding Member of the Russian Academy of Sciences in 1997.

Chapter 19
Valentin Glushko, N–1, and NPO Energiya

At the end of the day on 15 May 1974, Pilyugin called me on the Kremlin line.

"Vasiliy Mishin is leaving you. You're going to get a new designer, but this time a general [designer] rather than a chief [designer]."

"Who?"

"Glushko."

I was not surprised and didn't repeat my question. Just two years before, the very same thing happened in the movie *Taming the Fire* [*Ukroshcheniye Ognya*].[1] After the death of the main character of the film (chief designer

From the author's archives.

Boris Chertok with actor Kirill Lavrov (right), who played the role of Bashkirtsev in the movie *Taming the Fire*.

---

1. The movie was released in 1972. Chertok has much to say about the movie later in this chapter.

of rockets Bashkirtsev, in whose character the informed viewer recognized Korolev), chief designer of engines Ognev took his place. The brilliant actor Kirill Lavrov played the role of Bashkirtsev, while Igor Gorbachev played Ognev. In the film, the relationship between Bashkirtsev and Ognev was portrayed with greater warmth than in real life. In this regard, Isayev, who advised the creators of *Taming the Fire* along with me, said that it was simply not possible to show in a film the degree of complexity that really existed in the relationship between Korolev and Glushko.

"Let's make them good friends," he proposed. Daniil Khrabrovitskiy and I agreed.

I wasn't about to grill Pilyugin about how he had learned this sensational news and who had made this decision. Pilyugin had good connections in the Central Committee *apparat*, and he had total confidence in the information he reported. Nevertheless, I didn't dare pass on such earth-shattering news for our staff to any of my close friends.

The next day began with the usual hurly-burly of routine business, testing incidents, production problems and telephone calls to subcontractors, and disruptions of delivery dates. No one knew yet about the change of leadership. There was not a single telephone call "from the top," and no one was summoned.

On the way to the dining hall for our managerial staff I asked Mishin's secretary, "Where's Vasiliy Pavlovich?"

"He's been at the ministry all morning," answered Nina Petrovna.

We all sat wedged around the dining table in silence. Could it be that everyone already knew, as I did, but didn't dare be the first to say anything?

And, even so, I telephoned Pilyugin after lunch to recheck. He was offended.

"So, you don't believe me? Valentin has already consulted with me regarding the N-1. He doesn't want to continue this project. He asked how I feel about shutting down the N-1. I said that I had a lot of production stock for the control system, that I'm responsible for reliability and don't see any reason why we need to halt a project that has thousands of organizations involved in it. I recommend that you not waste any time and call Glushko yourself. I advised him to talk it over with you before he shows up at your firm."

After a minute's hesitation I dialed Glushko's number on the Kremlin line. He was clearly happy to hear from me and asked, "If it's not too much trouble, ride over to my office. I'll be waiting."

From many years of personal dealings with Glushko, from the stories of his close associates, based on the complexities of the relationship between Glushko and Korolev and his blatant dislike for Mishin, I knew that this man's nature was far from "sugar and spice." How was he going to behave himself when he was in charge of a staff where the memory of Korolev was sacredly cherished and where Vasiliy Mishin had already been in charge for more than eight years?

On the road to Khimki, in my mind I ran through convincing arguments in defense of the N-1 that I would tell Glushko in our meeting. But would he want to listen? Ultimately, it wasn't a minister or the VPK that would have to make such a decision, but the Politburo. Glushko knew how to show exceptional perseverance. This was well known. If he had ventured to mention the idea of shutting down the N-1 project to Pilyugin, then very likely he had already spoken with Keldysh, and perhaps with Ustinov as well.

In searching for the entrance gates to the grounds of OKB-456 (now KB Energomash), I relied on my memory. More than 30 years earlier I had worked briefly on these grounds at Factory No. 84. Beginning in 1939, this factory had been working on mastering the production of Douglas DC-3 twin-engine passenger airplanes. These airplanes were put into series production on the basis of a license purchased from the Americans and were called PS-84s—after the factory number. Vladimir Myasishchev was in charge of reworking the American drawings and converting inches into millimeters until mid-1938 when he was arrested as a political prisoner and he once again ended up working under Tupolev, who had also been arrested and sent to the NKVD's forced labor *sharashka* known as TsKB-29.[2] Consequently, the airplane had no chief designer. In 1942, the aircraft was assigned the designation Li-2 for the surname of the chief engineer of Factory No. 84, Boris Lisunov.

I first passed through the factory entryway in late 1939, on my way to the OKB of Chief Designer Viktor Bolkhovitinov. In those days there was no rocket technology here. Bolkhovitinov's OKB soon moved out of Factory No. 84 to Factory No. 293, built right here in Khimki. Factory No. 84 got rid of Bolkhovitinov's bothersome planners, who proposed ideas for airplanes that were too original and interfered with the series production of the American Douglas DC-3.[3]

I, a Moscow Power Engineering Institute diploma student, had reached an agreement with Bolkhovitinov for the development of electrical equipment with an alternating current system for a brand-new bomber airplane. A year later I defended a classified diploma with distinction and came to work for Bolkhovitinov, who had already moved to Factory No. 293. However, officially

---

2. The NKVD was a precursor of the KGB. In the late 1930s and through World War II, it operated a set of prison camps where incarcerated designers and scientists worked on specific military and civilian engineering projects. The most famous of these was known as TsKB-29 and headed by the Soviet aviation designer Andrey Nikolayevich Tupolev. For the most well-known account of the Tupolev *sharashka*, see L. L. Kerber, *Stalin's Aviation Gulag: A Memoir of Andrei Tupolev and the Purge Era*, ed. Von Hardesty (Washington, DC: Smithsonian Institution Press, 1996).

3. For Chertok's description of work at Bolkhovitinov's design bureau, see Chertok, *Rockets and People, Vol. I*, Chapters 9 through 13.

I went to work at Bolkhovitinov's OKB, passing through the entryway of Factory No. 84. Valentin Petrovich Glushko had been in charge here since 1946. Aircraft production had been shut down. The factory was converted into the largest firm in Europe involved in the development and manufacture of liquid-propellant rocket engines (ZhRD).[4]

Once again I looked around the grounds for the building housing the office of the chief designer, who would be my new boss. True, this time rather than standing in line at the access control office, I drove through the gate in my service vehicle. Without a hitch the secretary invited me into Glushko's office. For the first time I looked at Glushko as my future boss, and not as an esteemed subcontractor of Korolev.

It seemed to me he looked younger [than his age] when he quickly stood up and came out from behind his large desk to greet me. A scarcely discernible reserved smile lit up the regular and fine features of his face. In his splendidly fitting suit and tie of matching austere color, his whole slim figure radiated amiability and calm assurance.

"I haven't thrust myself on you in Sergey Pavlovich's place," said Glushko. "But we are obliged to comply with the Politburo's decision. As soon as the minister's order is issued, I will come over to you right away. This could even happen tomorrow. You are one of the leading managers of OKB-1. If I am not mistaken, we first met 30 years ago. Since then our paths have crossed enough times for us to trust one another. I am justified in counting on your help. I have laid down the condition that OKB-1 be merged with OKB-456 and that the new organization be called the Energiya Scientific Production Association (NPO Energiya). The Central Committee agreed with my proposals. I do not intend to meddle with your staff, to bring about a new order. First and foremost, effort needs to be spent on making a transition toward developing a series of new heavy launch vehicles instead of the N-1."

"What does 'instead of' mean?" I couldn't keep quiet.

"This means that work on the current version of the N-1 will be terminated and we will have to quickly develop a series of new launch vehicles with reliable

---

4. Factory No. 84 was originally established in June 1932 in Khimki for the repair of civilian aircraft. This is where Chertok worked briefly. In October 1941, as a result of the Nazi invasion, the factory was evacuated to Tashkent. In April 1942, the Soviet aviation industry established a new factory on the same premises of the old evacuated factory, known as Factory No. 456. The new factory was responsible for repairing military aircraft (such as the Li-2, Pe-2, and TB-3) for the war effort. In January 1946, the factory was made a branch of the design bureau of the famous aviation designer Sergey Ilyushin, but later in the year, in June 1946, all work on the premises was reoriented to the manufacture of liquid-propellant rocket engines. Glushko's wartime team from Kazan moved to the new facility in November and December 1946 to establish OKB-456.

engines. I do not intend to introduce radical changes into the space program. You have taken on big commitments with the orbital stations, spacecraft, and the joint project with the American Apollo—I am going to support this in every way possible; I hope that we have complete mutual understanding there. But you will admit that landing one man on the Moon 10 years after the Americans is stupid. We must have our own permanent base with a rotating team of real scientists on the Moon. To achieve this we need other launch vehicles. Mishin wasn't removed at my initiative, but I do not want to work with him. I hope that he understands this. Everyone else must do his duty responsibly. I hope that you, Pilyugin, Ryazanskiy, and Kuznetsov will support the project. I have already discussed this with each of them."

Glushko said all of this calmly, firmly, and confidently, excluding the very possibility of any doubts.

Nevertheless, I said, "We have developed proposals for a lunar base calling for the use of several N-1s with new reusable engines. We believe that with the same funding that was allocated for N1-L3, the base could be created in four or five years."

"You can't build a lunar base using rotten engines," Glushko interrupted me.

Glushko's attitude toward the subject under discussion and toward his conversation partner could be determined not so much by his words as by his face and eyes. I had learned this back when I met him in Germany. If his face became impenetrable and his eyes glazed over, it was better not to continue the conversation. I shouldn't have mentioned the lunar base to be created using the N-1.

I understood that the conversation was over, I thanked him for his confidence, and we said our good-byes. The entire appointment lasted 20 minutes. After driving away from the KB Energomash grounds, I got the driver confused trying to find the entrance to my former home Factory No. 293, which General Designer Petr Grushin, creator of the antimissile missile, now headed.[5] By some quirk of fate, this took place on the very same grounds where they had designed the first rocket interceptor for German bombers.[6] Now Petr Grushin was producing missiles one after the other—but these were interceptors of American intercontinental ballistic missiles.[7]

---

5. Grushin headed MKB Fakel—*Mashinostroitelnoye konstruktorskoye byuro Fakel* (Torch Machine Building Design Bureau).

6. This is a reference to the BI rocket-plane.

7. Grushin's OKB-2 (later MKB Fakel) developed the V-1000 missile that was part of the System A antiballistic missile system, the first experimental system of its kind. OKB-2 also developed missiles for later antiballistic missile systems, such as the 5V61 for System A-35, the 5Ya27 for the abandoned S-225 system, and the 51T6 exoatmospheric missile for System A-135.

ON 21 MAY 1974, A GOVERNMENT DECREE WAS ISSUED and then a minister's order regarding Glushko's appointment as general designer and director of NPO Energiya. What made 66-year-old Glushko agree with a proposal that dramatically altered his biography as an unadulterated engine specialist? He must have understood that among our staff, where the memory of Korolev was fresh, he would not be met with an enthusiastic reception. He took a lot of risks. The nation's nuclear missile shield depended on his engines. No, he did not abandon his own OKB-456 engine facilities. Glushko retained Energomash, having incorporated it into the new NPO Energiya. For an aspiring, ambitious, and extremely dedicated engineer and scientist, it is possible that this was not a misstep, but the logical conclusion of a dream from his distant youth about interplanetary flights. To become not just another subcontractor, but a general designer of interplanetary rocket-space complexes—how can one turn down an offer like that? I wasn't the only one who decided to help him rather than line up in opposition. Without any sort of collusion, that's what all of Mishin's former deputies thought.

The day after the minister's order came out, Glushko assembled all of the deputies of the chief designer at TsKBEM and laid out his concept for the development of cosmonautics. The N-1 did not have a place in this concept.

On 24 June 1974, Glushko summoned the chief designer of the N-1, Boris Dorofeyev, and asked him to prepare an order calling for the termination of the N-1 project. Dorofeyev refused. Then Glushko composed and signed the order himself. Neither the Council of Chief Designers nor the internal technical management gathered for a meeting beforehand. Dorofeyev's refusal was the only demonstration of public disobedience among the managers at TsKBEM.

Glushko called in an inner circle of planners to develop specific proposals for new launch vehicles. Managers, who associated with them owing to their professional obligations, understood that he was preparing for decisive actions against the N-1. But for thousands of people who had been associated with this "crucial government program" for many years, the order was an unexpected shock. Before the order came out, even my department had maintained the hope that the top managers—Afanasyev, Ustinov, and finally Keldysh—would not allow such a reprisal against the N-1 and would find some sort of compromise.

"Our new boss, it turns out, is a brave man," N-1 patriots in confidence chuckled, literally through their tears. "He, like one of Nekrasov's women, will stop a horse running at full tilt and will go into a burning house."[8]

---

8. Nikolay Alekseyevich Nekrasov (1821–1877) was a famous Russian poet known particularly for his works dealing with Russian peasantry. His work was deeply influenced by his love for his mother, and he expressed much love and empathy for all women in much of his canon.

Actually, it was much more formidable with the stroke of a pen to shut down the N-1 projects under way at hundreds of enterprises than it was to stop a horse. Once such a shutdown occurred, it was necessary to enter "houses" inflamed with rebellion. The protest was particularly intense at the Progress Factory in Kuybyshev and at its branch at the firing range, which was created solely for the sake of the N-1. There they had completed preparation of launch vehicle N-1 No. 8, on which all conceivable measures had been implemented. The most important of these was the installation of the Kuznetsov's newly modified engines. Each of the engines had previously undergone firing tests. Nikolay Kuznetsov's firm had developed a reusable engine, which our engine specialists—Raykov, Yershov, and Khaspekov—had nothing against.

At a meeting in early 1974, Raykov even joked, "Boris Yevseyevich, your KORD specialists are going to be left without a job. At last, Kuznetsov has made the engines so reliable that they don't need KORD."

It took 10 years for Kuznetsov to create a fully reliable engine "from scratch." The new engines also had a new designation. The first four N-1 rockets had engines with the designations 11D51, 11D52, and 11D53—for the first, second, and third stages, respectively. Beginning with No. 8L, engines with the designations 11D111, 11D112, and 11D113 were supposed to be installed.[9]

First and foremost, they revamped the turbopump assembly (TNA). They eliminated flame erosion and the breakdown of the oxygen pump by reducing the axial force on the radial support bearings. They improved the thermal protective coating on the turbines and elements of the oxidizer line, replaced the material of the seals, and improved the startup and shutdown automatics. Rather than a "two-out-of-four" or "two-out-of-six" selective method, a high degree of reliability was ensured by implementing tests of a complex of high-efficiency measurement and diagnostic methods for the analysis of dynamic processes. Bitter experience had taught that not a single defect, even the most insignificant one, should go without investigation, without conducting the necessary measures and subsequent checks under stringent conditions. They conducted 220 firing rig tests on 76 newly modified engines, during which they surpassed the design specifications requirements. Tests confirmed the reliability of repeated startup on 24 engines. On one of the engines they performed 10 firings without overhaul. During repeat firings the processes in the engines remained stable and did not depend on the number of previous startups. Beginning with N-1 No. 8L, each

---

9. The older engines were known as NK-15 (11D51), NK-15V (11D52), and NK-19 (11D53). The newer engines were known as NK-33 (11D111), NK-43 (11D112), and NK-39 (11D113).

series-produced engine that was to be installed on a rocket underwent inspection-sample tests from the batch and firing-acceptance tests; it was then sent to be installed without preliminary reworking.

Our chief engine specialist Mikhail Melnikov, who recently had been considerably more wrapped up in nuclear power problems than liquid-propellant rocket engines, nevertheless found time to keep an eye on the work going on in Kuznetsov's department.

"If five years ago we had had the engines that Kuznetsov has now put into series production, our history would have taken a different turn."

Melnikov expressed this thought having joined Bushuyev and me for an evening stroll along Academician Korolev Street in Moscow when we were discussing Glushko's order to shut down the N-1 project.

"And where were you, our chief engine 'ideologue,' five years ago? Why did you agree to the installation of unreliable engines?" I asked in exasperation. "You and Mishin were both elated that the engine had unique parameters and didn't think about the fact that you also needed to demand unique reliability."

In those days there were a great many such recriminations and conversations on the subject of "What will become of the N-1 now?"

After Glushko's order, a resolution calling for the operations to be halted and financing to be cut off for the N-1 program for the entire industry simply didn't ensue. The Central Committee and VPK *apparat* timidly hinted that this matter still hadn't been studied "at the very top." In order to stop this work, the reason needed to be named, losses needed to be added up, a decision needed to be made to write off five billion rubles of expenditures, and, perhaps, even to name and punish the guilty parties.

"One person guilty of disrupting the program has already suffered," they poked fun at us behind the scenes at VPK. "That's Vasiliy Mishin. After removing him from the job, they're not going to punish him any more. And all of you who are still there, if you raise a ruckus about N1-L3 you might suffer. Think about it, you've got enough work."

Outrage over Glushko's order was vented in crowded smoking rooms, among friends in their free time, and in the offices of managers, for whom in the past few years the N-1 had remained their primary *raison d'être*. Many people found themselves in a ridiculous situation: the staffs of the Progress Factory in Kuybyshev, which was the head factory for the manufacture of the entire launch vehicle, and in raw stock had already reached launch vehicle No. 14; at the M. V. Frunze Motor Factory, which after enormous difficulties had mastered the series production of rocket engines; and at Kuznetsov's OKB-276, which had finally developed reusable engines. The rig tests conducted in Kuybyshev and with particular partiality at NII-229 in Zagorsk proved that as a result of more than a decade of work, the series production of oxygen-kerosene engines, unique in terms of their parameters, had been set up and that these were not just prototypes.

Nikolay Kuznetsov flew to Moscow to meet with his minister, Petr Dementyev. Dmitriy Kozlov spoke his mind in this regard to Deputy Minister Viktor Litvinov, the former director of Progress, and to the minister himself, Sergey Afanasyev.

Several days after Glushko's order came out, I rode over to the ministry. The *apparat* clerks who had been drawn into the planning, coordination of production, and concurrence of recriminations on N1-L3 were in a state of shock. The movement of papers between desks and offices suddenly stopped. That same day I was asked to stop by the VPK. My acquaintances in the Kremlin *apparat* were frankly outraged by the fact that Glushko had allowed himself to issue such an order before the VPK decision came out.

Boris Shchegolkov, one of the old, experienced developers of the aviation industry, who worked in the VPK *apparat*, boasted, "I am the only non-Party person in the VPK *apparat*. They keep me because I know the industry better than the majority of people sitting here and have since before the war."

Shchegolkov didn't conceal his outrage.

"At the beginning of the war at the aviation factory in Moscow we worked almost around the clock. Every single minute was valuable. You yourselves remember: 'Everything for the front, everything for victory!' And suddenly—the order. Shut down production, dismantle the equipment, load it onto special trains, and evacuate to the east.[10] This was unexpected and psychologically difficult to endure. But we didn't simply escape to the east; we had a clear order: immediately upon arrival at the new location, set up airplane production, even if it's in an open field. But what is Glushko allowing himself to do? Simply shut down thousands of machine tool stations like that, and what are you going to start up tomorrow? In the old days heads would roll for stunts like this."

But not a single head rolled. Everyone understood that Glushko would not have decided to issue such an order if he hadn't obtained the minister's consent, and most likely Ustinov's as well. Before he had cooled off after his conversation over the Kremlin line with Glushko, Pilyugin telephoned me.

"I found out from Finogeyev, and he found out from your guys about Glushko's order. Who acts like that? You understand, don't you, that an order

---

10. Because of the Nazi invasion of the Soviet Union in June 1941, over 1,500 Soviet industrial enterprises were evacuated in the summer and autumn of 1941 to the eastern Soviet Union and Central Asia. See Sanford R. Lieberman, "The Evacuation of Industry in the Soviet Union during World War II," *Soviet Studies* 35, no. 1 (January 1983): 90–102.

like that affects all the other firms more than yours? My factory is swamped with orders for the N-1. I've disrupted other projects for the sake of the N-1. What am I supposed to do with tons of instruments and cables? What are you thinking there?"

IT ISN'T OURS TO DIVINE THE FUTURE. But from the future, which becomes the present, we can examine the past. Assessing the behavior of individual people and staffs, one realizes that we really did make history. If during the launch of the first *Sputnik* in 1957 we still did not fully recognize the value of such events, then just five years later—from state leaders and chief designers to thousands of engineers, workers, and soldiers who worked in design bureaus, laboratories, shops, and firing ranges, who to this day remain unknown to history—they understood that they were making history. They understood this just as clearly as a soldier during the Great Patriotic War recognized that he was defending his fatherland and giving up his life, not for foreign, unknown interests, but for his own nation, city, village, and family.

We knew the history that we had made. We tried to plan the future so as to correct the past. Everything in the plans, schedules, and deadlines was broken down year by year, month by month, and day by day. The workday was planned down to the minute. The preparation, launch, and flight of a rocket was calculated and forecast with an accuracy down to tenths of a second. Having been in the recent past, which just yesterday was our future, and once again looking into this future, which has become the past, we, like chess players, felt vexed as a result of our bad decisions and sorted through dozens of options in order to find the one that would bring victory.

My own notes, the stories of friends and acquaintances, and rare authoritative memoirs of that time have corroborated individual events and what at that time seemed like everyday life. Now, looking at my comrades and myself from today's perspective, I realize that we were involved in tremendous achievements. Episodes that had seemed workaday were great events. However, strict standards forbid the historian describing the past from reflecting on the pages of his work. What would have been, if....

However, the majority of people allow themselves to reflect about what would have been if an hour, a day, a month, or a year ago he or she had acted in one way rather than the other. Before beginning the next game, a chess player who has lost a match must thoroughly analyze the preceding game, find his mistake, and finish playing that match with himself proceeding from the assumption that he has made a stronger move.

It is more difficult for a field commander, who knows full well how he must act to prevent his troops from taking a drubbing and to save thousands of lives, but despite his predictions he is ordered "from the top" to act otherwise.

There are many examples of this in Marshal Zhukov's *Remembrances and Contemplations* [*Vospominaniya i razmyshleniya*].[11]

In 1974 we could still turn the tables in the Moon race. Four failed N-1 launches had provided a wealth of experience for the creation of a reliable launch vehicle. In late 1974, preparation was under way for the launch of N-1 No. 8 with new reusable engines, which had undergone technological firing tests (OTI). Hundreds of modifications had been performed on the launch vehicle based on the results of the previous four launches and also devised "just in case...." The future lunar base, the enormous MKBS, the expedition to Mars, the space radio telescopes with antennas hundreds of meters in diameter, and the communications satellites weighing many tons stationkeeping in geostationary orbit—all of this in thoroughly tangible designs was associated with the N-1. Only now did it begin to occur to us that along with the N-1, we were really losing opportunities for interplanetary flight and other less fantastic projects.

Signing the order calling for the termination of the N1-L3 projects, Glushko knew something that we, those involved in this work, didn't know at that time. In early May 1974, Ustinov gathered his inner circle in his office to decide the fate of the N1-L3. They were faced with preparing a verdict, which first needed to be reported to the Politburo and then formalized by a resolution of the Central Committee and Council of Ministers. Keldysh, Smirnov, Afanasyev, Tyulin, Serbin, Komissarov, and Mozzhorin were invited to the meeting. The only "outsider" was Minister of the Aviation Industry Dementyev.

"It's time to tell the Politburo the truth!" said Ustinov as he opened the meeting, each participant of which would have to answer to history for the possible consequences of the decision to be made. Not one of the N1-L3 creators was invited. Mishin's fate had been predetermined. Ustinov didn't invite Nikolay Kuznetsov because it wasn't difficult to surmise his position. Pilyugin, who was the closest of the chief designers to Ustinov back then, might speak out of turn and destroy the assumed unity. Ustinov could disregard the opinion of the military in this case. There were clearly no lunar program enthusiasts among them.

Many years later, Mozzhorin said, "Everyone in attendance spoke in favor of terminating the projects and closing the subject. Keldysh had no serious

---

11. G. K. Zhukov, *Vospominaniya i razmyshleniya* (Moscow: Novosti, 1969). Several updated editions of the memoirs have been published, most recently in 1992. Although not well known in the West anymore, Georgiy Konstantinovich Zhukov (1896–1974) remains the greatest Soviet war hero of the 20th century. He was a career military man who rose through the ranks to become a marshal of the Soviet Union and was one of the most decorated generals in the history of both Russia and the Soviet Union.

science programs in reserve that justified the continuation of expenditures on such a powerful launch vehicle. He believed that the Moon no longer held its previous interest for scientists. As far as Mars was concerned, we needed to develop a reusable space transport system (MKTS) and, with its help, begin construction on a large station in near-Earth orbit."[12]

After Keldysh spoke, everyone, except for Mozzhorin, came out in favor of shutting down operations on the N-1, even Dementyev and Afanasyev. These two ministers should have been frightened by the prospects of terminating work in which tens of thousands of people were involved. These ministers would have to find work for them.

Serbin, who had always been highly favorable towards Chelomey and had protected him, had at least received moral compensation. In due time, Chelomey's project—the super-heavy UR-700 launch vehicle—was shut down because work on the N-1 had already gained so much ground. Smirnov and his deputy Komissarov guessed what Ustinov wanted. Now it was easier and (for each of them personally) safer to shut down the N-1 than to risk continuing operations with unpredictable repercussions. Mozzhorin turned out to be the only one opposed to shutting down N-1 operations. He spoke in favor of continuing the launch vehicle's developmental testing program. Mozzhorin attempted to prove the need for the launch of N-1 No. 8, having alluded to the fact that new reusable engines had been installed on it.

"We are gaining the opportunity to test not just the first, but the second and third stages as well. After the Americans halt operations on the Saturn V, the N-1 will be the only super-heavy launch vehicle of similar class in the world. We must not under any circumstances miss this opportunity."

"And you guarantee that the fifth launch will be a success?" asked Ustinov.

"As you know, only an insurance policy gives full guarantees," Mozzhorin said, recalling Voskresenskiy's favorite aphorism.

For some reason this really infuriated Komissarov.

"Just look how he disrespects all of us. He's sprawled out in the chair and is lecturing us like little boys. I don't think that he has lived up to our hopes as director of the head institute."[13]

Ustinov stopped Komissarov: "Boris Alekseyevich, don't get personal, just go ahead and talk about the technology."

---

12. MKTS was the generic abbreviation Russians used to denote concepts for a next-generation reusable vehicle.

13. This "head institute" was TsNIImash. Mozzhorin directed TsNIImash from 1961 to 1990.

Winding up the meeting, Ustinov said that everyone, except Mozzhorin, had come out in favor of shutting down the project. We needed to prepare a well-reasoned resolution of the Central Committee and Council of Ministers.

"The next morning," Mozzhorin continued his story, "I hadn't yet managed to get into my daily business, when Minister Afanasyev telephoned."

"What are you doing?"

"I'm sitting and thinking, when are they going to take me off the job for what I said yesterday."

Afanasyev's reaction was unexpected: "You were great! You said the right thing," Afanasyev commended.

Someday future generations "sorting out the rubble of our times" will create a film series telling the history of three super-heavy launch vehicles—the Saturn V, N-1, and Energiya. Showing similar shadowy meetings will be just as essential as spectacular frames of launching rockets to understand our anything-but-simple history.

The time had come to let off steam, to discuss the problem of "where are we going?" If not the N-1, then what instead? On 28 June 1974, the minister approved the organization layout of NPO Energiya, in which there was no longer a post for chief designer of the N-1.

At Glushko's recommendation, they inserted chief designer posts for areas of endeavor directly subordinate to him. These chief designers were as follows:

- Yakov Kolyako—for multipurpose heavy launch vehicles;
- Igor Sadovskiy—for reusable transport space systems;
- Yuriy Semyonov—for orbital stations of all designations; and
- Ivan Prudnikov—for the lunar complex.
- Konstantin Bushuyev was appointed director and chief designer of the Apollo-Soyuz project.

In addition to the chief designers, the following posts were directly subordinate to Glushko:

- First Deputy Director and General Designer Yuriy Trufanov
- First Deputy Director and Director of the Factory of Experimental Machine Building Viktor Klyucharev
- First Deputy Director for Reconstruction, Building, and General Matters Georgiy Sovkov
- First Deputy General Designer and Head and Chief Designer of KB Energomash Vitaliy Radovskiy
- First Deputy Director and Head of KB Energomash and Director of the Experimental Factory of Power Machine Building Stanislav Bogdanovskiy
- Deputy General Designer for Coordination and Control Mikhail Khomyakov
- Deputy Director for Safety Anatoliy Kalygin

- Deputy Director for Personnel Georgiy Paukov
- Deputy Director for Flight Testing Support Mikhail Samokhin

Thus, Glushko saddled himself with an enormous load of administrative activity, which he had never liked and for which he displayed no talent. Moving into Korolev's office in Podlipki, Glushko left Khimki and his assistant Mikhail Yaremich. This staff employee of the security services had protected Glushko back in the days of his time in the Kazan *sharaga*—the special prison of the NKVD.[14] He regarded Glushko with a certain reverence. "I try to lessen Valentin Petrovich's burden and protect him from petty everyday and administrative concerns. He doesn't like them and doesn't know how to deal with them," confided Yaremich. Just three years later, Glushko was relieved of his post as director of NPO Energiya, retaining the position of general designer. Vakhtang Vachnadze became director of NPO Energiya in 1977.[15]

The NPO's main scientific design work was concentrated in thematic complexes. All complex managers, including the deputies of the general designer, were subordinate in the structural scheme to NPO Energiya First Deputy General Designer and Director Yuriy Trufanov, who until then had worked as chief engineer of the Third Main Directorate of our ministry.[16] Viktor Legostayev, manager of design and research Complex No. 3 for control systems, and Viktor Kalashnikov, manager of design Complex No. 4, were directly subordinate to me.

Other complexes were under the management of the following:
- Georgiy Degtyarenko—theoretical design;
- Viktor Ovchinnikov—on-board systems;
- Anatoliy Abramov—deputy general designer for the engineering launch site and experimental units;
- Mikhail Melnikov—for on-board power systems;
- Anatoliy Severov—for materials science;
- Anatoliy Rzhanov—for ground experimental testing;

---

14. *Sharaga* was the nickname given to the NKVD-organized prison camps during the Stalinist era. The diminutive *sharashka* is also often used.

15. Vakhtang Dmitriyevich Vachnadze (1929–) served as director of NPO Energiya from 1977 to 1991. Prior to that he had been a senior official at the Factory of Experimental Machine Building (ZEM), the production facility at OKB-1, and then chief of the Third Main Directorate of the Ministry of General Machine Building.

16. The Third Main Directorate at the ministry was the functional department in charge of space projects. Yuriy Nikolayevich Trufanov (1925–2008) had a long and illustrious career, serving at various times at OKB-23 (under Myasishchev) and OKB-52 Branch No. 1 (under Chelomey), at the Ministry of General Machine Building (under Afanasyev), at NPO Energiya (under Glushko), at NPO Lavochkin (under Kovtunenko), and at NPO Molniya (under Gleb Lozino-Lozinskiy).

- Yevgeniy Shabarov—for the preparation and performance of flight testing; and
- Aleksey Yeliseyev—for crew training and flight control.

Dmitriy Kozlov, meanwhile, achieved a complete—not just actual but also official—separation from the center. The independent Central Specialized Design Bureau emerged at the facilities of the TsKBEM branch in Kuybyshev, where Dmitriy Kozlov was named chief designer and head.[17] At the Progress Factory there, a small branch headed by Boris Penzin was spun off from the large one that Kozlov managed.

In order to familiarize my comrades with the new structure, I assembled "triangles" of complexes and departments and gave the following speech: "Korolev was the organizer of OKB-1, which has left its mark in history forever. Mishin transformed OKB-1 into TsKBEM. Both Sergey Pavlovich and Vasiliy Pavlovich were called chief designers. A new government resolution has made Valentin Petrovich Glushko head of our organization. And we have been transformed into the Energiya Scientific-Production Association, for which I congratulate you all and report the most preliminary information about changes in our subject matter and prospects.

"The heavy launch vehicle or launch vehicles will remain in first place. This means new developments in place of the N-1. What will actually become of the N-1, I don't know. I venture only to express my own personal point of view. We've come such a long way that it's cheaper to continue and bring the project to real results than to terminate it. We produced the N1-L3M design. At the end of this year, there is a real chance of launching N-1 No. 8. I am confident that after one or two launches the rocket will begin to fly. Then in three, at the most four, years we will be able to solve two problems: execute a lunar [landing] expedition and establish a lunar base—and thus upstage the Americans. They have terminated their lunar program, and we technically, ideologically, and politically can prove that we are capable of much more.

"The structure even has Chief Designer Prudnikov, who is responsible for lunar vehicle and lunar base designs. For us, there are basically no tasks in this field that are beyond our understanding. We understand full well what we need to do and how. We can solve the engineering, design, and process problems in two or three years. If the N-1 were to begin to fly, then with the two- or three-launch scenario we could land at least three Soviet cosmonauts on the Moon in three years, and in five years—we would have a permanent base there, and you never know, we could invite an American astronaut as a guest. If we try to

---

17. TsSKB achieved complete independence from NPO Energiya on 30 June 1974.

execute this task using new launch vehicles, then add a minimum of eight years to today's date of 1974 and we have 1982. But it will take at least another five to six billion rubles over and above the expenditures for the scenario using the N-1.

"The new structure will contain a new field of endeavor, which has been assigned to Sadovskiy—reusable space transport systems. They are supposed to become the response to the Americans' Space Shuttle. My opinion is that if they really pile this work on us, the lunar problem will go onto the back burner or will be forgotten altogether. The most dangerous thing is if the Americans take up this project in earnest. From the information available, we know that NASA has been working successfully on a specific design for three years now.[18] Our comrades who have visited the United States for the Apollo-Soyuz project have become acquainted with this system. After the Americans officially publicized its main parameters, some young and zealous guys from the Institute of Applied Mathematics (IPM) figured out in advance the possible orbits of the Space Shuttle allowing for possible maneuvers in the atmosphere at 2,000 kilometers clear of ballistic orbit. They scared Keldysh. Keldysh reported to Ustinov, and then to Brezhnev. It turned out that the Space Shuttle, flying far from our borders, having lulled the missile defense (PRO) and air defense (PVO) into a false sense of security, could suddenly execute a maneuver—a 'dash to the north,' and, flying over Moscow, could drop a 25-ton thermonuclear bomb with an explosive yield of at least 25 megatons there.

"I recently had the occasion to attend a meeting where they discussed the matter of whether it was at all worth our while to produce an MKTS in the American version. At this meeting, Valentin Petrovich spoke to the effect that this project would take away so much manpower and resources from us that the lunar programs would be unrealistic. He also said that he feared for the DOS projects.

"To this, Keldysh retorted that, after putting the Space Shuttle into service, the United States might obtain a decisive military advantage in a plan to deliver a preemptive nuclear strike against vitally important objectives on Soviet territory. And if so, then like it or not, we would be forced to develop an analogous system.

"Now, instructions have already been given to prepare a draft resolution for this work. Considering Keldysh's position, I predict that this work will soon be included in our plans, evidently with the participation of the aviation industry.

"Instead of being threatened with the termination of their projects, everyone working on DOSes and Soyuzes is being threatened with an increase in the

---

18. U.S. President Richard M. Nixon formally announced the Space Shuttle program on 5 January 1972.

volume of their work. In a year we will be faced with rendezvous and docking with Apollo.[19] Here, we're betting not simply on the prestige of the Soviet Union, but on our technical and scientific standing at the international level. In addition to these considerations of personal prestige, we need to consider that success in this program could lead to a thaw in the atmosphere of the Cold War. The Americans beat us in the Moon race, and then they drove their own lunar program into a dead end. It's not out of the question that they want to continue together with us.

"Keep in mind that Valentin Petrovich warned me: despite the fact that, structurally, our fields of endeavor are involved with piloted programs (DOSes, Soyuzes, Apollo-Soyuz), and have their own chief designers—Semyonov and Bushuyev—he wants personally to grapple with the main control problems and in critical situations to make decisions as the general designer. Each of you, who will be reporting to him, either with or without me, must be completely, down to the smallest detail, competent in the problems for which you are responsible. I am already convinced that Glushko understands electricity well enough. He will read our reports and design materials with partiality. Before the documents go to the general designer for signature, reread them five times each and don't feel sorry for the originators. After you, I don't want to receive comments about an unnecessary comma.

"For the first three months of work in his new capacity, Glushko hasn't begrudged time for the development of proposals for a prospective program of Soviet cosmonautics. Essentially, decisions concerning the creation of DOSes and transport vehicles were made before he came to us. They should have been refined, achieving greater sophistication, reliability, and service life. Above all, the transition from vehicle 7K to 7K-S, controlled by an on-board digital computer, should be refined. And there is also the Apollo-Soyuz international project. We planned to launch three Soyuzes and DOS No. 4 before the end of 1974. In 1975, we were supposed to continue preparations and then dock with the Americans. All of this was taking a lot of attention and time. But the ideas for these operations originated back with Korolev, and Mishin continued and developed them. Glushko could in no way call himself the general designer of these projects. That is why he devoted a great deal of time to the development of a completely new program, in which launch vehicles created based on *his* ideas moved into the foreground, and engines with a power the world had never seen before were developed for them. The fate of the N-1 was predetermined, but the MKTS might get in the way of his ambitious creative

---

19. The docking was planned for July 1975.

From the author's archives.

Shown here are Thomas Stafford (left), Nikolay Anfimov (center), and Boris Chertok in Moscow in 2005 to commemorate the 30th anniversary of the Apollo–Soyuz Test Project.

ideas. He needs to hurry. He's already 66 years old. He's already a two-time Hero of Socialist Labor. But that's not the main thing—these sorts of rockets and engines must go down in the history of technology so that no one will have any doubts as to their true chief creator. As today, no one doubts that the true chief designer of the R-7 and Vostok vehicle was Korolev."

The spate of new assignments, which required continuous effort, gradually dampened the anguish over the N-1. In a family with few children, the loss of a single child can inflict very heavy injury on the parents. In a large family, the necessity for day-to-day worry over the remaining children softens the grief. Each day it was necessary to deal with the problems of the upcoming Apollo-Soyuz docking, testing of the new DOS, *Salyut-4*, and preparation of the latest *Soyuz-15* for launch to Chelomey's Almaz station. Moreover, that hot summer, every now and then, rebellious thoughts crept in about vacation.

Since no government resolution had been issued on the complete termination of operations on the N-1, in smoking rooms and during our time off, timid thoughts were being expressed about how the "powers that be" would come to their senses and make Glushko reexamine his irreconcilable stance.

There were also brave people who appealed to the Central Committee with letters signed by several authors in this regard.

The Party committee of the Sixth Scientific-Testing Directorate of NIIP-5, in violation of all traditions of military discipline, held an all-night meeting expressing outrage about the termination of the N-1 project.[20] The result was a letter from military testers addressed to the Presidium of the Twenty-fifth Congress of the Communist Party.[21] The letter presented arguments for continuing debugging of the N-1, citing the opinions of specialists from the developer organizations. The firing range testers weren't asking for much: "Give us the opportunity to test rockets No. 8, No. 9, and No. 10, which are already prepared."

Of course, the letter didn't arrive before the Congress. The Party *apparat* understood full well: decisions had already been made at such a level that to take up the time of congressional delegates and even of the Presidium served no purpose. The headstrong military testers, who had devoted perhaps the best years of their lives to Tyuratam, Baykonur, the town of Leninsk, and to perfecting the grandiose N-1, were told that now their main mission was the MKTS program. The MIK, the launch site, and a lot of other facilities needed to be rebuilt for it.

At his own initiative, the irrepressible Andronik Iosifyan also appealed to the Central Committee with a letter. He considered the termination of the N-1 project to be an error of principle. But an acquaintance from the Central Committee *apparat* simply telephoned him over the Kremlin line and asked him to stop by and pick up his letter.

GLUSHKO'S ORDER ON THE TERMINATION OF THE N-1 PROJECT was not borne out by a ministerial order or by a VPK decision. The situation heated up. Conversations circulated to the effect that the government was not going to shut down the N-1. On Friday, 13 August 1974, three months after Glushko was named general designer and director of NPO Energiya, Ustinov decided to verify "on site" the mood of the "people." One could understand Ustinov's concern.

It was high time to undertake a new program in place of the landing expedition to the Moon that never happened. A month after his appointment to the post of general designer, Glushko promised to develop new promising proposals for the Moon, orbital stations, and space transport systems. Work

---

20. The Sixth Scientific-Technical Directorate at Tyuratam constituted the military staff at the firing range responsible for preparing and launching the N-1.

21. The Twenty-fifth Congress of the Communist Party was held between 24 February and 5 March 1976.

on N1-L3 at NPO Energiya was virtually halted, and what were the subcontractors, who had enormous amounts of process stock, to do? It was time to listen to the chief designers and report to the Politburo.

No one could accuse me of being superstitious. On the contrary, I was often accused of completely disregarding well-known folk omens. I made fun of drivers' fears when a black cat crossed the road in front of them; I never missed the opportunity to kid members of the launch team, who up until the last day feared that a woman would show up at the launch site; and I chuckled when someone proposed knocking on wood to ward off trouble or spitting over one's left shoulder. But somewhere in my subconscious I had an awareness when it came to two dates: 13 August 1937—the most probable date of the crash of Sigismund Levanevskiy's airplane—and 27 March.[22] I remember: 27 March 1942—the day of my mother's death; 27 March 1943—the day of Grigoriy Bakhchivandzhi's death; 27 March 1968—the death of Gagarin. Perhaps 13 August 1974 would be the date of the ultimate death of the N-1.

On 12 August 1974, Valentin Glushko personally telephoned the main managers of NPO Energiya and courteously requested that they make themselves completely available the following day, 13 August: "Dmitriy Fedorovich is coming here for a serious conversation." Glushko asked me to prepare a speech about the special features of the control system for the new Soyuz modification—vehicle 7K-S, or "article 11F732." He said nothing about who would be participating in the upcoming meeting.

At 10 a.m. on 13 August, in the large office of our former chief, now our general [designer], the managerial staff of NPO Energiya and its chief designers assembled: Barmin, Pilyugin, Ryazanskiy, and Viktor Kuznetsov. Afanasyev came, too, as well as his deputies, Tyulin and Litvinov. Smirnov's deputy Komissarov represented the VPK. Posters hung on the walls—pictures of the new launch vehicles, RLA-120, RLA-135, and RLA-150. A small group of planners had toiled under Glushko's personal unremitting supervision for the past two months on the designs of these launch vehicles.

Ustinov arrived accompanied by Serbin and Strogonov. Before Ustinov appeared, we didn't take our seats, but huddled together talking about matters that weren't work related. He strode in, as usual, quickly and energetically. When he saw me he extended his hand, and after a firm handshake, asked, "So, how's the 'old guard'?"

"We're hanging in there," I answered.

"You shouldn't just hang in there; you need to move forward."

---

22. See Chertok, *Rockets and People, Vol. I*, Chapter 7, for Levanevskiy.

Ustinov himself opened the meeting.

"I am very glad that I once again find myself in this group and in this historic office where Sergey Pavlovich Korolev used to work. The other day in the Politburo we had a serious conversation about our space problems. The Politburo requested that an objective assessment be made of why we have not landed Soviet cosmonauts on the Moon. It was mentioned in the Politburo that in view of the successful landings of the Americans, the task of exploring the Moon has become crucial for us. No matter what other problems we solve, this will remain primary and general, but in a new capacity. Today I would like to speak and to consult on a whole complex of problems. Your work is very broad here. How to organize the work so that it will not drag out for decades, so that it won't be handed down to our grandchildren. Let them go much farther than we. It is for us to decide what we will be doing in the next few years.

"I would by no means curtail operations on the Soyuz project. These vehicles, both unpiloted and piloted, must stay with your team. This is your project and it must not be abandoned. The Salyut-Soyuz system is very promising. Don't even think of abandoning it. We must examine the possibility of creating specialized modules for this system. Please don't forget, under any circumstances, about those projects that have already been successfully concluded."

These were Ustinov's opening remarks. I don't think that I am the only one from the "old guard" who viewed his speech as a warning to Glushko not to take it into his head to scrap and revamp a field of endeavor that Korolev had established and in which we had achieved universally acknowledged success under Mishin.

Ustinov continued, "How shall we approach the solution of the general problem? It might be worked out so that in 10 years you will again say that it's not working out with the Moon. But we must have it so that each year, do you understand, each year something big happens. I know that the first Council of Chiefs [meeting], in which the new assignments were preliminarily discussed, has already taken place. I specifically selected this day in order to also hear about these plans, which you are getting ready to approve in the next council.

"I believe we are justified in sparring between two historic council [meetings]. It's just that we need to spar about specific things. Not go off into the next century. Leave this job to the science fiction writers. If we are going to conduct business like you did with the N-1, insisting on launching in spite of reliability—we will obtain corresponding results."

Afanasyev, who habitually made notes on a notepad, raised his head as Ustinov was saying this, and making eye contact with me, gave me a piercing look. He recalled our argument in November 1972 before the launch of N-1 No. 7: "You and Dorofeyev are crawling on your bellies toward the 'launch' button. Go ahead and launch. I give you my word: one more failure and they might terminate the N-1."

Yes, perhaps the minister was right then, I thought, having met his piercing glance. If back then we had firmly said, "No, let's wait for the new engines," the fate of the N-1 might have shaped up differently. But, who knows? With the persistence of a schoolteacher, Ustinov continued to hammer us all with truths that were obvious, but so difficult to implement.

"You, specifically you, the creators of new space systems, must develop a general line and stick to it as strictly as possible. I propose that you listen to Valentin Petrovich."

Glushko talked for more than two hours, spelling out his doctrine in detail for the next few years. Above all, Glushko proposed developing a series of heavy and super-heavy launch vehicles made from standardized blocks. All of the launch vehicles were assigned the designation RLA—rocket-flying apparatus.[23] The lightest launch vehicle was the RLA-120. With a launch mass of 980 tons, this launch vehicle inserted a payload with a mass of 30 tons, 10 tons more than Chelomey's UR-500K-Proton, into Earth orbit. The most powerful launch vehicle, RLA-150, was capable of inserting a payload with a mass of 250 tons into orbit. Glushko approached the chalkboard and, on an area free of posters, he wrote:

RLA-120—1979 (30 tons in orbit).
POS—1979.[24]

Unlike the DOS, the POS was a permanent orbital station rather than a long-duration station. In 1980 and 1981, it was proposed that the POS be expanded using specialized modules. Instead of the UR-500K, Glushko proposed using the new RLA-120 launch vehicle for the assembly of the permanent orbital station.

Today we know that the construction of a permanent orbital station actually began in 1986 rather than 1979.[25] The RLA-120 simply didn't appear. The *Mir* station, now known throughout the world, began to be created during Glushko's lifetime with the help of Chelomey's Proton—the UR-500K.

Glushko wrote two more lines on the board:

---

23. It's worth nothing that the abbreviation RLA—*Raketnyy letatelnyy apparat*—was used by Glushko in the early 1930s at the Gas Dynamics Laboratory (GDL) to denote early rudimentary rockets.

24. POS—*Postoyannaya orbitalnaya stantsiya*.

25. The *Mir* core module was launched in February 1986.

RLA-135—1980 (100 tons in orbit).
Expedition to the Moon—1981.

And then further down:

RLA-150—1982 (250 tons in orbit).
Flights to Mars—1983.

"We need 12 billion rubles for the whole program. If you help us," said Glushko, addressing Ustinov directly. "I can with a great degree of confidence affirm: an expedition to Mars in the 1980s is a realistic mission. But before Mars we must build a permanent base on the Moon. We have such a design; we are certain of its feasibility. But we need reliable launch vehicles. Carrying out such missions using the N-1 means suffering a catastrophe."

By the end of the report Glushko's calm demeanor had changed. He turned quite red and finished his speech with emotion that was unusual for him. It was the first time I had seen him so stirred up.

Ustinov began to ask questions.

"Your heaviest vehicle has 28 chambers, and you yourself criticize the N-1, which has 30 chambers on the first stage."

"That's no big deal," answered Glushko. "Our old *Semyorka* had 32 chambers, and everyone's accustomed to that. We noticed, by the way, that a chamber is one thing, but an engine is something else entirely. I propose four-chamber engines. In actuality there are only seven engines on the first stage."[26]

"Please note the fundamental difference between this layout and that of the N-1. We are proposing a block principle. Rockets differ from one another in terms of the number of identical blocks on the first stage, and when necessary on the second stage as well. A decisive advantage of the block principle is the ability to manufacture each block at the factory and to transport it in assembled form to the firing range. We can conduct flight testing on the engines as part of the lightest single-block rocket and use this invaluable experience for multiblock rocket complexes without the risk of destroying a launch site. Each block should first undergo firing tests."

---

26. As Glushko first conceived it in 1974, the first stage of the RLA-150 would have been constructed from six boosters derived from the first stage of the RLA-120. These boosters would serve as strap-ons to a central core stage powered by liquid oxygen and liquid hydrogen.

"Is it necessary to insert 250 tons? Isn't that an awful lot compared with the Americans? They flew to the Moon and now they can't find any work for their Saturn. And it only inserted 140 tons."

"This isn't our concern," answered Glushko. "Let them have the headache, and we'll pass them by. And after this they will fall behind in pursuit of us. Or they will propose collaboration."

"And will it be *tsiklin* or hydrogen in the second stage?"[27]

"For the time being we are conducting calculations on *tsiklin*. We have too little experience with hydrogen. We can promise, but disrupt all of the deadlines."

"Let's get this straight—you clashed with Korolev because you refused to make powerful engines for the N-1 running on oxygen and kerosene. And now that Korolev is no longer around you are proposing that we agree to engines that you flat out rejected when Korolev was alive?" There was a clearly psychological subtext to Komissarov's question.

"Korolev and I clashed not because I was fundamentally opposed to creating powerful engines running on oxygen and kerosene. In the early 1960s we did not have the necessary experience to create such engines within the timeframe that the government resolution called for. From my perspective, this would have been a gamble. We were all working hard back then. Only now do we have the confidence that the creation of super-powerful oxygen-kerosene engines with stable combustion in the chamber, operating on a gas generator layout, is feasible. We selected the optimal four-chamber system for a super-powerful engine. The engine design makes it possible to rock the chamber for flight control, rather than throttling them, as was done on the N-1 to the detriment of the performance index. Special control thrusters will not be needed for control.

"And how will you respond to the American challenge when it comes to the reusable space transport system, the MKTS?"

"For this we are making a medium-sized vehicle. The first phase of the MKTS is a space airplane. It could appear in 1982. But this is under the condition that [the] aviation [industry] will be working [with us]. We are not going to build the airplane ourselves. We will ensure the insertion of the airplane on RLA-135. Two airplanes need to be built right away."

"What do the deadlines you're proposing depend on?"

---

27. *Tsiklin* (or sintin) is the name of an advanced synthetic hydrocarbon fuel based on furfural and propylene. Although much more expensive, it is more efficient than "ordinary" kerosene.

Suddenly Radovskiy wedged his way into the fray: "The deadlines depend on the engine specialists. All of the RLAs are supposed to have oxygen engines, which aren't yet available."[28]

No response to this remark ensued. A 10-minute break was announced. After the break the meeting continued with a very aggressive speech by Barmin.

"Valentin Petrovich's proposals, which we have listened to today, constitute already the third version in the past two months. Valentin Petrovich is getting further and further away from the realities of our century and pulling us into the 21st century. There has been no analysis of our previous errors. Moreover, the errors are being repeated. We need to start building a program with the spacecraft and missions that we need, rather than with launch vehicles. Let's be frank. For all his genius, Korolev began the lunar program proceeding from the launch vehicle rather than from lunar vehicles. During his own lifetime, he understood that there wasn't enough energy to launch a landing expedition to the Moon. Modifications began on the N-1. We added six engines to the first stage. Next, we realized that this still wasn't enough. We understood that the expedition design needed to be altered. We wanted to correct the error by using a two-launch scenario for the L3M. And quite recently everyone agreed with this. Instead of that, today a series of entirely new launch vehicles is being proposed. Nobody needs a launch vehicle for a 250-ton payload. The Americans are making the Space Shuttle because they only need one heavy launch vehicle, one that's multipurpose to boot. Today, 140 organizations are working with us on the lunar base project. We can create it if we don't fritter away our resources on unrealistic launch vehicle designs. The 12.5 billion rubles that Glushko mentions is two times less than what is really required for such a program. Multiblock configurations for launch vehicles are unsuitable. The selection that Valentin Petrovich is proposing to us is wrong. After lengthy research, Korolev selected the optimal configuration for the N-1. He purposely rejected multiblock rockets. The N-1 needs to undergo serious updating, instead of reinventing the wheel. We have already spent four billion rubles on the N-1, and we must use them. Betting on engines with a thrust of 1,000 to 1,200 tons is tempting, but completely unrealistic in terms of deadlines. Take it from me, I am not the only one who has a great deal of experience—we all do. *Tsiklin* is proposed for the second and third stages. A kilogram of *tsiklin* costs 50 rubles, while a kilogram of hydrogen costs less than

---

28. Viktor Petrovich Radovskiy (1920–2001) was Glushko's most senior deputy. During the period when Glushko was general designer of NPO Energiya, Radovskiy effectively headed (as chief designer) KB Energomash, i.e., the former OKB-456, which had been subsumed under the Energiya umbrella.

30 rubles. Hydrogen is the future of our rocket-power generation. Valentin Petrovich's lunar program stubbornly ignores both hydrogen *and* my proposals for the construction of a lunar base.[29] We need to build a base on the Moon. To build it we need a reusable space transport system using an updated N-1. NPO Energiya will not pull off the program that Glushko is proposing before the end of the century. We need to create a system capable of taking 40 tons of real payload and return at least 20 tons to Earth."

Barmin stood up, walked up to the chalkboard, and crisscrossed through all the lines containing information about the RLA series of launch vehicles. Above, he wrote: "Uprated N-1 + reusable."

Serbin asked Barmin a question, "And how many more years will your uprating of the N-1 take?"

"I don't want to answer for the developers, who are sitting here in silence. Most likely, Valentin Petrovich forbade them to defend the N-1, but the uprated launch vehicle could fly in a year and a payload needs to be prepared for it. And what Valentin Petrovich is proposing will hold us back on the lunar program by another six or seven years. I should warn about one more danger. Prominent psychotherapists are telling us that the human mind outside of Earth's magnetic field might experience changes. The Moon has no magnetic field, and therefore staying there for many months is fraught with psychological problems."

Having considered Barmin's words regarding our silence as a hint at our unwillingness to speak out against our new boss, Ustinov turned to us, smiling, "I have no doubt that you all want to select the best scenario for carrying out this crucial government mission. Your statements must be bold and critical, but well reasoned. Without a fundamental Party relationship to the matter at hand we will kill any project. Speak courageously, sensibly, and authoritatively."

"Permit me to display my courage," requested Pilyugin.

"In my opinion, Nikolay Alekseyevich, you never lost it," retorted Ustinov.

"Dmitriy Fedorovich, I am going to speak regarding control problems. Let others talk about everything else. So, today we are confident in the N-1 control system. During the last launch, although we only got to work for a little while, we confirmed that the new system with the on-board computer reliably controls the rocket. Over the last year and a half, we have done a lot more and can demonstrate that control reliability will be ensured, at least for the first three stages. We gained a wealth of experience with the booster stages

---

29. By this time, Barmin's design bureau had been working on plans for long-term lunar bases under such code names as *Bolshoye koltso* (Big Ring), *Kolumb* (Columbus), *Dal* (Distance), and *Osvoyeniye* (Mastery).

during the L1 launches.[30] Therefore, here too we are confident that we will solve the problem. The transition proposed to us today for a series of new launch vehicles will initially require us to curtail current production, discard production stock, then design, and develop, and once again set up production using a new manufacturing process. We will not have an RLA in any version before 1979. We are wasting five or six years."

Glushko appeared calm and unflappable. He was catching his breath after a difficult report and was sitting with an air of detachment, as if the speech had been about things that had nothing to do with him.

After Pilyugin, Ryazanskiy took the floor.

"I totally disagree with what Barmin said. We need a rocket like the RLA-120 capable of inserting 30 tons. We have managed to do a lot for the Moon. For the L1, Zond, Mars, and Soyuz programs we developed radio complexes, which can be modified for any program. We need to create a full-fledged Mission Control Center as soon as possible."

Yuriy Semyonov defused the situation somewhat trying to remind those assembled about the problems of orbital stations.

"We need to ensure the reliable operation of systems in orbit for decades. The Americans are announcing publicly that they are already working on such long-duration systems. We should not postpone this work; otherwise we will once again be playing catch-up. Orbital stations can become permanent only with systems that are reliable in terms of service life."

I began my speech by walking up to the chalkboard and erasing the X that Barmin had placed on number 30, the payload that the RLA-120 launch vehicle proposed by Glushko was capable of inserting. However, I left the bold X that Barmin had used to cross out the number 250. I devoted the main part of my speech to information about the status of the on-board digital computers and hardware components of the radio electronics.

"In order to have a permanent orbital station, a long-duration lunar base, much less an expedition to Mars, we need hardware with a guarantee of failure-free operation for at least three to five years. For the time being, our radio electronic industry is promising to provide them, but it says that this will require three years of testing. We will also spend two or three years creating instrumentation for this hardware. On balance, it will be at least five to six years, allowing for ground developmental testing. Another way would

---

30. This is a reference to the N1-L3's Block D upper stage, which was also used as an upper stage for the Proton-K rocket.

be multiple redundancy. But this will require an increase in masses, volumes, and, again, power generation."

After the meeting Feoktistov said to me, "You made two errors in your speech. When you left the X on number 250, you displeased Glushko, and when you began linking reliability testing with deadlines, you irritated Ustinov because you hit on one of his 'hot-button issues.' He understands full well that it takes time to achieve a high degree of reliability, but this contradicts his own requirement to shorten the deadlines."

Indeed, after the loss of DOS No. 3 in 1973, Ustinov had this to say at a meeting in the Central Committee: "Keep in mind: we are not rushing you, but we do demand the most thorough testing of these complex and expensive mechanisms at the factory, at the KIS [monitoring and test facility], and at the TP [engineering facility]. But we also cannot allow liberties to be taken with deadlines...."

Bushuyev told in detail about the progress of negotiations with the Americans on the Apollo-Soyuz project, about the attitudes of the American side, and he confirmed that they were burning with the desire to collaborate with us. The curtailment of the lunar program led them into a crisis, from which they were trying to emerge by developing the Space Shuttle.

Mozzhorin was on vacation, so Avduyevskiy spoke on behalf of TsNIImash.[31]

"The Space Shuttle is advantageous for returning very expensive technology from space for reuse. If we follow this trend, we will need to rebuild all of our space programs. Barmin is correct when he says that we need to proceed from the final objectives, and not turn the development of launch vehicles into a self-contained main task."

Our new first deputy general designer Yuriy Trufanov could not criticize Glushko—otherwise he would not be the first deputy.

"We must master Sun-synchronous orbits," he said. "Once we have solved this problem, we will have global monitoring over the entire planet with the aid of the modules of the orbital station."

I was anxious to hear the minister's speech. How would he respond to the proposal to do away with the N-1? Would he really support the new rocket series? Ultimately he would have to answer to the Politburo!

"It is difficult to give a weighty assessment of these materials today," began Afanasyev. "I am forced to admonish the head institutes of the ministry:

---

31. Vsevolod Sergeyevich Avduyevskiy (1920–2003), a specialist in high-speed aeromechanics, served as first deputy director of TsNIImash from 1973 to 1987.

From the author's archives.
From left to right are Sergey Afanasyev, Valentin Glushko, and Mstislav Keldysh, three of the most powerful men in the Soviet space program in the 1970s. They are attending a meeting at TsNIImash in Kaliningrad (now Korolev).

TsNIImash and NIITP.[32] For some reason they adopted a wait-and-see attitude, instead of immediately getting their main subdivisions involved in these research projects. It would be foolish to think that the general designer's team of 40,000 alone can do everything that he has said here.

"The report proposes solving all the problems almost simultaneously. This is a mistake. We need to introduce a rational phase-by-phase approach. We will manage to find such a solution if we quash our ambitious desires to seize everything at once and to promise unrealistic deadlines.

"Today a version of a launch vehicle for a 30-ton payload is taking shape. We need this launch vehicle first and foremost for the crucial intelligence-gathering purposes of the Ministry of Defense in Sun-synchronous orbits.

---

32. NIITP—*Nauchno-issledovatelskiy institut teplovykh protsessov* (Scientific-Research Institute of Thermal Processes) was the new name for the old NII-1, famous for its interwar and wartime research on rocket propulsion.

Its integral tanks with a diameter of 6 meters will require completely new technological fittings, and the welding of very thick materials will have to be mastered. I have consulted with Boris Yevgenyevich Paton. He encouraged me that in the near future this problem will be solved. 'We will learn how to weld 6-meter tanks,' Paton assured me. But then an engine is proposed right off the bat with 1,200 tons of thrust. I have a great deal of respect for Valentin Petrovich as our nation's, and perhaps also the world's, greatest scientist and engine-building specialist, but I think that he is profoundly mistaken when he assures us that such an engine can be produced in two years. The ministry has already been tasked with producing a piloted reusable system on par with the U.S. Shuttle. This is a crucial and very difficult task. It's time for us to master [liquid] hydrogen. Here, we're behind the Americans. In his proposals the honorable Valentin Petrovich for some reason insists on walking away from hydrogen and is pushing *tsiklin* on us. The ministry does not agree with this. We insist on developing a liquid-propellant rocket engine that operates on oxygen and hydrogen, and we will support such projects in every way possible.

"The time has come to bring in other design organizations. I consulted with Pilyugin. He can confirm that he fully agreed to take on the production of the control system for a reusable spacecraft. The development of a glider needs to be assigned to the aviation industry. For the time being, I would leave the X that Barmin placed over 250 tons. Barmin is right in this case. We know what the situation is in our country. We need to restructure ourselves toward assembly in orbit and achieve a very high degree of reliability in docking. This will be a lot less expensive than producing another super-heavy launch vehicle. They are assuring us that the N-1 launch facilities can be used for the new series. No one has verified this in detail. Barmin maintains that this is impossible. This needs to be carefully examined. There was no Soviet man on the Moon. This is the fault of OKB-1 and our fault in general. A lunar base—in my opinion this is not a priority mission. It needs to be transferred to research work. Barmin's strong suit is that he knows how to build a cooperative network. Let's hand this project over to him especially since he'll take it, and just let him.

"We need to distribute our forces sensibly. Today in the report we did not see a year-by-year distribution of expenditures and working capacity. How much does all this enjoyment cost? As I see it, MOM alone will have to double its budgetary allocations for this new program, and every bit of all the capital investments will go here. We just put missiles into service in silos in order to ensure parity, and now they already need to be upgraded. Do you know how much that costs? Please don't forget that your organization is also responsible for the 8K98 [or RT-2] combat missiles and upgrading them. And no one has yet taken away Valentin Petrovich's duties as chief designer of the engines for Yangel's and Chelomey's combat missiles.[33]

"Today we have 40,000 people at NPO Energiya, and 30,000 are working on its projects at the Progress Factory, for a total of 70,000! We intend to set up engine production in Omsk.[34] This means that another 20,000 people will be working on Energiya's projects. The main problem in Omsk is the firing test rigs. What is to be done with the N-1 launch pad? If you get it into your head to seriously redesign it, new capital funds will be needed. Have you thought about this? The most important and urgent task is Apollo-Soyuz. Here, the main thing is reliability and quality. The workforce hasn't been entirely successful with this.

"What shall we do in the near future? We need to launch DOS No. 4. We're really behind schedule with DOS No. 5. They're telling us that big changes have been made on it and that it's going to be a new station. The problem of modular construction is being solved on it. For production here, in Podlipki, and in Fili this is additional work, but once it has been decided, it will have to be done. But if we put a new station into production, then why one? We need to make a sixth, and perhaps also a seventh. We can't allow a failure. We haven't landed on the Moon, so at least we should always have orbital stations circling Earth. ZIKh will make the hulls. But I can't transfer systems configuration over to ZIKh—this is Energiya's business. I have inspected the 7K-S spacecraft. Chertok assured me that a wonderful job has been done on the control system. However, the spacecraft is not equipped for docking. I warned: we need to make a new transport vehicle right away. They say that the 7K-T is obsolete. We don't have a chance with Chelomey's TKS. We must by all means debug the 7K-S in the transport version. I consider today's conversation preliminary. We need to rework the entire prospective program taking our comments into consideration and only then can it be put before the Council of Chiefs."

In Smirnov's absence, Boris Komissarov spoke as VPK deputy chairman.

---

33. KB Energomash developed engines for the following Yangel ICBMs: the R-16 (RD-218 and RD-219 engines), the R-36 (RD-251 and RD-252), the MR UR-100 (RD-268), the R-36M (RD-264), and the R-36M2 (RD-274). The organization did not develop any engines for Chelomey's combat missiles, although it did produce the RD-253 engine for the Proton-K booster as well as derivatives of the RD-253 such as the RD-275.

34. OKB-456 had originally established a branch at Omsk (its Branch No. 3) in December 1958 for the manufacture of engines for the R-16 ICBM. The branch was dissolved in 1968. Ten years later, series production of the RD-170 engines for the 11K25 launch vehicle were set up at the Polet Production Association (PO Polet) in Omsk. Because of the need for mass production of these engines (as well as the RD-171), Glushko reestablished a branch at Omsk in June 1983.

"The program has not been coordinated with the general contractor—the Ministry of Defense—or with the Academy of Sciences. I do not understand why you absolutely have to insert 25 tons into Sun-synchronous orbit. Our heaviest reconnaissance satellite weighs no more than 12 tons.

"The Americans are planning to have modules weighing no more than 14 tons. The Ministry of Defense doesn't need 30 tons today. We need to tell it straight—we disgraced ourselves with the N-1 and now you propose a new gamble with the RLA. Space is space, but we need to keep our feet on the ground. Live by general toil and trouble; don't lose contact with real opportunities. In the plan for updating the lunar projects we were about to execute an on-orbit docking using two N-1 launch vehicles. Now the general designer is proposing that this docking take place on the ground and that a new launch vehicle with a liftoff mass of 6,000 tons be developed; in other words, this means two N-1s! This project is a mistake. We need to pray for the N-1 to lift off. They crashed one, restored it, and now what—are we going to start tearing it apart with our own hands? Who is going to undertake such a bold move? In terms of market value in our branch of industry a ruble is equivalent to a dollar. I'd like to see the President of the United States go before Congress and say, by the way, you need to write off 4 billion dollars for a launch vehicle and allocate another 12.5 billion dollars to NASA for a new launch vehicle, for unknown reasons. The whole world would make fun of him. And here, nobody is even threatened with a reprimand for such unauthorized activity."

Ivan Serbin took the floor.

"The discussion has shown that the program has not been elaborated to the point where we can make a decision. We don't have much time. We must decide how to get the maximum use out of 70,000 people, and not a faceless crowd, but highly qualified specialists. The program was preliminarily esti- mated at a little over 12 billion rubles. But we simply do not have that kind of money. And if we did, then it would be very difficult to use it up. The Council of Chief Designers shouldn't convene yet. We need to have comparative data on expenditures for each area of endeavor, rather than a single horrifying sum just for the RLA. Now many enthusiasts have come out in favor of a reusable system. This is good. But the second stage is an airplane. And without the Ministry of the Aviation Industry you won't be able to cope with this project. We can't allow such lack of discipline that Almaz and DOS are running in parallel. Neither you nor Chelomey are private firms where everyone thinks 'I'll do what I want to.' It's time for this to end. Such a major plan needs to be thoroughly elaborated with the subcontractors. Without them you're not going to do anything. And you also need to develop your experimental facilities for them. You didn't take that into consideration in your expenses."

It was time to wrap up the meeting. Ustinov understood this and recommended that Glushko respond to the main critical comments. Glushko started, and rather than a calm speaker, I saw in him a focused prizefighter in the ring, who after a knockdown was once again going over for a decisive attack.

"We have been talking today about an unfinished program, and we are in the process of searching. We have familiarized you with the status of affairs. Actually, we must compare and provide evidence that the proposals are optimal. I have met with the military twice. We talked for a long time, and I asked for their help in developing plans. In particular, General Karas promised to send us his recommendations by 15 August. The Ministry of Defense ardently supports the station's modular structure and 30-ton payload. We are in constant contact with subcontractors and competitors.

"Now let's turn to Barmin's speech, in which he so vehemently defended the N-1 and proposed, in terms of new projects, confining ourselves just to the reusable system. I maintain that the N-1 transports air. Compare its weight characteristics with Saturn V. The dry weight of a unit of volume of the first stage of the N-1 is two and a half times worse than the Saturn V, the second stage is five times worse, and the third stage is three and a half times worse. This is when the volumes of the stages themselves are almost equal. I didn't want to mention the errors committed in gas dynamics. Let it be known to you that just due to pressure drop under the aft end of the first stage we lose more than 750 tons. In order to compensate for such a loss, we need to install five more engines. Vladimir Pavlovich [Barmin], do you want your launch site to be destroyed again? Let's stand around with our fingers crossed, as they suggested today. Do we really need a launch vehicle that transports air and has bad engines to boot? Regarding Barmin's speech on the lunar base, I agree that the construction of 'Barmingrad' be classified as research work.[35] But it is our job to create the first base on the Moon for three to five persons for two to three weeks. And we are prepared for this work. Vladimir Pavlovich frightened us here saying that the Moon has no magnetic field and this is very dangerous for the human psyche. Such speeches show that mental deviances happen on Earth even with the presence of a magnetic field."

Glushko had hit Barmin "below the belt," but none of the high-ranking judges had interrupted him. He continued to speak rapidly and even passionately, which to my memory happened very rarely with him.

---

35. This is, again, a reference to ongoing planning at Barmin's design bureau for permanent bases on the Moon.

"We will show what launch vehicle weights are needed on Earth so that on the Moon a base for three or four people might operate. We don't just need spacesuits, we need cubic capacity, and special equipment, which we must first test and debug on the POS. I emphasize, on the *permanent*, not long-duration, orbital station. In order to create a POS we also need a new launch vehicle. The UR-500K with its 18 to 20 tons is inadequate. We need a minimum of 30 tons of payload to begin with. And this is our mission, which must not be buried in long-term research projects. This is a priority research and development project, if anything, instead of the MKBS.

"I regret that not everyone understands the idea of a super-heavy launch vehicle. We are not making this launch vehicle—it's coming about on its own, we're putting it together from modules which have already been optimized on lighter rockets. Six modules make up the first stage. The second stage is a single oxygen-hydrogen block standardized for the entire launch vehicle series. This is standardization and modularity, which we have been talking about so heatedly today. And we are not going to refuse to have anything to do with hydrogen. But for the time being we don't have it, so we have to use *tsiklin*.

"Yes, producing these launch vehicles costs a lot of money. But we gain a lot in standardization. One shouldn't be afraid that some factories are going to 'coast.' We intend to schedule the project so that production doesn't go idle anywhere, so that people fly into space each year.

"Now we are already working on the 7K-S vehicle in the transport version. It has a new and much more advanced control system. Chertok didn't have time to tell about its main feature. On the 7K-S he wants to try out control using on-board computers. We still lag behind the Americans in this. We'll begin with unpiloted vehicles. Klyucharev must master the new androgynous docking assembly.[36] We're using it for docking with the Americans, and then we'll put it on the 7K-S and the DOSes. These vehicles will load Klyucharev down completely. DOS No. 5 is the workload for ZIKh, and I would vote for No. 6 if a gap in production were to occur at ZIKh. Progress [Factory] can start mastering the production process of the 6-meter tanks right away. We and our subcontractors are really are up to our ears in work. But I don't see any other way to get ahead of the Americans. We have capabilities that we haven't yet discovered and haven't used. You caught us when development and testing of the programs was in full swing. I agree to postpone the Council of Chiefs

---

36. This is a reference to the Androgynous-Peripheral Docking Assembly (*Androginno-periferiynyy agregat stykovki-75* or APAS-75), which dispensed with the earlier probe-and-drogue docking system in favor of identical docking units on both spacecraft.

[meeting] for a week or two, but no more. We need to boost all cooperation as soon as possible. We have a lot of resources."

Toward the end of his speech Glushko was excited and flushed, as if he'd just taken a bath. He took a handkerchief and wiped the beads of sweat off his forehead, but he didn't sit down. Evidently he was gathering his thoughts to continue his speech. Taking advantage of the pause, Ustinov decided that it was time to wrap up the meeting, which had run over. He understood that he wasn't going to get any interesting new information and that he ought not to get mixed up in arguments between chief designers. He said, "Thank you, Valentin Petrovich! I am very happy that we had such a good turnout for the meeting today and that we have enlightened one another a bit. You didn't have time and weren't able to say everything. I too am unable to tell everything definitively. We need to give some serious thought to a lot of new things and about a lot of things in general. But we have missions, which are already completely spelled out, which we are obligated to fulfill in the next year. I am referring first and foremost to Apollo-Soyuz. God forbid that we should disgrace ourselves before the world public. Valentin Petrovich, I request that you personally take over supervision of this project. This work must be performed brilliantly. Changes have taken place in the United States. The new president has announced that he intends to continue his predecessor's line.[37] The Americans are going to study our work intensely and literally examine it as if it were under a microscope. You must keep a firm hold on our technical and ideological positions.

"The Americans are already asking us, 'So what shall we do next?' We aren't going to be able to avoid answering that question for long. For the time being we are saying that we're using Soyuz. It's not turning out very well. Thus, we're losing initiative, or more accurately, we're giving it away. They're observing, examining, studying, and analyzing everything with their own satellites. They know our military complexes better than we do. Our firing ranges and launch sites, every liftoff, every road, every building—it's all being monitored from space. We've agreed on a Soyuz-Apollo docking. Well, we'll dock once, maybe twice. There will be a bit of hype on both sides. And then what? Where are your proposals? We don't have any ideas about ways for further collaboration. NASA Administrators George Low and James Fletcher aren't dying to come over here for no good reason.[38] They are receiving our people, and how are we

---

37. Richard M. Nixon resigned as President of the United States on 9 August 1974. He was replaced by former Vice President Gerald R. Ford.

38. At the time (1974), James Chipman Fletcher (1919–1991) was the NASA Administrator, while George Michael Low (1926–1984) was a Deputy Administrator.

responding? I'm convinced we have got to reciprocate. Actions speak louder than words; and that's also true in the field of science. We need actions. I request that you formulate a strategic plan and draw up proposals.

"For the time being we are relying on the Soyuz spacecraft; I understand this is reality, as they say, it's what we've got on hand. We need to diligently work on its reliability. We need to launch the new Salyut no matter what.[39] We need to work on DOS No. 5. You are the ones who got it up and running—make it more reliable. But tell me exactly what is DOS No. 6? Is it a repeat of No. 5 or something new? Get to the bottom of that. When Mishin was in charge no one was able to clearly define the DOS series for me. Moreover, you know, and this is no secret, that Chelomey and Mishin proposed terminating DOSes altogether, leaving only Almaz, and then focusing on Chelomey's Transport Supply Vehicle.

"Don't abandon upgrading the R-7. Progress Factory has fully mastered it. This rocket is your bread and butter. Just like the UR-500K is now. In the next two or three years these launch vehicles will determine our space plans.

"But what's next? Designs have been proposed (and I know, they've gone a long way) for an expedition to Mars and for a lunar base. Here, collaboration with the Americans is possible. Don't throw the opportunity away; we will support you. Bushuyev is meeting with them. Courage, Konstantin Davidovich. Try to be diplomatic, as you know how; get a feel for their attitudes.

"We're placing a big stake on your organization. Very big. We deliberately created such a powerful merger and placed a very experienced chief in charge, who, as they say, had been through fire, water, and brass trumpets. As you just heard, your general designer already has forty thousand persons directly subordinate to him. And if you add to that the immediate subcontracting organizations, this number exceeds 250,000. This is an enormous workforce! You are capable of developing an efficient, realistic program. Break it down deadline by deadline into phases. Everything won't pan out right away; we understand this. But keep in mind that it matters to us, how this pans out and at what cost. We will ask the Central Committee for what we need, but we will need some justification.

"When I looked at the N-1 launch complex, it took my breath away. Our job is not just to admire, but also to make sure that these facilities operate. We will try to provide you with everything that you need. But you, too, need to think and consider so that your own conscience is not tormented over the

---

39. This was a reference to DOS-4, which was later launched as *Salyut-4* on 26 December 1974.

resources that nation is so generously giving, tearing them away from the people's needs.

"Now one more problem is cropping up—'the shuttle.' I understand this is a very difficult matter—and above all for airplane designers. The government just adopted a colossal aviation resolution. It spells out the workloads for all the aviation design bureaus and factories. We lag behind in terms of both military and civilian airplanes. They have resolved to eliminate this gap. If we go to aviation with the shuttle, we still don't know where it will be put.

"I think that today's conversation has been useful for everyone. We need to find a common line with the Ministry of Defense and the Academy of Sciences. Sergey Aleksandrovich [Afanasyev], you will call a meeting of your ministerial organizers, and then the heads of other ministries, who will be involved in these projects. In the next few days we need to determine a group of our comrades who are capable of preparing a detailed draft of a resolution and who are very objective. The resolution will define our strategic line. This work needs to be approached with a great sense of duty to the Party and the state.

"I am giving you a month, perhaps two, but no more, to prepare this resolution. All the issues must be given high-quality treatment. I thank you for the frank conversations we had today."

THE NEXT DAY, 14 AUGUST 1974, Glushko called us together to share his thoughts and hear our considerations on the results of this fateful, as I now view it, meeting. It seemed to us that Glushko had failed to achieve his desired goals. Had Korolev been in his place, I have no doubt he would have looked worried and upset. Despite his theatrical flair, Korolev couldn't conceal his internal state.

Bright and early, Glushko met us looking chipper, well groomed, and anything but dispirited. As always, in a well-fitting suit with a matching tie, he exuded confidence that his position was right. Once again sorting through my memory of the first six chiefs, I would say that Glushko emanated the pride and well-born manner of a gentleman. He did not like to switch over to the familiar *ty*. He didn't tolerate any hints of chummy behavior.

"Receive with indifference both flattery and slander and don't argue with a fool...," recited Glushko, as if summarizing the conversations from the day before.[40] It wasn't until the last years of his life that he began to display excessive irritability. After he first arrived among his new staff it was as though he

---

40. This is the last line of the poem "Exegi Monumentum" (1836) by Aleksandr Sergeyevich Pushkin (1799–1837).

wanted to show that class couldn't be learned; one needed to be born that way. I remember how Barmin, after one of those difficult conversations with Korolev, remarked to our staff, "None of you has any class. Sergey, who when necessary knows how to play the Russian gentleman, does not encourage tact and good manners in his minions."

Korolev's great internal work and relentless pondering were clearly visible to those around him. He knew how to look an interlocutor in the eye, as if pouring his own will and energy, his own conviction, into him. When dealing with Korolev, I paid attention to his face, eyes, and voice. His suit didn't affect me at all. That wasn't the issue. The seriousness with which he posed the problem (which sometimes seemed not even to be worth his attention), the sharp words, and the emotionally strong language were overwhelming.

Glushko was always well groomed, impeccably dressed, and proper. In the discussion of a problem and also in documents, he demanded solid logic, clarity, and accuracy in the wording. Sometimes documents that were brought to him for his signature were retyped many times, just because the originator was unable to reconcile the clarity of the statement with the syntax of the Russian language or hadn't observed scrupulous precision in the name of the addressee. In this regard he was meticulous, even relentless.

Concealed behind his external civility was a strong will in defense of his positions and convictions. Without resorting to strong language, he could reach logical constructions that were very offensive to his opponent. Sometimes he was uncompromising where it seemed a hard-line attitude would harm both him and the matter in question.

With any of the "non-chief" designers or subcontractors, Korolev could have a quarrel using very strong language. But amazingly, no matter how much he cursed at somebody, they weren't offended. I remember him yelling at Aleksey Bogomolov, "Little boy! Get out of here! I don't want to work with you anymore!"[41] After this tongue-lashing, Bogomolov smiled and knew that the next day he and Korolev would be talking on equal footing, as if nothing had happened.

Without raising his voice and without resorting to strong language, Glushko was capable of showing a person that he or she was working irresponsibly and shouldn't be trusted with anything serious. I don't recall an instance in which Korolev might have displayed indifference or aloofness in business meetings with me, with any other of his colleagues, or subcontractors. If he didn't feel like talking to you, he simply said, "Not now, look, I've got so much mail.

---

41. See Chertok, *Rockets and People, Vol. III*, pp. 236–238.

Figure it out yourself." Or, "Don't bother me, I'm about to have a difficult conversation with Keldysh (or with the minister, or with Ustinov)."

One of the chief designers once complained to me, "When I proposed a harebrained idea to Korolev, he listened to me as if he was interested and then, after glancing at the clock, he said that I was an old fool and had robbed him of 30 precious minutes. But then he grabbed the telephone and called the deputy chairman of the VPK asking him to meet with me because the proposal was interesting, but had nothing to do with his line of work."

Ten years later in that same office, Glushko sat in Korolev's place. I was giving him a report, not on a harebrained idea, but on the absolutely specific timeline of the [Apollo-Soyuz] joint project, which was at odds with those deadlines that he had advocated in the draft government resolution without having first consulted with me. He looked through me with such a fixed, glassy stare that I lost any desire to persuade him. And I left. The dates that he had signed off on, of course, we failed to meet. Glushko turned out to be innocent, and the collegium reprimanded me....

Neither Korolev nor Glushko had any close friends at work (at least that's the way it seemed to me and to others) with whom they could confide their innermost thoughts and ideas. Both men had very strong and very different personalities. But one thing united them: both belonged to the generation who were children during the civil class war and both had given up their youth to heroic labor for the sake of a great goal. They had been exposed to most horrible tests, both moral and physical, and through all of this they had not altered their dreams; they had maintained their singleness of purpose and their belief in their own strength.

HERE I CONSIDER IT FITTING to tell about the idealization of heroes in movies. In 1970, at the request of the management of *Mosfilm*, I was engaged as a consultant to work on the film *Taming the Fire*. Screenwriter and director Daniil Khrabrovitskiy by that time was already a well-known screenwriter of the films *Vse nachinayetsya s dorogi* [*Everything Begins with a Journey*], *Chistoye nebo* [*Clear Blue Sky*], and *Devyat dney odnogo goda* [*Nine Days of One Year*]. The main characters of these films were strong people, true heroes. From the first days of my acquaintance with Khrabrovitskiy we developed a good, trusting relationship.

I became enthralled with the idea of showing Khrabrovitskiy the nuts and bolts of our work—the "creative kitchen" and, above all, the extraordinarily interesting character of Chief Designer Korolev. While I was reviewing and modifying the first, naïve version of the screenplay, no major disagreements occurred. Usually I said, "It doesn't happen like that" or "That never happened." Khrabrovitskiy replied that it needed to be that way or else they wouldn't release the film. When I became exasperated that the main hero Bashkirtsev (based on Korolev) dies not in the Kremlin hospital but on the side of a dusty road, Khrabrovitskiy calmly replied, "And do you think that Chapayev died the way it was portrayed in the celebrated film?[42] When we were still kids we marveled over *Bronenosets Potemkin* [*Battleship Potemkin*], but the most famous scenes—the massacre on the Odessa Steps—have nothing in common with real history. I don't need to tell you that all the episodes in the famous films *Chelovek s ruzhyem* [*Man with a Gun*], *Lenin v oktyabre* [*Lenin in October*], and *Lenin v 1918* [*Lenin in 1918*] reflect the spirit of the time, the epoch, but have nothing in common with what really happened and how, aside from the calendar dates. I hope that after the Twentieth Party Congress you understood this.[43] There are only two people close to Lenin in the films—Stalin and Sverdlov.[44] And where are the rest of the heroes and real leaders of the uprising?

"I am making an artistic film, not a documentary. You must help us by showing us the technology, the creative process, and people's behavior in extreme situations. Don't impose documentary authenticity on me. There is a documentary film studio for that. For the time being they are forbidden to show the actual creators of the technology. They have their main heroes—the cosmonauts and scientists who sit in the presidiums and in public press conferences. In my film the main heroes are the creators, you and your comrades—all under fictitious names, so that no one except Korolev is recognizable. Lev Tolstoy thought up Pierre Bezukhov, Andrey Bolkonskiy, and Natasha Rostov.[45] They didn't exist. But the Battle of Borodino, Napoleon, Kutuzov, and the Moscow fire were real. Therefore, we accept the authenticity of Tolstoy's heroes. Your rockets were and are real. They launched a man into space. People will also believe in my characters. We will show that you experienced failures, accidents, heated arguments, and differences of opinion. That is the truth about which nothing was to be said or written. If the main characters were given the names of real heroes who are still alive, then we would have to stick to the facts in everything and speak about actual events, and this is forbidden. The censors won't tolerate my naming any of you. Therefore, even unclassified Korolev is Bashkirtsev rather than Korolev, Glushko is Ognev instead of Glushko,

---

42. *Chapayev* (1934) is a Soviet film about the legendary Red Army commander Vasiliy Ivanovich Chapayev, who became a hero during the Russian Civil War. A poll of film critics in 1978 named the film as one of the 100 best films in world history.

43. The Twentieth Party Congress in 1956 was when Khrushchev for the first time openly condemned the massive and horrendous crimes committed under Stalin.

44. Yakov Mikhaylovich Sverdlov (1885–1919) was a noted Bolshevik and ally of Lenin who played a key role in the October Revolution.

45. These are major characters from *War and Peace* [*Voyna i mir*], first published in 1869.

Ustinov is Loginov, and Nedelin is Vladimirov. I made a concession to you only in Voskresenskiy's case—his first name is still Leonid, but changed his surname to Sretenskiy."

When it came to selecting and approving the actors, I backed away more and more from my dogmatic commitment to the truth. I tried to interject into the screenplay a hint of the repression to which Korolev and Glushko were subjected in their time, but another consultant—Deputy Commander-in-Chief of the Strategic Rocket Forces Colonel General Mikhail Grigoryev—laughed at me.[46] He said, "Boris Yevseyevich, I respect you very much as a specialist, but I am astonished by your political naiveté. Who in our time will tolerate this?! I won't begrudge the funds to show real launches, and we're concocting bunkers and building sets of control rooms, about which we are still only dreaming—this will all happen. But recollections about the Purges have nothing to do with the objectives of the film. And if we want the people to see our film, then don't argue."

Khrabrovitskiy very much wanted to show Korolev's romantic youth involved with gliders and GIRD.[47] I introduced him to Isayev. Khrabrovitskiy was literally spellbound by Isayev's tales about his youth, his passion for Magnitogorsk, and then for airplanes and rocket engines. In the last edition of the screenplay, Khrabrovitskiy synthesized the image of the main hero so that it had parts of Korolev, Isayev, and Tikhonravov (whom I also introduced to Khrabrovitskiy), who was infatuated with the future of cosmonautics.[48] Khrabrovitskiy himself fabricated the personal life of his main hero from beginning to end. It has absolutely nothing to do with the biography of Korolev or Isayev.

Under commission from *Mosfilm*, Isayev developed and, at his own production facilities, manufactured an authentic rocket for the historic frames of the very first steps of rocket technology. The launches of Isayev's movie rockets thrilled the film's creators. This was, very likely, a reproduction of the way it all began that was close to historical authenticity. But Isayev's movie rockets proved to be much more reliable than the Korolev-Tikhonravov rockets in the 1930s.

---

46. Mikhail Grigoryevich Grigoryev (1917–1981) served as the First Deputy Commander-in-Chief of the Soviet Strategic Rocket Forces from 1968 to 1981.

47. GIRD—*Gruppa izucheniya reaktivnogo dvizheniya* (Group for the Study of Reactive Motion).

48. Mikhail Klavdiyevich Tikhonravov (1900–1974) was one of the pioneers of Soviet cosmonautics, having contributed to the development of the first Soviet rocket to use liquid propellants, the *Katyusha* solid-propellant rockets, the first launch vehicle studies in the postwar era, the first satellite studies, the development of the Vostok and Luna spacecraft, the early design of the N-1 rocket, and conceptions of piloted Mars spaceships conceived in the 1960s.

I was exasperated about the very warm relationship between the main hero Bashkirtsev, for whom Korolev was the prototype, and Ognev—the chief designer of engines, meant to be Glushko. Two outstanding actors— Kirill Lavrov and Igor Gorbachev—played the close friends.[49] Not only did Gorbachev (Ognev) not clash with Lavrov (Bashkirtsev), but he admired him and esteemed his talent. Khrabrovitskiy countered my objections that the characters in the film bore no resemblance to those in real life, by saying that the audience must see good-hearted, sympathetic, highly intellectual heroes in the people making history, not cold technocrats. In the film, Gorbachev succeeded in doing just that. In no way could his hero be suspected of being guilty of one of the most prevalent human vices: envy.

"It is unfortunate," I tried to argue to Khrabrovitskiy, "that scientists, including great ones, chiefs and generals, are not devoid of this feeling. In their environment, showing envy of the success of an outsider, no matter how quiet it is kept, is particularly dangerous."

"It is impossible for envy to exist between real friends Bashkirtsev and Ognev. They are genetically stripped of this feeling," objected Khrabrovitskiy.

Isayev didn't back me up in arguments with Khrabrovitskiy over the relationship between Korolev/Bashkirtsev and Glushko/Ognev. After familiarizing himself with the screenplay and listening to my comments, Isayev unexpectedly displayed the talent of a movie critic.

"The screenwriter has the right to idealize the heroes. It's not necessary to give a detailed description of all their weaknesses. When we defend our designs, we have to glamorize them. The experts know this and tolerate it, keeping in mind that they will be modified during the operating process. The film has the advantage that it isn't modified after it goes on the screen. So, let's allow Khrabrovitskiy and his heroes all their sins."

At my recommendation, the three of us got together on neutral territory in a quiet corner of the Botanical Garden to discuss the problem of the relationship between the main characters.

"What are you trying to prove?" Isayev asked me. "The acrimonious conflict between Korolev and Glushko occurred sometime in 1960, and not without some help from Vasiliy Mishin. But before then, from the time they worked at NII-3, then in Kazan, and in Germany during the production of all the rockets up to and including the *Semyorka*, they were kindred spirits. Both of

---

49. Kirill Yurevich Lavrov (1925–2007) was a famous Soviet stage and film actor who appeared in over 70 movies during his lifetime. Igor Olegovich Gorbachev (1927–2003) was a stage and film actor who also taught drama and acting in Leningrad.

them have personalities that are too complex for literary heroes, much less for cinema. Korolev is even more understandable, although he was not just the 'founder of practical cosmonautics', as they now write, but a great performing artist. If fate had taken a different turn, he could have also become a military leader, or director of a major factory, or perhaps even a minister. In a word, he was a natural leader who needed to continually overcome difficulty. If he had been a commander, he would have moved the army into frontal attacks, without regard for losses, leaving garrisons of the remaining enemy in the rear—if only he could be the first to seize or liberate a city. And unremittingly—onward once again.

"Glushko doesn't have Korolev's artistry or his talent as a commander. If it weren't for his purposeful devotion since his youth to rocket engines for the sake of interplanetary flights, he might have become a scientist, even a loner astronomer, chemist, radio physicist, I don't know what else, but [he would have been] very devoted. After developing a new theory in great detail, he will not back down from his principles and will defend them very passionately.

"In history, they were both destined to become chief designers. Before this, they endured the school of 'enemies of the people' together. This brought them together. Although even while imprisoned in Kazan, Korolev could barely acknowledge the authority of chief designer Glushko, who was also imprisoned there.[50] After their release, both were sent to Germany at the same time. But Glushko had the rank of colonel, while Korolev was a lieutenant colonel. Later, Korolev officially outranked Glushko. He was head chief designer, he was the technical manager for all the State Commissions, and he was head of the Council of Chief Designers. Korolev was hungry for power, and Glushko was hungry for fame. At Korolev's funeral, we walked out of the House of Unions together. Glushko said in dead earnest, 'I am ready to die in a year if they give me a funeral like that.'

"Glushko throws himself into his work, but he dreams of fame, even posthumous fame. Korolev didn't spare himself either, but he needed fame while he was alive."

Our meeting in the Botanical Garden created an atmosphere ripe for revelations and reminiscences. Isayev and I had arranged to skip out of work for the afternoon, and Khrabrovitskiy needed to recharge to work on his screenplay

---

50. For a brief period, from 1944 to 1945, Korolev served as Glushko's deputy at OKB SD—*Opytno-konstruktorskoye byuro spetsialnykh dvigateley* (Experimental Design Bureau for Special Engines)—which was the cover name for the facility where they jointly designed rocket-assisted takeoff units for various Soviet military aircraft.

and direction. Isayev took advantage of the opportunity to tell us about what he described as a heart-to-heart conversation with Glushko.

This conversation took place at the firing range on 24 October 1968—Isayev's 60th birthday. The next day Isayev began to tell me about it, but the circumstances prevented me from hearing out his confession. We were preparing for Beregovoy's launch, and at that time I wasn't interested in hearing what Glushko discussed with Isayev. Now I shall try to reproduce Isayev's story from memory.

"At the firing range at that time we were preparing the first piloted Soyuz launch after the death of Komarov. Beregovoy was supposed to fly, and the day before I had turned 60. My guys tried to organize a party, but I begged off. In the morning we had to get up early for liftoff. And there was the prelaunch State Commission [meeting]. We had first launched an unpiloted vehicle.[51] If everything went fine with it, a day later a piloted vehicle was supposed to lift off to dock with the unpiloted one. Before this, after calling 'for all the top ranking people' to show up, more brass than necessary flew in from Moscow. Over the course of the day they came to see me at the hotel one at a time and in groups. I held up as best I could, but by evening, when the stream of guests ended, I felt more tired than after sorting out failures on the test stand. I could barely keep my eyes open, and all of a sudden Glushko arrived. He brought his own bottle. Courteously, as only he knows how, he apologized, but said very adamantly that two engine specialists, he and I, had both turned 60 this year and he would not leave until I drank with him to the success of our cause.

"From previous encounters and from common acquaintances I knew that he didn't drink at all, but that evening I was immediately no longer sleepy when Glushko poured himself and me a glass as equals. Little by little we almost finished the bottle. True, it was top-notch vodka, *Posolskaya* (Ambassadorial), and there were enough snacks left on the table (the guys had intended to drop in for breakfast early that morning). We talked a bit about our problems and discussed all the brass from the minister to Ustinov, and somehow of its own accord the conversation came around to the N-1. Before this I had been on an excursion to the big MIK. Vanya Raykov showed me and explained everything there.[52] I must admit that when I saw 30 chambers on the first stage, it made me a bit nervous. But after Raykov's confession about how the developmen-

---

51. *Soyuz-2* (7K-OK No. 11) was launched at 1200 hours Moscow time on 25 October 1968.

52. Ivan Iosifovich Raykov (1918–1999) was one of the leading rocket engine specialists working for Korolev (and later, Mishin). Like Mishin, Chertok, Isayev, and many others, he had worked at the famous NII-1 institute during World War II.

tal testing of the engines was going in Kuznetsov's shop, I thought that you wouldn't be able to pull this huge thing off without Korolev. This gossip has nothing to do with your screenplay, Daniil Yakovlevich. For you it all ends with the death of Bashkirtsev. But it's a shame. There should be another series about the Moon."

"I remember how Glushko changed when I asked him, not very effectively, his opinion on the N-1. The calm, almost amicable conversation dropped off. He even changed outwardly. He straightened up in his chair and began to berate me as if I was to blame for the fact that Korolev had made that vehicle. I had nothing to do with that whole affair. Then Glushko very much wanted me to take his side in this conflict, if only as an engine specialist, and realize that he was right. According to him, Korolev very much wanted him to produce an oxygen engine with 145 to 150 tons of thrust within inconceivably short deadlines. From the very beginning he did not understand why Korolev just simply refused to go with the cluster configuration, which had ensured success for the *Semyorka* and which by that time Chelomey was already using in the *Pyatisotka* [Proton]. At that time, he, Glushko, was still afraid of oxygen-kerosene engines due to their propensity toward high frequency. Moreover, Glushko maintained that he had proposed a compromise to Korolev: reconfigure the rocket so that the engine clusters would be arranged in separate blocks using the cluster configuration that they had optimized on the R-7. Then each six-engine block could be tested out in stand-alone mode on a test rig. And finally, he persuaded him to agree to high-boiling propellant components. In this case, Glushko set about creating an engine with 600 tons of thrust within five years.[53] At that time at the hotel Glushko assured me that Korolev, under Mishin's influence, did not agree to any of the compromises. Both Korolev and Mishin placed their bets on Kuznetsov, and they simply took him, Glushko, off the N-1 rocket project.

"Projects for Yangel and Chelomey compelled him to create a large-scale test rig facility for high-boiling component engines. Glushko promised Korolev that he would get involved with a high-power oxygen engine, but later. At the time, in 1961, there was no such window for oxygen, and in terms of the deadlines, it was much easier to produce a high-power engine running on tetroxide and *geptil*. In order to show that we could produce high-power engines, he accepted Chelomey's proposal. He was already finishing up developmental testing of engines with 640 tons of thrust for the UR-700. No one was driving him.

---

53. This was the RD-270 (or 8D420) engine with a sea-level thrust of 640 tons. Its development was terminated in 1969.

There was still no trace of Chelomey's rockets, but he had an engine. And if we had been working on the N-1 since 1961, then we could have delivered the engines as early as 1966.

"I knew the story behind the development of the *Semisotka* [UR-700] and 600-ton engines. We were all exasperated by the redundancy of the N-1. But that evening Glushko vented his resentment to me; he wanted to prove that if Korolev had agreed at that time, seven years ago, then we would still have had the hope of catching up with the Americans. And the first stage of the N-1 would not have become a warehouse of questionable engines. Instead of a calm discussion, Korolev handed over all the information to Mishin for analysis. And as for Mishin, right off the bat he rejected everything that didn't conform to his idea of controlling the rocket by changing the thrust of opposing engines."

Puffing on one of his favorite *Belomor* cigarettes, Isayev spoke so intelligibly, graphically, and convincingly, that Khrabrovitskiy, who was not well versed in engine matters, listened to him without interrupting and without asking questions. I was the one who interrupted him.

"Everything that you are telling us is top secret, and we ask Daniil Yakovlevich never to mention this. But to understand the complexity of the relationship between Korolev and Glushko, let it be taken into consideration."

I tried to critique the screenplay for other obvious departures from the actual biographies of the heroes. Ada Rogovtseva played Natasha—the girl whom Bashkirtsev loved in his distant youth, whom he never stopped loving, but forgot for the sake of a rocket.[54] The first rocket edged out his first love. After becoming famous and settling down in the House on the Embankment, Bashkirtsev feels that he can no longer live without this woman.[55]

"Now you know, there's absolutely nothing akin to Korolev's biography here," I admonished Khrabrovitskiy. "Moreover, Ada Rogovtseva, that is, Natasha, is a charming woman; she raises a son on her own, and in actual fact Korolev had, and, thank God, has a living and healthy daughter Natasha."

"You keep on arguing with me because you know how things really were," Khrabrovitskiy said. "I am not at all obliged to reverently adhere to the real characters and biographies. The heroes of the film are mine, not yours, and the moviegoers will believe me because they will love these heroes. I deliberately idealize people and I want them to be that way. These shouldn't be varnished

---

54. Ada Nikolayevna Rogovtseva (1937–) is a famous Soviet (and Ukrainian) stage and film actress who has been in over 70 movies. In 2007, then-President of Ukraine, Viktor Yushchenko, awarded Rogovtseva the rank of "Hero of Ukraine" for her contributions to theater and film.

55. An apartment house on the Bersenevskaya Embankment in Moscow, completed in 1931 as the Government Building, was a residence of the Soviet elite.

ideals, but the viewer should love each of my heroes. Our film has no evildoers, traitors, executioners, prostitutes, or spies. I admire all of you just as you are, but I want to make you even better. I see this as my mission."

The wonderful actors such as Kirill Lavrov, Igor Gorbachev, Ada Rogovtseva, Vsevolod Safonov, Igor Vladimirov, Andrey Popov, and Innokentiy Smoktunovskiy did their part, as did the fact that *Taming the Fire* was shot on location. The *Semyorka* launches and crashes were the real thing, from documentary footage. In the feature film they had a much stronger impact on the viewer than in the documentary format.

A small group of consultants and several big-shot officials from the ministry and VPK, invited by Khrabrovitskiy at our insistence, watched the still-raw film for the first time on a small screen at the *Mosfilm* studio. No one could remain indifferent. All of us were disturbed by the question: how would the powers that be feel about the film? For the first time on the screen the fire of failed launches raged, rather than just those successful liftoffs known to the viewer.

"You know, Daniil Yakovlevich," Isayev turned to Khrabrovitskiy after the screening, "you managed to show so convincingly the process of 'taming the fire' on the screen that I was more concerned and experienced a more intense thrill than when I was at the firing range for the actual launches. Even the real crashes affected me less because I was not as anxious over my own fate as I was today for your heroes."

In the depths of his soul Isayev remained an inveterate romantic. He possessed a blend of creative obsession, natural simplicity, and humor that Korolev and Glushko lacked. But he belonged to the very same generation. Therefore, the romantic idealization and artistic ennoblement of their characters impressed him.

Khrabrovitskiy was happy and touched. Grigoryev and I advised him, "In order to get the green light for the film to be released, you need to show it to Ustinov. He will decide who else you need to invite."

The management of *Mosfilm* took our advice and went to Ustinov. Grigoryev also telephoned him. He explained that Marshal Nikolay Krylov had commissioned him to be a consultant and among the consultants he mentioned Isayev and me, and Vladimir Patrushev, the chief of the First Directorate of the firing range, who directed the launches in the film footage. Ustinov accepted the invitation and came for a screening with a small group of Central Committee staff. On the advice of the Central Committee, Khrabrovitskiy did not call Mishin, Glushko, or other chiefs.

With Ustinov's permission, Isayev, Grigoryev, and I were invited to the closed screening. Before *Taming the Fire*, they showed the American film *Marooned*—an artistic interpretation of the possible consequences of the failure of a spacecraft's descent engine.[56] The three astronauts are deprived of the possibility of returning to Earth. Oxygen supplies are rapidly dwindling; they are faced with an agonizing death. We have always feared such a situation more than any other space emergencies. A Soviet spacecraft tries to save the Americans, but the rendezvous process failed. The U.S. Air Force frantically prepares a small super-secret winged spacecraft. They rush through the idea of using a small "shuttle" as the rescue vehicle. To add drama to the action, the oldest member of the American crew is ejected into space to prolong the lives of the younger crewmembers. All the heroes of the American film were quite positive, but they didn't have to act; the bulk of the time was devoted to showing technology, not people. The U.S. Air Force's secret spacecraft saves the crew of a spacecraft similar to the Apollo.

In *Taming the Fire*, at my prompting, they emphasized the organizational role of the high-ranking Party-economic manager. As best I could, I told People's Artist of the USSR Popov about Ustinov's role in our affairs.[57] In the film my tip proved to be rather transparent. The screening was a success. Ustinov was clearly moved. He gave Khrabrovitskiy a firm handshake, congratulating him on his success. Turning to us, the consultants, he said, "Your influence is palpable. We are still just dreaming about such equipment in the bunker. Thank you for giving pointers, it means there's already a mockup. And during Korolev's lifetime we couldn't make peace between him and Glushko. If they had been such friends as Bashkirtsev and Ognev, a lot of things would have been different for us."

"I don't think that you would have been so preoccupied with the fate of the N-1," said Isayev suddenly.

"Yes, perhaps, you're right," replied Ustinov with a melancholy smile.

Ustinov said that Leonid Ilyich Brezhnev and other members of the Politburo must absolutely see this film. A screening was organized, and the film appeared uncensored on the nation's screens. By that time, Isayev was no longer among the living, and I was unable to share my impressions with him. In 1972, the film *Taming the Fire* received the Crystal Globe—the main prize at the Karlovy Vary International Film Festival—and, in 1973, first prize at the All-Union Film Festival in Alma Ata.

Two years after the film's release, when Glushko was appointed general designer of NPO Energiya, I was asked, "What is this? At your insistence Mishin

---

56. *Marooned* (1969) was directed by John Sturges and starred Gregory Peck and Gene Hackman among others. It was based on the 1964 novel of the same name by Martin Caidin.

57. Andrey Alekseyevich Popov (1918–1983) was a Soviet theater and film actor who gained fame in such movies as the Russian production of *Othello* (1955) and *Oblomov* (1980).

became the chief after Korolev's death, and according to the film, which was shot four years ago, the chief engine specialist, that is to say, Glushko, takes Korolev's place. How were you able to foresee this back then? So you wanted to correct your mistake through the film?"

I laughed it off: "First they showed the film to Ustinov, and then to Brezhnev. After that they mulled it over for two years, and as you see, they made the decision. This is the great power of art."

For Isayev and me, our participation in the work on the movie became a sort of diversion, a respite from our very stressful everyday routine. We were able to correct history and people at our discretion. Together, Isayev and I talked Khrabrovitskiy into continuing the space epic and making an exciting science adventure film about the Moon race. Isayev's death dashed our dreams. After *Taming the Fire* Khrabrovitskiy managed to make two more films: *Tale of the Human Heart* [*Povest o chelovecheskom serdtse*], devoted to cardiac surgeons, and *Poem About Wings* [*Poema o krylyakh*], in which the main heroes were Tupolev and Sikorskiy.[58] At the screening of the latter film at the House of Film, I reminded Khrabrovitskiy about our dream. He promised to give it some more thought. Perhaps he did, but the cardiac surgeons were unable to save his life.[59]

AFTER OUR DIGRESSION about the film *Taming the Fire*, let's return to Glushko's office and to our conversation in August 1974.

"Barmin's position is extremely disturbing to me," said Glushko. "Has Barmin maybe been reborn in the past few years? Instead of his ostensible work, he's been carried away with the effect of the magnetic field on the human mind. He argues with a straight face that going beyond the limits of the magnetic field risks mental breakdown. It seems to me that Barmin doesn't want to work in our cooperative network. We need a backup for his organization in the development of ground-based launch systems so that our work doesn't suffer—on a competitive basis. I propose that we give some thought to competitions not just for the ground systems. Why not work on going to the Moon at the same time? I'm certain that there are also developers who will be able to propose interesting designs for the competition. I'm certain that Solovyev's design bureau can solve launch

---

58. Andrey Nikolayevich Tupolev (1888–1972) and Igor Ivanovich Sikorskiy (1889–1972) were contemporaries and giants of Soviet aviation. Sikorskiy immigrated to the United States in 1919, where he had a long and illustrious career as a designer of helicopters.

59. Khrabrovitskiy died on 1 March 1980.

problems as well as Barmin's.[60] Or Viktor Kuznetsov's. He's your friend, Boris Yevseyevich. Kuznetsov wants to have a tranquil life working on his old gyroscope production stock. With that kind of attitude it's difficult to expect much from him. Give some thought about whom we could give the gyroscope order to instead of Kuznetsov, also on a competitive basis. It would also be good to set up competition for the entire series of reusable transport systems for the Moon. But we have to start with Barmin. Let him realize that he's not the center of the universe, that there are groups who are proposing better designs.

"Next. We need to have Guskov back up Ryazanskiy on the whole radio complex.[61] Instead of Mnatsakanyan's *Igla*, it's high time we began development of a backup system. Why haven't you tested Bogomolov's *Kontakt* (Contact) system yet?[62] We particularly need this kind of competition for computers.

"Lidorenko's electrochemical generators are clearly inferior to the *Minsredmash* proposal for the L3.[63] You weren't afraid and took the generators offered by this ministry. Why can you do it there, and not in other places? Can you explain this to me?"

"A competition system is fine for architecture," I tried to object. "There, during the drawings phase, one can argue and select beautiful designs. In our technology, until we come up with the first experimental prototypes, it is difficult to bring out an error-free design. In order to back up development before the actual model-testing phase, we will have to increase expenditures and extend deadlines by 150 to 200 percent. We need to test not one, but a minimum of two versions. Such an idea will hardly be successful without guarantees for funding. We'll give it some thought, but without a VPK decision there won't be a bidding process. We won't be funding our main subcontractors; the budget will."

"And you're going to leave that for me."

---

60. Vsevolod Nikolayevich Solovyev (1924–) served as the chief designer of KB Transmash—*Konstruktorskoye byuro transportnogo mashinostroyeniya* (Design Bureau for Transport Machine Building)—from 1963 to 1991. Beginning in the 1970s, this organization became Barmin's competitor for designing launch complexes for Soviet missiles and launch vehicles. It designed the fully automated launch complex for the Zenit-2 rocket.

61. Gennadiy Yakovlevich Guskov (1918–2002) was chief designer of NII Mikropribor from 1967 to 1975. He later headed NPO Elas, which designed microchips and microelectronic components for various military and civilian applications.

62. *Kontakt* was the rendezvous radar system developed for the L3 piloted lunar landing project for use between the LOK and the LK.

63. *Minsredmash* was the ministry in charge of developing nuclear weapons.

From our side, Anatoliy Abramov was overseeing Barmin's projects.[64] Having worked at one time in the field of diplomacy, he was viewed by our organization as a diplomat and master of reconciling confrontational situations, including those between Korolev and Barmin.

"Vladimir Pavlovich's speech was strange," he said. "The very form of such a statement was off the wall and shocked everyone. All of us around this table have seen and heard all kinds of speeches over the past 20 years. But never have they been so spiteful. However, we must take into consideration the fact that it is unrealistic to entrust the modification of the N-1 launch site for any other rocket to anyone besides Barmin. Barmin understands this full well and knows that the minister will back him up. If you do not object, Valentin Petrovich, I will try again to speak with him."

We all understood that regardless of his authorization, Abramov would still have a talk with Barmin, just as I did not need permission to meet and have candid conversations with Pilyugin, Kuznetsov, and Ryazanskiy.

IT WAS MOST DIFFICULT FOR THE ENGINE SPECIALISTS. Melnikov, Sokolov, and Raykov were supposed to concisely explain to Nikolay Kuznetsov and his deputies, with whom over these years they had not only argued until they were blue in the face but had also already begun to work well together, why work was being shut down on engines for the N-1. In the gravest of situations, none of them dreamed that now it would come to the termination of the project and complete breakdown. But why? They could only answer that such was the order of Glushko, who had been appointed general designer. There had not yet been any ministerial orders, much less any governmental resolutions calling for the termination of operations on Kuznetsov's engines for the N-1.

Several days later Bushuyev, Pilyugin, and I had to hear out Barmin one more time when we met at a gathering of our academic department at the Institute of Machine Science on Griboyedov Street. Barmin was offended by Glushko's remarks to him in front of Ustinov concerning his intention to take away the lunar base.

"You know better than I that from the very beginning Glushko was against the N-1. He proposed his own high-boiling component engines to Korolev, and you, Mishin, and Korolev only required oxygen. After having a run-in with Glushko, you had Kuznetsov begin developing a liquid-propellant engine from scratch. You aired your dirty linen in this regard at the Defense Council

---

64. Chertok is alluding to the fact that Abramov was the person at NPO Energiya in charge of ground systems development, which was subcontracted to Barmin's design bureau.

that Khrushchev convened in Pitsunda.[65] We hadn't allowed such a thing in our own small council. I believe that Glushko ruined our old Council of Chief Designers. Sergey had a strong character; I don't have to tell you that. Khrushchev personally tried to make peace between them. Nothing came of it. (Khrushchev's attempt to reconcile Korolev and Glushko is described in volume two of Sergey Nikitich Khrushchev's book *Nikita Khrushchev: Crises and Rockets*.)[66] Glushko could no longer influence the development of the N-1.

"Mishin, with our general assistance, made a mess of this grandiose project. No one bothered to explain to our people why Soviet cosmonauts didn't visit the Moon. Abroad they know full well that we were in the process of preparing an enormous rocket. They wrote openly about our failures.[67] Only our people aren't supposed to know the truth. At diplomatic and other types of meetings with foreign dignitaries and leaders of fraternal parties, Brezhnev was also asked, 'What's going on with the Moon?' Ustinov evidently thought for a long time, sought a convenient excuse, and then Keldysh suggested, 'The most relevant space program now isn't the Moon, but the reusable space transport system.' This system is strategic, and we must give the Americans an appropriate response. And so as not to put an end to the lunar program, they report to the Politburo, or perhaps they have already reported, that an end hasn't been put to the lunar program, and in fact, a powerful concentration of forces has been created in the form of NPO Energiya. Heading the enterprise is Korolev's old compatriot, prominent scientist and engine specialist Glushko. Now Glushko is dreaming of going down in history not only as a great engine specialist, but also as a great rocket engineer. Today's Politburo has long forgotten about Glushko's differences of opinion with Korolev.

"The priority task when a project has been terminated is to manage to report to your superior that the necessary measures have been taken to strengthen management. And if someone asks Ustinov what the main ministry is doing—after

---

65. This is a reference to a famous meeting held in February 1962 at the holiday resort of Pitsunda where a number of major decisions were taken on the development of strategic missile systems.

66. Sergey Khrushchev, *Nikita Khrushchev: Krizisy i Rakety: vzgliad iznutry*, 2 vols. [*Nikita Khrushchev: Crises and Rockets: A View from the Inside*] (Moscow: Novosti, 1994). A slightly different English translation of the combined two volumes was later published in the United States. See *Nikita Khrushchev: Creation of a Superpower* (University Park: Pennsylvania State University Press, 2000).

67. The failures of the N-1 rocket were generally known from open sources in the West beginning in the fall of 1969. See, for example, Stuart Auerbach, "Soviet Moon Rocket Exploded in Test," *Washington Post* (18 November 1969): A1; "Soviets Suffer Setbacks in Space," *Aviation Week and Space Technology* (17 November 1969): 26–27; "Disaster at Tyuratam," *Time* (28 November 1969): 27.

all, the government had created the Lunar Council—then one could report that Minister Afanasyev turned out not to be up to the task.[68] But not right away. You need a one- or two-year wait until you can remove the minister—until the Space Shuttle begins to fly. When it comes to light that the lunar program has been scuttled, and the reusable system still hasn't been created, then the minister can be held responsible, especially since he's not just a minister, but also the former chairman of the Lunar Council. And if they make me modify the launch facilities for another launch vehicle, then ultimately I'll do it. Just don't let Glushko hope that this is going to be minor repairs. Modifying the launch facilities will take three or four years."

ACTUALLY, IT WASN'T THREE OR FOUR YEARS. The decision of the Central Committee and Council of Ministers about the termination of operations and writing off the expenditures for the N1-L3 project didn't appear until February 1976. They wrote off expenditures of 6 billion rubles at 1970s prices. On 17 February of that same year, 1976, a decree was issued calling for the creation of the MKTS, the basis of which was the new super-heavy launch vehicle. This decree appeared four years after a similar decision of U.S. President Richard Nixon calling for the creation of the Space Shuttle space transportation system. Nixon's decision put an end to the possibility of the continued use of the Saturn V launch vehicle, which had demonstrated its reliability to the whole world during the lunar expeditions.

The decree of the Central Committee and USSR Council of Ministers, dated 17 February 1976, "On the creation of the MKTS consisting of a booster stage, orbital aircraft, interorbital tug vehicle, system control complex, liftoff/landing and repair/recovery complexes, and other ground-based facilities supporting the insertion of payloads up to 30 tons in northeast orbits to an altitude of 200 kilometers and the return from orbit of cargoes weighing up to 20 tons" finally put an end to the N1-L3 program. It also put an end to projects dealing with the lunar base.

Work on the Energiya-Buran program required such a mobilization of efforts throughout the entire nation that the RLA launch vehicle series project,

---

68. The Lunar Council was an interdepartmental body established to supervise the progress of the N1-L3 program. It was originally established by VPK decree on 31 July 1964 (when it was known as the "Council on the N-1 Complex"). The Council was originally headed by S. A. Zverev, the then-chairman of the State Committee for Defense Technology. Once the space program was transferred to the new Ministry of General Machine Building in 1965, Afanasyev replaced Zverev as chairman.

about which Glushko had delivered his speech in 1974, remained on paper.[69] The Energiya launch vehicle distinguished itself favorably from the American Space Shuttle in that it could carry not only the Buran spacecraft, but also any payload with a mass up to 100 tons, into Earth orbit. To control the flight of the Space Shuttle complex the Americans created a system in which the entire payload was placed on board the piloted spacecraft. We remained faithful to the classic format. The Energiya launch vehicle had its own system that provided control for the insertion into space of any payload. Unlike the American Space Shuttle, the Buran orbital vehicle did not control flight during the insertion flight segment.

Up until the late 1960s, Glushko remained an opponent of producing powerful engines operating on oxygen-kerosene and oxygen-hydrogen propellant components for the N-1. Fifteen years after his falling out with Korolev, Glushko decided to prove that only his school (GDL—OKB-456—KB Energomash) was capable of producing the best super-powerful oxygen-kerosene engine in the world. After Glushko's appointment as general director of NPO Energiya, Vitaliy Radovskiy became chief designer at KB Energomash in Khimki. He was tasked with creating the unique (in terms of its performance data) RD-170 oxygen-kerosene engine for the first stage of the Energiya launch vehicle. However, Glushko retained conceptual management and the right to personally make crucial decisions in critical situations. A government decree assigned the development of the RD-0120 oxygen-hydrogen engine for the second stage of the launch vehicle to Aleksandr Konopatov, the chief designer of KB Khimavtomatiki in Voronezh.[70]

The production of actuators to pivot the engine chambers on the first and second stages and engine control servo system drives were assigned to Complex No. 4 (which was part of my group), under the management of Vadim Kudryavtsev. Rather than being an outside observer, in my line of duty, I was a participant in the developmental testing of the stage-one and stage-two propulsion systems and their integration with the rocket and control system. During the process of testing the engines, a well-known dialectical postulate about the "transformation of quantity into quality" manifested itself to the full extent. The engine capacities, their dimensions and masses, moments of inertia, and accuracy of the deviations required for control exceeded many times everything that we had dealt with in our previous "actuator" work. It

---

69. For an excellent and detailed account of the Energiya-Buran project, see Bart Hendrickx, *Energiya-Buran: The Soviet Space Shuttle* (New York: Springer, 2007).

70. KB Khimavtomatiki was the new name of OKB-154, the old Kosberg design bureau.

was not possible to solve new problems using classical methods of the theory of automatic control.

Glushko happened to be the general designer of a rocket, the second stage of which used hydrogen as propellant. This was the very same hydrogen that Glushko had considered unacceptable for use due to its very low boiling temperature and low density. Directives ordering the creation of new, powerful engines that were called for by the government decree of 1962 were fulfilled 20 years later under a new decree. Glushko not only rejected his previous anti-hydrogen dogmas, but also as the head general designer he took on the solution of new tasks using cryogenic components—oxygen and hydrogen.

The first stage of the Energiya consisted of four blocks, each with one four-chamber RD-170 engine having a sea-level thrust of 740 tons. For the second stage they used four single-chamber RD-0120 engines, each with a thrust of 200 tons. The bitter experience of explosions and fires on the N-1 launch vehicle was fully taken into consideration during the development of the Energiya and, above all, of its engine systems. Glushko presented the ministry and later the VPK an ultimatum: the firing range needed a test rig for full-scale firing tests on a flight-ready model of Energiya.

Those opposed to the construction of a rig, a very expensive structure, argued that unlike the N-1, the engines of Energiya were reusable. They undergo in-process firing tests and then are installed on the rocket without being overhauled. The test rig was an extravagance that Glushko had contrived to gain time. It was obvious to everyone that the RD-170 engine was going to fall through, and here Glushko found a way to gain an additional couple of years to find a way out of this dead-end situation. The support of Ustinov, who at that time was a Politburo member and minister of defense, ensured a decision in favor of building the unique test rig/launch facility.[71]

The development of the RD-170 engine for the first stage of the Energiya began back in 1976. Just five years later the first engine arrived in Khimki for integrated firing tests. And from the very first firing there was one failure after another on the test rig. The most severe was the failure in June 1982 during a test on the first stage of a Zenit rocket, which had the very same RD-170 engine as the Energiya.[72] The explosion of the engine was so powerful that

---

71. This was a special facility as Site 250 at Baykonur known as the UKSS—*Universalnyy kompleks stend-start* (Universal Rig-Launch Complex)—which doubled as both a test stand and a launch site.

72. The Zenit used a slightly different version of the RD-170 known as the RD-171. For more information, see Hendrickx, *Energiya-Buran.*

it destroyed the only test rig in the rocket industry created especially for the ground-based developmental testing of heavy rockets.

Even our most revolutionary engine specialist, Mikhail Melnikov, was reeling.

"Glushko took a stab at a problem that is more than we or the Americans can handle at the current level of technology. This is like what happened with controlled thermonuclear reaction. It was 25 years ago that Kurchatov announced that we were on the verge of learning how to control a thermonuclear reaction and would make humankind very happy. So far, nothing has come of it. And then Glushko rushed to make an announcement about an engine with a thrust of almost 800 tons and with a closed-cycle configuration to boot."

It wasn't just the unique Energiya-Buran rocket space complex program that was on the line. Seventy-five-year-old Glushko was threatened with a technical defeat rather than an administrative one. But not only did he refuse to budge from his positions, he displayed amazing performance and an unyielding sense of purpose and tenacity. After each failure, it is necessary to find the causes, perform modifications, and prove one's case not just to the skeptics in one's own organization, but also to high-ranking interdepartmental commissions. By the way, Arkhip Lyulka was the only one on this commission who was not a harsh critic, but was a well-intentioned aide and consultant.

It wasn't until December 1984 that completely successful tests were conducted confirming the engine's stated parameters and reliability. By this time, Konopatov's first hydrogen engines had also arrived. And we, the control specialists, were convinced of the reliability of our new, absolutely unique and powerful digital control surface actuators.

And now it was once again 15 May! But this time, it was 1987. Exactly 30 years had passed since the launch of the world's first intercontinental *Semyorka*. (At that time, the launch had been a failure.) The super-heavy rocket, called Energiya at Glushko's recommendation, lifted off for the first time, not from a standard launch system, but from a test rig/launch facility, for which Glushko had battled so fiercely. The reliability of the launch vehicle was confirmed on the first attempt. The torments of many years of ground developmental testing had not been in vain.[73]

The first successful flight of the American Space Shuttle, which had spurred us to begin making our own Energiya-Buran reusable space system, took

---

73. It should be noted that the payload for the first Energiya launch, the *Polyus/Skif-DM* laser station prototype, failed to reach orbit on account of a malfunction in the control system. On this launch, the payload was supposed to provide the final boost to orbital velocity.

place on 12 April 1981—10 years after development had begun. From the last launch of N-1 No. 7 to the first launch of the new super-heavy launch vehicle, 15 years had passed!

On 15 November 1988, the Energiya-Buran reusable rocket-space complex brilliantly executed its first and last flight. This was the second launch for the Energiya. The Buran reusable orbital vehicle was flying for the first time. After making two passes around the globe in unpiloted mode, Buran landed at the airfield with amazing precision under conditions of very strong crosswind. The two flights of the Energiya launch vehicle were truly a triumph for the engine and control specialists. Neither Glushko nor Pilyugin was present for the first and last launch of the Energiya-Buran reusable rocket-space complex.[74]

Over the first three years of this 15-year period, i.e., from 1972 to 1975, it was possible using the already available production stock for the N-1 launch vehicle and the new batch of engines (by 1974 around 100 units had been manufactured) to produce a reliable launch vehicle, compared with the performance characteristics of the modern Molniya and Proton launch vehicles. Over this same three- to five-year period (to be on the safe side we'll add another two years), our domestic technology was fully capable of creating spacecraft and modules for an expedition to build a lunar base.

Having created the Salyut and then the *Mir* orbital stations, we had ensured the permanent presence of a human being in Earth orbit in space. The resources invested in the Energiya-Buran reusable space system would have been more than enough to create a lunar base. And then…then, beginning in 1980, Soviet (and then Russian) cosmonauts would not only have been continuously in Earth orbit, but also on the Moon.

After 1975, after completing the Apollo-Soyuz project, the Americans finally halted operations on the Saturn launch vehicle, switching NASA's main forces to the production of the Space Shuttle system. We rushed to catch up with them, having completely shut down the N1-L3 project, and following their example, we invested enormous resources into a reusable transport system. In 1988, we proved that our Energiya-Buran reusable rocket-space complex was technically as good as the American Space Shuttle. By the Americans' own admission, economically, the Space Shuttle reusable transport system did not live up to their expectations. It cost more to insert payloads into space using the reusable system than using expendable launch vehicles. That's where we beat out the Americans!

---

74. Glushko and Pilyugin passed away on 10 January 1989 and 2 August 1982, respectively.

"Every cloud has a silver lining." The termination of the N1-L3 project and the five-year time lag on the MKTS made us continue our work on orbital stations at a faster pace and perfect nonreusable transport systems using our tried-and-true R-7 and UR-500K launch vehicles. Despite the woes that befell our cosmonautics after the collapse of the USSR, and the general Russian economic crisis, we kept the piloted *Mir* station in orbit and continued to remain "ahead of the whole planet." The American Shuttle learned how to approach our *Mir* and dock with it.[75] Engineers from both nations worked together to solve this problem. If someone had mentioned the possibility of such a turn of events even in 1975 when the decision was made concerning an "appropriate" strategic response, in the best-case scenario he or she would have been considered delusional.

In August 1965, the Belgian newspaper *Latern* published an article by Wernher von Braun with the catchy headline "In 1970 Your Ticket to the Moon Will Cost 5 Billion Francs."[76] We actually could have built a base on the Moon by 1985. And then a ticket to visit our base would have cost around 100 million dollars.

In 1965, Wernher von Braun gave the following prediction: "As long as we use nonreusable launch vehicles to transport passengers, potential clients will have to pay 5 million dollars when flying from Earth into orbit and 50 to 100 million dollars when visiting the Moon, which will take place from 1970 to 1975."

From 1969 to 1972, the actual cost to the United States of sending one man to the Moon and returning him from the Moon was more than 1 billion dollars.[77] A trip into orbit aboard the Shuttle for one individual in a seven-person crew in 1997 cost not 5 million, as von Braun predicted, but 75 million dollars. If one were to sell tickets, a three-day Earth orbit on our Soyuz would cost 15 million dollars. But given the acute need for funds, the Russian Space Agency and RKK Energiya have established a rate of 20 million U.S. dollars for an eight- to ten-day trip for space tourists on the Soyuz and International Space Station.

In 1964, Korolev said that it wouldn't be long before it would be possible to make a trip into space on a trade union pass. Alas! The optimistic predictions of von Braun and Korolev failed to materialize before the end of the 20th

---

75. The Space Shuttle docked with the *Mir* space station for the first time during the STS-71 mission from June to July in 1995.

76. According to the rates in 1965, 1 dollar was equal to 50 Belgian francs.

77. NASA reported a figure of 25.4 billion dollars in 1973 for the total Apollo program, which included seven attempted landings, including one failed mission.

century. Korolev, Glushko, and von Braun were not only engineers and realists, but they were also dreamers. Technically, their dreams and predictions could have been fully realized before the end of the 20th century.

After the reliability of Kuznetsov's engines was proven, after the creation of the world's most powerful engine, the RD-170, and the RD-0120 hydrogen engine in Voronezh, after two spectacular flights of the Energiya launch vehicle, and after proving that long-term resident cosmonauts on *Mir* were capable of working, there was no more doubt: we could have created a habitable base on the Moon before the end of the 20th century, and with the participation of the U.S. and European countries—no doubt whatsoever!

THE SUMMER OF 1988 WAS NOTABLE for particular space activity on the *Mir* orbital station. The first flight of the Energiya in conjunction with the Buran was being prepared for autumn. All the hardware was manufactured and delivered. In short supply was a "weightless" intellectual product—software. Glushko continued to amaze everyone. He patiently interrogated my comrades, our subcontractors, and me, attempting to understand what was causing the difficulties in producing and developing this product, which was unconventional for previous rocket technology. Unlike many other older chiefs, Glushko very much wanted to gain insight into the true nature of the new software problem. It seemed to me it would take two or three more meetings and he would understand the difficulties that had cropped up as a result of our having entrusted spacecraft control to computers. It didn't turn out that way.

One typical workday he was working alone in his office. Taking advantage of his right to enter unannounced, Mikhail Yaremich stopped by to report about the completion of an assignment.[78] He saw Glushko, who had made a feeble attempt to stand up. He couldn't explain what had happened. An ambulance took Valentin Petrovich to a hospital on Michurinskiy Prospekt. A month later, we were reassured that everything would be all right, but with the proviso: "Bear in mind his age. Anything could happen."

On 2 September 1988, Glushko turned 80. Semyonov, Vachnadze, Ryumin, Yaremich, and I came to the hospital to wish him a happy birthday. When we entered his ward, he was sitting in a chair dressed in clothes that were certainly not hospital garb. Each of us said something, told him happy birthday, and wished him a speedy recovery. Glushko listened, nodded slightly, without smiling; he looked detached, as if he were thinking about something completely different. The time allotted for visits quickly ran out.

---

78. Mikhail Ivanovich Yaremich was Glushko's long-time personal and security aide.

Senior veterans of the Soviet space program gather at the unveiling of a memorial plaque in honor of Valentin Glushko at his former workplace in Building 65 at NPO Energiya. From left to right are M. S. Khomyakov, V. M. Filin, A. I. Ostashev, N. I. Zelenshchikov, B. Ye. Chertok, O. D. Baklanov, V. M. Karashtin, and M. N. Ivanov.

His illness progressed. He managed to ask Yaremich and Stanislav Petrovich Bogdanovskiy, the director of Energomash's Experimental Factory, who visited him six days before his death, that his body be cremated and his ashes be delivered into space—to Mars or Venus. Glushko passed away on 10 January 1989. His request about the cremation raised no objections in the top-ranking Party organs. But no one could fulfill his last wish. The urn containing his ashes was buried at Novodevichye Cemetery. Fastened to his granite gravestone was a stylized image of the last great creation of Soviet cosmonautics—the launch vehicle Energiya gushing a fiery plume with the Buran orbital vehicle perched on its back.

AFTER THE COLLAPSE OF THE SOVIET UNION, the main portion of its scientific and technical inheritance and industrial potential of the rocket-space sector remained in Russia. The mass breakdown of economic contacts with the former Soviet republics and the actual loss of effective government support threatened the scientific and technological potential of domestic rocket technology and cosmonautics.

History assigned a mission to the leaders of the rocket-space schools—survive no matter what; preserve and pass on to new generations not only technology, but also the best of the traditions and human aspirations that united and contributed to the immensely rapid development of cosmonautics. Fifty years after the launch of the first artificial satellite, the two leading space powers, the United States of America and Russia, have no great strategic programs. Humankind really needs Korolev, Glushko, and von Braun. Hundreds of modern-day managers will never replace them.

Epilogue

The world in the 21st century continues to change at a scorching pace. Today's reader working in any of the new fields of technology has very little time for reading all four volumes of my memoirs. I am counting on the attention of those who were there at the turn of the millennium, who are trying to make sense of the past and are not indifferent to the future.

The second half of the 20th century is replete with truly revolutionary scientific research, discoveries, and engineering achievements. World War II and the Cold War years gave rise to aerospace, nuclear, radio engineering, and computer technologies, and they became a great material strength. Just in the two decades after the war, space was transformed into a real necessity. The race between the two great powers to explore space was more risky and arduous than the rivalry between Spain, Portugal, and England during the Age of Exploration.

In the 20th century the rate of scientific discoveries increased hundreds of times. Historians believe that the total achievements of scientific and technical progress over the past 50 years have exceeded everything that was done in the preceding 5,000 years. The "hot" and "cold" world wars have receded into the past, but myriad local wars continue. They stimulate some fields of science and technology, slow down others, and devour enormous resources, which could be spent on further breakthroughs into the secrets of nature, on discoveries, and on enriching human knowledge. The thirst for knowledge did not die even in the darkest periods of human history. This is a powerful driving force. I was one of the warriors at the very leading edge of scientific and technical progress, and working there was enthralling. Writing memoirs about this bustling time has proved more difficult than being directly involved in the dynamics of the process.

I do not regret that I was born in the Russian Empire, grew up in Soviet Russia, achieved a great deal in the Soviet Union, and continue to work in Russia. Hundreds of thousands, even millions of my contemporaries lived "not by bread alone." Those who revile their native land's past in pursuit of big news stories and careers and try to trample underfoot everything that our people have created forget that they owe their very existence here on Earth to a heroic generation that saved human civilization. Yes, we made many mistakes. But those who excel in the cynicism of subverting everything that happened "after 1917," under the cover of the hastily hammered together philosophy of utilitarian pragmatism, will not shy away from the criminal plundering of the riches created by the people for the sake of their own enrichment.

From the author's archives.

Boris Chertok.

The most difficult thing for me, the author of these memoirs, was performing flight control on an imaginary time machine. Where and for how many lines should I pause? What route shall I take next? It is up to the reader to judge how successful my choices have been. Taking advantage of my rights as an author, I would like to quickly sail through the history of astronautics in the second half of the 20th century. In the process of this cursory perusal I would like to show the errors that we in the USSR, and in Russia, and also that the Americans made when producing space technology. At the beginning of the Space Age, fully competent and active developers of actual rocket-space systems pondered over its future, rather than outsider pundits. It is very interesting to contrast what they dreamed of with what actually came about, what they worked on, and what considerable funds were spent on. I will say, right off the bat, that both we and the Americans were quite wrong in our predictions. We have a legitimate excuse—the tragedy of the collapse of the Soviet Union, which protracted into a 10-year permanent political, social, and economic crisis. The Americans had no such legitimate excuses. It is all the more amazing that they made so many more errors in their prognoses. Therefore, let's start with them.

The United States entered the Space Age on 1 February 1958, when a Jupiter-C launch vehicle (a modification of the Redstone combat missile) inserted *Explorer 1*—a satellite with a mass of 14 kilograms—into low near-Earth orbit. A group of German specialists headed by Wernher von Braun developed the Redstone and Jupiter-C in the United States. I will remind the reader that the Soviet Union inserted the world's first artificial satellite (with a mass of 86 kilograms) into space and a second one carrying the famous dog Layka in 1957. After the Redstone came modifications of American combat missiles Thor, Atlas, and Titan II, which were used as space launch vehicles. The first American Mercury single-seat spacecraft were inserted into ballistic trajectories using the Redstone and into Earth orbits using Atlas-D launch vehicles. Launches of Gemini two-seat spacecraft were the preparatory stage of the Apollo program. The Titan II launch vehicle inserted these vehicles into Earth orbit. The flight of the first U.S. astronaut [in orbit], John Glenn, took place 10 months after the flight of Yuriy Gagarin. The new Saturn I, Saturn IB, and Saturn V were designed from the very beginning as space launch vehicles rather than strategic weapon delivery vehicles.

Rockets from the Saturn series were designed above all for the Apollo program of piloted lunar vehicles. It was assumed that after the first lunar expeditions were completed and the Saturn V launch vehicle was updated, it would be used for new missions—the creation of a habitable base on the Moon and the beginning of piloted flights to other planets. However, after the conclusion of the Apollo program on 7 December 1972, the Saturn V was used just one time, without its third stage, to insert the *Skylab* experimental orbital station.[1] The Saturn IB completed its last flight in 1975 as part of the Apollo-Soyuz program.

After 1975, the United States abandoned piloted flights until the reusable Space Shuttle space transport system was put into service. The Delta, Atlas-Centaur, Titan II, and Titan III launch vehicles were subsequently used only to insert unpiloted spacecraft of various applications. America's rejection of the tried-and-true, reliable Saturn V launch vehicle seemed strange. I believe it was a mistake. American historians of astronautics whom I have met have been unable to give a clear explanation as to why, despite previous plans, they "laid to rest" the excellent Saturn V launch vehicle.

In 1965, the United States prepared a prognosis of the development of astronautics until the year 2001. These data were presented at a high-level symposium in March 1966 in Washington, DC. In 1967, we received the opportunity to familiarize ourselves with the American plans in documents classified "secret" or "for official use only," despite the fact that in the United States, materials from the symposium were available in open publications. The majority of our specialists assessed the American prognoses as overly optimistic,

---

1. The final Apollo mission, *Apollo 17*, began on 7 December 1972. The crew of astronauts Eugene A. Cernan, Ronald E. Evans, and Harrison H. "Jack" Schmitt returned to Earth on 19 December 1972 after Cernan and Schmitt completed three extended excursions on the lunar surface.

but no one dared call them absurd. The argument was primarily about the reality of the dates. We believed that even working with us, the Americans could fulfill a significant portion of these plans, but around five years later than planned. And without us, one needed to add another five years or so.

As it is impossible to discuss in detail our rivals' prognoses for all areas of astronautics, I shall touch on the epochal ones. The Americans intended to put small, continuously operating orbital laboratory stations (like our *Salyuts*) into service in 1972; an orbital complex with chemical engines in 1973; ones with nuclear engines in 1974; a large orbital research laboratory in 1976; a piloted orbital global communications, information, and surveillance center in geostationary orbit in 1984; and an orbital manufacturing complex in 1987. Piloted flights to other planets would have begun with the landing of a human being on the Moon in 1969. From 1975 to 1978, there were plans to create a continuously operating lunar scientific station, a manufacturing base using local resources, and a lunar interplanetary spaceport!

NASA managers, the directors and vice presidents of leading aerospace corporations, reputable scientists, employees of the Department of Defense, and even members of Congress delivered reports about the captivating prospects for colonizing almost all of near-solar space. The boundaries of American interests extended far beyond near-Earth space. He who masters space will master the world—the prognoses of 1966 were built on this principle.

The Americans planned a heliocentric expeditionary flight using nuclear rocket engines for 1981 and a Mars reconnaissance station, Mars surface landing, and study and colonization of its satellites for 1984 to 1986. A piloted flight with a possible landing on Venus was supposed to take place before 1988. In 1966, American scientists still did not know what Venus's atmosphere was like and what the conditions of its surface were. Beginning in 1967, one Soviet automatic Venera spacecraft after another reported that our idea of life was not compatible with the conditions on Venus.

During the period from 1990 to 2000, they planned to create scientific research stations on the satellites of Jupiter and Saturn. They didn't forget about Mercury either. They planned to create a station on Mercury to study the Sun, and by the end of the century—mines and enterprises to extract and process metallic ores. Numerous flights of automatic vehicles—interplanetary reconnaissance probes—were supposed to precede all of these piloted expeditions.

Now we know that this prognosis panned out only in terms of the first lunar expeditions and automatic reconnaissance vehicles. The Americans fulfilled President Kennedy's national challenge to land on the Moon. The role of the lunar expeditions for the United States consisted not just in gaining scientific and technological priority, particularly over the Soviet Union. This red-letter day rallied the nation as a unified sociocultural whole.

Examples of the flights of the first Soviet cosmonauts from 1961 to 1965 and of the American lunar expeditions from 1969 to 1972 graphically showed that such achievements are truly a powerful stimulus for unifying society; each citizen has the opportunity to be proud of the achievements of his or her country. After such triumphant victories, public opinion magnanimously pardons optimists for their prognostic errors.

The future programs of piloted orbital flights and exploration of the Moon and planets depended on having a refined Saturn V launch vehicle by 1975, bringing its payload mass to 160 tons, a launch vehicle successor to Saturn with a payload mass of 320 to 640 tons (developed by 1989), and a reusable aerospace delivery vehicle.

They intended to make broad use of impulse nuclear and thermonuclear rocket engines as the primary propulsion systems. These would shorten the flight time to planets severalfold compared with chemical fuel engines. Their plans also called for prosaic near-Earth space systems for the purposes of meteorology, communications, navigation, global surveillance, and monitoring ecological safety.

To a great extent, the prognosis of 1966 panned out regarding the flights of interplanetary automatic vehicles. American scientists made sensational discoveries every year while studying Mars, Jupiter, Saturn, their moons, and even the most distant planets of the solar system. In near-Earth space, new, strictly utilitarian commercial benefits and prospects for achieving military superiority in space were discovered. Fans of piloted flights to the planets had to "come down to Earth."

The situation during the years 1971 to 1973, when the Space Shuttle program was being considered, required that the managers responsible for decision-making carefully add up the total cost of the program and the annual budgetary limits for the various attractive versions of reusable systems. Ten years later, in 1976, the Americans once again mobilized scientists to draw up a forecast for the development of space technology for the period from 1980 to 2000. This was a much more serious collective scientific work concerning all areas of science and technology supporting the development of astronautics.

For piloted Earth-orbit flights, the idea of doing away with expendable launch vehicles gained a foothold. The main difference in the plans and corresponding decisions of 1966 and 1975 was that in 1975 there was a much more refined technical base, created for the Apollo program and for military space, scientific, and economic programs over the past decade.

Citing the space successes of the USSR, the Pentagon demanded that more funds be allocated to military space programs. They had yet to be formulated, but ideas were already "in the air" regarding the future Strategic Defense Initiative (SDI).

In 1975, the main criterion for selecting proposals based on prognoses for all fields supporting the advancement of space technology was the cost (in dollars) of inserting units of mass into low-Earth orbit. As far as delivery vehicles were concerned, all subsequent decisions were made in favor of the Space Shuttle. Moreover, it was assumed that it would be substantially improved compared with the design that was already being implemented. All plans were based on the overly optimistic estimates of the cost of inserting a payload into space and also on the fact that the Space Shuttle would not only insert but could also return expensive space hardware to the ground for repair and relaunch.

NASA's preliminary estimates showed that compared with an expendable launch vehicle such as the Saturn IB, the cost of insertion into low-Earth orbit decreased, at first threefold or fivefold, and then tenfold. While neglectful economic estimates had been allowed in 1966, in the 1970s they were performed more meticulously. It is all the more surprising that the Americans, knowing how to count money much better than we, predicted a completely ridiculous cost for the insertion of a unit of payload mass by the year 2000.

For various scenarios using the Space Shuttle, the cost vacillated in a range from 90 to 330 dollars per kilogram. Moreover, it was assumed that the second-generation Space Shuttle would make it possible to lower these numbers to 33 to 66 dollars per kilogram.

American economists erred by a factor of 60 to 100! Such mistakes are simply inconceivable when calculating the technical parameters of space systems. If American economists could commit such mistakes, should one reproach our domestic economist-reformers, who consider U.S. economists overly authoritarian? Powerful modern computer technology has sharply increased the confidence level and reliability of scientific and engineering calculations. Sometimes practical results are even better than calculations because input data with considerable margins have been loaded into the computer. Economic calculations for large systems in principle will be erroneous if the main baseline parameters are subjective considerations, the political situation, or an ad hoc social mandate.

The American scientists' prognoses in 1966 and 1967 for the piloted flight programs proved true only with regard to the first lunar expeditions and the creation of the Space Shuttle reusable piloted transport system. For the sake of this system they didn't just mothball the reliable Saturn V launch vehicles. The launch complexes at Cape Canaveral and at the John F. Kennedy Space Center were modified for the Shuttles, and they were no longer suitable for Saturns. The actual dates for creating a lunar base and for an expedition to Mars were moved far beyond the year 2001. The thrilling prospect of colonizing the planets of the solar system (before the end of the 20th century), which was elaborated in detail in 1966, in my view, in the best-case scenario, needed to be postponed to the second half of the 21st century.

The first flight of the Space Shuttle reusable space transport system took place on Cosmonautics Day, 12 April 1981.[2] To be fair, I must say that in terms of fundamental scientific research, the Americans surpassed their own prognoses. After spending more than 2 billion dollars, they used the Space Shuttle to insert the automatic Hubble satellite into space; this is a large, even by Earth-based standards, telescope for astrophysical research. The information obtained using the Hubble over the years of its service was many times greater than the information that the field of astrophysics had possessed before this.

In the early 1970s, after six piloted lunar expeditions, the construction of a permanently operating lunar base and an expedition to Mars before the beginning of the 21st century seemed quite feasible not just to scientists, but also to the clear-eyed managers of aerospace corporations. The main factor precluding the implementation of even these two very realistic programs was the turn of U.S. politics toward the militarization of space. Somewhat later, the whole array of military space programs to intimidate a potential enemy was called the Strategic Defense Initiative (SDI). The main objectives and missions of the SDI program were considerably clearer and more necessary to the Pentagon, to large corporations, and to the majority of Congress than was the aspiration of romantic scientists for interplanetary travels.

In the late 1960s, the USSR and the United States adhered to doctrines of nuclear deterrence. Their gist was based on the following concept: both sides possess such means that if one of the sides were to use nuclear weapons first, then the retaliatory strike would force the aggressor to incur exorbitantly high expenses relative to the possible gain. Such a balance was based on the common sense of the sides. Both great superpowers agreed in principle that deterrence based on mutual vulnerability was not only expedient, but also necessary.

However, such an approach created a threat for the main producers of combat missile systems, nuclear warheads, nuclear submarines, and airplanes carrying nuclear weapons. Actually, if so much weaponry were produced that by design each of the opposing sides knew it was capable of destroying the other many times over, then the amount of orders, and consequently the profits and super-profits, would decrease sharply in the near future. Moreover, politicians who realized the senselessness of the continued buildup of strategic weapons began negotiations to limit and reduce them. The Soviet

---

2. This was the STS-1 mission with astronauts John W. Young and Robert L. Crippen piloting the Space Shuttle *Columbia* on a two-day mission.

Union spent enormous resources and paid a high price to achieve quantitative and qualitative parity with the strategic rocket forces of the United States. American strategists, having realized that the Soviet Union had achieved parity, discovered a way to inflict heavy economic damage on it without resorting to nuclear attack. If there were more than enough intercontinental rockets and nuclear warheads, then it was necessary to invest many billions of dollars in creating an effective defense, rather than in the buildup of means for nuclear missile attack. Theoretically it wasn't difficult to justify the need for creating fundamentally new systems to protect the United States. American propaganda loudly declared that Soviet missile weaponry was creating an increasingly greater threat to the viability of American forces of deterrence and the structures controlling them.

At the same time that the United States was spending over 25 billion dollars on the Apollo lunar program alone, the USSR continued to work intensively on new types of intercontinental missiles and on the creation of new classes of submarines equipped with state-of-the-art ballistic and cruise missiles.

The Pentagon exaggerated the achievements of our missile technology, counting on securing a sharp increase in budgetary allocations for the SDI program from Congress. They reported to Congress and to the President of the United States that by the mid-1970s Soviet missiles had become considerably more powerful and more accurate, which would enable them to quickly and effectively undermine the capability of U.S. ground forces for a retaliatory strike. According to the calculations of U.S. military economists (I was unable to find our own authoritative data), on average, the Soviet Union spent 40 billion dollars per year each on strategic offensive programs, and also on active and passive defensive programs. This did not take into account the many billions allocated for conventional armaments. In the Americans' view, the Russians, despite their peaceful assurances, were adhering to doctrines for achieving their objectives by delivering a preemptive strike.

Given such a terrible prospect, could the United States allow itself to invest funds in colonizing the Moon, Venus, Mars, Mercury, and the moons of Saturn and Jupiter? It's unclear when and what would happen there. But if, instead of the fanciful plans of eggheads dreaming of strolling along the "dusty lanes of distant planets," you could mobilize scientists and industry, using the very latest achievements of world science, to develop advanced technologies and systems to protect against Soviet missiles, then you could kill three birds with one stone:

- First, save the United States from the threat of nuclear annihilation if the USSR attacked first.
- Second, draw the USSR into a new arms race—not of offensive weapons, but defensive ones. This would require expenditures that the Soviet

economy would be unable to sustain, and the United States would win a non-nuclear victory.

- Third, rather than single one-of-a-kind space objects, create new types of defensive weaponry that require the mass production of weaponry to destroy the striking power of the attacking side. And this would require enormous capital investments, as well as hundreds of thousands of new jobs, and would bring enormous profits for companies capable of mastering very advanced technology.

The systemic concept of SDI looked very enticing. It called for the stage-by-stage development and deployment of antiballistic missile complexes. It all began with space systems for monitoring and tracking targets during the powered flight segment, in space, and during entry into the atmosphere. Each enemy missile flight segment requires the development of its own monitoring and striking systems, including space-based systems, exoatmospheric interceptors, and ground-based antiballistic missiles. To destroy thousands of missiles and warheads flying toward the United States, it was suggested that conventional smart projectiles be used on the first stages, and thereafter a wide array of all sorts of laser weaponry. For "death rays" they designed space-based military neutral particle accelerators and space- and ground-based lasers. They also proposed the creation of super-high-velocity guns, first based on the ground and then in space. Engineer Garin, the main character of Aleksey Tolstoy's famous novel *Hyperboloid of Engineer Garin*, works alone to create a portable device—the source of a beam that could burn through any obstacle in its path.[3] Fifty years after the appearance of this talented science fiction detective, it turned out that it was really possible to create such a beam. But to do this required not one ingenious inventor, but thousands of engineers, physicists, and the most sophisticated manufacturing technology. Automated ground-based combat control and communication systems would be needed to control thousands of automatic vehicles on duty in space and a multitude of projectiles and combat platforms attacking the missiles of a potential enemy. They must receive advance information from numerous ground-based radar stations and surveillance satellites and, after processing the information, transmit commands to the weapon.

The integrated systemic design called for the development of super-high-speed computers, fundamentally new optical and microwave sensors to detect and track targets, high-capacity nuclear power energy sources to supply power

---

3. Aleksey Tolstoy's *Giperboloid inzhener Garina* was first published in serialized form from 1925 to 1927 in the journal *Krasnaya nov* [*Red Virgin Soil*].

to accelerators and lasers, space-based platforms with all kinds of projectiles, and many other elements of new systems that were appealing to scientist-inventors and engineers. For scientific creativity and corporate profitability, prospects had been opened up that were beyond their wildest dreams in the field of the peaceful exploration of space. Stunning "Star Wars" images filled movie and television screens.

After achieving worldwide celebrity for the United States, the Saturn V launch vehicle proved unnecessary for the SDI program. There were no payloads for it. In the view of the SDI creators, the Shuttles could handle everything that needed to be preliminarily inserted in space. Thus, the Americans themselves closed the door on piloted flights to the Moon and planets. All the prognoses and actual designs for this subject have been left for historians and posterity, if they are lucky enough in the 21st century to bring back to life the attempts to conduct interplanetary expeditions.

The new space initiative of President George W. Bush, made public in 2006,[4] calls for a return to the Moon, the construction of a lunar base, and an expedition to Mars. The exact dates of the flight have not yet been mentioned, but there is no place for an updated Saturn V and Space Shuttle in these prospective programs. Space transport systems are once again under development using the wealth of past experience.[5]

After the collapse of the USSR and the signing of various international agreements, the SDI program had to be curtailed. In any case, only scientific research has been continued. However, the broad capabilities of space technology have found practical application in local wars. If the main objective of the space vehicles of the SDI program was to protect the territory of the United States against Soviet missiles, then in the local wars in the Persian Gulf region in 1991, during the NATO offensive in Yugoslavia in 1999, and in the war in Iraq, space technology supported the conduct of combat actions in three areas: on land, on the sea, and in the air.

According to the latest data, more than 100 automatic space vehicles took part in the military operations in the Balkans. They conducted optical-electronic, radar, and radio reconnaissance; provided navigational support for

---

4. Chertok means 2004.

5. President George W. Bush announced his Vision for Space Exploration (VSE) during a speech given on 14 January 2004. According to the original plan, humans were to return to the Moon by 2018 and set up a permanent base. Such a base could eventually be used for future missions to Mars. A new, crewed space transportation system, known as Constellation, would use elements of the Space Shuttle design. The Constellation program, however, was effectively canceled by President Barack Obama, although some elements (such as the Orion vehicle) could still be built.

combat aviation, and high-precision cruise missiles; and gave meteorological support and communications for troop control at strategic and tactical levels.

At the end of the Cold War, the United States had achieved its primary strategic objective: the collapse of the Soviet Union and the neutralization or utilization for its own interests of Russia's scientific and technical potential. Having remained the sole superpower for a while, the United States is rushing to turn our planet and near-Earth space into a zone of American interests.

Instead of resuscitating programs for interplanetary flights, NASA has come up with the idea of creating a large near-Earth orbital station. Russia's indisputable achievements in this field were the reason for this. I wrote earlier about how and why we got ahead of the Americans in the creation of Long-Duration Orbital Stations.

LET'S RETURN TO THE SOVIET UNION and have a look at what we planned during the last years of Korolev's life and the two decades after him. Unlike the Americans, we did not predict the future until the year 2001; rather, we began at once to design this future.

In 1959, the R-7 rocket had just learned how to fly. After many failures, we finally delivered a pendant of the USSR to the Moon with a direct hit and astounded the world, having transmitted the first authentic, if not very clear, images of the far side of the Moon. That same year of 1959, with Korolev's approval, Mikhail Tikhonravov's group, which included Maksimov, Dulnev, Dashkov, and Kubasov, designed a heavy interplanetary spacecraft.[6] Work on the design of a single-seat Vostok had just begun, and these zealots had already designed the equipment layout for a three-seat vehicle weighing 75 tons, 12 meters long, and 6 meters in diameter. A year later they modified the design: they added a nuclear reactor to the vehicle as a power source. After getting involved in the design process, Feoktistov and Gorshkov increased the number of crewmembers to six. Three or four people could land on the surface of Mars and travel in special planetary rovers.

In 1964, on the advice of the chairman of the State Committee on Defense Technology, Sergey Zverev, the Scientific-Research Institute of Transport Machine Building (NIItransmash) became involved in the design of planetary rovers.[7] The main specialty of this NII was tank building. Korolev personally visited NIItransmash. Director Vladimir Stepanovich Starovoytov

---

6. The generic name of this project, which continued through the 1960s, 1970s, and 1980s, was Heavy Interplanetary Ship (TMK).

7. Sergey Alekseyevich Zverev (1912–1978) served as chairman of the State Committee on Defense Technology from 1963 to 1965.

introduced him to Aleksandr Levonovich Kemurdzhian, whom they asked to switch from a tank to a planetary rover. Eight years later Kemurdzhian had managed to create lunar rovers that could be controlled from Earth. From 1970 to 1973, two lunar rovers traveled a total of 47 kilometers on the surface of the Moon.

Work on the Mars expedition project continued after Korolev. Failed launches of the N-1 rocket did not dampen the enthusiasm of Korolev's "Martians." Mikhail Melnikov's team, together with the organizations of the Ministry of Medium Machine Building, achieved the first encouraging successes in the development of space nuclear reactors as primary power sources. Thermionic generators were sources of electric power for electric rocket engines, which had a performance index five times greater than chemical engines. The results of broad research on nuclear power sources and electric rocket engines inspired confidence in the reality of interplanetary expeditions.

Glushko, who had come to lead Korolev's team, rather than shut down the project, supported Fridrikh Tsander's rallying cry well known to the leading lights—"Onward to Mars!" Under Glushko, the Mars vehicle design was enriched for reliability with a second nuclear reactor. After operations on the N-1 and N-1M were shut down completely in 1976, Glushko insisted on using the Vulkan launch vehicle, designed to insert a payload of up to 230 tons into near-Earth orbit.

The expedition project based on the Vulkan gave rise to acute "allergy" attacks in our ministry and in the cabinets of the VPK. For this reason, the planners of interplanetary expeditions switched to the Energiya launch vehicle, capable of inserting up to 100 tons of payload into Earth orbit. The very extensive experience of assembling large structures in space, which was accumulated during the creation of orbital stations, inspired confidence that an expedition could be assembled in Earth orbit in increments of 100 tons each, provided with everything it needed, and sent to Mars.

Everyone who has returned from space talks about how beautiful our Earth is. But both cosmonauts and unpiloted surveillance and reconnaissance satellites see that on our blue planet, small wars continue unabated. Even without space-based reconnaissance, it is well known that wars in Afghanistan and Chechnya and the destruction in Yugoslavia and Iraq have cost tens of times more money than needed for an expedition to Mars.

After the collapse of the USSR and the beginning of the implementation of a "market economy" in Russia, cosmonautics not only lost government support, but also encountered the concealed and open opposition of the reformers who ended up in power. After the death of Valentin Glushko, from 1991 through 2005 Yuriy Semyonov occupied the post of general director and general designer of NPO Energiya. In 1994, this state organization was converted into the publicly traded corporation S. P. Korolev Energiya Rocket-Space Corporation.[8]

Unlike its predecessors, the managers of Russia's rocket-space enterprises had to work under "new economic conditions" and above all solve the problem of survival. The chief and general designers had attained great achievements during the epoch of the centralized mobilized economy. However, during that time, not one of them had to fear for the very existence of the enterprise and its staff. The omnipotent Central Committee could remove a chief designer from the job and replace him with a more obedient one. As I recall, in the 45 years after the war this very seldom happened. But before 1992, no one even dreamed that enormous staffs could be deprived of the means to sustain them and pushed to the verge of a squalid existence. The struggle for survival—the new sphere of business for the managers of all enterprises and organizations of the once powerful military-industrial complex—demanded enormous efforts. Not everyone managed to endure. Despite the fierce struggle for survival that the management of RKK Energiya faced, the Mars expedition projects continued to be updated. True, this was only on paper.

Well, but what about the Moon? After the American expeditions to the Moon we considered it quite realistic to even the score by establishing a permanently operating lunar base. Proposals for the delivery of a nuclear power plant to the Moon seemed quite feasible. The plant would power a factory for the production of oxygen from lunar rocks and provide life support for all the systems for scientific research.

Back in Mishin's time, the staff of TsKBEM and specialists under Barmin's supervision at KB OM had been working on the development of a design for the lunar base relying on the N-1M launch vehicle.[9] Funding for these projects came from the budget of the Ministry of General Machine Building.[10] I have already mentioned that Glushko objected to continuing these projects in

---

8. The S. P. Korolev Energiya Rocket-Space Corporation (*Raketno-kosmicheskaya korporatsiya 'Energiya' imeni S. P. Koroleva*, or RKK Energiya) was established by an order of the president of the Russian Federation on 29 April 1994.

9. KB OM—*Konstruktorskoye byuro obshchego mashinostroyeniya* (Design Bureau of Machine Building)—was the new designation for Barmin's old design bureau, originally known as GSKB Spetsmash. As of 2011, KB OM was known as the V. P. Barmin Scientific-Research Institute of Launch Complexes, which is a branch of the larger TsENKI—*Tsentr ekspluatatsii obyektov nazemnoy kosmicheskoy infrastruktury* (Center for the Operation of Ground Space Infrastructure Objects), the consolidated organization that manages all ground infrastructure for the Russian space program.

10. The implication here is that the project was not funded by the primary clients of the Soviet space program, the missile and space forces.

Barmin's shop and persuaded the ministry and the VPK to completely transfer these projects to NPO Energiya.

Glushko entrusted the management for developing the Zvezda lunar expedition complex to two quite distinguished figures of Korolev's school. Konstantin Bushuyev was in charge of developing vehicles for the flight to the Moon and return to Earth, while Ivan Prudnikov was in charge of the lunar village, which called for a habitation module, a nuclear power station, a laboratory module, a factory module, and a driver-operated lunar rover with an operating radius of up to 200 kilometers.[11] Bushuyev, who held the high-activity post of director of the Soviet part of the Apollo-Soyuz program, had a difficult time making the transition to the placid design work on the lunar base after the program's brilliant conclusion in 1975.

During this period I was so loaded down with updates on the Soyuzes and off-nominal situations on the Salyuts that I didn't have time to respond to Bushuyev's and Prudnikov's requests to delve into the details of their projects and render active assistance in designing the control and electric power systems.

In the winter of 1977, during one of our "nightcap" strolls along Academician Korolev Street shrouded in a frosty fog, Bushuyev complained that he didn't believe in his current design for the lunar expedition complex.

"No one but Valentin Glushko is interested in this work," said Bushuyev. "The ministry and the VPK say that we need to catch up with the Americans in terms of a reusable transport system. With [Yuriy] Semyonov in charge, you all don't have time for anything but orbital stations and Soyuzes. Igor Sadovskiy has gotten carried away with the Soviet version of the Shuttle and considers our work on the Moon to be frivolous. The Central Committee wants to perform as many piloted launches as possible in order to outdo the Americans in terms of the number of cosmonauts. We are planning an expedition counting on having at least 60 tons in lunar orbit and landing cargoes of 22 tons each on the surface of the Moon. If we hadn't stopped upgrading the N-1, we would have optimized the hydrogen Block S_R instead of Blocks G and D. Then two launches for such a payload would have been sufficient. In all: 8 to 10 launches of the upgraded N-1—and we would have a base for six persons on the Moon."

The next morning, I dropped everything and I went to Bushuyev's office and listened to his comments on the wall charts and diagrams of the lunar base/station project.

---

11. Ivan Savelyevich Prudnikov (1919–) served as chief designer at NPO Energiya from 1974 to 1982, specializing in human lunar spacecraft.

Boris Chertok (left) and Konstantin Bushuyev, one of the leading deputies at OKB–1 who was in charge of the development of piloted spacecraft.

"Now you believe that, given our capacity of 43,000 people and with a half million subcontractors, in around five years we can produce all the vehicles and modules and upstage the Americans, who out of their own stupidity terminated the Saturn—for the long run if not forever?"

Bushuyev and Prudnikov convinced me of the feasibility of the project, even if the new Vulkan launch vehicle never appeared.

On the morning of 26 October 1978, Bushuyev had a toothache, and he went straight from his home to the polyclinic. For some reason, before the dentist would see him, he was advised to have an electrocardiogram. Sitting calmly in an armchair waiting for the results of his EKG, he died.

Prudnikov, having realized the hopelessness of continuing the projects on the lunar colonies, switched to a more relevant activity for that time—developing the design for a military space station.

In 1978, after reviewing the lunar expedition projects based on the use of Vulkan launch vehicles, an expert commission chaired by President of the USSR Academy of Sciences Mstislav Keldysh considered them irrelevant and found that they distracted the staff of NPO Energiya from the main mission of vital importance to the state, creating the Energiya-Buran reusable space transportation system.

The launch vehicle for the Buran was the Energiya rocket, which completed its first successful flight on 15 May 1987. Glushko made his last attempt to save the lunar base projects, using the Energiya rocket, but he received no support "from the top."

Our project for a lunar expedition in 1973 using upgraded N1-L3M rockets could have been the first attempt at equalizing the score in the Moon race. The lunar base projects of 1976 through 1978 were the second attempt. Both proposals were shut down "from the top." Thirty years have passed. Today we are even further from the possibility of creating a lunar base than we were in 1978.

On the occasion of Vladimir Barmin's 90th birthday, a commemorative meeting was held at the firm named after him.[12] Among those invited, I gave a speech with my memories of Barmin and made sure to mention his enthusiasm for the lunar base project. After a session in the company museum among the brilliantly executed mockups of the launch systems of various rockets, which I had had the occasion to see in reality over the years, in the farthest corner of the exhibit I discovered a mockup of the lunar colony, "the Barmingrad."

IN THE HISTORY OF SPACE EXPLORATION, there are dates that it has become tradition to celebrate, both nationally and internationally. Russia still remembers 4 October 1957 and 12 April 1961. We rarely think about 20 July 1969, the date of the first landing of an Earthling on the Moon, although this event also ranks among the great scientific and technical accomplishments. In addition to such generally recognized anniversary dates, there are many events, forgotten by or simply unknown to the broad public, that are dear to a small group of individuals directly involved in them.

On 20 February 1986, the first, core module of the *Mir* station was launched and the construction of a habitable space station began. Two months before the launch of *Mir*, at the large "Council in Fili" (at the Khrunichev Factory), which Minister of General Machine Building Oleg Baklanov[13] conducted, I reported about the software arrearages and the missed deadlines for the delivery of the latest innovation in control technology for the space station: powered control moment gyroscopes. So that the beginning of construction on the station would not be delayed, instead of installing them on the core module, Sheremetyevskiy and I proposed installing six control moment gyroscopes on the *Kvant* module, which we were getting ready to launch after we made sure that the main core module was operating normally.

---

12. Barmin's 90th birthday was celebrated on 17 March 1999.

13. Oleg Dmitriyevich Baklanov (1932–) served as minister of general machine building from 1983 to 1988. Later, he was one of the architects of the coup against Soviet Communist Party General Secretary Mikhail Sergeyevich Gorbachev in August 1991.

The *Mir* control system was fundamentally new. The dates for the station launch were not so much determined by its manufacture as by its ground-based debugging. My comrades, our subcontractors, and I reported optimistically, but inwardly each of us was heartsick. The skepticism regarding our proposal—to launch the core module, and then deliver and hook up the main attitude-control system (the control moment gyroscopes) a couple of months later—was understandable.

After an uproarious discussion during a 3-hour meeting, ZIKh Director Anatoliy Kiselev invited all of us to dinner.[14] It would be unfair to complain about the array of drinks and hors d'oeuvres spread out over the tables in the next room. After our emotional conversations at the meeting, I relaxed and didn't stop my friends when they promptly filled my wineglass.

Suddenly, over the general noise, I heard someone say my name, and my comrades sitting next to me started to nudge me hard.

"Answer the minister," I heard someone whisper.

Oleg Baklanov, who was sitting an another table, had turned to me, and now for the third time was asking me: "So tell me honestly, Boris Yevseyevich, will we fulfill the mission or are we just warming up? Before the Party Congress we don't just need a successful launch, but steady work in space.[15] Today I learned that the dates and reliability of the orbital station depend on a fundamentally new control system."

I stood up and loudly reported: "We will fulfill the mission. And the station will not only be in operation for the congress, but for three years after that."

At that time three years seemed like the limit of a guaranteed service life. Twenty days after inserting the core module into orbit we were confident that we could reliably control the station. The very first *Mir* crew was Leonid Kizim and Vladimir Solovyev. They arrived on board on 15 March 1986.

Gradually the station configuration was completely transformed. The core module became overgrown with the modules *Kvant*, *Kvant-2*, *Kristall*, *Spektr*, and *Priroda*. The total mass of the orbital complex grew from 25 tons to 136 tons. The total volume of the pressurized compartments was 400 cubic meters. Absolute world records were set on the station for the continuous length of time spent by a human being under spaceflight conditions. Valeriy Polyakov

---

14. Anatoliy Ivanovich Kiselev (1938–) served as director of ZIKh from February 1975 to June 1993. Later, he was director of the M. V. Khrunichev State Space Scientific-Production Center before retiring in 2001.

15. The Twenty-seventh Congress of the Communist Party was held between 25 February 1986 and 6 March 1986.

became the absolute world record holder. He spent 438 days continuously on *Mir*, and his total time for two flights was 679 days.[16]

Sergey Avdeyev set the record for the cumulative duration of his time in space, 748 days.[17] American astronaut Shannon Lucid set the women's record for spaceflight duration on *Mir*, 188 days.[18] Twenty-eight long-duration primary expeditions were conducted on *Mir* and 25 visiting expeditions on Soyuz and Space Shuttle vehicles. One hundred and four cosmonauts and astronauts worked as part of the crews. Given a total station mass of 135 tons, the mass of the scientific equipment comprised 11.5 tons. During *Mir*'s time in service the processes of rendezvous, docking, and the delivery of cargoes and fuel by Progress cargo vehicles was refined and brought to a high degree of reliability. Domestic vehicles delivered 150 tons of cargo. In all, more than 220 organizations of the former USSR were involved in the creation and operation of the *Mir* station.

On 25 June 1997, due to the error of people involved in the rendezvous control loop, cargo vehicle *Progress M-34* collided with *Mir*. This was the first "space battering ram." After similar off-nominal situations, airplanes "deviate toward the ground." After being rammed, *Mir* remained functional.

Along with the piloted and unpiloted transport systems, *Mir* was a one-of-a-kind space complex. *Mir* was the pride of Russia. The Energiya Rocket Space Corporation, the actual owner of *Mir*, had every right to be proud of it, but no one from the Russian elite—"you greedy hordes around the throne"[19]—was interested in its continued operation in space.

Instead of the three years promised in 1986, *Mir* survived 15 years! The Americans, who did not have our unique experience, were able to create the big International Space Station only with our help. And we sank our superiority in the ocean with our own hands because the Russian economy denied

---

16. The second space mission of Valeriy Vladimirovich Polyakov (1942–) lasted 437 days, 17 hours, and 58 minutes. He was launched on *Soyuz TM-18* on 8 January 1994 and returned on *Soyuz TM-19* on 22 March 1995, having stayed on board *Mir* as part of three different Primary Expeditions (*Ekspeditsiya osnovnaya* or EO), EO-15, -16, and -17. He spent 241 days in space during an earlier mission to *Mir* in 1988–1989.

17. This record was superseded on August 16, 2005, by cosmonaut Sergey Konstantinovich Krikalev (1958–), whose cumulative time spent in space stands at 803 days, 9 hours, and 39 minutes, accumulated on six different missions between 1988 and 2005.

18. On 16 June 2007, Lucid's record was broken by NASA astronaut Sunita Williams (1965–) on ISS Expedition 15, which lasted 196 days, 17 hours, and 17 minutes.

19. This is a line from the poem "Death of a Poet" ["Smert Poeta"] by Mikhail Yuryevich Lermontov (1814—1841).

cosmonautics the funds for subsistence. "Russia cannot be understood with the mind alone...."[20]

Russia's utmost misfortune is that not just *Mir*, but all of Russian science and the enormous technical potential of its defense technology did not fit together with the philosophy of the mafia-style preeminence of utilitarian/pragmatic self-interest. *Mir*'s fight for life was one of the episodes of Russia's general decline over the last decade of the 20th century.

At the meeting of the Russian Academy of Sciences dedicated to its 275th anniversary, the M. V. Lomonosov Gold Medal was awarded to Aleksandr Isayevich Solzhenitsyn.[21] Speaking from the academy's podium, Solzhenitsyn said: "Under the conditions of the only pirate nation in human history under a democratic flag, when the concerns of those in power are only about power itself, and not about the nation and the people inhabiting it, when the national wealth went to enriching the ruling oligarchy made up of countless cadres from the supreme, legislative, executive, and judicial authorities, it is difficult to come up with a reassuring prognosis for Russia!"[22]

Among the many foreign guests who gave salutatory speeches on the occasion of the 275th anniversary, only the president of the Chinese Engineering Academy noted the great achievements of Soviet and Russian scientists in space.

At the beginning of the 21st century, China managed to put a man in space using its own resources.[23] The Chinese economy's rate of development is astounding. Rocket technology and cosmonautics are priority industries in China. I believe that in the next 10 to 15 years China will take the place of the world's second superpower, including in the field of cosmonautics.

---

20. This is the first line from the poem of the same name composed by Fedor Ivanovich Tyutchev (1803–1873), one of the most memorized and quoted Russian poets of the 19th century. He was a contemporary of other Russian romantic poets such as Aleksandr Pushkin and Mikhail Lermontov.

21. Aleksandr Isayevich Solzhenitsyn (1918–2008) was one of the most famous Soviet dissident writers in the post-Stalin era. He wrote the earliest published accounts of life in the Gulag such as *One Day in the Life of Ivan Denisovich* (1962) and the three-volume *Gulag Archipelago* (1973). He was awarded the Nobel Prize in literature in 1970 but was sent into exile from the Soviet Union in 1974. For most of that time, Solzhenitsyn lived in the United States, until he returned to Russia in 1994.

22. A. I. Solzhenitsyn, "Nauka v piratskom gosudarstve" ["Science in a Pirate State"], *Nezavisimaya Gazeta*, 3 June 1999. The meeting was held the day before. Chertok quotes from text that is also reproduced at *http://vivovoco.rsl.ru/VV/PAPERS/ECCE/LOMOSOLJ.HTM*, last accessed 11 August 2011. The M. V. Lomonosov Gold Medal is the highest award given by the Russian Academy of Sciences. The award was established in 1956 and has been given annually to one Russian and foreign scholar.

23. China launched its first citizen in space, the fighter pilot Yang Liwei, into orbit on 15 October 2003.

From the author's archives.

Yakov Kolyako and Viktor Frumson at Red Square.

I SHALL RETURN NOW TO THE 30TH ANNIVERSARY of the first launch of the N-1 rocket. This event was described in a separate chapter of my book.[24] The management of the Energiya corporation supported the initiative of former N-1 chief designer Boris Dorofeyev and decided to make a gift to all those involved in the rocket's creation who were still living. Dorofeyev, with the help of Viktor Frumson, organized the showing of a once top-secret documentary film dedicated to the history of the rocket's creation and to all four launches. Frumson was the organizer and was involved in the creation of the full-length film, which is of exceptional historical value. The corporation's management granted permission to invite into our large, 400-seat auditorium not only those still working, but also those who had retired from the enterprise and representatives of other organizations involved in N-1 projects.

Because 21 February 1999 fell on a Sunday, the film screening was scheduled for 2 p.m. on 22 February. The hour-long film covered the history of the N1-L3, from the first resolution to the last tragic launch in November 1972. The film took us back to the past, and each of us experienced it in his or her own way. The last frame faded from the screen, and a hush fell over the packed auditorium. The last launch needed just 7 seconds more for the second stage to start up and for the

---

24. See Chapter 10 of this book.

flight to continue, which could have altered the subsequent fate of the N-1! The film ended with an optimistic text, which a professional narrator read with élan. The authors of the text didn't know the future yet.

Discussion of the film had not been planned, but Vasiliy Mishin expressed his version of the demise of the N1-L3 program. The upshot of his speech was that there is no need to seek out the guilty parties personally.

"The nation's economy was not ready to carry out such an expensive program."

Sergey Kryukov took

From the author's archives.

Vasiliy Mishin, shown here in 1992, by which time his role in the Soviet human lunar program was publicly known.

exception with Mishin: "You can't write off the N1-L3 tragedy to the weakness of our economy. We found financing for the Energiya-Buran program. Those funds would have been quite enough to update the N1-L3 and for successful expeditions to the Moon."[25]

The discussion ended, but we were in no hurry to break up. I can't remember now who from among the veterans walked up to me then and said: "It brought tears to my eyes when I was watching. You promised in your fourth book to tell about the history of the Moon race. Why didn't you speak out now?"

"I really do hope to tell about that in the book, but right now a 3- to 5-minute speech wouldn't turn out well."

The festivities on the occasion of the 30th anniversary of the first N-1 launch were limited to the film screening described above.

The events dedicated to the 30th anniversary of the first landing of an Earthling on the Moon were supposed to take place in Europe and in America in July 1999. The publisher of the German translation of my first volume of

---

25. Both Mishin and Kryukov have written major works on the history of the Soviet human lunar program. See V. P. Mishin, "Pochemu my ne sletali na lunu?" ["Why Didn't We Land on the Moon?"], *Kosmonavtika, astronomiya* no. 12 (1990): 1–64; S. S. Kryukov, *Izbrannyye raboty: iz lichnogo arkhiva* [*Selected Works: From the Personal Archive*] (Moscow: MGTU im. N. E. Baumana, 2010).

Rockets and People telephoned me from Germany asking me to take part in a big radio show dedicated to the history of the Moon race. I was to come to Cologne in July for it. I asked him to pass on to the organizers of that radio program that as long as NATO was bombing the European nation of Yugoslavia using the latest achievements of aviation and cosmonautics, I could not accept such an offer.[26] Moreover, I had no desire to appear in foreign mass media and tell about the glorious past of domestic cosmonautics against the background of its very uncertain present and of the gloomy prognosis for its future. Even here, in Russia, not everyone understands me if I quote the classic words from the popular film: "I'm offended on behalf of the nation."[27] And there's no way they'll understand this in the West.

Over the course of many decades, during periods of the worst shocks, we did not lose our optimism and confidence in the future. That same confidence did not leave the creators of the N1-L3 even after the decision to shut down operations on this program. To this day, people continue to argue about whether this decision was a mistake. Today, I am answering for myself: we committed many mistakes in the process of the Moon race. Mistakes also occurred in Korolev's time. His premature departure from life deprived him of the opportunity to correct the mistakes, including those that he himself made. At his initiative, at the very beginning of the design process on the two-launch version of the lunar expedition, we reworked it into a single-launch version, simultaneously modifying the N-1 launch vehicle to increase the payload capacity from 75 to 95 tons. Theoretically, a launch vehicle capable of inserting 75 tons into near-Earth orbit could come out a year before the one modified to insert 95 tons.

"Stop!" my opponents would object. "We had three accidents due to unreliable engines. And if testing had started a year earlier, the engines would have been even less reliable."

"Right! That's our mistake. That's not Korolev's fault. He left this life believing that the engines would be reliable."

Three years after Korolev's death, flight tests began on the unreliable engines, and this was a fatal error. History has shown that the engines developed at N. D. Kuznetsov's design bureau in Kuybyshev were successfully brought to such a degree of reliability that 25 years later the Americans considered it

---

26. The NATO bombing of the former nation of Yugoslavia took place between 24 March and 11 June 1999.

27. This is a line from the Soviet film *Beloye solntse pustyni* [*White Sun of the Desert*, 1970], directed by Vladimir Yakovlevich Motyl (1927–2010). It is one of the most famous films in the history of Soviet cinema, and many of the characters' lines have become firmly rooted in Russian conversational language.

feasible to use them to update their launch vehicles.[28] At the turn of the century a proposal came out to upgrade our most reliable Soyuz launch vehicle, the R-7: on the central block (the second stage), Glushko's engine, which had a ground thrust of 85 tons, would be replaced with Kuznetsov's engine, which had a thrust of 160 tons and was left over from the production stock for the N-1.[29] The old tried-and-true *Semyorka* with this engine would make it possible to insert into space a piloted vehicle with a mass of 11 tons rather than 7. The future piloted Soyuz vehicles and Progress cargo transporters would make a quantum leap. But that is in the future!

But meanwhile I'm sometimes asked: "How would Korolev have acted in the situation with the N-1 after four failures if he had lived another eight years?"

I can't answer for Korolev. As Korolev's comrade-in-arms I can answer this question as I see fit. It was easier for us to do this because we knew that future which remained unknown to him. Korolev always analyzed and corrected mistakes. Most likely, he would not have allowed flight tests to begin. Yes, he would have had to "hold his nose"—drive through the review of the lunar program in the administration in terms of dates, objectives, and missions.

But there could also have been a different scenario: after realizing the unreliability of the rocket as a whole, after the first two launches Korolev would forbid the continuation of flight tests. One would like to think with all the antagonism in his relationship with Glushko, he would have come to an agreement with him about technical assistance for the modification of the engines, which Glushko called "rotten." Now we know that Kuznetsov brought them to a very high level of reliability, but this happened when Korolev's former best friend—Valentin Glushko—became general designer of NPO Energiya.

Glushko received a unique opportunity: to correct—albeit late, but radically—the errors that Korolev, Mishin, and we, their deputies, had committed. Undoubtedly, the great 20th-century rocket-engine specialist was able to gain detailed insight into the promising outlook of Kuznetsov's engines. But now Glushko himself was supposed to go against his own ambition. Essentially, Glushko was unwilling to remain the general designer of a rocket that he had not been involved in developing. I am confident that Korolev's staff would have supported Glushko if he had begun to upgrade the N-1 in his role as general designer. Glushko was the only one who could convince

---

28. Orbital Sciences Corporation's Taurus II launch vehicle will use Kuznetsov's NK-33 rocket engines (originally slated for use on the N-1) on its first stage. In its "American" version, owned by Aerojet, the engine is known as AJ26-58.

29. The most recent such proposal is known as the Soyuz-2.1v, a light-class launch vehicle that will make use of a single NK-33-1 on the core block.

first Keldysh and then Ustinov that there was no point in burying the N-1 and that the lunar program needed to be implemented from 1977 through 1980 using the new N1-L3M configuration or any other one. Today we understand that this was quite realistic. But Glushko decided to start with new launch vehicles, new engines, and a new big system. Under his leadership, the new Energiya launch vehicle really was created and it had new RD-170 liquid-oxygen–kerosene engines that were the most powerful in the world. There were great difficulties in the creation of this engine. During firing rig tests, one failure after another would occur. Many highly placed skeptics simply didn't believe that it was possible to solve the problems facing the staff of the Energomash Design Bureau and Glushko himself. Bringing the engine to the highest degree of reliability by the beginning of flight tests was Glushko's personal achievement.[30]

But this took another 13 years! What else can be said in defense of Glushko? He was under very strong pressure "from the top"—they said we didn't need the Moon; we needed a reusable transport system that was as good as the American Space Shuttle. Fourteen years after shutting down the N1-L3 program, such a system was created.

After Buran, nobody in the world ever made a reusable spacecraft capable of landing at an airfield in unpiloted, automatic mode again and again with uncanny precision.[31] On 15 November 1988, after two orbits around Earth, at 0924 hours and 42 seconds, ahead of the calculated time by just one second, Buran touched down on the takeoff and landing strip at the airfield especially created for it, and after running 1,620 meters, it stopped in the center with a deviation of just 3 meters from the center line. And this was despite a stormy cross-headwind. The miss in terms of the longitudinal axis was just 15 meters!

But a year after the first brilliant flight, no use was made of Energiya or Buran. One of the Buran vehicles was installed as a space attraction next to a restaurant on the Kremlin quay of the Moscow River.[32] And what happened to the Energiya launch vehicle? We feverishly hunted for payloads for it. And actually, very interesting prospective projects materialized, which could have led to new achievements in the field of fundamental astrophysics research,

---

30. See Bart Hendrickx, "The Origins and Evolution of the Energiya Rocket Family," *Journal of the British Interplanetary Society* 55 (2002): 242–278.

31. The U.S. Air Force's X-37 Orbital Test Vehicle completed a fully automated landing on a runway at Vandenberg Air Force Base in California on 3 December 2010 after over seven months in Earth orbit.

32. This was Buran model OK-M, originally used for static and precision testing, which now resides on the Frunze embankment of the Moscow River in the M. Gorky Central Park of Culture and Leisure.

global communication systems, information systems development, and also monitoring in the interests of the national economy and national security.

In July 1989, Central Committee General Secretary Mikhail Gorbachev was supposed to fly to Paris for the celebration of the 200th anniversary of the French Revolution. High-level negotiations were planned with the President of France, including negotiations for joint space projects. A month before the very high-level visit, I flew to Paris as part of a government delegation. My task was to persuade French specialists and bureaucrats to take part in creating a global communication system using a heavy universal space platform (UKP) with a mass of 18 tons, which only the Energiya rocket could insert into geostationary orbit.[33]

The French listened politely but just as politely implied that they did not have the funds for such promising projects, and France could serve its current interests with its own Ariane rocket.

At the same time as the French, we were also courting the Germans. First we invited specialists from leading corporations to Moscow. It seemed that the ice was breaking. Then the Bosch Corporation invited us to Backnang, where the company's radio electronics division was located.[34] Our delegation included the managers of the five leading Soviet radio electronics firms, with whom we had cooperated on the design of the UKP in geostationary orbit.

Throughout the week we familiarized the Germans with information, which they received with genuine interest. The specialists of the firm were extremely interested in a joint project, but the upper management of the corporation, who had spared no expense for our delegation on receptions and far-flung excursions, did not want to risk investing capital in a project that, based on a very optimistic business plan, would not return a profit until five years later.

In 1989, the new general designer of NPO Energiya, Yuriy Semyonov, exhibited a truly combative nature. He attained consideration and approval of proposals for the UKP in the Defense Council. A draft decision of the USSR Council of Ministers appeared, which N. I. Ryzhkov was supposed to sign shortly.[35] The ministry and Military-Industrial Commission declared that the

---

33. UKP—*Universalnaya kosmicheskaya platforma.*
34. Backnang is about 50 kilometers northeast of Stuttgart.
35. Nikolay Ivanovich Ryzhkov (1929–) was a close associate of Gorbachev's who served as chairman of the Council of Ministers from 1985 to 1990.

work on the UKP ranked third in terms of importance after Buran and the *Mir* orbital station.[36]

Almost at the same time as the UKP, NPO Energiya and the Academy of Sciences were jointly developing the design of a space radio interferometer. The spacecraft, equipped with a uniquely precise parabolic antenna with a diameter of 25 meters, was to be inserted into elliptical orbits with an apogee of up to 150,000 kilometers. Only the Energiya rocket was capable of doing this. Corresponding Member (now Academician) Nikolay Kardashev was responsible for the scientific part of the project.[37] We flew to the Netherlands together. The European Space Research and Technology Center (ESTEC) is located there in the city of Noordwijk. In Noordwijk, and later in Paris, a special competitive commission declared that our radio interferometer would make it possible to study the finest structure of the universe right down to the "last boundaries of creation." The universe was ready to reveal its secrets, but for this we needed to find approximately 1 billion dollars.... We didn't find it. We even "teamed up" with the Europeans.

Yes, we could have implemented many projects. By all appearances, they were pipe dreams.... But why not fantasize a little? If Defense Minister Ustinov had not allowed the invasion of Afghanistan and had given half of the funds spent on that war to cosmonautics, the nation would not only have saved 15,000 lives—we would have built a permanently operating base on the Moon. The mistakes of the government and politicians cost the people hundreds and thousands of times more than the biggest space programs.

Very interesting projects for other payloads appeared for the Energiya launch vehicle, including military space complexes. It was assumed that the reusable Energiya-Buran system would become the main system for the insertion of reconnaissance satellites and military orbital stations, including those equipped with laser weaponry. The Soviet Union had the opportunity to ensure its superiority not only in the field of ground-based and sea-launched nuclear missiles, but also in space in the event of "Star Wars." However, the main customer of the Energiya-Buran complex—the Ministry of Defense—abandoned the system and its military application.

---

36. This heavy standardized communications satellite proposal that Chertok mentions was approved by a decree of the President of the USSR on 5 February 1991. Chertok was one of its main architects at NPO Energiya; the project was later named *Globis*. After the collapse of the Soviet Union, work on the project was stopped by mid-1993.

37. Nikolay Semenovich Kardashev (1932–) is a famous Russian astronomer specializing in experimental and theoretical astrophysics and radio astronomy. He became an Academician in 1994.

The development of the Energiya-Buran system involved 1,206 enterprises and organizations from almost 100 ministries and agencies. The nation's largest scientific and production centers were involved. In all, more than a million people worked on this large nationwide program over a period of 18 years!

In December 1991, the State Council of Russia abolished the Ministry of General Machine Building, which had been responsible for cosmonautics. Everything came tumbling down in no time. A space disaster had occurred through no fault of scientists, generals, chief designers, and managers of the rocket-space industry. Of all the major space developments of our organization that I was directly involved in, and of which I can rightfully be proud in front of my descendants, at that time only *Mir* was temporarily spared and was fighting for its life. The old saying "misery loves company" inspired a certain grain of optimism.

In connection with the 275th anniversary of the Russian Academy of Sciences, it was noted that recent years had inflicted on it the most fundament shakeups in its entire history from the times of Peter the Great.[38] The Academy had endured because it was created under conditions that were very difficult for the nation, but historically favorable for the prosperity of science and industry.

The Council of Chiefs, which included many academicians, did not withstand the government's pressure. On 3 October 2001, it made the decision to terminate the flight of the *Mir* station.[39] In order to reliably scuttle the fully operational station, two Progress cargo vehicles had to be docked to it.

The station celebrated its 15th anniversary on 20 February 2001 without a crew. On 19 March, an orbit exit program was loaded into its on-board computer complex. On the night of 23 March, hundreds of people gathered at TsUP. At 9 p.m. Moscow time, 40 tons of fragments that hadn't burned up in the atmosphere fell into the Pacific Ocean. I couldn't bring myself to watch the death of the station at TsUP. The legendary *Mir* complex had ceased to exist. I was later told that everyone stood up, a hush fell over the room, and they observed a minute of silence. Many had tears in their eyes. "The king is dead. Long live the king!" Thus, two years after the funeral of *Mir* we could console ourselves. All the "Mirites" were switched over to the construction of the International Space Station.

Of all the endeavors of the military-industrial complex, the rocket-space industry, inextricably tied with science, proved its resiliency under the conditions of the Russian national crisis. The backbone of the industry, which was put

---

38. The 275th anniversary was celebrated in 1999.
39. Chertok probably means 3 October 2000.

in place by the pioneers of rocket science and technology, industrial organizers, and millions of workers—true zealots of science and technology—contributed to the solution of extremely complex problems. The answer to the question "to be, or not to be" for Russian cosmonautics can only be affirmative. I am confident that this is exactly how the tens of millions of Russians who blazed the trail to new civilization with their labor will answer.

Afterword

To my readers, about the future of space exploration:

The beginning of the era of practical space exploration dates back to 4 October 1957: the date that the USSR launched the world's first artificial satellite. In the years since then—in less than the lifetime of one generation of humanity—a breakthrough was made into a new sphere of activity. A completely new branch of science, technology, industry, and culture was created.

The 20th century gave humankind the theory of relativity, quantum mechanics, nuclear energy, spaceflight, unusual progress in aviation technology, information science, the automotive industry, and many other things. What will the 21st century bring humanity?

The most important achievements in space exploration belong to the second half of the 20th century. Everything that is happening at present—in the first decade of the 21st century—is, so far, based on the scientific and technical discoveries and achievements of the 20th century.

On Errors in Predictions

One can predict scientific and technical developments 10 to 15 years in advance more or less accurately, but making predictions up to the mid-21st century is exceptionally difficult. Any prediction will be, to a certain extent, biased and nonobjective, including predictions about space exploration. I would like to call the reader's attention to an interesting fact. In 1966, at a symposium of the American Astronautical Society, U.S. scientists and specialists presented their predictions on the development of space technology. Of greatest interest was the general presentation by one of the theoreticians of the former German rocket center in Peenemünde, K. A. Ehricke, "Solar Transportation."[1] Ehricke

---

1. Krafft Arnold Ehricke (1917–1984) was a well-known German propulsion engineer who worked with Walter Thiel at Peenemünde. After immigrating to the United States following World War II, he had an illustrious career in government and private industry. In his later years, he was a vocal advocate of industrial exploitation of the Moon.

envisaged the events of the next 35 years and painted a picture of real—from the viewpoint of American scientists—achievements of space technology by 2001. None of the scientists doubted Tsiolkovskiy's prediction, made at the beginning of the 20th century, that humankind would not remain forever in its cradle on Earth, but would settle the entire solar system.

"In the fall of 2000, the interplanetary flight corridors from Mercury to Saturn are alive with manned vehicles of relatively luxurious and sophisticated design…. On Mars, a long range program has just been started to induce in the circumpolar regions of the northern and southern hemisphere, large scale culture of special Mars-hardened plants…." And many other highly interesting predictions and proposals, which are no less relevant today, yet still very far from being realized.[2]

For space exploration at the beginning of the 21st century, the cost of sending 1 kilogram of payload into space is on the order of 10,000 dollars. I can only echo the challenge by Elon Musk of "500 dollars per pound of payload," but for now, I do not see any real technological breakthroughs toward achieving this in this next decade.[3]

That which we call "common sense" allows us to assert that Tsiolkovskiy's proposed human colonization of the solar system will begin only through the establishment of a lunar base.

Today's unpiloted, automatic satellite telescopes, equipped with remote research equipment and data transmission systems, have enriched humankind by producing a greater number of discoveries over the last 30 years in the fields of planetology and the workings and creation of the universe than were made over all the preceding millennia. Dozens of modern countries that have joined the "space club" consider it necessary to have an astronaut of their own, their own communications satellites, and—even better—their own launch vehicles and launch sites. And yet it is unfortunate that we do not know the names of the scientists who use the achievements of space exploration for knowledge, for studying the world, and for discoveries. The mass media in the countries that

---

2. Abridged quote taken from the book *Kosmicheskaya era; prognozy na 2001 god* [*The Space Age. Predictions for 2001*], ed. V. S. Yemelyanov, translated from English (Moscow: Mir, 1970). The original English was published as *Space Age in Fiscal Year 2001: Proceedings of the Fourth AAS Goddard Memorial Symposium*, 15–16 March 1966, Washington, DC, eds. Eugene B. Konecci, Maxwell W. Hunter II, and Robert F. Trapp (Tarzana, CA: American Astronautical Society Publications Office, 1967).

3. Elon Musk (1971–) is a South African–born Canadian entrepreneur who was the cofounder of PayPal and is currently CEO of SpaceX, a private company that has been developing the Falcon series of orbital launch vehicles. On 8 December 2010, SpaceX became the first private company to launch an object into orbit.

lead the field of science (including the United States and Russia) describe the flights of cosmonauts and astronauts on the ISS but rarely mention the discoveries of scientists who work with the data from the Hubble orbital telescope or the automatic instruments on the Cassini probe, or many other spacecraft.

Modern science and technology in the 21st century have approached a boundary that, when overcome, will change much in the living conditions of humanity. This boundary is direct technological intervention by people in the structure of matter at the atomic/molecular level. We do not yet know who thought up, devised, and created the program to combine atoms and molecules in such a way as to create life. Romantics and fans of outer space still hold out hope that extraterrestrial intelligence helped. We will probably not find it by the end of the 21st century.

In the 21st century, humankind must acknowledge planet Earth's uniqueness in the entire observable universe in order to unite the efforts of all the leading countries to preserve her. *Homo sapiens* is a completely exceptional phenomenon, falling outside of the scope of observations by spacecraft. This "wise man" must use the force of intellect to reliably defend the planet from the folly of unwise *Homo sapiens*.

From the author's archives.

Boris Chertok shown here with Metropolitan Kirill (Cyril), the Russian Orthodox bishop who is the Patriarch of Moscow and all of Russia. The picture was taken in 2005 at the Bauman Moscow Higher Technical School at the Korolev Readings.

The State and Space Exploration

The future of space exploration can be predicted together with an analysis of national and state sociopolitical strategy. The United States, even with all its internal problems, by the 2030s will remain the most powerful country in the world in military terms and the most advanced in the field of science and technology. NATO is a reliable tool that allows the United States to use not only its own scientific-technical potential, but Europe's as well. Priorities in a very broad spectrum of programs will be the space strategy for the next 20 to 30 years.

The operation of the ISS will be supported through the transport systems of Russia and Europe. The ISS on its own is no longer particularly interesting to the United States. In 10 to 15 years, having broken the flight record of Mir, the ISS will be scuttled. Russia, Europe, and Japan are currently unable to support the operation of the ISS without the economic support of the United States.

For Russia, future programs of new technologies in the rocket-space industry are problems that are not just scientific and economic in nature. As a result of liberal market reforms, the Russian defense industry was deprived of many thousands of qualified workers and engineers. On the other hand, we provided the United States and Europe with personnel. The "dictatorship of the proletariat" is no longer possible in Russia; there is simply nobody to implement this dictatorship. From the standpoint of democracy, today the most democratic country in the whole world is the United States. If one compares Russian and American democracy, of course everything falls in favor of the American version.

There is a shortage of "golden hands" of highly qualified workers and luminous brains of enthusiastic engineers; overcoming this shortage is a problem Russia faces but the United States does not.

Russia, the United States, China, and India have approved programs for the next 10 years. With adjustments for the global economic crisis, they will be implemented.

In order to study the universe, a new space observatory will be launched to take the place of the famous Hubble telescope, which will exist for five more years without maintenance provided by the Space Shuttle.[4] New automatic spacecraft will continue research and will enrich science with a broad spectrum of new discoveries made on the planets of the solar system, primarily the moons of Jupiter and Saturn. NASA's powerful scientific apparatus will

---

4. The James Webb Space Telescope, an international collaboration between NASA, the European Space Agency, and the Canadian Space Agency, is the planned successor to the Hubble Space Telescope. This infrared space observatory is planned for launch in 2018.

develop not only the technology, but also the strategy for future space exploration. Unfortunately, Russia lacks such a state-level apparatus that has similar intellectual potential.

Round-the-clock information from Earth remote sensing satellites provides reliable meteorological forecasts, warnings about emergencies, monitoring of humanmade catastrophes, violation of environmental regulations, etc. High-resolution monitoring of strategically important regions will be carried out by secret military spy satellites. Optical-electronic digital systems guarantee resolution on the order of centimeters with real-time processing. The United States will be the first to create systems that combine data from Navstar GPS navigation satellites with low-orbit spy satellites and satellite communications and guidance systems. Joint processing of information from satellites on three levels—low-orbit, navigational, and geostationary—will make it possible to guide all types of transport: ground, air, and sea.

The American government agency NASA is vested with a great deal of authority. All federal expenditures on space exploration, with the exception of purely military expenditures, are implemented through NASA or under its supervision. NASA's annual budget for 2010 exceeds Russia's space budget by almost tenfold. Given these initial conditions, there is no doubt that in the next 10 to 15 years, the United States will create a new launch vehicle and piloted spacecraft for a flight to the Moon, lunar landing module, and cargo delivery system for a lunar base.

Over the course of the next 20 to 25 years, China will invest enormous resources under the slogan "Catch up to and overtake America and Russia in the field of space exploration." China is building a socialist society with "Chinese characteristics." Chinese Communists were able, in a short amount of time, to convert a backward agrarian country with partial literacy and a population of 1.5 billion into a state that mastered all types of modern technology and mass production of competitive goods from the latest computers to tennis shoes. China's latest strategic tasks are to create a society based on a "knowledge economy." In the past 15 years, China has solved economic and technological tasks in scopes and within timeframes that are impossible for other states. China will become not only a secondary power capable of achieving real "supremacy in space," but it will strive to ideologically capture the basic positions of world space exploration, and I think it will be successful. One of the deciding factors guaranteeing China's phenomenal successes is the ideological and political unity and true, rather than rhetorical, enthusiasm in mastering knowledge and high technologies.

Go to any Russian modern electronics shop. There is a wide selection for any taste and any wallet. But you will not find a single one of even the simplest electronic gadgets that was "Made in Russia." Ninety percent were "Made in

China." The Chinese strategy for creating advanced technologies is a reliable foothold for future implementation of the principle of "supremacy in space."

Russia still does not have a development strategy that will unite society. For 15 years of criminal reforms under the motto of the omnipotence of the free market, Russia's defense industry, mechanical engineering, and agriculture were destroyed, and the Army has been thrown into disarray. Basic survival relies on the sale of natural wealth: primarily oil, gas, and timber. The super-profits from natural resources have created new elites, a class of super-rich and a blatantly corrupted bureaucracy. Why should this elite care about the country's development of space exploration? In order for Russian space exploration to still be at least in the top five in the future, we need radical, stringent sociopolitical reforms. And not just for the sake of space exploration.

Proceeding from such unhappy thoughts, I believe that by 2030, Russia must devote most of its attention to programs of unconditional space security (satellites for all types of communications and Earth remote sensing [ERS], including intelligence, missile-defense systems, GLONASS, and meteorological systems).[5]

Space programs for ensuring security and high defense capability for the country must have a single general manager, who is responsible not only for the development and data of spacecraft, but for the whole system right up to immediate reports to the higher military-political leadership of the country about the real results of the use of space-based intelligence data.

Modern technology makes it possible to observe tanks, artillery, armored personnel carriers, and other equipment from space in real time.

Space exploration and rocket technology are bound by common production organizations, testing technology, and cosmodromes. Russia's future space programs will, in large part, be determined by the timeframe for creating a new heavy launch vehicle to replace the Proton that is just as reliable. One assumes that it will be the Angara.[6] Ten years will be spent on this. The United States will create a heavy and super-heavy vehicle in the next 8 to 10 years.

---

5. Russians typically use the abbreviation DZZ—*Distantsionnoye zondirovaniye zemli* (Remote Sensing of Earth)—as a shorthand for remote sensing. GLONASS (*Globalnaya navigatsionnaya sputnikovaya sistema* or Global Navigation Satellite System) is the Russian equivalent of the Global Positioning System (GPS). The system, comprised of *Uragan* (Hurricane) or 11F654 satellites, was originally conceived and developed during Soviet times. The first three satellites in the GLONASS system were launched on 12 October 1982. The system was officially declared operational on 24 September 1993, although a fully operational system requires a complement of 24 satellites.

6. Angara is the name of a family of new Russian launch vehicles developed by the M. V. Khrunichev State Space Scientific-Production Space Center.

Geostationary Orbit

In the 21st century there will be an intensified economic and political battle for room for communication satellites in geostationary Earth orbit (GEO). A spacecraft inserted into GEO has an orbital period equal to the rotational period of Earth, and the plane of orbit is virtually coincident with the plane of Earth's equator. The point under the satellite has its own geographical longitude—the working point—and zero latitude.

The first spacecraft were inserted into GEO in the 1960s.[7] Since that time, a total of 800 spacecraft have been inserted into GEO, and each year, on average, 20 to 25 new ones are inserted. According to data from 2008, more than 1,150 objects were in geostationary orbit. Among them were about 240 controlled spacecraft, while the remainder are spent upper stages and other items.

On average, the mass of the payload carried into near-Earth orbit by the launch vehicle makes up 3 to 4 percent of the launch mass of the vehicle. For geostationary orbit, the mass of the spacecraft makes up only 0.3 to 0.5 percent of the launch mass of the vehicle and the upper stage. Launching a spacecraft into GEO, as a rule, is done using a three-stage vehicle with the subsequent use of upper stages. Geostationary orbit, as the most advantageous location for placing satellite communications systems, will exhaust its resources in the next 20 years.

Strict international competition is unavoidable. One possible solution could be the creation in GEO of a heavy multipurpose platform. With coverage of nearly 1/3 of the surface of the planet, such a multipurpose platform will be able to replace dozens of modern communications satellites. The platform will require a high-capacity solar power plant. To support dozens of modern communications satellites, the platform will require a capacity of 500 to 1,000 kilowatts.

Large parabolic antennas or active phased arrays are capable of creating any given value of equivalent isotropically radiated power (EIIM) at Earth's surface and receiving information from subscribers on Earth, using devices no larger than the best modern mobile phones.[8] The capability of placing hundreds of relays for various ranges on a heavy geostationary platform makes it possible for the owners of such platforms to sell all types of communications trunks for any region on Earth.

Heavy multipurpose platforms will be commercially advantageous and will facilitate the global information rapprochement of peoples. Humankind

---

7. The first spacecraft launched into geostationary orbit was *Syncom-3*, which launched on 19 August 1964.

8. EIIM—*Effektivnaya izotropno izluchayemaya moshchost.*

needs the development and creation of such geostationary systems not in the distant future, but in the next 25 to 30 years.

The problem of creating and operating heavy geostationary platforms can be quickly solved if there is cooperation between Russian and European technology. However, space stations in GEO can be used for military purposes, too, to suppress an aggressor in local conflicts and in situations such as "Star Wars." (More about that later.)

In the early 1990s, Russia developed a real design for the world's first heavy universal platform for GEO. The mass of the proposed platform, according to the design, was 20 tons.[9] Insertion into orbit was slated for the Energiya launch vehicle, which had successfully passed its flight tests. In 1989 and 1990, RKK Energiya, with the support of the Military-Industrial Commission of the USSR Council of Ministers, made proposals to Germany, France, and the European Space Agency regarding cooperation and joint work to create the universal heavy space platform in GEO. In those years, only Russia, possessing the unique Energiya vehicle, could perform this task. The detailed development of the platform design and the technology for insertion were of great interest to the leading German and French corporations. Joint work was begun. However, the liberal market reforms of the 1990s destroyed the organization and deprived the Energiya vehicle's manufacturers of any state support. After the loss of the launch vehicle, the proposal for work on the heavy space platform became pointless.

Because of Russia's geographical situation, apart from using geostationary orbit, which does not provide communications to Arctic regions, it is necessary to create a group of three satellites in geosynchronous elliptical orbits such as the Molniya, which provide coverage of 100 percent of the territory, including the Arctic.

Russia's inventory of scientific and technical developments will still ensure the capability to implement a multifunctional space-based communication system for any point in the country. The prerequisite is the creation of a new launch vehicle and transport system for the creation in GEO of the multi-purpose platform.

Star Wars

In the hot days of the Cold War, in the second half of the 20th century, American propaganda for "supremacy in space" introduced the term "Star

---

9. The in-orbit mass of these *Globis* communications satellites would have been 13.8 tons (phase I) and 17.8 tons (phase II).

Wars." This concept had nothing to do with actual stars. Various media outlets used the term "Star Wars" to describe the missile-defense program, the fight against space-based military systems, and any other actions using outer space for military purposes. The overt and classified programs of "Star Wars" were limited to near-Earth space and (in the future) to creating military bases on the Moon.

The use of weapons based on new physics principles was proposed as the main means of waging the battle to achieve military supremacy in space and to destroy the nuclear-missile potential of the enemy. The achievements in physics in the 20th century made it possible to claim that the hyperboloid of Engineer Garin could truly move from the pages of Aleksey Tolstoy's excellent novel to become a real "Star Wars" weapon.[10] Almost 100 years were necessary to turn a charming fantasy into reality.

Yet another effective means of blinding and defeating ground-based air-defense systems, missile-defense systems, and various radio-electronic troop command and control systems would be the use of powerful super-broadband emitters. Powerful generators of directed electromagnetic energy could be installed on geostationary space platforms and, in the future, could also be installed at a lunar military base.

Practically all types of modern-day weapons, systems for controlling air traffic, oceanic ships, and ground-based combat equipment, and all types of data transmission and processing, use microelectronic devices. By the end of the 21st century, electronics will be based on semiconductors operating with a low level of voltage and current. The absolute value of currents and voltages, as microminiaturization progresses, will reach very small amounts. With the use of nanotechnology in information technology, the values for currents and voltages will only get smaller.

The effect of ultra-broadband electromagnetic pulses produces induced currents of comparatively high voltage in all electronic devices and, in practical terms, causes them to fail. It is well known that powerful electromagnetic pulses are created by the explosion of nuclear warheads. Therefore, the electrical lines for controlling communications and all the electronics of modern-day missile launchers are appropriately hardened against a retaliatory strike. Powerful unidirectional electromagnetic strikes could be made from space without the use of nuclear weapons. It is practically impossible to protect the entire mass of communications and control electronics from this.

---

10. This is a reference to Aleksey Nikolayevich Tolstoy's 1927 novel *Giperboloid inzhenera Garina* [*The Hyperboloid of Engineer Garin*].

The formation of artificial radiation belts around Earth could be a "Star Wars" weapon. In the late 1950s and early 1960s, the U.S. and USSR conducted experimental nuclear explosions in near-Earth space (at altitudes of 100 to 400 kilometers).

Studies conducted by the United States and Soviet Union showed that one nuclear device detonated at an altitude of 125 to 300 kilometers with a yield of approximately 10 kilotonnes is enough to disable all forms of radio communication, in all ranges, thousands of kilometers from the explosion site, for many hours. A nuclear explosion in near-Earth space will lead to the creation of such highly concentrated plasmas that for several hours, all forms of radar and radio communication are ruled out. For several hours, the use of conventional weapons will be paralyzed.

Judging by the experience of the 20th century, one can also assert that people in the 21st century will create new types of space-based weaponry that we cannot even imagine today, just as the people of the early 20th century were incapable of creating systems like GPS and GLONASS. However, the creation of ray, beam, and electromagnetic types of weapons is fully realizable in the coming decades.

The Moon and Mars

In 1986, Congress and the U.S. President created a national commission on developing the future space program for the next 50 years.[11] The main recommendation of this commission was a challenge to create a permanent (inhabited) base on the Moon in the first decade of the 21st century.

The first decade of the 21st century has come to a close, and the Americans did not begin constructing a lunar base. In my personal opinion, if the United States intends to build a base on its own—and it is capable of doing so—a realistic start date would be 2020. The creation of a permanent active lunar base with a staff of 8 to 12 persons will require another 10 to 15 years.

In the last century, Russia projected the construction of a base that was jokingly named "Barmingrad" after the chief designer.[12] Construction on the Moon does not require any sort of new scientific discoveries. Present-day technology is fully capable of supporting colonization of the Moon. But there are sociopolitical, economic, and international problems that any country wishing to have its own base on the Moon will encounter.

In light of this, one may predict that Russia is not capable of independently creating its own base in the next 20 years. Construction of a lunar

---

11. The text of the report was published as *Pioneering the Space Frontier: The Report of the National Commission on Space* (Toronto: Bantam Books, 1986).
12. This is a reference to Vladimir Pavlovich Barmin (1909–1993).

base is possible, if it is a national, multiyear program on a scale exceeding the transformation of the Sochi region into a Winter Olympics base and resort comparable to the Cote d'Azur. It is likely that China will create its base five years before Russia does. The fourth colonizer of the Moon will be India. It is unlikely, but theoretically possible, that Russia and Europe will combine their technical and economic resources to build an international lunar base. One example of united technological and economic resources is the ISS.

Unlike the ISS, lunar bases can have three purposes: scientific, industrial/technological, and military/strategic. Creation of a single lunar base for Earth will be possible only if the world overcomes its divisions into military-political groups. Taking into account the possibilities for strategic use of the Moon, one cannot rule out the possibility that NATO countries will combine their resources. Combining the leading countries of Europe with the lunar programs of the United States could reduce the timeframe by three to five years.

The Moon is planet Earth's domain. The Moon is a planetary body on which people could live, using local lunar resources. It is fully accessible for humankind and will not require any new scientific discoveries.

For 3 or 4 billion years, the Moon was tied to Earth by the laws of celestial mechanics. In the 20th century, 12 men landed on the Moon. In the 21st century, for the first time, the Moon and Earth will be tied together by a reliable transport system for delivering technical cargo and the constant bidirectional traffic of a human transport system.

In the first half of the 21st century, NATO will be preserved and new military-political factions may arise. From the standpoint of "space supremacy" for each such faction, in the event of "Star Wars," the prospect of building a base on the visible side of the Moon that has powerful ray and ultra-broadband weapons is enticing. Future optical-electronic and radar systems will make it possible to conduct continuous monitoring of everything taking place on dry land, in the ocean, in the air, and in near-Earth space. In the event of military conflicts, lunar bases can carry out local strikes pre-empting the use of nuclear weapons. The economic crisis of 2008 to 2010 showed that modern states are capable of negotiating in good faith and even combining their economic efforts. Perhaps in 5 to 10 years, they will join forces in order to colonize the Moon.

For the world's astronomers and astrophysicists, the creation of observatories on the dark side of the Moon is quite alluring. The Moon will serve as a screen, protecting the observatory's equipment from noise that reduces the resolution capability of modern land-based observatories. Radio observatories on the dark side of the Moon will be equipped with extra-large parabolic antennas and phased arrays. For fans of the search for signals from extraterrestrial civilizations, research will be transferred to the Moon.

From the author's archives.

Boris Chertok with his sons Mikhail (left) and Valentin on his 95th birthday on 1 March 2007.

TODAY'S MASS MEDIA, and sometimes even well-known scientists and politicians, make announcements about human expeditions to Mars that will take place in the next few decades. Mars fanatics and ambitious government bureaucrats tout human flights to Mars as being basically the main prospect for space exploration in the 21st century. One has to admit that, from a technical standpoint, human flights to Mars could, in fact, be implemented in the 21st century. However, it is very difficult to prove that it is necessary to include human flights to Mars in future programs for the 21st century. Indeed, why invest a minimum of 300 to 500 billion dollars, paying for the labor of hundreds of thousands of workers, engineers, and scientists, if all the questions that interest Earthlings can be answered by the Martian robots that are controlled by scientists on Earth? The automatic spacecraft orbiting Mars and the Mars rovers that traverse the surface have convincingly shown that there is no life on the surface of Mars. By the end of the 21st century, at least 8 to 10 more Mars rovers will land on the planet. They will conduct detailed, unhurried research on the atmosphere, the climate dynamics, and the planet's soil. New information will be obtained without enormous risk to the lives of expedition crewmembers. Cosmonauts on a Martian expedition would have to spend almost a year in weightlessness on the way there. Immediately after landing on Mars, they would prepare for the return flight, which would be riskier. (Unlike for orbital stations, Earth cannot provide assistance.) It is my firm conviction that human flights to Mars in the 21st century are technically possible, but unnecessary. The ambitious goal does not justify the enormous expense and risk.

Revolutionary Discoveries and Technologies

New breakthrough space programs, in terms of the timeframe for their implementation, their scope, and their contribution to "common human values," will largely be determined by the breakthrough discoveries in other areas of science and technology.

For the second half of the 21st century, we can—with some degree of certainty—expect discoveries that make it possible to produce controlled thermonuclear reactions, new materials, and previously unimaginable technical devices. Energy sources based on thermonuclear reactors of various capacities will allow all types of transportation to be made completely electrical.

The demand for hydrocarbon fuels (oil and gas) will drop a hundredfold. Accordingly, the era of development and production of a wide variety of reliable, cheap, and available thermonuclear power sources will dawn.

Alchemists of the Middle Ages tried to obtain gold by mixing mercury with copper shavings. Physical chemists of the 21st century will create materials that have the properties of superconductors at high temperatures. This will be the greatest revolution in electrical engineering. At the same time, new magnetic materials will be created. Electrical catapults will replace solid-propellant and liquid-propellant rocket engines for launches from Earth or the Moon. High-thrust electrical rocket engines using thermonuclear energy sources will replace chemical engines for many space exploration tasks.

Revolutionary achievements in creating the structure of photoconverters of solar energy into electrical energy will increase their efficiency from 10 percent to 50 to 60 percent. This will make it

From the author's archives.

Boris Chertok with his granddaughter Dasha.

possible, if there are difficulties using thermonuclear energy, to create high-capacity ground-based solar power stations. The electrical output per unit area of a solar array on a spacecraft will increase by three to five times.

In the late 20th and early 21st centuries, a technological and information revolution took place. Even in the middle of the 20th century, most scientists did not believe that any person could place in his pocket a device that could store all the information of the Russian State Library and the libraries of the British Museum and the U.S. Congress. Today's electronic devices allow anyone, without leaving home, to read and even copy the contents of books of the main libraries of the world. At the beginning of the 20th century, this would have been pure fantasy.

The information revolution of the late 20th century has, in some way or other, touched each inhabitant of Earth. Even the science fiction writers of the early 20th century did not predict its scale.

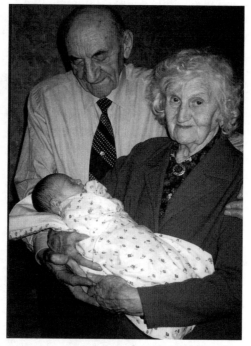

From the author's archives.
Will he fly to Mars? Boris Chertok and his wife Yekaterina Golubkina in 1998 with their great-grandson Mikhail Borisovich.

Index

Note: A page number in italics indicates a page with an image of the named person, object, or place.

The NASA History Series

Reference Works, NASA SP-4000:

Grimwood, James M. *Project Mercury: A Chronology.* NASA SP-4001, 1963.

Grimwood, James M., and Barton C. Hacker, with Peter J. Vorzimmer. *Project Gemini Technology and Operations: A Chronology.* NASA SP-4002, 1969.

Link, Mae Mills. *Space Medicine in Project Mercury.* NASA SP-4003, 1965.

Astronautics and Aeronautics, 1963: Chronology of Science, Technology, and Policy. NASA SP-4004, 1964.

Astronautics and Aeronautics, 1964: Chronology of Science, Technology, and Policy. NASA SP-4005, 1965.

Astronautics and Aeronautics, 1965: Chronology of Science, Technology, and Policy. NASA SP-4006, 1966.

Astronautics and Aeronautics, 1966: Chronology of Science, Technology, and Policy. NASA SP-4007, 1967.

Astronautics and Aeronautics, 1967: Chronology of Science, Technology, and Policy. NASA SP-4008, 1968.

Ertel, Ivan D., and Mary Louise Morse. *The Apollo Spacecraft: A Chronology, Volume I, Through November 7, 1962.* NASA SP-4009, 1969.

Morse, Mary Louise, and Jean Kernahan Bays. *The Apollo Spacecraft: A Chronology, Volume II, November 8, 1962–September 30, 1964.* NASA SP-4009, 1973.

Brooks, Courtney G., and Ivan D. Ertel. *The Apollo Spacecraft: A Chronology, Volume III, October 1, 1964–January 20, 1966.* NASA SP-4009, 1973.

Ertel, Ivan D., and Roland W. Newkirk, with Courtney G. Brooks. *The Apollo Spacecraft: A Chronology, Volume IV, January 21, 1966–July 13, 1974.* NASA SP-4009, 1978.

Astronautics and Aeronautics, 1968: Chronology of Science, Technology, and Policy. NASA SP-4010, 1969.

Newkirk, Roland W., and Ivan D. Ertel, with Courtney G. Brooks. *Skylab: A Chronology.* NASA SP-4011, 1977.

Van Nimmen, Jane, and Leonard C. Bruno, with Robert L. Rosholt. *NASA Historical Data Book, Volume I: NASA Resources, 1958–1968.* NASA SP-4012, 1976; rep. ed. 1988.

Ezell, Linda Neuman. *NASA Historical Data Book, Volume II: Programs and Projects, 1958–1968.* NASA SP-4012, 1988.

Ezell, Linda Neuman. *NASA Historical Data Book, Volume III: Programs and Projects, 1969–1978.* NASA SP-4012, 1988.

Gawdiak, Ihor, with Helen Fedor. *NASA Historical Data Book, Volume IV: NASA Resources, 1969–1978.* NASA SP-4012, 1994.

Rumerman, Judy A. *NASA Historical Data Book, Volume V: NASA Launch Systems, Space Transportation, Human Spaceflight, and Space Science, 1979–1988.* NASA SP-4012, 1999.

Rumerman, Judy A. *NASA Historical Data Book, Volume VI: NASA Space Applications, Aeronautics and Space Research and Technology, Tracking and Data Acquisition/Support Operations, Commercial Programs, and Resources, 1979– 1988.* NASA SP-4012, 1999.

Rumerman, Judy A. *NASA Historical Data Book, Volume VII: NASA Launch Systems, Space Transportation, Human Spaceflight, and Space Science, 1989–1998.* NASA SP-2009-4012, 2009.

No SP-4013.

Astronautics and Aeronautics, 1969: Chronology of Science, Technology, and Policy. NASA SP-4014, 1970.

Astronautics and Aeronautics, 1970: Chronology of Science, Technology, and Policy. NASA SP-4015, 1972.

Astronautics and Aeronautics, 1971: Chronology of Science, Technology, and Policy. NASA SP-4016, 1972.

Astronautics and Aeronautics, 1972: Chronology of Science, Technology, and Policy. NASA SP-4017, 1974.

Astronautics and Aeronautics, 1973: Chronology of Science, Technology, and Policy. NASA SP-4018, 1975.

Astronautics and Aeronautics, 1974: Chronology of Science, Technology, and Policy. NASA SP-4019, 1977.

Astronautics and Aeronautics, 1975: Chronology of Science, Technology, and Policy. NASA SP-4020, 1979.

Astronautics and Aeronautics, 1976: Chronology of Science, Technology, and Policy. NASA SP-4021, 1984.

Astronautics and Aeronautics, 1977: Chronology of Science, Technology, and Policy. NASA SP-4022, 1986.

Astronautics and Aeronautics, 1978: Chronology of Science, Technology, and Policy. NASA SP-4023, 1986.

Astronautics and Aeronautics, 1979–1984: Chronology of Science, Technology, and Policy. NASA SP-4024, 1988.

Astronautics and Aeronautics, 1985: Chronology of Science, Technology, and Policy. NASA SP-4025, 1990.

Noordung, Hermann. *The Problem of Space Travel: The Rocket Motor.* Edited by Ernst Stuhlinger and J. D. Hunley, with Jennifer Garland. NASA SP-4026, 1995.

Astronautics and Aeronautics, 1986–1990: A Chronology. NASA SP-4027, 1997.

Astronautics and Aeronautics, 1991–1995: A Chronology. NASA SP-2000-4028, 2000.

Orloff, Richard W. *Apollo by the Numbers: A Statistical Reference.* NASA SP-2000-4029, 2000.

Lewis, Marieke, and Ryan Swanson. *Astronautics and Aeronautics: A Chronology, 1996–2000.* NASA SP-2009-4030, 2009.

Ivey, William Noel, and Ryan Swanson. *Astronautics and Aeronautics: A Chronology, 2001–2005.* NASA SP-2010-4031, 2010.

Management Histories, NASA SP-4100:

Rosholt, Robert L. *An Administrative History of NASA, 1958–1963.* NASA SP-4101, 1966.

Levine, Arnold S. *Managing NASA in the Apollo Era.* NASA SP-4102, 1982.

Roland, Alex. *Model Research: The National Advisory Committee for Aeronautics, 1915–1958.* NASA SP-4103, 1985.

Fries, Sylvia D. *NASA Engineers and the Age of Apollo.* NASA SP-4104, 1992.

Glennan, T. Keith. *The Birth of NASA: The Diary of T. Keith Glennan.* Edited by J. D. Hunley. NASA SP-4105, 1993.

Seamans, Robert C. *Aiming at Targets: The Autobiography of Robert C. Seamans.* NASA SP-4106, 1996.

Garber, Stephen J., ed. *Looking Backward, Looking Forward: Forty Years of Human Spaceflight Symposium*. NASA SP-2002-4107, 2002.

Mallick, Donald L., with Peter W. Merlin. *The Smell of Kerosene: A Test Pilot's Odyssey*. NASA SP-4108, 2003.

Iliff, Kenneth W., and Curtis L. Peebles. *From Runway to Orbit: Reflections of a NASA Engineer*. NASA SP-2004-4109, 2004.

Chertok, Boris. *Rockets and People, Volume I*. NASA SP-2005-4110, 2005.

Chertok, Boris. *Rockets and People: Creating a Rocket Industry, Volume II*. NASA SP-2006-4110, 2006.

Chertok, Boris. *Rockets and People: Hot Days of the Cold War, Volume III*. NASA SP-2009-4110, 2009.

Laufer, Alexander, Todd Post, and Edward Hoffman. *Shared Voyage: Learning and Unlearning from Remarkable Projects*. NASA SP-2005-4111, 2005.

Dawson, Virginia P., and Mark D. Bowles. *Realizing the Dream of Flight: Biographical Essays in Honor of the Centennial of Flight, 1903–2003*. NASA SP-2005-4112, 2005.

Mudgway, Douglas J. *William H. Pickering: America's Deep Space Pioneer*. NASA SP-2008-4113, 2008.

Project Histories, NASA SP-4200:

Swenson, Loyd S., Jr., James M. Grimwood, and Charles C. Alexander. *This New Ocean: A History of Project Mercury*. NASA SP-4201, 1966; rep. ed. 1999.

Green, Constance McLaughlin, and Milton Lomask. *Vanguard: A History*. NASA SP-4202, 1970; rep. ed. Smithsonian Institution Press, 1971.

Hacker, Barton C., and James M. Grimwood. *On the Shoulders of Titans: A History of Project Gemini*. NASA SP-4203, 1977; rep. ed. 2002.

Benson, Charles D., and William Barnaby Faherty. *Moonport: A History of Apollo Launch Facilities and Operations*. NASA SP-4204, 1978.

Brooks, Courtney G., James M. Grimwood, and Loyd S. Swenson, Jr. *Chariots for Apollo: A History of Manned Lunar Spacecraft*. NASA SP-4205, 1979.

Bilstein, Roger E. *Stages to Saturn: A Technological History of the Apollo/Saturn Launch Vehicles*. NASA SP-4206, 1980 and 1996.

No SP-4207.

Compton, W. David, and Charles D. Benson. *Living and Working in Space: A History of Skylab*. NASA SP-4208, 1983.

Ezell, Edward Clinton, and Linda Neuman Ezell. *The Partnership: A History of the Apollo-Soyuz Test Project*. NASA SP-4209, 1978.

Hall, R. Cargill. *Lunar Impact: A History of Project Ranger*. NASA SP-4210, 1977.

Newell, Homer E. *Beyond the Atmosphere: Early Years of Space Science*. NASA SP-4211, 1980.

Ezell, Edward Clinton, and Linda Neuman Ezell. *On Mars: Exploration of the Red Planet, 1958–1978*. NASA SP-4212, 1984.

Pitts, John A. *The Human Factor: Biomedicine in the Manned Space Program to 1980*. NASA SP-4213, 1985.

Compton, W. David. *Where No Man Has Gone Before: A History of Apollo Lunar Exploration Missions*. NASA SP-4214, 1989.

Naugle, John E. *First Among Equals: The Selection of NASA Space Science Experiments*. NASA SP-4215, 1991.

Wallace, Lane E. *Airborne Trailblazer: Two Decades with NASA Langley's 737 Flying Laboratory*. NASA SP-4216, 1994.

Butrica, Andrew J., ed. *Beyond the Ionosphere: Fifty Years of Satellite Communications*. NASA SP-4217, 1997.

Butrica, Andrew J. *To See the Unseen: A History of Planetary Radar Astronomy*. NASA SP-4218, 1996.

Mack, Pamela E., ed. *From Engineering Science to Big Science: The NACA and NASA Collier Trophy Research Project Winners*. NASA SP-4219, 1998.

Reed, R. Dale. *Wingless Flight: The Lifting Body Story*. NASA SP-4220, 1998.

Heppenheimer, T. A. *The Space Shuttle Decision: NASA's Search for a Reusable Space Vehicle*. NASA SP-4221, 1999.

Hunley, J. D., ed. *Toward Mach 2: The Douglas D-558 Program*. NASA SP-4222, 1999.

Swanson, Glen E., ed. *"Before This Decade Is Out . . ." Personal Reflections on the Apollo Program*. NASA SP-4223, 1999.

Tomayko, James E. *Computers Take Flight: A History of NASA's Pioneering Digital Fly-By-Wire Project*. NASA SP-4224, 2000.

Morgan, Clay. *Shuttle-Mir: The United States and Russia Share History's Highest Stage*. NASA SP-2001-4225, 2001.

Leary, William M. *"We Freeze to Please": A History of NASA's Icing Research Tunnel and the Quest for Safety*. NASA SP-2002-4226, 2002.

Mudgway, Douglas J. *Uplink-Downlink: A History of the Deep Space Network, 1957–1997.* NASA SP-2001-4227, 2001.

No SP-4228 or SP-4229.

Dawson, Virginia P., and Mark D. Bowles. *Taming Liquid Hydrogen: The Centaur Upper Stage Rocket, 1958–2002.* NASA SP-2004-4230, 2004.

Meltzer, Michael. *Mission to Jupiter: A History of the Galileo Project.* NASA SP-2007-4231, 2007.

Heppenheimer, T. A. *Facing the Heat Barrier: A History of Hypersonics.* NASA SP-2007-4232, 2007.

Tsiao, Sunny. *"Read You Loud and Clear!" The Story of NASA's Spaceflight Tracking and Data Network.* NASA SP-2007-4233, 2007.

Meltzer, Michael. *When Biospheres Collide: A History of NASA's Planetary Protection Programs.* NASA SP-2011-4234, 2011.

Center Histories, NASA SP-4300:

Rosenthal, Alfred. *Venture into Space: Early Years of Goddard Space Flight Center.* NASA SP-4301, 1985.

Hartman, Edwin P. *Adventures in Research: A History of Ames Research Center, 1940–1965.* NASA SP-4302, 1970.

Hallion, Richard P. *On the Frontier: Flight Research at Dryden, 1946–1981.* NASA SP-4303, 1984.

Muenger, Elizabeth A. *Searching the Horizon: A History of Ames Research Center, 1940–1976.* NASA SP-4304, 1985.

Hansen, James R. *Engineer in Charge: A History of the Langley Aeronautical Laboratory, 1917–1958.* NASA SP-4305, 1987.

Dawson, Virginia P. *Engines and Innovation: Lewis Laboratory and American Propulsion Technology.* NASA SP-4306, 1991.

Dethloff, Henry C. *"Suddenly Tomorrow Came . . .": A History of the Johnson Space Center, 1957–1990.* NASA SP-4307, 1993.

Hansen, James R. *Spaceflight Revolution: NASA Langley Research Center from Sputnik to Apollo.* NASA SP-4308, 1995.

Wallace, Lane E. *Flights of Discovery: An Illustrated History of the Dryden Flight Research Center.* NASA SP-4309, 1996.

Herring, Mack R. *Way Station to Space: A History of the John C. Stennis Space Center.* NASA SP-4310, 1997.

Wallace, Harold D., Jr. *Wallops Station and the Creation of an American Space Program*. NASA SP-4311, 1997.

Wallace, Lane E. *Dreams, Hopes, Realities. NASA's Goddard Space Flight Center: The First Forty Years*. NASA SP-4312, 1999.

Dunar, Andrew J., and Stephen P. Waring. *Power to Explore: A History of Marshall Space Flight Center, 1960–1990*. NASA SP-4313, 1999.

Bugos, Glenn E. *Atmosphere of Freedom: Sixty Years at the NASA Ames Research Center*. NASA SP-2000-4314, 2000.

No SP-4315.

Schultz, James. *Crafting Flight: Aircraft Pioneers and the Contributions of the Men and Women of NASA Langley Research Center*. NASA SP-2003-4316, 2003.

Bowles, Mark D. *Science in Flux: NASA's Nuclear Program at Plum Brook Station, 1955–2005*. NASA SP-2006-4317, 2006.

Wallace, Lane E. *Flights of Discovery: An Illustrated History of the Dryden Flight Research Center*. NASA SP-2007-4318, 2007. Revised version of NASA SP-4309.

Arrighi, Robert S. *Revolutionary Atmosphere: The Story of the Altitude Wind Tunnel and the Space Power Chambers*. NASA SP-2010-4319, 2010.

General Histories, NASA SP-4400:

Corliss, William R. *NASA Sounding Rockets, 1958–1968: A Historical Summary*. NASA SP-4401, 1971.

Wells, Helen T., Susan H. Whiteley, and Carrie Karegeannes. *Origins of NASA Names*. NASA SP-4402, 1976.

Anderson, Frank W., Jr. *Orders of Magnitude: A History of NACA and NASA, 1915–1980*. NASA SP-4403, 1981.

Sloop, John L. *Liquid Hydrogen as a Propulsion Fuel, 1945–1959*. NASA SP-4404, 1978.

Roland, Alex. *A Spacefaring People: Perspectives on Early Spaceflight*. NASA SP-4405, 1985.

Bilstein, Roger E. *Orders of Magnitude: A History of the NACA and NASA, 1915–1990*. NASA SP-4406, 1989.

Logsdon, John M., ed., with Linda J. Lear, Jannelle Warren Findley, Ray A. Williamson, and Dwayne A. Day. *Exploring the Unknown: Selected Documents in the History of the U.S. Civil Space Program, Volume I: Organizing for Exploration*. NASA SP-4407, 1995.

Logsdon, John M., ed., with Dwayne A. Day and Roger D. Launius. *Exploring the Unknown: Selected Documents in the History of the U.S. Civil Space Program, Volume II: External Relationships*. NASA SP-4407, 1996.

Logsdon, John M., ed., with Roger D. Launius, David H. Onkst, and Stephen J. Garber. *Exploring the Unknown: Selected Documents in the History of the U.S. Civil Space Program, Volume III: Using Space*. NASA SP-4407, 1998.

Logsdon, John M., ed., with Ray A. Williamson, Roger D. Launius, Russell J. Acker, Stephen J. Garber, and Jonathan L. Friedman. *Exploring the Unknown: Selected Documents in the History of the U.S. Civil Space Program, Volume IV: Accessing Space*. NASA SP-4407, 1999.

Logsdon, John M., ed., with Amy Paige Snyder, Roger D. Launius, Stephen J. Garber, and Regan Anne Newport. *Exploring the Unknown: Selected Documents in the History of the U.S. Civil Space Program, Volume V: Exploring the Cosmos*. NASA SP-2001-4407, 2001.

Logsdon, John M., ed., with Stephen J. Garber, Roger D. Launius, and Ray A. Williamson. *Exploring the Unknown: Selected Documents in the History of the U.S. Civil Space Program, Volume VI: Space and Earth Science*. NASA SP-2004-4407, 2004.

Logsdon, John M., ed., with Roger D. Launius. *Exploring the Unknown: Selected Documents in the History of the U.S. Civil Space Program, Volume VII: Human Spaceflight: Projects Mercury, Gemini, and Apollo*. NASA SP-2008-4407, 2008.

Siddiqi, Asif A., *Challenge to Apollo: The Soviet Union and the Space Race, 1945–1974*. NASA SP-2000-4408, 2000.

Hansen, James R., ed. *The Wind and Beyond: Journey into the History of Aerodynamics in America, Volume 1: The Ascent of the Airplane*. NASA SP-2003-4409, 2003.

Hansen, James R., ed. *The Wind and Beyond: Journey into the History of Aerodynamics in America, Volume 2: Reinventing the Airplane*. NASA SP-2007-4409, 2007.

Hogan, Thor. *Mars Wars: The Rise and Fall of the Space Exploration Initiative*. NASA SP-2007-4410, 2007.

Vakoch, Douglas A., ed. *Psychology of Space Exploration: Contemporary Research in Historical Perspective*. NASA SP-2011-4411, 2011.

Monographs in Aerospace History, NASA SP-4500:

Launius, Roger D., and Aaron K. Gillette, comps. *Toward a History of the Space Shuttle: An Annotated Bibliography*. Monographs in Aerospace History, No. 1, 1992.

Launius, Roger D., and J. D. Hunley, comps. *An Annotated Bibliography of the Apollo Program*. Monographs in Aerospace History, No. 2, 1994.

Launius, Roger D. *Apollo: A Retrospective Analysis*. Monographs in Aerospace History, No. 3, 1994.

Hansen, James R. *Enchanted Rendezvous: John C. Houbolt and the Genesis of the Lunar-Orbit Rendezvous Concept*. Monographs in Aerospace History, No. 4, 1995.

Gorn, Michael H. *Hugh L. Dryden's Career in Aviation and Space*. Monographs in Aerospace History, No. 5, 1996.

Powers, Sheryll Goecke. *Women in Flight Research at NASA Dryden Flight Research Center from 1946 to 1995*. Monographs in Aerospace History, No. 6, 1997.

Portree, David S. F., and Robert C. Trevino. *Walking to Olympus: An EVA Chronology*. Monographs in Aerospace History, No. 7, 1997.

Logsdon, John M., moderator. *Legislative Origins of the National Aeronautics and Space Act of 1958: Proceedings of an Oral History Workshop*. Monographs in Aerospace History, No. 8, 1998.

Rumerman, Judy A., comp. *U.S. Human Spaceflight: A Record of Achievement, 1961–1998*. Monographs in Aerospace History, No. 9, 1998.

Portree, David S. F. *NASA's Origins and the Dawn of the Space Age*. Monographs in Aerospace History, No. 10, 1998.

Logsdon, John M. *Together in Orbit: The Origins of International Cooperation in the Space Station*. Monographs in Aerospace History, No. 11, 1998.

Phillips, W. Hewitt. *Journey in Aeronautical Research: A Career at NASA Langley Research Center*. Monographs in Aerospace History, No. 12, 1998.

Braslow, Albert L. *A History of Suction-Type Laminar-Flow Control with Emphasis on Flight Research*. Monographs in Aerospace History, No. 13, 1999.

Logsdon, John M., moderator. *Managing the Moon Program: Lessons Learned from Apollo*. Monographs in Aerospace History, No. 14, 1999.

Perminov, V. G. *The Difficult Road to Mars: A Brief History of Mars Exploration in the Soviet Union*. Monographs in Aerospace History, No. 15, 1999.

Tucker, Tom. *Touchdown: The Development of Propulsion Controlled Aircraft at NASA Dryden*. Monographs in Aerospace History, No. 16, 1999.

Maisel, Martin, Demo J. Giulanetti, and Daniel C. Dugan. *The History of the XV-15 Tilt Rotor Research Aircraft: From Concept to Flight*. Monographs in Aerospace History, No. 17, 2000. NASA SP-2000-4517.

Jenkins, Dennis R. *Hypersonics Before the Shuttle: A Concise History of the X-15 Research Airplane*. Monographs in Aerospace History, No. 18, 2000. NASA SP-2000-4518.

Chambers, Joseph R. *Partners in Freedom: Contributions of the Langley Research Center to U.S. Military Aircraft of the 1990s*. Monographs in Aerospace History, No. 19, 2000. NASA SP-2000-4519.

Waltman, Gene L. *Black Magic and Gremlins: Analog Flight Simulations at NASA's Flight Research Center*. Monographs in Aerospace History, No. 20, 2000. NASA SP-2000-4520.

Portree, David S. F. *Humans to Mars: Fifty Years of Mission Planning, 1950–2000*. Monographs in Aerospace History, No. 21, 2001. NASA SP-2001-4521.

Thompson, Milton O., with J. D. Hunley. *Flight Research: Problems Encountered and What They Should Teach Us*. Monographs in Aerospace History, No. 22, 2001. NASA SP-2001-4522.

Tucker, Tom. *The Eclipse Project*. Monographs in Aerospace History, No. 23, 2001. NASA SP-2001-4523.

Siddiqi, Asif A. *Deep Space Chronicle: A Chronology of Deep Space and Planetary Probes, 1958–2000*. Monographs in Aerospace History, No. 24, 2002. NASA SP-2002-4524.

Merlin, Peter W. *Mach 3+: NASA/USAF YF-12 Flight Research, 1969–1979*. Monographs in Aerospace History, No. 25, 2001. NASA SP-2001-4525.

Anderson, Seth B. *Memoirs of an Aeronautical Engineer: Flight Tests at Ames Research Center: 1940–1970*. Monographs in Aerospace History, No. 26, 2002. NASA SP-2002-4526.

Renstrom, Arthur G. *Wilbur and Orville Wright: A Bibliography Commemorating the One-Hundredth Anniversary of the First Powered Flight on December 17, 1903*. Monographs in Aerospace History, No. 27, 2002. NASA SP-2002-4527.

No monograph 28.

Chambers, Joseph R. *Concept to Reality: Contributions of the NASA Langley Research Center to U.S. Civil Aircraft of the 1990s*. Monographs in Aerospace History, No. 29, 2003. NASA SP-2003-4529.

Peebles, Curtis, ed. *The Spoken Word: Recollections of Dryden History, The Early Years.* Monographs in Aerospace History, No. 30, 2003. NASA SP-2003-4530.

Jenkins, Dennis R., Tony Landis, and Jay Miller. *American X-Vehicles: An Inventory—X-1 to X-50.* Monographs in Aerospace History, No. 31, 2003. NASA SP-2003-4531.

Renstrom, Arthur G. *Wilbur and Orville Wright: A Chronology Commemorating the One-Hundredth Anniversary of the First Powered Flight on December 17, 1903.* Monographs in Aerospace History, No. 32, 2003. NASA SP-2003-4532.

Bowles, Mark D., and Robert S. Arrighi. *NASA's Nuclear Frontier: The Plum Brook Research Reactor.* Monographs in Aerospace History, No. 33, 2004. NASA SP-2004-4533.

Wallace, Lane, and Christian Gelzer. *Nose Up: High Angle-of-Attack and Thrust Vectoring Research at NASA Dryden, 1979–2001.* Monographs in Aerospace History, No. 34, 2009. NASA SP-2009-4534.

Matranga, Gene J., C. Wayne Ottinger, Calvin R. Jarvis, and D. Christian Gelzer. *Unconventional, Contrary, and Ugly: The Lunar Landing Research Vehicle.* Monographs in Aerospace History, No. 35, 2006. NASA SP-2004-4535.

McCurdy, Howard E. *Low-Cost Innovation in Spaceflight: The History of the Near Earth Asteroid Rendezvous (NEAR) Mission.* Monographs in Aerospace History, No. 36, 2005. NASA SP-2005-4536.

Seamans, Robert C., Jr. *Project Apollo: The Tough Decisions.* Monographs in Aerospace History, No. 37, 2005. NASA SP-2005-4537.

Lambright, W. Henry. *NASA and the Environment: The Case of Ozone Depletion.* Monographs in Aerospace History, No. 38, 2005. NASA SP-2005-4538.

Chambers, Joseph R. *Innovation in Flight: Research of the NASA Langley Research Center on Revolutionary Advanced Concepts for Aeronautics.* Monographs in Aerospace History, No. 39, 2005. NASA SP-2005-4539.

Phillips, W. Hewitt. *Journey into Space Research: Continuation of a Career at NASA Langley Research Center.* Monographs in Aerospace History, No. 40, 2005. NASA SP-2005-4540.

Rumerman, Judy A., Chris Gamble, and Gabriel Okolski, comps. *U.S. Human Spaceflight: A Record of Achievement, 1961–2006.* Monographs in Aerospace History, No. 41, 2007. NASA SP-2007-4541.

Peebles, Curtis. *The Spoken Word: Recollections of Dryden History Beyond the Sky.* Mongraphs in Aerospace History, No. 42, 2011. NASA SP-2011-4542.

Dick, Steven J., Stephen J. Garber, and Jane H. Odom. *Research in NASA History*. Monographs in Aerospace History, No. 43, 2009. NASA SP-2009-4543.

Merlin, Peter W. *Ikhana: Unmanned Aircraft System Western States Fire Missions*. Monographs in Aerospace History, No. 44, 2009. NASA SP-2009-4544.

Fisher, Steven C., and Shamim A. Rahman. *Remembering the Giants: Apollo Rocket Propulsion Development*. Monographs in Aerospace History, No. 45, 2009. NASA SP-2009-4545.

Gelzer, Christian. *Fairing Well: From Shoebox to Bat Truck and Beyond, Aerodynamic Truck Research at NASA's Dryden Flight Research Center*. Monographs in Aerospace History, No. 46, 2011. NASA SP-2011-4546.

Electronic Media, NASA SP-4600:

Remembering Apollo 11: The 30th Anniversary Data Archive CD-ROM. NASA SP-4601, 1999.

Remembering Apollo 11: The 35th Anniversary Data Archive CD-ROM. NASA SP-2004-4601, 2004. This is an update of the 1999 edition.

The Mission Transcript Collection: U.S. Human Spaceflight Missions from Mercury Redstone 3 to Apollo 17. NASA SP-2000-4602, 2001.

Shuttle-Mir: The United States and Russia Share History's Highest Stage. NASA SP-2001-4603, 2002.

U.S. Centennial of Flight Commission Presents Born of Dreams—Inspired by Freedom. NASA SP-2004-4604, 2004.

Of Ashes and Atoms: A Documentary on the NASA Plum Brook Reactor Facility. NASA SP-2005-4605, 2005.

Taming Liquid Hydrogen: The Centaur Upper Stage Rocket Interactive CD-ROM. NASA SP-2004-4606, 2004.

Fueling Space Exploration: The History of NASA's Rocket Engine Test Facility DVD. NASA SP-2005-4607, 2005.

Altitude Wind Tunnel at NASA Glenn Research Center: An Interactive History CD-ROM. NASA SP-2008-4608, 2008.

A Tunnel Through Time: The History of NASA's Altitude Wind Tunnel. NASA SP-2010-4609, 2010.

Conference Proceedings, NASA SP-4700:

Dick, Steven J., and Keith Cowing, eds. *Risk and Exploration: Earth, Sea and the Stars*. NASA SP-2005-4701, 2005.

Dick, Steven J., and Roger D. Launius. *Critical Issues in the History of Spaceflight*. NASA SP-2006-4702, 2006.

Dick, Steven J., ed. *Remembering the Space Age: Proceedings of the 50th Anniversary Conference*. NASA SP-2008-4703, 2008.

Dick, Steven J., ed. *NASA's First 50 Years: Historical Perspectives*. NASA SP-2010-4704, 2010.

Societal Impact, NASA SP-4800:

Dick, Steven J., and Roger D. Launius. *Societal Impact of Spaceflight*. NASA SP-2007-4801, 2007.

Dick, Steven J., and Mark L. Lupisella. *Cosmos and Culture: Cultural Evolution in a Cosmic Context*. NASA SP-2009-4802, 2009.